INFORMATION ENGINEERING

INFORMATION ENGINEERING

Strategic Systems Development

Clive Finkelstein
Information Engineering Services Pty Ltd

Addison-Wesley Publishing Company

Sydney • Wokingham, England • Reading, Massachusetts
Menlo Park, California • New York • Don Mills, Ontario • Amsterdam
Bonn • Singapore • Tokyo • Madrid • San Juan • Milan • Paris

The programs in this book have been included for their instructional value. They have been tested with care but are not guaranteed for any particular purpose. The publisher does not offer any warranties or representations, nor does it accept any liabilities with respect to the programs.

Many of the designations used by manufacturers and sellers to distinguish their products are claimed as trademarks. Addison-Wesley has made every attempt to supply trademark information about manufacturers and their products mentioned in this book. A list of the trademark designations and their owners appears on page xviii.

Cover designed by The Art of Business, Singapore.
Typeset by Colset Pte Ltd, Singapore.
Printed in Singapore.

First printed 1992.

National Library of Australia Cataloguing in Publication Data
Finkelstein, Clive
   Information engineering, strategic systems development.
   Includes index.
   ISBN 0 201 50988 1.

   1. Strategic planning. 2. Information technology. 3. System development.
   4. System analysis. 5. System design. 6. Title.
   004.2

Library of Congress Cataloging in Publication Data
Finkelstein, Clive.
   Information engineering: strategic systems development/Clive
Finkelstein.
      p.   cm.
   Includes index.
   ISBN 0-201-50988-1
   1. Strategic planning. 2. Information technology. 3. System development.
   4. System analysis. 5. System design. 6. Title.
QA76.9.S88F53   1992   91–40735
004.2′1 – dc20   CIP

I dedicate this book to my wife Jill and our daughter Kristi.

PREFACE

Strategic planning and systems development are both disciplines which historically have been applied independently of each other. Today they are merging. Each is vital to an organization's future: both economically and competitively. Information technology is now recognized as having the potential to create competitive advantage; information systems must be capable of supporting the strategic plans of an organization. The time has long passed when systems development or strategic planning can be accomplished without an acknowledgement of the importance of each discipline to the other.

Corporate strategic planning is normally used by senior management. Other managers in the organization also use strategic planning principles at the business unit or program level, or at the functional area level, both in implementing the plans set by senior management, and in defining plans for their areas of responsibility.

Strategic plans, developed at all levels of the organization, provide direct input for the development of information systems that are needed to support those plans. The MIS department therefore needs to be closely involved in the development of strategic plans so they can provide the necessary decision support capability through the information systems that are developed. Further, MIS participation in strategic planning allows the competitive advantages arising from information technology to be introduced into those plans.

To date, strategic planning used by MIS staff has focused on systems strategic planning: so defining hardware and software support needed for the future. In many organizations today these decisions are made without an understanding of factors that link corporate strategic planning to systems strategic planning, and vice versa. This must change. MIS staff, and also managers and user staff at all levels, must work together more closely. The result is the definition of executive information systems (EIS), decision support systems (DSS), and also operational systems.

Because systems are defined by the users from a business perspective, they exhibit a higher quality than is achieved by the traditional systems development methods. And by using relational data base management systems, fourth generation languages, object-oriented languages, computer-aided software engineering (CASE) and other software tools, these systems are being developed faster and with lower on-going maintenance costs. Many organizations, government and commercial, now use information technology for competitive advantage. These will be the survivors in the competitive environment of the 1990s. Increasingly, they are using the techniques of Information Engineering.

The evolution of information engineering

The initial concepts of Information Engineering were first developed in 1972, and were refined over the period 1976–1981. Since then, Information Engineering has been used to design and build information systems that reflect the business needs of organizations more effectively than other techniques such as Business Systems Planning (BSP) or software engineering. It has evolved into two main variants. The first uses existing functions of an organization as the starting point; data needed by the functions are then defined. This approach is more DP-driven than the second variant. In this DP variant, the business knowledge is incorporated from users often by interview; but significantly there is subjective interpretation of the users' input by DP personnel. This is sometimes referred to as 'conventional Information Engineering' [1], or 'DP-driven Information Engineering', and is supported by many of the Information Engineering software products on the market today [2].

The second variant is the subject of this book. It starts with the strategic plans set by management at all levels of an organization. From these plans are defined the data, and later the functions, needed to support those plans. This approach is more user-driven than the DP variant. It is sometimes referred to as 'enterprise Information Engineering' [3], or 'business-driven Information Engineering' [4]. With this business-driven variant, managers and users trained in Information Engineering apply the techniques directly, rather than by interview; the defined business knowledge is objectively interpreted by software to identify the functions and systems needed to achieve the strategic plans. The business-driven Information Engineering variant is supported by some Information Engineering expert systems software products available today, as discussed in this book [5].

About this book

The book focuses on strategic planning and on systems development. It provides a step-by-step method for strategic planning at all levels of an organization, either government or commercial. It shows how to identify competitive threats, and also opportunities that offer competitive advantage. This leads to the development of proactive, competitive strategic plans that provide clear direction for the future.

These plans provide input for the definition of strategic, tactical and operational models. These are data models that identify data required at all levels of the organization; they may be implemented as centralized or distributed data bases, using relational or non-relational DBMS products as required. Object-oriented systems can be directly derived from these data models using process modeling concepts; these systems may be implemented with object-oriented languages, or instead by using conventional third or fourth generation languages.

The resulting information systems support the strategic plans as executive information systems or decision support systems that provide information for decision-making. The operational systems needed to run the organization, and provide the information used by these EIS and DSS, are also developed using methods in the book.

This book is not theoretical. It uses a practical, *how-to* approach which can be used in any organization. It offers a step by step method to help you apply information technology in your own environment. It is organized in four parts.

- **Part 1** contains Chapter 1. This provides an overall introduction to the strategic systems development methodology. It introduces strategic planning and Information Engineering, and then indicates how the book can be used by its different reader audiences.

- **Part 2** provides an introduction to the data modeling and process modeling principles used by Information Engineering. An understanding of these concepts is essential: they are used extensively throughout the book.

- **Part 3** describes corporate strategic planning, applied at the business unit or program level, and also at the corporate level. This uses a strategic planning approach which can be applied at all management levels in both commercial or government organizations, so providing immediate feedback for development and refinement of strategic plans.

- **Part 4** covers systems development, based on strategic plans developed in Part 3. It uses data modeling concepts from Part 2 to develop the strategic, tactical and operational models which represent the various levels of the strategic plan. Process modeling is used to derive object-oriented logic from these data models. This derived logic is implemented using conventional or object-oriented languages, whether third or fourth generation, and by using relational or other DBMS products.

The book can be read completely, or instead in sections according to your specific interests. To help you, Chapter 1 first provides an introduction to strategic planning and to systems development. It then describes the structure of the book in detail, discussing sections of interest to different readers. From this you can decide how you wish to read it.

This book is intended for use by senior and middle managers and their staff, and by MIS staff, in a project environment. It is designed so that it can also be used in conjunction with education courses, presented either in a tertiary environment or as public seminars. In a tertiary environment it is intended to be used at undergraduate or postgraduate levels in management and business-oriented disciplines, and in computer science and information technology fields. It can also be used in conjunction with inhouse courses conducted within an organization, as a catalyst for development of strategic systems that relate directly to the organization.

The methods described in this book lead not only to development of strategic systems which offer competitive advantage: when used in a project environment these methods introduce a corporate culture. The systems are defined from the perspective of the business, rather than the computer: the business knowledge of managers and users is thus essential. Senior and middle managers, their staff and MIS all learn how to work together in a strategic planning environment – with benefit to their organization, and their careers. This results not only in development of strategic systems today, but also the ability to change systems rapidly in the competitive environment of tomorrow.

Acknowledgements

In my earlier book [6] I acknowledged the contributions made by many people in the years since 1972 that I have spent developing and refining Information Engineering. The material covered in this book represents extensions to the techniques; many of these were developed from late 1988 based on the use of Information Engineering by large corporations.

Part 3 discusses a variety of tools and techniques that can be used for strategic planning: as methods, charts, graphs or matrices. Many tools and techniques have evolved over the years as they have been used for strategic analysis by various authors. They have been further modified for use in strategic management planning as described in this book. As a consequence, the true origin of some tools has been lost. *Where known, I have tried to give full acknowledgement to the original authors; where specific references are not provided, I hereby acknowledge the work of those authors.*

In particular I would like to thank Professor Bill Birkett in Sydney, whose initial work in developing the Practical Strategic Planning workshop as part of Information Engineering in 1983 provided inspiration, and some of the source material, for the strategic management planning method in Chapters 10-12. I also want to thank my good friend Gordon Miles of Information Engineering Services Limited in Auckland, for his work in developing the goal analysis technique in Chapter 9.

In the USA, I would like to thank Frank Davis, previously of the US Navy and now US Air Force, for his continued support and encouragement throughout the 80s. His efforts, plus those of Russ Richards of the Defense Information Systems Agency, have lead to use of the business-driven Information Engineering methods described in this book by the US Department of Defense. My thanks also go to Dean Mohlstrom, Glen Hughlette, Jim Lair, Tim Rinaman and the staff at Information Engineering Systems Corporation of Alexandria, VA, who use these methods every day in support of their numerous US and Canadian corporate clients: helping them to structure themselves to compete in the turbulent 90s and beyond.

Finally, my greatest thanks go to my wife, Jill, and our daughter Kristi, without whose continuing love and support none of this would have been possible.

Clive Finkelstein
Melbourne, Australia
March 1992

Publishers acknowledgement

The publishers wish to thank the following companies for permission to reproduce material from published sources: Dartmouth Publishing Company, John Wiley & Sons, Inc. and Nolan, Norton & Company.

References

[1] Coleman, D. S. (1991). *Information Engineering Styles in Conflict*, Database Newsletter: Boston, MA Vol 19, No 2.

[2] IEW/ADW from Knowledgeware (Atlanta, GA) and IEF from Texas Instruments (Dallas, TX) are typical CASE tools for the DP-driven variant of Information Engineering.

[3] Mohlstrom, D. (1991). *Business-Driven Information Engineering: Achieving Effective Strategic Management*, CASE Trends: Shrewsbury, MA Vol 3, No 3.

[4] Coleman, D. S. (1991). *Information Engineering Styles in Conflict*, Database Newsletter: Boston, MA Vol 19, No 2.

[5] IE: Expert from Information Engineering Systems Corporation (Alexandria, VA) and ISM from Infonetics (Sydney, Australia) both support the business-driven variant of Information Engineering.

[6] Finkelstein, C. (1989). *An Introduction to Information Engineering*, Addison-Wesley: Reading, MA.

CONTENTS

PART ONE

Introduction

CHAPTER 1

Introduction to Strategic Systems Development

This book integrates corporate strategic planning with systems development and data base design, so that the resulting strategic information systems provide direct support to management for decision-making. It describes a methodology that is used for strategic systems development: using strategic management planning and systems development methodologies of Information Engineering. This integration of strategic planning and systems development draws on business and strategic planning expertise of managers and their staff, and systems development and data base design expertise of DP staff.

Strategic systems development requires both a knowledge of Information Engineering, as well as an understanding of strategic planning principles and practice. The required Information Engineering concepts are presented in Part 2; strategic planning principles are covered in Part 3. These are used together for systems development in Part 4. This chapter provides an overall introduction to the later parts of the book. We will start with strategic planning.

1.1 STRATEGIC PLANNING

There has been much research into and application of strategic planning in the last thirty years. Traditionally, strategic planning has focused on three main disciplines [1, 2, 3]:

- Strategy formulation, also called strategy content.
- Strategy implementation, also called strategy process.
- Strategic management, or the management of strategy.

More and more, it has become evident that the complexity of organizations precludes separation into these three categories. They are all interrelated: each provides feedback to, and receives feedback from, the other disciplines. They represent a life cycle for strategic planning (see Figure 1.1). Recognizing this interdependence and complexity, this book attempts to integrate the three disciplines with a methodology that we will call **strategic management planning**. This permits strategic management of strategic planning and implementation, with rapid feedback for refinement of the strategic plans.

Strategic management planning uses an approach that also focuses on the development of organization structures and information systems (manual or automated) that directly support the strategic plans: at the business unit level, and at the corporate level. We will first discuss traditional strategic planning based on the above three disciplines in more detail. We will then consider some of the problems encountered, before addressing strategic management planning.

1.1.1 Traditional strategic planning

Strategic planning, as we know it today, is generally accepted to have had its genesis in the 60's with the works by Chandler (*Strategy and Structure*) [4], Ansoff (*Corporate Strategy*) [5] and Andrews (*The Concept of Strategic Management*) [6]. These books resulted in an explosion of research into strategic planning. As new approaches were developed and applied to organizations, significant results were achieved. In this book we collectively refer to these approaches as the **traditional strategic planning** methods.

There were successes, but there were also failures as the body of experience grew. These failures were often due, in many respects, to problems associated with different requirements at separate stages in the strategic planning life cycle. These problems are discussed in Chapter 8, and are illustrated in Figure 1.1. They are summarized below.

- The evaluation of a strategic plan is difficult, often possible only by the pilot introduction of a new plan using part of the organization as a guinea pig. After assessing the results of the pilot, adjustments are made to the plan before it is introduced corporate-wide.
- A greater problem is the time horizon before useful feedback is available for refinement of the plan. With pilot introduction, six to twelve

Strategic Planning Life Cycle

Problems with Traditional Strategic Planning	
Strategic Planning	Limited strategic alternatives
Strategic Implementation	Ineffective communication
	Misinterpretation
Strategic Management	Long feedback cycle (3–5 years)
	Ineffective performance monitoring

Figure 1.1   **The problems with traditional strategic planning.**

months' operation under a new strategic plan may be required before an evaluation can be made. An assessment after the plan has been introduced corporate-wide may need one to two years' further operation before effective overall evaluation is possible.

• The necessary changes to the plan then take more time: the result is a three to five year time horizon between strategic plans. But we live in a changing world. Tomorrow's competitive environment will not allow us the luxury of this start-stop approach to planning. Evolutionary, incremental adjustment to a plan over a short time period, through progressive refinement, is needed.

• Integrating information systems with an organization's strategic plan; providing information needed by management for decision support, is another problem. Traditional systems development methods normally focus too low, mainly at the operational level, for decision support systems to be developed which are useful to management. Management and DP staff must work closely together to define decision support needs: but they have difficulty communicating, because of the jargon and different backgrounds of each group.

Discussing the consequences of all of these problems, Gray [7] indicates that:

> 'Strategic planning as many text books describe it may not be around for much longer but not for the reasons most critics give. If formal strategic planning vanishes in a few years, it will be because wherever it is undertaken it either

gets better or it gets worse, depending on how well it's done: if you do it poorly, either you drop out or you rattle around in its mechanics; if you do it well, you evolve beyond strategic planning into strategic management.'

Nolan, in discussing the transformation of organizations to compete in the 21st century, comments [8]:

'As the heartbeat of business quickens, we can no longer enter upon orderly phases of strategic planning every five years or so, followed by periods of implementation. Strategy must be monitored continuously, and implementation altered as strategies are adjusted.' He goes on to say that: *'Transformation entails changing everything about the business, while incorporating information technology at the same time.'*

1.1.2 Strategic management planning

Strategic management planning allows continual evaluation and refinement of the strategic plan at all stages of its development. It leads to precise implementation of the plan, with the development of information systems that support the plan exactly through the use of strategic systems development. The result is more effective decision support to management than is achieved by traditional strategic planning and systems development methods. The methodology is based on much of the work by Drucker [9], and also by Porter [10, 11].

Figure 1.2 illustrates strategic management planning. Feedback using this methodology is rapid, effective and precise, with clear communication

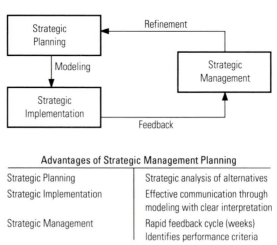

Figure 1.2 Advantages of strategic management planning.

and exact implementation. Wrong interpretation by lower level managers during implementation that often presents problems in traditional strategic planning, can be identified and resolved early.

Managers at all levels are able to interpret the strategic directions from their perspective, using modeling (as described in Part 2) to aid strategic thinking. Feedback from more detailed modeling at tactical and operational levels is available for strategic management review. All levels of the organization thus participate. There is clear identification of the benefits that address specific needs at each level. A corporate culture develops: planning becomes a normal part of each manager's job. There is also rapid feedback to senior management of new innovative opportunities. The result is integration at all levels of the organization: with its data, information and systems (both manual and automated) and new organization structures able to be integrated to achieve the strategic directions.

Because of its utility and advantage of rapid feedback, strategic management planning is also used for continuing assessment and refinement of the plan in response to perceived competitive threats or opportunities. This allows the organization to respond rapidly to highly competitive situations if necessary. Where rapid response is not required, this method also allows management to introduce controlled, evolutionary changes which have already been evaluated and highly refined before introduction to the organization.

Instead of using pilot introduction for evaluation of the defined strategic plan, strategic management planning uses the technique of **goal analysis** to provide rapid feedback that helps management to identify gaps or missed opportunities in the plan. This is achieved in days, rather than months as required by traditional strategic planning. Goal analysis can be applied not only at the highest corporate level, but also at lower management levels to ensure the correct implementation of the plan. It is described in Chapter 9.

Strategic management planning is also integrated with systems development to develop strategic information systems which directly support the strategic plan. This is one of the responsibilities of the Chief Information Officer (CIO) [12]. Direct strategic plan input is used in Parts 3 and 4 to develop strategic, tactical and operational models (see Figure 1.3), designed by managers and staff charged with the responsibility for implementing the plan. Because these models are developed by business experts based on directions defined in the plan, they result in information systems that exhibit higher quality than systems traditionally developed by DP professionals.

Figure 1.3 shows the progressive development of these models using strategic, tactical and operational modeling methods of Information Engineering. This is discussed in Chapter 7, and in Part 4.

Strategic modeling from the strategic plans of a project area identifies a number of tactical areas. If the project area is the corporation, the strategic model is the foundation of a corporate data model: a major focus

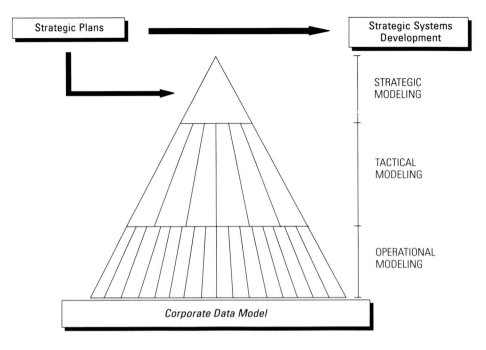

Figure 1.3   Strategic plans identify strategic systems.

of the CIO. Tactical modeling of priority tactical areas identifies operational systems. Priority operational systems are then taken to full data detail through operational modeling. These all expand the corporate data model to tactical and operational detail in those areas. Process modeling derives procedures from data models, to implement manual or automated procedures as operational systems. But priority systems can be implemented long before the corporate data model is completed, as illustrated in Figure 1.4. This is an example of *rapid application development*.

This approach allows priority areas to be selected, and taken to full operational detail in individual implementation projects for business units as shown in Figure 1.4. A high degree of concurrent development is the result. The corporate data model progressively expands based on this modeling feedback as discussed earlier; the concurrent business unit projects also apply the same methods to define and implement the operational data bases and systems that they require. The result is the early delivery of priority systems, and progressive evolution of the corporate data model as more projects move through to operational detail. Both of these are important objectives of the CIO.

Systems development previously has worked on individual application systems. The later integration of these separate systems has been diffi-

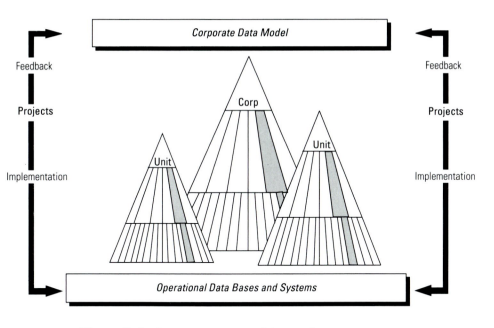

Figure 1.4 Progressive project delivery of priority systems.

cult. Bridges between systems have had to be built to enable them to work together; or instead significant changes have had to be made in existing systems. This has often been compared to fitting together a complex jigsaw puzzle . . . without an understanding of the overall jigsaw picture.

The strategic model provides that overall picture: either corporate-wide or for specific business unit projects. The tactical models are sections of the jigsaw picture that should be put together first. Operational models are completed sections. The process models show how the pieces in these sections fit internally, and also how those sections are externally interfaced, or integrated, with other tactical and operational models and their process models. This is achieved using strategic systems development as described in this book. Corporate and business unit strategic plans provide input to the analysis, design and generation methods used by Information Engineering, shown in Figure 1.5.

Strategic systems development is based on Information Engineering; we will discuss this shortly. Systems that have been developed with this approach can use the best hardware or software technologies available. They can be implemented using either traditional or relational Data Base Management Systems (DBMS or RDBMS). They use third, fourth or fifth generation languages: either conventional or object-oriented. The resulting systems can be implemented on mainframes, minis or micros: either centralized or distributed. These information systems can accommodate

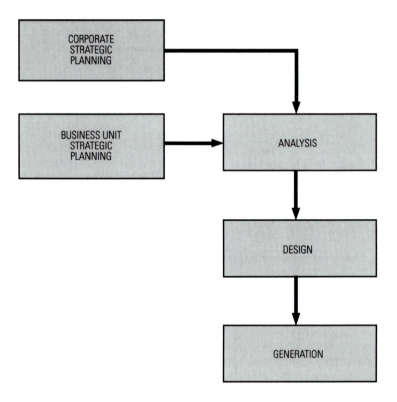

Figure 1.5 Strategic plans provide input to development.

business and technological changes more readily than systems developed using traditional systems development methods based on Business Systems Planning (BSP) [13] or Software Engineering [14, 15]. As summarized by Smith [16]:

> 'The original BSP technique resulted in models (or architectures) too fuzzy or high-level to be implemented. Systems builders simply did not know how to transform the BSP study into actual data structures and working code.'

1.2 INFORMATION ENGINEERING

Information Engineering is a set of techniques which enable managers and users, with no computer experience, to work in a design partnership with data processing staff. Together they can design manual or automated systems that satisfy the information and processing needs of the managers and users.

We will use the term **users** in this book to refer collectively to these managers and users. Those users with detailed expertise in particular parts of the business we refer to as **business experts**. We will refer to systems analysts and business analysts collectively as **analysts**.

My earlier book, *An Introduction to Information Engineering* [17], provides a more extensive introduction to this subject. It defines the term as:

> *'Information Engineering is an integrated set of techniques, based on corporate strategic planning, which results in the analysis, design and development of systems which support those plans exactly. Information Engineering is applied by managers and users with no knowledge of computers, but instead with an expert knowledge of their business – in conjunction with expert systems which provide rapid feedback to management for refinement of the strategic plans.'*

The availability of managers and users with an expert knowledge of their business (the business experts) is an essential requirement. When these experts obtain rapid feedback from an evolving design, they refine their strategic and business plans accordingly. This feedback is provided in small projects by analysts experienced in Information Engineering. In large projects, which may cover major parts of an organization, the availability of expert systems software to provide automated support to the Information Engineering methodology is essential.

Systems developed using Information Engineering are represented as blueprints of the data needed by users to carry out their jobs. This offers a visual representation of data. This blueprint is referred to as a **data model**. Strategic, tactical and operational models discussed earlier are all examples of data models at different organizational or project levels. These data models can be defined by business experts without requiring any knowledge of computers. They illustrate detailed business knowledge of the experts. They are an exact specification of business requirements for development of systems.

1.3 ANALYSIS AND DESIGN METHODS

Information Engineering focuses on the information needs of an organization, rather than on its current procedures. It helps to identify the data that are fundamental to the operation of the organization, from which information needed by managers is derived. Data indicate *what* details the operational levels of an organization need, or what details are needed to measure achievement of specific *goals* or *objectives* set by management.

There may be many ways in which the data may be used, or may be processed. These indicate *how* the data are used: they are called *procedures*. Similarly there may be many ways which indicate *how* defined goals or objectives may be reached: these are called *strategies*. Strategies may comprise one or many procedures.

Many DP methods have been developed for the analysis and design of systems based on procedures. These include systems analysis and Business Systems Planning. They also include structured analysis and structured design. Because of their emphasis on procedures, these are all called **process-driven methods**.

In contrast, Information Engineering focuses on data rather than on procedures: it is therefore called a **data-driven method**. Other data-driven methods are based on the Warnier-Orr [18], and also Jackson [19], systems development methodologies. Each of these methods can be utilized by analysts for the analysis and design of both small and large systems. Information Engineering is, however, unique – as it can also be applied by users with no computer experience. They use it to analyze and design corporate-wide systems based on strategic plans set either for specific divisions or business units, or for the entire organization. They use it also to design the most effective organization structures based on those strategic plans.

It is now widely accepted that the data of an organization change more slowly than its procedures. Consequently systems designed based on data-driven methods have been found to be much more stable than systems designed using process-driven methods.

With Information Engineering, business experts define high-level information models, as well as detailed data models. The analysts design systems from these data models, rather than by interviewing the users (the traditional way to design systems using process-driven methods). They design and develop systems and data bases needed to satisfy the information defined by the data models.

Expert systems software generates the data bases automatically for a variety of DBMS (Data Base Management System) products. Analysts can then use systems development facilities and languages provided with these DBMS products to design and develop menus, screens, reports and programs to process the data stored in the data bases.

The quality of the systems developed using Information Engineering in this way has been found to be much higher than those developed using process-driven methods: due to the rapid feedback which the users receive. Interestingly, systems are also developed much faster because of the greater business understanding of the users. The users know the business. Analysts know computers. Each draws on the expertise of their respective disciplines. The result is a *design partnership*: the users provide the business design;

analysts provide the computer design. This is achieved by data modeling, covered in Part 2.

1.4 HOW TO USE THIS BOOK

We earlier discussed that strategic systems development integrates strategic planning and systems development. To address such a broad spectrum, as well as satisfying the specific interests that you may have, this book can be used in two ways:

- It can be read in Chapter sequence to gain an overall understanding of the strategic systems development methodology.
- It can be used as a Reference text in a project: read in sections according to the specific background and interests of the reader.

The book addresses three classes of reader:

- **Class 1:** Managers and users with no computer expertise: who are required to define or implement strategic plans and who want to use information technology for competitive advantage – using strategic plans as catalysts for the development of information systems that support those plans.
- **Class 2:** Project managers, middle managers and data administrators: charged with project responsibility to design and develop information systems directly based on those strategic plans.
- **Class 3:** Systems analysts, business analysts, data base administrators (DBAs) and programmers: charged with project responsibility to implement the information systems designed from strategic plans.

Each chapter is discussed in detail below, with its intended readership shown in square brackets as: [All] – essential reading for all readers; or with the class number – for example, [1, 2] for class 1 and 2 readers. *Class 2 readers should read every chapter.*

1.4.1 Part 1 – Introduction

This part contains one chapter, that is intended to be read by all classes of reader.

- **Chapter 1:** [All] introduces strategic systems development, strategic planning and Information Engineering methodologies. It indicates how the book can be used to satisfy different reader objectives.

1.4.2   Part 2 – Information engineering concepts

This provides an introduction to the data modeling and process modeling principles used by Information Engineering. An understanding of Chapters 2–4, and Chapter 7, is essential: these chapters should be read by all.

- **Chapter 2:** [All] introduces the Information Engineering terminology that is used for entities and attributes.

- **Chapter 3:** [All] provides an introduction to data mapping conventions. It shows how associations are used in a data map to represent strategies. It introduces the development of a data map from management statements of policies and strategies.

- **Chapter 4:** [All] introduces the concepts of business normalization – covering first, second, third, fourth and fifth business normal forms. This is used as a business technique for detailed strategic, tactical and operational modeling.

- **Chapter 5:** [2, 3] introduces process modeling concepts. It describes how logic is derived from a data model. While data redundancy is eliminated by business normalization, process modeling eliminates redundant logic. This is common, reusable logic – implemented as generic procedures or as object-oriented code.

- **Chapter 6:** [2, 3] shows that data flow diagrams can be derived from a data model. This is the reverse of the approach used by software engineering. The data map, together with procedure maps, represents the program module structure. Procedure maps are expressed in pseudocode: they can be implemented using procedural or non-procedural languages, either third, fourth or fifth generation and using either conventional or object-oriented approaches. Examples based on SQL are used to illustrate typical logic derived from data and procedure maps.

- **Chapter 7:** [All] discusses the stages of Information Engineering. It describes strategic, tactical and operational modeling – and the catalyst which is provided to modeling by strategic planning.

1.4.3   Part 3 – Strategic planning

This describes strategic management planning in detail, applied at the business unit or program level, and also at the corporate level. This is of particular interest to managers and users with no computer experience (Class 1 readers). It is essential reading also for Class 2 readers.

- **Chapter 8:** [1, 2] provides an overview of strategic management planning. The Management Questionnaire, used in all Information

Engineering projects to capture details of the current strategy, is described.

- **Chapter 9:** [1, 2] covers the technique of goal analysis used to evaluate strategic plans. It illustrates the application of this technique using responses from a typical Management Questionnaire.

- **Chapter 10:** [1, 2] discusses the steps involved in an internal appraisal, at either the business unit or corporate level of an organization, to identify its strengths and weaknesses. This addresses identified deficiencies in the existing strategic plan.

- **Chapter 11:** [1, 2] describes steps involved in carrying out an external appraisal of competitors. This is used to identify opportunities and threats which may impact the strategic plan defined in the earlier chapters.

- **Chapter 12:** [1, 2] next sets new, proactive strategic plans to achieve competitive advantage. Strategic gap analysis uses the internal appraisal (from Chapter 10) and the external appraisal (from Chapter 11) first to identify any performance gaps. Strategic alternatives are defined to address these gaps. Alternatives are selected to pursue feasible opportunities, or resolve potential difficulties that arise from competitor threats. The strategic rationale is documented with contingencies underlying the strategic plan. Strategies are refined and objectives are defined. The result is a refined strategic plan that incorporates the strategies from Chapter 9, and includes additional strategies which offer significant competitive advantage.

- **Chapter 13:** [1, 2] uses the strategic plan to develop a corporate strategic model. This identifies data entities that provide information needed by management based on the plan, and which offer great flexibility for proactive management.

- **Chapter 14:** [1, 2] focuses on defining an organization structure appropriate to the strategic plan. The corporate strategic model allows priority strategic functions to be identified. Different organization structures are defined; these are evaluated against the strategic model. Management flexibility is added to this model: through generic performance monitoring and documentation capabilities able to be used dynamically by management to monitor any areas of interest. From the strategic statements and objectives of Chapter 12, strategic attributes are identified to prepare for strategic implementation in Part 4, to support achievement of the plan.

1.4.4   Part 4 – Systems development

This covers systems development, based on strategic plans developed in Part 3. It uses data modeling concepts from Part 2 to develop the strategic, tactical and operational models which represent the various levels of the strategic plan. It is of specific interest to systems analysts, business analysts, DBAs and programmers (Class 3 readers). It is essential reading for Class 2 readers.

- **Chapter 15:** [2, 3] illustrates the development of a project strategic model based on priority strategic functions identified by management. It shows initial definition and evolution of a data model from the mission statement of a priority area.

- **Chapter 16:** [2, 3] expands the strategic model from Chapter 15 to tactical model detail, based on markets, products and services, and channels of the priority area.

- **Chapter 17:** [2, 3] discusses analysis of data models to identify priority systems for early development and delivery. It illustrates the development of a project plan from the data model, to manage the subsequent development activity.

- **Chapter 18:** [2, 3] expands the tactical model from Chapter 16 into operational model detail. It discusses three data modeling approaches: top-down, sideways-in and bottom-up. It shows cross-checking of the operational model using the source documents, enquiries, reports and file or data base formats of existing systems.

- **Chapter 19:** [2, 3] next uses process modeling to identify priority operational systems and project plans for their development. It shows the development of both high-level and detailed process models. This is a user-driven method for the design of object-oriented systems, for rapid development and easy maintainability.

- **Chapter 20:** [2, 3] discusses software development tools. It provides an overview of tools used with ORACLE RDBMS: SQL*Forms, SQL*Plus and SQL*Menu by Oracle Corporation. Similar tools are used with INGRES RDBMS: INGRES/QBF (Query-By-Forms), INGRES/MENU, INGRES ABF/4GL (Applications-By-Forms) and INGRES/Windows 4GL by Ingres Corporation are also overviewed. These tools are typical of many DBMS systems development products today; they are used in Chapters 21 and 22 to implement operational data bases and systems.

- **Chapter 21:** [2, 3] describes the design and development of data entry screens. It shows the generation of SQL data base tables from an operational model, and the generation of default screens from that data base using SQL*Forms, and also QBF. These default screens are then refined for data entry use.

- **Chapter 22:** [2, 3] shows design and development of application screens, linked with data entry screens into application systems using

SQL*Forms with process models from Chapter 19. The resulting systems are then linked by SQL*Menu to produce complex analysis systems. Capacity planning of designed data bases, and performance analysis of designed transactions and systems, is carried out.

- **Chapter 23:** [All] provides a summary of the book. This chapter brings together the various concepts covered in earlier chapters, emphasizing both the technology-independent and the technology-dependent aspects of strategic systems development. It can be read immediately after this Chapter 1 (if you wish) to gain an overall perspective of Information Engineering.

1.4.5 Appendices

- **Appendix 1:** provides a tutorial introduction to SQL, for readers who are not familiar with this non-procedural language.
- **Appendix 2:** provides the full documentation of the Cluster Report discussed in conjunction with IE: Expert in Chapter 17.

1.5 SUMMARY

In this chapter we discussed strategic planning and systems development. We saw that traditional strategic planning has suffered from many problems. Those problems due to ineffective communication, or misinterpretation, of the directions set by management are magnified by a long feedback cycle before information is available for refinement of the strategic plans: typically 3–5 years.

We discussed that strategic management planning emerged to address these problems. Continual evaluation and refinement of the plan at all stages of development, and also during implementation, is a characteristic of strategic management planning. Feedback is available to management within weeks, and sometimes even in days. This feedback is achieved through modeling at three levels of a project area: through strategic, tactical and operational modeling. The project area can be a complete corporation, or a business unit, department, section, functional area, or an application area.

We also discussed systems development: the process-driven methods of Business Systems Planning (BSP), systems analysis, structured analysis and structured design; and the data-driven methodologies of Jackson, of Warnier-Orr, and of Information Engineering. We discussed that business changes bring about changes in procedures more often than changes in the data on which the business is based. Systems developed using the process-driven methodologies may have to change greatly. But the systems developed using data-driven methodologies can accommodate business changes with less disruption, as they are based on a more stable foundation: data.

We saw that strategic management planning, when used with Information Engineering, results in strategic systems development. This is the subject of the book.

The chapter concluded with a guide to reading the book, based on the background and experience of different readers. Three classes of reader were addressed:

- Managers and users with business knowledge, but no computer expertise.

- Project managers, middle managers and data administrators who have been given the project responsibility to design and develop information systems based on strategic plans.

- Systems analysts, business analysts, DBAs and programmers charged with the project responsibility to implement information systems that have been designed from strategic plans.

References

[1] Fahey, L. and Christensen, H. K. (1986). Evaluating the Research on Strategy Content, *Journal of Management*, Vol 12, No 2.

[2] Huff, A. S. and Reger, R. K. (1987). A Review of Strategic Process Research, *Journal of Management*, Vol 13, No 2.

[3] Schendel, D. E. and Hofer, C. W. (1979). *Strategic Management: A New View of Business Policy and Planning*, Little, Brown & Company: USA.

[4] Chandler, A. D. (1962). *Strategy and Structure: Chapters in the History of the American Industrial Enterprise*, MIT Press: Cambridge, MA.

[5] Ansoff, H. I. (1965). *Corporate Strategy*, McGraw-Hill: New York, NY.

[6] Andrews, K. R. (1971). *The Concept of Corporate Strategy*, Irwin: Homewood, IL.

[7] Gray, D. H. (1986). *Uses and Misuses of Strategic Planning*, Harvard Business Review: Boston, MA (Jan–Feb).

[8] Nolan, R. L. (1987). What Transformation Is, in *Stage by Stage*, Nolan, Norton & Co: Boston, MA Vol 7, No 5.

[9] Drucker, P. (1974). *Management: Tasks, Responsibilities, Practices*, Harper & Row: New York, NY.

[10] Porter, M. E. (1980). *Competitive Strategy*, Free Press, MacMillan Publishing: New York, NY.

[11] Porter, M. E. (1985). *Competitive Advantage*, Free Press, MacMillan Publishing: New York, NY.

[12] EDP Analyzer, (1984). *The Chief Information Officer Role*, Canning Publications, Vol. 22, No. 11.

[13] *Business Systems Planning: Information Systems Planning Guide*, IBM Corporation: White Plains, NY (1981) IBM Reference No. GE20-0527.

[14] Yourdon, E. and Constantine, L. (1978). *Structured Design: Fundamentals of a Discipline of Computer Program Systems Design*, Prentice-Hall: Englewood Cliffs, NJ.

[15] De Marco, T. (1982). *Software Systems Development*, Yourdon Press: New York, NY.

[16] Smith, W. G. (1990). The Requirements for an IRM Environment, Data Base Advisor, Part of Data Base Newsletter: Boston, MA (May–June).

[17] Finkelstein, C. (1989). *An Introduction to Information Engineering*, Addison-Wesley: Reading, MA.

[18] Orr, K. (1977). *Structured Systems Development*, Yourdon Press: New York, NY.

[19] Jackson, M. (1975). *Principles of Program Design*, Academic Press: New York, NY.

PART TWO

Information
Engineering Concepts

CHAPTER 2

Introduction to Data Modeling

This chapter describes terminology used in an Information Engineering project for data modeling. An appreciation of these terms is essential for an understanding of the book, and for effective participation in a project.

2.1 DATA MODELING

Data modeling is a process used to identify, communicate and record details about data and the relationships which exist between data. Several data modeling approaches exist, including: entity-relationship modeling (E–R) [1, 2]; extended entity-relationship modeling (EER) [3, 4]; semantic modeling [5]; and binary modeling [6]. We will use a business data modeling approach [7], with its own terminology and conventions. These terms include: **data entities** (which represent data to be stored for later reference); **data attributes** (which indicate specific details contained in entities); and **data associations** (which indicate relationships that exist between entities). These are abbreviated to entities, attributes and associations.

In a computer system which is subsequently developed from a data model, entities are implemented as records or as tables, depending on the DBMS products used. Attributes are implemented as fields within a record, or as columns within a table. Associations are implemented as data base relationships, or as tables joined via common keys. We will use **entity**, **attribute** and **association** when we refer to data in its logical form; we will

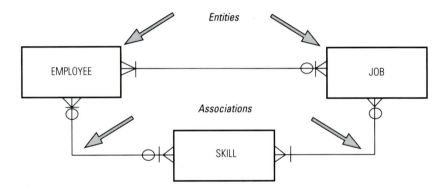

Figure 2.1 An Information Engineering data map.

use **record** or **table, field** or **column** and **relationship** or **join** respectively when we refer to data in its physical form in a computer system.

Entities may contain data of interest to different parts of an organization. We will call each of these parts a **functional area**. A functional area may contain many entities. It may be as large as a division or business unit, or as small as a branch, a section, a work unit or a function.

A data model comprises both a graphical representation, called a **data map** as well as detailed reports of defined entities, attributes and associations. A data map shows entities as boxes, with the name of the entity written within the box in capitals and in the singular. Associations are shown as lines joining entity boxes. Associations are named, but (distinct from the DP variant of Information Engineering) the name of the association is not written on a data map. A typical data map is illustrated in Figure 2.1.

Attributes are not shown on a data map. They are written in the singular in lower case italics and recorded in an **entity list**. This is one of the data modeling reports which, together with the data map, comprise the data model.

Data modeling uses a process called **business normalization**. This is a set of rules which helps to identify required entities, attributes and associations. It concentrates on placing attributes in the entities where they belong, so that the data can be used most effectively. Business normalization is used to identify data needed by current systems. It also can be used to help identify data required by proposed future systems in the project area. Business normalization is described in Chapter 4.

2.2 DATA ENTITIES

As we saw, entities represent data to be stored for later reference. For example, for employees who occupy jobs in an organization, we are interested in details about those employees and their jobs. EMPLOYEE and JOB represent two data entities – we may want to store these details for reference many times. Entities are always written in the singular and in capitals.

Specific details such as *employee name* and *employee address*, or *job title* and *job salary* are attributes of EMPLOYEE and JOB respectively. It is sometimes difficult to distinguish between an entity and an attribute, however. As a general rule, an entity suggests additional detailed information that we need. For example we may require details about employees such as *employee name* and *employee address*. EMPLOYEE therefore is an entity. But further details about a name are not needed: *employee name* is thus an attribute of EMPLOYEE; not another entity.

We must be able to identify uniquely each occurrence of an entity. This is achieved by an identifying attribute, called a **primary key**. Sometimes two or more attributes may have to be combined to establish uniqueness: called a **compound primary key**. For example, each employee in an organization has a unique employee number. This ensures that employee details relate to the correct employee, and that the correct salary is paid to that employee. We would therefore define the attribute *employee number* as the primary key of EMPLOYEE. To show that it is a key, the attribute name is suffixed with a # (hash or pound); to show that it is in fact a primary key, it is also underlined thus: *employee number#*. A primary key may be a number, or a name, or a code – but it must be unique. This means we could not use *employee name#* as a primary key. If we did, we would not be able to employ more than one John Smith!

There are six main types of entities used in a data model. These are:

- Principal entities
- Secondary entities
- Intersecting entities
- Type entities
- Role entities
- Structure entities

The type, role and structure entities above are called **meta-entities**: they are used to provide information about the other entities listed above them.

2.2.1 Principal entities

A **principal entity** is an entity of interest to a number of different functional areas in an organization. It may be stored and updated centrally, but accessed from different areas. Some areas may have authority to update details held in a principal entity; others may only be allowed to refer to occurrences of the entity, but not change data held within it. For example, EMPLOYEE would be a principal entity: several departments may need to refer to details about employees. These may be the Sales, Personnel and Executive Management Departments.

We discussed that the primary key of EMPLOYEE is *employee number#*. A principal entity often uses only one primary key as a unique identifier. The entity and the attributes within it (see earlier) can be written in an entity list as:

EMPLOYEE   (employee number #, employee name, employee address)

2.2.2 Secondary entities

A **secondary entity** contains details of interest to only part of an organization. It is linked to a principal entity. It removes from that entity the attributes of interest only to one or two functional areas, rather than all areas who are interested in the principal entity.

Data maps which include secondary entities permit a more precise representation of the data important to different parts of the organization. Specific business expertise can be incorporated more accurately. Application systems can be developed faster and more correctly from a data map if secondary entities are used as they indicate necessary program logic more clearly.

For example, secondary entities are used if an organization wants to keep specific details separate for certain types of employees – such as quota and sales to date for each sales person. SALES PERSON is therefore a secondary entity. It contains the attributes of: *sales person quota* and *sales person sales to date* which are of interest to the sales department. Similarly, details of interest to executive management – such as *manager reporting level* and *manager title* – are held in a MANAGER secondary

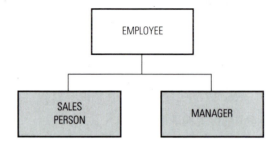

Figure 2.2   A data map with secondary entities.

entity. Each Department needs common attributes in the principal entity EMPLOYEE, such as *employee name* and *employee address*. This is illustrated in Figure 2.2.

Secondary entities are related to principal entities and so have the same primary key. Thus the primary key of SALES PERSON and of MANAGER is also *employee number#*. The employee number can thus be used to obtain details common to all employees, as well as details specific to sales persons and to managers. These entities and their attributes would be written in entity list form as:

EMPLOYEE   (employee number#, employee name, employee address)

SALES PERSON   (employee number#, sales person quota, sales person sales to date)

MANAGER   (employee number#, manager title, manager reporting level)

2.2.3 Intersecting entities

In data modeling we will find situations between two entities, such as EMPLOYEE and JOB, where a **many to many** association exists. That is, an employee may have one or many jobs, and a job may be held by one or many employees. This is shown in a data map by crows feet (which indicate **one or many**) at each end of the association line joining the related entities (see Figure 2.3).

A many to many association is difficult to implement in an application system: it is hard to determine which jobs an employee has carried out, or which employees have occupied a job. To resolve this, an intermediate entity is created which cross-references employees and jobs. This is called an **intersecting entity**. It is often named by combining the names of the two entities related by the many to many association, such as EMPLOYEE JOB as shown in Figure 2.4.

An intersecting entity may have a combined primary key made up from the primary keys of the two entities in the many to many association; or it may instead be given a single, unique primary key. If EMPLOYEE has the primary key of *employee number#* and JOB has the primary key of *job number#*, then the primary key of EMPLOYEE JOB is combined as

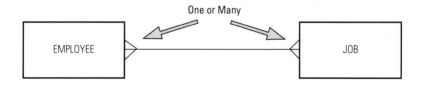

Figure 2.3 A many to many association.

Figure 2.4 An intersecting entity resolves a many to many association.

employee number#, *job number#*. This is a **compound primary key**. It can be used as a cross-reference. Or instead, a single unique primary key of *employee job number#*, or alternatively *position number#* may be defined.

A compound primary key that includes employee number allows all jobs that have been held by the employee to be easily determined. Similarly, if a job number is included, all employees holding that job can be found. Other details relevant for a specific job held by a particular employee may be the date the job was first occupied by the employee and the salary paid. Thus the attributes *employee job start date* and *employee job salary* would also be held in the intersecting entity EMPLOYEE JOB, as follows:

EMPLOYEE JOB   (employee number#, job number#, employee job start date, employee job salary)

Given an employee number and a job number, the start date and the salary paid can be found for that employee.

2.2.4 Type entities

We know that a principal entity can have a number of types, which are shown in a data map as secondary entities (see Figure 2.2). A **type entity** is used to indicate that a number of types exist for the principal entity, and is linked to the principal entity as shown in Figure 2.5. A type entity is a meta-entity, as it contains information about other entities.

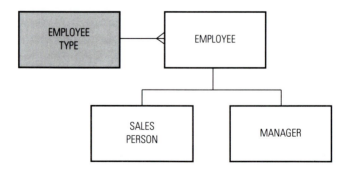

Figure 2.5 A type entity indicates types exist for a principal entity.

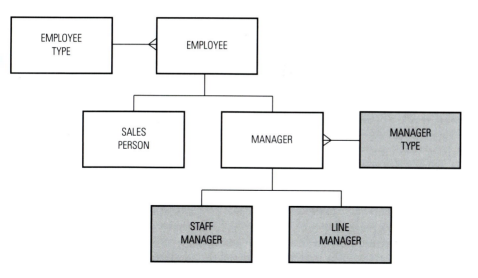

Figure 2.6   A secondary entity may have types.

A secondary entity can also have types. There may be several types of managers, such as STAFF MANAGER and LINE MANAGER. This is indicated by a type entity linked to a secondary entity, as shown in Figure 2.6 with MANAGER TYPE. In this figure the principal entity EMPLOYEE is known as a typed principal entity, while the secondary entity MANAGER is known as a typed secondary entity.

Generally a type entity indicates that a specific occurrence of an entity can have only one secondary entity associated to it. In Figure 2.5 this is implied by the association between EMPLOYEE TYPE and EMPLOYEE. The crows foot at the end closest to EMPLOYEE indicates one or many: no crows foot at the end closest to EMPLOYEE TYPE indicates one. This means that a specific employee type can have one or many employees, but that an employee can be of only one type. It means that an employee can be either a sales person, or a manager, but not both. Similarly in Figure 2.6 a manager can be either a staff manager, or a line manager, but not both.

A type entity is implemented in an application system as a table. This indicates the number and names of all secondary entities related to a typed principal entity (or to a typed secondary entity). In data modeling there is no limit to the number of secondary entities for a type entity, apart from physical constraints imposed by the computer hardware and software selected to implement the application system.

A type entity has a primary key, usually named by suffixing the word 'number' or 'id' (for 'identifier') after the entity name, as in *employee*

Table 2.1 Contents of EMPLOYEE TYPE table for Figure 2.5

Employee type number	Employee type name
0	Employee
1	Sales person
2	Manager

type number# or *employee type id#*. It has a second attribute, such as *employee type name* which contains the name of the secondary entity identified by the type number and can have others. Thus the contents of the EMPLOYEE TYPE table in Figure 2.5, for the secondary entities shown, would be as illustrated in Table 2.1.

A typed principal entity (or typed secondary entity) is usually given a type number of 0 (zero). In an application system, each type of employee can thus be easily identified. *Employee type number* represents the employee record code if using traditional file access methods or DBMS products, or employee table number if using relational DBMS products. When later implemented in a data base it may also contain other attributes, such as the geographic location of specific files or tables in a distributed data base environment, and the number of occurrences (data volume) in each file or table.

Because a type entity is linked to a typed principal or typed secondary entity, its key is also included in the relevant entity, such as *employee type number#*. It is called a **foreign key** in that entity, as it relates it to the type entity where the key exists as a primary key. To distinguish them from primary keys, foreign keys are not underlined. The entities in Figure 2.5 therefore contain the following attributes, with a foreign key in EMPLOYEE:

EMPLOYEE TYPE   (employee type number#, employee type name)

EMPLOYEE   (employee number#, employee name, employee address, employee type number#)

2.2.5 Role entities

Figure 2.5 – where an employee can be either a sales person, or a manager, but not both – indicates a very restrictive employment strategy. Taken literally, it means that once hired as one type of employee, that person cannot change to the other. But over time an organization may promote sales persons to managers, and vice versa. This is shown in Figure 2.7 by a crows foot at each end of the association line between EMPLOYEE TYPE and

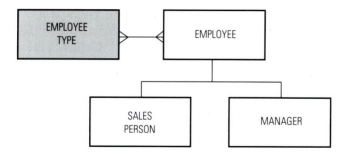

Figure 2.7 A principal entity can be of more than one type.

EMPLOYEE, where an employee type has one or many employees, and an employee can be one or many employee types.

We now know that a many to many association between two entities is decomposed into an intermediate, intersecting entity. Where the many to many association is between a principal (or secondary) entity and a type entity, the intersecting entity which results is called a **role entity**. It is usually named by adding the suffix 'role' to the name of the principal (or secondary) entity, as we can see with EMPLOYEE ROLE in Figure 2.8. A role entity is a meta-entity, as it provides information about the entities it interrelates: the relevant type and principal entities.

As it is an intersecting entity, EMPLOYEE ROLE has a compound primary key. This comprises the primary keys used for the principal and type entities, such as *employee number#*, *employee type number#*. The foreign key in the principal entity (*employee type number#* in EMPLOYEE) is moved out of that entity when it is part of the primary key of EMPLOYEE ROLE.

EMPLOYEE ROLE may contain other details of interest, such as the date an employee was first appointed to a role, and the person's evaluation

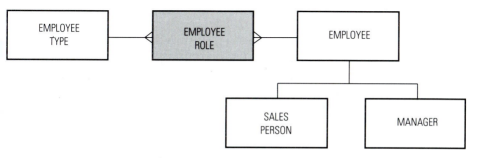

Figure 2.8 Role entity if principal is more than one type.

rating in that role. This indicates additional attributes of: *employee role start date* and *employee role rating* in EMPLOYEE ROLE, and is written in entity list form as follows:

EMPLOYEE TYPE   (employee type number#, employee type name)

EMPLOYEE   (employee number#, employee name, employee address)

EMPLOYEE ROLE   (employee number#, employee type number#, employee role start date, employee role rating)

2.2.6 Structure entities

We have so far seen examples where *all* occurrences of one entity are related to *all* occurrences of a different entity. For example, the associations between EMPLOYEE, JOB and EMPLOYEE JOB in Figure 2.4 apply to all employees and all jobs. There are many cases, however, where an association exists only between specific occurrences of an entity or entity type. An example is: employees who report to another employee, who is a manager. Managers also report to other managers. This indicates the presence of two recursive associations as shown in Figure 2.9. Similarly, a manager may be responsible for many sales persons, who in turn may have many managers (over time). This is shown by the many to many association in Figure 2.9 between SALES PERSON and MANAGER.

In this example we have considered only two types of employees: sales persons and managers. But line managers may report to staff managers (see Figure 2.6). And what of sales persons for which these different types of managers are responsible – either directly (as line managers) or indirectly (as staff managers). There may also be many other types of employees who are interrelated.

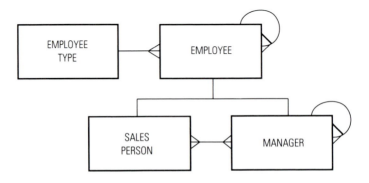

Figure 2.9 Recursive associations.

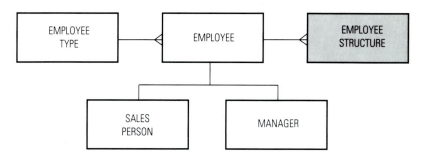

Figure 2.10   A structure entity for EMPLOYEE.

To represent these rather complex associations, we use a **structure entity**. This is a table which allows us to record the associations between occurrences of the same entity or entity type. It is linked to the relevant principal entity and is named by appending 'structure' to the principal entity name (see Figure 2.10). A structure entity is a meta-entity, as it provides information about occurrences of other entities that are interrelated.

A structure entity usually has two primary keys: the primary key of the principal entity and that of its type entity – each of which is further duplicated as a foreign key. In Figure 2.10, EMPLOYEE STRUCTURE therefore has primary and foreign keys of *employee number#*, *employee type number#*, as follows:

EMPLOYEE STRUCTURE   (employee number#, employee type number#, employee number#, employee type number#)

This allows an employee of one type to be related to an employee of the same or another type. Other forms of the structure entity may include the duplicated primary key of the principal entity only; or instead the duplicated primary key of the type entity only – this latter example representing a **type structure** entity. Another structure entity form includes a reason for the interrelated entity occurrence and a relevant date, as: *employee relationship reason* and *employee relationship start date* – dependent now on all four keys in EMPLOYEE STRUCTURE above.

A structure entity is usually implemented as a table. For example Table 2.2 illustrates some typical employee relationships which would be stored in a structure entity. On the right-hand side it lists all employees who report to Manager 1358. Managers 1362 and 1556 also have other sales persons reporting to them. We can see how an employee occurrence is related to other types of employees. The left-hand side thus indicates 'is responsible for', while the right-hand side indicates 'reports to'.

Table 2.2   A table to implement a structure entity

Employee number	Employee type number	Employee number	Employee type number
1358	Manager	1362	Manager
		1460	Sales person
		1556	Manager
		1661	Sales person
1362	Manager	262	Sales person
		1132	Sales person
		1441	Sales person
1556	Manager	1333	Sales person
		1512	Sales person

Note: This table is incorrect: it shows *employee type number* columns with 'Manager' and 'Sales person' as character values, not numbers of 2 and 1 respectively from Table 2.1. We will however use these character values for illustrative purposes in Table 2.2.

2.3 DATA ATTRIBUTES

We saw several examples of attributes when we discussed entities above. We saw that attributes become data fields in a file or data base record, or columns in a table. We will now consider attributes in more detail.

There are two main types of attributes, **keys** and **non-keys**. To ensure a unique name is used for each non-key it is normally preceded by the name of the entity in which it resides.

2.3.1 Keys

A key must have a unique name, but it can reside in many entities. Each of those entities is thus potentially related through the presence of common keys, such as:

- Primary keys
- Foreign keys
- Compound keys
- Candidate keys

Primary keys

A **primary key** uniquely identifies an entity. To show that it is a key, the attribute name is suffixed with a # (hash or pound). It is underlined to indicate that it is a primary key, such as *employee number#*. An entity always has at least one primary key, but can have many – as discussed below under Compound Keys. Primary keys are listed before other attributes in an entity.

Secondary entities usually have the same primary key as the principal entity to which they belong. Thus SALES PERSON, MANAGER and EMPLOYEE all have the same primary key: *employee number#*.

A primary key is implemented as a unique index to a file, data base record or table. This allows the specific employee details to be found for a given employee number.

Foreign keys

A **foreign key** in one entity is used to identify another entity to which the first entity is related. The foreign key may exist in that second entity as either a primary key, or as another foreign key. A foreign key must, however, exist in at least one entity as a primary key. It indicates the potential existence of associations between entities which have the same key.

As for a primary key, a foreign key is suffixed with a # (hash or pound) but is *not* underlined. Foreign keys are generally always listed after all other attributes, as with *employee type number#* in EMPLOYEE and EMPLOYEE TYPE:

EMPLOYEE TYPE   (employee type number#, employee type name)

EMPLOYEE   (employee number#, employee name, employee address, employee type number#)

As for primary keys, foreign keys are also implemented as unique indexes to files, data base records or tables. This allows related entities to be located which have the same foreign or primary key.

Compound keys

A **compound key** occurs when there are two or more primary keys in an entity, as with intersecting entities and structure entities. More than one key is needed to establish uniqueness. For example, we can determine specific details about an employee in a particular job if we have a compound primary key which is made up of *employee number#*, *job number#* in EMPLOYEE JOB. This establishes uniqueness.

Candidate keys

There may be more than one key attribute which can be used to identify an entity uniquely. Each is therefore referred to as a **candidate key**. For example, a job may be uniquely identified by *job number#*, or by *job title#*. Both are candidate keys. The specific attribute chosen from these candidates then becomes the primary key, such as *job number#* in our previous examples.

2.3.2 Non-keys

Distinct from keys (which can reside in many entities) a non-key can reside in only one entity if it has been correctly normalized (see Chapter 4). It must have a unique name, which it usually takes from the name of the entity in which it resides. There are several types of non-keys. These are:

- Selection attributes
- Group attributes
- Repeating group attributes
- Derived attributes
- Non-key attributes

Selection attributes (secondary keys)

A **selection attribute** is used to locate an entity when a key is not unique, such as an *employee name*. It may also be called a **secondary key**, which has been carried over from data processing terminology. In spite of its DP name it is classified as a non-key attribute, rather than a key attribute such as a primary or foreign key. As more than one employee may have the same name, *employee name* can be used to locate each employee with that name. Another example is *postcode* or *zipcode*. When used for employees, all persons living in the same postal area can be located. A selection attribute is also called an alternative access key.

When written in an entity list, a selection attribute or secondary key is indicated by surrounding it with single square left and right brackets, such as [*employee name*] and [*employee postcode*]:

EMPLOYEE (employee number#, [employee name], employee address, [employee postcode])

It is implemented in an application system as a non-unique index (duplicates are allowed) for the relevant file, data base record or table.

Group attributes

A *group attribute* is a non-key. It indicates a group of more detailed attributes which reside within it, to be defined in detail at a later time. For example an attribute *address* may be made up of *street number, street name, suburb* and *city. Address* is therefore a group attribute. It can be used to refer to all of these detailed address attributes.

In an entity list, a group attribute is indicated by surrounding it with single left and right curved brackets, such as (*employee address*):

EMPLOYEE   (employee number #, [employee name], (employee address), [employee postcode])

Repeating group attributes

A **repeating group** is also a non-key. It indicates that there may be one or several occurrences of the relevant attribute(s) in an entity. For example, an employee may receive several pay rises (over a period of time) while in the same job. If we need to keep each salary paid and the date payment commenced, then *employee job salary commencement date* and *employee job salary amount* is a repeating group in entity EMPLOYEE JOB. A repeating group is indicated in an entity list by surrounding it with *double* left and right curved brackets, such as:

EMPLOYEE JOB   (employee number #, job number #, employee job start date, ((employee job salary commencement date, employee job salary amount)))

Derived attributes

Some attributes are derived from other attributes. Depending on how frequently a derived attribute is referenced, and the amount of processing needed to derive it, it may not be stored. If its reference is infrequent and it requires little derivation processing, it is derived whenever needed. However if it needs much processing and it is frequently referenced, it may still be stored. It is derived only when the values involved in its derivation change.

Regardless of whether a derived attribute is stored or not, it still exists and **must** be represented in data modeling. We indicate a derived attribute by surrounding it by single left and right curly braces, such as {*sales person sales to date*}:

SALES PERSON   (employee number #, sales person quota, {sales person sales to date})

This is derived from the total of all sales made by a sales person to the current date.

Non-key attributes

If a non-key is not a selection attribute (secondary key), a group attribute or a repeating group attribute, then it is called a **non-key attribute**. This indicates that it is a fundamental data attribute.

A non-key attribute is written in an entity list with no special symbols. The example of MANAGER, next, indicates that *manager title* is a secondary key (because of the single left and right square brackets), while *manager reporting level* has no special symbols surrounding it and so is a non-key attribute:

MANAGER   (employee number #, [manager title], manager reporting level)

In discussing data modeling, we used two forms of documentation: the data map and the entity list. Together these comprise a data model. We discuss data map conventions in detail in Chapter 3. The conventions for writing entity lists are covered next.

2.4 ENTITY LIST DOCUMENTATION CONVENTIONS

An entity list is a convenient shorthand way of documenting entities and attributes. It is a useful notation for writing the results of data modeling sessions. It may be used for direct input to software which automates data modeling.

ENTITY   (primary key 1#, primary key 2#, . . .
           [selection attribute 1], [selection attribute 2], . . .
           (group attribute 1), (group attribute 2), . . .
           ((repeating group 1)), ((repeating group 2)), . . .
           {derived attribute 1}, {derived attribute 2}, . . .
           non-key attribute 1, non-key attribute 2, . . .
           foreign key 1#, foreign key 2#, . . .)

When identifying attributes in data modeling, the rightmost curved bracket surrounding all of the attributes is sometimes left off. This indicates that there are more attributes still to be identified in later modeling sessions. Using these documentation conventions, each of the earlier entity examples are listed below, in the entity list for the data map in Figure 2.11.

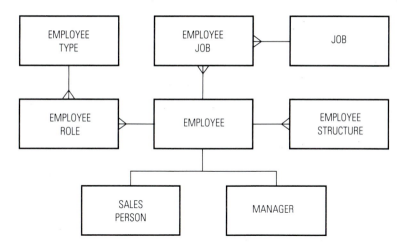

Figure 2.11   The data map for all entities discussed in this chapter.

EMPLOYEE TYPE	(employee type number #, employee type name)
EMPLOYEE ROLE	(employee number #, employee type number #, employee role start date, employee role rating)
EMPLOYEE	(employee number #, [employee name], (employee address), [employee postcode])
SALES PERSON	(employee number #, sales person quota, {sales person sales to date})
MANAGER	(employee number #, [manager title], manager reporting level)
EMPLOYEE STRUCTURE	(employee number #, employee type number #, employee number #, employee type number #)
EMPLOYEE JOB	(employee number #, job number #, employee job start date, ((employee job salary commencement date, employee job salary amount)))
JOB	(job number #, [job title], job standard salary)

While the sequence of attributes in the entity list is useful, the only real requirement is that keys are indicated with a # suffix, primary keys are underlined, and each type of attribute is indicated by its surrounding brackets (or none, for non-key attributes).

We have now covered the basic data modeling terminology relating to entities and attributes in an Information Engineering project. We have seen examples of entity lists and data maps. However the associations used in these data map examples were only conceptual: for example we did not use any of the symbols on the association lines as illustrated in Figure 2.1. We need now to consider the terminology and conventions used to represent associations. This is the subject of the next chapter.

2.5 SUMMARY

In this chapter we defined the terminology used in data modeling. We discussed data entities, used to represent data stored for later reference. Data attributes provide specific details about entities. Associations are used to indicate how entities are related.

A data model comprises a data map and its entity list. The data map is a schematic representation of entities and associations. The entity list documents entities and the attributes that reside within them.

We saw that there are a number of types of entities in a data model:

- Principal entities, that contain data to be shared by all authorized areas.
- Secondary entities, that contain data of interest only to some areas.
- Intersecting entities, formed by decomposing many to many associations.
- Type entities, that indicate the secondary entities for a principal entity.
- Role entities, for principal and secondary entities of more than one type.
- Structure entities, for recursive associations as interrelated occurrences of principal or secondary entities.

We saw that type, role and structure entities are meta-entities: they provide information about other entities.

We discussed the different types of attributes:

- **Keys:** Primary keys, compound keys, foreign keys, and candidate keys.
- **Non-keys:** Selection attributes (also called secondary keys), derived attributes, group attributes, repeating group attributes and non-key attributes.

We concluded the chapter by defining the entity list documentation conventions.

References

[1] Chen, P. (1976). The Entity Relationship Model: Toward a Unified View of Data, *ACM Trans. on Database Systems*, pp. 9–36.

[2] Dampney, C. N. G. (1987). Specifying a Semantically Adequate Structure for Information Systems and Databases, *Proc of 6th Int'l Conf on E-R Approach*, New York, pp. 143–164.

[3] Kozaczynski, W. and Lillien, L. (1987). An Extended Entity-Relationship (E^{2}R) Database Specification and Transformation into the Logical Relational Design, *Proc of 6th Int'l Conf on E-R Approach*, New York, pp. 497–513.

[4] Teory, T. J, Yang, D. and Fry, J. P. (1986). A Logical Design Methodology for Relational Data Bases Using the Extended Entity-Relationship Model, *Computing Surveys*, Vol 18, No 2 (June 1986) pp. 197–222.

[5] Rolland, C. (1988). Recent Techniques for Information Modeling, *Proc of Joint Int'l Symp. on Information Systems*, Sydney, pp. 345–360.

[6] Thompson, P. S. (1987). The Object and Role of Binary Modeling, *Proc of 6th Int'l Conf on E-R Approach*, New York, pp. 55–64.

[7] Finkelstein, C. (1989). *An Introduction to Information Engineering*, Addison-Wesley: Reading, MA.

CHAPTER 3

Data Mapping Conventions

We discussed in Chapter 2 the conventions used to represent entities and attributes in an entity list. This is one of the documentation components of a data model. The data map is the other component. We saw examples of data maps used to illustrate the different entity types. Data maps allow strategic alternatives to be shown visually and assist management at different levels to refine their strategic and business plans. This chapter discusses the documentation conventions used for data maps in more detail. We will use these conventions extensively in later chapters of the book.

3.1 DATA ASSOCIATIONS

We saw that associations represent relationships which exist between entities. They are shown in a data map as lines joining related entity boxes. While entities and the attributes within them indicate *what* data are available, associations indicate *how* the data are used. They are used to represent strategies in strategic planning, and at a detailed level indicate procedures in daily operational processing.

3.1.1 Association degree

An association has two characteristics, degree and nature. Association degree is sometimes called association cardinality by other data modeling

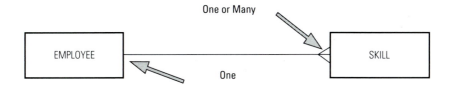

Figure 3.1   An association degree example.

Figure 3.2   Many to many association example.

Figure 3.3   Many to many association becomes an intersecting entity.

methods. In Chapter 2 we saw basic examples of association **degree** when we used a crows foot to represent many and no crows foot to represent one, as in Figure 3.1 which shows an association between EMPLOYEE and SKILL. Both ends of the line represent a relevant association degree. This indicates that an employee has one or many skills, and that a skill is held by one employee. Figure 3.2 represents a refinement on this data map: it indicates that while an employee has one or many skills, a skill may be held by one or many employees.

We saw in Chapter 2 that when a many to many association exists, as in Figure 3.2, it results in the creation of an intersecting entity (EMPLOYEE SKILL) with two one to many associations as shown in Figure 3.3.

3.1.2   Association nature

Association nature indicates whether an association between entities is optional, mandatory or optional becoming mandatory. This is represented at each end of an association line: with a circle if it is optional, a vertical bar if it is mandatory, and both a circle and a vertical bar if it is optional becoming mandatory. This enables us to add a refinement to the data map in Figure 3.1, illustrated now as Figure 3.4.

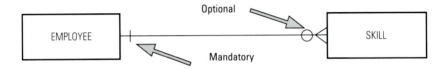

Figure 3.4 An example of association nature.

Figure 3.5 A variation on the association nature of Figure 3.4.

In discussing association nature, we use the word **may** to indicate optional, and **must** to indicate mandatory. Figure 3.4 therefore indicates that an employee **may** have zero, one or many skills, and that a skill **must** be held by one (and only one) employee. A variation on this is shown in Figure 3.5 which indicates that while an employee initially may have no skills, eventually the employee must have one or many skills. An association nature of optional becoming mandatory suggests a time element: we use the word **will** to show the imperative of time. Let us consider another example, based on a further variation of Figure 3.4.

Figure 3.6 indicates that a skill must be held by one or many employees. As we saw earlier, a many to many association results in an intersecting entity in Figure 3.7, but note where the association nature at each end of the line has been placed. The association degree and nature which was at the SKILL end of the line in Figure 3.6 is now at the EMPLOYEE SKILL end in Figure 3.7. In each figure it is at the end of the relevant line **furthest** from EMPLOYEE. It shows that an employee has one or many skills, and that this is optional becoming mandatory. However in Figure 3.7 we are explicitly referring to the skills held by a specific employee (shown by the mandatory one at the EMPLOYEE end of the line). Figure 3.7 also indicates that a skill *must* be held by one or many employees (mandatory one or many at EMPLOYEE SKILL). Each has a specific skill in which we have an interest (mandatory one at SKILL).

Figure 3.6 Another example of association nature.

Figure 3.7 Association natures for an intersecting entity.

Unlike some data modeling approaches, the modeling method described in this book uses only one association line to represent different interpretations in various areas of the business, based on the policies and strategies relevant to those areas. These multiple policies or strategies are documented by textual description of the association purpose and relevant strategies.

3.2 | POLICIES AND STRATEGIES

In this section we will see how the association conventions used for degree and nature can illustrate different business policies and strategies, using some of the principles we have covered so far.

3.2.1 Representing strategies

The association between EMPLOYEE and SKILL tells us much about how we manage employees and their skills. For example, it can be used to illustrate the following employee skills strategy (keyed to Figure 3.7 by comments in brackets):

> 'We hire employees who presently have none of our skills, but we will train them (optional becoming mandatory, one or many at EMPLOYEE SKILL). Each employee must have demonstrated an ability to be trained, however (shown by mandatory one at EMPLOYEE). We must have at least one employee, but we need many (mandatory many at EMPLOYEE SKILL) for each skill (mandatory one at SKILL).'

This employee skills strategy shows that training is important for the organization. However it is also a restrictive strategy. It states that there *must* be at least one employee for each skill. But what if the organization has to introduce a new skill?

The mandatory one to mandatory many association between SKILL and EMPLOYEE SKILL indicates that we cannot even plan for a new skill until we have at least one employee with that skill. How does that happen?

Figure 3.8   A different employee skills strategy.

Must we hire a new employee who already has that skill? This implies that we do not train and promote from within for new skills, but always hire from outside.

In Figure 3.8 the nature of the SKILL to EMPLOYEE SKILL association has been changed at the EMPLOYEE SKILL end now to optional becoming mandatory. An important variation on the earlier employee skills strategy is now suggested, as follows (with changes shown in brackets):

> *'We hire employees who presently have none of our skills, but we will train them. Each employee must have demonstrated an ability to be trained. For new skills we need to develop, we will train our present employees where possible so that eventually we will have at least one employee, but we need many (optional becoming mandatory many at EMPLOYEE SKILL) for each skill. We only hire from outside for new skills which are not economical to mount training programs for our present employees.'*

This demonstrates the ability of data mapping to illustrate quite complex strategies. It can be used as a catalyst for strategic thought. We will see later in this chapter how we can use the principles introduced so far to develop data maps using statements of management policy and strategy as input, rather than as output as we have seen so far.

It also shows that an association can be interpreted to represent different strategies. Managers should be given the opportunity to express their different views so that the correct interpretation and strategy can be agreed and implemented. A different interpretation due to an early misunderstanding can be very expensive to correct after the application system has been developed.

Another benefit stems from using associations to represent strategies: strategic alternatives can be evaluated using a data map. This was illustrated in the variations between Figures 2.5 and 2.6. We can consider variations without having to test those alternatives using part of the organization as a guinea pig (as often used with strategic planning in the past). If appropriate, alternatives are developed further using strategic, tactical and operational modeling. The feedback to management from this more detailed modeling may suggest other refinements needed before the strategy is introduced into the organization.

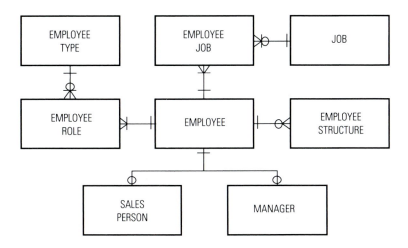

Figure 3.9 A data map can illustrate policies.

3.2.2 Representing policies

We can now provide a more explicit data map than the one developed in Chapter 2 and illustrated as Figure 2.11. Association nature has been added to each association line, now shown as Figure 3.9. This section shows how a data map can be used to illustrate different management policies.

Figure 3.9 also shows a fundamental convention with principal entities, secondary entities and type entities. Secondary entities (for example, SALES PERSON and MANAGER) are always related to their principal entity by an optional one (at the secondary entity) to mandatory one association (at the principal entity, EMPLOYEE). A principal entity is related to its type entity by optional becoming mandatory many (at the principal entity – EMPLOYEE or at the role entity – EMPLOYEE ROLE) to mandatory one (at the type entity – EMPLOYEE TYPE).

This data map includes several related entities. While an association between two entities illustrates a strategy, a data map made up of a number of related entities covers a number of strategies. It thus represents a higher strategic level: a **policy**. A policy provides broad guidelines for the management and control of a number of strategies. For example, Figure 3.9 may represent the following employment policy (comments are keyed to the figure, in brackets):

EMPLOYMENT POLICY

'An employee (mandatory one at EMPLOYEE), when hired, must be assigned to a job but may occupy many jobs over time (mandatory many at

EMPLOYEE JOB). A job (mandatory one at JOB) may initially be vacant, but each job will be filled by an employee (optional becoming mandatory at EMPLOYEE JOB). There are many employees in a job over time (many at EMPLOYEE JOB).

We will have many employees who are either sales persons or managers (mandatory one at EMPLOYEE TYPE to optional becoming mandatory many at EMPLOYEE ROLE). An employee may be either a sales person or a manager (mandatory one at EMPLOYEE to optional one at SALES PERSON and also at MANAGER). That employee can be both a sales person and a manager at the same time, or over time, but must be at least one (mandatory one at EMPLOYEE to mandatory many at EMPLOYEE ROLE).

We may need to know the sales persons who report to each manager, and we may also be interested in managers who are (or have been) sales persons (mandatory one at EMPLOYEE to optional many at EMPLOYEE STRUCTURE).'

The last paragraph in this statement expresses the intent of the EMPLOYEE STRUCTURE entity as illustrated in Table 2.2.

The interpretation of the employment policy above is subjective. Each manager expresses a relevant interpretation, then all managers discuss the implications of any differences. They change the data map, or refine the policy statement, or both.

We are beginning to see some of the power of using data maps to illustrate different interpretations of policies and strategies. We will shortly consider other examples, but we need to understand the principles of entity dependency, first.

3.3 | ENTITY DEPENDENCY

An important property of associations is that they enable **entity dependency** to be determined. For two entities related by an association, one entity is classed as an owner entity. The other entity is a member entity, which is dependent on the owner entity.

Entity dependency is important. It shows a degree of control (or lack of control) which may be essential for management or audit purposes. It may indicate required data, needed for business reasons. It also enables project plans to be derived from a data map and suggests a sequence of implementation for development purposes. Entity dependency leads to a determination of entity ownership.

Ownership is established by examining the degree and nature of an association. A mandatory nature is stronger than optional becoming mandatory, while an optional nature is weakest. Similarly an association degree of one is stronger than a degree of one or many. An entity which has manda-

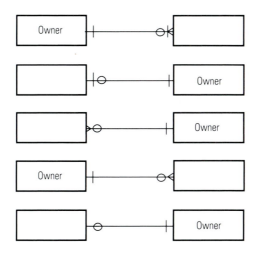

Figure 3.10 Valid associations – entity dependency is clear.

tory one at its end of the association is the strongest combination. That entity owns its related entity, which would therefore be a member entity in that association.

Entity dependency allows associations to be classified as valid, cautionable or unimplementable.

3.3.1 Valid associations

A **valid association** is one where the ownership is clear. There are in all ten valid associations (sometimes also called dominant). Five are shown in Figure 3.10; the other five valid associations are mirror images of this figure. In every case ownership is established by the mandatory one association, which is strongest.

3.3.2 Cautionable associations

Cautionable associations are ambiguous, but dependency assumptions can be made. There are eight cautionable associations: four are shown in Figure 3.11; the other four cautionable associations are mirror images.

The clear ownership indicated by mandatory one, which we saw existed for valid associations in Figure 3.10, is not present with cautionable associations in Figure 3.11. An assumption can be made, however, to remove ambiguity: the *assumed* owner is indicated by 'Owner?' for each of the cautionable associations in this figure.

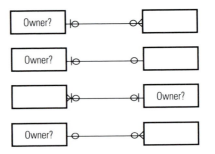

Figure 3.11 Cautionable associations.

With Figure 3.11 both ends of each cautionable association are weak. But an *optional becoming mandatory* nature is stronger than *optional*, and so can be used to establish dependency. It is assumed to be *mandatory* for this purpose. Similarly *optional one* is stronger than *optional many* and is assumed to be *mandatory* for dependency purposes.

3.3.3 Unimplementable associations

An **unimplementable association** is one where the entity ownership cannot be determined by any assumption. There are four types of situations which result in unimplementable associations. These are: where nature or degree have not been fully defined; or where they are the same at each end (see Figure 3.12); where there is a *many to many* association (Figure 3.13); or where an *optional one to mandatory many* association occurs (Figure 3.14).

In Figure 3.12 associations which have not been completely defined as to nature and degree at each end cannot be used to establish dependency. They must first be fully defined. Additionally the *one to one* associations in this figure, which are equal at both ends, can potentially be merged into one single entity. They indicate incorrect or incomplete modeling. Alternatively (if correct) they highlight potential conflicts in the organization. We will see examples of these in later chapters of the book.

Figure 3.13 shows *many to many* associations which are unimplementable. Entity dependency can only be determined when these are decomposed into two *one to many* associations, with an intersecting entity and the nature and degree defined for each end of the two associations. The decomposition of a *many to many* association can be carried out schematically on the data map as we have seen, or can be achieved through the process of business normalization.

Undefined Associations

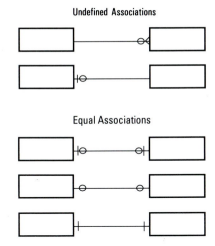

Equal Associations

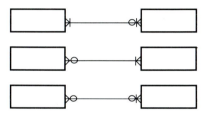

Figure 3.12   Undefined or equal associations are unimplementable.

Figure 3.13   *Many to many* associations are unimplementable.

Figure 3.14   *Optional one to mandatory* is unimplementable.

Figure 3.14 illustrates a further example which is unimplementable because we are unable to establish dependency. This is due to the association nature of *optional*. If this association is correct it suggests there are other entities at a more detailed level which we have not identified yet.

An example is illustrated in Figure 3.15. This indicates that a job *must* have *mandatory one or many* employees assigned to it. However an employee *may* (*optional*) be assigned to *one* job (or none). But this raises many questions. Which employees are assigned to a job? Which are not?

Figure 3.15 An unimplementable optional one association.

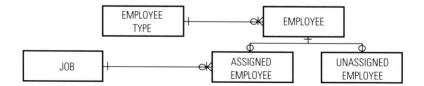

Figure 3.16 Resolution of association in Figure 3.15.

How do we distinguish between an assigned employee and an unassigned employee?

Ah . . . a clue! There is missing underlying detail. EMPLOYEE is a principal entity, but we now have two secondary entities: ASSIGNED EMPLOYEE and UNASSIGNED EMPLOYEE, also. The problem is resolved in Figure 3.16. The association is between ASSIGNED EMPLOYEE and JOB. UNASSIGNED EMPLOYEE has no association at all with JOB until the person becomes an assigned employee.

Figure 3.16 also shows the conventions we discussed earlier for principal entities, secondary entities and type entities. Secondary entities (for example, ASSIGNED EMPLOYEE and UNASSIGNED EMPLOYEE) are always related to their principal entity by an *optional one* (at the secondary entity) to *mandatory one* association (at the principal entity). A secondary entity is always dependent on the principal entity, which we now see is its owner. ASSIGNED EMPLOYEE also has another owner: JOB. Further, a principal entity is dependent on its type entity by *optional becoming mandatory many* (at the principal entity) to *mandatory one* (at the type entity). EMPLOYEE TYPE we now see is the owner of EMPLOYEE.

3.4 ENTITY CYCLE

Entity dependency allows us to identify potential problems in data mapping due to circular references, also called entity cycles. An **entity cycle** occurs when entity *A* is dependent on entity *B*, which is dependent on entity *C* . . . which depends on entity *A*, as illustrated in Figure 3.17.

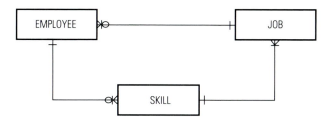

Figure 3.17 An entity cycle.

Figure 3.17 illustrates a circular reference: JOB depends on SKILL, which depends on EMPLOYEE, which depends on JOB. It illustrates an entity cycle which is only too real for teenagers looking for their first job after leaving school:

An employee is dependent on a job, and that job is the only way a person can develop a specific skill needed by the job. Yet the skill must already be held for an employee to be employed in the job.

This example has occurred mainly because of incomplete definition of *many to many* associations which exist, such as between EMPLOYEE and JOB. By decomposing this into an intersecting entity the cycle is broken as shown in Figure 3.18. This may represent a real-life solution with the teenager developing some skills as an employee in a related job, or perhaps as a trainee or an apprentice.

Many examples of entity cycles occur in real life: we phone a company for assistance, but we are directed to another department. They pass us on to another area, who direct us to the first location we phoned. We have been given the run-around: sometimes called 'passing the buck'. It indicates that no clear customer assistance policy has been implemented by the organization concerned. Often a cycle is broken by more explicit associations between secondary entities.

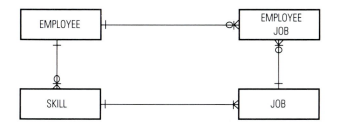

Figure 3.18 Resolution of the entity cycle in Figure 3.17.

We can use these principles of entity dependency to establish reporting structures in an organization. They can be used to show management control, and also audit control. They can help avoid circular references. They lead to a determination of implementation sequence and project plans for development purposes. We will see an application of these principles in the closing section of this chapter.

We have seen how we can use a data map to uncover strategic alternatives and so refine relevant strategies. We will now reverse this process. We will see how a data map can be developed based on existing management statements. This will allow us to express strategic and business plans schematically; for their interpretation, evaluation and refinement where necessary.

3.5 DEVELOPING A DATA MAP

Our example is based on employees and skills as covered earlier in this chapter. We will use statements of management policy to develop a data map progressively to illustrate these principles. You will remember in Figures 3.7 and 3.8 we discussed how associations can be used to illustrate alternative strategies. In Figure 3.9 we saw that a related group of entities and their associations illustrate policies. We will use policy statements to identify related groups of entities and statements of strategy to refine the associations between those entities.

We start with the employment policy of a typical organization, expressed perhaps simplistically, but nevertheless memorably.

> *We assign persons to jobs so that the right person, with the right skills, is placed in the right job.*

We will use this policy statement as a catalyst to identify potential entities. These are suggested by nouns, expressed either explicitly or implicitly. In this example they are clear: we are interested in persons, jobs and skills. Policies can indicate data subjects that represent groups of entities, or can suggest specific entities. This example indicates specific entities; Chapters 13 and 14 discuss data subjects. We show them in data map form in Figure 3.19 as entities, where each entity name is expressed in the singular.

These three entities express the policy. They are related in some way, according to employment strategies such as:

SKILLS DEVELOPMENT STRATEGY
A job demands many skills. These skills may be held by more than one person.

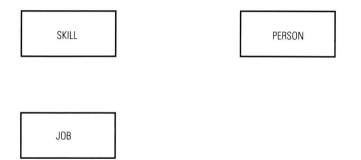

Figure 3.19   Embryonic data map from a statement of policy.

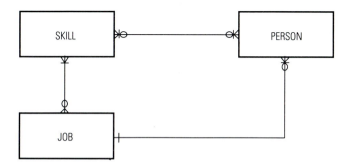

Figure 3.20   Initial data map for skills development strategy.

Personnel who already have the skills required by a job will be assigned to that job in preference to personnel without those skills.

Personnel without the necessary skills will be trained to an appropriate level of skill demanded by a job before they are assigned to that job.

These strategies define associations between the entities as illustrated in Figure 3.20. They are expressed initially as *many to many* associations.

As we have seen, we decompose these *many to many* associations into intersecting entities with *one to many* associations. This is illustrated in Figure 3.21.

This data map shows a more detailed expression of the skills development strategy. It leads us to refine the earlier statement as follows:

REFINED SKILLS DEVELOPMENT STRATEGY

A person will (eventually, through training) have one or many skills. A skill will (also as a result of training) be held by one or many persons.

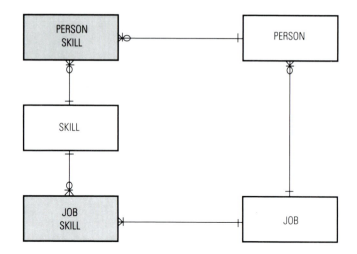

Figure 3.21 Data map clarifying skills development strategy.

A job must have one or many skills which are needed for effective execution of that job, but we may not have the skills needed to carry out that job until persons have been trained to a suitable standard.

A person must be assigned to a job where that person's skill is satisfactory.

We have uncovered additional data which is needed: data about training. This implies still further entities, such as: COURSE and TRAINING CLASS. COURSE is related to SKILL, as it is used to develop skills in persons. PERSON is also related to COURSE through TRAINING CLASS, for those persons assigned to a training class in a course which will develop appropriate skills. Figure 3.22 illustrates this expansion of the data map as a result of the refined strategies above.

We express greater detail which emerges in data map form. The expanded data map then leads us to express a further strategy – one which addresses skills training:

SKILLS TRAINING STRATEGY

Persons who are not yet qualified for a job are classed as trainees. Each trainee will be scheduled to attend training classes in an appropriate course which will develop the required skills. The class instructor will evaluate the trainee's skill development and report to the manager of the trainee when a suitable skill level has been reached. The trainee will then be considered a qualified employee and will be promoted into the job.

This skills training strategy indicates that we are interested in several types

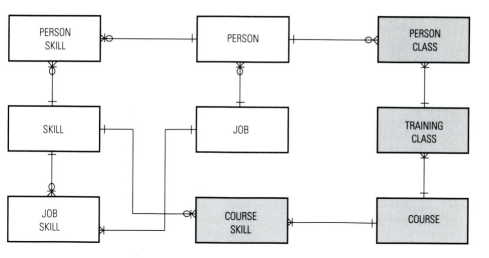

Figure 3.22 Expanded data map from refined strategy.

of persons: trainees, class instructors, managers, and qualified employees. These are secondary entities of PERSON. The interrelationships between trainees, their class instructors and their managers are represented in a structure entity: PERSON STRUCTURE. This results in an expanded data map which is now illustrated in Figure 3.23.

This example shows how the use of data mapping provides immediate feedback to management. They test alternatives, using the data map as a catalyst. They refine their thinking and strategic directions. Data models enable management and staff to express their business expertise precisely. Data processing staff can develop computer support systems that meet their information needs exactly.

However we have only used one part of the data model: the data map. The entity list is also a powerful catalyst, particularly when the process of business normalization is used. This leads us to the next chapter.

3.6 | SUMMARY

In this chapter we covered the conventions used for data mapping. We discussed the characteristics of associations: their degree (also called cardinality); and their nature.

We saw that a crows foot on the association line represents a degree of *one or many*; no crows foot represents an association degree of *one*. A

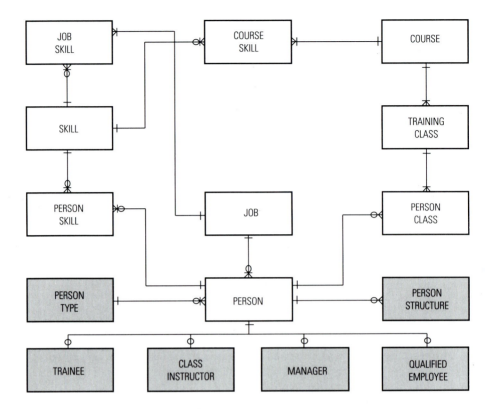

Figure 3.23   Data map including skills training strategy.

circle on the line represents an association nature of *optional*; a bar shows a nature of *mandatory*; a bar together with a circle represents *optional becoming mandatory*. These are interpreted as *may*, *must* and *will* respectively. They will later be used to define conditional logic in procedures.

We discussed that statements of policy define related groups of entities illustrating **what** data each policy represents. Strategies define **how** a policy is implemented; they are shown as associations between entities. We saw that a data map can thus be used to illustrate, interpret and also refine, statements of both policy and strategy.

We saw that only one association line is drawn between two related entities, but the line is used to represent many ways in which the related entities are used. An association represents strategies, and also procedures. The first are defined in textual descriptions of the relevant strategies; the second in textual purpose descriptions of the association. An unlimited number of strategies and procedures can thus be represented by a single association line.

We discussed the concepts of entity dependency, and saw that valid associations can be used to identify owner and member entities unambiguously. We saw that cautionable associations are ambiguous; they need further interpretation to identify their owner and member entities. Unimplementable associations require further modeling. The concepts of entity dependency are used to identify separately implementable systems and subject data bases from a data map. They are used also to derive project plans from a data map. We will discuss these aspects further, in Chapter 17.

We discussed the problems of entity cycles, which often represent incomplete business controls in real life. We saw that entity cycles are often resolved by further modeling; this can clarify the additional business controls needed.

We concluded the chapter by developing a data map directly from statements of policy and strategy. We saw how the data map is used to refine those statements, so leading to a more detailed data map. This continues until the data map and associated policy and strategy statements have been expressed in sufficient detail to represent the business area being examined. Managers and users thus decide when their data and information needs have been correctly represented.

CHAPTER 4

Business Normalization

There are two formal approaches to normalization: we will refer to them in this book as **traditional normalization** and **business normalization**. A normalized data model is easier to implement and maintain in a computer application. Traditional normalization is based on original work by Codd [1, 2, 3] and on excellent work done by many others [4, 5, 6]. It has been used mainly by data administrators and analysts. Business normalization however is also applied by users who have no computer knowledge, but who have business expertise.

The data mapping conventions in Chapter 3 allow entities and associations to be shown schematically. Business normalization provides a set of rules which help us identify attributes that represent business knowledge about data within an organization. It is a process which places each attribute in an entity where it is dependent on the entire primary key of that entity, and on no other key.

We saw in data mapping that a *many to many* association results in an intersecting entity being defined, with two *one to many* associations. A *many to many* association is due to repeating groups in the related entities. Business normalization provides one step which removes repeating groups, and other steps which uncover additional entities. In so doing, much business knowledge is discovered which may not have been apparent just from a data map.

THE RULES OF BUSINESS NORMALIZATION

Each rule in business normalization is called a business normal form. There are five rules and we will discuss each of these rules in turn. We will apply them to an unnormalized entity, progressively decomposing it to fifth business normal form.

4.1.1 First business normal form (1BNF)

The first rule of business normalization identifies and removes repeating groups into another entity. As a many to many association in a data map is decomposed into an intersecting entity, so also repeating groups in an entity are moved to another entity. The rule for **first business normal form (1BNF)** is defined in Box 4.1.

Box 4.1
First business normal form (1BNF)

Identify and remove repeating group attributes to another entity.
The primary key of this other entity is made up of a compound key, comprising the primary key of the entity in which the repeating group originally resided together with the repeating group key itself, or instead another unique key based on the business needs. The name of the new entity initially may be based on a combination of the name of the repeating group and the name of the entity in which the repeating group originally resided. It may later be renamed according to its final attribute content after business normalization is completed.

Consider the following unnormalized entity in entity list format:

EMPLOYEE   (employee number #, [name], (address), [postcode], ((skill number #, [skill name], skill level)), sales quota, [manager title], job name, salary)

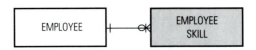

Figure 4.1   First business normal form data map (1BNF).

Each employee is identified by *employee number*#, with selection attributes (secondary keys) of [*name*] and [*postcode*] and a group attribute of *(address)*. A repeating group of skill details and other attributes of sales quota and the title of the employee's manager also exist in this entity, together with the name and salary of the job.

Based on the 1BNF rule, identification of repeating groups is easy: the skill details are already surrounded by (repeating) double left and right brackets. These skill attributes are moved into a new entity, called EMPLOYEE SKILL according to the 1BNF rule, and with a compound key of *employee number*#, *skill number*#:

EMPLOYEE	(employee number#, [name], (address), [postcode], sales quota, [manager title], job name, salary)
EMPLOYEE SKILL	(employee number#, skill number#, [skill name], skill level)

These two entities are now in 1BNF. We can represent them in a data map as shown in Figure 4.1. We have expressed the EMPLOYEE–SKILL association to indicate a strategy that an employee *will* (*optional becoming mandatory*) have one or many skills.

If the repeating group had not already been identified with double brackets we would still have been able to locate it with the 2BNF rule. The ability to cross-check data interpretation is an important characteristic of normalization.

4.1.2   Second business normal form (2BNF)

Second business normal form (2BNF) is based on partial dependencies, defined in Box 4.2. We will apply this rule to the 1BNF entities in the entity list: EMPLOYEE and EMPLOYEE SKILL. (For those readers familiar with traditional normalization, the 2BNF rule achieves Boyce-Codd normal form here, instead of after 3NF.)

We first look at compound key entities to decide whether any attributes depend on only part of the compound key. Yes, the attribute *skill name* in EMPLOYEE SKILL is dependent on only part of the compound key *employee number*#, *skill number*#. It is wholly dependent on *skill number*#, but not dependent at all on *employee number*#. The name we

Box 4.2
Second business normal form (2BNF)

Identify and remove those attributes into another entity which are only partially dependent on the primary key and also dependent on one or more other key attributes, or . . . which are dependent on only part of the compound key and possibly one or more other key attributes.

give to a skill has nothing to do with a specific employee. We therefore move *skill name* into a new entity, SKILL, whose single primary key is *skill number#*. *Skill level* is, however, wholly dependent on *both skill number#* and on *employee number#*. It therefore remains in EMPLOYEE SKILL.

EMPLOYEE   (employee number#, [name], (address), [postcode], sales quota, [manager title], job name, salary)

EMPLOYEE SKILL   (employee number#, skill number#, skill level)

SKILL   (skill number#, [skill name])

The data map now shows three entities, with degree and nature as illustrated in Figure 4.2. The new entity, SKILL, is shaded for emphasis. In fact, this data map tells us that there was originally a *many to many* association between two entities EMPLOYEE and SKILL. But because the attributes of SKILL were buried within EMPLOYEE as a repeating group, we did not even see the existence of SKILL until EMPLOYEE was in 1BNF. There was an implicit SKILL entity which we had missed. If we had correctly defined it we would have seen that this entity also had a repeating group: ((*employee number#*)) to indicate that one or more employees may have

Figure 4.2   Second business normal form data map (2BNF).

the same skill. It does not matter which repeating group we start with: 1BNF and 2BNF together will give us the same intersecting entity EMPLOYEE SKILL.

We have now seen one example of an important principle: business normalization helps us to discover data that we may not originally have identified. It also helps us to check the accuracy of data definition and data representation.

4.1.3   Third business normal form (3BNF)

While 2BNF was concerned with partial dependencies, the rule for **third business normal form (3BNF)** separates out attributes that are not even partially dependent on the primary key – as defined in Box 4.3.

Box 4.3
Third business normal form (3BNF)

Identify and remove into another entity those attributes which are dependent on a key other than the primary (or compound) key.

The 3BNF rule removes every attribute from an entity that is not dependent at all on the primary key of the entity in which it resides. Do any of the attributes of the 2BNF entity list satisfy this rule? Look at the EMPLOYEE entity again.

Yes, the name of a job is not dependent at all on *employee number#*. It is dependent only on a primary key of *job number#*. It therefore is moved out of EMPLOYEE and into a new entity JOB which has this primary key. But is that satisfactory? At least while it was in EMPLOYEE we knew the name of each employee's job. We have lost that information – unless we also leave *job number#* in EMPLOYEE as a foreign key. We can use this key to access the appropriate JOB entity occurrence to find out the name of the job. The entity list is shown next.

EMPLOYEE   (employee number#, [name], (address), [postcode], sales quota, [manager title], salary, job number#)

EMPLOYEE SKILL	(employee number#, skill number#, skill level)
SKILL	(skill number#, [skill name])
JOB	(job number#, job name)

Is it now in 3BNF? Yes, but only if an employee's salary is determined entirely by the primary key of *employee number#*. But in most organizations salary is determined also by the job, and so is dependent on a compound primary key of *employee number#, job number#*. In fact, when a person changes jobs there will likely be a different salary: we now see that we missed the fact that both *salary* and *job name* should have originally been shown as a repeating group ((*salary, job name*)); the 3BNF rule cross-checked the accuracy of their earlier definition in the unnormalized EMPLOYEE entity.

So salary (as defined) does not satisfy the 3BNF rule: it is only partially dependent on *employee number#*. It is also dependent on *job number#*, so satisfying the 2BNF rule. We therefore need to define a new entity, EMPLOYEE JOB, with these key attributes as a compound primary key. As a result we now no longer need the foreign key of *job number#* in EMPLOYEE: we can find each job for an employee from the EMPLOYEE JOB compound key – given an employee number.

The entities are now in 3BNF. We will have a final 3BNF entity list after we ensure that there is a unique name for each non-key attribute. We qualify each attribute, where necessary, with the name of the entity in which it resides.

We find an interesting thing happens: *salary* is now called *employee job salary* in EMPLOYEE JOB; it does not reside in EMPLOYEE and so is no longer considered to be *employee salary*. But what about other salaries? Is there a *job base salary*? Or an *employee base salary*? Or an *employee skill salary* that pays an incremental amount according to skills? Or a sales quota salary, perhaps called *commission salary*? None of these questions arose with the unnormalized entity, as *salary* was mentally interpreted based on each person's own experience. But we now see that salary was a **homonym** (the same name used for different data). The same name was used for all of these other salary attributes. The users can now consider their business needs more completely. They decide on attributes they need today, but they also decide on attributes needed for tomorrow: they design for the future. We will assume that they agree on the following:

EMPLOYEE	(employee number#, [employee name], (employee address), [employee postcode], employee sales quota, [employee manager title])
EMPLOYEE SKILL	(employee number#, skill number#, employee skill level)
SKILL	(skill number#, [skill name])

EMPLOYEE JOB	(employee number #, job number #, employee job salary)
JOB	(job number #, job name)

The above result is interesting. For example a person has (over time) more than one salary, and perhaps more than one job. We discussed earlier that we missed showing a repeating group of ((*salary, job name*)) in the original definition of the unnormalized entity. The 1BNF rule would have identified an intersecting entity of EMPLOYEE JOB with the attribute *employee job salary*. But we achieved the same result with the 2BNF and 3BNF rules, and we have also considered homonyms. Are all attributes correctly in 3BNF now? Not yet, as we will see next.

We have applied the 1BNF, 2BNF and 3BNF rules to all entities. Now we will do a further cross-check: we will fully apply these rules to each attribute in turn – starting with EMPLOYEE.

Is *employee name* a repeating group (1BNF)? Do we need: prior married names; names changed by deed poll; or alias names? No. (The latter would be very important if the data were to be used for law enforcement.) Is *employee name* only partially dependent on *employee number#* (2BNF)? No. Does it depend on another key; not on *employee number#* (3BNF)? No. If the answer is No to each of these cross-checking questions, then the *attribute employee name* is correctly in 3BNF.

What about *employee address*: is it a repeating group (1BNF)? Do we need several work addresses, and current or prior home addresses? Yes. Do the addresses depend also on other keys (2BNF)? Yes, on date, called *address date#*. This has uncovered an additional EMPLOYEE ADDRESS entity:

EMPLOYEE ADDRESS	(employee number #, address category #, address date #, employee address)

Is *employee sales quota* a repeating group (1BNF)? Yes. Is it partially dependent on another key (2BNF)? Yes, it depends also on a date key – called *quota period#*. Is it dependent not at all on *employee number#*, but on another key (3BNF)? No. (But this raises the question of job quotas, product quotas and territory quotas that are important to the Sales Department. For simplicity we will not discuss these issues here.) This has uncovered the EMPLOYEE QUOTA entity:

EMPLOYEE QUOTA	(employee number #, quota date #, employee sales quota)

These are further examples of using business normalization to help check the accuracy of data definition and data representation. They uncovered business knowledge that we had missed. But we will not use these additional entities: for simplicity Figure 4.3 now shows the entity list as a 3BNF data map, with only the earlier new entities (shaded).

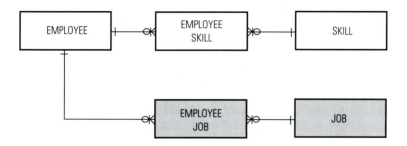

Figure 4.3 Third business normal form data map (3BNF).

However we have not yet finished normalizing these entities. They are in 3BNF, but there is much logic still locked in these entities. This would not be uncovered until we started programming to process the attributes of *sales quota* and *manager title*. When is sales quota relevant for an employee? Does it apply to all employees? And what do we mean by manager title? Is it really what it seems to be: the title of the employee's manager? 4BNF will help us answer these questions.

4.1.4   Fourth business normal form (4BNF)

Fourth business normal form is concerned with secondary entities that belong to a principal entity. These are sometimes also called subtype entities. The rule for **fourth business normal form (4BNF)** is defined in Box 4.4.

Box 4.4
Fourth business normal form (4BNF)

An entity is said to be in fourth business normal form when it is in third business normal form, and its attributes depend not only upon the entire primary (compound key) – but also on the value of the key, or when an attribute has been relocated from an entity where it is optional, instead to an entity where it is wholly dependent on the key and must exist, and so is mandatory.

The 4BNF rule helps us answer the questions about *sales quota* and *manager title*. We see that each attribute is dependent on *employee number#* (that is, it is in 3BNF) but it also depends on the type of employee – whether a sales person or a manager. It is dependent also on *employee type number#*.

These attributes apply to different types of employees and indicate the existence of secondary entities: SALES PERSON and MANAGER, with a type entity: EMPLOYEE TYPE. The secondary entities are 4BNF. EMPLOYEE is a principal entity and is 3BNF. The 4BNF entity list for EMPLOYEE is:

EMPLOYEE TYPE   (employee type number#, employee type name)

EMPLOYEE   (employee number#, [employee name], (employee address), [employee postcode], employee type number#)

SALES PERSON   (employee number#, sales person quota)

MANAGER   (employee number#, [manager title])

We would also have identified these 4BNF entities using only the second part of the 4BNF rule. *Sales quota* and *manager title* are optional attributes in EMPLOYEE. They don't apply to all employees. They are mandatory only when they reside in SALES PERSON and MANAGER respectively – which are therefore in 4BNF. Figure 4.4 now shows the complete 4BNF data map for all of the EMPLOYEE entities. We now see that secondary entities (see Chapter 2) are the data map representation of 4BNF.

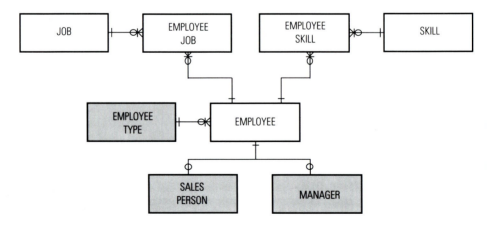

Figure 4.4 **Fourth business normal form data map (4BNF).**

4.1.5   4BNF indicates program logic

In developing application systems to process this 4BNF data model (made up of the data map and entity list) we need to provide program logic to add, read, update and delete (or archive) details held as attributes in each entity. We now see that the data map not only indicates the data: it also illustrates the program structure. It suggests that we need program modules which will process:

- Details common to all employees
- Details specific to sales persons
- Details specific to managers
- Details of jobs and the employees in each job
- Details of skills and the skills held by each employee

With the greater business detail provided in the data map and entity list, required employee program logic is now obvious:

- *Details common to all employees*
  For all employees
    then (common employee logic)

- *Details specific to sales persons*
  If employee is a sales person
    then (logic for sales persons)

- *Details specific to managers*
  If employee is a manager
    then (logic for managers)

Program logic for jobs and employees in jobs is also obvious:

- *Details of jobs and the employees in each job*
  For each job
    then (job logic)

  For each employee in a job
    then (employee job logic)

So also is program logic for skills and employee skills:

- *Details of skills and the skills held by each employee*
  For each skill
    then (skill logic)

  For each employee with a skill
    then (employee skills logic)

This logic was certainly not obvious by looking at the unnormalized EMPLOYEE entity that we started with. It demonstrates how a data model in 4BNF can readily be converted into program code to handle all required data maintenance logic (add, read, update, delete etc). This is discussed further in Chapters 5 and 6.

4.1.6   Fifth business normal form (5BNF)

We have so far considered dependencies for every occurrence of one entity with all occurrences of another entity. But what about dependencies between some occurrences only, of an entity or entity type. In other words, what about recursive (or involuted) associations as illustrated in Figure 2.9? This leads us to the rule of **fifth business normal form (5BNF)**, as defined in Box 4.5.

Box 4.5
Fifth business normal form (5BNF)

An entity is in fifth business normal form if its dependencies on occurrences of the same entity or entity type have been moved into a STRUCTURE entity.

A structure entity (such as the one we covered in Chapter 2) is a 5BNF entity. It occurs when associations exist between occurrences of the same entity or entity type, as we saw with the recursive associations and the *many to many* associations in Figure 2.9. The entity EMPLOYEE STRUCTURE is defined in 5BNF as follows:

EMPLOYEE STRUCTURE   (employee number#, employee type number#, employee number#, employee type number#)

An Employee Structure table allows us to indicate related employee occurrences, as discussed in conjunction with Table 2.2. We saw that a 5BNF structure entity enables us to maintain details of all managers and sales

Table 4.1   Typical content of a 5BNF structure entity

Employee number	Employee type number	Employee number	Employee type number
1358	Manager	1362	Manager
		1460	Sales person
		1556	Manager
		1661	Sales person
1362	Manager	262	Sales person
		1088	Support person
		1132	Sales person
		1441	Sales person
1556	Manager	1333	Sales person
		1495	Support person
		1512	Sales person
1088	Support person	1460	Sales person
		1661	Sales person
		1132	Sales person
		1441	Sales person
1495	Support person	1460	Sales person
		1661	Sales person
		1333	Sales person
		1512	Sales person
1088	Support person	1495	Support person

Note: As for Table 2.2, Table 4.1 shows employee type names, rather than employee type numbers. We will use this incorrect representation for illustrative clarity, however.

persons who report to a specific manager. This principle is extended further in Table 4.1.

We can determine which other employees these persons are related to by adding additional employee types as secondary 4BNF entities, as illustrated in Table 4.1. This expands on Table 2.2 by including SUPPORT PERSON entities who report to managers and assist sales persons or other support persons. In Table 4.1 two support persons both assist sales persons 1460 and 1661 – as well as supporting those sales persons in their specific work groups, who report with them to the same manager.

We can now see the reporting and support structure for each type of employee very clearly, and can change it as appropriate. But we can also include other knowledge in this entity, not apparent from the data model alone. This can be expert knowledge. For example, what if support person 1495 is sick? Who supports sales persons 1460 and 1661? Support person 1088, who is also responsible for their support. But what of sales persons 1333 and 1512? Do they have no support? The last row of Table 4.1 tells us that 1088 also supports 1495; 1088 has similar skills to 1495, and so can provide support for 1495.

In Chapter 2 we saw that extra structure attributes can be used. An additional attribute *employee relationship reason* would be useful here. We could enter a reason for this row as: 'Senior support person with similar skills'. (But the reverse is not true: there is no similar row with 1495 on the left and 1088 on the right.) This previously was expert knowledge known only to these two support persons and their managers, but it is knowledge now available in the EMPLOYEE STRUCTURE entity to all.

We are interested in certain employees who are managers, sales persons or support persons, but we do not have to include every employee belonging to these types in this table. Other employee types may also have been excluded from the table. A 5BNF structure entity, implemented as a 5BNF table, allows us to include associations only between those specific entity occurrences that are of interest.

Figure 4.5 now provides the complete data map, including all 4BNF entities and the 5BNF EMPLOYEE STRUCTURE entity followed by the complete entity list. We have defined no additional attributes for the SUPPORT PERSON entity other than the primary key. These figures show that the original EMPLOYEE unnormalized entity has been decomposed to a fully normalized data map and entity list of 10 entities in 4BNF and 5BNF.

At the end of Chapter 3 we used data mapping to represent an employment policy, with skills development and skills training strategies. Our example showed several types of persons: trainees, class instructors, managers and qualified employees. In this chapter we used business normalization to develop a data map, by normalizing entities in an entity list.

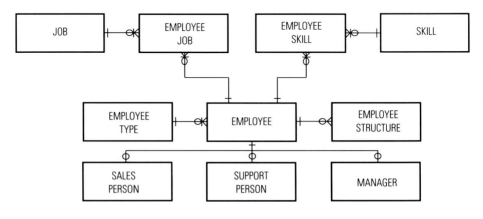

Figure 4.5   The EMPLOYEE data map in 4BNF and 5BNF.

While Chapter 3 discussed persons, and Chapter 4 considered employees, PERSON and EMPLOYEE are **synonyms**; and were used to represent the same data. We could add the person types (from Chapter 3) to the data map in Figure 4.5 as employee types. PERSON TYPE, PERSON and PERSON STRUCTURE from Figure 3.23 therefore become the respective EMPLOYEE type, principal and structure entities.

EMPLOYEE TYPE	(employee type number #, employee type name)
EMPLOYEE	(employee number #, [employee name], (employee address), [employee postcode], employee type number #)
SALES PERSON	(employee number #, sales person quota)
MANAGER	(employee number #, [manager title])
SUPPORT PERSON	(employee number #)
EMPLOYEE STRUCTURE	(employee number #, employee type number #, employee number #, employee type number #)
EMPLOYEE SKILL	(employee number #, skill number #, employee skill level)
SKILL	(skill number #, [skill name])
EMPLOYEE JOB	(employee number #, job number #, employee job salary)
JOB	(job number #, job name)

Table 4.1 could be expanded with these additional employee types. This would enable us to indicate class instructors who are responsible for specific trainees, and identify the managers also of those trainees. Thus EMPLOYEE STRUCTURE can be used to implement the trainee evaluation and manager notification responsibilities of class instructors according to the skills training strategy of Chapter 3.

4.2 SUMMARY

In this chapter we covered the five rules of business normalization.

- First business normal form (1BNF) removes repeating groups to another entity. This entity takes its name, and primary (compound) key attributes, from the original entity and from the repeating group.

- Second business normal form (2BNF) removes attributes, that are partially dependent on the primary key, to another entity. The primary (compound) key of this entity is the primary key of the entity in which it originally resided, together with all additional keys on which the attribute is wholly dependent.

- Third business normal form (3BNF) removes attributes, not dependent at all on the primary key, to another entity where they are wholly dependent on the entire primary key of that entity.

- Fourth business normal form (4BNF) removes attributes, dependent on the value of the primary key or that are optional, to a secondary entity where they wholly depend on the value of the primary key, or where they must (mandatorily) exist in that entity.

- Fifth business normal form (5BNF) exists as a structure entity if recursive, or other, associations exist between occurrences of secondary entities, or if recursive associations exist between occurrences of their principal entity.

We saw that first, second and third business normal form are most effective when they are applied by users with a detailed business knowledge of the data: they cross-check data meaning. We also saw that homonyms (the same name used for different data) can be identified by applying the 1BNF, 2BNF and 3BNF rules fully, to each attribute at a time. This is a further cross-check of the accuracy of data definition: it identifies current and future user information needs that may otherwise have been missed. This also helps identify synonyms.

We also discussed that program logic is more obvious when a data model has been taken down to fourth business normal form. We saw that fifth business normal form not only allows any predefined associations between occurrences of entities to be stored in a structure entity; it also allows expert knowledge to be captured. This knowledge can be based on details not represented in the data model, and so may not otherwise be available. Once it has been stored in a structure entity, this expert knowledge is available to all who are authorized to use it.

References

[1] Codd, E. F. (1970). *A Relational Model for Large Shared Data Banks*. CACM, 13 (6), pp. 377–387.

[2] Codd, E. F. (1979). Extending the Database Relational Model to Capture More Meaning. *ACM Trans on Database Systems*, Vol 4, No 4, pp. 397–434.

[3] Codd, E. F. (1988). Domains, Keys, and Referential Integrity in Relational Databases. *InfoDB* – Colin J White Consulting: San Jose, CA.

[4] Date, C. J. (1986). *An Introduction to Database Systems – Volume 1*. Fourth Edition. Addison-Wesley: Reading, MA.

[5] Fagin, R. (1979). Normal Forms and Relational Database Operators. Proc. *ACM SIGMOD International Conference on Management of Data.*

[6] Kent, W. (1983). A Simple Guide to Five Normal Forms in Relational Database Theory. *CACM 26, No. 2.*

[7] Finkelstein, C. (1989). *An Introduction to Information Engineering.* Addison-Wesley: Reading, MA.

CHAPTER 5

Process Modeling

The previous chapters covered the major concepts used in data modeling. This chapter introduces the principles of process modeling. Business normalization eliminates data redundancy through data normalization. We will see in this chapter that process modeling is used to solve a similar problem: it eliminates logic redundancy through logic normalization. This is achieved through development of generic procedures which represent common, reusable logic routines. These are implemented using either object-oriented programming or conventional programming techniques. Required programs are built from existing, tested, generic procedures which have been developed from a data model, so that program logic does not have to be rewritten each time. We will start by examining some of the problems that are associated with traditional program development.

5.1 | TRADITIONAL PROGRAM DEVELOPMENT

There are two areas which have an impact on program development productivity today. Redundant logic, which arises from redundant data, and embedded logic which results from incompletely normalized data.

5.1.1 Redundant logic

Different versions of the same data may exist redundantly throughout an organization. Each redundant version should be maintained up-to-date.

76

This maintenance processing involves creation (adding new occurrences of data), retrieval (which does not change the data), updating (to incorporate changes in each redundant version) and eventually deletion (when a data occurrence is no longer required). To ensure accuracy of each data version, a change made to one version must also be made to every other redundant version. Redundant data thus requires redundant processing.

Redundant processing is reflected also in redundant programs, written to process each data version. Each of these programs must be maintained. A greater problem arises if a change must be made not just to the data content (that is, redundant processing), but to the format of the data. Each of these programs represents redundant logic: each program which processes the data must thus be examined and probably also changed. So redundant data results in redundant program development, and in redundant program maintenance.

We saw that business normalization eliminates redundant data. One data version is thus made accessible to all who are authorized to reference or change it. Any changes made to the data are therefore immediately available to all. The many programs previously written to maintain each data version are now no longer required. As only one copy of the data now exists, only one set of programs is needed: to create, retrieve, update or delete occurrences of the single data version. This results in a significant improvement in program development and maintenance productivity.

Business normalization therefore eliminates both redundant data and logic. But this program logic can be even further refined, through process modeling as we will soon see. The logic needed to process a specific data version can be derived from that data. This introduces the concept of logic normalization, a topic we will address later in the chapter.

5.1.2 Embedded logic

To discuss problems of embedded logic, we will consider the 3BNF employee record illustrated in Figure 5.1. This record contains details which are common to all employees – shown as Employee Information in the figure. It contains details specific to salespersons (Salesperson Information) and also to managers (Manager Information). For managers there is also

EMPLOYEE INFORMATION	SALESPERSON INFORMATION	MANAGER INFORMATION	MANAGER TYPE INFORMATION	
			STAFF MANAGER	LINE MANAGER

Figure 5.1 A 3BNF Employee Record.

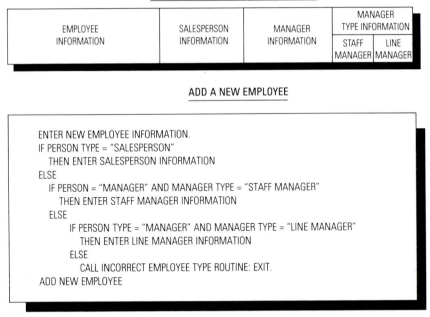

Figure 5.2 illustration contains:

PROCEDURE CODE FOR 3NF DATABASE

EMPLOYEE INFORMATION	SALESPERSON INFORMATION	MANAGER INFORMATION	MANAGER TYPE INFORMATION	
			STAFF MANAGER	LINE MANAGER

ADD A NEW EMPLOYEE

```
ENTER NEW EMPLOYEE INFORMATION.
IF PERSON TYPE = "SALESPERSON"
   THEN ENTER SALESPERSON INFORMATION
ELSE
   IF PERSON = "MANAGER" AND MANAGER TYPE = "STAFF MANAGER"
      THEN ENTER STAFF MANAGER INFORMATION
   ELSE
      IF PERSON TYPE = "MANAGER" AND MANAGER TYPE = "LINE MANAGER"
         THEN ENTER LINE MANAGER INFORMATION
      ELSE
         CALL INCORRECT EMPLOYEE TYPE ROUTINE: EXIT.
ADD NEW EMPLOYEE
```

Figure 5.2   Pseudocode program logic to add a new employee.

information for different types of managers (Manager Type Information), depending on whether the individual is a staff manager or a line manager.

The logic required to add a new employee record must also include logic for entering the specific information for each type of employee. Consequently a program written to add a new employee must accept the information common to all employees. It must then carry out tests to identify each particular type of employee, so that additional information specific to that employee type can be entered. An example of such program logic is illustrated in Figure 5.2, written in the form of pseudocode. This shows that we must test for each type of employee and accept entry (from a display screen, for example) of the relevant information for that employee type. Only then can we add the new employee record to the employee file or data base.

But what if we later have other types of employees? What changes must be made? The Employee record may need to include information on other employee types. This can be added at the end of the record, or between existing employee type information in the record. However many programs which access the record may also be affected by these record format changes. This depends on the particular file access method or data base management system utilized, and the extent to which programs can be written independent of physical file or data base formats: this is called **data independence**.

The program logic in Figure 5.2 must also be updated to test for additional types of employees added to the record format. Relevant information for each type of employee can then be entered to be included in the employee record. But not only will program logic need to be changed to add new employee types: every other program that operates against the employee record must be examined to determine whether its logic is affected also by the additional employee information. New data will of course require specific program logic for processing. However other program logic, which has nothing to do with the new data, may also be affected.

We will see that process modeling, with generic procedures, minimizes the impact of data changes through a high level of data independence, regardless of the file access method or DBMS architecture used.

5.1.3   Object-oriented programming

Object-oriented programming has emerged recently as a technique which can be used to reduce redundant logic: program code can be developed that is reusable. This code is packaged with its data so that together they represent an object: whenever the data is referenced, the relevant code is executed. Object-oriented programming is thus a packaging technique, rather than a coding technique. It uses concepts of encapsulation and inheritance.

Encapsulation places 'a wall of code around each piece of data' [1]. Conventional programming requires the programmer to define all processing to be carried out against data. In contrast, encapsulation ensures that access to the data is handled by procedures developed to mediate specific access to that data. This is not the same concept used for subroutines or functions in conventional programming. Encapsulation packages code and data together as an object so that a programmer need not be aware at all of the internal processing carried out by that object. While a function or a subroutine is called to initiate processing, the processing of an object is invoked by passing a message to it.

Inheritance enables an object to inherit characteristics of a higher-level object. This capability is not provided by conventional languages. Common code is automatically broadcasted to classes of code developed by several members of a programming team. Instead of writing code from scratch, these programmers reference a class that already exists in a library: they describe only how a new class differs from the existing class. Other characteristics are then automatically inherited from the existing class.

Together, encapsulation and inheritance have a dramatic effect on the reusability of code. But it is difficult to identify code to be made reusable.

Process modeling offers an identification method. Once this reusable code has been so identified, object-oriented programming (or instead conventional programming) can be used to implement it.

5.2 PROCESS MODELING CONCEPTS

The Employee record shown in Figures 5.1 and 5.2 in 3BNF can be drawn as a data map in 4BNF and 5BNF, as discussed in Chapter 4. This is illustrated in Figure 5.3.

Common employee information resides in the 3BNF principal entity EMPLOYEE. Information specific to each type of employee resides in a 4BNF secondary entity: SALES PERSON is one such example. There are two types of managers: MANAGER therefore has a type entity related to it, called MANAGER TYPE. The 4BNF secondary entities of STAFF MANAGER and LINE MANAGER are also related. MANAGER is therefore called a typed secondary entity and is also in 4BNF.

5.2.1 A simple procedure map

Using the data map in Figure 5.3, we will now define the steps involved in adding a new record for a LINE MANAGER employee. These steps are illustrated in the form of a procedure map in Figure 5.4. This is a schematic representation of program logic, used in process modeling. In the

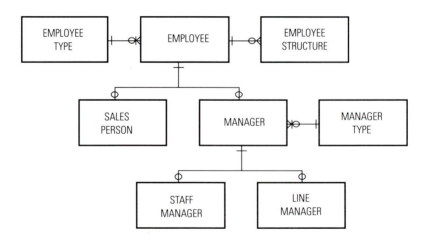

Figure 5.3 Employee data map in 4BNF and 5BNF.

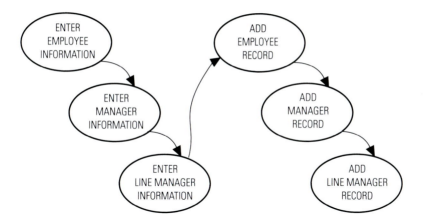

Figure 5.4   A procedure map showing unconditional logic.

following paragraphs we will discuss some of the basic process modeling principles.

A procedure map illustrates program logic schematically. It represents the processing associated with one (or several) **business events**. For example, Figure 5.4 is a procedure map for the business event: 'Add New Line Manager'. A procedure map comprises ellipses, called **steps,** which represent the processing logic written inside the ellipse. Logic shown in a step is **always** executed unconditionally. No conditional logic is ever executed within a step: all conditions are tested outside the step as discussed shortly.

A step may be joined to one or several other steps by arrows. These arrows indicate the sequence of execution, subject to any conditions associated with each arrow. We first enter (from a display screen, for example) the information which is common to each EMPLOYEE. Then we can enter information specific to a MANAGER. Next we enter that information which is unique to a LINE MANAGER. Only then can we add the EMPLOYEE record, followed by the MANAGER and then the LINE MANAGER records. (This logic is in fact in error: we will discuss this error in the next topic.)

Figure 5.4 shows unconditional execution of steps. A procedure map also enables conditional logic to be illustrated. One execution path (as indicated by arrows) is taken when a condition is true: a different path may be taken when the condition is false. We will use this principle to refine the logic illustrated above.

5.2.2   Conditional logic in a procedure map

As you have no doubt already found, the error in Figure 5.4 is due to an assumption that no record presently exists for the line manager whose new

"ADD NEW EMPLOYEE" PROCEDURE MAP

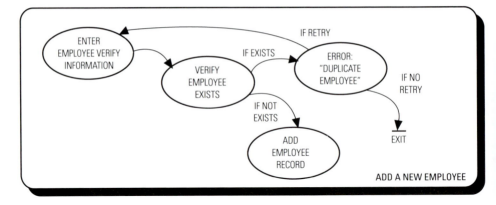

Figure 5.5 A procedure map to 'Add New Employee'. This illustrates the verification of an employee record, before adding that record.

record is to be added. In order to avoid a duplicate record being added we need to include a condition which tests whether a specific record exists. This is called **verifying a record,** and the logic is illustrated in Figure 5.5. This shows that conditions can be written on the procedure map at a point where an arrow which relates to that condition exits from the ellipse. Where several arrows exit from a step ellipse, each is followed in turn – moving around in a clockwise direction starting from the point of arrow entry into the ellipse from the preceding step.

In this example, the 'Verify Employee' Exists step is entered after the 'Enter Employee Information' step has been executed. After execution, we move around the ellipse clockwise from the point of entry until we reach the first exiting arrow.

If a condition is written in conjunction with an exiting arrow, the path indicated by that arrow is only taken if the condition is true. Otherwise that path is ignored and the next exiting arrow is examined. If no condition is written on the procedure map in conjunction with an arrow, that path is followed unconditionally.

Thus the path to the Error: 'Duplicate Employee' step is taken only if an employee record is found to exist by the 'Verify Employee Exists' step. To determine the record existence, the logic within that step may have attempted to read the specific record occurrence or to examine an index. If the record exists, the condition is true and the path is taken. Otherwise it is false: the path is not taken – we continue moving clockwise around the ellipse to the next exiting arrow.

If a record exists, the Error: 'Duplicate Employee' step is next executed.

This step may display the error message – Error: 'Duplicate Employee' on a display screen for the operator. Then we again move clockwise around this error step ellipse until the next exiting arrow is encountered. This has the condition 'If Retry' associated with it. The error may have been due to an incorrect employee number. It may be rectified by reentering the correct employee number. The exiting arrow shows this by leading back to the step 'Enter Employee Information'.

If the operator does not wish to retry (the error may be genuine and the required record already exists), the condition If 'No Retry' on the next exiting arrow is satisfied. This leads to a bar at the end of the arrow: it indicates EXIT; that is, no further processing is carried out for the specific employee record. Control therefore returns to the starting step: 'Enter Employee Information.' The next employee record which is to be added is then entered.

If no conditions were satisfied on moving clockwise around an ellipse, or if the last step at the end of a hierarchical series (or tree) of steps is executed and there are no other exiting arrows, we move back up the tree to the last exit point from a step. We continue moving clockwise from that point around the higher step. Thus we return to the point of exit from the 'Verify Employee Exists' step.

The next exiting arrow has the condition 'If Not Exists' associated with it. It leads to the step: 'Add Employee Record.' If the specific employee record does not exist, no error will occur from adding a record. The step therefore adds the employee record.

The last step in a tree has been executed. There are no other exiting arrows, so we move back to the starting step: 'Enter Employee Information'; to enter and process the next employee record.

A procedure map provides a clear representation of program logic for transaction-oriented, for batch-oriented, for real-time event-driven, or instead for embedded systems. It shows processing carried out for a business event by steps. Logic executed within an event is unconditional. All conditional logic is associated with exiting arrows from a step. These indicate the conditional execution paths of the subsequent steps to be executed.

The visual schematic logic in a procedure map can also be formally expressed as language-independent pseudocode. Figure 5.6 details the logic that is represented by the 'Add New Employee' procedure map in Figure 5.5.

This representation of procedure map and associated pseudocode offers us a significant advantage over other logic documentation methods such as program flow charts, action diagrams, data flow diagrams or structure charts (see Chapter 6). In conjunction with a data map in 4BNF and 5BNF, procedure maps enable us to identify common, reusable logic modules. These common logic modules are defined through **logic normalization**. They are called **generic procedures**.

ADD NEW EMPLOYEE PROCEDURE

```
ENTER EMPLOYEE VERIFY INFORMATION
VERIFY EMPLOYEE RECORD EXISTS
IF EMPLOYEE EXISTS
    THEN DISPLAY ERROR "DUPLICATE EMPLOYEE"
    IF NO RETRY IS REQUESTED
        THEN EXIT
    ELSE
        CALL VERIFY EMPLOYEE
    ELSE
        ADD EMPLOYEE RECORD
```

Figure 5.6   Pseudocode for procedure map in Figure 5.5.

5.3 | LOGIC NORMALIZATION

Business normalization groups attributes into entities where they are wholly dependent on the entire primary key of an entity. The definition of 4BNF secondary and 5BNF structure entities leads to greater business detail than traditional normalization.

Business normalization leads eventually to **logic normalization**: the logic required to process an entity exists in only one place, where it is wholly dependent on the attributes within that entity. It therefore can be used as common, reusable procedures: the intent of object-oriented programming. Logic normalization identifies reusable code through the development of generic procedures. This can be implemented by object-oriented or conventional programming techniques.

5.3.1   Generic procedures

A generic procedure is one where the same logic is used in conjunction with a number of different procedures. For example, the logic in Figure 5.5 – with some changes – is required not only when adding a record, but also when reading, updating or deleting a record. This is common logic which may be defined in a generic procedure. Logic in Figure 5.5 that is generic is indicated by shading in Figure 5.7. In its present form this logic is specific to addition of a record. We will first use it to introduce some of the concepts relating to generic procedures. We will then refine it as a generic procedure.

We can extract the shaded logic in Figure 5.7 into a separate procedure, called from the original procedure. This is shown as pseudocode in Figure

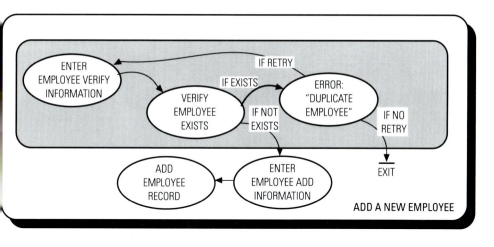

Figure 5.7   Potential generic logic is indicated by shading.

5.8. The 'Verify Employee' procedure is called (invoked) from the 'Add Employee' procedure. On return from this procedure a flag indicates whether a verify error occurred – that is, whether the record already exists. If an error was detected, the 'Add Employee' procedure exits immediately for the current employee. Otherwise the record is added.

When called, the 'Verify Employee' procedure first sets the error occurred flag to False. The employee verify information – such as an employee number – is entered from a display terminal, for example. This is used to determine (verify) whether the relevant employee record exists. If it does exist, the error message 'Duplicate Employee' is first displayed. If the operator indicates that no retry is requested, the error occurred flag is set to True and the procedure terminates. This flag is then tested in the 'Add Employee' procedure as discussed above. If a retry is requested, the 'Verify Employee' procedure is invoked recursively: the 'employee verify information' is reentered; the specified employee is again verified.

ADD EMPLOYEE PROCEDURE   VERIFY EMPLOYEE PROCEDURE

```
CALL VERIFY EMPLOYEE
IF ERROR OCCURRED
    THEN EXIT
ELSE
    ENTER EMPLOYEE ADD INFORMATION
    ADD EMPLOYEE RECORD
```

```
SET ERROR OCCURRED FLAG FALSE
ENTER EMPLOYEE VERIFY INFORMATION
VERIFY EMPLOYEE RECORD EXISTS
IF EMPLOYEE RECORD EXISTS
    THEN DISPLAY ERROR (DUPLICATE EMPLOYEE)
    IF NO RETRY IS REQUESTED
        THEN SET ERROR OCCURRED FLAG TRUE
    ELSE
        CALL VERIFY EMPLOYEE
```

Figure 5.8   Pseudocode for Verify Employee in Figure 5.7.

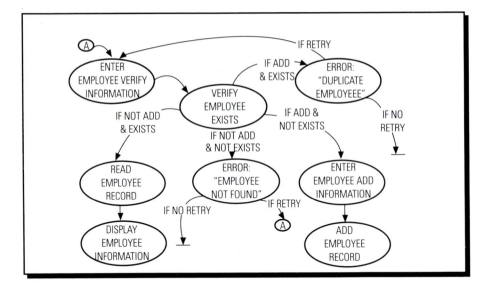

Figure 5.9 Correct procedure map for Verify Employee.

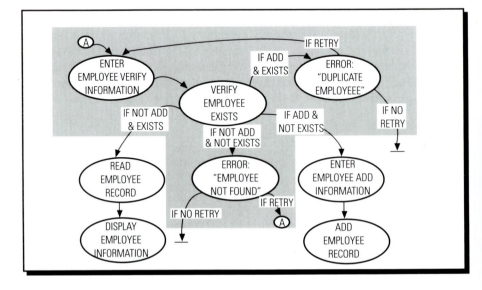

Figure 5.10 Generic logic is indicated by shading.

We discussed earlier that the 'Verify Employee' procedure only supports addition of a record. An error occurs in an add operation if the nominated record exists: a duplicate record would be added. However this is a valid condition for a read, update or delete operation. Only if the record exists can it be read, or updated, or deleted. An error is indicated if the record *does not* exist for these operations; this is shown by an error message, such as 'Record Not Found'.

A more correct procedure map is illustrated in Figure 5.9. If the operation is ADD and the record exists, the 'Duplicate Employee' error message is displayed. If no retry is requested, the procedure exits (terminates): otherwise the verify is retried with another nominated record. If no error occurs, the 'employee add information' is entered. These are attributes to be stored in the record for a new employee. The record is then added.

If the operation is NOT ADD (that is, read, update or delete), and the employee does not exist the 'Employee Not Found' error message applies. Retry can be requested or not, as discussed for add. Otherwise no error occurs and the record is read. It can then be displayed on a screen, for example. Logic common to this 'Verify Employee' procedure for add, read, update and delete operations is illustrated by shading in Figure 5.10. This is generic logic.

The logic illustrated in Figure 5.10 is expressed as pseudocode in Figure 5.11.

VERIFY EMPLOYEE PROCEDURE

```
SET ERROR OCCURRED FLAG FALSE
ENTER EMPLOYEE VERIFY INFORMATION
VERIFY EMPLOYEE RECORD EXISTS
IF (ADD AND EMPLOYEE EXISTS)
        THEN DISPLAY ERROR (DUPLICATE EMPLOYEE)
                IF NO RETRY IS REQUESTED
                    THEN SET ERROR OCCURRED FLAG TRUE
                ELSE
                    CALL VERIFY EMPLOYEE
IF (NOT ADD AND EMPLOYEE DOES NOT EXIST)
        THEN DISPLAY ERROR (EMPLOYEE NOT FOUND)
                IF NO RETRY IS REQUESTED
                    THEN SET ERROR OCCURRED FLAG TRUE
                ELSE
                    CALL VERIFY EMPLOYEE
```

Figure 5.11   Pseudocode for Verify procedure in Figure 5.10.

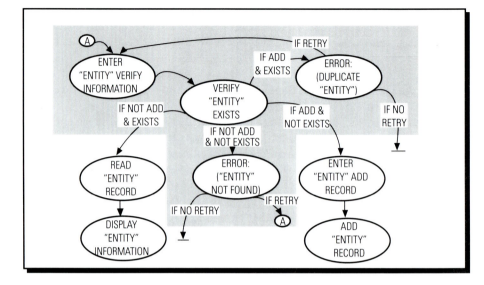

Figure 5.12 A generic Verify 'Entity' procedure map.

While Figures 5.10 and 5.11 show the logic for verifying an employee record, exactly the same logic applies when verifying the existence of any entity. This is illustrated in Figure 5.12, where the specific entity to be verified is indicated by the term 'ENTITY'.

Pseudocode for the generic procedure in Figure 5.12 is documented in Figure 5.13.

When this generic procedure is called from another procedure, at least two parameters are passed to it. One is the name of the entity to be verified. The other parameter is the operation to be carried out. For example, to verify the existence of an EMPLOYEE for an ADD operation, the generic Verify 'Entity' procedure in Figures 5.12 and 5.13 is invoked as follows:

```
Call Verify (EMPLOYEE, ADD)
```

These parameters are inserted dynamically in the generic Verify 'Entity' procedure. They verify the existence of the EMPLOYEE entity for an ADD operation. If it does not exist, the error message:

```
'DUPLICATE EMPLOYEE'
```

is displayed. However, if this procedure is called for any operation other than ADD (such as READ, or UPDATE, or DELETE), the error message

VERIFY "ENTITY" PROCEDURE

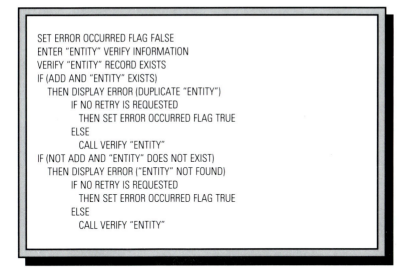

```
SET ERROR OCCURRED FLAG FALSE
ENTER "ENTITY" VERIFY INFORMATION
VERIFY "ENTITY" RECORD EXISTS
IF (ADD AND "ENTITY" EXISTS)
   THEN DISPLAY ERROR (DUPLICATE "ENTITY")
        IF NO RETRY IS REQUESTED
           THEN SET ERROR OCCURRED FLAG TRUE
        ELSE
           CALL VERIFY "ENTITY"
IF (NOT ADD AND "ENTITY" DOES NOT EXIST)
   THEN DISPLAY ERROR ("ENTITY" NOT FOUND)
        IF NO RETRY IS REQUESTED
           THEN SET ERROR OCCURRED FLAG TRUE
        ELSE
           CALL VERIFY "ENTITY"
```

Figure 5.13 Pseudocode for the procedure in Figure 5.12.

displayed instead is:

'EMPLOYEE NOT FOUND'

This generic procedure can be called from another procedure. As part of a procedure to read a record, for example, the existence of the record must first be verified. Thus a Read 'Entity' procedure can call the generic 'Verify Entity' procedure. The Read 'Entity' procedure therefore is also generic (see Figure 5.14).

Similarly, a Display 'Entity' procedure can call the generic Read 'Entity' procedure (which calls the generic Verify 'Entity' procedure). The Display 'Entity' procedure is thus generic as well. These generic procedures are illustrated in procedure map and pseudocode form in Figure 5.14.

The Verify 'Entity' procedure is shown in this figure as a heavy-line ellipse. While a step is indicated by a thin-line ellipse – with the name of the step written within it – a procedure map is shown as a heavy-line ellipse, but with the procedure name written within it. A Read 'Entity' generic procedure calls a Verify 'Entity' generic procedure, shown by shading in the figure, and is called by a Display 'Entity' generic procedure.

The Display 'Entity' generic procedure in turn can be invoked by a Change 'Entity' generic procedure as illustrated in Figure 5.15. After the

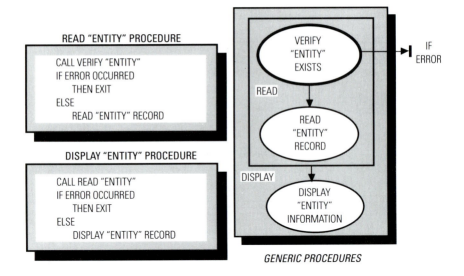

GENERIC PROCEDURES

Figure 5.14 Read and Display generic procedures.

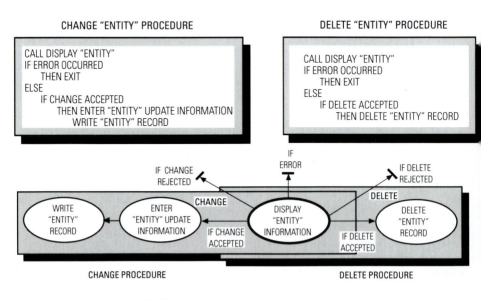

Figure 5.15 Change and Delete generic procedures.

required record is displayed, and before a change is applied, the operator is asked if the change is to be accepted. The specified record may have not been the particular record required, or the change may not be relevant for other reasons. If the operator rejects the change, the procedure terminates. Otherwise all updates are made to the record displayed on the screen. The updated record is written back, so replacing the previous version of the record.

The Display 'Entity' generic procedure is also invoked by the Delete 'Entity' generic procedure in Figure 5.15. The operator is similarly asked whether the displayed record is to be deleted. Again the record may not be the specific one required, or should not be deleted for other reasons. If the operator rejects the delete, the procedure terminates. If it is accepted, the displayed record is physically deleted.

Each of these generic procedures is illustrated together in Figure 5.16. This shows the invocation of generic procedures by other generic procedures.

We can now use these generic procedures in a higher-level generic procedure: Process 'Entity'. This is illustrated in Figure 5.17 together with the relevant pseudocode. As with the procedures described above, it also has two parameters. These are the name of the entity, and the operation that is to be applied (such as ADD, READ, CHANGE, DELETE or DISPLAY).

We have now covered many of the principles of process modeling and of generic procedures. The procedure mapping conventions are summarized in Box 5.1: some are not discussed until Chapter 6. We will use these concepts to develop quite complex procedures in that chapter. We will relate procedure maps to data flow diagrams, and will also implement them using a fourth generation language such as SQL.

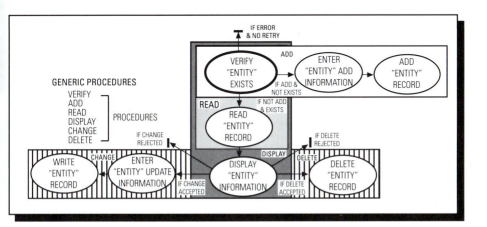

Figure 5.16 Summary of generic procedures.

GENERIC PROCEDURES

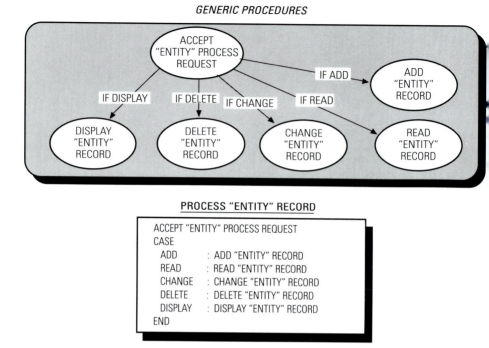

PROCESS "ENTITY" RECORD

```
ACCEPT "ENTITY" PROCESS REQUEST
CASE
    ADD      : ADD "ENTITY" RECORD
    READ     : READ "ENTITY" RECORD
    CHANGE   : CHANGE "ENTITY" RECORD
    DELETE   : DELETE "ENTITY" RECORD
    DISPLAY  : DISPLAY "ENTITY" RECORD
END
```

Figure 5.17 A generic Process procedure.

5.4 | SUMMARY

In this chapter we discussed some problems with traditional program development: due to redundant logic, and also embedded logic. This leads to high maintenance workloads when changes in data formats are made to files or data bases; many program changes must also be made. These problems are not adequately resolved by data independence facilities provided by DBMS products. Nor are they solved by traditional normalization to third normal form (3NF), or by business normalization to the third business normal form (3BNF) level.

Only when data are normalized to fourth and fifth business normal form (4BNF and 5BNF) are the problems of redundant logic and embedded logic adequately addressed. These business normalization forms also result in logic normalization: logic required to process an entity exists in only one place, where it is wholly dependent on the attributes of that entity. This is reusable logic; implemented by conventional programming, or by object-oriented programming methods.

Object-oriented logic exhibits characteristics of: encapsulation, where code is packaged with the data; and inheritance, where common logic in a higher-level object is inherited by all lower-level objects, unless overridden by the programmer.

We were introduced to conventions used by procedure maps in process modeling. A procedure map represents the processing associated with one (or several) business events. Ellipses illustrate steps, representing code executed unconditionally. All conditional logic is tested outside a step; the conditions control propagation to other steps in a defined execution sequence.

Logic normalization results in the development of generic procedures. This is generic logic to verify, add, read, display, change or delete data entities. It is coded as object-oriented logic, packaged with each relevant entity; or can be coded using conventional programming techniques.

Reference

[1] Cox, B. (1987). *Object Oriented Programming*. Addison-Wesley: Reading, MA.

Box 5.1

Procedure mapping conventions

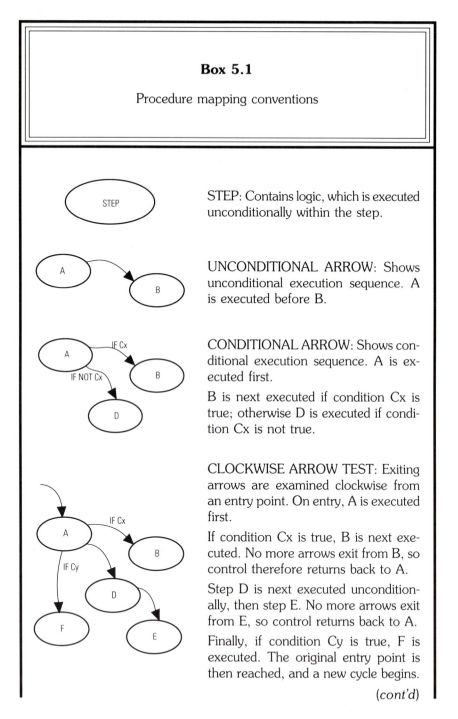

STEP: Contains logic, which is executed unconditionally within the step.

UNCONDITIONAL ARROW: Shows unconditional execution sequence. A is executed before B.

CONDITIONAL ARROW: Shows conditional execution sequence. A is executed first.

B is next executed if condition Cx is true; otherwise D is executed if condition Cx is not true.

CLOCKWISE ARROW TEST: Exiting arrows are examined clockwise from an entry point. On entry, A is executed first.

If condition Cx is true, B is next executed. No more arrows exit from B, so control therefore returns back to A.

Step D is next executed unconditionally, then step E. No more arrows exit from E, so control returns back to A.

Finally, if condition Cy is true, F is executed. The original entry point is then reached, and a new cycle begins.

(cont'd)

Box 5.1 (cont.)

Procedure mapping conventions

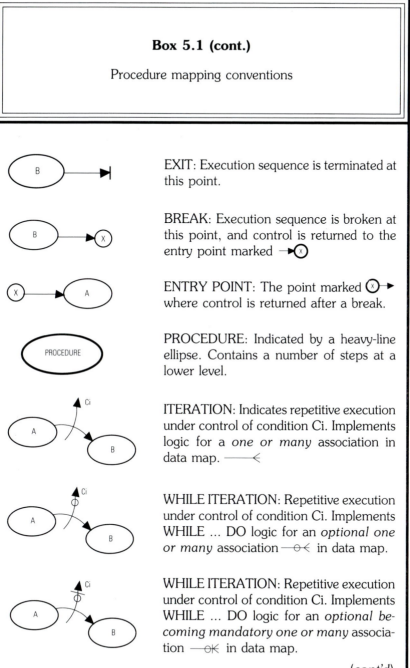

EXIT: Execution sequence is terminated at this point.

BREAK: Execution sequence is broken at this point, and control is returned to the entry point marked →Ⓧ

ENTRY POINT: The point marked Ⓧ→ where control is returned after a break.

PROCEDURE: Indicated by a heavy-line ellipse. Contains a number of steps at a lower level.

ITERATION: Indicates repetitive execution under control of condition C_i. Implements logic for a *one or many* association in data map. ——<

WHILE ITERATION: Repetitive execution under control of condition C_i. Implements WHILE ... DO logic for an *optional one or many* association —o< in data map.

WHILE ITERATION: Repetitive execution under control of condition C_i. Implements WHILE ... DO logic for an *optional becoming mandatory one or many* association —o< in data map.

(cont'd)

Box 5.1 (cont.)

Procedure mapping conventions

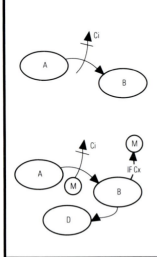

REPEAT ITERATION: Repetitive execution under control of condition Ci. Implements REPEAT ... UNTIL logic for a mandatory one or many association in data map. —K

CONDITIONAL RETURN: As for BREAK, iteration is broken at the point M. Control returns to the iteration test at M→

CHAPTER 6

Implementing Process Models

Process modeling derives procedural logic from a data model. Structured analysis, part of software engineering, uses Data Flow Diagrams (DFD's) and mini-specs to document logic. This chapter shows both the similarities and differences which exist between procedure maps and DFDs: it illustrates that, like procedure maps, DFDs can also be derived from a data model. But when data maps and procedure maps are both used, the need for structure charts (developed using structured design) is eliminated. The data map with its derived procedure maps represent the program module structure.

The chapter shows how procedure maps can be expressed as procedural logic using pseudocode, for implementation by third, fourth or fifth generation languages. It also shows their implementation using a non-procedural language such as SQL.

6.1 DATA FLOW DIAGRAMS AND DATA MODELS

A Data Flow Diagram is used by structured analysis to document the movement of data in an organization [1, 2, 3, 4, 5]. In this section we will examine how a DFD can be used in conjunction with a data model to represent processing of data. We will start with a DFD to represent processing of an Employee Adjustment Request, illustrated conceptually in Figure 6.1.

DATA FLOW DIAGRAM TO PROCESS EMPLOYEE ADJUSTMENT REQUEST

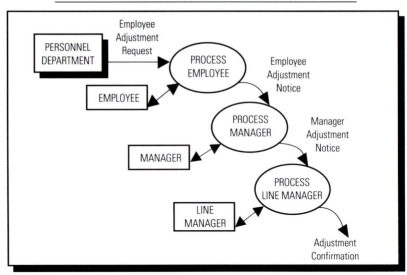

Figure 6.1   Employee Adjustment Request DFD.

This DFD has not been leveled in order to show characteristics of DFDs and procedure maps more clearly. We will look at leveling later in this chapter.

External entities such as the Personnel Department are represented by squares (not to be confused with the term 'entity' used in data modeling terminology). Processes, or **process 'bubbles'**, are represented by ellipses (not to be confused with 'steps' in process modeling). Data, referenced by processes, are shown as **'data stores'** and are represented by rectangles.

The DFD in Figure 6.1 shows acceptance of an Employee Adjustment Request from the Personnel Department (an **'external entity'** in DFD terminology). This request is first processed by referencing the Employee data store (indicated by the 'Process Employee' bubble and the 'Employee' rectangle). An Employee Adjustment Notice is produced by this process, which then flows to the next process bubble: 'Process Manager'. In turn, this references the 'Manager' data store. The Manager Adjustment Notice that is produced next flows to the 'Process Line Manager' bubble. This references the 'Line Manager' data store. The Adjustment Confirmation is finally produced.

We will take this DFD and map it onto the data model from Figure 5.3; illustrated in Figure 6.2.

This indicates that DFD data stores, when normalized correctly, correspond to entities of a data model. Furthermore, process bubbles

PROCESS EMPLOYEE ADJUSTMENT REQUEST

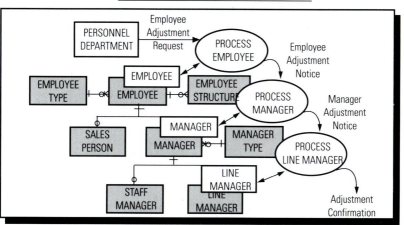

Figure 6.2   Mapping a DFD to a data model.

GENERIC EMPLOYEE PROCESSING PROCEDURE MODEL

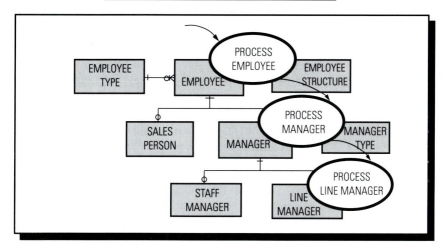

Figure 6.3   A procedure map for the DFD in Figure 6.2.

potentially correspond to the steps of a procedure map. Figure 6.3 shows a procedure map developed from the data model of Figure 5.3 which carries out processing similar to the DFD in Figures 6.1 and 6.2. It is a procedure map based on the generic *Process* procedure of Figure 5.17, showing an unconditional execution path.

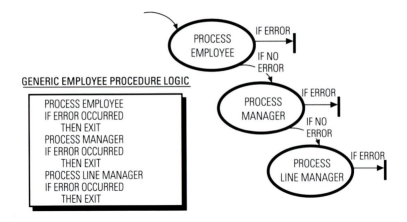

Figure 6.4 Pseudocode for procedure map in Figure 6.3.

Figure 6.4 illustrates in pseudocode the simple logic expressed in the procedure map of Figure 6.3. A data flow, moving from one process bubble to another, corresponds to the execution sequence of a procedure and indicates an access path through the data model. However, there are distinct differences between DFDs and procedure maps as discussed next.

6.1.1 DFD data consistency

In Figure 6.1 the flow of data from one process to the next did not occur because of redundant data, but because of necessary data transformations to be carried out by each process on the data. Often data must also flow between processes to ensure that any redundant versions are kept consistent and up to date: this is **DFD data consistency**. The flow of data within a procedure map which has been developed from a data model in 4BNF and 5BNF is significantly decreased because the data exist in a single version.

6.1.2 Conditional logic

A DFD shows data flow, not conditional logic. That logic is locked within each DFD process and is expressed by structured analysis as mini-specs, or pseudocode. In contrast, conditional logic is clearly shown in a procedure map by conditional execution paths.

A procedure map contains certain details similar to a Data Flow Diagram, and so can be used to represent DFDs. We saw that DFD processes contain embedded conditional logic, while the logic in each step of a procedure map is executed unconditionally. Conditional logic is shown as part of the procedure map, and can be translated directly into pseudocode. Thus a procedure map can represent both a DFD and its mini-specs. Furthermore, with the use of generic procedures, a procedure map (and hence DFD) can be derived directly from a data map as we saw in Figures 6.3 and 6.4.

This is the reverse of current structured analysis practice, which recommends that a DFD be developed first based on the current system physical environment. This DFD is called the Old Physical Model. It is then expressed in logical, rather than physical, terms and so becomes the Old Logical Model DFD. Next the New Logical Model DFD is defined for the new system to be developed, after which the New Physical Model DFD is determined for the new system physical environment.

A number of difficulties occur with this approach:

- DFDs are generally developed for operational application systems. These systems and their associated data may change in the future, based on new strategic directions set by management. The DFDs and application systems developed from them will also change.
- Old physical and old logical DFDs of operational systems may have much redundant data. Modern structured analysis specifies that data represented in data stores must be normalized. However, it is difficult to identify all the relevant data from only the procedural perspective of current operational systems.
- Moving from an old logical DFD to a new logical DFD can be difficult. The procedures needed to support new strategic directions set by management may not be obvious at the operational level of an organization, even if those new directions are communicated well by management.

In contrast, procedure maps are derived from data maps which reflect new strategic directions. These data maps may also suggest new strategies in support of new goals and objectives set by management and the strategies can lead to new procedures. The new logical DFDs (which are the objective of structured analysis) are analogous to and derived with precision from data maps which clearly represent managements' new directions.

6.1.3 Alternative access paths

A procedure map represents an access path through a data map. For example, Figure 6.3 showed an execution sequence (access path) which first processed data common to all employees: this was contained in the principal entity EMPLOYEE. Next processing specific to managers (in MANAGER) was carried out. Finally processing for line managers (in LINE MANAGER) was completed.

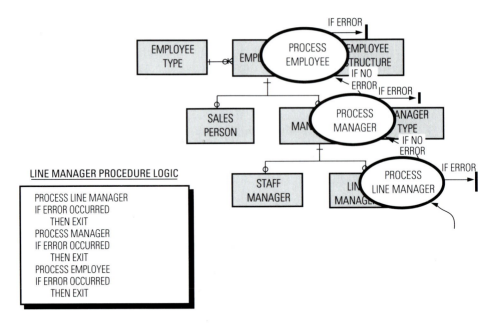

Figure 6.5 Specific-to-general (that is, 'expert') processing.

This is a **general-to-specific** processing strategy: from the principal entity (which exists for every employee) down the hierarchy of entities only for those employees who are managers, and more particularly line managers. It shows a processing strategy that may be appropriate for operators not familiar with manager and line manager employees. This strategy is sometimes called a **novice** processing strategy.

Alternatively we could have elected to use a **specific-to-general** processing strategy for experienced operators who already know that certain employees are line managers, and so can directly carry out relevant line manager processing first. This is sometimes called an **expert** processing strategy: experienced operators move directly to a detailed level of processing without having to pass first through intermediate steps. An example of this processing strategy is illustrated in Figure 6.5.

6.1.4 Leveling of procedures

We can use the *Process* procedure to build progressively more complex procedures, made up of a number of generic procedures. This leads to a leveling of procedures that are referred to as **high-level procedures**. These provide a similar degree of abstraction to that used for leveling DFDs, as discussed earlier. This construction of high-level procedures may be indicated by a

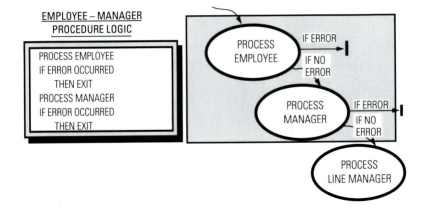

Figure 6.6   Employee–Manager higher-level procedure.

4BNF data map hierarchy as with the EMPLOYEE hierarchy in Figure 5.3. This is illustrated in Figure 6.6.

The two procedures: 'Process Employee' and 'Process Manager' have been consolidated in a higher-level procedure, called 'Process Employee–Manager'. When invoked, this initiates processing of both the EMPLOYEE and the MANAGER entities. We can develop from this a still more complex procedure, including the 'Process Line Manager' generic procedure in a higher-level procedure called 'Process Employee–Line Manager'. This is illustrated in Figure 6.7. The 'Employee–Line Manager' higher-level procedure thus represents leveling down through the hierarchy from EMPLOYEE to MANAGER to LINE MANAGER, and so reflects the general-to-specific novice processing strategy.

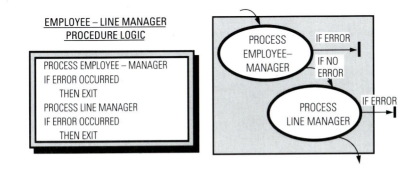

Figure 6.7   Employee–Line Manager higher-level procedure reflecting a 'novice' processing strategy.

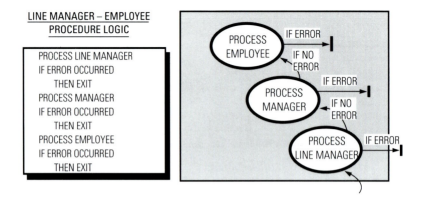

LINE MANAGER – EMPLOYEE
PROCEDURE LOGIC

PROCESS LINE MANAGER
IF ERROR OCCURRED
    THEN EXIT
PROCESS MANAGER
IF ERROR OCCURRED
    THEN EXIT
PROCESS EMPLOYEE
IF ERROR OCCURRED
    THEN EXIT

PROCESS EMPLOYEE   IF ERROR
                    IF NO ERROR
PROCESS MANAGER   IF ERROR
                    IF NO ERROR
PROCESS LINE MANAGER IF ERROR

Figure 6.8 Line Manager–Employee higher-level procedure reflecting an 'expert' processing strategy.

Similarly we can move up the hierarchy from LINE MANAGER to MANAGER to EMPLOYEE based on the specific-to-general, or expert processing strategy of Figure 6.5. This is shown in Figure 6.8.

These higher-level procedures can now be invoked to initiate processing of the generic procedures which comprise them, based on appropriate processing strategies. While the sequence of execution for the novice procedure in Figure 6.7 differs from the expert execution sequence in Figure 6.8, it is important to note that the processing logic is otherwise identical. These two higher-level procedures are shown in Figure 6.9.

We will now use the principles of alternative access path processing strategies, and of higher-level procedures, to consider more complex, iterative logic in procedure maps. We will relate these procedure maps also to their DFD counterparts. The procedure map conventions discussed in this next section are documented in Box 5.1.

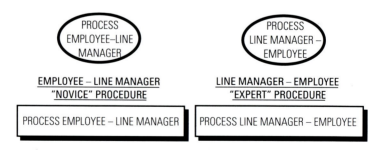

PROCESS EMPLOYEE–LINE MANAGER

EMPLOYEE – LINE MANAGER
"NOVICE" PROCEDURE

PROCESS EMPLOYEE – LINE MANAGER

PROCESS LINE MANAGER – EMPLOYEE

LINE MANAGER – EMPLOYEE
"EXPERT" PROCEDURE

PROCESS LINE MANAGER – EMPLOYEE

Figure 6.9 'Novice' and 'expert' higher-level procedures.

EMPLOYEE JOB SKILLS DATA MODEL

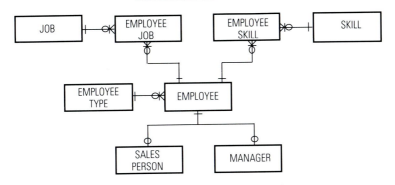

Figure 6.10   Data map of employees and skills.

6.1.5   Iterative procedure maps

We will use the data map from Figure 4.5 of employees and skills, repeated here as Figure 6.10. This will provide the basis for derivation of DFDs and procedure maps. The entity list for this data map is repeated from Chapter 4.

EMPLOYEE TYPE	(employee type number#, employee type name)
EMPLOYEE	(employee number#, [employee name], (employee address), [employee postcode], employee type number#)
SALES PERSON	(employee number#, sales person quota)
MANAGER	(employee number#, [manager title])
SUPPORT PERSON	(employee number#)
EMPLOYEE STRUCTURE	(employee number#, employee type number#, employee number#, employee type number#)
EMPLOYEE SKILL	(employee number#, skill number#, employee skill level)
SKILL	(skill number#, [skill name])
EMPLOYEE JOB	(employee number#, job number#, employee job salary)
JOB	(job number#, job name)

We will start with a DFD which documents the processing required to list employees having a given skill, as illustrated in Figure 6.11.

This was derived from the data map in Figure 6.10, as shown by Figure 6.12.

DATA FLOW DIAGRAM TO LIST ALL EMPLOYEES WITH A GIVEN SKILL

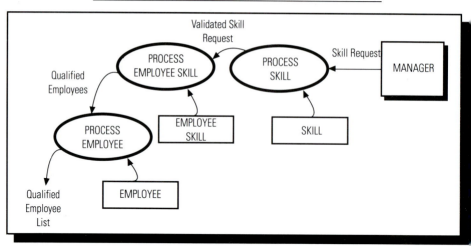

Figure 6.11 A DFD to list employees and their skills.

DERIVATION OF DATA FLOW DIAGRAM FROM EMPLOYEE JOB SKILLS DATA MODEL

"LIST ALL EMPLOYEES WITH A GIVEN SKILL"

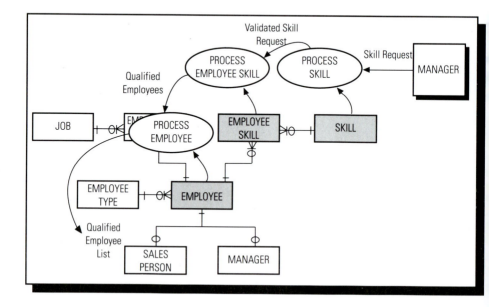

Figure 6.12 Derivation of DFD from data map.

PROCEDURE MAP TO LIST ALL EMPLOYEES WITH A GIVEN SKILL

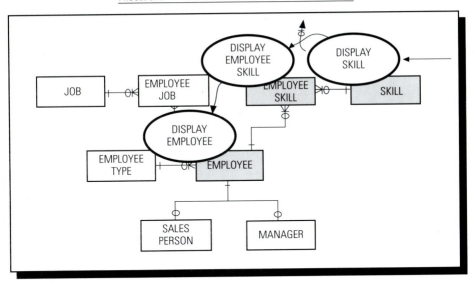

Figure 6.13 Procedure map for the business event: 'List employees with a given skill'.

We can similarly derive a procedure map for this processing, as shown in Figure 6.13. This illustrates processing for the business event: 'List all Employees with a Given Skill'.

We have been more explicit in the representation of the generic *Process* procedure in this figure: we now show the specific action within the procedure ellipse, such as in the 'Display Skill' procedure and the 'Display Employee Skill' procedure in Figure 6.13.

Notice the curved arrow on the execution path from the 'Display Skill' procedure to the 'Display Employee Skill' procedure. As defined in Box 5.1, this indicates processing iteration. It is determined directly from the *one to many* association between SKILL and EMPLOYEE SKILL in the data map. It indicates that procedures or steps following the curved line, to the end of the current execution tree (that is, 'Display Employee'), are executed as part of an execution loop.

The nature of a *one to many* association is repeated on the curved arrow. It shows the form of the loop. An association which is *optional* indicates WHILE . . . DO iteration: under certain conditions a related entity occurrence *may* exist; in this latter case the loop is not executed at all. An association which is *mandatory* shows REPEAT . . . UNTIL iteration: at least one iteration of the loop occurs; the association indicates that a related entity *must* exist. *Optional becoming mandatory* nature on the association

DISPLAY ALL EMPLOYEES WITH A GIVEN SKILL

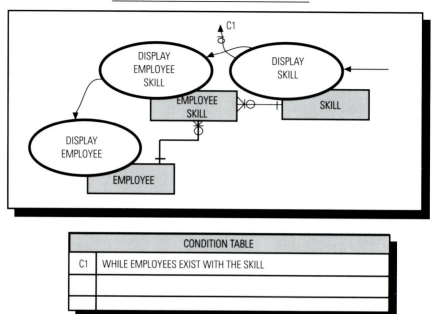

CONDITION TABLE	
C1	WHILE EMPLOYEES EXIST WITH THE SKILL

Figure 6.14 Processing iteration in a procedure map.

also indicates WHILE . . . DO iteration, but only under certain conditions which may, perhaps, indicate time dependency.

These iteration conditions can be written in full on the procedure map, or instead a code such as Cx (where x = a condition number) is written as shown in Figure 6.14. This code references a separate Condition Table that is associated with the procedure map. The detail of the condition is written in the Condition Table with the relevant condition number. The pseudocode for this procedure is shown in Figure 6.15.

```
DISPLAY SKILL
WHILE (EMPLOYEES EXIST WITH THE SKILL)
    DISPLAY EMPLOYEE SKILL
    DISPLAY EMPLOYEE
END WHILE
```

Figure 6.15 Pseudocode for the procedure map in Figure 6.14.

A Condition Table can be physically implemented as a table in a data base. This is very powerful: the Condition Table stores conditions as data. These conditions can therefore be easily changed to reflect changes in the business. Once changed, the new conditions are used in the procedure: so reducing program maintenance. To ensure appropriate program performance, relevant conditions are read from the Condition Table into memory at the start of program execution. These conditions can then be evaluated at CPU speed without I/O access overheads.

The logic represented in a procedure map and expressed in pseudocode translates very easily into third, fourth or fifth generation languages. We will illustrate this logic using SQL as a 4GL. For readers who are not familiar with SQL, Appendix 1 provides a tutorial. SQL is used extensively in the remainder of this book to show relevant logic: you may therefore wish to read Appendix 1 now.

Figure 6.16 shows a SQL SELECT command for the logic in Figures 6.14 and 6.15, based on the entity list for Figure 6.10. Each entity is implemented in SQL as a table, with each attribute within an entity implemented as a column in the relevant table. This shows a join of the SQL tables: SKILL, EMPLOYEE_SKILL and EMPLOYEE, with relevant columns projected as indicated in the SELECT clause.

Now consider the procedure map in Figure 6.17, which displays the processing logic for the business event: 'List the skills held by an employee'. This indicates a different processing strategy, shown by a different access path with entry not at SKILL (as for Figure 6.14) but instead at EMPLOYEE. The condition C2 on the procedure map is also included in the Condition Table. Compare Figure 6.17 now with Figure 6.14. We can see that the same generic *Process* procedures are used, but in a different execution sequence. This is one of the most powerful features of process modeling: code written for the generic *Process* procedures in Figure 6.14 is directly reusable also in Figure 6.17.

The logic of this procedure map is shown in pseudocode in Figure 6.18. As for Figure 6.15, this also includes a WHILE . . . DO loop: for the *optional becoming mandatory many* association between EMPLOYEE and EMPLOYEE SKILL.

```
SELECT    SKILL.skill_number, skill_name, employee_name,
            employee_skill_level
FROM      SKILL, EMPLOYEE_SKILL, EMPLOYEE
WHERE     SKILL.skill_number = EMPLOYEE_SKILL.skill_number
AND       EMPLOYEE_SKILL.employee_number =
            EMPLOYEE.employee_number;
```

Figure 6.16 Procedure map in Figure 6.14 expressed in SQL.

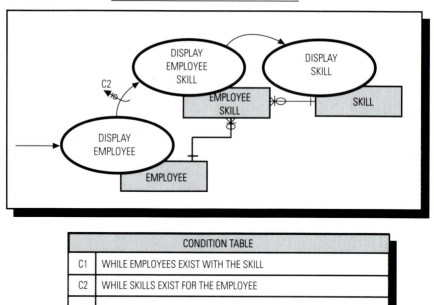

DISPLAY ALL SKILLS HELD BY AN EMPLOYEE

CONDITION TABLE	
C1	WHILE EMPLOYEES EXIST WITH THE SKILL
C2	WHILE SKILLS EXIST FOR THE EMPLOYEE

Figure 6.17   A different processing strategy, for the business event: 'List the skills held by an employee'.

Optional becoming Mandatory Many

```
DISPLAY EMPLOYEE
WHILE (SKILLS EXIST FOR THE EMPLOYEE)
     DISPLAY EMPLOYEE SKILL
     DISPLAY SKILL
END WHILE
```

Figure 6.18   WHILE . . . Do iteration for the *optional becoming mandatory many* association between EMPLOYEE and SKILL.

An SQL SELECT command for Figures 6.17 and 6.18 is documented in Figure 6.19. This determines whether an employee has any skills, by joining the EMPLOYEE and EMPLOYEE_SKILL tables. If an employee has no skills, a null result – that is, an empty result table – is presented; this implements the WHILE . . . DO processing iteration of Figure 6.18. Other-

```
SELECT    employee_name, SKILL.skill_number, skill_name,
              employee_skill_level
FROM      EMPLOYEE, SKILL, EMPLOYEE_SKILL
WHERE     EMPLOYEE.employee_number =
              EMPLOYEE_SKILL.employee_number
AND       EMPLOYEE_SKILL.skill_number = SKILL.skill_number;
```

Figure 6.19 SQL command for the procedure map in Figure 6.17.

wise all skills for an employee are retrieved by the join between EMPLOYEE and EMPLOYEE_SKILL, and by the join between EMPLOYEE_SKILL and SKILL.

If the EMPLOYEE to EMPLOYEE SKILL association was *mandatory many*, however, a REPEAT . . . UNTIL loop would be used; documented as pseudocode in Figure 6.20. This indicates a need for referential integrity.

6.1.6 Referential integrity

If the association between EMPLOYEE and EMPLOYEE SKILL is *mandatory many*, a referential integrity constraint is indicated. This association specifies that there must be a minimum of one skill for each employee. Complete support for referential integrity, as shown in Figure 6.20, is still lacking in some implementations of SQL on the market today. This constraint should be enforced by SQL when a new row is inserted in the EMPLOYEE table: at least one skill must also be inserted in the EMPLOYEE_SKILL table as a row for that employee.

The addition of skills for a new employee comprises the next example in Figure 6.21. This represents the business event: 'Add a New Employee and

Mandatory Many

```
DISPLAY EMPLOYEE
REPEAT
    DISPLAY EMPLOYEE SKILL
    DISPLAY SKILL
UNTIL (NO MORE SKILLS EXIST FOR THE EMPLOYEE)
```

Figure 6.20 Referential integrity of REPEAT . . . UNTIL iteration if a *mandatory many* association at EMPLOYEE SKILL exists in Figure 6.18.

ADD A NEW EMPLOYEE AND AT LEAST ONE SKILL

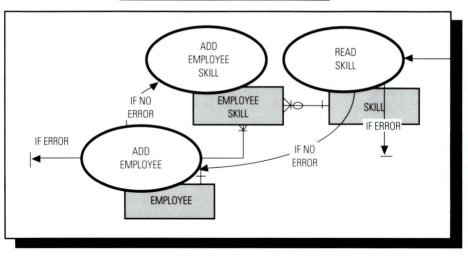

Figure 6.21 Addition of at least one skill for a new employee.

at least one skill'. We will see some of the problems created by the lack of referential integrity in SQL.

Figure 6.21 indicates that, if a specified SKILL is valid and an EMPLOYEE is added with that skill, unconditionally an EMPLOYEE SKILL occurrence must also be added; shown by the *mandatory one to mandatory many* association between EMPLOYEE and EMPLOYEE SKILL. This logic is shown in Figure 6.22. If the employee to be added is not a duplicate, then a skill for that employee must be added. Again, the same generic *Process* procedures used in Figures 6.14 and 6.17 are reused in Figure 6.21, showing now the 'Add' operation rather than the 'Display' operation.

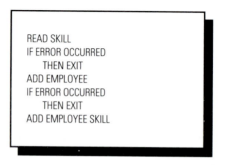

Figure 6.22 Pseudocode for Figure 6.21.

```
INSERT INTO     EMPLOYEE
VALUES          (6150, 'John Smith');

INSERT INTO     EMPLOYEE_SKILL
VALUES          (employee_number, skill_number, 3)
SELECT          employee_number, S1.skill_number
FROM            EMPLOYEE, SKILL S1
   WHERE EXISTS    (SELECT employee_number)
                   FROM    EMPLOYEE
                   WHERE   employee_number = 6150)
AND
   WHERE EXISTS    (SELECT S2.skill_number
                   FROM    SKILL S2
                   WHERE   S2.skill_number = 32);
```

Figure 6.23   SQL referential integrity errors for Figure 6.21.

Expressed directly in SQL using INSERT statements, the lack of referential integrity is obvious. This is shown in Figure 6.23. The result is cumbersome, and in error. This assumes the EMPLOYEE table was created with a unique index on *employee_number*. A new employee is added by the first INSERT statement; the second INSERT should not be executed, however, if any error occurs. An employee row cannot exist without at least one employee skill row: otherwise the result is data disintegrity.

Some SQL implementations provide a mechanism for testing SQL error return codes after each INSERT, but this is cumbersome and is dependent on that specific version of SQL. Embedded SQL commands in COBOL, PL/1 or C enable error conditions to be tested to enforce this referential integrity, but data model logic is thus implemented in programs rather than as part of the RDBMS.

SQL should be at least capable of accepting mandatory associations as shown in Figure 6.21, and enforcing the required referential integrity. The conditional association nature of optional, and of optional becoming mandatory, should also be expressed to SQL so that the referential integrity indicated by these associations is also observed.

Of course, no referential integrity problems exist for the example in Figure 6.24. This illustrates a SQL update command applied to a single table: it increases the quota of all sales persons by 10%.

We earlier discussed higher-level procedures in conjunction with Figures 6.6–6.9. These can be implemented in SQL using the SQL CREATE VIEW command. Views present a useful way to implement SQL logic associated with 4BNF secondary entities, and also 5BNF structure entities.

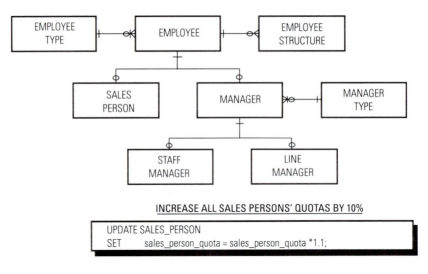

Figure 6.24 SQL update processing.

6.1.7 4BNF Secondary entities using SQL

The SQL CREATE VIEW command (see Appendix 1) allows complex SQL commands to be defined and given a view-name. Figure 6.25 shows the EMPLOYEE_SALES view, based on the join of EMPLOYEE and SALES PERSON. Only those employees who are sales persons are selected. SQL queries using this view follow in Figure 6.26.

The first of these examples selects all columns for employee number 8701. The second selects only those sales persons who have a sales quota exceeding 1,000. Both queries first result in a join of EMPLOYEE and SALES PERSON tables to select only those employees who are sales persons.

Consider now another view, EMPLOYEE_MANAGER, which is based on the join of EMPLOYEE and MANAGER as shown in Figure 6.27. A query based on this view is shown in Figure 6.28.

A view-name can be used in other commands as a simple table which exists logically, but is derived when the view-name is referenced. For integrity reasons many complex views cannot be updated (not 'updateable') and so cannot be used in conjunction with SQL INSERT, UPDATE or DELETE commands [6, 7].

Views not only simplify SQL queries for end-users: they also offer flexibility for data base administrators. If the processing overhead of frequent joins presents performance problems, the architectures supported by

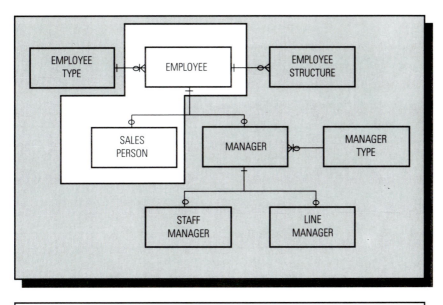

```
CREATE VIEW EMPLOYEE_SALES AS
(SELECT EMPLOYEE.employee_number, employee_name,
        employee_type_number, sales_person_quota
FROM    EMPLOYEE, SALES_PERSON
WHERE   EMPLOYEE.employee_number = SALES_PERSON. employee_number);
```

Figure 6.25   SQL CREATE VIEW for EMPLOYEE_SALES.

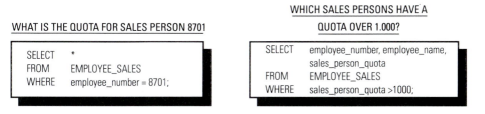

WHAT IS THE QUOTA FOR SALES PERSON 8701

```
SELECT   *
FROM     EMPLOYEE_SALES
WHERE    employee_number = 8701;
```

WHICH SALES PERSONS HAVE A
QUOTA OVER 1.000?

```
SELECT   employee_number, employee_name,
         sales_person_quota
FROM     EMPLOYEE_SALES
WHERE    sales_person_quota >1000;
```

Figure 6.26   SQL queries for the EMPLOYEE_SALES view.

many SQL implementations enable the tables or rows participating in a join to be physically clustered close together to minimize I/O accesses.

If this is not sufficient, a logical view can be implemented directly as a physical table. Thus 4BNF secondary entity tables or rows can be combined back into their associated 3BNF principal entity table, and implemented as one table. We saw in Chapter 5 that this can present maintenance problems

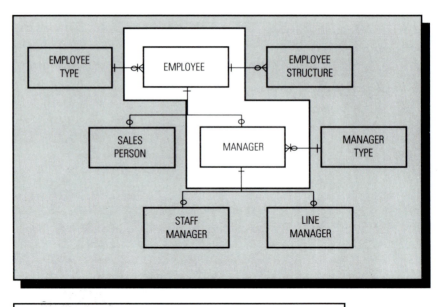

```
CREATE VIEW EMPLOYEE_MANAGER AS
(SELECT        EMPLOYEE.employee_number,
               employee_name, employee_type_number
FROM           EMPLOYEE, MANAGER
WHERE          EMPLOYEE.employee_number =
               MANAGER.employee_number);
```

Figure 6.27 SQL CREATE VIEW for EMPLOYEE_MANAGER.

WHO IS MANAGER #1234 ?

```
SELECT     *
FROM       EMPLOYEE_MANAGER
WHERE      employee_number = 1234;
```

Figure 6.28 SQL query for the EMPLOYEE_MANAGER view.

due to embedded logic, if entities are only in 3BNF. A SQL architectural solution is always preferable, as discussed above, but performance considerations may sometimes dictate this 3BNF consolidation approach.

We will now use SQL to implement the logic inherent in 5BNF entities.

6.1.8   5BNF structure entities using SQL

We saw that the STRUCTURE entity discussed in Chapter 2 is in fact a 5BNF entity as described in Chapter 4. Column names must be unique within a SQL table. Therefore the duplicate keys of a STRUCTURE entity are defined for SQL instead using foreign key alias names:

EMPLOYEE STRUCTURE   (employee number#, employee type number#, related employee number#, related employee type number#)

The typical content of an EMPLOYEE STRUCTURE table is illustrated in Figure 6.29.

We can define a SQL view which enables us to determine all employees who report to a manager. EMPLOYEE (which contains common employee columns such as employee name and address) and EMPLOYEE_STRUC-TURE are joined only for those employees who are of type 'MANAGER'.

Both of the queries in Figure 6.30 are based on the view illustrated in Figure 6.31. This view supports SQL query processing analogous to that used for a Bill of Materials product structure in manufacturing. The first

EMPLOYEE STRUCTURE DATA

Employee Number	Employee Type	Related Employee Number	Related Employee Type
1234	MANAGER	5678	SALES PERSON
		8901	SALES PERSON
		1733	LINE MANAGER
		2177	LINE MANAGER
		8791	SALES PERSON
2177	MANAGER	2177	SALES PERSON
		1336	SALES PERSON
		1733	SALES PERSON
		5678	SALES PERSON
7300	MANAGER	2177	LINE MANAGER
		1234	LINE MANAGER
		8701	LINE MANAGER
8701	MANAGER	8701	SALES PERSON
		8901	SALES PERSON
		1338	SALES PERSON

Figure 6.29   Content of the EMPLOYEE_STRUCTURE table.

WHO REPORTS TO MR. JONES (MANAGER 7300)?

```
SELECT    employee_number, employee_name, employee_type_number
FROM      MANAGEMENT
WHERE     employee_number = 7300;
```

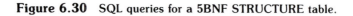

WHICH MANAGERS HAVE HAD SALES EXPERIENCE?

```
SELECT    employee_number, employee_name, employee_type_number
FROM      MANAGEMENT
WHERE     related_employee_type_number LIKE 'SALES PERSON'
AND       employee_number = related_employee_number;
```

Figure 6.30   SQL queries for a 5BNF STRUCTURE table.

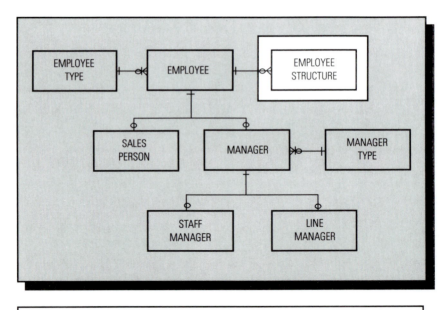

```
CREATE VIEW MANAGEMENT AS
(SELECT        *
FROM           EMPLOYEE, EMPLOYEE_STRUCTURE
WHERE          EMPLOYEE_STRUCTURE.employee_type_number = 'MANAGER'
AND            EMPLOYEE.employee_number =
               employee_structure.employee_number);
```

Figure 6.31   'Bill of Material' type logic using SQL.

```
CREATE VIEW SALES_REPORTING AS
(SELECT         *
FROM            EMPLOYEE, EMPLOYEE_STRUCTURE
WHERE           EMPLOYEE_STRUCTURE.related_employee_type_number =
                'SALES PERSON'
AND             EMPLOYEE_STRUCTURE.employee_number =
                EMPLOYEE.employee_number);
```

Figure 6.32 'Where-Used' type logic in SQL.

WHO DOES SALES PERSON# 1733 REPORT TO ?

```
SELECT      employee_number, employee_name, employee_type_number
FROM        SALES_REPORTING
WHERE       related_employee_number = 1733;
```

Figure 6.33 A Sales Reporting SQL query.

query extracts that section of the table in Figure 6.29 for Manager 7300. Line Managers 2177, 1234, and 8701 report to this manager. The second query in Figure 6.30 finds that Managers 2177 and 8701 have had prior sales experience.

The other perspective, analogous to the 'Where-Used' form of processing also used in manufacturing, is shown by the view in Figure 6.32 (see *Note* after Figure 6.29). This figure shows a Sales Reporting view, as shown by the query in Figure 6.33.

Figure 6.32 uses the SALES_REPORTING view first to select related employees who are sales persons. Figure 6.33 then selects related employee 1733, who reports as a sales person only to manager 2177. (Employee 1733 also reports to manager 1234, but as a line manager – not as a sales person.)

6.2 | BENEFITS OF PROCESS MODELING

Chapters 5 and 6 have introduced the principles of process modeling. This offers us the following advantages over traditional software engineering techniques:

- Procedure maps can be developed by users, or by computer professionals. The definition of data flow diagrams, action diagrams or structure charts, however, requires considerable DP expertise.

- Procedure maps show visual program logic. Different execution paths in a procedure map represent alternative processing strategies. This provides a flexible method for users to evaluate different business processing options.

- Procedure maps are derived directly from a data map. Data map associations show execution paths, iteration and conditional logic in the procedure map. Conditions are stored as data, so reducing program maintenance.

- Common logic modules can be readily identified from a data map. These can be implemented as generic procedures or as higher-level procedures, using conventional or object-oriented languages: either procedural or non-procedural. They represent reusable code.

- Procedure maps lead to high development productivity because of the expert business knowledge applied by the users, and through definition of generic procedures and higher-level procedures.

- Procedure maps show access paths through the data map. They can be used to identify transactions. They can also be used to derive data flow diagrams, action diagrams and structure charts from a data map.

- Pseudocode, and also program statements, can be translated directly from a procedure map. This program logic shows high levels of reusability through the use of generic procedures and higher-level procedures. Translation can be carried out manually, or automatically given appropriate CASE tool support. Alternatively pseudocode can be bypassed, with translation from a procedure map directly into program source code, in either third, fourth or fifth generation languages.

We have now discussed the derivation of procedure maps and DFDs from data maps. We have used SQL to implement logic represented by data maps and procedure maps. We are now ready to discuss the steps of a typical Information Engineering project.

6.3 SUMMARY

In this chapter we discussed the derivation of data flow diagrams, and also procedure maps, directly from a data map. We saw that procedure maps also illustrate conditional logic, and can be translated directly into pseudocode.

The processing strategy used in a procedure map is defined by access paths through the data map. Processing strategies required for different programs may only be different data map access paths: the same procedures are also used with other execution paths. Once generic *Process* procedures are coded for a data model, no additional programming may be needed for most data maintenance processing. In contrast, each new program is generally coded from scratch when using software engineering. Changes in business rules or conditions may result in changes to conditions stored as data in a Condition Table. Once changed in this table, program execution automatically changes to reflect the new business rules or conditions – so reducing program maintenance.

We concluded the chapter by illustrating SQL used for processing against a data map.

References

[1] De Marco, T. (1982). *Software Systems Development*, Yourdon Press, New York: NY.

[2] Yourdon, E. and Constantine, L. (1979). *Structured Design: Fundamentals of a Discipline of Computer Program Systems Design*, Prentice-Hall, Englewood Cliffs: NJ.

[3] Gane, C. and Sarson, T. (1977). *Structured Systems Analysis: Tools and Techniques*, Improved Systems Technologies, New York: NY.

[4] Jackson, M. (1975). *Principles of Program Design*, Academic Press, New York: NY.

[5] Martin, J. and Finkelstein, C. (1981). *Information Engineering*, Savant Institute, Carnforth: Lancs UK.

[6] Date, C. J. (1987). *A Guide to DB2* – 2nd Edition, Addison-Wesley, Reading: MA.

[7] Date, C. J. (1988). *A Guide to the SQL Standard*, Addison-Wesley, Reading: MA.

CHAPTER 7

Information Engineering Projects

This chapter introduces the Analysis Phase, which concerns us for much of this book. The Design and Generation Phases are discussed in Chapters 19–22.

7.1 THE ANALYSIS PHASE

The systems development Analysis Phase, using Information Engineering, moves through four main stages [1]. These are listed below, and are illustrated in Figure 7.1.

- Project scope
- Strategic modeling
- Tactical modeling
- Operational modeling

7.1.1 Project scope

The project scope establishes objectives and boundaries for the project. It identifies strategic directions for the project area; based on formal strategic plans, or on statements of direction defined in a management questionnaire. These statements, together with management participation, provide

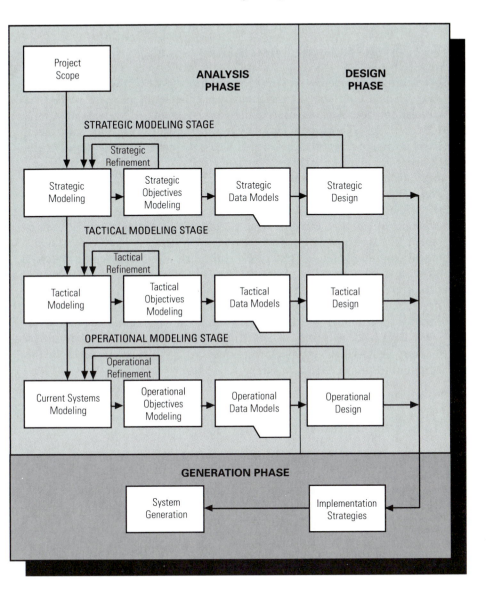

Figure 7.1   The Phases and Stages of Information Engineering [2].

the catalysts for strategic, tactical and operational modeling. We will see an example of such a management questionnaire in Chapter 8.

7.1.2 Strategic modeling

We call data of interest to senior management of a project area **strategic data**. That part of the organization managed by senior managers is called the **strategic project area,** or merely the **strategic area**. A strategic area may include all the organization if senior executive managers are involved. It may cover a specific division or business unit if only managers of that part of the business are involved. Strategic data that these managers need are derived from detailed data at lower tactical and operational parts of the strategic area. This leads us now to consider strategic modeling.

The process of identifying strategic data with senior managers of a strategic project area is called **strategic modeling**. Strategic data are represented in a **strategic data model**, also called a **strategic model**. A strategic model comprises high-level strategic entities of interest to senior management of a project area. These strategic entities are so called because they contain primary and foreign key attributes which establish associations between related entities. Strategic entities may contain high-level non-key attributes (strategic attributes) which generally represent aggregates derived from lower-level tactical entities. These strategic attributes may also be used to measure achievement of long-term goals. A strategic model leads to the definition of many tactical models.

7.1.3 Tactical modeling

The data of interest to middle management of a strategic area are called **tactical data**. The parts of an organization managed by middle managers are called **tactical project areas,** or just **tactical areas**. Tactical data, defined through tactical modeling, are often derived from more detailed data at lower operational parts of the tactical area.

The process of identifying tactical data with middle managers of a tactical area is called tactical modeling. Tactical data therefore are represented in tactical data models, called also tactical models. A tactical model comprises lower-level tactical entities of interest to the middle managers of a project area. These tactical entities contain non-key attributes (called tactical attributes) which provide detailed data of interest to these middle managers. Tactical attributes may include aggregates derived from lower-level operational entities, or may measure achievement of both strategic and short-term tactical objectives. A tactical model incorporates many operational models.

7.1.4 Operational modeling

The next definitions are now obvious. Data of interest to managers and staff at the operational levels of a tactical area are called **operational data**. These people belong to an **operational project area** (also called an **operational area**). Operational data represent data needed for day-to-day operation of the organization. Some operational data may be aggregated to provide tactical data.

The process of identifying operational data at operational levels is called **operational modeling**. Operational data are shown in **operational data models**, also called **operational models**. An operational model comprises operational level entities used day-to-day (called operational entities) containing detailed non-key attributes of interest to staff at the operational level of an organization. These are referred to as operational attributes. They may either be derived or non-derived. They may include attributes which measure achievement of both tactical and day-to-day operational objectives.

Operational modeling identifies data in existing systems, either manual or automated. It evaluates whether existing data are required also by data bases and systems identified during tactical and strategic modeling. Operational modeling is thus a quality assurance step as well as a detailed modeling step: it ensures that required data are incorporated from those existing systems which are to be replaced; or interfaces are developed to these systems if they are to be retained.

Operational modeling may include process modeling, to develop procedure maps and define generic and higher-level procedures from strategic, tactical and operational data maps. It may include the derivation from these data maps of DFDs, and transactions which indicate access paths through the data maps. This also leads to evaluation of the potential performance of defined systems prior to development, based on association frequencies of occurrence and on transaction volumes.

These definitions indicate a relationship between goals and objectives (defined in strategic plans), and data models (comprising data maps and underlying details of entities, attributes and associations).

7.1.5 Top-down development

The progressive application of strategic, tactical and operational modeling results in top-down development as illustrated in Figure 7.2. It shows the development of several tactical models from a strategic model, and the definition of a number of operational models from each tactical model.

Figure 7.3 indicates the progressive expansion of strategic models to tactical and then to operational models. A strategic model typically comprises 50–90 entities, which contain an average of two attributes per entity. These are mainly key attributes although non-key attributes may also exist.

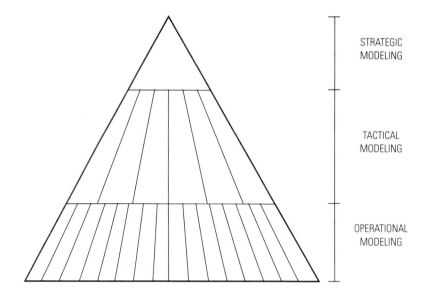

STRATEGIC
MODELING

TACTICAL
MODELING

OPERATIONAL
MODELING

Figure 7.2 Top-Down Development.

No. of Models	No. of Entities	Entity/Attribute Ratio
1 strategic model for each strategic area	50 – 90 entities per strategic model	1 : 2
approx 20 tactical models for each strategic model	10 – 20 entities per tactical model	1 : 5
	250 – 400 entities per strategic model	
approx 3 operational systems for each tactical model	2 – 5 entities per operational system	1 : 10
	400 – 1000 entities per strategic model	

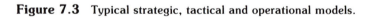

Figure 7.3 Typical strategic, tactical and operational models.

A strategic model may typically comprise perhaps twenty tactical models. Each of these tactical models comprises 10–20 tactical entities, with an average of five attributes per entity. As well as key attributes which establish the structure of each tactical model, also present are group attributes (still to be defined in detail at the operational level), selection attributes (secondary keys) and non-key attributes. At this stage of definition the strategic model will have expanded to 250–400 tactical entities.

At the operational level, each tactical model typically results in the definition of approximately three operational systems comprising 2–5 operational entities with an average of ten operational attributes. These are selection attributes and non-key attributes (derived or non-derived) which have been decomposed to a fundamental level of detail. They also include attributes to measure achievement of tactical and operational objectives. At this stage the strategic model will have expanded to 400–1,000 operational entities.

7.2 | STRATEGIC PLANNING

Managers of most organizations, both government or commercial, large or small, today recognize the importance and benefits of strategic planning. However achievement of these benefits has generally been less than their expectation. This is now recognized as being due to two critical factors: strategic implementation and strategic feedback. Traditional strategic planning is characterized by a feedback cycle typically of 3–5 years, as we saw in Chapter 1 and in Figure 1.1.

The strategic plans defined by management may consider several alternatives, limited perhaps to four or five major approaches. These are evaluated, and a selection is then made of those options which offer the best return commensurate with the cost of implementation and the risks involved. In Chapter 1 we discussed a guinea pig method for evaluation of a selected option. We saw the problems of feedback delays before refinement of the selected alternative could be undertaken.

Contrast this with **computer-aided strategic planning**, used in conjunction with strategic management planning and discussed extensively in Parts 3 and 4. Computer-aided strategic planning uses software to analyze data models, identifying alternative strategies that may have been overlooked. Some of these strategies may represent critical strategic gaps or strategic opportunities. They may indicate potential areas of competitive advantage, or instead may highlight areas of vulnerability. Software used for strategic analysis is discussed in Chapter 17. These software products include *IE: Expert* and also ISM [3].

Strategic alternatives may be evaluated through data modeling. Needed refinements can be made to the data model and evaluated, based on the rapid feedback obtained from modeling. Only after this refinement is an accepted strategic alternative introduced into the organization.

7.2.1 Strategic, tactical and operational statements

Strategic and tactical modeling focus on directions set by management for the future. Operational modeling focuses on existing systems which are to be replaced, or instead which may remain.

Strategic modeling statements
- Mission and purpose
- Concerns and issues
- Policies
- Goals and objectives
- Strategies and tactics

Tactical modeling statements
- Markets and channels
- Products and services
- Channels

Operational modeling documentation
- Existing systems or packages
- Source documents
- Report and screen formats
- File, data base and record formats

Management directions may be expressed formally in strategic plans, or informally in a management questionnaire. Or both may be used. These statements are catalysts which provide input for strategic and tactical modeling. Existing systems documentation provides input for operational modeling.

We have covered the basic concepts used by Information Engineering. We are now ready to apply them in practice, as we develop strategic, tactical and operational models for a typical organization. Part 3 presents the strategic management planning method in Chapters 8–12, used to develop strategic plans for any organizational level. Chapters 13-14 then show the development of a strategic model based on those plans.

Part 4 addresses systems development of priority areas selected by management from the strategic plans in Part 3. It illustrates the development of strategic, tactical and operational models for the selected priority area, followed by process modeling and then implementation in a relational data base environment.

7.3 SUMMARY

This chapter discussed the Analysis Phase of an Information Engineering project, which comprises: project scope; strategic modeling; tactical modeling and operational modeling.

The project scope establishes objectives and boundaries for the project. It identifies strategic directions using formal strategic plans and a management questionnaire. These provide catalysts for strategic and tactical modeling.

Strategic modeling develops a strategic model of entities and associations that represent information of interest to senior management of the project area. The strategic model may also contain strategic attributes for achievement of strategic goals. Many of these attributes are derived from more detailed tactical and operational data.

Tactical modeling develops tactical models that contain information of interest to middle management of the project area. These may contain non-derived attributes, or derived attributes from more detailed operational data.

Operational modeling develops operational models of fundamental data that already exist in current manual or automated systems, or may be required for new directions defined in strategic and tactical models. Operational models define interfaces to existing systems that are to be retained, or incorporate all of the data and processes for those systems that are to be replaced.

Process modeling is generally applied to operational models, for detailed processing of operational data. It can also be used with stable tactical or strategic models, to define detailed processing of derived tactical or strategic data.

References

[1] Finkelstein, C. (1989). *An Introduction to Information Engineering*, Addison-Wesley: Reading, MA.

[2] ibid.

[3] *IE: Expert*™ was developed and is supported by Information Engineering Systems Corp of Alexandria, VA, USA. ISM™ was developed and is supported by Infonetics Pty Ltd of Sydney, Australia. Chapter 17 covers these products.

PART THREE
Strategic Planning

CHAPTER 8

Introduction to Strategic Planning

In Chapter 1 we discussed traditional strategic planning and the problems encountered. We introduced an approach to bridge from strategic planning to systems development, called strategic management planning in this book. This permits strategic management of the process of planning and implementation, with rapid feedback for refinement and evolution of strategic plans. In this chapter we discuss the strategic planning research and experience that lead to the development of strategic management planning; building on the groundwork laid in Chapter 1.

In Chapters 9–12 we will use strategic management planning to formulate corporate and business unit strategies. In Chapters 13–14, and Part 4, we will use strategic systems development to identify data and information needed to implement the defined strategies, and operate the business at all management levels. The result is development of a strategic blueprint that can be used to define and evaluate the most appropriate organizational structures, together with the data bases and systems that provide the information needed for decision-making.

8.1 STRATEGIC PLANNING METHODS

The landmark works of Chandler [1], Ansoff [2] and Andrew [3] in the 1960s lead to an explosion in interest, research and application of strategic

133

planning. We will draw from this body of strategic planning research and experience to give insight into relevant concepts, principles and practice. We start by examining some of the methods used for strategic planning. We will discuss the traditional approach in the next section, and some of the problems that are associated with this approach. We then discuss the strategic management planning method. Many of the problems of traditional strategic planning are resolved through this latter approach.

8.1.1 Traditional strategic planning

Strategic planning research has generally been categorized into two main areas: strategic content research, and strategic process research. Strategic content addresses specifics of strategic decisions, while strategic process concentrates on how decisions are reached in an organizational environment.

Strategic content research examines the content of decisions regarding the goals, scope and/or competitive strategies of corporations, or of one or more of their business units. By 1986 research had moved on a long way – a summary by Fahey and Christensen [8] includes 91 references that added to the knowledge on strategic content. In discussing this research, they show that **goal content** focuses on survival, economic performance, social conduct; **scope content** addresses diversification, vertical integration, geographic expansion, strategic alliances, internal growth, and merger, acquisition or divestment; **competitive strategy** focuses on strategic groups and industry segmentation, stages of industry evolution, business unit performance factors (such as market share) and competitive response. These define *what* is to be achieved, and so provide useful input for data modeling. Strategic content research has therefore focused on the subject of strategic plans: merger, acquisition and divestment strategies; entry, exit and mobility barriers; differentiation of products or markets; turnaround strategies; and vertical integration strategies.

Strategic process research focuses on the actions that lead to, and support, strategy. This includes research into planning methods and decision-making, considering also alternative methods for generating and implementing strategy. These actions indicate *how* a strategy is to be achieved, and so provide input for process modeling. In 1987 Huff and Reger [5] summarized the research in this area, with 193 references for further reading. They classified these references into eight categories, in two divisions: strategy formulation and strategy implementation, with a ninth category that also integrates these divisions:

Strategy Formulation	Strategy Implementation
1 Planning Prescriptions	2 Systematic Implementation
3 Decision Aids	4 Evolutionary Prescriptions
5 Planning Practices	6 Structure Systems and Outcomes
7 Agendas and Attention	8 Contextual Influences
	9 Integrative

A problem that they noted was the parochial approach taken in much of this research. They also felt that work in other fields – such as organizational behaviour and organization theory, public administration, sociology, political science, international relations and education – had many insights to offer strategic planning research.

8.1.2   Strategy, structure and information

The main emphasis of Chandler's work [6], that '*structure follows strategy*', leads him to a discussion of four main strategies: volume expansion, geographic dispersion, vertical integration and product diversification. **Volume expansion** refers to increased sales in existing markets; **geographical dispersion** relates to entry into geographically different markets; **vertical integration** is achieved by an organization's absorption of its suppliers or customers; while **product diversification** is the development of new products. He argued that changes in strategy lead to changes in organizational structure: to utilize the organization's resources most effectively in implementing the strategy.

Galbraith and D. R. Nathanson [7] further discuss strategy formulation as the process of setting the basic mission of the organization, the objectives to be achieved, and major strategies and policies that govern the use of the organization's resources to achieve those objectives. They built on Chandler's work and later research into organizational structure. They found that single product businesses, and single dominant businesses such as the automobile industry, generally adopted a functional structure, while related businesses – with common customers, distribution channels, or technology – adopted a multi-divisional structure. The works of Chandler, Galbraith and Nathanson provided a focus for strategic modeling, and the design of organizational structure from strategic models as discussed in Chapter 14.

Organizational structure should reflect an organization's environment. Aldrich and Mindlin [8] discuss two methods of dealing with environmental impacts on organizations, arguing firstly that the environment is a source of information that can be used by organizational decision-makers as a '*basis for maintaining or modifying particular processes or structures*'. Secondly, they argue that the environment also is a source of resources that organizations both compete for, and share in. Uncertainty in the information available from the environment forces the organization to give up strict rules and procedures. Competition for resources results in dependencies, such as that between the suppliers who have control over a resource and customers who cannot substitute for, or do without that resource. Organizations that are dependent on the resources of their suppliers must take care of the relationships established with them. For example, the dependency that many countries of the world have on the oil resources of a few has a significant impact on international relationships, and on the range of feasible strategies in times of resource shortages and inflated prices.

Galbraith [9] discusses information processing strategies from an organizational, rather than a DP, perspective. He considers horizontal workflow across a functional division of labour, and also through hierarchical organization structures. Information overload in poorly designed organizations severely affects decision-making and organizational performance. He discusses four organizational design strategies that are used to control the effectiveness of information processing and decision-making:

- Creation of slack resources, by reducing the required level of performance. This reduces the amount of information and decision-making required to coordinate the resources needed to create the organization's products and services.

- Creation of self-contained tasks, where an organizational group has all of the information and resources needed to complete its designated tasks. Thus more decisions can be taken within the group, without reference to external areas.

- Investment in vertical information systems, where information is processed more automatically without overloading the decision-maker. This collects the information at its point of origin and directs it, at controlled times, to relevant places in the hierarchy.

- Creation of lateral relations, which employ lateral decision processes that cut across lines of authority. This moves decisions to lower levels of authority, while guaranteeing that all information is made available.

We will discuss some implications of these organizational design strategies further in Chapters 13 and 14. Galbraith emphasizes that these strategies represent an exhaustive set of alternatives:

> *'The organization must adopt at least one of the four strategies when faced with greater uncertainty. If it does not consciously choose one of the four, then the first, reduced performance standards, will happen automatically.'*

However, like many disciplines, strategic planning has become an end in itself, rather than a means to an end: that is, the planned development and implementation of strategy for the evolution of an organization. As so aptly summarized by Ackoff [10] in 1981:

> *'Most corporate planning is like a ritual rain dance: it has no effect on the weather that follows, but it makes those who engage in it feel that they are in control. Most discussions of the role of models in planning are directed at improving the dancing, not the weather.'*

As of 1979, 45% of organizations in the US Fortune 500 had used portfolio planning, as a part of strategic planning [11]. Some publications, emphasizing implementation and culture over planning, have reached the status of best-sellers [12]. However, in spite of this explosion of interest, there have been serious doubts about the role and benefits of strategic planning. The following pages develop this further.

Yip [13] argues that many of the problems that businesses experience in strategic planning can be traced to a mismatch of planning systems and organizational structure. He uses two companies, apparently similar, but which had divergent experiences with strategic planning – one positive, the other negative – to illustrate this. He identified three factors that affect an organization's need for strategic planning: demographic features; nature of the business; and nature of the market and environment.

He found three demographic features that are important to strategic planning:

- **Size:** The larger the size of an organization, the more need there is for a formal strategic planning system to achieve internal coordination and communication.
- **Diversity:** Greater diversity increases the need for strategic planning, until the diversity of the conglomerate with autonomous businesses is reached – where there is less need to run the business on an integrated basis, except financially.
- **Profitability:** The less profitable the organization, the greater is the need for strategic planning.

He found that the nature of the business affected strategic planning in five ways:

- **Number of important functions:** The need for more than one function to play a strategic role increases the need for a formal process that involves all functions.
- **Shared markets:** The need for synergy in sharing customers, programs and costs among products and markets increases the need for strategic planning.

- **Number of brands:** The fewer the number of brands (not products), the more important are coordinated strategic actions among product lines within a brand.

- **Complexity of markets:** More complex markets need a formal planning process to ensure that all essential aspects are considered.

- **Nature of strategic investment:** Fixed-asset investments require more elaborate planning than do more tactical expense investments, such as advertising.

The nature of the market and environment affected strategic planning in four ways:

- **Market growth rate:** Strategic planning is often used when markets stop growing, as in mature markets.

- **Competitive threat:** Competitive threat can change independently of market growth rate. Strategic planning addresses competitive threats at a strategic level; tactical planning addresses competition at a tactical or an operational level.

- **Environmental threat:** Environmental change, as well as competitive change, requires strategic planning to respond in the most appropriate way. These threats include legal, regulatory, economic, demographic and social sources.

- **Market cyclicality:** Greater cyclicality makes forecasting more difficult, requiring strategic contingency plans to be made.

All of these factors are important to an external appraisal of an organization and its competitors, as discussed in Chapter 11. Yip summarizes these in a matrix of structural factors and strategic planning features. These include strategic planning: objectives; process; subject matter; and output. He considers five strategic planning objectives: achieve competitive advantage; manage diversity; manage turbulence; achieve synergy; and create strategic change. Six strategic planning processes are: elaborate planning process; extensive data gathering and analysis; competitor orientation; multi-level and multi-stage planning processes; multi-functional process; and use of outsiders. Strategic planning subject matter is: total environment; long time horizon. Strategic planning output is: portfolio roles; scientific, precise goals; business unit reorganization; market redefinition; and strategic programs. In summary, he states:

> *'Large companies generally need a planning process that is relatively elaborate, that is multi-level and multi-stage, and that has outputs of scientific, precise goals and business unit reorganizations. Conversely, smaller companies*

generally do not need these planning features unless dictated by other structural factors.'

Langely [14] discusses some of the criteria for success in formal strategic planning. She emphasizes the importance of responsibility and follow-up. She goes on to say that:

> *'Successful strategic planning in all organizations depends on the CEO's ability to develop a coherent vision based on the input received, and then sell it to the rest of the organization . . . Strategic vision from above (is) crucial to the planning process . . . Strategic planning cannot provide this strategic vision on its own, (but) is totally useless without it.'*

Dutton and Duncan [15] emphasize a need to establish the link between an organization's strategic planning process and the initiation and implementation of strategic change. We will see that the establishment of that link is helped by strategic management planning.

Bourgeois and Brodwin, in discussing strategic implementation [16], provide very useful perspectives which will help us to understand some of the problems of past strategic planning and implementation efforts. They describe five models for strategic planning and implementation: the commander model; the change model; the collaborative model; the cultural model; and the crescive (growth) model. These are usefully described by relating them to the CEO's role, and to strategic questions asked by the CEO: summarized in the following table from their paper.

Model	CEO's Strategic Question	CEO's Role
Commander	*How do I formulate the optimum strategy?*	Rational Actor
Change	*I have a strategy in mind, now how do I implement it?*	Architect
Collaborative	*How do I involve top management to get commitment to strategies from the start?*	Coordinator
Cultural	*How do I involve the whole organization in implementation?*	Coach
Crescive	*How do I encourage managers to come forward as champions of sound strategies?*	Premise-setter and Judge

The Commander Model works best in organizations where the CEO wields great power and can command implementation, but it splits the organization into *'thinkers and doers'*. The Change Model starts where the commander model ends, using a number of behavioural science methods to increase the probability of successful implementation. The Collaborative Model uses group dynamics and brainstorming techniques to obtain input into the strategic planning process from managers with differing viewpoints. Each of these methods requires relatively low effort in formulation of strategy, but results in a high effort in implementation. Consequently their success has been limited.

The Cultural Model takes the participative elements of the collaborative model to lower levels of the organization. The CEO guides this effort by communicating and instilling his vision of the mission, allowing each individual to participate in designing his work procedures in concert with that mission. This method tries to incorporate some of the Japanese experience, and has been successful in breaking down the separation between thinkers and doers. It is characterized by high effort during formulation of strategy, but with low implementation effort, and rapid implementation.

The Crescive Model (named in their paper from the Latin *crescere*, to grow) builds on the experience of the cultural model. With this approach, strategy comes upward from the firing line, rather than dictated downward from the top. An environment is established to encourage innovation. The CEO then selects from the resulting projects or strategic alternatives that are proposed. This approach also requires high effort during strategy formulation, but it results in low implementation effort and rapid implementation. A key question is posed by Bourgeois and Brodwin:

> 'How can the CEO encourage a vigorous pace of innovation within the firm and still maintain an effective filter for screening out inappropriate or ill-conceived programmes? The answer to this question is, we believe, key to the next generation of strategic management.'

So how do all of the factors and observations that we have so far discussed relate to strategic management planning? The link is through strategic implementation. There are many criteria, detailed by Lorange [1], that are essential for successful implementation of a strategic plan. Strategic management planning evolved to address them:

- There must be potential benefits from planning for the CEO.
- Strategic planning must be explained, applied, and implemented in such a way that the relevant managers can understand it.
- Relatively complex planning tasks must be capable of being broken down into smaller elements.
- Identification of appropriate units of analysis in planning: that is, what parts of the business can be planned for and managed in a strategic manner.
- The degree to which the proposed innovation breaks with past experience and tradition: successful implementation occurs as a natural evolution of experience and understanding.

- There must be a well-defined, readily identifiable sponsor for each planning and implementation task.

- There must be a need that is clearly felt by the client. Each level of management must see benefits that address their relevant needs.

- Planning must be able to demonstrate some results relatively quickly; but as an initial effort, aspirations should not be set too high.

- There must be an early commitment to support and participate in the planning effort by all affected users. This includes corporate management, general line managers and the functional managers reporting to them.

- Finally, there must be a realistic assessment of resource needs. This includes making necessary staff and support facilities available, providing necessary budgets for training, meetings, equipment, implementation, and so on.

Lorange's criteria also apply to systems development projects, as embodied in strategic systems development. There are too many cases where these criteria have not been met: with the result that planning and implementation, with their consequent organizational and information systems changes, at best have not achieved their full potential benefit; and at worst have degenerated into complete disasters.

Strategic management planning and strategic systems development have evolved to address many of these problems. These methods, when used in the stages and steps described in this book, address Lorange's criteria. They address both the cultural and the crescive models defined earlier by Bourgeois and Brodwin, helping also to answer their question: '*How can the CEO encourage a vigorous pace of innovation within the firm and still maintain an effective filter for screening out inappropriate or ill-conceived programmes?*'

8.2 STRATEGIC MANAGEMENT PLANNING STAGES

Strategic management planning can be used at the business unit level or at the corporate level. As discussed in Chapters 1 and 7, we use the term strategic area to refer generally to the focus of a strategic planning exercise: we will call this exercise a **planning study**. Strategic management planning comprises four main stages:

- Identifying the current plan
- Evaluating the current plan
- Setting strategic directions
- Implementing the plan

8.2.1   Identifying the current plan

The current strategy used by the strategic area is obtained from existing documentation of its strategic plan. This is expanded upon by a management questionnaire, which is completed by all management participants of the planning study. Where an existing plan is not available, the questionnaire is used alone. The remainder of this chapter describes the content and use of the management questionnaire.

8.2.2   Evaluating the current plan

Goal analysis is used to evaluate the current strategy, as documented formally in the strategic plan. It is also used to analyze the management questionnaire responses, to identify problems or deficiencies in that plan which are perceived by the respondents. Goal analysis is described in Chapter 9. This uses typical questionnaire responses to illustrate application of the technique.

8.2.3   Setting strategic directions

Based on evaluation of the current strategy by goal analysis, specific areas which need improvement are examined further to determine the strategic direction to be taken for the future. Internal and external appraisals are applied at the business unit level (or program level for a government organization) and, if relevant, at the corporate level. An internal appraisal identifies the strengths and weaknesses of the organization: grouping related strengths which indicate comparative advantage, and also grouping weaknesses which suggest comparative disadvantage. An external appraisal is carried out on competitors: similarly identifying relevant comparative advantages and disadvantages. Likely actions taken by the organization and the effect on competitors (and the effect of competitors' actions on the organization), and the likely response of each to actions by the other, are evaluated to determine areas of competitive advantage.

8.2.4   Implementing the plan

Based on the directions embodied in the strategic plan, a strategic model is developed to represent the data and information needed to manage and operate the organization. This model is a strategic blueprint. It indicates data bases and information systems needed to support the plan, and can also be used to evaluate alternative organization structures. Chapters 13 and 14 describe the progressive development of a strategic model, and discuss the design of organization structures based on that model. Part 4 then describes the design and development of data bases and information systems that support the strategic plan.

8.2.5   Termination at earlier stages

An advantage of this approach is that the planning study progressively refines the plan through the first three stages, to the fourth stage – which focuses on implementation of that plan. Or it can be terminated partway through these earlier stages, moving directly then to the fourth stage.

For example, senior management can use the management questionnaire in Stage 1 to obtain feedback from lower level managers based on the current plan. The responses from the managers who will implement that plan can be used for its initial refinement if necessary. If the planning study is terminated at this point, the questionnaire is still able to provide direct (but raw) input in Stage 4 to implement the plan: strategic modeling can help evaluate organization structures; strategic, tactical and operational modeling can develop the associated information systems which support that plan.

Stage 2 can be used to evaluate both the current plan and the management questionnaire responses. Goal analysis identifies deficiencies in the plan that may need correction. It defines goals to be achieved, identifying issues that may impede their achievement. It then establishes strategies to overcome these issues. Functional responsibility for these strategies is then allocated to appropriate parts of the organization. Direct output of this Stage 2 is a clear job description of each functional position that is needed to implement the strategic plan. The planning study can terminate at this point if needed: the corrected plan is then available for input to Stage 4, for strategic modeling as before.

Stage 3 provides for further refinement of the current plan, or for definition of new strategic directions as required. This stage requires more time and effort than the earlier stages; it is essential if those stages show a need for strategic change. When developed, this plan provides input to strategic implementation in the fourth stage.

Stage 4 draws on the progressive definition of the strategic plan at each of the earlier three stages, and leads to the definition of an information system architecture necessary to support the plan. It can provide assistance for evaluation of alternative organization structures. Strategic modeling then leads to tactical and operational modeling: to develop and implement the information systems which directly support the new strategic plan.

8.3 STAGE 1 – IDENTIFYING THE CURRENT PLAN

Strategic directions are expressed in terms of strategic and tactical statements. These are introduced briefly here: they are described further in later chapters. These statements define the strategic plan. They form input to strategic, tactical and operational modeling. They lead to the design of information systems which support that plan. They are:

8.3.1 Strategic statements

- Mission and purpose
- Concerns and issues
- Policies
- Goals and objectives
- Strategies and tactics

8.3.2 Tactical statements

- Markets
- Products and services
- Channels

8.3.3 Obtaining management input

The current strategic plan may express strategic directions using statements similar to those above. Or the plan may be less formally presented: as management reports, or in documents for public consumption such as the annual report. Or it may not even exist in written form; it may only exist in the vision and direction of senior management. If the plan has been documented, that material defines the current strategy and can be analyzed for review by management. But if the plan exists only in the minds of senior managers, they must participate in the planning study.

8.3.4   The management questionnaire

The managers and staff participating in the planning study contribute much experience and wisdom. Staff at various levels of the organization may participate, as discussed in the following paragraph [19]:

> *'All staff use strategic planning, either explicitly or implicitly. It may not necessarily be called a strategic plan at the lowest parts of the organization. But all areas, and all individuals, work to strategic plans – either formally or informally expressed. They may be called targets. Or directions. Or they may be embodied in the job description which applies to the position occupied by an individual. For the manager of an area, this job description is a defacto strategic plan for the area to be managed. And of course, each job description is a strategic plan for the individual.'*

The management questionnaire is used to obtain input from all participants of the planning study. It has been designed to be completed not in committee, but personally by each individual free from any constraints or political inhibitions that may occur in a meeting of managers at different levels. The questions asked address factors that apply to the manager's specific responsibilities, and also to the strategic area.

The questionnaire is documented at the end of this chapter. It is provided as a guideline only. It can be tailored to each strategic area. Terminology may need to be changed and extra questions can be added. Some questions may need to be modified. But none should be deleted: all questions should be asked.

The questionnaire is distributed before the first meeting of the planning study, to allow adequate time for each person to complete the questions asked. The responses are then returned to a central point, where they are collated in a document which is presented to all participants at the first meeting.

The questions are summarized in the following page as strategic questions and tactical questions. Please take a moment now to read the questionnaire at the end of the chapter. Then turn back to this point for the summary of questions.

8.3.5 Strategic and tactical questions

Strategic questions

- Mission and purpose of the organization
- Mission and purpose of your area
- Concerns and issues
- Policies, objectives and strategies
- Priorities

Tactical questions

- Markets
- Products and services
- Channels

At the end of the questionnaire each respondent is asked for name, title and department or section. When questionnaires are consolidated, statements extracted from different responses are *not* attributed to their specific source: to encourage free comment. But a knowledge of the source may be appropriate to the central coordinating group if extra expansion is later needed of the points made.

The questionnaire provides input to the planning study. In Chapter 9 sample responses from a questionnaire are used to illustrate the application of goal analysis.

8.3.6 Benefits of the questionnaire

By using this questionnaire approach, several objectives are achieved:

- It provides early input to plan the best approach to be used for the planning study.
- It helps identify people who have been omitted, and who can contribute.
- It obtains different perspectives free from constraints imposed by management hierarchies: some managers may not be prepared to express certain statements verbally, or may only be prepared to make anonymous statements in the presence of their managers or their subordinates.
- It allows a consolidation of different perspectives, as a catalyst to the study.

- Each manager has a clear appreciation of the type of information needed for the study, and can prepare accordingly.

- Each manager, at all levels of participation, is involved and directly contributes.

- It provides direct input to strategic, tactical and operational modeling to develop information systems arising from the study.

8.3.7   A catalyst for strategic management

Through the questionnaire the participants can provide input to the strategic plan. It enables senior management to assess their staff's understanding of the plan. It provides clear input to later stages of the planning study. But it also offers a further benefit: the questionnaire responses can be used immediately for implementation in a strategic modeling project if the planning study is terminated at this point.

Following strategic modeling, the strategic model can progress both downwards and upwards in the organization. It moves downwards to tactical and operational modeling in priority areas identified during strategic modeling as shown in Figure 1.4. This leads to development of information systems which support the strategic plan. The strategic model also provides feedback to the planning study to refine the plan. This leads to strategic management.

If used this way, in conjunction with strategic modeling, strategic planning is far more productive. The strategic model forms a blueprint of the organization. It schematically represents the business in terms of its data, the information needed by management, the organization structure, and the strategies used to manage different parts of the business.

Managers adopt a strategic approach to the business at all levels in the organization. Strategic planning becomes a normal way of management life. The directed approach to strategic thought introduced by strategic management planning becomes a tool used by all managers on a day-to-day basis. It becomes a corporate culture. Managers use goal analysis to evaluate strategic plans at all levels of the business. They use strategic and tactical modeling to test new options. Their strategic plans are communicated fully and implemented exactly. The organization so moves beyond strategic planning to strategic management, as commented by Gray in the discussion associated with Figure 1.1.

This chapter concludes with the management questionnaire. This is a master copy, which can be reproduced for distribution to the planning study participants. It requires the mission statement for the relevant strategic area first to be inserted where indicated in the questionnaire, prior to its distribution. The next chapter uses typical responses from the management questionnaire to illustrate the application of goal analysis.

8.4 SUMMARY

In this chapter we discussed some of the research undertaken into strategic planning and strategic implementation. We saw that strategic planning is categorized into three main disciplines: strategic content, called strategy formulation; strategic process, called strategy implementation; and strategic management, called the management of strategy.

Galbraith and Nathanson discussed that strategy formulation requires setting the basic mission of the organization, defining the objectives to be achieved, and strategies and tactics to achieve those objectives. Aldrich and Mindlin discussed the critical roles that information sources and resource availability have on decision-making.

Yip emphasized that the problems of strategic planning are often due to a mismatch of planning systems and organizational structure. Langely addressed the strategic vision of the organization. Of Bourgeois and Brodwin's five models for strategic planning and implementation, we discussed that the Cultural and Crescive models are most effective.

These factors and observations lead to Lorange's analysis, emphasizing the criteria for successful implementation of strategic planning and systems development projects. These are: benefits to the CEO; the managers must understand the planning approach; complex tasks must be decomposed; easy selection of parts of the business to be examined; the ability for planning to build on past experience and understanding; there must be a visible sponsor for each task; the client and managers must have needs that can be addressed by the study; planning goals should be set to deliver early results; there must be a committment to support and participate by all affected users; and finally the resources needed for the study must be realistically assessed.

Strategic management planning evolved from Yip's factors and Lorange's criteria, following the Cultural and Crescive models of Bourgeois and Brodwin. It comprises three stages: 1) identifying the current plan; 2) evaluating the current plan; 3) setting strategic directions. The plan is implemented by using strategic modeling to define data and information needed for decision-making. The strategic model is then used to assess alternative organization structures, together with strategic systems development used to define required management information systems needed to support the plan.

Strategic management planning can use strategic modeling at any of its three stages, to develop a blueprint of the plan for evaluation by management. When used at Stage 1, the resulting strategic model is often seen to be reactive. At Stage 2, the current plan is refined using goal analysis. This plan, while improved over Stage 1, is still reactive. At Stage 3, opportunities and

competitive threats become apparent and the resulting plan is more proactive. The chapter then concluded with a discussion of the Management
Questionnaire for Stage 1.

References

[1] Chandler, A. D. (1962). *Strategy and Structure: Chapters in the History of the American Industrial Enterprise*, MIT Press: Cambridge, MA.

[2] Ansoff, H. I. (1965). *Corporate Strategy*, McGraw-Hill: New York, NY.

[3] Andrews, K. R. (1971). *The Concept of Corporate Strategy*, Irwin: Home-wood, IL.

[4] Fahey, L. and Christensen, H. K. (1986). *Evaluating the Research on Strategy Content.* In *1986 Yearly Review of Management*, Journal of Management, Vol 12, No 2, 167–183.

[5] Huff, A. and Reger, R. (1987). *A Review of Strategic Process Research, Journal of Management*, Vol 13, No 2, 211–236.

[6] Chandler, A. D. (1962). *Strategy and Structure: Chapters in the History of the American Industrial Enterprise*, MIT Press: Cambridge, MA.

[7] Galbraith, J. R. and Nathanson, D. R. (1978). *Strategy Implementation: The Role of Structure and Process*, West Publishing: St Paul, MI.

[8] Aldrich, H. and Mindlin, S. (1978). *Uncertainty and Dependence: Two Perspectives on Environment*, in L. Karpik (ed), *Organization and Environment*, Sage: Paris, France.

[9] Galbraith, J. (1973). *Designing Complex Organizations*, Addison-Wesley: Reading, MA.

[10] Ackoff, R. L. (1981). On the Use of Models in Corporate Planning, *Strategic Management Journal*, 2, 353–359.

[11] Haspelagh, P. (1982). Portfolio Planning: Uses and Limits, *Harvard Business Review*: Cambridge, MA (Jan–Feb).

[12] Peters, T. J. and Waterman, R. H., Jr. (1982). *In Search of Excellence*, Harper & Row: New York, NY.

[13] Yip, G. S. (1985). Who Needs Strategic Planning, *Journal of Business Strategy*, Vol 6, No 2.

[14] Langley, A. (1988). The Roles of Formal Strategic Planning, *Long Range Planning*, Vol 21, No 3.

[15] Dutton, J. E. and Duncan, R. B. (1987). The Influence of the Strategic Planning Process on Strategic Change, *Strategic Management Journal*, Vol 8.

[16] Bourgeois, L. J. and Brodwin, D. R. (1984). Strategic Implementation: Five Approaches to an Elusive Phenomenon, *Strategic Management Journal*, Vol 5, pp. 241–264.

[17] Lorange, P. (ed). (1982). *Implementation of Strategic Planning*, Prentice Hall: Englewood Cliffs, NJ.

[18] Finkelstein, C. B. (1989). *An Introduction to Information Engineering*, Addison-Wesley: Reading, MA.

[19] ibid.

8.5 | MANAGEMENT QUESTIONNAIRE

The management questionnaire which follows provides a catalyst for the planning study. The defined mission statement for the strategic area is first inserted on Page 1 of the questionnaire, which is then distributed to all participants 2–3 weeks prior to the first planning session. It may also be accompanied by the existing strategic plan.

Each respondent is asked to comment on the mission statement. Possible improvements to that statement are requested, as well as a definition of the mission of the respondent's own area. Any concerns, issues, strengths and weaknesses which affect achievement of that mission, either positively or negatively, are also requested. The questionnaire then asks for policies, objectives and strategies which apply to the area, prioritized from the individual's perspective. It requires the respondent to identify products and services produced by the area, and the markets (customers, or clients, or users) who use those products and services. It asks that the channels used to deliver or supply the products and services to the markets be documented.

The management questionnaire is completed from the perspective of each individual's responsibilities and environment. It is *not* intended to be completed by committee; but rather by each manager independently of all others. Anonymity is maintained so each person can provide maximum input to the project, free from any political or hierarchical constraints. Complete, candid replies to every question are thus very important: they are not intended to be part of a final, correct document, but to provide draft input to the planning study.

On receipt of the responses, they are analyzed. Every response to each question is first consolidated under the relevant question. Priorities assigned to policies, objectives and strategies are directly attached to each statement to which they refer. These consolidated responses are distributed to all study participants at the start of the first planning session, maintaining anonymity of all individual responses. They will form a catalyst for subsequent strategic planning and modeling sessions.

Box 8.1
Management questionnaire

STRATEGIC AND TACTICAL STATEMENTS
General

In developing information systems and decision support systems to assist management decision-making, it is important that they be based on our organization's needs for the future as well as today. To help in identifying those needs, please take a few moments to complete the following questionnaire from your own perspective. Unless otherwise indicated, you should answer the questions as they relate to your area of responsibility.

Mission and purpose

As an example, it could be said that our mission and purpose is:

NOTE: Include the agreed mission and purpose of the strategic area here, before distributing the questionnaire.

Please comment on this statement.

What should our mission and purpose be?

Mission and purpose of your area

Please write what you feel is the mission and purpose of your area or section, in achieving our overall mission and purpose. As a guide, it should address the questions:

What is the business (that is, main purpose) of your area now?

(cont'd)

Box 8.1 (cont.)
Management questionnaire

What will it be in the future?

What *should* it be in the future?

Concerns and issues

Please indicate the major concerns and issues in achieving the mission and purpose and serving your markets (of customers, clients or users). What are our strengths and weaknesses?

Concerns

Issues

Strengths

Weaknesses

Box 8.1 (cont.)
Management questionnaire

Policies, goals and strategies

To achieve your mission and purpose what policies, goals or strategies should be in place in your area?

(1)

(2)

(3)

(4)

(5)

(6)

(7)

(8)

(9)

(10)

(cont'd)

Box 8.1 (cont.)
Management questionnaire

Priorities

How do you rate the above policies, goals or strategies in terms of their importance in achieving your mission and purpose. Please indicate their relative position by giving them a priority rating from 1 to 10 (1 for the most important).

Policy, Goal or Strategy No.   **Priority Rating**
(from above)

(1)

(2)

(3)

(4)

(5)

(6)

(7)

(8)

(9)

(10)

Box 8.1 (cont.)
Management questionnaire

Markets

Who are our existing customers (or users, or clients) – that is, the users of our products and services?

Where are they located?

What do they need?

What do they consider value?

What are they prepared to 'pay'?

(cont'd)

Box 8.1 (cont.)
Management questionnaire

Products and services

Please give a brief description of our present products and services and, if relevant, any products or services which should or may be developed in the near future.

Present Products/Services

Future Products/Services

Channels

How are our products and services provided or distributed to their markets?

How should they and possible new products and services be distributed to present and future markets?

Additional Comments

Box 8.1 (cont.)
Management questionnaire

Questionnaire respondent

Organization _____

Name _____

Title _____

Dept/Section _____

Phone _____

Facsimile No _____

Date _____

CHAPTER 9

Evaluation of Current Strategy

This chapter discusses strategic thinking and strategic analysis, introducing a technique, called goal analysis, that can be used to evaluate strategic statements. In Chapter 8 we described the content, preparation and distribution of the management questionnaire as part of Stage 1 – Identification of Current Strategy. This chapter discusses Stage 2 – Evaluation of Current Strategy. Goal analysis is used to evaluate and refine responses from the questionnaire and can also be used in later stages of the planning study.

9.1 STRATEGIC THINKING AND STRATEGIC ANALYSIS

As part of the evaluation of current strategy, strategic thinking and strategic analysis are important disciplines. Through strategic thinking Kenichi Ohmae [1] discusses that:

> 'One first seeks a clear understanding of the particular character of each element of a situation and then makes the fullest possible use of human brainpower to restructure the elements in the most advantageous way'.

He suggests that the first stage is to 'pinpoint the critical issue in the situation'. This is the most important step in formulating a solution. To illustrate strategic thinking he uses **Issue Diagrams** to break a problem into its constituent symptoms or phenomena, then groups them based on common factors, abstracting groups that reflect common critical issues and finally formulating an approach to the problem. He extends this concept also to **Profit Diagrams** that provide an analytical approach to profit analysis of products.

Rowe, Mason, Dickel and Snyder [2] argue that the strategy of an organization is based on satisfying the hierarchy of organizational values, purposes, goals and objectives. The values and beliefs of the organization's leaders must become part of its corporate culture. Values *'used to guide the business must be appropriate to the time, place and conditions in which the business operates'*. Effective and operative values should be embodied in the organization's culture. A strategy must be consistent with the corporate culture to be successfully implemented.

Values are the foundation of the organization's mission, purpose, goals and objectives. Values and purposes define broad directions to be pursued. They should be timeless, but it should be recognized that they are seldom fully attained. The establishment of a grand strategy, definition of goals and objectives, evaluation and selection between strategic alternatives, and then the establishment of policies and plans represent the hierarchy of values referred to by Rowe *et al.*

Grand strategy addresses the total organization, its missions and purposes. They define goals as *'future states or outcomes of the organization to be obtained or retained'*, while objectives are defined as: *'precise, well-specified targets that are measurable and whose attainment is desired by a specific time'*.

9.2 | STAGE 2 – EVALUATION OF CURRENT STRATEGY

Critical success factors (CSFs) can be used to identify factors addressing organizational goals. Rockart [3] found that executives tend to think in terms of *'what it takes to be successful'* in their business rather than in terms of purposes, goals and objectives. He defined three main steps in evaluating answers to the question: *'what does it take to be successful in this business?'* These are: 1. Generate critical success factors; 2. Refine CSFs into objectives; 3. Identify measures of performance. This CSF analysis can be used in conjunction with goal analysis, as discussed in the remainder of this chapter.

Strategic thinking and strategic analysis are thus used to develop the strategic statements. Goal analysis [4] is used to evaluate these statements. We will discuss the application of this technique in conjunction with a mission statement from a fictional organization. This organization will be called the XYZ Corporation in our example. We will use fictional responses from managers of XYZ, taken from a hypothetical management questionnaire. The mission and the comments made by these managers do not represent any one particular organization, but reflect similar statements used by corporations in many different industries and countries.

9.2.1 Goal analysis

The goal analysis steps are illustrated in Figure 9.1. We first identify potential goals from the mission statement of XYZ Corporation and identify issues that may impede their achievement. Next we will define strategies to overcome those issues. The current functions of the organization are then identified. Strategies are allocated to appropriate functions, and any new functions needed to implement strategies are also defined. The functional responsibility for different strategies is then developed, as a potential job description for each functional position.

9.2.2 Mission and purpose of XYZ Corporation

Chapter 8 details questions which are included in a typical management questionnaire. The following mission statement of XYZ was included in the questionnaire prior to its distribution to these fictional managers. The initial comments made by two managers on this mission statement are documented in Response 9.1.

> **Response 9.1** Comments on mission and purpose
>
> **As an example, it could be said that our mission and purpose is:**
>
> *Develop, deliver and support products and services which satisfy the needs of customers in markets where we can achieve a return on investment at least 20% pa within two years of market entry.*
>
> **Please comment on this statement.**
>
> *Respondent 1: 'This mission statement provides us with criteria for selection of markets based on their return on investment. This depends on profitability and also market share. It requires us to track emerging new markets, but not enter them until we are sure that we can attain profitable market share with initial entry expenditure that will enable us to achieve the ROI goal within two*

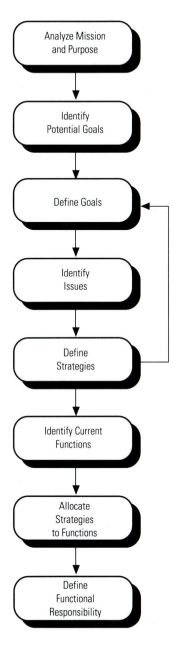

Figure 9.1   The steps of Goal Analysis.

years. Otherwise we will delay entry until those markets are sufficiently developed. It also implies that we will exit markets whose long-term ROI is expected to fall below this figure'.

Respondent 2: 'We must continually evaluate the performance of products and services in their ability to satisfy our customers' needs, and determine how those needs change over time. We must then change our products and services, or instead develop new products and services, so that they will continue to satisfy those needs of our customers. We will terminate any new or changed products and services whose profitability will not allow us to achieve the overall ROI criterion'.

9.2.3 Step 1 – Analyze mission and purpose

The mission and purpose statement, together with its comments from the management questionnaire, are used as a starting point. These are analyzed to identify major data subjects, which represent parts of the organization responsible for elements of the mission and purpose. Typically only four to six subjects will initially emerge. These are represented in a broad data map, showing interrelationships between the data subjects generally as *many to many* associations. This data map is thus a high-level schematic representation of the mission and purpose. It is called the **mission model**.

The mission statement and subsequent comments in Response 9.1 include nouns which indicate a number of high-level data subjects. The XYZ mission is to '*develop, deliver and support products and services*'. These are collectively referred to by XYZ as **products**: PRODUCT (in the singular) is the first identified data subject. These products must '*satisfy the needs of customers in markets*' – NEED, CUSTOMER and MARKET are also data subjects. The rest of the mission then defines an ROI performance criterion in relation to the other data subjects. PERFORMANCE is the fifth data subject.

We develop a mission model to show these data subjects, as illustrated in Figure 9.2. This shows a number of *many to many* association lines joining related data subjects. Associations in a mission model show association degree, but not the association nature. They will not be decomposed now, but will be left as *many to many* until Chapter 13.

Figure 9.2 shows associations between data subjects as defined by the XYZ managers. It indicates that a market has many needs, while a need may relate to many markets. A market also has many customers, while customers may participate in more than one market. A customer also has many needs, and purchases many products. A need, to be worth satisfying, must be held by more than one customer: a product is purchased by many customers. A product may address many markets, while a market will have many products.

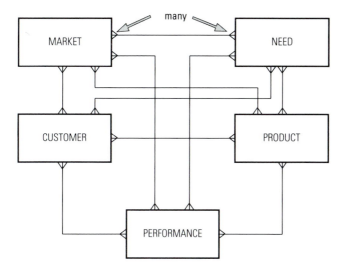

Figure 9.2 Mission model for XYZ Corporation.

The performance of all of these data subjects is important. There is therefore a *many to many* association between PERFORMANCE and each data subject. For example a product may have many performance criteria, while a performance criterion is used to evaluate the performance of many products. Similarly a performance criterion may be used to evaluate many customers, or many markets, or many needs. Each of these has many performance criteria which are used in their evaluation. Customers, needs, products markets and performance are all important aspects of Total Quality Management (TQM), as discussed later in Chapter 14.

9.2.4 Step 2 – Identify potential goals

Potential goals are next identified, expressed in terms of one or two descriptive words. These represent critical factors which influence the ability of the organization to obtain business, and grow in its identified markets. They are vital for the success and the survival of the business. They are therefore called **critical success factors (CSFs)**.

Response 9.2   Critical success factors of XYZ Corporation

- *Market Analysis*
- *Market Share*
- *Innovation*
- *Customer Satisfaction*

- *Product Quality*
- *Product Development*
- *Staff Productivity*
- *Asset Growth*
- *Profitability*

The critical success factors previously defined by senior management are documented in Response 9.2. Potential goals or CSFs include: Customer Satisfaction; Product Quality; Market Share; Revenue Growth; Net Income; Asset Growth; Staff Turnover; Staff Productivity.

Each potential goal is allocated to a data subject in the mission model as illustrated in Figure 9.3. Market Analysis is the first critical success factor (CSF) in Response 9.2. This regularly analyzes the needs, profitability and the current and potential size of markets. It has been defined as goal G1 in Figure 9.3. As it relates to MARKET and NEED it is attached to both of these data subjects. Market Share is the percentage share of each competitor in a market. It is goal G2 and is attached only to MARKET.

The next CSF is Innovation. This is goal G3 and has been attached to MARKET, to NEED and to PRODUCT. Goal G4: Customer Satisfaction, relates to CUSTOMER. G5 represents the Product Quality CSF and G6 is

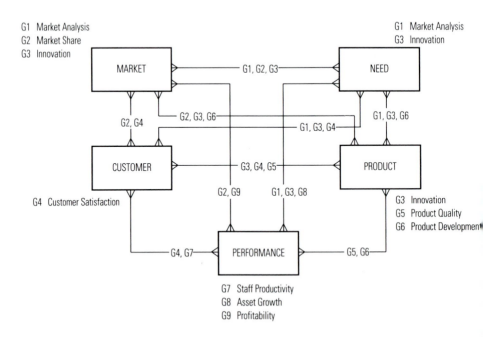

Figure 9.3   Goals attached to the mission model.

the Product Development CSF: these are both attached to PRODUCT. Finally G7: Staff Productivity, G8: Asset Growth and G9: Profitability are all attached to PERFORMANCE.

Goals are then attached to relevant associations between related data subjects. This will be of assistance later in the definition of these goals (Step 3) and the identification of potential issues (Step 4) which may affect achievement of the goals. For example: G1, G2 and G3 (Market Analysis, Market Share and Innovation respectively) relate to markets and their needs, and so are placed on the association between these two data subjects. G2 (Market Share) and G4 (Customer Satisfaction) relate to markets and also to customers and so are placed on the association between markets and customers. Goals attached to each data subject are examined for their relationships with other data subjects, and so are placed on relevant associations. You may wish to spend a moment considering why the XYZ managers, for specific associations, placed only some of the goals on some associations – but not all of the possible goals which are attached to their related data subjects.

9.2.5 Step 3 – Define goals

Each goal is next defined as a textual statement. The mission model in Figure 9.3, with goals attached to data subjects and to associations, is used as a catalyst for definition; together with the policies, objectives and strategies suggested by XYZ managers in the management questionnaire. These terms have different meanings to many people; we will see next that each has a very precise meaning when it is used with Information Engineering.

A **goal** represents a long-term target for achievement, while an **objective** is short-term: both are quantifiable. Each has three properties: a measure; a level; and a time [5]. The **measure** represents an attribute which holds the data that we want to measure. The **level** indicates the value we want to achieve. The **time** indicates when we want to reach that level. We will evaluate all goals and objectives in terms of these properties: unless all three are present they are not quantifiable.

Whereas goals and objectives indicate *what* we want to achieve, strategies and tactics define *how* we plan to achieve them. A **strategy** details a procedure which is carried out to achieve a goal or an objective. It may comprise many steps: each of which is called a **tactic**. There may be many possible procedures or steps that can be followed to achieve a goal or an objective: these represent alternative strategies or tactics. We also saw in Chapter 3 that strategies and tactics both relate to associations: they define how entities joined by those associations will be used or processed. But we cannot determine strategies or tactics until the relevant goals or objectives have been defined.

Finally, **policies** are qualitative. They indicate broad directions or the overall vision of management. They define boundaries of responsibility or interest, and are represented by related groups of entities and the associations which join them, as we also saw in Chapter 3. There can be many **issues** or **concerns** which relate to policies. These may indicate problems in following the policies, or may suggest opportunities that are available. Issues or concerns may also relate to goals and objectives: they also indicate problems or opportunities.

In this book we will refer to goals and objectives collectively as goals; strategies and tactics will be referred to as strategies; issues, concerns, problems and opportunities are referred to as issues. Policies, vision and boundaries are referred to as policies.

The policies, goals and strategies of the XYZ managers are shown in Response 9.3. The numbers below refer directly to the numbered statements in Response 9.3.

(1)   The first statement is in support of the Market Analysis goal (G1). This is a policy rather than a goal, as it is not yet sufficiently quantitative. It has a measure (*'analysis of market growth, market size and competition'*) but it does not indicate a level or time. It is qualitative in this form: *'regular'* is imprecise; the frequency and extent of market analysis are not indicated. While existing markets are known exactly, what are defined as *'emerging markets?'*. We would normally refine this statement now to provide the missing level and time, clarify the other questions, and define it as a goal. However we will leave that refinement for a later time.

(2)   This supports the Market Share goal (G2). It has a measure (*'market share'*) and time (*'within two years'*) but does not yet have a level. It is a policy, but could be restated as a goal by defining *'dominant market share'* level. A predefined market share may not be practical: dominance may differ in various markets. The statement should be refined to identify the criteria that determine the dominant share percentage of each market. The market exit policy is clear, but we should define what is meant by a *'satisfactory rate of return'*. It could then be restated as a quantitative goal.

(3)   This statement is really in support of both the Market Analysis and Innovation goals (G1 and G3 respectively), but is also qualitative. We need to define *'regular'* more precisely; there are no criteria suggested for determining *'growth and profit potential'*.

(4)   The Customer Satisfaction goal (G4) is addressed by this statement. Again, *'regular'* is not defined. And no criteria are suggested that allow us to measure *'satisfaction'*: is it measured by return business, by

survey, or complaints, or product returns? Nor is any level suggested that can be set as a target in a goal. This also is a policy.

(5) This policy focuses on the Product Quality goal (G5). It does not yet indicate what is used to measure *'reputation for product quality and service'*, nor what target level will achieve that measure. (We also will see in Chapter 10 that this policy is wishful thinking. XYZ does not provide outstanding product quality and service: rather, the opposite is true.)

(6) This supports the Product Development goal (G6). It can be left in this form, or may be quantified by setting a target of a specified number of new products or services to be developed within a year (say). But a defined target may inhibit development: criteria which can be defined to set targets dynamically may be more appropriate.

(7) This statement is readily quantified in support of the Staff Productivity goal (G7). A defined number of incentives, or instead training programs, can be set as a target to achieve each year. The staff turnover rate can be measured, and its change over time monitored. Incentive targets can be set for reduction in the staff turnover rate.

(8) The Asset Growth goal (G8) is supported by this policy statement. It establishes a performance monitoring policy so that all activities focus on contributing positively to the achievement of the return on investment defined in the XYZ mission.

(9) Similarly, this policy supports the Profitability goal (G9) and also the Asset Growth goal (G8). Goals 1–7 focus on identifying markets and needs, then developing, delivering and supporting products or services which satisfy those needs. Once a decision is made to enter markets, or to introduce new products that meet the needs of a market, this Goal 9 monitors profitability to ensure that we achieve or exceed the planned financial projections.

Response 9.3   Policies, goals and strategies of XYZ Corp.

Policy, Goal or Strategy

(1) *Market Analysis: Analyze existing and emerging markets on a regular basis to assess market growth, potential market size, and potential market competition.*

(2) *Market Share: Only enter markets where we expect to achieve dominant market share within two years of market entry. Exit markets where we are unable to achieve a satisfactory rate of return.*

(3) *Innovation: Track market needs on a regular basis to identify products or services which will address those needs in markets which have growth and profit potential.*

(4) ***Customer Satisfaction:*** *Regularly evaluate customer satisfaction of our products and services, and identify factors which will maintain or improve that satisfaction.*

(5) ***Product Quality:*** *Establish quality control programs which enhance and maintain our reputation for outstanding product quality and service in all our markets.*

(6) ***Product Development:*** *Carry out extensive research and development of new products and services, as indicated by identified needs and quality improvements in growth markets.*

(7) ***Staff Productivity:*** *Provide incentives, training programs and other initiatives that will improve and maintain high staff productivity and morale.*

(8) ***Asset Growth:*** *Monitor performance of all aspects of our business so that each activity has a favourable effect, directly or indirectly, on our mission ROI.*

(9) ***Profitability:*** *Monitor financial performance of all activities to ensure that profit and cash flow projections are achieved according to, or ahead of, plan.*

Response 9.3 provided some illustrative policies, goals and strategies. Each manager lists those statements which are most important, and indicates their relative priorities. Table 9.1 now places summarized statements from Response 9.3 in priority order, and also indicates the specific goals that each statement supports. This is used to identify the issues which affect achievement or implementation of the statements, addressing those of highest priority first.

9.2.6 Step 4 – Identify issues

Issues that affect achievement of a defined goal are next identified. These may indicate impediments to achievement, or instead catalysts for greater achievement. Typically only four or five major issues are identified per goal. As issues are determined, the relevant goal statement may need to be refined, or changed.

The defined issues from the XYZ managers have been extracted from the consolidated questionnaire. They are listed in Table 9.2 under each prioritized goal. Table 9.1 can be used for reference to the summarized statement for that priority, or to the complete statement as indicated by its number in Response 9.3.

9.2.7 Step 5 – Define strategies

For each issue identified for a goal, appropriate strategies are defined. These indicate how the goal should be reached, in the context of the relevant

Table 9.1 Prioritized policies, goals and strategies

Pty	Goal	No	Statement
1	Asset growth	G8	Monitor performance in all areas for effect on ROI.
2	Profitability	G9	Monitor financial performance to achieve or exceed plan.
3	Market share	G2	Enter markets for dominant market share in two years. Exit markets with unsatisfactory rate of return.
4	Market share Innovation	G3	Track market needs for products or services in markets which have growth and profit potential
5	Market analysis	G1	Analyze markets to assess growth, potential market size and potential market competition
6	Customer satisfaction	G4	Evaluate customer satisfaction and identify factors which maintain or improve that satisfaction.
7	Product quality	G5	Set quality control programs to achieve outstanding product quality and service in all markets.
8	Product development	G6	Carry out R&D of products and services to address needs and quality improvements in growth markets.
9	Staff productivity	G7	Provide incentives, training programs and other initiatives for high staff productivity and morale.

issue. They start with typical action words such as: Establish and Maintain; Ensure; Guide and Direct.

Table 9.2 lists the issues affecting each goal. Each group of issues relating to a goal are extracted for reference and discussion in the pages following the table, for progressive definition of strategies to address the identified issues.

Asset growth strategies

Asset Growth is the highest priority goal: '*monitor performance in all areas for effect on ROI*'. Table 9.2 indicates the relevant issues are:

- High proportion of investments in declining markets
- High market entry cost into markets found later to be marginal
- High debt levels for assets in sunset markets

Table 9.2 Issues for prioritized policies, goals and strategies

Pty	Goal	Concerns or Issues
1	Asset growth G8	High proportion of investments in declining markets High market entry cost into markets found later to be marginal High debt levels for assets in sunset markets
2	Profitability G9	Delayed financial reporting and poor financial control High interest costs and poor cash flow management Poor budget control
3	Market share G2	Market share statistics either unavailable or inaccurate Competitor activity analysis not available Market growth rates and total potential size not available Poor corporate image
4	Innovation G3	No monitoring of changes in technology Ineffective research capability and inadequate R&D funding Inability to attract and hold quality research staff
5	Market analysis G1	Demographic data, market sizes and profitability unavailable Market surveys are inaccurate or incomplete
6	Customer satisfaction G4	High level of customer returns and little repeat business Poor customer training, sales training and field support Unrealistic sales promises and customer expectations
7	Product quality G5	High product reject level and high product recall exposure High product maintenance and repair costs
8	Product development G6	Poor market introduction of new products High proportion of new products are rejected before market release as unprofitable
9	Staff productivity G7	Inadequate staff training Poor morale and high staff turnover

The issues for Asset Growth reflect a lack of adequate market analysis in the past. XYZ has entered markets, or continued in markets that have been found to be unprofitable. Many of these markets involved high entry or operation costs, with resulting high debt levels to maintain a market presence. XYZ should sell its interests in these markets and exit from them as soon as possible. The later goals address entry and operation in new markets that are more attractive for XYZ in the long-term, and result in asset growth. This leads to the definition of the following strategies:

Asset Disposal Strategy: Identify assets which cannot provide a return within two years consistent with the mission ROI, and dispose of them at the best possible price.

Market Exit Strategy: Identify markets which are unprofitable and in decline, and exit those markets at the lowest possible cost.

Profitability strategies

Issues identified in Table 9.2 directly affecting the Profitability goal (G9) *'monitor financial performance to achieve or exceed plan'* are:

- Delayed financial reporting and poor financial control
- High interest costs and poor cash flow management
- Poor budget control

These issues indicate that the financial control systems of XYZ must be improved if there is to be any improvement in its overall financial performance. The interest costs may be reduced by the *asset disposal* and *market exit* strategies defined above, but cash flow management and budget control must also be improved. The following strategies were defined by the XYZ managers:

Financial Reporting Strategy: Implement flexible financial reporting systems able to be introduced at any organizational level, that can provide profit and loss statements for any defined reporting frequency, with associated balance sheet statements.

Budget Control Strategy: Establish and maintain strong budgetary controls for all expenditure, linked directly to revenue achievement. All financial statements must clearly show actual revenue and expenditure against budget, and indicate percentage change from the previous reporting level.

Market analysis and market share strategies

Table 9.2 identified issues that affect achievement of the Market Share goal (G2): *'Enter markets for dominant market share in two years. Exit markets with unsatisfactory rate of return'*. These also indicate issues that relate to the market analysis goal (G1): *'analyze markets to assess growth, potential market size and potential market competition'*.

Market share issues

- Market share statistics either unavailable or inaccurate
- Competitor activity analysis not available
- Market growth rates and total potential size not available
- Poor corporate image

Market Analysis Issues

- Demographic data, market sizes and profitability unavailable
- Market surveys are inaccurate or incomplete

Because of the unavailability or inaccuracy of market survey and demographic data, the market share goal cannot be achieved. As a consequence, XYZ management have no effective information on which to base future market decisions. This is critical for the selection of markets that will enable it to achieve its mission ROI.

The strategies in support of the Asset Growth and Profitability goals discussed above were easy to decide: known solutions were available. These only required appropriate directions to be set by management. The issues associated with the Market Share and Market Analysis goals are more difficult: no obvious solutions are apparent. Strategies must be defined to identify alternative solutions first, so that management can then set relevant directions. Much time was spent in discussion before the following strategies were agreed upon.

Market Data Strategy: Identify organizations which can provide accurate market analysis, competitor analysis and demographic data, with market size, market growth, competitor activity and associated market share data.

Market Analysis Strategy: Based on organizations selected from the market data strategy, establish and maintain a regular market analysis capability so we can determine current and potential size of markets that management identify, together with their projected growth. Identify existing and potential competition in those markets, and their relative market shares.

Market Needs Analysis Strategy: For potential markets selected by management for possible entry, and for all markets where we operate, regularly determine the needs of existing and potential customers in those markets.

Innovation strategies

The issues affecting the Innovation goal (G3): *'track market needs for products or services in markets which have growth and profit potential'*, are listed next in Table 9.2:

- No monitoring of changes in technology
- Ineffective research capability and inadequate R&D funding
- Inability to attract and hold quality research staff

While the above *market analysis* and *market needs analysis* strategies enable XYZ to identify new markets to enter and determine their needs, their current R&D capability will not allow them to respond with appropriate products or services designed for those markets. The managers therefore defined the following innovation strategies:

> *Technology Monitoring Strategy: Monitor and evaluate all technologies that may be relevant to our business, as well as those specific to markets identified by management from the market needs analysis strategy.*

> *R&D Strategy: Establish and maintain a research and development capability that can design or enhance new or existing products and services based on the needs identified from the market needs analysis strategy.*

> *R&D Funding Strategy: Ensure that adequate funding of the R&D strategy is provided and establish an environment to attract and retain high quality R&D staff.*

Customer satisfaction strategies

Table 9.2 indicated issues associated with the Customer Satisfaction goal (G4): *'evaluate customer satisfaction and identify factors which maintain or improve that satisfaction'*.

- High level of customer returns and little repeat business
- Poor customer training, sales training and field support
- Unrealistic sales promises and customer expectations

The high level of returns and lack of repeat business may be symptoms of poor product quality. This is not helped by the poor field support also indicated. Strategies must be defined to determine whether product quality and field support are the cause. Strategies which will improve training may also help resolve the sales promise and customer expectation issues.

> *Customer Satisfaction Survey Strategy: Implement regular surveys of our customer satisfaction in selected markets, in conjunction with the market needs analysis strategy, to identify areas where we can improve; and also to determine customer needs which we do not yet address.*

> *Training Strategy: Establish and maintain sales training, support staff training and customer training programs that will maximize business opportunities and achieve satisfactory profit in all markets in which we operate.*

Product quality strategy

The Product Quality (G5) and Product Development (G6) goals are somewhat interrelated. The issues in Table 9.2 that apply to the product quality goal '*set quality control programs to achieve outstanding product quality and service in all markets*' are:

- High product reject level and high product recall exposure
- High product maintenance and repair costs

XYZ management are concerned about current quality control procedures. They define a new *quality control* strategy to reduce reject and recall levels. The R&D Department is also required to work with the Production Department, to identify ways in which maintenance and repair costs can be reduced.

> *Quality Control Strategy: Establish and maintain stringent quality control over all production, to achieve a significant reduction in reject and recall levels.*

> *Product Maintenance Improvement Strategy: Together with R&D, define, develop and implement design or production improvements which will result in a significant reduction in the cost of product maintenance and repair.*

Product development strategy

The issues in Table 9.2 for the Product Development goal (G6) '*carry out R&D of products and services to address needs and quality improvements in growth markets*' are:

- Poor market introduction of new products
- High proportion of new products rejected as unprofitable

These issues suggest that R&D may lack market awareness. They are delivering new products to the Product Development department that do not adequately address needs of the market, or which are unprofitable. The participation of R&D staff in the *quality control* strategy above should have a by-product effect: R&D staff will gain a better understanding of the problems encountered in the marketplace, for an improved market awareness.

> *Product Review Strategy: Establish criteria to evaluate all existing products and all new products under development for market acceptance and profitability. Ensure that existing products are withdrawn and new products are terminated which no longer satisfy those criteria.*

> *Product Release Strategy: Guide and direct product introduction strategies and associated advertising campaigns that emphasize the market needs addressed by those products, and their other benefits over existing products on the market.*

Staff productivity strategies

Table 9.2 highlighted the following issues arising from the Staff Productivity goal (G7) *'provide incentives, training programs and other initiatives'*:

- Inadequate staff training
- Poor morale and high staff turnover

Some of these issues have already had a negative effect on the Innovation, Product Quality and Customer Satisfaction goals. Strategies to address these issues focused on those specific goals. XYZ management defined additional strategies to improve staff productivity:

> *Career Planning Strategy: Establish and maintain a program of at least annual personal appraisal reviews which plan future job promotion and other career development moves with every employee on an individual basis. Reviews are to be seen as acknowledgements of personal performance improvement or rewards for excellent performance, rather than as punishment for poor performance.*
>
> *Staff Incentive Strategy: Together with the career planning strategy, provide incentive programs that reward and acknowledge high performers.*

9.2.8   Step 6 – Identify current functions

The current functions carried out by the organization are detailed. These are generally very easy to identify. They may later change as a result of the study and subsequent project. However at this point they will enable us initially to allocate functional responsibility for each strategy defined in support of each goal. The functions presently carried out within XYZ Corporation are:

- Corporate
- Finance
- Forecasting
- Marketing
- Sales
- R&D
- Production
- Purchasing
- Personnel

Strategy	Corporate	Finance	Mkt Research	Forecasting	Marketing	Sales	R&D	Product Mgt	Production	Purchasing	Education	Personnel		
Asset Disposal		•												
Market Exit					•									
Financial Reporting		•												
Budget Control		•												
Market Data			•											
Market Analysis			•											
Market Needs Analysis					•									
Technology Monitoring							•							
R&D							•							
R&D Funding	•													
Customer Satisfaction Survey						•								
Sales, Support & Customer Training											•			
Quality Control									•					
Product Maintenance Improvement									•					
Product Review								•						
Product Release						•								
Career Planning												•		
Staff Incentives												•		

Figure 9.4 Strategy–Function Matrix for XYZ Corporation.

These are documented as column headings in a matrix which lists the strategies carried out by the function. This is called the **strategy–function matrix** as illustrated in Figure 9.4.

9.2.9 Step 7 – Allocate strategies to functions

As each strategy is allocated to the function which has major responsibility for carrying out that strategy, a bullet or asterisk is placed in only one function column in Figure 9.4 except as follows:

- If a strategy cannot be allocated to any function which can focus adequately on that strategy, a new function is defined. Market Research, Product Management and Education are all new functions in Figure 9.4 that are needed to implement the strategies allocated to them. These functions had never been defined by XYZ before, but are needed to overcome the relevant issues discussed in Sections 9.2.6 and 9.2.7.

- If no strategies apply to a function, it may indicate: goals that have not yet been defined; or a function that exists at a lower level in the organization; or a function that is no longer relevant to the business.

- If a strategy applies to more than one function, it generally indicates a level of detail appropriate to a lower management level. A more general strategy should be defined that can be allocated to only one responsible function column.

The detailed strategies are later allocated when the goal analysis process is applied to a lower management level. Figure 9.4 shows the result of this strategy allocation for the XYZ Corporation.

Notice that no strategies have been allocated to the purchasing function. This function reports to the production manager. The function's responsibilities are later defined by the production manager as purchasing objectives to be achieved, so ensuring the *quality control* and *product maintenance improvement* strategies are implemented.

Notice also that no strategies were defined for the Forecasting function. Why? These were overlooked, as no forecasting issues were identified. On further investigation we find that XYZ carries out its forecasting well: this is one of its strengths. But it has been forecasting in declining markets. Most seriously, these forecasts had given management early warning of market decline, but no strategies had ever been defined to enter new markets.

The strategies above should be refined, or additional strategies defined, to capitalize on the forecasting strength of XYZ. We will not do that at this time, but will show how we can use the material developed to this point to define the responsibilities of each functional position. This also allows us to define functions and job responsibilities for new organization structures.

9.2.10   Step 8 – Define functional responsibility

The strategies allocated to each vertical function column in Figure 9.4 are extracted and documented for each function, to provide a statement of

Position: Financial Controller
Reports to: Managing Director

Goal	*Goal:* Concerns or Issues
Asset growth	*Monitor performance of all aspects of our business so that each activity has a favourable effect, directly or indirectly, on our mission ROI.* **Concerns or Issues:** • High proportion of investments in declining markets • High market entry cost into markets found later to be marginal • High debt levels for assets in sunset markets

(1)   **Asset Disposal Strategy:** Identify assets which cannot provide a return within two years consistent with the mission ROI, and dispose of them at the best possible price.

   Asset Disposal Objective: Following Board approval, dispose of all non-performing assets within 12 months.

Goal	*Goal:* Concerns or Issues
Profitability	*Monitor financial performance of all activities to ensure that profit and cash flow projections are achieved according to, or ahead of, plan* **Concerns or Issues:** • Delayed financial reporting and poor financial control • High interest costs and poor cash flow management • Poor budget control

(2)   **Financial Reporting Strategy:** Implement flexible financial reporting systems able to be introduced at any organizational level, and which can provide profit and loss statements for any defined reporting frequency, with associated balance sheet statements.

   Financial Reporting Objective: Implement financial reporting systems within 6 months that provide profit and loss, balance sheet and cash flow reporting within 1 day of the close of any defined financial period.

(3)   **Budget Control Strategy:** Establish and maintain strong budgetary controls for all expenditure, linked directly to revenue achievement. All financial statements must clearly show actual revenue and expenditure against budget, and indicate percentage change from the previous reporting level.

   Budget Control Objective: Implement budget control systems directly linked to financial reports according to the *budget control* strategy, within 6 months.

Figure 9.5   **Financial Controller Position Description.**

Goal	*Goal:* Concerns or Issues
Innovation	*Track market needs on a regular basis to identify products or services which will address those needs in markets which have growth and profit potential.* Concerns or Issues: • No monitoring of changes in technology • Ineffective research capability and inadequate R&D funding • Inability to attract and hold quality research staff

(4)   **R&D Funding Strategy:** Ensure that adequate funding of the R&D strategy is provided and establish an environment to attract and retain high quality R&D staff.

R&D Funding Objective: Within 3 months, determine funding requirements of R&D for the next 2 years.

Figure 9.5 (cont.)   **Financial Controller Position Description.**

functional responsibility. This forms the foundation of a job description for the manager responsible for the function.

For example, reading down the Finance function column, we see that it is responsible for the *asset disposal*, *financial reporting*, *budget control* and *R&D funding* strategies. Extracting these strategies from the earlier material, with their relevant goals and issues, we can prepare a function description for the Financial Controller: responsible for the Finance function. Each strategy is used to define specific quantifiable objectives which clearly indicate the result to be achieved by the strategy, as shown in Figure 9.5.

Notice that each objective in Figure 9.5 has a defined measure, level and time. These objectives are intended to be updated or replaced as each part of the relevant strategy is realized. For example the R&D objective ensures that the R&D funding requirements first be determined: these funding needs must be defined within 3 months. Management will then make a decision on the amount of funding to be provided to R&D, consistent with other strategies. This will lead to the definition of subsequent objectives: to ensure that the level of agreed funding is supplied; and to ensure that this funding is used effectively by the R&D Department.

Let us consider another example, for the new Market Research function. This is shown in Figure 9.6, which details the position description for the Market Research Manager.

The position description of the Market Research Manager indicates two objectives for each of three strategies. Similar position descriptions are

Position: Market Research Manager
Reports to: Marketing Director

Goal	*Goal:* Concerns or Issues
Market share	*Only enter markets where we expect to achieve dominant market share within two years of market entry. Exit markets where we are unable to achieve a satisfactory rate of return.* Concerns or Issues: • Market share statistics either unavailable or inaccurate • Competitor activity analysis not available • Market growth rates and total potential size not available • Poor corporate image

(1)   ***Market Data Strategy:*** Identify organizations which can provide accurate market analysis, competitor analysis and demographic data, with market size, market growth, competitor activity and associated market share data.

   Market Data Objective 1: Identify organizations within 1 month who are able to supply the information defined in the market data strategy.

   Market Data Objective 2: Of the organizations from *market data objective 1*, select two potential organizations within a further week who can satisfy our current and future requirements for market information.

(2)   **Market Analysis Strategy:** Based on organizations selected from the *market data* strategy, establish and maintain a regular market analysis capability so we can identify the current and potential size of markets that management identify, together with their projected growth. Identify existing and potential competition in those markets, and their relative market shares.

   Market Analysis Objective 1: Report quarterly for existing markets in terms of current and projected market size and market growth.

   Market Analysis Objective 2: Report quarterly for existing markets in terms of the market share of existing and potential competition in those markets.

(3)   **Market Needs Analysis Strategy:** For all potential markets which have been selected by management for possible entry, and for all markets where we operate, regularly determine the needs of existing and potential customers in those markets.

   Market Needs Objective 1: Report quarterly on the needs of existing and potential customers in markets where we currently operate, to indicate changes from previous periods.

   Market Needs Objective 2: For markets we are contemplating entering, report within 3 months on the identified needs of existing and potential customers in those markets.

Figure 9.6   **Market Research Manager Position.**

extracted for each management position to be established, based on the Strategy–Function matrix in Figure 9.4.

This completes goal analysis at the relevant management level. It is then applied at the next lower management level. Each strategy is examined similar to the approach described above for goals, to identify the lower level objectives that have been defined to ensure that the strategy is carried out: issues relating to those objectives are determined; then strategies; functional responsibility is allocated for lower level objectives and strategies; and last, functional descriptions are prepared for each lower level position. This progresses down through appropriate organization levels ensuring that all objectives and strategies, and similarly sub-objectives and tactics, are clearly defined and that responsibility is allocated for their implementation.

Goal analysis thus refines input obtained from the management questionnaire. It results in the development of goals, issues and strategies from the mission statement. These can form the initial strategic statements for input to a strategic modeling project. They can also be used as a catalyst for the definition of new strategic directions.

9.3 | SUMMARY

In this chapter we considered strategic thinking and strategic analysis. We discussed Rockart's critical success factor approach for definition of organizational goals. We saw that goal analysis progresses beyond Rockart's three CSF steps: 1) generate critical success factors; 2) refine CSFs into objectives; 3) identify measures of performance. It also can be used to define strategies, allocating those strategies to areas that will have functional responsibility for strategic implementation.

We worked through an example illustrating the steps of goal analysis, by its application to the XYZ Corporation. We analyzed the XYZ mission, developing a high-level mission model of major data subjects. We used this to identify critical success factors. We refined these CSFs into statements of goals, and then identified concerns or issues that affected achievement of the goals. We defined strategies to resolve those concerns or issues. We identified current functions of the project area, and allocated each strategy to a function that was responsible for its implementation. We finally developed statements of functional responsibility, in the form of job descriptions for the staff responsible for the functions. These defined specific, measurable objectives to be achieved.

The goal analysis technique can be used at any organizational level: it is most effective in defining new organization structures, or refining existing organization structures.

References

[1] Ohmae, K. (1982). The Mind of the Strategist, McGraw-Hill: New York, NY.

[2] Rowe, A. J., Mason, R. O., Dickel, K. E. and Snyder, N. H. (1990). *Strategic Management: A Methodological Approach (Third Edition)*, Addison-Wesley, Reading: MA.

[3] Rockart, J. F. (1979). Chief Executives Define Their Own Data Needs, *Harvard Business Review*: Cambridge, MA (March–April).

[4] Finkelstein, C. B. (1989). *An Introduction to Information Engineering*, Addison-Wesley: Reading, MA.

[5] Drucker, P. F. (1974). *Management: Tasks, Responsibilities, Practices*, Harper & Row: New York, NY.

CHAPTER 10

Internal Appraisal

Following evaluation of the current strategy in Chapter 9 using goal analysis, areas for improvement are indicated. New strategic directions may need to be established. This chapter, and Chapters 11–12, show how a strategic focus can be defined: identifying opportunities which build on strengths for competitive advantage, while avoiding those threats which attack weaknesses.

10.1 STAGE 3 – SETTING STRATEGIC DIRECTION

A corporate strategy should be comprehensive, and should include a plan that takes into account the resources available to the organization and the strategic advantage needed to achieve its basic mission. This is dependent on an organization's capability. Rowe, Mason, Dickel and Snyder [1] assess company capability with several techniques. A **company capability profile** examines strengths and weaknesses in four key areas: managerial, competitive (or marketing), financial, and technical. A profile is developed for a number of factors in these four areas, illustrating the degree of strength or weakness of each factor. They assess organizational performance with key performance indicators of: efficiency; effectiveness; equity; responsiveness. Other performance indicators are defined based on an organization's objectives.

Drucker [2] suggests eight key areas in which objectives must be set and performance measured: marketing; innovation; human organization; financial resources; physical resources; productivity; social responsibilities;

profit. Rowe *et al* assess performance indicators in Drucker's areas using their Key-Result Objective Analysis. They also discuss: WOTS-UP analysis (taken from Weaknesses, Opportunities, Threats and Strengths, with UP added to help remember the term); cost-benefit analysis; multi-attribute decision making; and computer simulation. These are used to help select a strategic thrust and strategic alternatives. Strategic alternatives are discussed further in Chapter 12. Strategic thrust addresses three questions which focus on whether the organization has, or can create:

- Cost advantages of products or services produced cheaper than competitors.
- Differentiation advantages: unique features, products or services for which customers will pay.
- Broad or narrow product or service range, forward or backward integration, geographic expanse, or industry segments in which it competes.

An organization's strategic thrust is developed in three steps (see Figure 10.1). The first step, the **internal appraisal**, is covered in this chapter: it identifies the strengths and weaknesses of the business. The second step, addressed in Chapter 11, is an **external appraisal** of the business: examining its competitors and the environment. Opportunities that offer competitive advantage are identified. Threats which may affect weaknesses of the business are evaluated: these indicate potential difficulties. A **strategic evaluation** is then undertaken in Chapter 12, to define a strategic direction

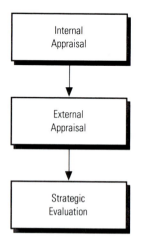

Figure 10.1 Setting strategic direction.

which emphasizes areas of competitive advantage while avoiding potential difficulties.

The above steps carried out in this Stage 3 represent the formal strategic planning stage summarized in Chapter 10 of my earlier book [3]. This is based on the *Practical Strategic Planning* method [4] developed as part of Information Engineering in the early 1980s. We will discuss each step in the following pages, then use the XYZ Corporation to illustrate their application.

10.1.1   Step 1 – Internal appraisal

An internal appraisal may be conducted at the business unit level for a commercial organization, or at the program level for a government organization. In this book we will use the term **business unit** to refer to both commercial business units and government programs. An internal appraisal is also carried out at the corporate level of both types of organizations.

Internal business unit appraisal

Business unit performance data   Performance data relating to the business unit (or program) is obtained for each functional area. This determines the resources needed (referred to as **resource contribution**), as well as the changes made to those resources by each functional area to produce its products or services (referred to as **resource conversion**). Performance indicators are defined in each area that are used to determine its strengths and weaknesses. Some typical examples in different functional areas follow.

- **Production:** Plant modernity; plant flexibility; productivity.
- **Marketing:** Product range; service organization; distribution; pricing structure.
- **Finance:** Profitability; low use of credit; cash flow.
- **Procurement:** Lines of supply.
- **Personnel:** Industrial relations; personnel development.
- **Public Relations:** Patent protection; tariff barriers; subsidies.
- **Structure:** Participative decision-making; information systems.
- **Management:** Innovative capability; performance indicators; depth.

Each performance indicator is ranked in the various functional areas of the business unit as strong, average or weak.

Business unit strengths   Performance indicators that have been assessed as strong (based on product or market goals or objectives set for the business unit in Stage 2 – see Chapter 9), are grouped together: these highlight the strengths of the business unit. Grouped performance indicators may suggest areas of distinctive competence of the business unit. These may give it a comparative advantage over other business units. These areas may be further refined in an external appraisal to gain competitive advantage for the organization.

Business unit weaknesses   Performance indicators assessed as average or weak (based also on product or market goals or objectives set for the business unit in Stage 2) are similarly grouped together. Grouped weak indicators that impede attainment of the defined goals or objectives, or impede comparative advantage, are identified.

Business unit resource commitments   The defined rankings of indicators as strong, average or weak are assessed in terms of the present commitment of resources to each functional area of the business unit. A **business unit resource deployment matrix** summarizes potential variations, shown in

BUSINESS UNIT RESOURCE DEPLOYMENT MATRIX

Business Unit: _____ Functional Area: _____

Grouped Performance Indicators	STRENGTHS		WEAKNESSES	
	Distinctive Competence	Comparative Advantage	Affecting Comparative Advantage	Warranting Remediation
A	√			
B	√	√		
C			√	
D				√
Existing Resource Commitment	$	$	$	$
Insensitivity to Resource Variation	$ + $ −	$ + $ −		
Required Resource Increment			$ +	$ +

Figure 10.2 Business unit resource deployment matrix.

Figure 10.2. For example, resources that have previously been committed to a functional area may not have been sufficient to convert a weak ranking to an average ranking. The sensitivity of areas of distinctive competence or comparative advantage to changes in allocation of resources is evaluated.

Following the internal appraisal of each relevant business unit, a similar approach is applied to the organization itself. This is the internal corporate appraisal.

Internal corporate appraisal

At the corporate level, senior management face the problem of generating financial resources and deciding on their allocation to specific business units or programs in the organization's strategic portfolio. Their interest thus is largely on financial performance indicators.

Corporate performance data   Performance data needed by senior management relates to the achievement of goals and objectives, the success of defined strategies, the financial condition of the organization as a whole and its potential for generating surplus financial resources, and the experience and capability of management at all levels of the organization. Financial management and managerial control indicators are particularly important at the corporate level. Performance in all of these areas is ranked as strong, average or weak.

Corporate strengths and weaknesses   Strengths and weaknesses identified at the business unit level, particularly those conferring or impeding distinctive competence or comparative advantage, are evaluated in terms of prior patterns of financial resource commitment. An assessment is made of the likely effect, on performance, of variations in financial commitment: such as developed at the business unit level in Figure 10.2. Distinctive competence or comparative advantage strengths are highlighted if they can be particularly influenced by changes in resource commitments and remedies are defined for those weaknesses which are likely to impede them. The financial position and capital structure of the organization is then assessed in terms of exposure to takeover or loss of corporate control. The importance of areas of *corporate* distinctive competence and potential comparative advantage to the likely attainment of corporate goals and objectives is evaluated.

Corporate resource commitments   The effect of change in allocation of financial and other resources on areas of distinctive competence or comparative advantage at the corporate level are evaluated, as well as their effect

CORPORATE RESOURCE DEPLOYMENT MATRIX

Organization: _____

Grouped Performance Indicators	STRENGTHS		WEAKNESSES	
	Distinctive Competence	Comparative Advantage	Affecting Comparative Advantage	Warranting Remediation
A	√			
B	√	√		
C			√	
D				√
Existing Resource Commitment	$	$	$	$
Insensitivity to Resource Variation	$ + $ −	$ + $ −		
Required Resource Increment			$ +	$ +

Figure 10.3 Corporate resource deployment matrix.

on weaknesses which represent potential difficulties. A **corporate resource deployment matrix,** as shown in Figure 10.3, can be used to summarize these commitments.

The result of this internal appraisal is a clear definition of:

- Strengths and weaknesses of each business unit.
- Business units with distinctive competence or comparative advantage.
- Strengths and weaknesses of the organization as a whole.
- Distinctive competence or comparative advantage of the organization.

Elsworth [5] is critical of the failure of many managers to integrate financial policies and corporate strategy, with the result that the strategic implications of financial policies are rarely evaluated. He argues:

> 'When apparently objective financial policies become arbitrarily imposed corporate goals, they lose their flexibility, become sacrosanct, and can even restrict a company's potential value'.

Financial policies affect the sustainable rate of growth of an organization. He goes on:

> 'To achieve the full competitive potential of an integrated, consistent strategy, top management needs to regain control over the formulation of financial policies to prevent capital market influences from overwhelming strategic operating considerations'.

Elsworth discusses that operating managers have little input into the corporate planning process. The financial resources allocated to them are thus predetermined, constraining business unit strategic planning flexibility, and leading to lost opportunity costs. He suggests a four step program to integrate financial policy with strategic planning at both the corporate and business unit levels:

- Identify the assumptions on which financial policy is based. Conduct an analysis of alternative financial policies that are specific to the organization, its business opportunities, and its level of risk.
- Motivate and direct financial officers to incorporate strategy in their financial policy proposals.
- Include operating managers in the financial policy debate.
- Avoid turning financial policies into corporate goals.

Elsworth indicates that this results in the following benefits:

- Achieves an open exchange between operating and financial managers that makes the conflict among policies more explicit, and results in a greater balance in the debate.
- Provides a vehicle for operating managers to voice their arguments and to vent the frustration they feel when faced with restrictive financial policies.
- Achieves a greater understanding by all of how the financial policies fit with the organization's strategy.
- Leads to a reduction in the tendency of operating managers to implicitly ration capital by refusing to sponsor sound investments for fear they would be rejected because of corporate capital constraints.
- Leads to a more ready acceptance of policy through operating management's participation in the decision-making process.

Marshuetz [6] describes how American Can allocates capital by centralizing its investment decisions, while decentralizing its operating decisions – so allocating funds for the best possible strategic use. American Can operates mainly in the packaging industry (metal cans, disposable cups, plastic toothpaste tubes), and in a number of other industries, including a retail record store chain (Musicland) and a mail-order business (Fingerhut). It distinguishes between decisions supporting daily operations, and those that determine the future of each of its businesses. Business unit managers present investment ideas formally during the strategic planning process. The impact of an investment can then be evaluated as for the strategic plan: measuring the investment's impact on the competitive position of the business, measured by the amount, timing and risk of the investment's cash flows.

We will now illustrate the application of Step 1 (see Figure 10.1), using an internal appraisal to determine strengths and weaknesses of XYZ Corporation. For brevity, we will concentrate only on an internal corporate appraisal. Strengths are identified which confer distinctive competence or comparative advantage on XYZ at the corporate level, together with weaknesses that represent corporate comparative disadvantages. Also for brevity we will omit an assessment of resource deployment as shown in Figures 10.2 and 10.3.

10.1.2 Internal appraisal of XYZ Corporation

The responses to the management questionnaire in Chapter 8 indicated a number of strengths and weaknesses of XYZ Corporation. These responses identified several performance indicators, including: capital resources; cash flow and profitability; sales and marketing; customer support; research and development; plant flexibility and productivity; product development; management and personnel; and computer support. We will discuss the strengths and weaknesses of each indicator in turn. They are summarized in Table 10.1. We will start by evaluating Capital Resources.

Indicator	Strengths	Weaknesses
Capital Resources	• Cash reserves and shareholder equity • Large investment in property • Flexible plant capability	• Investments in sunset markets • Poor market profitability analysis • Interest rate fluctuation exposure

XYZ Corporation is fortunate: it has strong shareholder equity and substantial cash reserves. It is cash rich. Its strength in property investment is due to its long standing management policy of investing a proportion of retained earnings in property for capital appreciation. It sells a wide range of manufactured products, with value-added services that also generate good returns. It has invested in plant and equipment that is very flexible, able to be changed easily to produce new products or offer new services for markets in which it participates. It would appear that XYZ Corporation has little to worry about the future.

However its weaknesses suggest troubled waters may lie ahead. We discuss these with management. We find that the capital appreciation of property has achieved a return on investment of 12% pa. This return is significantly below the mission ROI of 20%. Also, XYZ is very active in markets that are declining. Furthermore, initial entry into these markets was funded by debt at a time of low interest rates, to free up funds for property investment. These loans were long-term, but the interest rates were not fixed. As a result, today's high interest rates represent a large drain on profits. Let us examine cash flow and profitability further.

Indicator	Strengths	Weaknesses
Cash Flow and Profitability	• Stable sales and profit growth • Strong cash flow • Strong dividend policy • Property investment foçus	• Profit growth less than sales growth • Poor financial reporting and control • High interest cost in servicing debt • Poor cash flow management • Poor budget control (*'fat & happy'*)

XYZ is profitable, with a strong cash flow, and has paid consistent dividends to its shareholders. Although it is active in sunset markets, sales are still strong. But we see that the profit growth rate is less than the sales growth rate: this suggests that these sales are costing more to obtain. This may be due to high cost of sales, the high interest costs in servicing debt, or there may well be other reasons: these should all be investigated.

The indicated poor financial reporting and control, and poor cash flow management are serious concerns. XYZ has very poor debtor control: accounts receivable follow up is sporadic, with most accounts still outstanding after 60 days. It also has many bad debts as credit control is poor: many new customers are never given a credit check. Cash management is lax: funds are left in accounts that earn no interest, rather than take advantage of high money market rates available at call. And it has poor budget control.

As one responding manager has indicated, XYZ has become *'fat and happy'*. Its lack of financial control reflects the good fortune of yesterday.

Management are complacent. Although the company is still profitable and is cash rich, it is starting to bleed. It is a classic example of Galbraith's first organizational design strategy [7]: *'creation of slack resources'* (see Chapter 8). In fact, we will see XYZ has no real performance targets. But management are not even aware of the danger. Unless something is done quickly, XYZ will soon die. Let us investigate the problem further, first by looking at Sales and Marketing in more detail.

Indicator	Strengths	Weaknesses
Sales and Marketing	• Strong distribution channels • Large, dedicated sales force • High level of quota achievement • Good knowledge of current markets • Strong cash generation capability	• Poor corporate image • Inadequate advertising budget • Ineffective sales force incentives • Poor market analysis capability • Poor customer analysis capability • Poor competitive analysis capability

XYZ has strong distribution channels and a large sales force with good knowledge of the current markets. They generate substantial sales, regularly achieving their allocated sales quota. *'We have always met our quota without fail for the last ten years'*, says the sales manager proudly. But the indicated weaknesses are very worrying. The poor corporate image may be a result of limited advertising, or may be due to poor product quality. We also see that the high quota achievement is not really a strength, as sales force incentives are ineffective. It appears that the sales quotas are not aggressive enough, or the sales commission plan is inadequate, or both. *'If we use greater sales incentives, perhaps even higher sales can be achieved'* should be the real interpretation of the sales manager on the last decade of consistent quota achievement!

The real problem becomes apparent from the last three weaknesses: poor market, customer and competitor analysis. XYZ is so complacent in its traditional markets it does not realize that they are in decline, and danger lies ahead. But it does not even track its current markets, let alone identify potential new markets. It has no idea what its customers want. As the sales manager says: *'Of course our customers are happy; our quota achievement indicates that. If they weren't happy, they wouldn't buy our products, would they?'* As it does not track competitors: it is not aware that they will soon offer better products, of higher quality and at a lower price, in its traditional markets. The customers are not happy: if they had another alternative they would certainly not buy from XYZ. XYZ has been blinded by its past success, and is not aware it is missing opportunities in new emerging markets that have been identified by these competitors.

The competitors are small, but they know of the cash generation capability of the traditional markets. These are seen as *'cash cows'*, ready to be milked for profits. Their competitive strategy is simple. It is readily assessed by anyone with a knowledge of the market:

> *Use superior service, with new technology, high quality, low cost products to gain market share. As market share and profitability grow, use these profits to fund development of other products and services for new emerging markets.*

Warning signs are also apparent in the strengths and weaknesses relating to Customer Support. The sales force strength, and sales growth, are emphasized again. But we see that sales training and field support are inadequate. And because of the lack of customer focus, XYZ is not aware that its customers are definitely *not happy*. Until now, customers have had no choice but to continue to buy from XYZ. But they will soon have superior alternatives, the competitors are making sure of that! XYZ must use its large cash reserves to change or it may lose its traditional markets. But how? Can it develop new products and services for these emerging new markets itself? Can it change its production capability? Is management able to change? How capable are XYZ managers and their staff? Have they forgotten how to fight?

Indicator	Strengths	Weaknesses
Customer Support	• Dedicated sales force • Strong sales growth	• Lack of customer focus & marketing • Sales training is inadequate • Field support is inadequate

We will examine XYZ's plant flexibility and productivity, and its product development indicators. Finally we will evaluate their management and personnel performance indicator. We first evaluate Research and Development capability.

XYZ Corporation has a strong R&D capability for products and services that are appropriate to its traditional markets. Its R&D staff are experienced, and have a good knowledge of its current products and services; but this is offset by their lack of market awareness. Although it has the potential to use latest technology, we can see that it does not monitor developments in technology at all well. Over the years it has scaled down its R&D funding, seeing better returns in property. R&D staff see very little future for themselves with XYZ. As a result, it is losing its best people.

Indicator	Strengths	Weaknesses
Research and Development	• Latest technology potential • Modern R&D plant and equipment • Strong staff product skills	• Inadequate technology monitoring • Inadequate R&D funding • Unable to retain R&D staff • Lack of market awareness

Because of experience in manufacturing its present products, a Plant Flexibility and Productivity evaluation shows that plant operation is efficient with long production runs and a standard product range. But we see that product quality is poor, with a high reject rate and with many customer returns: its products are not reliable. Production incentives concentrate on running the plant at full capacity with long production runs. But quality control is poor.

Indicator	Strengths	Weaknesses
Plant Flexibility and Productivity	• Efficient plant utilization • Long production runs • Standard product range • Product runs can be changed easily	• Poor product quality, high rejects • Customization potential not used • Production not integrated with sales • Poor product reliability

Production is not integrated with sales. High inventory levels accumulate for some products because of the long runs, while other product inventories are allowed to fall dangerously low. Customers also request slight changes to products. Although these changes could easily be accommodated because of plant flexibility, such requests are discouraged: customized products affect standard production runs. *'We run our plant efficiently. We can't afford these special runs'*, says the production manager.

So we see that XYZ is more concerned with running its plant, than in meeting the needs of its customers with good quality, reliable products designed to satisfy their unique needs. This has helped contribute to its poor corporate image. What about the Product Development performance indicator?

Indicator	Strengths	Weaknesses
Product Development	• Rapid development capability • Product development skills • Flexible plant capability • Available plant capacity	• Lack of market awareness • Lack of product planning • Poor product selection • Under-utilized plant

XYZ has a capability to develop new products rapidly. Its staff have strong product development skills, flexible plant capability and available capacity. Even though the production manager prides himself on *'efficient plant operation with long production runs'*, we see that it is under-utilized. These long runs leave other parts of the plant idle: plant flexibility could use this idle plant to satisfy customers' special requests.

The issues discussed in Chapter 9 also partly help explain the lack of market awareness indicated above. Many products developed by R&D are not sufficiently profitable, or do not meet customers' needs. This is symptomatic of a larger problem, highlighted by the lack of product planning and poor product selection indicated above: again we can see that XYZ has lost touch with its markets and customers. Let us now look at Management and Personnel factors.

Indicator	Strengths	Weaknesses
Management and Personnel	• Managers promoted from ranks • Managers have product experience • Dedicated staff with unique skills • Efficient staff capability	• Poor management direction • Lack of business orientation • Managers fixed in their ways • Performance indicators not used • High staff turnover • Lack of specialized training

We can now begin to see part of the cause. As XYZ managers are promoted from the ranks, they certainly have good product experience. But their product strength is offset by a lack of business orientation. XYZ has no program of management or staff training; managers and staff are expected to *'learn on the job'*. The staff have unique skills, and they are good at what they do. But the management direction is poor, and performance indicators and incentives are not used.

These weaknesses all contribute to the high staff turnover. XYZ is losing a valuable resource: its people. It must change, to survive. But the general reaction of its managers is: *'Our people are good: they learn best on the job, not in a classroom. You know, we have always done it that way. We are the best in our field, so why should we change?'* These managers are fixed in their ways. They resist change; they have not learned how to manage change. While XYZ has been the best in its field, it has also been the only one in that field . . . until now. It soon will see why it must change. Before we address these problems, let us examine its Computer Support performance indicator.

Indicator	Strengths	Weaknesses
Computer Support	• Latest hardware and software • Distributed processing capability • Moving to relational data base • Wide computer literacy	• Data is inconsistent, or out-of-date • Data bases are not integrated • Sales and production not integrated • Sales and financial reports late

XYZ has the latest hardware and software. It uses centralized mainframes for high volume processing, with distributed departmental minis in the larger branch offices and distributed micros located in small outlying branches. Its staff have wide computer literacy, with extensive experience over many years.

XYZ is moving to a relational data base environment which it hopes will remedy its problems of out-of-date, redundant and inconsistent data. *'Relational data base will allow our sales and financial reports to be completed earlier, and will enable sales and production to be more closely integrated'*, says the CEO. We can see that the software salesman has sold his products well. But software alone is not the solution to XYZ's problems: most of the problems are due to poor strategic planning. This created no difficulty until now. XYZ has serious competition, and must change. It is a classic example of mismatched planning systems and organizational structure, discussed by Yip [8] in Chapter 8.

Continuing discussion of XYZ's out-of-date and inconsistent data, management had previously not determined how data base integration could be achieved. They now see that they must develop a data model of their business; this will help them to identify the data they need. They know that relational data base software can then be used with this data model, to manage the data. They now see that strategic management planning can help them plan for the future. They also see that strategic systems development will lead to data base integration, and will help them design and develop the information systems they sorely need.

The strengths and weaknesses above are summarized in Table 10.1. We will use this to identify strengths which offer XYZ distinctive competence, or potential comparative advantage, as described following the table.

Table 10.1   Strengths and weaknesses of XYZ Corporation

Indicator	Strengths	Weaknesses
Capital Resources	• Cash reserves and shareholder equity • Large investment in property • Flexible plant capability	• Investments in sunset markets • Poor market profitability analysis • Interest rate fluctuation exposure
Cash Flow and Profitability	• Stable profit growth • Strong cash flow • Strong dividend policy • Property investment focus	• Profit growth less than sales growth • Poor financial reporting and control • High interest cost in servicing debt • Poor cash flow management • Poor budget control ('*fat & happy*')
Sales and Marketing	• Strong distribution channels • Large, dedicated sales force • High level of quota achievement • Good knowledge of current markets • Strong cash generation capability	• Poor corporate image • Inadequate advertising budget • Ineffective sales force incentives • Poor market analysis capability • Poor customer analysis capability • Poor competitive analysis capability
Customer Support	• Dedicated sales force • Strong sales growth	• Lack of customer focus & marketing • Sales training is inadequate • Field support is inadequate
Research and Development	• Latest technology potential • Modern R&D plant and equipment	• Inadequate technology monitoring • Inadequate R&D funding

(*cont'd*)

Table 10.1 (Cont'd) Strengths and weaknesses of XYZ Corporation

Indicator	Strengths	Weaknesses
	• Strong staff product skills	• Unable to retain R&D staff • Lack of market awareness
Plant Flexibility and Productivity	• Efficient plant utilization • Long production runs • Standard product range • Product runs can be changed easily	• Poor product quality, high rejects • Customization potential not used • Production not integrated with sales • Poor product reliability
Product Development	• Rapid development capability • Product development skills • Flexible plant capability • Available plant capacity	• Lack of market awareness • Lack of product planning • Poor product selection • Under-utilized plant
Management and Personnel	• Managers promoted from ranks • Managers have product experience • Dedicated staff with unique skills • Efficient staff capability	• Poor management direction • Lack of business orientation • Managers fixed in their ways • Performance indicators not used • High staff turnover • Lack of specialized training
Computer Support	• Latest hardware and software • Distributed processing capability • Moving to relational data base • Wide computer literacy	• Data is inconsistent, or out-of-date • Data bases are not integrated • Sales and production not integrated • Sales and financial reports late

10.1.3 Distinctive competence

Those strengths which provide an organization with comparative advantage over its competitors should be emphasized, so diminishing the effect of its weaknesses. We will group together major strengths where XYZ exhibits distinctive competence, so offering it potential comparative advantage. This is illustrated at the end of the chapter, as Figure 10.4. We will discuss these advantages in the following pages, starting with its Cash and Capital Resources strengths.

Cash and capital resources

XYZ is cash rich: strengths in Table 10.1 which indicate cash generation, investment and capital resource capabilities together represent distinctive competence. This may give it a potential comparative advantage over competitors. This is called Comparative Advantage 1 (CA1) or CA1: Cash and Capital Resources below.

Indicator	CA1: Cash and Capital Resources
Capital Resources	• Cash reserves and shareholder equity • Large investment in property
Cash Flow and Profitability	• Stable profit growth • Strong cash flow • Strong dividend policy • Property investment
Sales and Marketing	• Strong cash generation capability
Computer Support	• Latest hardware and software

We saw earlier that XYZ needs to change. This requires capital resources, through equity, loans or asset sales. Capital Resources are represented above by strengths in cash reserves and investment in property. These tangible assets are reflected in a strong share price and high market valuation, with a large number of shares issued.

The Cash Flow and Profitability strengths show that XYZ has strong cash flow and so could service loans, but interest rates are currently very high. It has stable profit growth (but profit is not growing as fast as sales growth, as we have seen). Its shareholders have been treated well in the past by its strong dividend policy: it can therefore raise equity through new share issues. But its best funding alternative appears to be through asset sales. It has a large investment in property, but these investments only return 12% pa as we saw earlier: this is substantially below the mission ROI of 20%. Furthermore, property values are expected to fall in the near future due to high interest rates: people can no longer afford to borrow money for property.

Sales and Marketing above indicates a cash generation strength. The Computer Support indicator shows that XYZ has the latest hardware and software. We will see later that these will enable it to generate additional sales and profits in its traditional markets, and will also allow it to improve its management information systems. Let us now group together those strengths that relate to its sales and distribution capability.

Sales and distribution capability

XYZ has distinctive competence in Sales and Marketing, with strong distribution channels and a large, dedicated sales force with a good knowledge of the current markets. It achieves good sales, and most salespersons achieve their allocated sales quota. Its sales and distribution capability provide it with a second comparative advantage (CA2), shown next and also in Figure 10.4.

Indicator	CA2: Sales and Distribution Capability
Sales and Marketing	• Strong distribution channels • Large, dedicated sales force • High level of quota achievement • Good knowledge of current markets
Customer Support	• Dedicated sales force • Strong sales growth
Computer Support	• Distributed processing capability

We earlier saw that sales can potentially be increased further, by more aggressive sales incentives. Table 10.1 also showed weaknesses in customer support which can be improved. Its dedicated sales force is an advantage: sales growth is strong, but growth may be faster if better customer support is provided. Distributed processing strength, in computer support above, may offer opportunities also for improved customer support. And what about XYZ strengths in its R&D capability, and its plant flexibility?

R&D and plant flexibility

XYZ has a distinctive competence in its plant capability, which is extremely flexible. Given its strengths in R&D – modern R&D plant and equipment, staff product skills and potential to use the latest technology (although we saw earlier that it does not track changes in technology well) – it can improve existing products, or develop products for new markets. This is its third comparative advantage (CA3).

Indicator	CA3: R&D and Plant Flexibility
Capital Resources	• Flexible plant capability
Research and Development	• Latest technology potential • Modern R&D plant and equipment • Strong staff product skills
Plant Flexibility/Productivity	• Product runs can be changed easily
Product Development	• Rapid development capability • Product development skills • Flexible plant capability • Available plant capacity
Management and Personnel	• Managers have product experience • Dedicated staff with unique skills • Efficient staff capability

Product Development strengths above indicate a capability and skills that can allow new products to be developed rapidly. It has available plant capacity, but its Plant Flexibility and Productivity strength is not being used effectively. We see that product runs can be changed easily: it has a potential to customize products in response to customer change requests. Management and Personnel strengths indicate that the product experience of management, and the skills and efficiency of their staff, can also be used to improve the quality and reliability of products.

These three areas represent distinctive competence held by XYZ that potentially provide it with comparative advantage. To gain a better perspective, we also need to identify any comparative disadvantages.

10.1.4   Comparative disadvantages

Major weaknesses are also grouped in the same fashion at the end of this chapter in Figure 10.4. These indicate comparative disadvantages. For example, XYZ managers do not appear to be very effective: we earlier saw that they resist change and are fixed in their thinking. Management Effectiveness bears further examination.

Management effectiveness

We have seen a number of examples in the discussions earlier where management are not aware of changes that have occurred in XYZ's industry, in the business, and in its markets. This appears to represent XYZ's first comparative disadvantage: indicated as CD1 below, and summarized in Figure 10.4.

What may have been correct decisions years ago, have since been overtaken by events. The managers must change their approach. But if they

Indicator	CD1: Management Effectiveness
Capital Resources	• Interest rate fluctuation exposure
Cash Flow and Profitability	• Profit growth less than sales growth • Poor financial reporting and control • High interest cost in servicing debt • Poor cash flow management • Poor budget control ('*fat and happy*')
Sales and Marketing	• Inadequate advertising budget • Ineffective sales force incentives
Research and Development	• Inadequate R&D funding • Unable to retain R&D staff
Management and Personnel	• Poor management direction • Lack of business orientation • Managers fixed in their ways • Performance indicators not used • High staff turnover • Lack of specialized training
Computer Support	• Data is inconsistent, or out-of-date • Data bases are not integrated • Sales and production are not integrated • Sales and financial reports late

are unable to change, they must be replaced. For example, the exposure which XYZ has to fluctuations in interest rates reflects on management. This should be addressed: by paying out some loans from cash reserves, or by refinancing them with fixed interest loans; the company can certainly negotiate from a position of financial strength.

We saw that the high debt servicing cost may be part of the reason for a lower growth in profits compared to sales growth. However the other Cash Flow and Profitability weaknesses of financial reporting and control, cash flow management and budget control are all symptoms of poor management. These should have been corrected long ago. Managements' focus on property investment has resulted in a reduced allocation of funds to Sales and Marketing. The advertising budget is inadequate. Sales incentives are no longer effective. Similarly, Research and Development suffers from inadequate funding. As a result, XYZ is unable to retain valuable R&D staff.

The Management and Personnel weaknesses give us a better picture. Management no longer provide needed direction. They are inflexible: '*Change that? Why? We always do it that way!*' While they have good product experience – a strength in traditional markets – these markets are changing. Yet they lack business orientation and have little experience in managing change. Performance indicators are not used. Specialized training of management and of staff is lacking. These all contribute to the high turnover of personnel: their staff see no future for themselves at XYZ.

The computer support strengths (see Table 10.1) paradoxically show some of the dangers: XYZ has the latest hardware and software, uses distributed processing and is moving to relational data base. These are all admirable strengths, but they were easy decisions to make: they only required money! The weaknesses above give the picture. Hardware, software, distributed processing and data base, alone, will not resolve these problems. Integrated data bases can avoid data that are inconsistent and out-of-date. For example if sales and production are integrated, inventory problems discussed earlier can be avoided. And late sales and financial reports are ticking time bombs! Management base their decisions on late data; or worse, on incorrect data. Integrated data bases are essential to the coming competitive environment. But management did not set this as a direction, until now. This is a major weakness: XYZ is frittering away any computer support advantages it has.

The XYZ managers have become fat and happy. Fortunately they have been saved by its financial strength so far. But time is running out: its competitors are growing stronger each month. The weaknesses relating to market and customer analysis should be examined next.

Market and customer analysis

The capital resource weaknesses below (summarized in Figure 10.4) show that XYZ is active in markets that are in decline. However market profitability has not been analyzed: recent experience suggests that it is costing XYZ more to make sales.

Indicator	CD2: Market and Customer Analysis
Capital Resources	• Investments in sunset markets • Poor market profitability analysis
Sales and Marketing	• Poor corporate image • Poor market analysis capability • Poor customer analysis capability • Poor competitive analysis capability
Customer Support	• Lack of customer focus and marketing • Sales training is inadequate • Field support is inadequate
Research and Development	• Lack of market awareness
Plant Flexibility and Productivity	• Production not integrated with sales
Product Development	• Lack of market awareness • Poor product selection

Sales and marketing weaknesses have been grouped together, highlighting poor capabilities that it has in market analysis, customer analysis and competitive analysis. We see that it also has a poor corporate image. As discussed this may be due to its poor quality control and unreliable products, but it may also be due to its customer support weaknesses of inadequate sales training and field support, as well as a lack of customer focus and marketing. These all represent the second comparative disadvantage: CD2.

R&D staff lack market awareness, as we discussed in earlier, with the result that many products are terminated by product development because they are unprofitable, or are unsuitable to XYZ's traditional markets. Inventory problems were apparent in plant flexibility and productivity that are due to production not being integrated with sales.

Product quality and reliability weaknesses also indicate comparative disadvantage, as summarized in Figure 10.4 and discussed next.

Product quality and reliability

We can see relevant grouped weaknesses below. R&D does not monitor changes in technology adequately: technological developments can suggest changes to products that can improve product quality or reliability. Plant flexibility and productivity indicate that quality control is poor, so resulting in a high reject rate and unreliable products. While the plant is flexible, this potential is not being used for the manufacture of customized products to improve customer service. Together these represent the third comparative disadvantage of XYZ: shown in Figure 10.4, and next, as CD3.

Indicator	CD3: Product Quality and Reliability
Research and Development	• Inadequate technology monitoring
Plant Flexibility and Productivity	• Poor product quality, high rejects • Customization potential not used • Poor product reliability

The grouped strengths discussed earlier, which offer comparative advantage, have all been summarized in Figure 10.4. This shows three columns labelled CA1–CA3 that represent competitive advantages 1–3: defined by the legend at the foot of the table. The asterisk in a column indicates a grouped

Figure 10.4 Grouped strengths show distinctive competence, which offer comparative advantage. Similarly weaknesses, when grouped, indicate comparative disadvantage.

Strengths	Comparative Advantage			Weaknesses	Comparative Disadvantage		
	CA1	CA2	CA3		CD1	CD2	CD3
Capital Resources							
• Cash reserves & equity	*			• Active in sunset markets		*	
• Property investment	*			• Poor market analysis		*	
• Plant capability			*	• Interest rate exposure	*		
Cash Flow/Profit							
• Stable profit growth	*			• Profit growth < sales	*		
• Strong cash flow	*			• Poor financial control	*		
• Strong dividend policy	*			• High debt servicing cost	*		
• Property investment	*			• Poor cash flow mgt	*		
Sales & Marketing							
• Distribution channels		*		• Poor corporate image		*	
• Large sales force		*		• Low advertising budget	*		
• Quota achievement		*		• Poor sales incentives	*		
• Market knowledge		*		• Poor market analysis		*	
• Cash generation	*			• Poor customer analysis		*	
				• Competitive analysis		*	
Customer Support							
• Dedicated sales force		*		• Lack of customer focus		*	
• Strong sales growth		*		• Poor sales training		*	
				• Poor field support		*	
R&D							
• Technology potential			*	• Technology monitoring			*
• R&D equipment			*	• R&D funding	*		
• Staff product skills			*	• R&D staff retention	*		
				• Lack of market awareness		*	
Plant Productivity							
• Efficient plant utilization				• Product quality/rejects			*
• Long production runs				• No product customization			*
• Standard product range				• Prodn/sales not integrated		*	
• Easy product run changes			*	• Poor product reliability			*
Product Development							
• Rapid dev't capability			*	• Lack of market awareness		*	
• Product dev't skills			*	• Lack of product planning			
• Flexible plant capability			*	• Poor product selection		*	
• Available plant capacity			*	• Under-utilized plant			
Mgt and Personnel							
• Managers from ranks				• Management direction	*		
• Product experience			*	• Business orientation	*		
• Staff skills			*	• Inflexible managers	*		
• Staff capability			*	• Performance indicators	*		
				• High staff turnover	*		
				• Lack of training	*		
Computer Suppport							
• Latest hardware/software	*			• Data inconsistent	*		
• Distributed processing		*		• No database integration	*		
• Relational data base		*		• Sales/prodn integration			
• Computer literacy				• Sales/financial reports	*		

Comparative Advantage
CA1 = Cash and Capital Resources
CA2 = Sales and Distribution Capability
CA3 = R&D and Plant Flexibility

Comparative Disadvantage
CD1 = Management Effectiveness
CD2 = Market and Customer Analysis
CD3 = Product Quality and Reliability

strength which represents a comparative advantage. Some strengths and weaknesses are abbreviated, due to limited space.

The cash and capital resources strengths are CA1. Sales and distribution capability strengths are grouped in CA2. Similarly, the R&D and plant flexibility strengths are grouped in CA3. Similarly weaknesses show Comparative Disadvantage, grouped in columns CD1–CD3. The grouped weaknesses relating to management effectiveness are also shown by asterisks in CD1. The market and customer analysis weaknesses are grouped in CD2. Product quality and reliability are grouped in CD3.

10.2 SUMMARY

We started this chapter with brief reviews of Drucker's eight objectives for performance measurement, and approaches for assessment of company capability and performance indicators as used by Rowe, Mason, Dickel and Snyder. We discussed that the strategic thrust of an organization can be developed during Stage 3 (Setting Strategic Direction) of strategic management planning by three steps, internal appraisal, external appraisal and strategic evaluation.

This chapter covered the first step: Internal Appraisal. It overviewed internal appraisals carried out at the business unit level, and also at the corporate level. In applying this step to an internal corporate appraisal of XYZ Corporation, we saw that we first identify performance indicators in order to identify areas of distinctive competence and comparative disadvantages. Opportunities or threats that exist are identified through an external appraisal in Chapter 11. We can then evaluate the comparative advantages and disadvantages of XYZ Corporation in relation to its competitors.

References

[1] Rowe, A. J., Mason, R. O., Dickel, K. E. and Snyder, N. H. (1990). *Strategic Management: A Methodological Approach (Third Edition)*, Addison-Wesley, Reading: MA.

[2] Drucker, P. F. (1974). *Management: Tasks, Responsibilities, Practices*, Harper & Row: New York, NY.

[3] Finkelstein, C. (1989). *An Introduction to Information Engineering*, Addison-Wesley: Reading, MA.

[4] Birkett, W. (1983). *Practical Strategic Planning*, Information Engineering Press: Sydney.

[5] Elsworth, R. R. (1983). Subordinate Financial Policy to Corporate Strategy, *Harvard Business Review*: Cambridge, MA, (Nov–Dec 1983).

[6] Marshuetz, R. J. (1985). How American Can Allocates Capital, *Harvard Business Review*: Cambridge, MA (Jan–Feb 1985).

[7] Galbraith, J. (1973). *Designing Complex Organizations*, Addison-Wesley: Reading, MA.

[8] Yip, G. S. (1985). Who Needs Strategic Planning, *Journal of Business Strategy*, Vol 6, No 2.

CHAPTER 11

External Appraisal

We now need to carry out an external appraisal of competitors, highlighting opportunities where strategies can later be defined to focus on the strengths we identified in Chapter 10. Competitor threats that attack known weaknesses can also be identified: strategies can be defined later to avoid these threats. This later definition of strategies will be carried out in Chapter 12.

Because of the diversity of organizations, not all tools or techniques described in this chapter are relevant to every business; but the most appropriate of them can be selected for a specific organization.

11.1 STEP 2 – EXTERNAL APPRAISAL

Where strategic planning is applied at the corporate level, external appraisal examines the environment external to the organization itself. It focuses on various business units in terms of the broad markets they address and the products or services which they supply to their markets. If, on the other hand, strategic planning is used at the business unit level in a larger organization, an external appraisal focuses on the environment external only to that business unit. This includes other parts of the organization as well as areas outside the organization. The separate products and services, as well as the markets of each business unit, are evaluated in greater detail than at the corporate level.

Thus at the corporate level, external appraisal provides a broad delineation of markets, and of products and services that address those markets. But at the business unit level specific markets, products and services are defined in greater detail. At both levels the same external appraisal approach is applied. But before looking at these approaches, we need to discuss the concept of the **life cycle**.

11.1.1   Product and market life cycle

Both markets, and the products and services that address those markets, move through a number of life cycle stages as shown in Figure 11.1. These stages are used to assess the status of each related group of markets, and of products and services, during an external appraisal as described in the following pages. They are defined as:

- **Development:** Initial development and entry of new products and/or markets.

- **Growth:** Rapid growth of product, and market, sales and profitability.

- **Shakeout:** Entry of new competitors into markets, and departure of others.

- **Maturity:** Maintenance of sales and profitability in established markets.

- **Decline:** Product replacement, and decline of products and/or markets.

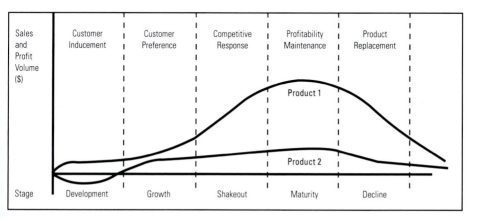

Figure 11.1   Product and Market Evolution.

11.1.2 Tenets of strategy

The external appraisal step evaluates a number of factors, called **tenets of strategy**. They include: thrust; scope; distinctive competence; competitive advantage; and synergy. **Thrust** gives direction to organizational activities, while **scope** indicates the breadth of interaction that an organization has with its environment. For internal appraisals earlier, we identified areas of distinctive competence in deployment, utilization or capitalization of resources: some may offer comparative advantage. An evaluation of **synergy** – joint effects flowing from advantages – is also important. Synergies developed in resource usage, or in market and product thrusts, or in support facilities, increase the strength of comparative advantages. Each advantage is evaluated against those of competitors. This identifies those areas which offer **competitive advantage**.

In identifying competitive advantage, an external appraisal is carried out initially at the business unit level. The following pages provide an overview of an external business unit appraisal, as well as an external corporate appraisal. We will then apply some of these principles to an external appraisal of XYZ Corporation.

11.1.3 External business unit appraisal

Business unit product/service evaluation   We first evaluate the products or services of each business unit in terms of the product life cycle introduced above: development; growth; shakeout; maturity; decline. The markets for products or services are then analyzed in terms of: size; stage of evolution; growth rate and potential; types of segmentation; size and growth rate of each segment; needs and characteristics of each market segment; and identification of those segments that are served well, and those served poorly. Each product or service is then related to its markets: in terms of its relative growth rate, and its share of its markets.

Business unit industry evaluation   The business unit is evaluated within its industry. First the industry life cycle stage is assessed, together with: the extent of competition; any barriers to entry; the nature of product differentiation; price/cost structures and their trends; communication and distribution systems; supply and labour characteristics; regulation of the industry; its capital structure; financing needs and sources; and the relative market power of competitors. Next the industry is related to its markets to assess under- or over-utilized capacity in the industry. The business unit is then related to the industry: in terms of its relative growth rate; its market share; and its ability to compete for resources and profitability.

Business unit competitor evaluation   Each competitor of a business unit ideally should first be evaluated by an internal appraisal, as described in Chapter 10. After identifying comparative advantages and disadvantages each competitor is assessed using an external appraisal: to evaluate its products or services, the markets in which it operates and its position in the industry. Likely actions that may be taken by competitors, and their effect on the business unit, are identified. Actions that may be taken by the business unit, and their effect on competitors, are also determined. Likely responses to these actions by competitors, and by the business unit, are considered. These are categorized either as threats or opportunities.

Business unit environmental evaluation   The effects of environmental factors are next considered. These may be categorized as: demographic; economic; social; cultural; political; legal or technological. Demographic factors are: the growth rate, birth rate, and age distribution of population segments; regional shifts; migration. Economic factors include: GNP trends; money supply; inflation rates; currency devaluation; interest rates; wage levels; unemployment levels. Social factors address: consumer activism; work and leisure; family formation; career and job sharing; life-style changes. Cultural factors include: modernization; affluence; rate of change; urbanization; literacy; respect for science and technology; affirmative action. Political factors are: government attitudes to business and the public sector; social priorities; economic priorities; free trade and tariffs. Legal factors relate to: anti-trust or trade practice legislation; consumer protection; tax laws; environmental protection. Technological factors include: research & development spending; energy; communication; transportation; computation; attitudes to invention and innovation. Relevant factors are categorized as threats or opportunities for the business unit, and for competitors.

Business unit competitive position   The analysis above is summarized in Figure 11.2 for each business unit, with notations in relevant cells indicating the competitive position of: the products and markets of the business unit; the industry; the competitors; the contributors of resources (financial, personnel, materials or other) to the business unit; and the environment. Identified threats and opportunities are also indicated in relation to each of these factors.

11.1.4   External corporate appraisal

Corporate industry evaluation   At the corporate level the industries in which the organization's business units operate are determined. The relative attractiveness of these industries is assessed by the same factors used above

Business Unit: _____

Factors	Competitive Position	Threats	Opportunities
Product / Market			
Industry			
Competitors			
Resource Contributors			
Environment			

Figure 11.2 Summary of Business Unit External Appraisal.

for the Business Unit Industry Evaluation. The relative competitive position of each business unit in the organization is next evaluated. The current portfolio position of the organization's business units is then assessed for each, according to industry attractiveness and competitive position.

Corporate competitor evaluation The organization is compared with immediate and major competitors in all relevant business units, as for Business Unit Competitor Evaluation above. The likely effect of competitors' actions, or their likely responses to the organization's actions, are assessed. Potential competition for financial resources in the capital market is assessed, as well as the likely effects of environmental factors or changes in the organization's business portfolio, those of its competitors, or changes in the supply of financial resources. Each of these are categorized as opportunities or threats.

Corporate competitive position This analysis is summarized in Figure 11.3 for the organization, indicating by notations in relevant cells its competitive position together with identified threats and opportunities.

Rowe, Mason, Dickel [1] and Snyder [2] outline an effective method for examination of the external environment. They describe environmental scanning, an approach for detailed analysis of threats and opportunities

Organization: _____ Evaluation Period: _____

	Portfolio Position	Threats	Opportunities
Industry Attractiveness			
Competitive Position			
Competitors			
Resource Generation			
Environment			

Figure 11.3 Summary of Corporate External Appraisal.

that an organization faces. Their Stakeholder analysis identifies stakeholders, then uncovers and ranks assumptions about them: it evaluates assumptions to be followed, to meet multiple external demands. They apply competitive analysis using Michael Porter's approach [3]. Finally technology analysis evaluates how effectively an organization responds to technological change.

Environmental scanning is subdivided into six key factors: economic; political; social; technological; competitive; and geographical factors. This is the first step in identifying threats and opportunities in the environment. Rowe *et al* evaluate these by developing an Environmental Threat and Opportunity Profile.

They use stakeholder analysis next, to identify stakeholders using checklists such as: owners and stockholders; corporate management; creditors; customers and clients; employees; suppliers; competitors; labour unions; sources of new technology; local communities; local, state and federal government; scientific labs; university researchers; public interest groups; the media. To uncover assumptions about stakeholders they ask:

> 'What are the most plausible assumptions the organization must make about each stakeholder in order for the strategy to be successful?'

They next classify these assumptions into two categories: supporting or driving force assumptions that indicate strategic opportunities, strengths, and favourable conditions; and the resisting or constraining force assumptions that lead to threats, weaknesses and adverse or dangerous conditions. They rate these assumptions for their importance and certainty using an assumption rating graph. The relative importance of assumptions is evaluated by an assumption force-field analysis: this plots the relative importance of supporting assumptions against resisting assumptions, because:

> 'a successful strategy will be one that effectively draws on the supporting assumptions and also reduces the potency of the resisting assumptions'.

Porter's competitive analysis [4] involves ten key factors that can be used to position a firm strategically in relation to its present and potential competitors:

- Potential rate of growth of the industry
- Threats of entry – determined by the barriers to entry
- Intensity of rivalry
- Pressure from substitute products
- Dependency on complimentary products and services
- Bargaining power of buyers
- Bargaining power of suppliers
- Technological sophistication of the industry
- Rate of innovation
- Management capability

In discussing technology, Rowe *et al* say that:

> 'technology is often the driving force of strategy. New products, new markets, new production processes and new distribution systems come from technology'.

To carry out technology assessment, they describe two steps: technology scanning; and technology evaluation. They finally compare the result of technology assessment with the result of competitive portfolio analysis (discussed later this chapter with Figure 11.10) to determine whether the organization's technology position is consistent with its competitive business position.

In discussing financial analysis in strategic planning, Rowe *et al* describe the ratios that can be used to evaluate financial well-being of an organization. These financial ratios can highlight a company's internal strengths and weaknesses, as well as evaluate an organization's position in an industry and in relation to competitors. They discuss four key financial analysis areas: profitability; liquidity; leverage; activity – with numerous examples to illustrate calculation and evaluation of the most commonly used ratios in each of these areas.

We are now ready to illustrate Step 2 by an external appraisal of XYZ Corporation. For brevity we will omit the External Business Unit Appraisal; we will concentrate mainly on an External Corporate Appraisal of XYZ and a selected group of its competitors.

11.2 EXTERNAL APPRAISAL OF XYZ

You will remember in Chapter 9, when evaluating current strategy of XYZ, that we defined functional responsibility for the market research manager (see Figure 9.6). A quarterly market analysis was commissioned from the selected Market Research firm. The result of their Product and Market Analysis is summarized in Figure 11.4.

In evaluating the markets and products of XYZ they assessed major markets, products and product groups to determine their life cycle stage; they evaluated current and new markets, and relevant products for those markets; and they evaluated these products against those offered by competitors in the same market segments.

Organization: _____ XYZ Corporation _____

Market: _____ CV Market _____ Life Cycle Stage: _____ Maturity _____

Life Cycle Stage	Competitive Position		
	Strong	Average	Weak
Development			
Growth			
Shakeout			
Maturity		Product Group A Product Group B	Major Product M Major Product X
Decline		Major Product N	Major Product P Product Group C

Figure 11.4 Life Cycle Evaluation Matrix.

11.2.1 Product and market analysis

Figure 11.4 is organized by market to assess its life cycle stage, and the stage of major products relevant to the market. The competitive position of major products and groups (identified by XYZ codes) are evaluated relative to competitors: as strong, average, or weak. Figure 11.4 shows that market CV is a mature market. The competitive position of XYZ Corporation's major products and product groups were assessed as average for product groups A and B: which are mature; and also for major product group N which is in the stage of decline. Major product M and X (maturity), major product P and product group C (decline) are assessed as weak.

At this point a **Product/Market Matrix** was used as shown in Figure 11.5. (This is also useful in Stage 3 for setting market and product strategic directions – see Chapter 12.) It shows that product groups A-G, and major products M-X, are used in the current market. New related product groups H-J, and major product Y can be developed for this market, as well as new, unrelated groups P-T and product Z.

New markets M1 and M2 are related to the current market. M3 is an unrelated market. The present groups A-D can also be used in market M1, with groups E-G in M2. These products will need some modification, and will need different pricing, to be acceptable to those markets. Products M-N can be sold in the new, unrelated market M3, but will need a substantial advertising campaign to penetrate it. Related product groups Q-S apply to M1, product W to M2, and groups R and U apply to market M3. Similarly, the new, unrelated product groups K-M apply to M1, product X applies to M2, and group T applies to M3.

A Product/Market Matrix as illustrated in Figure 11.5 can be used to examine a variety of market and product choices. For example, a decision

Organization: _____ XYZ Corporation

Products Markets	Present Product	New Product	
		Related Product	Unrelated Product
Current Market	Product Groups A-G Major Product M-X	Product Groups H-J Major Product Y	Product Groups P-T Major Product Z
New, Related Market	M1: Groups A-D M2: Groups E-G	M1: Groups Q-S M2: Product W	M1: Groups K-M M2: Product X
New, Unrelated Market	M3: Products M-N	M3: Groups R, U	M3: Group T

Figure 11.5 Product/Market Matrix used for evaluation.

may be to increase the amount of advertising to induce new uses for present products in current markets or to introduce present products to new, related markets.

Current markets, with either related or unrelated products, represent a market strategy of **horizontal diversification**. The organization can also provide its own markets, using divisions or subsidiaries as customers of other business units: this is referred to as **vertical integration**. Related markets and related products are examples of **concentric diversification**, such as with related marketing and production technologies. Related markets with unrelated products also represent concentric diversification; but in this case only related marketing technologies are relevant. Unrelated markets that use related products represent concentric diversification and related production technologies. And last, unrelated markets with unrelated products represent **conglomerate diversification**, such as through the purchase of other organizations. Generally the amount of risk and investment increases from the top left cell of the matrix to the bottom right cell.

The cells can be used as in Figure 11.5, or can represent classification, expression of preferences, or can be used as stimulus for analysis of opportunities for diversification. Product/Market Matrices are most relevant to organizations that have single product lines and are just beginning product diversification programs, or that are dominant product-line organizations with other products closely related to the main product line. This is certainly the case with the XYZ Corporation.

An analysis of each product in different market segments in its industry, relative to competitors, was carried out for XYZ. Products are positioned in an industry according to market segments relevant to that industry, and according to other products sold by industry competitors active in those same market segments. This is evaluated by a **Product Positioning Matrix** for the industry, developed as part of the product and market analysis carried out for XYZ and illustrated in Figure 11.6. This matrix contains any appropriate or available measure, such as dollar sales, unit sales, market share or profits. Figure 11.6 shows dollar sales by product and market, for example. Matrices also should be prepared for past or future periods, as well as for the present period.

Figure 11.6 shows that Competitor X and Y compete against XYZ Corporation in Major Products M, N, P and X and also in Product Groups A, B and C. X is apparently the major competitor for XYZ. It is competing strongly with its product group XA: its sales of $35.6M match XYZ group A sales of $35.8M. Sales of its product XN at $12.2M are almost double those of XYZ product N. Its group XC has sales of $20.2M: almost three times the sales of XYZ group C. Its product XM is gaining market share against Product M also: however XYZ sales of M at $31.6M are still 2.9 times the XM sales of $10.8M.

How should we respond to this competition? We must evaluate each

Sales by Product and Market for 1991

Industry: _____Industry SV_____ Period: _____1991_____

Organization:___XYZ Corporation_____ Market:_____CV Market_____

Competitor	Products	CV Market Segments					
		S1 ($M)	S2 ($M)	S3 ($M)	...	Sn ($M)	Total ($M)
XYZ	Products M	31.6					31.6
	N	6.6					6.6
	P		5.4				5.4
	X			5.9			5.9
	Group A		35.8				35.8
	B	5.1					5.1
	C			7.6			7.6
Competitor X	Products XM	10.8					10.8
	XN	12.2					12.2
	XP		2.5				2.5
	XX			2.1			2.1
	Groups XA		35.6				35.6
	XB	6.6					6.6
	XC			20.2			20.2
Competitor Y	Products YM	2.1					2.1
	YN	0.6					0.6
	YP		0.2				0.2
	YX			1.2			1.2
	Groups YA		2.1				2.1
	YB	0.5					0.5
	YC			2.3			2.3
	Totals	76.1	81.6	39.3			197.0

Figure 11.6 Product Positioning Matrix for XYZ.

competitor more closely. When considered together, the Life Cycle Evaluation Matrix (Figure 11.4), the Product/Market Matrix (Figure 11.5) and the Product Positioning Matrix (Figure 11.6) provide initial insight into the scope of each competitor's product and market strategy. These provide input to the Corporate Competitor Evaluation step which we will cover shortly, but we need more information. We will start with an evaluation of the industry.

11.2.2 Corporate industry evaluation

A **Directional Market Policy Matrix** can be prepared for each industry and market of interest to XYZ, shown in Figure 11.7 for the CV Market in

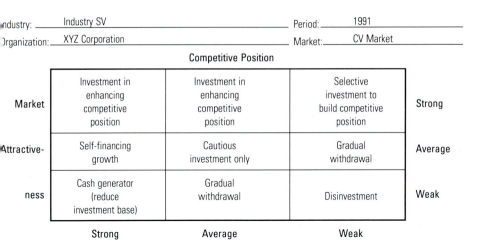

Figure 11.7 **Directional Market Policy Matrix.**

Industry SV. The position of an organization can be determined in each market, as well as the trends and strategies relevant to this position and the market, as discussed in the following paragraphs.

The Market Attractiveness vertical axis in Figure 11.7 can be quantified in many ways: taking into account factors such as those summarized in Figure 11.8. This allocates a score between 0 and 1 for each factor (1 being highest in attractiveness). This score is then weighted as a percentage, according to its perceived importance for the market being assessed. Figure 11.8 shows a score of 59.1, which is assessed as average: this positions the CV Market in the middle row of cells in Figure 11.7.

Organization:	XYZ Corporation	Market:	CV Market
Factor	**Score (0–1)***	**Weight (%)**	**Ranking**
Market Size	0.5	10	5.0
Market Growth	0.1	10	1.0
Segmentation	0.2	5	2.5
Price Differentiation	0.1	4	0.4
Profitability	1.0	30	30.0
Competitive Structure	0.5	30	15.0
Customer Financing	0.5	10	5.0
Technological Vulnerability	0	0	0.0
Environmental Risk	0.2	1	0.2
		100	59.1
*0 = Low; 1 = High			**(Average)**

Figure 11.8 **Market Attractiveness Assessment.**

Organization: XYZ Corporation   Market: CV Market

Factor	Score (0–1)*	Weight (%)	Ranking
Market Share	0.5	20	10.0
Breadth of Product Line	0.2	10	2.0
Pricing Structures	0.1	5	0.5
Distribution	0.1	5	0.5
Service	0.1	5	0.5
Sales Expertise	0.5	5	0.5
Scale of Production	0.5	30	15.0
Raw Materials Supply	0.4	10	4.0
Production Efficiency	0.5	10	5.0
		100	38.0

*0 = Low; 1 = High   (Average)

Figure 11.9 Competitive Position Assessment.

Similarly the Competitive Position axis in Figure 11.7 is quantified in Figure 11.9 by key market or industry success factors, and given a score between 0 and 1 (1 is highest) based on perceived importance of each factor in the relevant market.

The competitive position of each of XYZ's business units is weighted as a percentage, according to its perceived standing in relation to each factor. Figure 11.9 shows this evaluation with a ranked score of 38.0. This is assessed as average, and positions the CV Market in the middle column of cells in Figure 11.7.

As a result of assessment in Figures 11.8 and 11.9, the CV Market for XYZ is located in the middle cell of Figure 11.7. This advises 'Cautious investment only'. In Chapter 12 we discuss this further, with examples of different strategies relevant not only to this cell but also strategies for the other cells; so we can set appropriate strategic directions based on the assessed competitive position of each market.

The Competitive Position Matrix in Figure 11.7 can also be used to assess a number of related markets collectively. This uses different sized pies, showing the market size of markets CV, PQ and RS as illustrated in Figure 11.10. It is a variation on techniques used by Cash et al [5].

The large share held by XYZ in each market is shown as a white pie slice, while the shares held by competitors are shown as differently-shaded pie slices. We saw earlier that cautious investment only is recommended for the CV Market. From Figure 11.7 we see that the PQ Market is in the gradual withdrawal cell, while the RS Market falls in the disinvestment cell. Directional arrows in Figure 11.11 show alternative investment options for XYZ: to the left, to improve its competitive position (using technology or perhaps advertising); vertically, to improve market attractiveness relative to

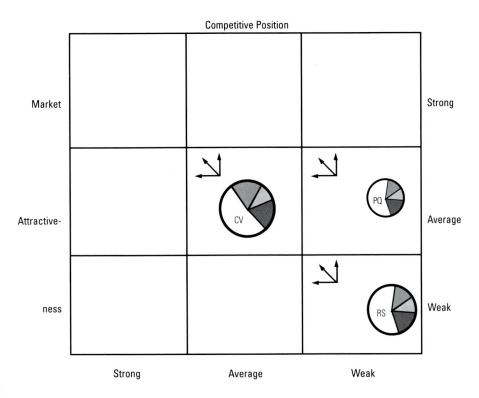

Figure 11.10   Market Share Directional Matrix.

other XYZ markets (by higher profitability); diagonally, to improve both attractiveness and competitive position of the market. Next we need to examine the competitors of XYZ Corporation more closely.

11.2.3   Corporate competitor evaluation

Following the corporate industry evaluation for XYZ Corporation, an analysis was also undertaken by the Market Research firm for each major competitor. This is summarized as comments in cells of a **Competitor Analysis Chart**. Figure 11.11 shows an analysis of XYZ's major competition in the CV Market of Industry SV: Competitor X. This table is used for a corporate analysis as shown in Figure 11.11, but also allows for analysis of specific business units and functional areas if relevant.

A profile of known **objectives** used by Competitor X was developed. It is a low cost, high quality supplier to allow it to gain market share in XYZ's most profitable markets. To achieve this, it has adopted the following **tenets of strategy** appropriate to market entry: its **thrust** is to develop low cost

Industry: _____SV Industry_____ Period: _____1991_____

Organization: ___X Corporation_____ Market: _____CV Market_____

Factor	Corporate	Business Unit	Functional Areas		
			Labour	Marketing	...
Objectives	• Low cost, high quality supplier • Gain market share in XYZ markets				
Tenets of Strategy 1 Thrust 2 Scope 3 Distinctive Competence 4 Comparative Advantage 5 Synergy	1 Low cost products 2 Profitable segments 3 Quality and service Custom products 4 Small and flexible Innovative Mgt 5 Changes fast				
Resource Commitments	• Low capitalization • Debt financing only				
Weakness/Threat 1 Internal 2 Competition 3 Environment	1 Stretched thin. Mgt is also R&D. 2 Depends on external sales force only. Limited advertising. 3 Sensitive to high interest rates.				
Potential reaction to XYZ attack on weaknesses/threats	Also drop prices and advertise expensively, so impacting profit.				
Exploitable Comparative Advantage	Unable to sustain long price war or concerted advertising campaign.				
Potential response to exploitation	Will take on equity partners for funding; vulnerable to takeover.				
Possibility of competitor attack	Will initiate price war itself if it has funds.				

Figure 11.11   **Competitor Analysis Chart.**

products; its **scope** is to attack only the most profitable segments for XYZ of the CV Market. It has distinctive competence in product quality and service that it delivers, and in the supply of customized products that satisfy the customers' needs better than do the products delivered by XYZ. It has **comparative advantage** of small size and flexibility, with innovative management. These strategies work together in **synergy**: X can determine emerging market changes, has good R&D and management, and can change fast.

An analysis of the **resource commitments** of X was undertaken by the Market Research firm. Figure 11.11 shows it has low capitalization, with funding through debt. This was obtained from the most recent annual corporate and financial returns reported by X. It indicates a serious financial vulnerability.

An *internal appraisal* was also carried out, based on informal discussions with present and past employees and also customers, of X. While obviously not able to be as complete as described for XYZ in Chapter 10, it highlighted that X has the following **weaknesses/threats**. It is stretched very thin, being a small company with few staff. While this is a strength in its ability to change fast, it has only limited financial and staff resources to handle large fluctuations in production and sales. Further, senior managers also carry out R&D: if these managers are too busy running the business, R&D suffers.

The *weakness/threat* relating to *competition* in Figure 11.11 reflects the fact that X has a small sales force: most of its sales are through an external sales organization. It uses limited advertising, relying on 'word-of-mouth' comments by satisfied customers. Its dependence on debt financing, with low capitalization and small cash reserves, indicates a serious *environmental* weakness: high interest rates will have a severe impact on it.

A competitive strategy that XYZ could adopt against X is to drop prices and increase advertising for selected products. When faced with this competition, the management of X would be expected to react by dropping their prices also, with expensive advertising. This *potential reaction to attack* will have a negative impact on its profits.

We saw in Chapter 9 that XYZ has large cash reserves. In contrast, X has limited funds available. This would become an **exploitable comparative advantage** (see Figure 11.11) if a price war and advertising campaign for selected products was sustained over a long period. Its **potential response to exploitation** in this way will be for management to sell part of the company: they will take on equity partners who will provide equity funding. X is a profitable, but closely-held company: the majority of shares are held by management. But its limited funding today makes it particularly vulnerable to takeover. Finally, if it can obtain sufficient funds, there is a strong **possibility of competitor attack** by X on XYZ in exactly the same way: it will initiate a price war to gain market share at the expense of XYZ. If it was to do this now, we saw in Chapter 10 that there is little that XYZ could do.

Organization: ___XYZ Corporation___

Market: ___CV Market___   Period: ___1990 – 1991___

Product	Sales ($M)		Cash Flow ($M)		Market Growth Rate (% pa)
	1990	1991	1990	1991	
Major Product M	29.2	31.6	3.8	4.5	4%
N	8.5	6.6	3.2	(0.5)	3%
P	4.1	5.4	2.2	2.3	2%
X	4.8	5.9	2.1	1.9	6%
Product Group A	21.3	35.8	2.5	3.1	5%
B	7.6	5.1	0.8	0.5	8%
C	8.3	7.6	0.6	(0.5)	4%
Totals	83.8	98.0	15.2	11.3	

Figure 11.12   Sales and cash flow by year for the CV Market.

So XYZ must act first! But if it is to start a price war, what products should be reduced in price? Which should be advertised? A wrong decision will cost XYZ a lot of money. If it is not careful, it may shoot itself in the foot!

A portfolio analysis is therefore appropriate for XYZ and for its main competitors. This helps define an organization's scope and can suggest strategic alternatives. The analysis of XYZ major products and product groups (see Figure 11.4), carried out by the market research firm for the CV Market, is summarized in Figure 11.12 for the period 1990–1991. This shows sales and cash flow in each year of threatened product groups A, B and C and major products M, N, P and X together with the annual market growth rate.

While total sales have increased from $83.8M to $98.0M in the two years, total cash flow has declined from $15.2M to $11.3M. Product group A and major products M, N, P and X generated $85.3M of these sales. The cash flow was affected by product groups B and C, but particularly by major product N whose cash flow decreased by $3.7M over the two years.

This is also carried out for each major competitor, in particular Competitor X. Detailed competitive sales and cash flow information is of course highly confidential. In the absence of these details from X, we use Figure 11.6, Sales by Product and Market.

Figure 11.13 summarizes these major products and product groups in terms of market share. This is expressed as a ratio of XYZ sales for 1991

Organization: _____XYZ Corporation_____

Market: _____CV Market_____ Period:_____1990 – 1991_____

Product	Relative Market Share *		Market Attractiveness	Competitive Position	Product Evolution Stage
	1990	1991	1991	1991	
Major Product M	3.8	2.9	75	21	Maturity
N	0.8	0.5	70	45	Decline
P	2.5	2.2	25	15	Decline
X	3.1	2.8	55	35	Maturity
Product Group A	1.5	1.0	85	52	Maturity
B	0.9	0.8	70	48	Maturity
C	0.5	0.4	30	30	Decline

*Relative market share   =   Sales of XYZ Product (from Figures 11.12 or 11.6)
                               Sales of Competitor X Product (from Figure 11.6)

Figure 11.13 Market and competitive position of XYZ products.

(from Figure 11.12 or 11.6) to sales of the relevant products of Competitor X (Figure 11.6). Market attractiveness and competitive position are calculated as for Figures 11.8 and 11.9 respectively. The product evolution stage is also indicated.

Figures 11.12 and 11.13 have been used to develop a **Portfolio Analysis Chart** of the CV Market for XYZ Corporation in 1991, as illustrated in Figure 11.14. Each product is shown as a circle, whose relative size represents the total dollar sales (from Figure 11.12) of the product in its market. Its competitive position in that market is shown on the X-axis as the market share of the product relative to the firm's largest competitor (from Figure 11.13). The business growth rate on the Y-axis shows the growth rate of the market in which the product competes (from Figure 11.12).

The top left quadrant represents products that are **stars** (terminology generally attributed to the Boston Consulting Group [9]). These are high growth, high market share products that may or may not yet be self-sufficient in cash flow: they may still need investment for the high growth experienced now, but should turn into surplus cash generators as growth slows. Products that fall in the bottom left quadrant are products that generate more cash than can profitably be invested in them (cash cows) and generally relate to mature products or markets. These products have a dominant share of a slowly growing market and generate surplus cash.

We can see in Figure 11.14 that product groups M, X and P are cash

Organization: _____ XYZ Corporation _____

Market: _____ CV Market _____ Period: _____ 1991 _____

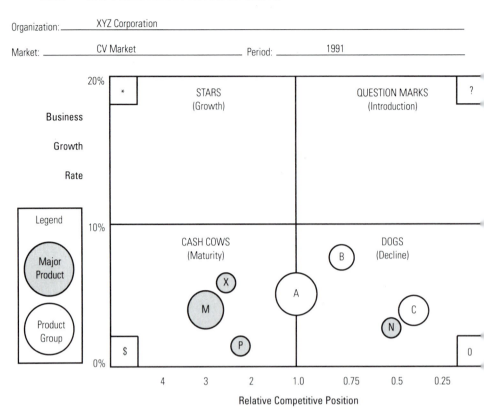

Figure 11.14   Portfolio Analysis Chart; (adapted from Cash *et al* [6, 7], and also from the Boston Consulting Group [8]).

cows, shown also by their cash flow contribution in Figure 11.12. Major product A, which generates most sales and is a major contributor to cash flow, falls on the line for relative competitive position 1.0: it is under threat from Competitor X with equal sales (see Figure 11.6).

The top right quadrant represents products that have a low market share in a fast growing market. These represent **question marks**; they generally relate to products or markets in the development stage. They result in low profits and cash flow, with high growth likely to require investment to maintain or increase their market share. Products in the bottom right quadrant are **dogs**: they have low share in a slowly growing market, or for a market in decline. To hold market share may require continuing reinvestment, plus additional investment. These represent dangerous cash traps. Figure 11.14 shows that major products B and C fall into this category, as well as product group N – confirmed by its disastrous cash flow decline in Figure 11.12.

Figure 11.14 gives us now a better perspective of the problems XYZ faces, alluded to in Chapters 9 and 10. It certainly has a number of products that are cash cows, but all are losing market share to competitors (see Figure 11.13). They may soon become dogs like products B and C, and also group N.

The Portfolio Analysis Chart can also be used to show the future position of each product assuming no change in strategy. Together these two matrices help to define the scope and competitive advantage of each product, as well as strategic issues facing the organization, such as:

- How to finance growth programs for stars.
- How to increase profitability of cash cows.
- How to reduce dogs.
- How to convert stars to cash cows.
- How to finance and convert question marks to stars.
- How to prevent question marks becoming dogs.
- How to prevent stars becoming question marks.
- How to prevent cash cows becoming dogs.

It can be argued that the Portfolio Analysis Chart in Figure 11.14 is too simplistic however: four cells do not allow adequate focus. Market growth rate may be an inadequate indicator of industry or market attractiveness: for example, a high market growth rate may be unprofitable because of over-supply. Market share may be an inadequate criterion of competitive position if it is difficult to define the market, and market shares, exactly.

The Market Share Directional Matrix in Figure 11.10 may be used instead, as described earlier. It can be used to show current market share, and also a forecast position based on appropriate market and product strategies. The size and shares of the pies, as well as the position of each product pie in the matrix, may vary for different scenarios. These allow an assessment to be made for XYZ, and for major competitors, of the scope and competitive advantage of different competing products. But this matrix does not readily show the position of new products, or of markets at an early stage of the life cycle, that may grow into new industries. Figure 11.15 is useful for this purpose.

In the **Product/Market Evolution Chart** in Figure 11.15, the XYZ market share pie slice is white (or shaded); the black pie slice indicates all other competitors. This format is useful when a business unit or organization has few products or market segments.

The Portfolio Analysis Chart (Figure 11.14) and the Product/Market Evolution Chart (Figure 11.15) identify unbalanced portfolios. A portfolio with too many losers (dogs), for example, may exhibit some or all of the

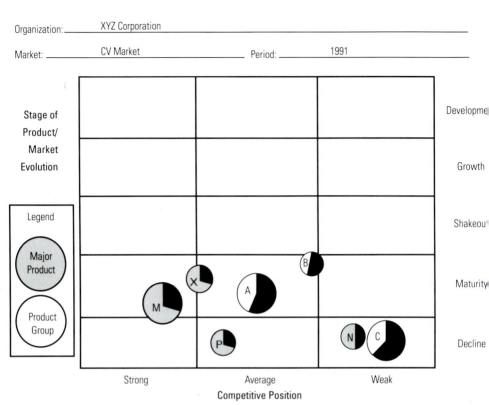

Figure 11.15 Product/Market Evolution Chart.

following symptoms: inadequate cash flow; inadequate profits; inadequate growth. A portfolio with too many question marks may also have inadequate cash flow or profits. In contrast, too many profit producers (cash cows) may have inadequate growth and excessive cash flow that is not being utilized effectively; too many stars may impose large cash demands for investment, excessive demands on management and unstable growth and profits.

A portfolio may have many desirable positions, depending on the organization. This is illustrated in Figure 11.16, based on Figure 11.7. Portfolio charts have many advantages: to plot directional movements of products in markets; to analyze competitors' moves and responses; to assess the fit of a business unit or organization about to be acquired by takeover; or to assess the business risk and financial risk associated with specific product and market portfolio positions.

We have now completed the corporate competitor evaluation of

Competitive Position

	Strong	Average	Weak	
Market	Winners	Winners	Question Marks	Strong
Attractive-	Winners	Average Businesses	Losers	Average
ness	Profit Producers	Losers	Losers	Weak

Figure 11.16   Portfolio Summary.

Competitor X. We are ready to determine the corporate competitive position of XYZ Corporation.

11.2.4   Corporate competitive position

The analysis described above allows a clear evaluation of an organization's strategic profile in relation to its competitors. A number of factors are important to consider in assessing an organization's corporate competitive position.

1. Product and market concentration   Dominant products or markets in relation to the organization's competitors are identified and measured in terms of:

- Sales by customer classification
- Sales by major product groups
- Sales by distribution channel
- Sales by price or quality category
- Sales by geographic distribution

Figure 11.6 analyzed sales by major product groups. X is the main competitor of XYZ Corporation: it has equal sales of product group A ($35.6M for X versus $35.8M for XYZ); twice XYZ sales of product N ($12.2M vs $6.6M); almost three times the XYZ sales of group C ($20.2M vs $7.6M);

XYZ Competitive Position Assessment

Industry: _____Industry SV_____ Period: _____1991_____

Organization: _____Competitor X_____ Market: _____CV Market_____

| Products | Sales | | XYZ Cash Flow | | Growth Rate | Evolution Stage | Comment |
	XYZ ($M)	X ($M)	1991 ($M)	91-90 ($M)			
Products M	31.6	10.8	4.5	0.7	4%	Maturity	Expand
N	6.6	12.2	(0.5)	(3.7)	3%	Decline	Exit
P	5.4	2.5	2.3	0.1	2%	Decline	Expand
X	5.9	2.1	1.9	(0.2)	6%	Maturity	Evaluate
Group A	35.8	35.6	3.1	0.6	5%	Maturity	Expand
B	5.1	6.6	0.5	(0.3)	8%	Maturity	Exit
C	7.6	20.2	(0.5)	(1.1)	4%	Decline	Exit
Totals	98.0	90.0	11.3	(3.8)			

Figure 11.17   Competitive positions of XYZ and X.

but one third the sales of product M ($10.8M vs $31.6M). These sales are summarized in Figure 11.17, and may be further analyzed by customer classification, distribution channel, price, quality or geographic distribution.

The Portfolio Analysis Chart for XYZ (Figure 11.14) showed that products M, X and P are cash cows, while group A is under attack and is in danger of becoming a dog. Groups B and C and product N are already dogs, reflected in their negative cash flow.

The Product/Market Evolution Chart (Figure 11.15) showed that products M and X are strong competitively, while product P and groups A and B are average. Group C and product N are weak competitively. Products P and N are in decline.

Figure 11.12 showed the cash flow from each of these products and groups for 1990 and 1991; cash flow results for Competitor X were not available. As well as the sales for XYZ and for X, Figure 11.17 summarizes XYZ cash flow for 1991 and the change from 1990 (that is, 1991–1990). The market growth rate (from Figure 11.12) and product evolution stage (from Figure 11.13) have also been consolidated in Figure 11.17 for a more detailed assessment of the competitive position of XYZ against X.

We can now see the impact of competition through the decline in cash flow over these two years: Group B cash flow has dropped by $0.3M; group

C by $1.1M; and product N by $3.7M. The latter two are in the stage of decline; group B is mature. XYZ should exit the market for these products and groups as indicated in the comment column of Figure 11.17, with priority on product N and group C – which are weak competitively.

Product M is strong competitively (Figure 11.15). It generated $31.6M sales of the total 1991 XYZ sales of $98.0M for the products we are examining. It is a large contributor to cash flow: in 1991 it generated $4.5M of the total XYZ cash flow of $11.3M (Figure 11.17); its cash flow contribution increased by $0.7M over the two years. Product P had sales of $5.4M, but with a relatively large cash flow contribution of $2.3M: an increase of $0.1M. It is average competitively. XYZ can focus on these two products to expand sales and cash flow. They are cash cows (Figure 11.14). Product P should also be examined to determine the reason for its high, relative cash flow contribution: this may give an insight into setting an appropriate expansion strategy.

Product X is also a cash cow. Its sales of $5.9M contributed $1.9M to cash flow, but this was a decrease of $0.2M over the previous year. Yet it is rated as between strong and average competitively (Figure 11.15). The growth rate of its market is the second highest at 6% and it is a mature product. Figure 11.17 indicates that this product needs further evaluation before an appropriate strategy can be set.

Group A is under attack. It has the largest sales ($35.8M of total sales of $98.0M) and is the second largest cash flow contributor ($3.1M). In spite of competition, cash flow increased by $0.6M over the two years. A strategy to defend against competition and expand sales and cash flow for this group should be established.

In Chapter 9 we defined a *market needs analysis strategy* for the market research manager as:

> 'For all potential markets which have been selected by management for possible entry, and for all markets where we operate, regularly determine the needs of existing and potential customers in those markets.'

This should be carried out for those products we wish to expand (products M and P, and group A), as well as those for evaluation (product X).

The above assessment will help XYZ to concentrate on those products and groups with the greatest positive contribution to cash flow, and therefore a potential effect on profit. The market analysis will help establish strategies to expand their sales and cash flow contribution. XYZ will also exit the market for negative cash flow contributors that are in decline, and are weak competitively. But how should its resources be allocated? This brings us to the next factor in assessing XYZ's corporate competitive position.

2. Resource allocation   The specific business units or activities which receive the greatest deployment of company resources are identified and measured in terms of:

- Distribution of assets among business units and activities
- Cash flows produced by each unit or activity
- Emphasis of discretionary resource allocations

We have examined the cash flows of the products and groups of interest. We first need to determine the funds, plant and equipment, raw materials and other assets that can be potentially released after exiting groups B and C, and also product N. These should be allocated to improve the sales and cash flow of those products and groups we wish to expand, if feasible. If this reallocation is not possible, these assets will represent an exit cost (hopefully only a one-time cost) for product rationalization.

We must also evaluate the impact of this rationalization on personnel. What are the likely costs of retraining or any possible redundancies? Are there any union constraints? What additional funds and personnel are needed to expand sales, and to support the expected increase in production volumes? What additional equipment, raw materials, support and other facilities are needed and what is their cost?

These are all questions which must be answered for each product exit or expansion strategy which is considered. Alternative strategies may need to be evaluated in terms of resources released on exit, and additional resources required for expansion. Strategies should also address competitive advantages that XYZ has over its competition: this is the next factor to consider in assessing the corporate competitive position of XYZ.

3. Major competitive advantages By comparing the organization with its major competitors, competitive advantages can be identified and measured – such as in:

- Market share
- Product quality
- Product price
- Product customer acceptance
- Profit margin
- Plant capabilities
- Managerial capabilities

Comparative advantages were identified for XYZ in Chapter 10. These are summarized in Figure 10.4. This indicates that XYZ has a financial comparative advantage in its cash and capital resources. It has a sales and distribution capability advantage, and advantage in its R&D capability and its plant flexibility. But these advantages are offset by comparative disadvantages in management effectiveness, market and customer analysis, and product quality and reliability. They are the main reason for the decline in market share and cash flow that we have seen in this chapter.

But in Figure 11.11 we saw that Competitor X is vulnerable: it has low capitalization with debt financing. However we also saw in Figure 11.17 that it achieved impressive sales against XYZ in 1991. Its total sales for these products were $90.0M, with $98.0M for XYZ. We don't have cash flow figures for X, but we know that it has lower costs than XYZ. It is therefore expected to have a comparable, or even greater, cash flow than the $11.3M cash of XYZ in 1991. We are also fairly sure that the decrease in XYZ cash flow of $3.8M experienced over the two years has resulted in a corresponding cash flow increase for X. The annual financial return for X shows that it is profitable, but not as profitable as it should be from this cash flow: due to its high interest payments for the debt financing it needed to develop products to compete against XYZ. Cash flow is funding its growth. Cash and capital resources gives XYZ a competitive advantage over X!

Figure 11.11 also indicated that X has only a small sales force: it depends on an external organization for the majority of its sales. In contrast, XYZ has a large sales force and a strong distribution capability. This is its second competitive advantage!

Both XYZ and X have flexible plants; but X has better quality control, and is already delivering customized products that the customers want. This product customization is one of the main reasons for its rapid growth. This gives it a competitive advantage over XYZ. While both have good R&D, that carried out by X depends on time availability of its senior managers: they are directly involved in R&D as well as running the business. Therefore a strong competitive attack on X, which will occupy the time of its managers, will also limit its ability to respond through new product design or enhancement.

The strategy of a price war and an aggressive advertising campaign, proposed when we discussed Figure 11.11, can use XYZ's financial and sales competitive advantages to finance an expansion of sales and cash flow for products M, P and X and for group A in their current market. Competitor X is likely to respond by also dropping prices and advertising expensively (see Figure 11.11). This will not only impact its profitability; it will also tie up its resources, so impacting its R&D capability and its ability to move into new markets. But we need to be careful how XYZ financial resources are applied: this is the next factor to be considered.

4. Financial strategies   The financial strategies of an organization and competitors are identified and measured, for example in terms of:

- Debt/equity ratio
- Current asset and liability ratios

- Dividend distribution
- Cash position

We saw in Figure 11.11 that Competitor X is under capitalized, and is unable to sustain a long price war or concerted advertising campaign. It will initially fund this from cash flow, but price cuts and advertising will erode this as a source of funding. It will have to take on equity partners to fund an extended competitive campaign. But the current investment climate does not favour investments in businesses like X. This will be a further drain on management time, in talking to potential investors: they will have many requirements for financial and other information about X. The longer this takes, the more vulnerable X will become. How will their management respond? At the same time, how will XYZ managers respond? In Chapter 10 they were '*fat and happy*': can they shake themselves out of their complacency? This is the next factor.

5. Executive management   The personal strategies of key executives, both of XYZ and of its major competitors, are important in assessing their competitive positions and likely actions. These strategies should be assessed in relation to:

- Risk orientation
- Time horizon
- Entrepreneurial nature
- Functional orientation (production, sales, finance, marketing etc)
- Consensus building

XYZ managers are risk averse; have a short time horizon; are not entrepreneurial and have too strong a functional orientation, having been promoted from the ranks. They are political, and consensus builders: the antithesis of the managers of X. Here X has a competitive advantage over XYZ. This is a potential difficulty that may result in a price war backfiring on XYZ, so draining its cash reserves. We need to watch this carefully when we define the strategic agenda for XYZ in Chapter 12.

The corporate competitive position of XYZ has been summarized in Figure 11.18, based on Figure 11.3. It shows the portfolio position: for the industry; for the competitive position of XYZ; for its competitors; for resource generation; and for environmental considerations. Any threats which indicate potential difficulties are also included, as are competitive advantages that indicate opportunities.

Industry attractiveness in Figure 11.18 has been summarized from Figure 11.10 for CV, PQ and RS Markets. We saw that Figure 11.7 advised: *cautious investment* for CV; *gradual withdrawal* for PQ; and *disinvestment*

Organization: ___XYZ Corporation___   Evaluation Period: ___1991___

	Portfolio Position	Threat to XYZ	XYZ Opportunity
Industry Attractiveness *Industry SV:* • CV Market • PQ Market • RS Market	• Cautious investment only • Gradual withdrawal • Disinvestment	• Strong competition • High market costs • Low cash flow • Strong competition • Low cash flow	• Strong cash flow • Competitors are weak financially

Competitive Position
CV Market:
• Resources
 	
• Sales & distribution
• Production
 	
• Management
	• Cash and capital reserves
	
	• Established supplier
	• Flexible plant capacity
	
	• *"Fat and happy"*
		
		• Quality products
		  from competitors
		• Entrepreneurial
		  competitors
			• Invest to improve
			  competitive position
			• Strong sales force
			• Custom products
			• Plant flexibility

Competitors *Competitor X:* • Resources • Sales & distribution • Production • Management	• Cash and capital reserves • Established supplier • Flexible plant capacity • Entrepreneurial	 • Custom products • Quality products	• Limited cash reserves • Funded by cash flow • Small sales force • External sales org. • Managers do R&D • Stretched thin
Resource Generation *Cash Flow:*	Major Product M N P X Product Group A B C	*Cash Contribution* • High XYZ cash flow • Cash drain for XYZ • Very high relative cash flow for XYZ • High XYZ cash flow • High XYZ cash flow • Cash drain for XYZ • Cash drain for XYZ	*Competitive Strength* • Strong; Expand • Weak; Exit • Strong; Expand • Cash flow decline • Strong; Evaluate • Under attack; Expand • Weak; Exit • Weak; Exit
Environment *Finance:*	XYZ Corporation Competitor X	• High interest rates • Equity funding for X	• Property disposal • Loan retirement • Price/advertising war • X is cash sensitive

Figure 11.18   Summary of Corporate External Appraisal.

for RS. The CV and RS Markets are under competitive threat; the PQ Market has high market costs. Both PQ and RS have low cash flows. The CV Market represents an opportunity for XYZ: it generates strong cash flows; and its competitors have limited cash resources.

The **Competitive Position** of XYZ in Figure 11.18 next indicates that cash and capital reserves give it an opportunity to invest in the CV Market to improve its competitive position; as does its strong sales force. The delivery of custom products, through plant flexibility, present it with another opportunity. However its competitors provide higher quality products. They also have flexible plants, and already deliver custom products. But XYZ managers are '*fat and happy*': there is a very real threat that they cannot change as fast as their entrepreneurial competitors.

In summarizing **Competitors**, we will only address Competitor X. It has limited cash reserves and equity, with debt financing, and is funded by cash flow. This represents an opportunity for XYZ. X has a small sales force, using an external organization to generate the majority of its sales. This also is an XYZ opportunity. X has flexible plant capacity, and already supplies high quality, customized products: a threat to XYZ. Its managers are entrepreneurial, but are stretched thin and also are involved in R&D: an XYZ opportunity again.

In **Resource Generation**, Figure 11.18 has focused only on cash flow: summarizing the competitive evaluation of XYZ products. Other resources which might be included are raw materials, personnel, plant and equipment. The *cash contribution* and *competitive strength* of each product or group has been summarized directly, rather than evaluate these indirectly in terms of threats or opportunities. We discuss these in Chapter 12.

Finally, **Environment** examines the effect of the current financial environment on XYZ and X. The high interest rates are a threat to XYZ, as we saw in Chapters 9 and 10. But they also affect Competitor X: unless it can obtain an equity partner, giving it access to low-cost equity funding; this would be a threat to XYZ. However, opportunities open to XYZ based on its cash and capital reserves are: the disposal of its property assets to retire present high interest rate loans; and investment in a price war to take advantage of the cash sensitivity of X – hopefully to drive it from the CV Market.

We will now consider the final factor in the corporate competitive position of XYZ.

6. Strategic evaluation   The methods used by the organization and its competitors in analyzing and evaluating their strategic profiles are also important, such as the:

- Timing of evaluations of strategies
- Methods of evaluating strategies

XYZ managers have not previously done any strategic planning. While they are acting now to rectify this omission, there is not much time. Competitor X, and the others, are growing stronger every month at the expense of XYZ. The strategies that were defined in Chapter 9 must be evaluated in terms of the internal appraisal carried out in Chapter 10, and the external appraisal completed in this chapter.

XYZ has identified a number of alternative strategies it could take in response to actions by competitors. It could choose to operate as a single business with no diversification, but instead respond aggressively to competition, as discussed. It can lower prices, and improve product quality and customer support to increase sales. Alternatively it could expand into new markets, while still responding aggressively to competition in present markets. Or it could move out of its present markets (leaving them to competitors) and move into new markets. It will certainly do this for products and groups it intends to exit. The option to move completely out of present markets would only be appropriate if they were loss-makers; but they are very profitable, as we have seen. These markets and products are in decline: XYZ will move out of them eventually; but not yet. If they were in the growth stage, it may be better not to respond as aggressively to competition: new entrants into a growth market help expand that market faster. We consider these and other strategic alternatives in Chapter 12.

11.3 | SUMMARY

We discussed tools and techniques in this chapter that are used for an external appraisal of competitors and the environment. We introduced the life cycle stages that products and markets move through: development; growth; shakeout; maturity; decline. Steps used for an external business unit appraisal, and an external corporate appraisal, were overviewed. We discussed environmental scanning and stakeholder analysis used by Rowe *et al*, and also competitive analysis as used by Porter.

These principles were used for an external corporate appraisal of XYZ Corporation. We first assessed the life cycle stage of XYZ's products. We developed a Product/Market Matrix of those products in current markets, and in new markets: related and unrelated, and for new related products and unrelated products. Sales by Product and Market were used to evaluate the positioning of products in market segments for XYZ; for its major competitor X; and for a minor competitor Y.

In a Corporate Industry Evaluation, a Directional Policy Matrix developed for XYZ for the CV market advised cautious investment. A Market Share Directional Matrix advised gradual withdrawal from the PQ market, and disinvestment from the RS market.

A Corporate Competitor Evaluation of competitor X indicated that it is a low cost, high quality supplier that is financially vulnerable. Using a Portfolio Analysis Chart we saw that product group A is under attack by X; its competitive product to A generates most of its cash flow. This was further confirmed by a Product/Market Evolution Chart.

A Competitive Position Assessment for XYZ identified those products that should be expanded, products that should exit their markets and those products that need further evaluation. These actions were assessed for resource allocation. An evaluation of XYZ competitive advantages indicated that its distinctive competence in both cash and capital resources; and in sales and distribution capability could be used to attack competitor X in a price war and aggressive advertising campaign for product group A. The financial vulnerability of X showed that this would affect the ability of X to compete.

References

[1] Rowe, A. J., Mason, R. O. and Dickel, K. E. (1986). *Strategic Management and Business Policy: A Methodological Approach (Second Edition)*, Addison-Wesley, Reading: MA.

[2] Rowe, A. J., Mason, R. O., Dickel, K. E. and Snyder, N. H. (1990). *Strategic Management and Business Policy: A Methodological Approach (Third Edition)*, Addison-Wesley, Reading: MA.

[3] Porter, M. (1980). *Competitive Strategy: Techniques for Analyzing Industries and Competitors*, Free Press: New York, NY.

[4] ibid.

[5] Cash, I. J., McFarlane, F. W. and McKenney, F. L. (1983). *Corporate Information Systems Management*, Irwin.

[6] ibid.

[7] Cash, I. J., McFarlane, F. W., McKenney, F. L. and Vitale, M. R. (1990). *Corporate Information Systems Management (Second Edition)*, Irwin.

[8] Boston Consulting Group. (1979). *Segmentation and Strategy. BCG Perspective No. 156*, Boston Consulting Group: Boston, MA.

[9] ibid.

CHAPTER 12

Strategic Evaluation

Having completed the assessment of strengths and weaknesses we are now ready to identify alternative strategies. We can then define a strategic agenda and set the strategic direction. The material covered in this chapter consolidates the stages described in Chapter 10 of my earlier book [1] on Strategic Gap Analysis, Strategic Alternatives, Strategic Selection and Strategic Statements. This is based on the Practical Strategic Planning method [2] of Information Engineering, developed in the early 1980s.

We discussed traditional strategic planning in Chapters 1 and 8, contrasting it with the strategic management planning method described in this book. Chapter 8 then identified the organization's current strategy; Chapter 9 evaluated and refined that strategy using goal analysis. If a new strategic direction was required, Chapter 10 discussed the steps involved in an internal appraisal and Chapter 11 described an external appraisal. These all provide input for strategic evaluation and depend on strategic management. The next section consolidates the key aspects of strategic management following its introduction at appropriate points in earlier chapters.

12.1 STRATEGIC MANAGEMENT

We saw that strategic management involves the setting of objectives, and the allocation of resources to enable those objectives to be achieved. Strategic management addresses an organization's internal and external relations:

both with the environment and with its competitors. At the functional area level it addresses the specific resource contributions or processing carried out by that area for its customers (users, clients, or other parts of the organization). The functional area may be involved in finance, treasury, marketing, distribution, purchasing, production, personnel, public relations, government and legal relations, or it may involve other functions. At the level of a program or business unit, strategic management addresses allocation of resources of all types: for use in resource transformation or processing in support of specific products or services, or product, market or industry segments. At the corporate level it is concerned with the arrangement and interaction of programs or business units, or instead of separate organizations or inter-organization ventures. Different tenets of strategy (see Chapter 11) are appropriate for these levels of strategic management.

Functional area strategies generally focus on efficiency or productivity in resource acquisition or use. Tenets of strategy of primary concern to these areas are: synergy, development or utilization of distinctive competences, and maintenance of competitive advantage. These strategies are likely to be constrained by strategies at the program or business unit level which are referred to collectively as business unit strategies.

The focus of business unit strategies is on how to compete in a particular industry, or a product or market segment. Distinctive competence and competitive advantage are of importance here. Synergy focuses on integration of different functional area activities within the program or business unit. Scope is of limited concern, concentrating mainly on market segmentation for a given product, rather than on the product range.

In contrast, corporate strategies focus on the mission of the organization. They define the various programs or businesses in which the organization should be active, and their interaction. For example, with related-product, multi-industry firms scope defines the limits of diversification. Competitive advantage is assessed in relation to an industry as a whole, or by industry – rather than in relation to specific competitors or products. Synergy may be sought among programs or businesses, but becomes less important where the product range is unrelated – except for financial and managerial capacity. As diversification proceeds, distinctive competence in financial and managerial capacity are particularly important.

The analysis carried out in Chapters 10 and 11 enabled us to define strategies for each level of the organization. We concentrated on internal and external corporate appraisals in those chapters in relation to XYZ Corporation. Chapter 11, for example, indicated that XYZ has distinctive competence in its cash and capital resources, but is weak in terms of its managerial capacity. Chapter 10 showed that its past financial management focus on property investment has not changed in the current competitive climate. If not addressed, this inaction in financial management will dilute XYZ's advantage in cash and capital resources. Its strategic thrust is important.

Thrust gives direction to an organization's activities. These can generally be categorized as: *stability*; *growth*; *reduction*; or a *combination*. A number of strategic alternatives exist within each of these categories. Each type of thrust will have an effect on the scope of an alternative, and on the contributions, inducements or balance established with resource contributors such as staff, suppliers, customers or financial institutions. We will use these categories of thrust to discuss strategic alternatives.

Strategic alternatives are also suggested from the four business strategies outlined by Kenichi Ohmae [3] that will allow a company to *'gain significant ground on its competitors at an acceptable cost to itself'*. They are described as: key factors for success, relative superiority, aggressive initiatives and strategic degrees of freedom. By identifying *key factors for success* in an industry or business, resources can be allocated *'where the company sees an opportunity to gain the most significant strategic advantage over its competitors'*. By exploiting any difference in competitive conditions between a company and its rivals, *relative superiority* is used as a business strategy. An *aggressive initiative* is *'an unconventional strategy aimed at upsetting the key factors for success on which a competitor has built an advantage'*. Innovations, such as opening up new markets or developing new products, are examples of business strategy based on *strategic degrees of freedom*.

When identifying strategic alternatives, the work of Michael Carley [4] is important. In discussing analytic rationality he considers five sequential activities that are undertaken by *'the idealized "rational man"'*. These activities underpin much of what is meant by rationality. He describes them as follows:

(1) A problem which requires action is identified, and goals, values, and objectives related to the problem are classified and organized.

(2) All important possible ways of solving the problem or achieving goals and activities are listed – these are alternative strategies, courses of action, or policies.

(3) The important consequences which would follow from each alternative strategy are predicted and the probability of those consequences occurring is estimated.

(4) The consequences of each strategy are then compared to the goals and objectives identified above.

(5) Finally, a policy or strategy is selected from which consequences most closely match goals and objectives, or the problem is most nearly solved, or most benefit is got from equal cost, or equal benefit at least cost.

The evaluation of strategic alternatives, and the selection of appropriate alternatives, is dependent on the judgement of management. Geoffrey Vickers [5] discusses that there are *'three kinds of judgement – value judgement, reality judgement and action judgement – in the making of business decisions'*. A reality judgement is made in the appreciation of a situation; a value judgement is made in assessing or evaluating that situation; an *action judgement*, he indicates: *'is called for by the interaction of value judgement and reality judgement, and is only selected by further use of the same criteria'*. He goes on to say: *'the higher the level of judgement involved, the less possible it is to find an objective test by which to prove that the judgement is good. The appraisal of judgement is itself an act of judgement.'* The difficulty in deciding on the most appropriate strategy from all of the alternatives considered is to reconcile the often conflicting values involved.

While the certainty of success following selection of any specific alternative cannot be guaranteed, the strategic analysis carried out through internal and external appraisal will help in making the appropriate reality and value judgements. The selected alternatives then represent the consequent action judgements.

12.2 STRATEGIC ALTERNATIVES

Given the selection of an appropriate thrust and scope, strategic management focuses on securing competitive advantage, commensurate with objectives, which capitalizes on distinctive competence and advantages of synergy. Strategic alternatives exist for each category of thrust, at the business unit and corporate levels of strategic management.

Rowe, Mason, Dickel [6] and Snyder [7] provide a comprehensive discussion of strategic alternatives, with examples taken from many case studies of organizations. *'A strategic alternative'*, they say, *'is a means of moving the company from a position of stability or status quo to a new strategic position'*. The following sections summarize the points made by them and by others, differentiating in particular between business unit and corporate alternatives.

12.2.1 Business unit strategic alternatives

Stability   At the business unit level, this category of thrust emphasizes continuation of the status quo: for example, marketing the same product in the same way to the same customers. The focus is on incremental improvement of functional area performance. Non-economic strategies for consolidation, such as patents, are appropriate. There are several indications which point to stability as an appropriate thrust:

- The organization is secure in its competitive advantage, and is meeting its objectives.
- There are no environmental resource threats.
- There is low environmental uncertainty.

Growth   A thrust which emphasizes growth is appropriate where there are abundant resources, environmental opportunities, or where change is occurring in a stable way. Growth may focus on increasing market share, maintaining market share in a growing market or increasing profitability.

A growth thrust based on **increasing market share** focuses on significantly changing the competitive position of the business unit. Indications that point to this thrust are:

- Ability to capitalize on existing competitive advantage.
- Access to capital for significant additional investment.
- Movement to a later stage in product or market evolution.
- Low possibility of competitor response.

A growth thrust based on **maintaining market share** in a growing market is indicated by:

- Products or markets at an early stage of evolution.
- A need to maintain investment, to sustain growth.
- A need to develop new competitive weapons as market evolution proceeds. For example, shifting from a production-based distinctive competence to marketing- and finance-based distinctive competences.
- Competitor activity.

A growth thrust for **increasing profitability** needs to monitor environmental trends, alter resource deployments as required, and pursue opportunities for synergy. Relevant to this thrust are the following indications:

- Last stage of product or market evolution, with no growth and with established competition.
- Little possibility of increasing market share.
- Low likelihood of improved return from increased investment.

Reduction   This thrust is relevant where there is a resource scarcity or concentration, where there are few opportunities for change, or few environmental opportunities. The reduction focus may be on: market concentration and asset reduction; turnaround; or on liquidation or divestiture.

A reduction thrust of **market concentration and asset reduction** is suggested where the scope is narrow, or where there is a decrease in resources allocated to the program or business unit. The focus therefore needs to concentrate on areas of market strength, or on a defensible niche. This thrust is indicated by:

- A weak competitive position.
- Products or markets that are in the stage of decline.
- A reasonable market share needed, to be able to concentrate on areas of strength or distinctive competence.

A **turnaround** reduction thrust focuses on reversing the fortunes of declining products: by increasing revenues, reducing costs, and/or reducing assets. This is indicated by:

- A strong possibility of improving long-term profitability of the business unit, or of improving its value as a 'going concern': so exceeding its liquidation value.
- Inefficient implementation or operation of the business unit being the cause of its decline.
- A possibility of remediation prior to bankruptcy.

A reduction thrust of **liquidation or divestiture** emphasizes the generation of cash flow, while withdrawing relevant products from the market, or while exiting the market. This is indicated by:

- A weak competitive position and low industry attractiveness.
- Low contribution to profitability through low margins.
- Achievement of objectives below the defined minimum threshold.
- Little possibility or advantage in turnaround. For example, there may be few implementation or operational inefficiencies that can be improved.

The final business unit thrust which may be considered is a combination of the above. This would be the overall result of a product or market rationalization. A combination thrust, in most cases, is impractical for specific products or markets. But the result of rationalization, overall, does involve a combination of the above thrusts. For example, a strategic thrust of stability may be appropriate for some products or markets, a growth thrust may be appropriate in other areas, while a reduction may be best for still other products or markets.

Each of these strategic alternatives will affect the objectives to be set for related groups of business units. The extent or speed of change may need to be constrained by objectives; they may be rendered unfeasible by other objectives. Criteria in definition of objectives are needed that will force a reassessment of strategy. For example, a growth thrust may need to change to a thrust of stability, if regulations apply to limit the establishment of product or market monopolies. Reduction should be reassessed if competition changes, such as by the exit of a major competitor of specific products or markets.

12.2.2 Corporate strategic alternatives

We saw earlier that the focus, at the corporate level of strategic management, is on the combination of programs or businesses to be maintained. The same thrusts apply as for business units, but with different emphasis and indications.

Stability This thrust continues to market the same set of products to the same markets in the same way, as discussed at the business unit level. Advantages are gained only in securing distinctive competences, and in pursuing synergy. The indications are:

- The organization is secure in its set of competitive advantages, and is meeting its objectives.
- Distinctive competences are fully utilized.
- There are no environmental resource threats.
- There is low environmental uncertainty.

Growth This thrust is appropriate where there are abundant resources, or where there is unstable change, strong competition, or environmental opportunity. The thrust may focus on internal growth, or on external growth.
  An **internal growth** thrust is indicated by:

- Volume growth in the present product line.
- Horizontal diversification into new product lines. This may be concentric, or conglomerate (see Chapter 11). For example, for:
  - Concentric diversification: develop products that serve similar customers or use similar technologies.
  - Conglomerate diversification: develop products or services that address different, unrelated customers; or use different, unrelated technologies in the present product line.

- Vertical diversification or integration. This can be forward, or backward:
  - Forward diversification: establish outlets for direct sale of products or services; for example, retail outlets.
  - Backward diversification: establish a supplier division or business unit for some or all resources.

There are several strategic alternatives based on an **external growth** thrust. These may address: the purchase of new product lines; horizontal concentric mergers; horizontal conglomerate mergers; or vertical integration through purchase, takeover, or merger. External growth diversification is indicated by:

- Growth or competitive advantage in the existing product range is limited.
- A need to capitalize on, or acquire, distinctive competence.
- A need to reduce dependence on a single product, so spreading the business risk in a volatile environment.
- Existence of environmental opportunities or incentives.
- Advantages of synergy in scope, management or other areas.
- A need to reduce resource dependence or allay competitive threats.
- Utilization of unused technological capacity, or excess funds.

In addition to the above, other indications for external diversification are:

- Availability of strategic resources: financial or otherwise.
- A need to acquire distinctive competence or an established competitive advantage.
- A need to acquire advantage more economically, or faster.

Including all of the above, other indications for conglomerate diversification are:

- A need to spread business and financial risk.
- Availability of financial or other strategic resources.
- Financial and managerial synergy.

Reduction   At the corporate level, a reduction thrust is relevant where resources are scarce and concentrated, where change is unstable, where there is high uncertainty, or where there is strong and effective competition. A performance improvement is needed. This may be achieved by improving performance of programs or business units, such as by cost or asset reduction. Or instead, performance of the portfolio of programs or business units may be improved by eliminating those that are unprofitable. The ultimate reduction alternative is by complete liquidation or merger of the organization. Strategic alternatives that apply here are: cutback or turnaround; divestment; or liquidation.

A corporate reduction thrust of **cutback or turnaround** is relevant if the product line has to be reduced; or if resource conversion and acquisition costs, or overheads, must be reduced. This is indicated by:

- Generally strong competition.
- Short term environmental pressures.
- Poor performance due to inefficient implementation or operation, or an over-extended product range.

A reduction thrust of **divestment** results in the sale of programs or business units, indicated by:

- Inadequate performance or profitability.
- Environmental threats, such as technological change, anti-trust or trade practice factors.
- A need to apply resources to more profitable opportunities.
- Difficulties in matching distinctive competences, or achieving synergy.

A reduction thrust of **liquidation** achieves the sale of the organization overall. This is indicated by:

- An inability to compete.
- Loss of distinctive competence.
- Forced sale through loss of control.
- Better opportunities for use of funds elsewhere.

A combination of the above strategic thrusts at the corporate level involves combining stability, growth and reduction for different programs or business units in the same organization. Alternatively they may be applied in combination to a single program or business unit.

Rowe *et al* offer fifteen questions that help management determine the most appropriate strategic alternatives:

(1) Is the strategy designed to increase market share?

(2) Are investments justified by increased market share, and will the assets used lead to real growth and positive return?

(3)   Will investment in operations and productivity lead to product leadership and result in positive cash flow?

(4)   Will asset management, productivity gains, and cost reductions achieve an appropriate return on assets?

(5)   Should short-term earnings and high positive cash flow and profitability be emphasized rather than market position?

(6)   Should products, business units or markets be liquidated or abandoned because of declining market share or intense competition?

(7)   Can new technology improve product quality, durability, serviceability, or other sources of competitive advantage?

(8)   Can a market be penetrated, or the market position of existing products be improved, by combining forces with another company?

(9)   Can better product distribution reach more domestic or foreign markets?

(10)   Can a sustainable competitive advantage be achieved with competitors, suppliers, or customers?

(11)   Should more funds be expended on R&D, advertising, or market research?

(12)   Can organizational restructuring emphasize profitable products or divisions?

(13)   Should business unit portfolios be changed to sustain competitive advantage?

(14)   Can new products or businesses be acquired to improve competitive position?

(15)   Do customers consistently perceive a difference between the organization's products and services and those of its competitors?

We have now discussed strategic alternatives that can be considered at the business unit and at the corporate levels. In Chapter 8, we completed the first stage of the strategic management planning method: Identification of Current Strategy. Chapter 9 covered the second stage: Evaluation of Current Strategy. In Chapter 10 we saw that the third stage – Setting Strategic Direction – comprised three steps:

- Step 1. Internal appraisal (Chapter 10)
- Step 2. External appraisal (Chapter 11)
- Step 3. Strategic evaluation (Chapter 12)

We are now ready to carry out Step 3. This requires an assessment of the current strategy (from Chapter 9), based on the internal appraisal and the external appraisal.

12.3 STEP 3 – STRATEGIC EVALUATION

We will first list the tasks involved in a strategic evaluation. We will then use each task in turn to evaluate the strategic direction set for XYZ Corporation. Strategic evaluation involves four tasks:

- Task 1. Strategic gap analysis, to define the strategic agenda.
- Task 2. Strategic alternatives, to identify relevant alternatives.
- Task 3. Strategic selection, to evaluate alternatives from the strategic agenda.
- Task 4. Strategic statements, to define the strategic direction.

12.3.1 Task 1 – Strategic gap analysis

Strategic gap analysis is carried out both at the business unit level, and at the corporate level. It involves the following subtasks:

- Subtask 1.1 Distinctive competences, leading to comparative advantages determined from the internal appraisal, are aligned with competitor weaknesses as assessed in the external appraisal. This indicates **feasible opportunities**.
- Subtask 1.2 Current strategies are aligned with weaknesses from the internal appraisal. Weaknesses then are aligned with threats from competitors, as indicated from the external appraisal, to identify **potential difficulties**.
- Subtask 1.3 Feasible opportunities and potential difficulties indicate **performance gaps**, where assumptions used for the current strategies no longer hold.
- Subtask 1.4 Additional strategies are defined to address performance gaps. With the current strategies, these set the **strategic agenda** of the organization.

Subtask 1.1 Feasible opportunities are analyzed in Figure 12.1. This examines distinctive competences of XYZ (determined in Chapter 10) of: (a) Cash and Capital Resources; (b) Sales and Distribution; (c) R&D and Plant Flexibility.

(a) XYZ Cash and Capital Resources give it comparative advantage in cash reserves and equity, property investment and cash flow. In contrast, its competitor X has limited cash reserves, with funding from

Opportunity Analysis

Organization: _____ XYZ Corporation _____ Evaluation Period: ___ 1991 _____

Distinctive Competence	Comparative Advantages	Competitor Weaknesses	Feasible Opportunities
(a) Cash & Capital Resources	• Cash reserves and equity • Large property investment • Strong cash flow	• Limited cash reserves • Funded by cash flow • X is cash sensitive	• Loan retirement • Property disposal
(b) Sales and Distribution	• Strong distribution channels • Large, dedicated sales force • Knowledge of current markets	• Small sales force • External sales org.	• Aggressive sales and advertising campaign
(c) R&D + Plant Flexibility	• Flexible plant capacity • Easy product run changes • Rapid development capability • Product development skills	• Managers do R&D • Stretched thin	• Customized products • Flexible job lots

Figure 12.1 XYZ Feasible Opportunities.

cash flow: it is cash sensitive. Loan retirement and property disposal are therefore feasible opportunities.

(b) XYZ distinctive competence in Sales and Distribution, with comparative advantage of a large, dedicated sales force with a knowledge of current markets – in contrast to X's small sales force and dependence on an external sales organization – highlights that an aggressive sales and advertising campaign is definitely a feasible XYZ opportunity.

(c) Further, advantages of flexible plant capacity and easy product run changes, with rapid development capability and product development skills give XYZ comparative advantages over X managers, whose limited resources mean that they are stretched thin: so affecting their ability to undertake R&D. This offers XYZ feasible opportunities with customized products and the ability to handle flexible job lots for its customers.

Subtask 1.2 Potential Difficulties are next analyzed in Figure 12.2. This examines the current strategies of XYZ (determined in Chapter 9): (a) Financial; (b) Market Research; (c) Innovation; (d) Customer Satisfaction; (e) Production; (f) Personnel.

(a) XYZ *Financial* strategies of asset disposal or exit from non-performing assets or markets address its identified weakness in interest rate exposure. Its poor financial and budget control weaknesses are

Difficulty Analysis

Organization: _____ XYZ Corporation _____ Evaluation Period: _____ 1991 _____

Current Strategies	Weaknesses	Threats from Competitors	Potential Difficulties
Financial • Asset Disposal • Financial Reporting • Budget Control	• Interest rate exposure • Poor financial control • Poor budget control	• Equity funding for X	• Delays in asset disposal
Market Research • Market Data • Market Analysis • Market Needs Analysis • Market Exit	• Inadequate advertising budget • Poor market analysis • Poor market and customer needs analysis • Investments in sunset markets	• Strong competition • Entrepreneurial competitors	• Pre-emptive price war and advertising campaign by competitors
Innovation • Technology Monitoring • R&D Funding	• Poor technology monitoring • Unable to retain R&D staff • Inadequate R&D funding	• Innovative products	• Equity R&D funding for competitors
Customer Satisfaction • Customer Survey • Sales, Support, Customer Training	• Lack of customer focus • Sales training is inadequate • Field support is inadequate	• Strong customer support	• Competitor initiatives in further customer support
Production • Quality Control • Product Maintenance • Product Review • Product Release	• Poor product quality • Poor product reliability • Poor product selection • Lack of market awareness	• Quality products from competitors • Custom products	• Production initiatives from competitors
Personnel • Career Planning • Staff Incentives	• No performance indicators • Ineffective sales incentives		• Ability of XYZ managers to improve their effectiveness

Figure 12.2 XYZ Potential Difficulties.

addressed by the financial reporting and budget control strategies. A threat from competitor X is that it may obtain equity funding to resolve its weakness in limited cash reserves (see Figure 12.1). This indicates a potential difficulty if XYZ has delays in asset disposal.

(b) The *Market Research* strategies focus on finding market research organizations to carry out market analysis and market needs analysis, to address the XYZ weaknesses in poor market and customer analysis. This was used in Chapter 11 to analyze markets and competitors. It is also necessary for market exit from sunset markets; and in preparation of advertising campaigns that emphasize market needs satisfied by XYZ products. XYZ has strong competitors: this is a threat. It would be a potential difficulty if X obtained equity funding to launch a pre-emptive price war and advertising campaign.

(c)   *Innovation* strategies of XYZ in Figure 12.2 focus on technology monitoring, and also on R&D funding. This addresses weaknesses in the ability to hold R&D staff, by poor technology monitoring and inadequate funding. Its competitors are innovative. In the past they have taken XYZ products, identified weaknesses and improved on the products significantly: this represents a threat. Equity R&D funding for competitors is a potential difficulty: this would enable them to develop additional innovative products.

(d)   *Customer Satisfaction* strategies of XYZ use a customer survey to determine needs, together with sales, field support staff and customer training for customer service improvement. Its weaknesses in a lack of customer focus, inadequate sales training and field support are addressed. Its competitors offer strong customer support: a threat that raises a potential difficulty of competitor initiatives in further customer support.

(e)   The XYZ *Production* strategies of quality control, product maintenance, product review and product release focus on its weaknesses of poor product quality, reliability, selection and lack of market awareness of R&D and product development staff. The threat of quality competitive products that are customized to customers' needs leads to a potential difficulty in production initiatives from competitors.

(f)   XYZ has set *Personnel* career planning and staff incentive strategies to overcome its weaknesses of no performance indicators and ineffective sales incentives. There are no perceived threats, but the ability of XYZ managers to improve their effectiveness is a potential difficulty.

Subtask 1.3   Performance Gap Analysis is summarized in Figure 12.3. This aligns potential difficulties with feasible opportunities to identify performance gaps. Figure 12.1 indicated feasible opportunities; Figure 12.2 identified potential difficulties.

Opportunities for asset and property disposal are offset by potential difficulties if there are delays in disposal. This indicates a performance gap which would result in delays in loan retirement, with continuing loan servicing costs. The opportunity for a sales and advertising campaign of selected products may be offset by a pre-emptive competitor campaign, or by competitor initiatives of further customer support. Performance gaps are

Organization: _____ XYZ Corporation _____ Evaluation Period: _____ 1991 _____

Feasible Opportunities	Potential Difficulties	Performance Gaps
• Asset and property disposal	• Delays in asset disposal	• Delays in loan retirement
• Aggressive sales and advertising campaign	• Pre-emptive price war and advertising campaign • Competitor initiatives in further customer support	• Delays in initiating sales and advertising campaign • Effective market and customer needs analysis
• Customized products • Flexible job lots	• Production initiatives from competitors • Equity R&D funding for competitors	• Ability of XYZ to improve product quality and reliability • Ability of XYZ to retain R&D staff
	• Ability of XYZ managers to improve effectiveness	• Ability of XYZ to change its management and staff culture

Figure 12.3   XYZ **Performance Gap Analysis.**

indicated of possible delays in initiating the sales and advertising campaign, and a need for effective market and customer needs analysis to select relevant products and emphasize benefits of interest to XYZ customers. Customized product and flexible job lot opportunities could be offset by new production initiatives from competitors, or by competitor equity R&D funding. XYZ has performance gaps in its ability to improve its product quality and reliability, and its ability to retain R&D staff. Finally, the potential difficulty in the ability of XYZ managers to improve their effectiveness indicates a performance gap: whether XYZ can change its management and staff culture to one that is more entrepreneurial and aggressive remains to be seen.

Subtask 1.4   The current strategies defined in Chapter 9 are summarized in Figure 12.4. Figure 12.2 evaluated these strategies in terms of weaknesses, and determined that they are still relevant. The external appraisal in Chapter 11 showed that additional strategies were needed in relation to competitors. Following performance gap analysis in Figure 12.3, we can now define these new strategies: they are summarized in Figure 12.5. The current strategies (Figure 12.4) and the new strategies (Figure 12.5) form the Strategic Agenda.

Figure 12.3 indicates that asset and property disposal, if delayed, will result in delays in loan retirement. Figure 12.4 shows that the current asset disposal strategy is correct. The performance gap analysis highlights that specific objectives must be set to ensure timely disposal. This will be addressed in Task 4, later in the chapter.

Figure 12.3 identified an opportunity for customized products and flexible job lots. This may be affected if new production initiatives are introduced by competitors, or if they obtain equity R&D funding. It also depends on whether XYZ can improve its product quality and reliability (defined by its current production strategies – see Figure 12.4), and its ability to hold R&D staff. Figure 12.5 defines new *Production* strategies for *Custom Product Analysis* and *Custom Product Development*.

Figure 12.3 also identified an opportunity for a sales and advertising campaign. This may be pre-empted by competitors or they may instead introduce new customer support initiatives. Effective market and customer needs analysis, and custom product analysis, is essential before initiating this campaign. Delays in obtaining analysis information, or in the initiation of a campaign increase XYZ's exposure to a pre-emptive action by its competitors. Figure 9.6 (in Chapter 9) defined two specific objectives for the *market needs analysis* strategy of the Market Research Manager:

- **Market Needs Objective 1:** Report quarterly on the needs of existing and potential customers in markets where we currently operate, to indicate changes from previous periods.

- **Market Needs Objective 2:** For markets we are contemplating entering, report within 3 months on the identified needs of existing and potential customers in those markets.

Organization: _____ XYZ Corporation _____ Evaluation Period: ____ 1991 _____

Current Strategy	Strategy Description
Financial Asset Disposal	Identify assets which cannot provide a return within two years consistent with the mission ROI; and dispose of them at the best possible price.
Market Exit	Identify markets which are unprofitable and in decline, and exit those markets at the lowest possible cost.
Financial Reporting	Implement flexible financial reporting systems able to be introduced at any organizational level, and which can provide profit and loss statements for any defined reporting frequency, with associated balance sheet statements.
Budget Control	Establish and maintain strong budgetary controls for all expenditure, linked directly to revenue achievement. All financial statements must clearly show actual revenue and expenditure against budget, and indicate percentage change from the previous reporting level.

Figure 12.4   **Current strategies for XYZ Corporation.**

Current Strategy	Strategy Description
Market Research Market Data	Identify organizations which can provide accurate market analysis, competitor analysis and demographic data, with market size, market growth, competitor activity and associated market share data.
Market Analysis	Based on organizations selected from the market data strategy, establish and maintain a regular market analysis capability so we can determine current and potential size of markets that management identify, together with their projected growth. Identify existing and potential competition in those markets, and their relative market shares.
Market Needs Analysis	For potential markets selected by management for possible entry, and for all markets where we operate, regularly determine the needs of existing and potential customers in those markets.
Innovation Technology Monitoring	Monitor and evaluate all technologies that may be relevant to our business, as well as those specific to markets identified by management from the Market Needs Analysis strategy.
R&D	Establish and maintain a research and development capability which can design or enhance new or existing products and services based on the needs identified from the Market Needs Analysis strategy.
R&D Funding	Ensure that adequate funding of the R&D strategy is provided, and provide an environment to attract and retain high quality R&D staff.
Customer Satisfaction Customer Satisfaction	Implement regular surveys of our customer satisfaction in selected markets, in conjunction with the Market Needs Analysis strategy, to identify areas where we can improve; and also to determine customer needs which we do not yet address.
Training	Establish and maintain sales training, support staff training and customer training programs which will maximize business opportunities and achieve satisfactory profit in all markets in which we operate.
Production Quality Control	Establish and maintain stringent quality control over all production, to achieve a significant reduction in reject and recall levels.
Product Maintenance Improvement	Together with R&D, define, develop and implement design or production improvements which will result in a significant reduction in the cost of product maintenance and repair.
Product Review	Establish criteria to evaluate all existing products and all new products under development for market acceptance and profitability. Ensure that existing products are withdrawn and new products are terminated which no longer satisfy those criteria.
Product Release	Guide and direct product introduction strategies and associated advertising campaigns which emphasize the market needs addressed by those products, and their other benefits over existing products on the market.

Figure 12.4 (cont.)   **Current strategies for XYZ Corporation.**

Organization: _____ XYZ Corporation _____ Evaluation Period: _____ 1991 _____

Current Strategy	Strategy Description
Personnel Career Planning	Establish and maintain a program of at least annual personal appraisal reviews which plan future job promotion and other career development moves with every employee on an individual basis. Reviews are to be seen as acknowledgements of personal performance improvement or rewards for excellent performance, rather than as punishment for poor performance.
Staff Incentives	Together with the career planning strategy, provide incentive programs which reward and acknowledge high performers.

Figure 12.4 (cont.)   **Current strategies for XYZ Corporation.**

These are too passive: an additional objective is needed to provide required information to initiate the sales and advertising campaign. This will be defined in Task 4, later. But the sales and advertising campaign is a new

Organization: _____ XYZ Corporation _____ Evaluation Period: _____ 1991 _____

New Strategy	Strategy Description
Production Custom Product Analysis	Identify products with a need for customization and/or flexible job lot sizes, based on the current Market Needs Analysis and Customer Satisfaction strategies.
Custom Product Development	Establish a product customization capability and the ability to handle flexible job lot sizes, based on the Production strategies.
Market Research Product Pricing	Set aggressive price reductions in key cash flow products of Competitor X based on the Market Analysis strategy, to encourage similar price reductions by X. Reduce XYZ costs for these lower-priced products to maintain profitability.
Advertising	Develop an advertising campaign which emphasizes: price reductions from the new Product Pricing strategy; product customization and flexible job lot capability from the new Production strategies; and also needs and benefits highlighted by the current Product Release strategy and the Market Needs Analysis strategy.
Acquisition Competitor Acquisition	Initiate discussions with Competitor X to determine its likely acquisition cost. If acceptable to both, acquire it: if possible at less cost than the proposed campaign.

Figure 12.5   **New strategies for XYZ Corporation.**

opportunity: Figure 12.5 documents new *Market Research* strategies of *product pricing* and of *advertising*. Note that the product pricing strategy must be accompanied by cost reductions, to maintain XYZ profitability. It is designed to initiate similar price reductions by Competitor X, to negatively affect funding of its operation through cash flow.

The final performance gap in Figure 12.3 indicates the most serious problem that XYZ faces: *its ability to change its management and staff culture*. Culture changes happen not by dictate, but by example. In contrast, Competitor X managers and staff already have the entrepreneurial attributes which XYZ hopes to acquire. This raises a possibility: the pricing strategy above is designed to bring about the financial demise of Competitor X, if at all possible. But it will cost XYZ money. Figure 12.1 showed that X has limited cash reserves: it is vulnerable to takeover. An alternative strategy, based on *Acquisition* of Competitor X, is defined in Figure 12.5.

If the shareholders of Competitor X do not agree to a takeover by XYZ, or if the price is too high, the sales and advertising campaign must be initiated. This will reduce the cash flow available to X for its operation. If the campaign is effective and continues for long enough, the effect on cash flow should reduce the value of X. It will likely result in agreement from its shareholders for the company to be acquired. Once acquired, X will be merged with XYZ. Selected X managers can be placed in positions of authority to help bring about a change in culture of XYZ. Merging products and technology with those of XYZ will also improve the overall product range.

The strategies in Figure 12.4 are passive: they are reactive. It is now clear that Strategic Gap Analysis focuses on change: the resulting strategies (see Figure 12.5) are proactive. Together, these strategies form the strategic agenda. However we also must determine whether there are strategic alternatives we have missed. This is the next task.

12.3.2   Task 2 – Identification of strategic alternatives

We saw earlier in this chapter that there are four major directions of thrust: stability; growth; reduction; combination. Stability is appropriate only if the organization is secure in its competitive advantage: this does not apply to XYZ. Growth is relevant to capitalize on existing competitive advantage: XYZ has cash and capital for investment. Reduction is appropriate for products or markets that are weak competitively, and in the stage of decline: this also applies to XYZ. We first need to examine the business unit strategic alternatives open to it.

Figure 11.17 determined that products M and P, and group A, are cash cows: they should be expanded. XYZ and Competitor X had almost equal sales of group A in 1991. Group A is X's highest selling product, and is the second highest cash flow generator for XYZ. A price war on this product may invoke a similar price reduction from X, so affecting its cash flow. Figure 12.6 indicates a growth thrust of investment to increase market share of these products. But XYZ must also invest in reducing the cost of group A, to increase its profitability. When its price is reduced for the price war, XYZ can still maintain its present level of profit. A reduction thrust of market concentration in Figure 12.6 focuses the CV Market on the cash cow products above.

The corporate alternatives indicate both internal growth and external growth strategies: internal growth, by horizontal concentric diversification into new product lines for similar customers and technologies; external growth, by purchasing X to acquire its distinctive competence in entrepreneurial management and technology. If the price is not too high, X should be purchased before the price war; otherwise it should be taken over when its value has been reduced due to cash flow decline.

Figure 12.6 indicates reduction thrusts of divestment and cutback: disposal of assets and property whose return on investment is below the

Organization: _____XYZ Corporation_____   Evaluation Period: ____1991____

Thrust	Strategic Alternative
Growth Business Unit Market share	Invest to improve market share of cash cow products M and P, and group A, in CV Market.
Profitability	Invest to reduce costs and improve profitability of group A in CV Market.
Corporate Internal growth	Horizontal concentric diversification into new product lines for similar customers and technologies.
External growth	Acquire distinctive competence in entrepreneurial management, and technology. Takeover Competitor X, before the price war if feasible.
Reduction Business Unit Concentration	Focus on cash cow products M and P, and group A, in CV Market.
Corporate Divestment	Dispose of assets and property with return on investment below mission of 20%.
Cutback	Terminate poorly competitive products N, and groups B and C, in CV Market

Figure 12.6   Strategic alternatives for XYZ Corporation.

mission ROI of 20%; cutback by terminating under-performing products. Figure 11.17 showed that XYZ should exit the CV Market for product N, and for groups B and C. These products are loss-makers under severe competitive attack, in the stage of maturity or decline. (Product X may be expanded, or terminated, based on the evaluation recommended in Figure 11.17.)

12.3.3 Task 3 – Selection of strategic alternatives

These strategic alternatives are next evaluated against all items on the strategic agenda in terms of: the tenets of strategy; likely resource commitments involved; the modes of strategy; assumptions regarding organizational and environmental aspects; alternative assumptions; most likely threats or weaknesses associated with each alternative. The advantages and disadvantages associated with each strategic agenda item are included in a **Strategic Alternative Evaluation Matrix**, as illustrated in Figure 12.7.

The alternatives for each agenda item are evaluated in terms of: feasibility – feasible, or not feasible; advantages – few, or many; disadvantages – few, or many; threat exposure – low, medium or high. The likelihood, and the risk, of achieving the desired outcome – as well as the likelihood of failure due to incorrect assumptions – each is assessed as low, medium or high (likelihood, risk or failure).

The **performance gaps** listed in Figure 12.7 relate to loan retirement for turnaround of ROI on assets and property: a reduction thrust. The assumption is that current interest rates will remain high, but its success is threatened by inaction of XYZ managers – assessed as low risk. Another low risk gap is delay in the sales campaign, for internal growth to increase market share of group A; this gap will occur if there are delays in achieving the required cost reduction of group A so that current profit margins are maintained with a reduced sales price for the campaign.

The market and customer needs analysis performance gap, essential to increase market share for growth of group A and other products, indicates that $100,000 has been committed as fees to the firm currently used for market research: XYZ is weak in its own needs analysis capability. This gap is assessed as low risk. But not so for the next gap: XYZ's ability to improve its product quality and reliability. Present product quality is poor, assuming current XYZ production facilities are used. $2.5M has already been committed to the Development Department for quality and reliability improvement to support a growth thrust for increased market share; but it may not be sufficient. A lack of ability to achieve required quality improvements is seen as a likely outcome: assessed as a high threat. The allocation of $3.2M for R&D staff retention represents low risk for internal growth: the first task

Organization: _XYZ Corporation_ _____ Area: _____ Industry SV _____ Period: _1991_

Strategic Agenda Item	Indicated Alternatives	Comm. Resrce	Tenets Strategy	Assump-tions	Threats / Weakness	Evaluation
Performance Gaps	Affects:					
• Delay in completing loan retirement	• ROI Turnaround		Reduction	Current interest	• XYZ mgt inaction	Low risk
• Delay in initiating sales campaign	• Internal growth		Growth	Group A target	• Grp A cost reduction	Low risk
• Effective market and customer needs analysis	• Market share	$0.1M	Growth	Current research	• Poor needs analysis	Low risk
• Ability to improve quality and reliability	• Market share	$2.5M	Growth	Current product'n	• Product quality poor	High threat
• R&D staff retention	• Internal growth	$3.2M	Growth	Quality	• Poor qual.	Low risk
• Culture change	• Turnaround	$0.5M	Reduction	Current XYZ mgt	• XYZ mgt effect'ness	High threat
Potential Difficulties	Affects:					
• Delays in asset and property disposal	• ROI Turnaround		Reduction	Curr. mkt demand	• XYZ mgt inaction	Low risk
• Pre-emptive campaign	• Internal growth		Growth	X no cash	• X equity	Med threat
• Competitor customer support initiatives	• Market share		Growth	Current activity	• X cust. support	Med threat
• Competitor production initiatives	• Market share		Growth	Current activity	• XYZ prod quality	Med threat
• Equity funding for competitors	• Market share		Growth	X no fund	• X equity	Med threat
• Ability of managers to improve effectiveness	• Turnaround		Reduction	Current XYZ mgt	• XYZ mgt inaction	High threat
Feasible Opportunities	Affects:					
• Dispose of assets and property	• Divestment		Reduction	Current demand	• XYZ mgt inaction	Feasible
• Sales and advertising campaign	• Market share	$2.2M	Growth	Group A target	• Pre-emptive X campaign	Feasible
• Customized products	• Market share	$4.5M	Growth	Current research	• Poor mkt analysis	Feasible
• Flexible job lots	• Market share	$1.2M	Growth	Current product'n	• Poor mkt analysis	Feasible

Figure 12.7   Strategic alternative evaluation matrix for XYZ.

is to work with product development to identify ways in which quality improvement can be achieved. A total of $5.7M will thus be allocated to this quality threat.

Finally, $0.5M has been committed to training and other measures to change the culture of XYZ managers and staff. A turnaround in management effectiveness is vital if XYZ is to compete effectively in the difficult times ahead. Assuming the current managers remain, this is seen as a high threat. The threat may be reduced if Competitor X is taken over, and X managers are given authority to bring about the required culture change. As the CEO of XYZ says: *'If you can't beat 'em, buy 'em!'*

The **potential difficulty** in Figure 12.7 of delays in asset and property disposal for ROI turnaround, assuming the current property market demand, is seen as a possible threat due to XYZ management inaction. But this is seen as low risk as the CEO has shown he means business. He has set clear disposal objectives which are easily measured (see Task 4): if they are not sold promptly: *'It's your head!'*

A pre-emptive price campaign, or new initiatives in customer support or production by competitors, are all quite possible assuming current competitor activity. XYZ is already planning to move in these directions; but because they attack its weaknesses these pre-emptive moves are seen as medium threats. So also is the possibility that Competitor X will obtain equity funding, so removing its cash weakness. Again, the ability of XYZ managers to improve their effectiveness is a potential difficulty seen as a high threat.

Feasible opportunities evaluated in Figure 12.7 indicate commitments of: $2.2M to the Sales Department for the planned campaign; $4.5M to the Production Department for plant changes to produce customized products, and $1.2M for production changes to support flexible job lots required by customers. In spite of the threats listed, these are all achievable based on the financial resources committed: they are assessed as feasible.

As an alternative to evaluating gaps, difficulties and opportunities as discussed above, factors can be weighted numerically if appropriate to the organization. Different weights allow a 'what if' analysis to be carried out of the sensitivity of the evaluation result to changes in different factors. A strategic choice must be made from these alternatives. Strategic choice involves establishing indicators of relative desirability or relative value. This is mostly subjective: it relies on the creativity, insights, judgement and experience of the managers involved in the strategic planning process. At the business unit level a number of factors may influence a strategic choice:

- The extent to which a strategic alternative is likely to contribute to objectives.
- Confidence in the analytic process by which alternatives are generated.
- Political pressures and relative power within a program or business unit.
- Constraints or prescriptions imposed by the corporate level.
- The need for: a proactive or reactive stance; adaptive or entrepreneurial initiatives; risk or caution.
- The situation in which the program or business unit is located, which may preclude certain alternatives.

At the corporate level the choice is more difficult. Management should try to develop an 'ideal', or a 'balanced' portfolio – against which specific portfolios can be evaluated. The ideal portfolio tries to balance: the degree of business risk associated with program or business unit portfolios and their competitive position strategies; the financial risks associated with the organization's resource generation strategy; and its current and potential cash flow and profitability. While this ideal portfolio can be used for selection among different alternatives, it should be recognized that the ideal is rarely achieved.

12.3.4   Task 4 – Definition of strategic statements

The rationale on which statements of strategy are based is documented as illustrated in Figure 12.8. This details the assumptions used (from Figure 12.7 and elsewhere), with the reasoning involved and the conclusions reached. If these assumptions change, the documented reasoning may lead to different conclusions, so requiring a change in the strategic direction and hence in the statements.

A Statement of Strategy includes strategic contingency plans, such as in Figure 12.9. These plans suggest alternative strategies if the assumptions and reasoning (from Figure 12.8 and elsewhere) on which agreed strategies are based prove incorrect or dubious. They also specify key environmental indicators that warrant strategy review. For example, at the end of 1989 the world inflation rates were 4.6% in USA; 3.0% in Japan; and 8% in Australia [8]. This should be contrasted with inflation rates at the start of the decade. In Jan 1980 inflation was 13.92% in USA; 6.23% in Japan; and 10.53% in Australia. (In fact, in Dec 1986 US inflation was only 1.1%, while negative rates were achieved in Japan over the period Jan–Mar 1987.) Changes in the inflation rate have a significant impact on pricing in the SV Industry. Pricing strategies appropriate to XYZ Corporation for the early 1990s would have had a disastrous affect on profit if applied in the high inflation environment at the start of the 1980s.

Another environmental indicator is exchange rates: these directly affect the cost to XYZ of imported raw materials, and the price and competitiveness of its exported products in foreign markets. The exchange rate on Dec 31, 1989 was $US1.00 = ¥113.6 in Japan; $US1.00 = $A1.26 in Australia (Jan 1980: $US1.00 = ¥239.75; $US1.00 = $A0.90). The price of gold is also a useful indicator. On Dec 31, 1989 gold was $US402.80 per ounce, equivalent to $A510.20 (Jan 1980: $US526.50; $A476.58).

Economic indicators affecting the ROI of assets and property are world stock market indicators. We saw in Chapter 10 that XYZ's property ROI is only 12%; substantially below the mission ROI of 20%. Other assets

Organization: __XYZ Corporation__   Area: __Industry SV__   Period: __1991__

Factor	Assumptions	Reasoning	Conclusions
Interest rates	• High interest rates affect current investment yield. • Property ROI is 12%.	• Higher returns can be achieved from increased CV market share, and in purchasing competitors.	• Dispose of assets and property with ROI<20%. • Retire loans. Invest in: market share; other assets; competitors.
Current demand	• Current demand is high for property and other XYZ assets.	• Use property and asset sales to retire loans, and invest for better ROI.	• Sell property and other assets *promptly* in current demand environment.
Current activity	• Competitor X is gaining market share at expense of XYZ profitability.	• Competitor X is attacking cash cow products of XYZ.	• XYZ must maintain, or increase, market share of its cash cow products.
X has low equity	• Low Competitor X equity limits ability to compete in a sustained price war.	• High Competitor X equity is essential to resist competitive attack.	• XYZ must move fast, before Competitor X can obtain equity funding.
Group A target	• Group A is high revenue product for X, and is a high cash flow earner for XYZ.	• Group A is a strong cash flow contributor to X. • If attacked, X is expected to follow suit. This will affect its cash flow.	• XYZ to initiate sales and advertising campaign. • Initiate aggressive price reductions for group A.
X has low cash	• Group A sales and cash flow provide funding for Competitor X.	• Cash flow funding needed by X for its operation.	• Reduction in X cash flow reduces its competitive ability, reduces its value, and leaves it vulnerable to takeover by XYZ.
Current research	• XYZ is poor in market and customer needs analysis capability.	• XYZ must know market and customer needs, to increase market share.	• Focus sales campaign on market & customer needs. • Commission Market Research firm for prompt needs analysis.
Current prod'n	• XYZ current production is for standard products and long production runs, to achieve plant efficiency.	• Customized products and flexible job lots essential for customer satisfaction, to gain market share.	• Current plant is under-utilized, but flexible. • Current plant can support customized products.
Current Mgt	• XYZ managers are bureau-cratic, ineffective, and fixed in their ways.	• Management must change emphasis, if XYZ is to compete effectively.	• Aggressive, business-oriented, entrepreneurial managers needed, to change XYZ culture.

Figure 12.8 **Strategic Rationale.**

Organization: _____XYZ Corporation_____   Area: _____Industry SV_____   Period: _____1991_____

Contingency Factor	Alternative Strategy
Assumption/Reason	
Interest rates	Review yields on assets and property if loan interest rates drop.
Current demand	Review likely asset and property sale prices if current demand drops.
Current activity	Review competitive position of products if competitor activity drops.
X has low equity	Review Competitor X threats if equity is obtained, but not from XYZ.
Group A target	Review competitive position of products if sales of group A change.
X has low cash	Review Competitor X status if sales of XYZ cash cow products change.
Current research	Monitor market research progress, with incentive for early completion.
Current prod'n	Review market and customer needs, for additional product needs.
Current Mgt	If X taken over, appoint selected X managers to achieve culture change.
Environment	*End 1989*
Inflation Rates	USA (Nov) 4.6%; Japan (Dec) 3.0%; Australia (Sep Qtr) 8%
Exchange Rates	$US=¥ 113.6; $US=$A 1.26
Gold	(Dec 31) $US 402.80; $A 510.20
Stock Markets	(Dec 31) US Dow 2753; Japan Nikkei 38,916; Australia All Ords 1649
Interest Rates	Australia (Dec 31): 90 day bills 17.55%; Prime rate 20.5%

Figure 12.9 Strategic Contingencies.

are shares on the world stock markets, acquired at the start of the 80s bull market and still greatly above their purchase prices. On Dec 31, 1989 the US Dow Jones index was 2,753; the Nikkei Dow in Japan was 38,916; the Australian All Ordinaries index was 1,649. On Jan 1, 1980 the Dow stood at only 838; the Nikkei Dow index was 6,569; and the All Ordinaries was 513 – a remarkable decade of growth: even allowing for falls since the market crash of Oct 19, 1987. On that day, the Dow Jones fell 508 points to 1,738. On Oct 20 the Nikkei Dow fell 3,836 to 21,910 and the All Ordinaries fell 516 to 1,549. By the end of the decade both the Dow and Nikkei indices had posted new record highs, but the Australian All Ordinaries index had languished around the crash level. The Nikkei index did not begin its eventual fall until 1990. Fortunately, XYZ's portfolio is largely in US shares.

The most critical indicator for XYZ is interest rates: listed at the end of Figure 12.9. Loans were taken out with Australian banks in 1980 to purchase shares and property. Prevailing Australian interest rates have a significant impact on its profitability: they are based not on a fixed interest rate, but float at 2% above the prime overdraft rate. The 90 day Australian bank bill rate on Dec 31, 1989 was 17.55%: the prime rate was 20.5% – *setting the interest rate on its loans at a profit-draining 22.5%!* These loans were taken out in Jan 1980, when 90 day bills were 10.075% and the prime rate was 11.5%: the interest rate then was a more comfortable 13.5%. In hindsight, the original decision to borrow for stock market and property investment was brilliant: XYZ's assets increased in real value over the decade (allowing for inflation) by almost an order of magnitude.

While it was a correct decision then, however, now is the time to sell: property and shares are still at very high values; the 1991 recession had not yet affected these prices greatly. But the capital is better invested in industries XYZ knows best: to arrest its shrinking market share for cash cow products in the present sunset markets, and to diversify into new growth markets. As the CEO so aptly put it: *'Its time to get back to the knitting!'*

Objectives defined from the strategic rationale, allowing for defined contingencies, are documented as shown in Figure 12.10. This identifies the responsible manager for each relevant strategy. For each objective set for the strategy, a description is provided with the specific factors or values used to measure achievement of the objective: called the **measure**. The **level** defined for satisfactory achievement is also indicated and the **time** by which the level should be reached. This target level optionally may include minimum and maximum levels, as relevant for each objective.

The Performance Gap Analysis in Figure 12.3 confirmed that the asset disposal strategy (see Figure 12.4) was correct. An asset disposal objective set for the Financial Controller was defined (in Figure 9.5): *Following Board approval, dispose of all non-performing assets within 12 months.* But no guidance was given in the discussion of Chapter 9 to identify non-performing assets. We can now refine and quantify the original objective.

Organization: XYZ Corporation   Area: Industry SV   Period: 1991

Responsible Manager: Financial Controller

Strategy: Asset Disposal

Description: Identify assets which cannot provide a return within two years consistent with the mission ROI, and dispose of them at the best possible price.

Objective	Description	Measure	Level	Time
Property Disposal	Sell Australian and US property at the best market price, to liquidate at least 90% of our portfolio within 3 months, and *all* property within 6 months.	Total asset sale price	• >=90% property • 100% property	3 mths 6 mths
Share Disposal	Sell the Australian and US share portfolio at best price, to liquidate *all* Australian shares within 1 month, and more than 90% of US shares within 3 months. *All* US shares must be liquidated within 6 months.	Total asset sale price	• All Aust shares • >90% US shares • 100% US shares	1 mth 3 mths 6 mths

Figure 12.10   Asset disposal objectives.

Figure 12.10 shows the strategy now with two objectives that are directly measurable:

At least 90% of US and Australian property is to be sold within 3 months; all Australian shares are to be sold at the best price within one month; with more than 90% of US shares to be sold within 3 months. All property and shares must be sold within 6 months.

We earlier saw that speed is equally as important as sale price: these objectives emphasize action! The specific assets to be disposed have been identified; for these two objectives the quantifiable measure is total asset sale price achieved. Similarly, Figure 9.6 defined the *Market Needs Analysis* strategy set for the Market Research Manager, with two objectives:

(1)   Report quarterly on the needs of existing and potential customers in markets where we currently operate, to indicate changes from previous periods;

(2)   For markets we are contemplating entering, report within 3 months on the identified needs of existing and potential customers in those markets.

In our earlier discussion of Figure 12.3 we saw that the sales and advertising campaign depended on information from the *Market Needs Analysis* strategy: we discussed then that these objectives were too passive. We have refined the definition of each objective in Figure 12.11, and set quantifiable measures. We have also defined an additional sales campaign objective. We are concerned with: the timeliness of report delivery; changes from previous periods; group A sales and market share for XYZ and Competitor X; and sales growth rates of competitors in new markets XYZ is contemplating entering. These objectives are all documented and quantified.

For each objective, or a related group of objectives from the strategies in Figure 12.4, strategic statements are defined in Figure 12.12. This shows a typical statement for the Financial Controller. It is more detailed than the statement in Figure 12.10. That latter figure defined each objective in support of the *Asset Disposal* strategy. Figure 12.12 also details factors that are important to the Property Disposal objective of that strategy: another figure details the Share Disposal objective. The strategy statement is repeated, with the defined objective and the agreed measure, level and time. This then provides more detail for the specific objective. The following factors should be incorporated:

- Describe each of the tenets, or components, of strategy.
- Indicate resource commitments, sequence, priorities, and time frame.

rganization:_____XYZ Corporation_____ Area:_____Industry SV_____ Period:___1991_____

esponsible Manager:_____Market Research Manager_____

trategy:_____Market Needs Analysis_____

escription: _____For potential markets selected by management for possible entry, and for all markets where we_____

_____operate, regularly determine the needs of existing and potential customers in those markets._____

Objective	Description	Measure	Level	Time
Needs of Current Markets	• Within 1 month of the close of each quarter, report on the needs of existing and potential customers in markets where we currently operate.	Report completion date	• Report delivery	Qtr + 1 month
	• In each quarterly report, include percent revenue change from previous periods against key needs indicators.	Percent change in revenue	• Report delivery	Qtr + 1 month
Sales Campaign	• For group A in the CV Market, report within one month on total market sales – together with total sales and percent market share for each of XYZ and Competitor X.	Group A sales report completion	• Report delivery	<1 mth
Needs of New Entry Markets	• For markets we are contemplating entering, report within 3 months on the identified needs of existing and potential customers in those markets.	Report completion date	• Report delivery	Reqst + 3 mths
	• In each new market, include five year projected sales growth rates of the market, and of each market player.	5 yr sales growth rate	• Report delivery	Reqst + 3 mths

Figure 12.11   **Market needs analysis objectives.**

- Indicate how the strategy will lead to achievement of objectives.
- Indicate how the strategy is to be pursued: for example, by economic, legal, social, or political means.
- Be as precise as possible.

The implementation of the stated Property Disposal objective involves several steps that represent strategies dependent on that objective: each strategy is a more detailed tactic. The thrust of the objective is: reduction of property assets. The scope is defined as: all Australian and US property. The mode is: sell at best market price. Time is of the essence: at least 90% is to be sold within 3 months (first) with all property sold within 6 months (second) as indicated in the objective statement. This is the highest priority.

XYZ's competence in: capital and cash resources is indicated; other objectives would highlight different distinctive competences. Objectives for

Detailed Objective Definition

Organization: _____XYZ Corporation_____ Area: _____Industry SV_____ Period: ___1990___

Responsible Manager: _____Financial Controller_____

Strategy: _____Asset Disposal_____

Description: _____Identify assets which cannot provide a return within two years consistent with the_____

_____mission ROI, and dispose of them at the best possible price._____

Objective: _____Property Disposal_____

Description: _____Sell Australian and US property at the best market price, to liquidate at least 90% of_____

_____our portfolio within 3 months, and *all* property within 6 months._____

Measure: _____Total asset sale price for Australian and US property_____

Level: _____>=90% property_____ Time: _____<= 3 months_____

_____100% property_____ Time: _____<= 6 months_____

Factor	Tactics	Mode	Time	Seq	Pty
Thrust	• Reduction of property assets	Sell at best market price	• 90% in 3 mths	1	1
Scope	• All Australian and US property		• Rest in 6 mths	2	
Distinctive Competence	• XYZ has capital assets in property and shares, and has cash reserves	Use capital: • To acquire competit. X	Within: • 1 year	1	1
Comparative • Advantages • Disadvantages	• Competitors weak in equity and cash • Competitors strong in innovation, and in entrepreneurial management	• To acquire others that meet ROI	• 2 years	2	2
Synergy	Will use capital & cash resources to: • Improve prod quality and reliability • Increase market share in CV market • Acquire competitors in CV market • Concentric horiz. diversification in *growth* markets for XYZ products	Improving: • Cust satisf. • Profitability • Our culture • Future ROI potential	Within: • 6 mths • 1 year • 1 year • 2 years	1 2 2 3	1 1 1 2
Resource Commitment	Available from Asset Disposal strategy • Proceeds from property and share sales *less* (working capital + 50%)	• For future growth	• Over 1st 2 years	1	1

Figure 12.12 Statement of strategy for asset disposal.

the sales campaign strategy, for example, would indicate a distinctive competence in its sales force and distribution capability. Comparative advantages and disadvantages highlight relevant factors for the listed competences. The mode indicates that capital from the property sales will be used: to acquire Competitor X within 1 year (first, as highest priority); and then to acquire other competitors that meet the ROI criterion within 2 years (second, as lower priority).

The synergy of the Property Disposal objective in Figure 12.12 is next indicated. XYZ's capital and cash resources (from the property disposal and share disposal objectives – see Figure 12.10), plus its cash reserves, will first be used to improve product quality and reliability within 6 months, for improved customer satisfaction: this is the highest priority. Second, it will use its resources to increase market share in the CV market within 1 year for improved profitability: this is also the highest priority. Equal second (that is, concurrently) XYZ will acquire competitors in the CV market that meet the ROI criterion, and also increase market share. This is of equal highest priority, and will be carried out in 1 year. The intent is to use the competitors to achieve a change in culture of XYZ managers and staff. Third, but of lower priority, XYZ will diversify into growth markets to achieve an improved future ROI within two years. This expansion is by concentric horizontal diversification: same products; same technology; in new growth markets.

The total resources available from the asset disposal strategy, to invest in the above synergistic tactics for future growth over the first two years of the new strategic plan, are – proceeds from property and share sales: less the cash required by the business for its working capital needs plus an additional 50% of working capital as a safety margin.

Figure 12.12 is thus a clear definition of the property disposal objective. It shows its thrust and scope; indicates related distinctive competences, comparative advantages and disadvantages; shows supporting tactics which provide synergy for achievement of the objective; and defines the total resources *available* from the objective to implement the tactics. (Alternatively, this indicates the total resources *allocated* to the objective). These tactics lead to the definition of detailed sub-objectives, for staff nominated to implement each tactic. Thus, for implementation: each strategy leads to detailed tactics; and each objective expands through tactics to sub-objectives – as indicated following Figure 9.6, briefly, in Chapter 9.

A detailed objective statement not only clearly defines each objective as above: it also sets parameters for performance monitoring and forecasting, and for administrative, functional and operational planning. In turn, forecasts and plans arising from objectives set the parameters for budgeting. These statements result not only in a clear definition of responsibilities and achievements for implementation of strategies; they also lead to precise definition and development of computer systems that provide the information feedback needed by management to evaluate the effectiveness of the defined strategies. The definition and development of these systems is carried out by strategic, tactical and operational modeling. The next chapter illustrates how strategic modeling is used to identify strategic information systems from the statements we have developed. XYZ Corporation needs these systems so that it can implement its strategic plan: it will use information technology to achieve competitive advantage.

Our focus to this point has been at the corporate level, and also at the business unit or program level. Strategic planning for a functional area in a business unit or a program follows the same approach, but with a different emphasis.

12.3.5 Functional area strategic planning

Strategic management of a functional area involves the management of relations with its resource contributors, by formal or informal organization structures using technologies relevant for the functional area to convert the resources from those contributors into appropriate products or services for its markets (either internal or external). This is carried out within constraints defined for the business unit or program: allowing for competition for the specific resources, and also allowing for environmental factors.

A number of strategic alternatives can be established for each functional area, associated with particular technologies. For example Marketing alternatives include: geographic coverage of national, regional or local markets; or in consumer, industrial or wholesale markets; or through multiple or single distribution channels; or by market development to stimulate demand or increase market share; or through promotional media such as newspapers, billboards, radio or TV; or by customization of product lines, such as standard, modified, or custom products; or by undercutting, matching or overpricing products. Production alternatives include: degree of integration as full, partial or none (assembly); plant size, with one large plant or several small plants; production scheduling, via inventory or by customer order; maintaining high, or low inventories; and with high, moderate or low quality control. Procurement alternatives are: high or low inventory levels; many or few suppliers; and short term or long term contracts.

Finance alternatives are: source of funds as debt, equity or retained earnings; high, low or no dividends; high or low asset backing. Personnel factors that indicate alternatives are: high or low job specialization; close or loose supervision; with union or non-union representation; and economic or non-economic incentives. Public relations alternatives include: generalized or specific service; building or preventative image; press, personal or contact

Organization:_____ Business Unit:_____

Functional Area	Development	Growth	Shakeout	Maturity	Decline
Production					
Marketing					
Procurement					
Personnel					
Finance					
Public Relations					
Gov't Relations					

Figure 12.13 Functional area product life cycle matrix.

media; government relations are: proactive or reactive; and either affiliated or independent mode.

The strategic alternatives available to, or relevant to a functional area are likely to vary depending on the product life cycle stage. For example, different functional areas are likely to assume different types of importance at different stages of the cycle. This may be represented in a functional area product life cycle matrix, as shown in Figure 12.13.

We will complete this chapter with three reference boxes. These provide a summary of the steps for strategic planning at the corporate level (Box 12.1) and at the business unit level (Box 12.2). The strategic management planning steps followed for a functional area are similar to those for corporate planning, and for business unit planning. These steps are summarized in Box 12.3.

Box 12.1
Corporate strategic planning summary

Step 1 – Internal appraisal

1.1 Identify performance data for goals, objectives and strategies of the organization, and its management and financial condition: ranked as strong, average or weak.

1.2 Evaluate strengths conferring distinctive competence, or comparative advantage, and identify those affected by prior financial resource commitments.

1.3 Define remedies for weak indicators that impede attainment of goals, objectives or comparative advantage, and so are potential difficulties.

1.4 Evaluate changes in resource commitment for effect on distinctive competences or comparative advantages, or weaknesses (see the Corporate Resource Deployment Matrix in Figure 10.3).

Step 2 – External appraisal

2.1 Evaluate the life cycle position of the organization's industries; evaluate relative competitive position of business units in their industries; assess current portfolio position of the business units for industry attractiveness and competitive position.

2.2 Compare the organization with competitors; assess effect of actions and responses on each; assess competition for financial resources; assess effect of environment on: business portfolio of the organization, on competitors, or on changes in the supply of financial resources. Categorize each as an opportunity or threat.

2.3 Indicate the competitive position of the organization, and of each competitor, for opportunities and threats (see External Corporate Appraisal, in Figure 11.3).

Box 12.1 (cont.)
Corporate strategic planning summary

Step 3 – Strategic evaluation

3.1   Strategic gap analysis

3.1.1   Align distinctive competences (from the internal appraisal) with competitor weaknesses (from the external appraisal) to identify feasible opportunities (see Opportunity Analysis, in Figure 12.1).

3.1.2   Align current strategies with weaknesses (from the internal appraisal); then align weaknesses with threats from competitors (from the external appraisal) to identify potential difficulties (see Difficulty Analysis, in Figure 12.2).

3.1.3   Align feasible opportunities with potential difficulties to identify performance gaps, where assumptions used to define current strategies may no longer hold (see Performance Gap Analysis, in Figure 12.3).

3.1.4   Define further strategies to resolve performance gaps. Current strategies (see Figure 12.4) and new strategies (see Figure 12.5) form the Strategic Agenda.

3.2   Identification of strategic alternatives

3.2.1   Identify alternative strategies for thrust tenets of: stability; growth; reduction; combination (see Strategic Alternatives, in Figure 12.6).

3.3   Evaluation and selection of strategic alternatives

3.3.1   Evaluate each strategic alternative against strategic agenda items for: tenets of strategy; resource commitments; modes of strategy; organization assumptions; environmental aspects; alternative assumptions; threats; weaknesses.

3.3.2   Establish indicators of relative value for a strategic choice. Develop an 'ideal' portfolio to evaluate each portfolio for:

(cont'd)

Box 12.1 (cont.)
Corporate strategic planning summary

competitive position; financial risks; current and potential cash flow; profitability; need for a proactive or reactive stance, adaptive or entrepreneurial initiatives, risk or caution.

3.4 Definition of strategic statements

3.4.1 Document the rationale on which the strategic direction is based (see Strategic Rationale, in Figure 12.8).

3.4.2 Identify alternative strategies to be used if assumptions and reasoning behind the strategic direction are incorrect; identify environmental indicators that are to be monitored (see Strategic Contingencies, in Figure 12.9).

3.4.3 Document objectives from the strategic rationale, allowing for contingencies; identify the responsible manager for each relevant strategy; define measure, level and time for each objective (see Objectives, in Figures 12.10 and 12.11).

3.4.4 Define detailed objective statements, including: tenets of strategy; sequence, priorities, time frame; distinctive competences, comparative advantages and disadvantages; tactics for objective achievement; resource commitments (see Detailed Objective Definition, in Figure 12.12).

Box 12.2
Business unit strategic planning summary

Step 1 – Internal appraisal

1.1 Identify performance data of resources needed for the business unit (or program), and determine strengths and weaknesses: ranked as strong, average or weak.

1.2 Evaluate strengths of the business unit to identify areas of distinctive competence that may give it comparative advantage over other business units.

1.3 Define remedies for weak indicators that impede attainment of goals, objectives or comparative advantage, and so are potential difficulties.

1.4 Evaluate changes in resource commitments for their effect on areas of: distinctive competence; comparative advantage; or weakness (see Business Unit Resource Deployment Matrix, in Figure 10.2).

Step 2 – External appraisal

2.1 Evaluate life cycle position of the business unit's products and services. Analyze their markets by: size; life cycle stage; growth rate and potential; segmentation; segment size and growth; needs and characteristics; segments served well or poorly. Relate each product or service to its markets, by: relative growth rate; market share.

2.2 Evaluate business unit in its industry by: life cycle; extent of competition; barriers to entry; product differentiation; price/ cost structures or trends; communication and distribution; supply and labour; industry regulation; capital structure; finance needs and sources; power of competitors. Evaluate under- or over-capacity of the industry. Relate business unit to the industry, by: relative growth rate; market share; resource competitiveness; profitability.

(cont'd)

Box 12.2 (cont.)
Business unit strategic planning summary

2.3 Evaluate each competitor for: strengths and weaknesses, distinctive competences, comparative advantages, potential difficulties; products; services; markets; industry position. Identify actions, effects and responses of business unit and competitors. Categorize each as an opportunity, or a threat.

2.4 Evaluate effect of changes in the environment: demographic; economic; social; cultural; political; legal or technological – on the business unit and competitors. Categorize each factor as an opportunity or a threat.

2.5 Evaluate competitive position of business unit by: its products; markets; industry; competitors; resource contributors; environment. Identify relevant opportunities and threats (see External Business Unit Appraisal, in Figure 11.2).

Step 3 – Strategic evaluation

3.1 Strategic gap analysis

3.1.1 Align distinctive competences (from the internal appraisal) with competitor weaknesses (from the external appraisal) to identify feasible opportunities (see Opportunity Analysis, in Figure 12.1).

3.1.2 Align current strategies with weaknesses (from the internal appraisal); then align weaknesses with threats from competitors (from the external appraisal) to identify potential difficulties (see Difficulty Analysis, in Figure 12.2).

3.1.3 Align feasible opportunities with potential difficulties to identify performance gaps, where assumptions used to define current strategies may no longer hold (see Performance Gap Analysis, in Figure 12.3).

3.1.4 Define further strategies to resolve performance gaps. Current strategies (see Figure 12.4) and new strategies (see Figure 12.5) form the Strategic Agenda.

Box 12.2 (cont.)
Business unit strategic planning summary

3.2 Identification of strategic alternatives

3.2.1 Identify alternative strategies for thrust tenets of: stability; growth; reduction; combination (see Strategic Alternatives, in Figure 12.6).

3.3 Evaluation and selection of strategic alternatives

3.3.1 Evaluate each strategic alternative against strategic agenda items for: tenets of strategy; resource commitments; modes of strategy; organization assumptions; environmental aspects; alternative assumptions; threats; weaknesses.

3.3.2 Establish indicators of relative value for strategic alternatives. Evaluate for: contribution to objectives; confidence in analytic process; political pressures; relative power; corporate constraints or prescriptions imposed; precluded alternatives; need for a proactive or reactive stance, adaptive or entrepreneurial initiatives, risk or caution.

3.4 Definition of strategic statements

3.4.1 Document the rationale on which the strategic direction is based (see Strategic Rationale, in Figure 12.8).

3.4.2 Identify alternative strategies to be used, if assumptions and reasoning behind the strategic direction are incorrect; identify environmental indicators that are to be monitored (see Strategic Contingencies, in Figure 12.9).

3.4.3 Document objectives from the strategic rationale, allowing for contingencies; identify the responsible manager for each relevant strategy; define measure, level and time for each objective (see Objectives, in Figures 12.10 and 12.11).

3.4.4 Define detailed objective statements, including: tenets of strategy; sequence, priorities, time frame; distinctive competences, comparative advantages and disadvantages; tactics for objective achievement; resource commitments (see Detailed Objective Definition, in Figure 12.12).

Box 12.3
Functional area strategic planning summary

Step 1 – Current strategies

1.1 Establish constraints set by business unit or corporate strategies, including the effect of the product life cycle situation.

1.2 Identify current functional area strategies, by the management questionnaire or as otherwise documented.

Step 2 – Internal appraisal

2.1 Identify performance data for the functional area in terms of: conditions of resource acquisition, technologies that are used for resource acquisition or conversion, structural arrangements, and management of the functional area.

2.2 Develop factors for each category in step 2.1 to be used as performance indicators. Rank performance in each indicator as: strong, average or weak.

2.3 Align those indicators rated as strong against the overall strategic objective of the functional area from steps 1.1 and 1.2. Identify those factors that indicate distinctive competence. Assign rankings to those distinctive competences that confer comparative advantage.

2.4 Align those indicators rated average or weak on the overall strategic objective of the functional area. Identify those factors that may impede attainment of objectives, or of comparative advantage. Identify remedies for these factors and determine their feasibility.

2.5 Assess the extent to which synergy is possible, or achieved, within operations of the functional area. Categorize any discrepancy between possible and achieved synergy as strong, average or weak. Identify areas of weakness that warrant remediation.

2.6 Determine whether the ranking in steps 2.2–2.5 is due to past patterns of resource allocation within the functional area, and

---

Box 12.3 (cont.)
Functional area strategic planning summary

---

evaluate the effect of changing these patterns (use a Functional Area Resource Deployment Matrix, similar to Figure 10.1).

2.7   Document the result of the internal appraisal as for Figures 10.3 and 10.4.

Step 3 – External appraisal

3.1   Evaluate each resource in its market, analyzing the market by: size; stage of evolution; growth rate and potential; types of segmentation; size and growth rate of each segment; needs and characteristics; segments served well, and those served poorly. Relate resource usage to market variables such as size of usage relative to the market, or growth of usage relative to market growth.

3.2   Evaluate the industry in which resource suppliers are located by: analyzing structure, conduct and performance of the industry; determining under- or over-utilized capacity; evaluating the functional area's pattern of resource usage, and conditions of resource acquisition, within the industry.

3.3   Evaluate major competitors for each type of resource by: analyzing patterns of resource usage; and modes of resource acquisition (such as political, legal, economic, social). Analyze strengths and weaknesses of each competitor in relation to resource acquisition.

3.4   Identify actions, effects and responses of the functional area and competitors. Categorize each as an opportunity or a threat.

3.5   Evaluate the effect of environmental changes on: the market; the industry; on competitors and on the resource position of the functional area. Categorize each change as an opportunity or a threat.

3.6   Evaluate the competitive position of the functional area,

(cont'd)

Box 12.3 (cont.)
Functional area strategic planning summary

---

together with threats and opportunities, similar to External Business Unit Appraisal, in Figure 11.2.

Step 4 – Strategic evaluation

4.1 Strategic gap analysis

4.1.1 Align distinctive competences (from the internal appraisal) with resource competitor weaknesses (from the external appraisal) to identify feasible opportunities (similar to Opportunity Analysis, in Figure 12.1).

4.1.2 Align current strategies with weaknesses (from internal appraisal); then align weaknesses with threats from resource competitors (from external appraisal) to identify potential difficulties (similar to Difficulty Analysis, in Figure 12.2).

4.1.3 Align feasible opportunities with potential difficulties to identify performance gaps, where assumptions used to define current strategies may no longer hold (similar to Performance Gap Analysis, in Figure 12.3).

4.1.4 Define further strategies to resolve performance gaps. Current strategies (see Figure 12.4) and new strategies (see Figure 12.5) form the Strategic Agenda.

4.2 Identification of strategic alternatives

4.2.1 Identify alternative functional area strategies as discussed in Functional Area Strategic Planning earlier, in terms of the product life cycle (see Functional Area Product Life Cycle Matrix, in Figure 12.13).

4.3 Evaluation and selection of strategic alternatives

4.3.1 Evaluate each strategic alternative against strategic agenda items for: tenets of strategy; resource commitments; modes of strategy; organization assumptions; environmental aspects; alternative assumptions; threats; weaknesses.

Box 12.3 (cont.)
Functional area strategic planning summary

4.3.2   Establish indicators of relative value for functional area strategic alternatives. Evaluate for: contribution to objectives; confidence in analytic process; political pressures; relative power; business unit constraints; precluded alternatives; need for proactive or reactive stance, adaptive or entrepreneurial initiatives, risk or caution.

4.4   Definition of strategic statements

4.4.1   Document the rationale on which the strategic direction is based (similar to Strategic Rationale, in Figure 12.8).

4.4.2   Identify alternative strategies to be used, if assumptions and reasoning behind the strategic direction are incorrect; identify environmental indicators that are to be monitored (similar to Strategic Contingencies, in Figure 12.9).

4.4.3   Document objectives from the strategic rationale, allowing for contingencies; identify the responsible manager for each strategy; define measure, level and time for each objective (similar to Objectives, in Figures 12.10 and 12.11).

4.4.4   Define detailed objective statements, including: tenets of strategy; sequence, priorities, time frame; distinctive competences, comparative advantages and disadvantages; tactics for objective achievement; resource commitments (similar to Detailed Objective Definition, in Figure 12.12).

12.4 SUMMARY

The strategic statements developed in Chapter 9 using goal analysis were found to be reactive. This Chapter 12 brought together the internal appraisal (see Chapter 10), with the external appraisal (see Chapter 11) to evaluate and set strategic direction. The result was a more proactive plan.

We discussed the strategic alternatives available to an organization at the business unit or program level, and also at the corporate level. We considered different thrusts that could be adopted, of: stability; growth; reduction; or a combination of these thrusts. The indicators for each directional thrust were detailed.

The chapter then introduced the four tasks to be carried out for strategic evaluation to set strategic direction: 1. strategic gap analysis; 2. assess strategic alternatives; 3. make a strategic selection; and 4. define strategic statements.

(1) **Strategic gap analysis** involves four subtasks: a) distinctive competences (from the internal appraisal) are aligned with competitor weaknesses (from external appraisal) to identify feasible opportunities; b) weaknesses (internal appraisal) are aligned with competitor threats (external appraisal) to identify potential difficulties; c) feasible opportunities and potential difficulties were used to identify performance gaps; d) additional (proactive) strategies were defined to address these performance gaps. The current and additional strategies thus form the strategic agenda.

(2) **Strategic alternatives** were assessed for the strategic agenda. A combination of strategic thrusts was found to be most appropriate for XYZ Corporation: stability, for mature products secure in their competitive position; reduction, for products that were weak competitively and in a declining market; and growth, for products that were profitable, in a mature market, and under attack.

(3) The **selected strategic alternatives** focused on the financial weakness of Competitor X. A price war and advertising campaign targeted at the major cash flow product of X was assessed to have most potential affect on its operation and funding. A concurrent strategy to attempt acquisition of X was also selected.

(4) Following strategic selection in 3, the final task documented the strategic rationale and defined strategic contingencies. Current strategies and objectives defined using goal analysis in Chapter 9, plus all new proactive strategies from Chapter 12, were also documented. The quantified measures, levels and times, and detailed definition of each objective, were then completed.

The chapter concluded with a discussion of functional area strategic planning, and with three summary boxes covering the steps discussed in Chapters 10–12: Box 12.1 for corporate strategic planning; Box 12.2 for business unit strategic planning; and Box 12.3 for functional area strategic planning.

References

[1] Finkelstein, C. (1989). *An Introduction to Information Engineering*, Addison-Wesley: Reading, MA.

[2] Birkett, W. (1983). *Practical Strategic Planning*, Information Engineering Press: Sydney.

[3] Ohmae, K. (1982). *The Mind of the Strategist*, McGraw-Hill: New York, NY.

[4] Carley, M. (1980). *Rational Techniques in Policy Analysis*, Heinemann: London, UK.

[5] Vickers, G. (1960). Judgement, as Chapter 4 in *Towards a Sociology of Management*, Chapman and Hall: London, UK.

[6] Rowe, A. J., Mason, R. O. and Dickel, K. E. (1986). *Strategic Management and Business Policy: A Methodological Approach (Second Edition)*, Addison-Wesley, Reading: MA.

[7] Rowe, A. J., Mason, R. O., Dickel, K. E. and Snyder, N. H. (1990). *Strategic Management and Business Policy: A Methodological Approach (Third Edition)*, Addison-Wesley, Reading: MA.

[8] Source: Hongkong Bank of Australia Ltd. The Financial Markets in the 1980s, Australian Business: Sydney (Jan 17, 1990).

CHAPTER 13

Developing a Strategic Model

A strategic model schematically documents the data and information needed by senior managers of the strategic area to implement the strategic plan and operate the business. This chapter illustrates development of a strategic model from the strategic plan which was developed in earlier chapters.

13.1 INTRODUCTION

As indicated in Chapter 8, a strategic model can be developed from responses obtained through the management questionnaire. However these responses in their raw form, as we have seen, are at best incomplete or ambiguous; at worst they merely reflect the problems of the past. They may be quite inappropriate to the future. After goal analysis the refined responses offer better input for strategic modeling.

Chapter 10 completed an internal appraisal of the organization, either at the corporate level or at the business unit level as appropriate. This appraisal used known strengths to identify distinctive competences. The external appraisal of competitors, in Chapter 11, identified strengths and weaknesses of those competitors. These strengths, aligned with weaknesses of the organization in Chapter 12, identified potential threats. Similarly the distinctive competences of the organization, when aligned with competitor weaknesses, indicated feasible opportunities.

It was not until Chapter 12 that we saw that the strategic plan developed in the earlier chapters was passive, or instead reactive. It was not aggressive enough for competitive advantage. Strategic gap analysis aligned feasible opportunities and potential difficulties to identify performance gaps. Strategies were defined to close those gaps and to focus on competitive advantages: these strategies were more proactive. Alternative strategies were identified and evaluated. The strategic rationale behind the plan was documented. Contingencies, objectives and detailed objective definitions were also documented. The strategic plan was thus fully defined, refined and documented: so offering accurate input to strategic modeling.

13.2 STRATEGIC MODELING

We briefly saw in Chapter 1 that strategic modeling develops a schematic blueprint of the information and data needed to manage an organization, based on its strategic plan. Data from operational levels of the business are used to derive information needed for decision-making by management. As an architect's plan provides a schematic blueprint for the construction of a building, so a strategic model is a blueprint for construction of the information systems needed by management. The architect's plan leads to detailed construction blueprints to be used by the builder; so also, the strategic model leads to detailed tactical and operational data models, and process models, for the design and development of application systems. It is also used to evaluate appropriate organization structures. We will progressively develop a strategic model for the XYZ Corporation in the following pages. In Chapter 14 we will discuss possible organization structures.

The starting point for strategic modeling is the mission statement for the strategic area. For XYZ Corporation, this was included as part of the management questionnaire in Chapter 8:

> *XYZ Corporation Mission*
> *Develop, deliver and support products and services which satisfy the needs of customers in markets where we can achieve a return on investment at least 20%pa within two years of market entry.*

In Chapter 9 we used goal analysis to evaluate and refine the questionnaire responses, defining current strategies based on this mission. These were summarized in Figure 12.4. Chapter 12 identified performance gaps and defined additional strategies in Figure 12.5. These two tables have been consolidated as Figure 13.1; they provide direct input to the strategic modeling steps.

Organization: _____XYZ Corporation_____ Evaluation Period: ____1991_____

Strategy	Strategy Description
Financial	
Asset Disposal	Identify assets which cannot provide a return within two years consistent with the mission ROI, and dispose of them at the best possible price.
Market Exit	Identify markets which are unprofitable and in decline, and exit those markets at the lowest possible cost.
Financial Reporting	Implement flexible financial reporting systems able to be introduced at any organizational level, and which can provide profit and loss statements for any defined reporting frequency, with associated balance sheet statements.
Budget Control	Establish and maintain strong budgetary controls for all expenditure, linked directly to revenue achievement, All financial statements must clearly show actual revenue and expenditure against budget, and indicate percentage change from the previous reporting period.
Market Research	
Market Data	Identify organizations which can provide accurate market analysis, competitor analysis and demographic data, with market size, market growth, competitor activity and associated market share data.
Market Analysis	Based on organizations selected from the market data strategy, establish and maintain a regular market analysis capability so we can determine current and potential size of markets that management identify, together with their projected growth. Identify existing and potential competition in those markets, and their relative market shares.
Market Needs Analysis	For potential markets selected by management for possible entry, and for all markets where we operate, regularly determine the needs of existing and potential customers in those markets.
Product Pricing	Set aggressive price reductions in key cash flow products of Competitor X based on the Market Analysis strategy, to encourage similar price reductions by X. Reduce XYZ costs for these lower-priced products to maintain profitability.
Advertising	Develop an advertising campaign which emphasizes: price reductions from the Product Pricing strategy; product customization and flexible job lot capability from the Production strategies; and also needs and benefits highlighted by the Product Release strategy and the Market Needs Analysis strategy.
Innovation	
Technology Monitoring	Monitor and evaluate all technologies that may be relevant to our business, as well as those specific to markets identified by management from the Market Needs Analysis strategy.
R&D	Establish and maintain a research and development capability which can design or enhance new or existing products and services based on the needs identified from the Market Needs Analysis strategy.
R&D Funding	Ensure that adequate funding of the R&D strategy is provided, and provide an environment to attract and retain high quality R&D staff.

Figure 13.1   **Strategies for XYZ Corporation.**

rganization: _____ XYZ Corporation _____ Evaluation Period: ___ 1991 _____

Strategy	Strategy Description
Customer Satisfaction Customer Satisfaction	Implement regular surveys of our customer satisfaction in selected markets, in conjunction with the Market Needs Analysis strategy, to identify areas where we can improve; and also to determine customer needs which we do not yet address.
Training	Establish and maintain sales training, support staff training and customer training programs which will maximize business opportunities and achieve satisfactory profit in all markets in which we operate.
Production Quality Control	Establish and maintain stringent quality control over all production, to achieve a significant reduction in reject and recall levels.
Product Maintenance Improvement	Together with R&D, define, develop and implement design or production improvements which will result in a significant reduction in the cost of product maintenance and repair.
Product Review	Establish criteria to evaluate all existing products and all new products under development for market acceptance and profitability. Ensure that existing products are withdrawn and new products are terminated which no longer satisfy those criteria.
Product Release	Guide and direct product introduction strategies and associated advertising campaigns which emphasize the market needs addressed by those products, and their other benefits over existing products on the market.
Custom Product Analysis	Identify products with a need for customization and/or flexible job lot sizes, based on the Market Needs Analysis and Customer Satisfaction strategies.
Custom Product Development	Establish a product customization capability and the ability to handle flexible job lot sizes, based on the Custom Product Analysis strategies.
Personnel Career Planning	Establish and maintain a program of at least annual personal appraisal reviews which plan future job promotion and other career development moves with every employee on an individual basis. Reviews are to be seen as acknowledgements of personal performance improvement or rewards for excellent performance, rather than as punishment for poor performance.
Staff Incentives	Together with the career planning strategy, provide incentive programs which reward and acknowledge high performers.
Acquisition Competitor Acquisition	Initiate discussions with Competitor X to determine its likely acquisition cost. If acceptable to both, acquire it: if possible at less cost than the proposed campaign.

Figure 13.1 (cont.)   **Strategies for XYZ Corporation.**

We will develop a strategic model in this chapter that will permit XYZ to respond rapidly, through its data bases and systems, to the competitive environment of the 90s and into the 21st century. In Chapter 14 we provide additional flexibility in the strategic model for performance monitoring. We will use this strategic model, developed from the strategic statements in Figure 13.1, to evaluate alternative organization structures that will enable XYZ Corporation itself, also to respond rapidly to change.

13.2.1   Step 1 – Identify data subjects

In this chapter we will use a variation of the five strategic modeling steps described in Chapter 17 of my earlier book. As the first step we will take the data map of major data subjects which was developed as the mission model in Chapter 9.

This data map of data subjects (Figure 9.2, repeated as Figure 13.2) was defined from the mission statement of XYZ. It shows five data subjects: MARKET, NEED, CUSTOMER, PRODUCT and PERFORMANCE, and the *many to many* associations relating them.

These data subjects in Figure 13.2 are decomposed to identify data entities in the second step.

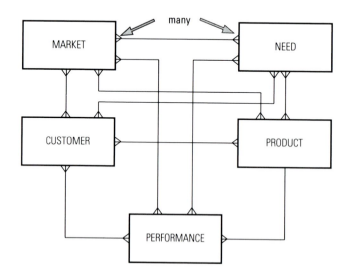

Figure 13.2   Mission model of XYZ (from Figure 9.2).

13.2.2   Step 2 – Identify data entities from mission

Data entities are determined by the graphical application of business normalization (see Chapter 4) to the mission model, using the following three steps:

2(a)   Every *many to many* association is replaced by an intersecting entity, together with two, *one to many* associations (1BNF and 2BNF rules).

2(b)   Subtype (secondary) entities are defined (4BNF rule).

2(c)   Structure entities are defined for recursive associations (5BNF rule).

Applying rule 2(a), the *many to many* association in Figure 13.1 between MARKET and NEED results in the intersecting entity MARKET NEED, shown in Figure 13.3. Data defining the needs of each market are represented by this entity: it represents the Market Needs Analysis function of XYZ Corporation. An intersecting entity is defined between MARKET and CUSTOMER, as MARKET CUSTOMER: this represents the Customer Marketing function. Similarly, MARKET PRODUCT is Product Marketing; CUSTOMER NEED represents the Customer Support function; PRODUCT NEED is the Product Development function; CUSTOMER PRODUCT represents the Sales and Distribution function. Every intersecting entity in Figure 13.3 is shaded: representing major tactical functions that are needed to support the related data subjects, to achieve the goals and objectives defined in Chapters 9 and 12.

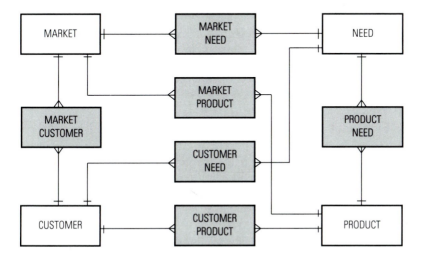

Figure 13.3   Intersecting data entities, showing major functions.

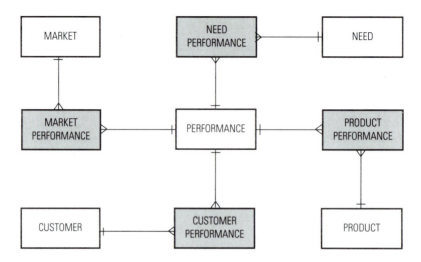

Figure 13.4 Performance entities from the mission model.

PERFORMANCE is also related in a *many to many* association with each of the entities in Figure 13.2: representing performance monitoring responsibilities of management. Using rule 2(a) again, the *many to many* association between PERFORMANCE and CUSTOMER is replaced by CUSTOMER PERFORMANCE as shown in Figure 13.4: this represents Customer Performance Monitoring, responsible for Customer Support.

Applying rule 2(a) further, Quality Control Performance Monitoring is indicated (in part) by PRODUCT PERFORMANCE. Market Analysis Performance Monitoring is indicated by MARKET PERFORMANCE. NEED PERFORMANCE represents the Market Research Performance Monitoring function. These performance entities are all of interest to senior management: they represent management performance monitoring functions, leading to the definition of detailed objectives for achievement by middle management.

PERFORMANCE is also related to each of the intersecting entities for tactical functions in Figure 13.3, indicating tactical performance monitoring functions. These functions lead to definition of objectives for achievement by tactical management responsible for the relevant tactical functions. For example, a *many to many* association exists between MARKET NEED and PERFORMANCE. This is MARKET NEED PERFORMANCE, representing the Market Needs Analysis tactical performance monitoring function.

So also MARKET CUSTOMER PERFORMANCE represents the Customer Marketing Performance Monitoring function; MARKET PRODUCT PERFORMANCE is the Product Marketing Performance Monitoring function; CUSTOMER NEED PERFORMANCE is the Customer

Support Performance Monitoring function; PRODUCT NEED PER-FORMANCE is the Product Development Performance Monitoring function; CUSTOMER PRODUCT PERFORMANCE represents Sales and Distribution Performance Monitoring. We have not shown these tactical performance monitoring entities in a data map, however: we will see in Chapter 14 that all intersecting performance entities can be represented by a generic performance monitoring data model.

We have seen that the intersecting entities, identified above by the 1BNF rule, suggest possible functions. These are summarized in the next step.

13.2.3 Step 3 – Identify preliminary functions

Tactical functions identified from Figure 13.3, management performance monitoring functions from Figure 13.4 and the tactical performance monitoring functions discussed above, together with their relevant intersecting entities, can be summarized in an initial **Entity/Function Matrix** as shown in Table 13.1.

This table is *not* a complete definition of functions at this stage of strategic modeling: rather, it allows preliminary selection of functions for more detailed modeling in areas of major interest to management. It will guide us in the further identification of data entities: using the strategies in Figure 13.1 as input for additional strategic modeling, and applying the 4BNF and 5BNF rules above. We will discuss implementation of these functions in potential organization structures in Chapter 14.

13.2.4 Step 4 – Identify data entities from strategies

We saw in earlier chapters that XYZ is weak in market analysis and market research. Its senior managers have decided to focus first on the functions of Market Needs Analysis and Customer Marketing in Table 13.1, for initial strategic modeling. In Figure 13.3 we saw that the data subjects MARKET, CUSTOMER and NEED are related to the intersecting entities in Table 13.1 for these functions. This part of the strategic data map is illustrated in Figure 13.5.

The *many* associations are now defined as *optional* (by a circle), or *optional becoming mandatory* (by a circle and a bar), near the *many* end of the association. For example, a market (to exist) *will* have *one or many* needs – but XYZ may not be able to address all of those needs; a need *may*

Table 13.1   Initial entity/function matrix for XYZ Corporation

Intersecting Entity	Associated Function
Tactical Entities	**Tactical Functions**
MARKET NEED	Market Needs Analysis
MARKET CUSTOMER	Customer Marketing
MARKET PRODUCT	Product Marketing
CUSTOMER NEED	Customer Support
PRODUCT NEED	Product Development
CUSTOMER PRODUCT	Sales and Distribution
Management Performance Entitles	**Management Performance Functions**
CUSTOMER PERFORMANCE	Customer Performance Monitoring
PRODUCT PERFORMANCE	Quality Control Performance Monitoring
MARKET PERFORMANCE	Market Analysis Performance Monitoring
NEED PERFORMANCE	Market Research Performance Monitoring
Tactical Performance Entitles	**Tactical Performance Functions**
MARKET NEED PERFORMANCE	Market Needs Analysis Performance Monitoring
MARKET CUSTOMER PERFORMANCE	Customer Marketing Performance Monitoring
MARKET PRODUCT PERFORMANCE	Product Marketing Performance Monitoring
CUSTOMER NEED PERFORMANCE	Customer Support Performance Monitoring
PRODUCT NEED PERFORMANCE	Product Development Performance Monitoring
CUSTOMER PRODUCT PERFORMANCE	Sales and Distribution Performance Monitoring

indicate *zero, one or many* markets of interest to XYZ. A market *will* have *one or many* customers; a customer *will* belong to *one or many* markets. A customer *will* have *one or many* needs; a need of interest to XYZ *may* be held by *zero, one or many* customers.

Three strategies in Figure 13.1 are relevant to Figure 13.5 – the *Market Analysis, Market Needs Analysis* and *Customer Satisfaction* strategies, repeated for reference as follows:

> ***Market Analysis:*** *'Based on organizations selected from the market data strategy, establish and maintain a regular market analysis capability so we can determine current and potential size of markets that management identify, together with their projected growth. Identify existing and potential competition in those markets, and their relative market shares.'*

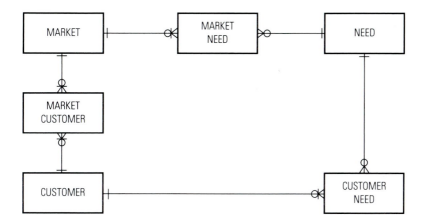

Figure 13.5 Partial strategic data map for market analysis and market research.

Market Needs Analysis: 'For potential markets selected by management for possible entry, and for all markets where we operate, regularly determine the needs of existing and potential customers in those markets.'

Customer Satisfaction: 'Implement regular surveys of our customer satisfaction in selected markets, in conjunction with the market needs analysis strategy, to identify areas where we can improve; and also to determine customer needs which we do not yet address.'

We will examine the *Market Analysis* strategy first. Markets are made up of customers, as shown in Figure 13.5. The customers of XYZ are organizations, and also individual personal customers. Organizations are private sector customers such as companies, or public sector customers such as government departments. We can show these types of customers in a 4BNF data map in Figure 13.6.

The *Market Analysis* strategy refers to competition: competitors compete with XYZ for customers. Private sector organizations, public sector organizations, competitors and XYZ itself all are organizations of interest. Personal customers are not only individuals, but also joint persons such as husband and wife, or family units: collectively referred to as 'personal organizations'. In fact, XYZ uses the term 'organization' to refer to all of the above. (If XYZ operated in the legal or law enforcement industries, we instead might use the term: LEGAL ENTITY, rather than ORGANIZATION. A person is a legal entity, referred to as a 'natural person'. A company, partnership or government department is also a legal entity: referred to as a 'corporate person'.)

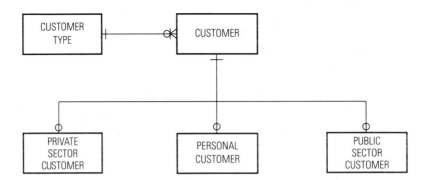

Figure 13.6   Initial data map for customers.

XYZ is interested in 'organizations'. Rather than model customers as illustrated above – which excludes competitors – the XYZ managers decide to view organizations from a different perspective, as shown in Figure 13.7.

This partial data map of organizations is still not satisfactory: it does not allow us easily to determine the role of each organization in its dealings with XYZ. For example, we indicated that private and government organizations are customers. But competitors are not customers. (Or perhaps they may be, in some circumstances.) And XYZ is not a customer: it is a supplier to its customers. Further, some customers are also suppliers to XYZ. How can we represent all of these different roles?

The clue is in the question. We know that organizations have many roles: as customers, suppliers, or competitors; and some organizations can have different roles at the same time. These roles may be carried out with formal or informal agreements: formally by a customer sales agreement, or informally by a customer sales order; by a supplier purchase agreement, or

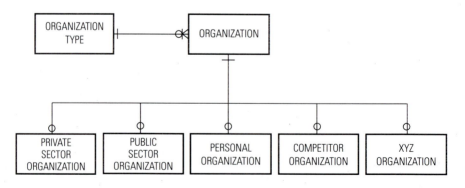

Figure 13.7   Data map for organizations.

a supplier purchase order; or by a support services agreement (supporting a customer, or supported by a supplier).

We map this in Figure 13.8 with different organizations related according to role: using a *mandatory one to mandatory one or many* association between the ORGANIZATION and ORGANIZATION ROLE principal entities; and a similar association between the AGREEMENT and ORGANIZATION ROLE principal entities. An organization, to be of interest to XYZ, *must* have one or many defined roles: as a customer, as a supplier, or as a competitor. So that mutual responsibilities are well defined, XYZ management have specified that an agreement (whether formal or informal) *must* exist for XYZ to do business with its customers or suppliers: there are many agreements, for different roles. Indirect agreements also exist for competitors: these are support services agreements between XYZ and its market research firm, selected (in Chapter 9) to provide market research information about XYZ's competitors. Figure 13.8 shows these associations.

The ORGANIZATION secondary entities: PRIVATE SECTOR ORGANIZATION, PUBLIC SECTOR ORGANIZATION and PERSONAL ORGANIZATION are defined as discussed earlier. The ORGANIZATION ROLE secondary entities are defined as: CUSTOMER, SUPPLIER and COMPETITOR. Rather than define secondary entities for formal and informal agreements, we define: CUSTOMER SALES

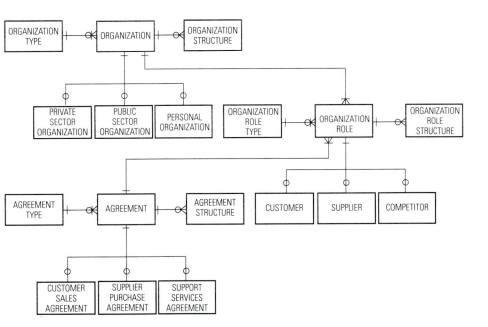

Figure 13.8 Organization Role partial strategic data map.

Table 13.2   Customer, supplier and competitor roles

	ORGANIZATION ROLE STRUCTURE		
Organization	**Organization Role**	**Related Organization**	**Related Organization Role**
XYZ Corporation	Supplier	KLM Limited	Customer
		MNO Incorporated	Customer
		PTC Corporation	Customer
XYZ Corporation	Customer	Brink Incorporated	Supplier
		PMM Corporation	Supplier
XYZ Corporation	Competitor	MPP Incorporated	Competitor
		PXM Limited	Competitor
		Brink Incorporated	Competitor

AGREEMENT; SUPPLIER PURCHASE AGREEMENT; and SUPPORT SERVICES AGREEMENT as explicit secondary entities of AGREEMENT. These entities are defined by applying the 4BNF rule of business normalization: rule 2(b) earlier.

Figure 13.8 also includes three additional entities: ORGANIZATION STRUCTURE; ORGANIZATION ROLE STRUCTURE; and AGREEMENT STRUCTURE. These result from applying rule 2(c) to decompose recursive associations between occurrences of principal and/or secondary entities. The examples discussed in Tables 13.2 and 13.3 illustrate the power of these 5BNF entities. Table 13.2 shows the role of organizations in their dealings with XYZ: as customers, suppliers or competitors. Table 13.3 lists related organizations: parent companies, subsidiary companies and major shareholders. We will examine some of the data that typically reside in these 5BNF tables.

Table 13.3   Related organizations

	ORGANIZATION STRUCTURE		
Organization	**Organization Type**	**Related Organization**	**Related Organization Type**
ABC Corporation	Parent Company	KLM Limited	Subsidiary Company
		MNO Incorporated	Subsidiary Company
		PTC Corporation	Subsidiary Company
		Brink Incorporated	Subsidiary Company
PXM Limited	Parent Company	MPP Incorporated	Subsidiary Company
		PMM Corporation	Subsidiary Company
MNO Incorporated	Major Shareholder	PXM Limited	Parent Company

We can see in Table 13.2 that XYZ is a supplier to KLM Limited, MNO Incorporated and PTC Corporation, each of which thus has a role as a customer. Similarly XYZ is a customer to Brink Incorporated and PMM Corporation: who are its suppliers. Finally, XYZ competes with MPP Incorporated, PXM Limited and Brink Incorporated.

We see from this table that Brink Incorporated is both a supplier and a competitor of XYZ Corporation. XYZ's supplier purchase agreement with Brink thus may need special confidentiality and restraint clauses, to protect XYZ from predatory withholding of supplies because of Brink's conflicting role also as a competitor. But this is not the only danger to XYZ, as Table 13.3 indicates.

We can see that Brink is a subsidiary company of ABC Corporation. However ABC is also the parent of KLM, MNO and PTC: we saw in Table 13.2 that these companies are all customers of XYZ. Their customer sales agreements should include confidentiality clauses to prevent them from supplying confidential information about XYZ to Brink, which is a sister company. Similar clauses should be included in the supplier purchase agreements between XYZ and PMM Corporation, as PMM and MPP Incorporated – another competitor of XYZ – also have the same parent: PXM Limited. Finally, we can see that MNO is a major shareholder of PXM: MNO as a customer therefore also has a conflicting indirect interest in competitor MPP.

XYZ's performance in delivering goods and services under a customer sales agreement may be dependent also on the performance of suppliers in providing raw materials to XYZ based on supplier purchase agreements. A similar approach to that in Table 13.2 can be used with the 5BNF entity AGREEMENT STRUCTURE, indicating that certain customer and supplier agreements are related.

Data which is in 5BNF (as in Tables 13.2 and 13.3) is not fixed: it is very dynamic – particularly in the competitive environment of the 1990s and beyond – with mergers, takeovers and share acquisitions. Restraint, conflict of interest and confidentiality clauses would all normally be part of any legal agreements, and must be worded to address this dynamic environment.

These examples are obvious: 5BNF has done nothing new except to make this data more accessible and able to be analyzed. But the examples used here illustrate a number of principles: structure entities contain dynamic data, generally external to the modeled area of the business, representing vital expert knowledge. (We saw other examples of 5BNF entities used to record expert knowledge in Chapter 4). If this expert knowledge is captured and analyzed such as discussed using 5BNF, it can offer great competitive advantage. We will see other examples as we continue strategic modeling using the XYZ strategies.

We now need to include the Organization Role entities from Figure 13.8 in the Market Analysis data map in Figure 13.5. We also need to examine the *Market Analysis* and *Market Needs Analysis* strategies from Figure 13.1 further:

> **Market Analysis:** *'Based on organizations selected from the market data strategy, establish and maintain a regular market analysis capability so we can determine current and potential size of markets that management identify, together with their projected growth. Identify existing and potential competition in those markets, and their relative market shares.'*

This suggests an association between MARKET and ORGANIZATION ROLE, shown in Figure 13.9: each organization active in a market exists as a customer, supplier, competitor, or any combination of these. A market will have *one or many* organization roles, where each role relates to one market. There may be secondary market entities of interest to XYZ; but we will only consider the principal entity MARKET.

> **Market Needs Analysis:** *'For potential markets selected by management for possible entry, and for all markets where we operate, regularly determine the needs of existing and potential customers in those markets.'*

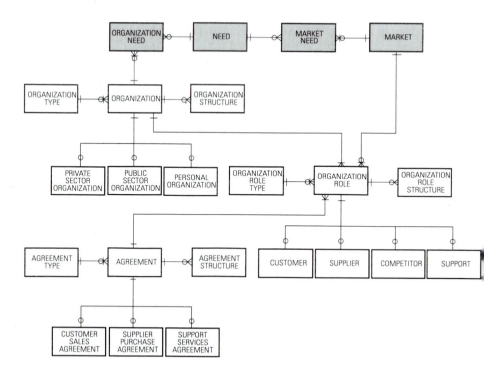

Figure 13.9 Market analysis and market research strategic map. New entities are shown shaded.

Needs are also important, related to markets as in Figure 13.5. This further modeling is shown shaded in Figure 13.9. The needs of each market can be determined: these needs can then be related to each organization. A market is linked to organizations who participate in it as customers, suppliers or competitors (see ORGANIZATION ROLE).

Let us now look at the *Customer Satisfaction* strategy again:

> **Customer Satisfaction:** *'Implement regular surveys of our customer satisfaction in selected markets, in conjunction with the market needs analysis strategy, to identify areas where we can improve; and also to determine customer needs which we do not yet address.'*

This suggests the entity SURVEY and the intersecting entity MARKET SURVEY. The association between MARKET and ORGANIZATION ROLE now enables us to survey not only customers, but also suppliers. Furthermore, during those surveys we can also obtain details of customers' and suppliers' needs, and their activity with competitors.

The entity PERFORMANCE is also suggested by the strategies above; modeled in a preliminary form in Figure 13.4. However we will defer modeling of performance until Chapter 14.

The regular market analysis required by these strategies, together with projected growth rates, indicate that time is important. Rather than model time directly, we will introduce a more flexible representation: PERIOD. A time period is defined with a start date and time, and a duration – from which is derived the end date and time of the period. A duration of zero indicates a point in time. Or instead a start date and time is defined, together with an end date and time – from which the duration can be derived. By also indicating the unit of measure for a time period, the duration can be expressed in years, months, weeks, days, hours, minutes or seconds. Different time periods of interest can thus be defined: for accounting, reporting or performance periods. These are all secondary entities of period.

This offers great flexibility. For example, accounting periods are normally monthly. But this enables us to define differing accounting periods in parts of the organization as required: quarterly, weekly, or daily accounting periods. Similarly, reporting periods can be defined differently as required. Performance can also be monitored according to different time periods again: either daily, hourly . . . or every nanosecond in real-time or process control systems, for example.

This leads us to the next priority area of concern to XYZ management: the *Financial* Strategies defined in Figure 13.1. The first relates to *Asset Disposal*:

> **Asset Disposal:** *'Identify assets which cannot provide a return within two years consistent with the mission ROI, and dispose of them at the best possible price.'*

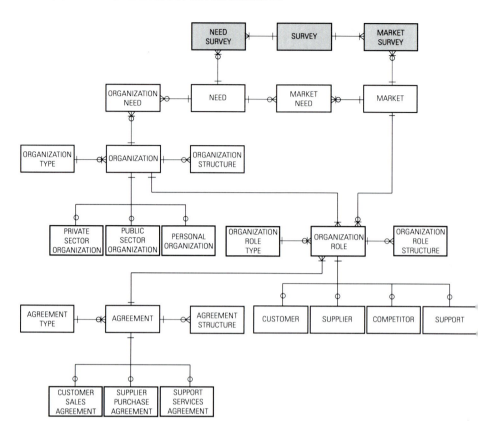

Figure 13.10 Customer satisfaction surveys included in strategic map. New entities are shown shaded.

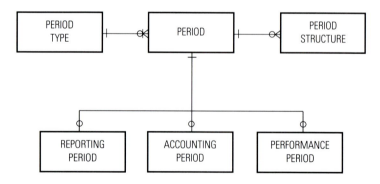

Figure 13.11 Time can be modeled flexibly by using PERIOD.

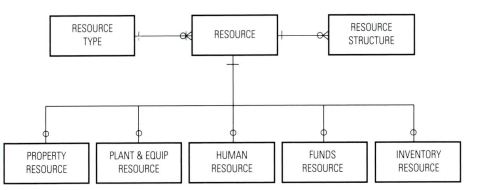

Figure 13.12   Data map for resources.

Assets are resources: generally property, or plant and equipment. Resources that do not achieve the mission ROI of 20% should be sold. Other resources are: human resources, funds and inventory. These are all secondary entities of RESOURCE. They are related in a 5BNF RESOURCE STRUCTURE entity. This identifies those resources which are used together, such as plant and equipment, raw materials (from inventory), funds and human resources used to produce products. These are illustrated in Figure 13.12.

Resources must be managed to ensure they provide a satisfactory return on the funds invested in them. This return is indicated in the financial balance sheets for XYZ. The *Financial Reporting* strategy defined in Figure 13.1 is important:

> **Financial Reporting:** *'Implement flexible financial reporting systems able to be introduced at any organizational level, and which can provide profit and loss statements for any defined reporting frequency, with associated balance sheet statements.'*

Balance sheets show assets and liabilities, reflected in the resources of an organization. Profit and loss statements show revenue and expenses: revenue is obtained from sale or usage of products from inventory; expenses reflect use of resources. Flexible financial reports must be available at any organizational level, and for any defined period: yearly, quarterly, monthly, weekly . . . or even daily if required. Budgets are also important:

> **Budget Control:** *'Establish and maintain strong budgetary controls for all expenditure, linked directly to revenue achievement. All financial statements must clearly show actual revenue and expenditure against budget, and indicate percentage change from the previous reporting period.'*

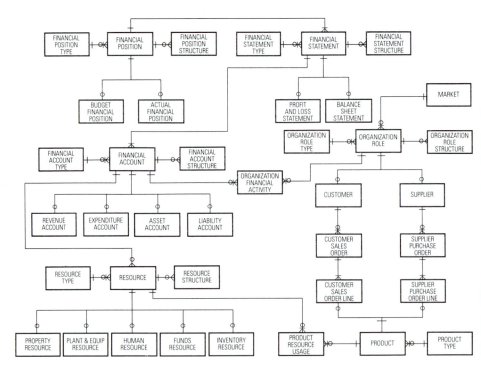

Figure 13.13 Financial strategic map. All entities are new, except for OR-GANIZATION ROLE and MARKET.

The actual financial position at any organizational level in each period, as shown by the financial statements, is compared to the budget financial position for that period. The variance of actual against budget, and the percentage change from the previous period, are of interest to management. These financial strategies are modeled in Figure 13.13.

A financial statement has one or many financial accounts. Resources are charged to financial accounts: as revenue, expenditure, assets or liabilities. Resources are used by products: in their production, support, delivery, maintenance or storage – as shown by the PRODUCT RESOURCE USAGE intersecting entity: this represents the Production function. Organizations are involved in product orders: either as customers or suppliers; through customer sales orders or supplier purchase orders – comprising order lines for required products. ORGANIZATION FINANCIAL ACTIV-ITY is an intersecting entity: charging supplier or customer orders to expenditure or revenue financial accounts as relevant. This represents the Production function also, for suppliers, or the Sales and Distribution function for customers.

This strategic map supports the Financial strategies in Figure 13.1. Financial statements can be prepared for any period, to reflect the financial activity of any organization: a customer or a supplier, or (from the ORGANIZATION ROLE to ORGANIZATION association in Figure 13.10) any part of XYZ itself. ORGANIZATION STRUCTURE (in Figure 13.5) allows any level of an organization to be defined, or any organization structure, and its hierarchical reporting structure. The ORGANIZATION FINANCIAL ACTIVITY entity charges each activity, based on the role of the relevant organization, to an appropriate financial account. These accounts are summarized in FINANCIAL STATEMENT; actual position is compared against budget position in FINANCIAL POSITION. The Financial strategies are thus supported.

MARKET has a *one to many* association with ORGANIZATION ROLE. We can thus determine the financial activity of all organizations in a market (customers, suppliers, and even competitors). Given that relevant information about customers and suppliers is available, the strategic map in Figure 13.13 also supports the *Market Exit* financial strategy in Figure 13.1:

> **Market Exit:** *'Identify markets which are unprofitable and in decline, and exit those markets at the lowest possible cost.'*

The strategic map grows as we progressively define intersecting and principal entities, together with associated type, secondary and structure entities. Data entities represent specific parts of the business, and the data needed to manage them. Intersecting entities at this level represent major business functions, as we have seen: at more detailed levels they represent tactical and operational systems. The associations joining data entities represent: communication paths, reporting paths, or strategies and procedures defined to run the business. A strategic map, developed from a strategic plan, is thus a blueprint of the business; it also indicates the data and functions needed to operate the business. In Chapter 14 we will use it to evaluate alternative organization structures.

As the strategic map becomes more detailed, we will find it useful to abstract it to a higher level: as a **subject map**. This form of the strategic map includes only principal and intersecting entities. Type, secondary and structure entities are subsumed into their relevant principal entity, shown by a solid border. They can all be fully displayed at the strategic map level when required. Figure 13.14 illustrates the subject map for XYZ, based on the principal and intersecting entities from Figures 13.10 and 13.13.

We can clearly see representation of the *Market Needs Analysis* strategy in Figure 13.14, shown by the MARKET, SURVEY, NEED and ORGANIZATION principal entities, and their corresponding intersecting entities. The *Market Analysis* strategy is shown by MARKET, ORGANIZATION, AGREEMENT and ORGANIZATION ROLE.

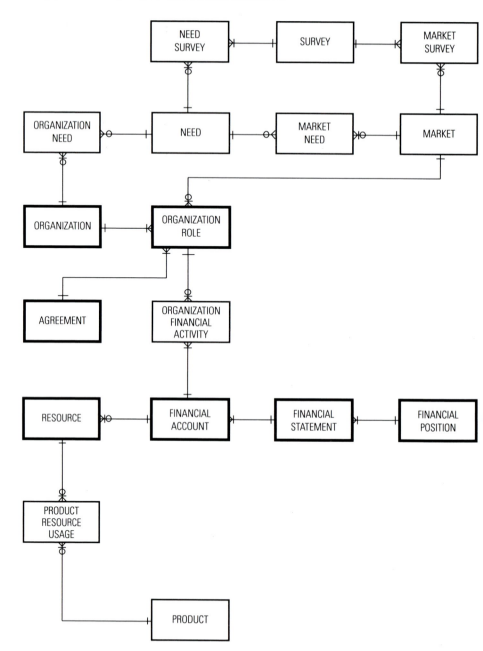

Figure 13.14 XYZ subject map for market analysis, market research and finance. A solid border for an entity indicates that more detailed type, secondary and structure entities exist.

The *Financial* strategies from Figure 13.1 are shown in Figure 13.14 by principal entities FINANCIAL POSITION, FINANCIAL STATEMENT, FINANCIAL ACCOUNT and RESOURCE. The intersecting entity OR-GANIZATION FINANCIAL ACTIVITY represents the Sales and Distribution function and the Production function, which also includes PRODUCT RESOURCE USAGE.

The remaining *Customer Satisfaction* and *Market Research* strategies in Figure 13.1 still need to be addressed, as well as the *Innovation, Production, Personnel* and *Acquisition* strategies. We will progressively add these to the subject map in Figure 13.14, showing the relevant strategic map detail only when necessary. We will start with the Market Research proactive strategies of *Product Pricing* and *Advertising*.

> **Product Pricing:** *'Set aggressive price reductions in key cash flow products of Competitor X based on the Market Analysis strategy, to encourage similar price reductions by X. Reduce XYZ costs for these lower-priced products to maintain profitability.'*

The main factor in setting price reductions for key cash flow products is still to maintain profitability. This implies close financial control of products. The intersecting entity PRODUCT FINANCIAL ACTIVITY represents the Product Financial Control function between FINANCIAL ACCOUNT and PRODUCT. Financial statements of product profitability are thus obtained as Product Profit and Loss statements, and also Product Balance Sheet statements if relevant. A budget financial position can be set for each future period (as annual, monthly or other period budgets), and later compared to the actual financial position achieved in those periods. This is shown in Figure 13.15.

> **Advertising:** *'Develop an advertising campaign which emphasizes: price reductions from the Product Pricing strategy; product customization and flexible job lot capability from the Production strategies; and also needs and benefits highlighted by the Product Release strategy and the Market Needs Analysis strategy.'*

The *Advertising* strategy in Market Research emphasizes needs and benefits satisfied by products, as well as the flexibility and customization from the Production strategies. PRODUCT NEED is thus indicated in Figure 13.15, representing part of the Product Development function. Notice that this NEED entity is shown with a *shaded border* for the entity box. This indicates that NEED has been defined elsewhere in the subject map, where it appears with an unshaded border.

Figure 13.15 shows ADVERTISING CAMPAIGN. The Advertising function shown by PRODUCT ADVERTISING is associated with the

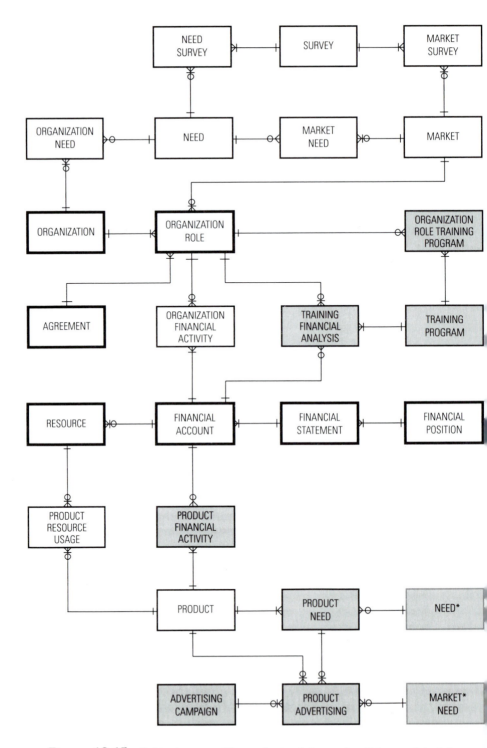

Figure 13.15 Subject map with product pricing, advertising and training strategies included. New entities are shaded. Asterisk entities are repeated.

ADVERTISING CAMPAIGN, PRODUCT, PRODUCT NEED and MAR-KET NEED entities: the latter with a *shaded border* as it is defined else-where. The *optional becoming mandatory* nature of these associations reflects management direction that there *will* eventually be advertising for every product, in some form.

The *Training* Customer Satisfaction strategy relates to training of sales and support staff for their role in providing support to customers, and also direct training of customers.

> *Training:* '*Establish and maintain sales training, support staff training and customer training programs which will maximize business opportunities and achieve satisfactory profit in all markets in which we operate.*'

Sales and support staff are collectively represented by the entity SUPPORT, added as another secondary entity to ORGANIZATION ROLE (Figure 13.10), shown shaded in Figure 13.16.

Figure 13.15 includes TRAINING PROGRAM. Training programs are carried out for customers and support staff, as indicated by the inter-secting entity ORGANIZATION ROLE TRAINING PROGRAM. This is the Training function to manage ORGANIZATION ROLE and TRAIN-ING PROGRAM. It can be used not only for training customers, and sales and support staff, but also for training staff who deal with suppliers – or for training suppliers themselves, if relevant. Further, we see from above that we can train sales and support staff about competitors and their products: this knowledge will enable XYZ staff thus to be more effective in selling to, or supporting, customers.

We need to manage training programs financially in relation to markets, as indicated by the last part of the strategy. MARKET is related to

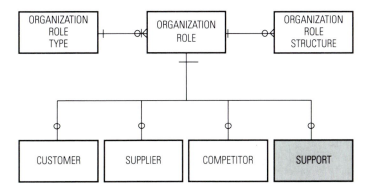

Figure 13.16 Data map showing the support organization role.

ORGANIZATION ROLE as we saw in Figures 13.13 and 13.14. The intersecting entity TRAINING FINANCIAL ANALYSIS supports this direct financial analysis in Figure 13.15.

We will now examine Innovation strategies from Figure 13.1, shown in Figure 13.17.

> **R&D:** *'Establish and maintain a research and development capability which can design or enhance new or existing products and services based on the needs identified from the market needs analysis strategy.'*

This strategy establishes the R&D function to design products which satisfy specific market needs. The intersecting entity PRODUCT DESIGN PROJECT represents this at the subject map level, with associations to PROJECT, MARKET NEED, PRODUCT NEED and also PRODUCT as shown in Figure 13.17.

> **R&D Funding:** *'Ensure that adequate funding of the R&D strategy is provided, and provide an environment to attract and retain high quality R&D staff.'*

This implies financial management and control of projects, as indicated by PROJECT FINANCIAL CONTROL. As funds and staff are resources, it also implies PROJECT RESOURCE USAGE. These intersecting entities represent R&D functions of Project Financial Management and Project Resource Allocation (see Figure 13.17).

> **Technology Monitoring:** *'Monitor and evaluate all technologies that may be relevant to our business, as well as those specific to markets identified by management from the market needs analysis strategy.'*

Technologies are of interest. We saw that market needs indicate appropriate product needs: not all of the required needs may be addressed by current technologies. New technologies may be necessary, with new product solutions to satisfy those needs. Projects are established for those technologies that address specific needs. The entity PROJECT NEED TECHNOLOGY, with associations to TECHNOLOGY, PROJECT and NEED represents the Technology Monitoring function of R&D. Figure 13.17 also includes these entities.

> **Product Maintenance Improvement:** *'Together with R&D, define, develop and implement design or production improvements which will result in a significant reduction in the cost of product maintenance and repair.'*

This implies product financial control at the strategic level, shown in the subject map of Figure 13.17 by PRODUCT FINANCIAL ACTIVITY and

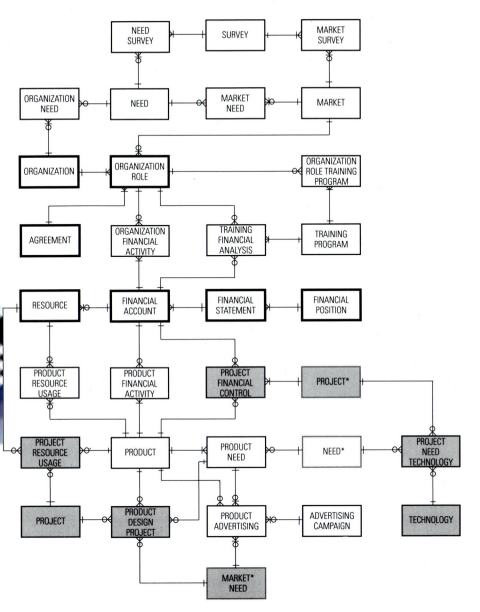

Figure 13.17 Subject map with R&D. New entities are shaded. Asterisk entities are repeated.

PRODUCT RESOURCE USAGE. This strategy will lead to the definition of more detailed entities at the tactical level. With PRODUCT DESIGN PROJECT and PROJECT FINANCIAL CONTROL, this addresses the *Product Review* strategy, one of the Production strategies from Figure 13.1.

> *Product Review: 'Establish criteria to evaluate all existing products and all new products under development for market acceptance and profitability. Ensure that existing products are withdrawn and new products are terminated which no longer satisfy those criteria.'*

The Product Release strategy next, is also supported:

> *Product Release: 'Guide and direct product introduction strategies and associated advertising campaigns which emphasize the market needs addressed by those products, and their other benefits over existing products on the market.'*

PRODUCT ADVERTISING has already been defined in Figure 13.17, associated with PRODUCT, PRODUCT NEED, MARKET NEED and ADVERTISING CAMPAIGN. However the *Custom Product Analysis* and *Custom Product Development* strategies next, will require some further definition of PRODUCT.

> *Custom Product Analysis: 'Identify products with a need for customization and/or flexible job lot sizes, based on the Market Needs Analysis and Customer Satisfaction strategies.'*

> *Custom Product Development: 'Establish a product customization capability and the ability to handle flexible job lot sizes, based on the Custom Product Analysis strategies.'*

XYZ produces not only standard products, but also custom products, as shown in Figure 13.18. This requires different processes and production management at tactical and operational levels. We will not develop the strategic map to that level now, but the STANDARD PRODUCT and CUSTOM PRODUCT secondary entities are included with PRODUCT. A custom product may be based on a standard product, but with specific customization. PRODUCT STRUCTURE is also useful to show these interrelationships.

PRODUCT will therefore be shown on the subject map with a heavy border, to indicate the existence of these type, secondary and structure entities. Later, during tactical and operational modeling, additional secondary entities of ASSEMBLY, SUBASSEMBLY and COMPONENT ITEM could be added. PRODUCT STRUCTURE would thus not only show custom

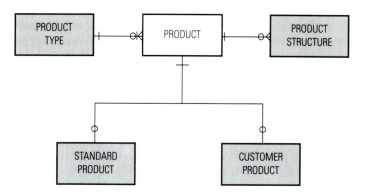

Figure 13.18   Data map for products.

products which are based on (related to) standard products: it can be used to define the Bills of Material to produce each product from relevant assemblies, subassemblies and component items. It can also provide a 'where used' capability, to identify the products in which specific items, subassemblies or assemblies are used.

We will leave strategic modeling of the remaining *Quality Control* Production strategy until we address the question of performance monitoring in Chapter 14. We will now address the *Personnel* strategies.

> *Career Planning:* 'Establish and maintain a program of at least annual personal appraisal reviews which plan future job promotion and other career development moves with every employee on an individual basis. Reviews are to be seen as acknowledgements of personal performance improvement or rewards for excellent performance, rather than as punishment for poor performance.'

> *Staff Incentives:* 'Together with the career planning strategy, provide incentive programs which reward and acknowledge high performers.'

These strategies relate to the performance of personnel. During tactical and operational modeling they can be defined in relation to PERSON. But it is not appropriate to move to that detail at this time. At the strategic level, persons are represented by the secondary entity HUMAN RESOURCE. This suggests human resource performance monitoring, which we will also address shortly.

The remaining strategy in Figure 13.1 is the *Acquisition* strategy:

> *Competitor Acquisition:* 'Initiate discussions with Competitor X to determine its likely acquisition cost. If acceptable to both, acquire it: if possible at less cost than the proposed campaign.'

This is a tactical strategy, focused on acquiring Competitor X. The cost of acquisition should be less than the proposed advertising campaign, if possible. This implies more detailed tactical modeling involving ADVERTIS-ING CAMPAIGN, RESOURCE, and the financial entities of Figure 13.13. No new entities are added to the strategic map.

We have now modeled most of the strategies in 13.1, and have developed a strategic map, a blueprint of data and information needed to manage and operate an organization. It is ready for more detailed defini-tion in Chapter 14, to allow flexible performance monitoring in any areas identified by management. We will then use the strategic model to define appropriate organization structures for XYZ. We will summarize Chapters 13 and 14, and also earlier chapters of this Part 3, at the end of Chapter 14.

CHAPTER 14

Defining Organization Structure

This chapter shows how the strategic map which we developed for XYZ Corporation in Chapter 13 can be used to evaluate different organization structures. It describes the definition of strategic attributes that complete the strategic model, ready for strategic implementation. This is carried out by tactical, operational and process modeling to design and develop detailed data bases and information systems needed to support managers and staff at all levels of the organization.

But first we will discuss the concepts of dynamic modeling: this advanced modeling technique leads to the development of information systems that offer great power and flexibility to management for performance monitoring. It provides a vital mechanism to support the rapid organizational change that will be the norm of the 1990s and beyond.

14.1 DYNAMIC MODELING

Dynamic modeling refers to the development of strategic, tactical and operational models that are defined in generic terms, allowing relevant systems to be implemented rapidly and also to be modified dynamically during operation. We saw one example of this capability when we discussed structure entities: these allow expert knowledge about interrelated entity occurrences to be introduced during system operation (see Tables 13.2 and 13.3). Other examples are performance monitoring and documentation.

Performance monitoring occurs in every organization. It is either managed explicitly to achieve acceptable performance in areas indicated by management, or (as we saw with Galbraith [1] in Chapter 8) by its omission it leads to reduced performance standards. Areas where performance is to be monitored are not fixed: the focus for performance monitoring will change many times over the life of an organization. We need to be able to define performance criteria dynamically, and attach these criteria to any data we wish to monitor.

Product specifications are examples of static documentation which must be managed. **Dynamic documentation** is also important, but is not well managed. For example, an order may have special comments or instructions which must be followed, or a product may require reference to special notes at a particular point. In real life, we write notes to each other to ensure these things are done. These notes are dynamic, such as yellow 'sticky notes' which are attached temporarily for reference. An electronic 'sticky notes' capability would be particularly useful. We will develop a generic model, which will allow us to define performance criteria, or provide notes, that can be dynamically associated with any data in the resulting data bases and systems developed using the methods described in this book.

In my earlier book [2], I discussed the use of objectives for performance monitoring and exception reporting. Figure 11.5 of that book shows a typical decision early warning graph for management. This is repeated here as Figure 14.1.

This plots the value of a performance criterion (Y-axis) against a time period (X-axis). In each period, managers define upper and lower performance values indicating a range of acceptable performance. A target value in the range is also defined for achievement at each period. An actual performance value falling outside the defined range for a period is unacceptable: the responsible manager is notified on an exception basis. Figure 14.1 is one form of performance graph. Other forms include average control charts and range control charts used for Total Quality Control (TQC) and Total Quality Management (TQM). This is discussed shortly.

Figure 14.1 shows that the actual values can also indicate a trend towards unacceptable performance after several periods. Resources such as people, funds or equipment may be needed to change this performance trend in real life. There may be a lead time before these resources can be allocated to the problem area, called the **resource lead time**; further time may be needed before they have an effect on the performance trend, called the **resource lag time**. Together with a **safety factor**, the sum of these is the total elapsed period before a decision to apply the resources will take effect: called the **decision early warning period**. The trend in Figure 14.1 allows an early decision to be made, so that the allocated resources will take effect just before performance moves outside the acceptable range.

Addison-Wesley Publishing Company

One Jacob Way

READING, MASSACHUSETTS 01867

(617) 944-3700

November 13, 1992

Belden Menkus
Journal of Systems Management
P.O. Box 129
Hillsboro, TN 37342

Dear Belden,

Allow me to introduce myself, my name is Tiffany Moore. I am the Marketing Assistant in the Corporate & Professional Publishing Group at Addison-Wesley. Please feel free to contact me directly for future review copies as well as any questions about this book.

I am pleased to present you with Clive Finkelstein's *Information Engineering*. Strategic planning and systems development are both disciplines that are merging today. Information technology is now recognized as having the potential to create competitive advantage; therefore systems must be capable of supporting the strategic plans of an organization.

Information Engineering uses a practical, "how-to" approach for tying strategic planning to MIS at all levels of an organization, both commercial and government. This is a step-by-step method to help your readers apply information technology in their own environment.

The cost of the book is $50.50 and the ISBN # is 0-201-50988-1. If you would like to provide your readers with ordering information our toll free phone number is (800) 238-9682. If you do mention this book in any publication I would appreciate receiving a tear sheet. Please call me if you have additional questions at (617) 944-3700 x2714.

Sincerely,

Tiffany A. Moore
Marketing Assistant
Corporate & Professional Publishing Group

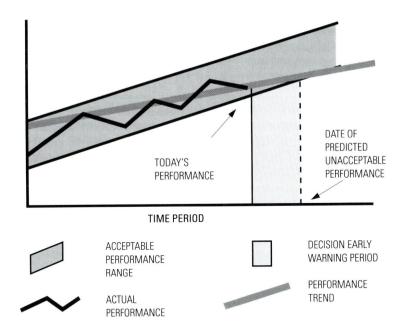

Figure 14.1   A decision early warning trend analysis graph.

Performance criteria are based on objectives set by management. A PERSON may have many objectives, and is to be notified if performance against objectives is unacceptable. An OBJECTIVE will have *one or many* PERFORMANCE CRITERION used in its measurement. OBJECTIVE PERFORMANCE reflects the fact that a performance criterion may apply to more than one objective. This entity provides the data for the decision early warning graph in Figure 14.1. It contains attributes: *upper value, lower value, target value, actual value, early warning period, early warning units*, all prefixed by the qualifier *objective performance*. The *actual value* is derived by a procedure, which depends on the performance criterion. A procedure may be manual or automated, involving tasks carried out in a defined sequence. PROCEDURE and TASK are both secondary entities of the entity PROCESS. PROCESS STRUCTURE indicates how tasks are used in procedures. Figure 14.2 shows the data map defined for performance monitoring to this point.

PROCESS STRUCTURE is the procedure manual of tasks for manual processes; it is the job control library, and also the program library for automated processes. A procedure may be a computer job, with programs as the tasks of that job in a job control library. A program is also a procedure, with subroutines as tasks. In turn, these are procedures with program instructions as tasks: all in a program library.

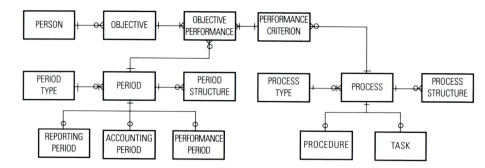

Figure 14.2   A performance monitoring data map (incomplete).

An objective is defined by a person (a manager), with relevant performance criteria. Values for performance monitoring are defined (in OBJECTIVE PERFORMANCE). Each performance criterion is further defined in terms of the process used to derive an actual value for the criterion. This process is invoked for each performance period automatically, deriving the actual value for that period. This value is compared against the target value and range. If unacceptable, the relevant person is notified.

The decision early warning trend analysis graph in Figure 14.1 assumes a controlled, predictable process. In contrast, many processes are uncontrolled and unpredictable. A different approach to that described above is appropriate to these processes. Dr W. A. Shewhart, in his work at Bell Laboratories in the 1920s, developed a theory that he used to predict the limits of variation – summarized in three rules:

(1)   All processes display variation;
(2)   Some processes display controlled variation;
(3)   Other processes display uncontrolled variation.

Shewhart's methods were refined by Dr W. Edwards Deming, leading to a new management philosophy. In the late 1940s and early 1950s Deming was invited many times to Japan to conduct a series of seminars and lectures. As described by McConnell [3], he told the Japanese that:

> *'If they adopted his approach to quality all their problems would be over in but a few years and they would take their place among the world's most prosperous nations. The rest is history.'*

In Australia his method is known as Total Quality Control (TQC) applied through Total Quality Management (TQM); in the USA it is called the Deming Method; in Japan it is known as Company Wide Quality Control. Deming indicated that:

'Good quality does not necessarily mean high quality. It means a predictable degree of uniformity and dependability at low cost, with a quality suited to the market.'

Shewhart's average control charts and range control charts, and the work of Deming, are outside the scope of this book. McConnell's book is an excellent reference to the use of these charts. These can be modeled similarly to OBJECTIVE PERFORMANCE described above, and used in conjunction with Generic Performance Monitoring discussed shortly.

We saw in Table 13.1 that there are many intersecting entities used for performance monitoring. Other entities are suggested by the Quality Control, Career Planning and Staff Incentives strategies from Figure 13.1 that we left until this section. During tactical and operational modeling we will see other intersecting entities for performance: in fact we can suffix almost any entity with the word 'performance', and it will suggest other performance monitoring which is relevant. How can we model this dynamic situation? The answer is to model the data as meta-data.

We are interested in data, stored as tables in a data base as shown in Figure 14.3. Each entity is a data base table; each attribute is a column of rows in the table for the entity. A performance criterion represents object data which is attached to any row in any column and table of interest; the process attached to the performance criterion indicates the logic that is to be associated with that object data. Rows that apply to the criterion are defined according to specific data base conditions that are associated with the object data. This approach permits performance criteria to be defined dynamically. The data, logic and conditions associated with OBJECT DATA in Figure

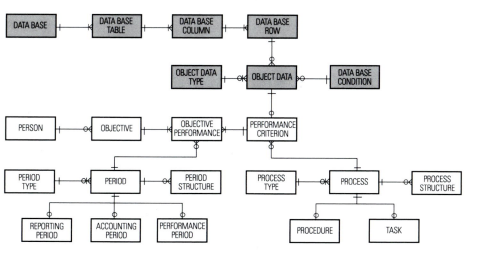

Figure 14.3 Dynamic performance monitoring data map.

14.3 can be implemented using process modeling (see Chapters 4 and 5) with either conventional or object-oriented programming techniques.

In addition to PERFORMANCE CRITERION, other secondary entities can be defined. One example relates to SECURITY CONTROL. Passwords, or other security controls, can also be defined dynamically; they can be attached to any data base, table, column, row or condition as relevant.

We can now implement generic performance monitoring, as illustrated by the following scenario.

14.1.1   Generic performance monitoring

The Production Manager of XYZ Corporation has instituted changes to reduce the production reject rate for Product A from a range of 3%-5% rejects at present, down to 0.5%-2.5% within the next 6 weeks, for quality control purposes. He needs to monitor reject rates of Product A over this time to determine whether the changes are having an effect. He will register performance criteria based on the PRODUCT entity.

We will see in Part 4, after operational modeling, that the PRODUCT entity contains the primary keys: *product id#*, *period id#*, and the non-key attributes: *product total accepted this period, product total rejected this period*. From these are calculated the derived attributes: {*product reject percent this period*}, {*product reject change percent from previous period*}.

XYZ Corporation uses SQL. The Production Manager is not a computer expert, so he uses a systems analyst to write SQL queries for him. He enters a procedure using SQL commands to calculate these values, names this procedure 'Product Reject Monitoring', and saves it. He specifies conditions which define the products to be monitored in an SQL WHERE clause, names and saves it as the 'Product Reject Monitoring' condition.

At his terminal he calls the Performance Registration System (developed from the data map in Figure 14.3). After entering his password, he first registers the Product Reject Objective and registers two performance criteria associated with it. These he calls: 'Product Rejects' and 'Product Reject Change Rate'. He attaches these to the 'Product Reject Monitoring' procedure defined earlier.

The system knows he is authorized to use the Production data base: it displays the names of all tables he is authorized to use. He selects PRODUCT. The column names of PRODUCT are displayed: he first selects {*product reject percent this period*} for the Product Reject criterion, and then {*product reject change percent from previous period*} for the 'Project Reject Change Rate' criterion. For each criterion he registers the 'Product Reject Monitoring' condition to identify the products which are to be monitored. He has now completed registration. He can change conditions

Table 14.1 Performance monitoring values for Product Rejects

<table>
<tr><td colspan="6" align="center">**Decision Early Warning Values**</td></tr>
<tr><td colspan="3">Objective: *Product Reject Objective*</td><td colspan="3">Manager: *Production Manager*</td></tr>
<tr><td colspan="3">Criterion: *Product Rejects*</td><td colspan="3">Procedure: *Product Reject Monitoring*</td></tr>
<tr><td colspan="3">Condition: *Product Reject Monitoring*</td><td colspan="3">Frequency: *Weekly*</td></tr>
</table>

Period	Range Upper Value	Lower Value	Target Value	Warning Period
1	5.0	3.0	4.0	5 weeks
2	4.5	2.5	3.5	5 weeks
3	4.0	2.0	3.0	5 weeks
4	3.5	1.5	2.5	5 weeks
5	3.0	1.0	2.0	5 weeks
6	2.5	0.5	1.5	5 weeks
7	2.0	0.5	1.0	5 weeks

that control application of criteria at any time, by modifying the WHERE condition for 'Product Reject Monitoring', stored as data in the table for DATA BASE CONDITION.

He next specifies the frequency of performance monitoring as 'weekly', and then enters the upper and lower value, the target value, and the early warning period and units for each future performance period, as illustrated in Table 14.1.

This specifies the values for seven periods. The upper value for the product reject rate in period 1 is 5.0%; the lower value is 3.0%; the target value is 4.0%; the early warning period is 5 weeks. He wants to be notified *immediately* if the actual value that is automatically calculated for period 1 is greater than 5% or less than 3%. If there is a trend (based on past reject rates) which suggests that the reject rate will move outside the range in the next 5 weeks, he is to be given early warning for a resource allocation decision to change the trend: the resources have a two week lead time, and take two weeks to have an effect (lag time). This leaves one week as a safety margin. He progressively reduces the upper and lower values, and the target value, in each period in expectation of the decreasing reject rates based on his earlier decision: if the actual reject rate falls outside these values he wants to be notified immediately; if the decreasing trend is slower than expected he will be given early warning to allocate more resources. If the downward trend is faster than anticipated, he will also be given early warning: more resources may have been allocated than are necessary. He may be able to utilize them better by allocating those excess resources elsewhere.

The decision early warning graph is displayed for his confirmation (but without actual values yet, of course) as illustrated in Figure 14.4. He can

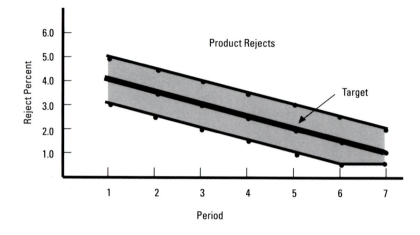

Figure 14.4   Performance monitoring graph for Table 14.1.

modify values directly on the graph using a mouse. If he anticipates a change in resource lead time, or in resource lag time in any period, he can vary the early warning period in Table 14.1 at will.

The result is the dynamic definition and introduction of performance monitoring at any time, whenever required by management. Once registered, performance criteria remain active for automatic monitoring within the defined ranges, or are deactivated and later reactivated at will. For example, unacceptable performance at one level may cause the automatic activation of detailed monitoring at a lower level, to identify possible causes of the poor performance. The manager is not only given early notification of a problem for correction before it becomes serious, he is also given all relevant information on that problem to help him reach a decision.

Figure 14.3 illustrated flexible performance monitoring. It enables performance criteria to be defined dynamically, attached to object data in rows of columns and tables representing data to be monitored. Equally, the ability to attach notes, or other documentation, dynamically to any object data is also useful. This documentation may be textual, graphical, audio or video as shown in Figure 14.5.

We will include these documentation entities with the performance monitoring data map of Figure 14.3, showing the result as a subject map for performance and documentation as illustrated in Figure 14.6.

The flexibility of dynamic modeling is now apparent. Data base definition entities of tables, columns and rows in Figure 14.6 contain the names of all data to be dynamically managed. This data base definition normally is part of the catalog of all RDBMS data base software used for implementation. If that catalog is accessible by programs, it can be used in place of the

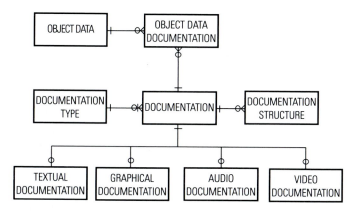

Figure 14.5 Data map for a dynamic documentation capability.

entities above; otherwise these entities offer a DBMS-independent approach to defining data for dynamic management. Let us now develop the strategic map further.

The strategies in Figure 13.1 did not address concerns that were related to location. As a result, no reference to location appeared in the XYZ subject map in Figure 13.7. In the competitive environment which XYZ finds itself, the location of customers, suppliers and others may well be important, but

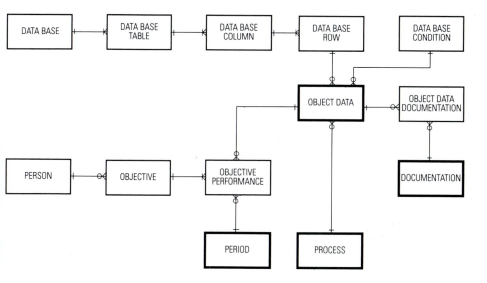

Figure 14.6 Subject map for dynamic performance monitoring, with dynamic documentation capability – able to be attached to any rows, in any column and table, based on defined conditions.

may not emerge until more detailed modeling is carried out at the tactical and operational levels. We will look at some implications of location next.

To support customers, for example, we need to know their locations so we can ensure adequate support staff are available. A customer may have many branch offices, each at a different location. An association from LOCATION to ORGANIZATION ROLE thus exists, as shown in Figure 14.7. Each organization role is specific to one location; but a location may have many organizations, each carrying out an organization role.

LOCATION, in Figure 14.7, has secondary entities for LOGICAL LOCATION, GRID LOCATION and GEOGRAPHIC LOCATION; LOCATION STRUCTURE is a 5BNF entity. This is very powerful, and offers great analysis flexibility. For example, used for demographics: a geographic location is defined as a city; a logical location is a page in the city street directory; a grid location is a square on that page. Or instead, the address of a building is its geographic location; a logical location can be a floor of the building; a grid location is a point on a floor.

Alternatively, a non-contiguous area can be defined as a logical location. An example is the central business district (CBD) of selected cities: as

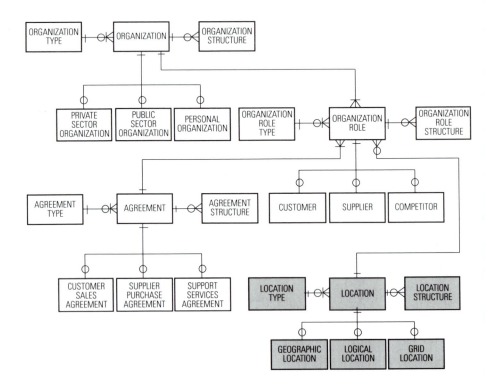

Figure 14.7 Modeling locations of interest.

a logical location this can be referred to as the '(city-name) CBD location'. The geographic and grid locations for each city can thus be related to its CBD location in LOCATION STRUCTURE. This offers great benefit in consolidated analysis. For example, financial analysis by location can provide financial reports not only for each geographic location, but can also report on the CBD of relevant cities, and can also consolidate these reports for all CBD's.

Location has been added to the subject map and the XYZ strategic model has been documented as a subject map in its final form in Figure 14.8. Now we can identify strategic functions from the subject and strategic maps more precisely; we can also use these to evaluate alternative organization structures.

14.2 DEFINING ORGANIZATION STRUCTURE

A strategic map is a schematic representation of data and information that are needed to manage and operate an organization. This applies regardless of whether systems that provide the data and information are manual or automated. Now, rather than using the guinea pig approach discussed in Chapter 1, we can use the strategic map as a model of the organization. This will enable us to design data bases and information systems, and also design appropriate organization structures. We address data bases and information systems in Part 4. We will cover organization structure design now. As we saw with product and market life cycles in Chapter 11, organizations also move through different life cycle phases. We will start with the concept of the organization life cycle.

14.2.1 Organization life cycles

Different organization structures are appropriate, depending on the size and nature of an organization, and its position in the organization life cycle [4, 5, 6]. Rowe *et al* [7] discuss that an organization moves through several phases in its life cycle. These are summarized below, with reference to relevant organizational structures in Charts 14.1–14.5.

Phase 1. The entrepreneurial organization

This is called the **Initiation Phase**. The organization is very young, and small. It has an entrepreneurial management style and informal management structure (see Chart 14.1).

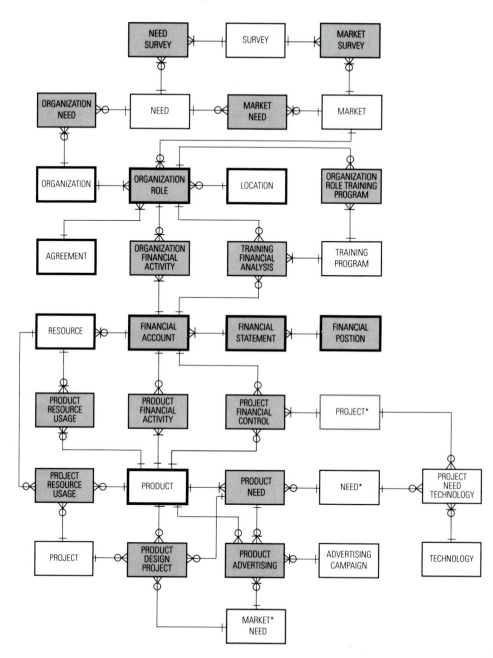

Figure 14.8 XYZ subject map, following strategic modeling. Shaded entities are all associated with PERIOD. Heavy border entities indicate type, secondary and structure entities also exist. Asterisk entities have been repeated.

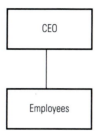

Chart 14.1   Organization chart for an entrepreneurial firm (Phase 1).

The main emphasis is on creating products and markets. But as the business grows, the founders are increasingly burdened with more and more management responsibilities. The entrepreneurial skills needed to establish the firm are no longer effective. This leads to crisis; the organization needs managers who can introduce control. The organization moves to Phase 2.

Phase 2. The bureaucratic organization

This is called the **Formalization Phase**. It introduces a bureaucratic structure (see Chart 14.2), with analytic or directive management. The controls that are applied in this phase achieve needed efficiencies in the operation of the organization, and in its centralized and effective management.

As the organization grows, however, lower level executives who have more knowledge of their operations and markets than do top management demand greater freedom in decision-making than is offered by the centralized hierarchy. This generally leads to the divisional structure of Phase 3a.

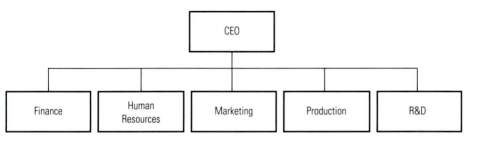

Chart 14.2   Organization chart for a bureaucratic firm (Phase 2).

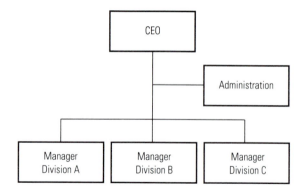

Chart 14.3   Organization chart for a divisional firm (Phase 3a).

Phase 3a. The divisional organization

This is often called the **Expansion Phase**. It uses a divisional structure for
decentralized decision-making, with analytic decentralized management (see
Chart 14.3). Greater responsibility is given to the managers of plants and
market territories; this tends to result in strong market expansion. But when
senior managers feel they are losing control over diversified operations, they
attempt to regain control over the organization; leading to an extension of
the divisional structure in Phase 3b.

Phase 3b. The coordinated organization

This is called the **Coordination Phase**. It uses an extension of a divisionalized
structure, with strategic business units (SBU) or product groups (see Chart
14.4). Centralized control is still retained with SBU and product group structures, but with decentralized decision-making. Autonomous field managers
are required to coordinate plans, money, personnel (that is, resources) and
technology with the rest of the organization. This divisional structure,
with SBUs and/or product groups, offers improved efficiencies – without
creating more staff (as distinct from line) positions as does a strictly divisional structure. But these structures are less adaptive to change, leading to
Phase 4.

Phase 4. The participative or matrix organization

This is called the **Participation Phase**. It uses participative and/or matrix
management (see Chart 14.5). Organizations in this phase are often able

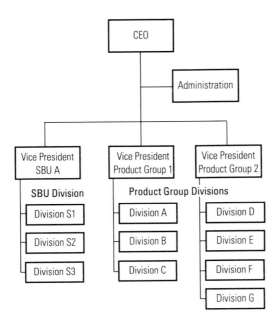

Chart 14.4   Organization chart for a coordinated firm (Phase 3b).

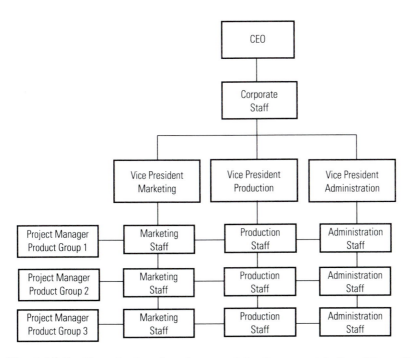

Chart 14.5   Organization chart for a participative or matrix firm (Phase 4).

to introduce rapid changes, without the disruption that change brings to organizations in the earlier phases.

Rapid changes in technology or other environmental factors make an adaptability to change the most important single determinant of survival for the firm. This is the environment that organizations in the 21st century will find themselves.

14.2.2   Organizational transformation

The evolution from one organizational life cycle phase to another phase is referred to as **organizational transformation**. The transformation of the bureaucratic organization to a more viable form for competing in the 21st century, using information technology, is discussed by Richard Nolan (1987) [8].

> *'The deregulation of industries is a logical consequence of the shift from an industrial economy to an information-service economy . . . We believe that transformation involves not incremental change, but major changes on many levels at once. From our client-centred experience, we have pulled together a five step cycle for accomplishing transformation:*
>
> *(1)   Downsize*
>
> *(2)   Discover growth*
>
> *(3)   Restructure*
>
> *(4)   Reward performance*
>
> *(5)   Validate.'*

Nolan argues that downsizing (in his Step 1) leads to a better balanced ratio of people and technology and that it enables: *'the same amount of work to be performed with only 50 to 60 percent of the people required in a functional hierarchy.'* The focus today on growth strategies (Step 2) that are centred around the customer, the market and on adding value for the customer involves intangibles, while the bureaucratic form of organization was designed to manufacture tangible products. *'But as we move into a service economy, the focus shifts to producing intangibles such as quality, usefulness, and uniqueness.'*

Discussing restructuring (Step 3), Nolan observes that: *'One emerging organizational form better suited to today's complex, global businesses is the network.'* This involves *'groups of knowledge workers assembled to treat a particular task or activity related to carrying the organization's growth strategy forward. Decision-making authority and accountability rest with these coalitions, each of which embraces the overall business vision.'* These coalitions lead to *'a fluidity and dynamism not found in the less flexible bureaucracy.'*

To assist in this restructuring, he points to other papers on organizational design [9] and information technology architecture [10]. His network organization with coalition groups equates conceptually to the participative or matrix organization illustrated in Chart 14.5. This chart shows projects (coalitions) focused on a product group basis; but projects can be established, on a formal or informal basis, to focus on any areas of interest.

Performance should not be tied to traditional reporting or budgeting structures as in the past. The actual performance resulting from each person's efforts should be monitored and rewarded (Nolan's Step 4) more effectively. Finally, the new organizational structures must be validated as completely as possible before implementation (Step 5). He summarizes:

> *'For the executive, transformation means that managing information technology has changed from a spectator sport to a participatory sport.'*

Transformation is difficult; if managed poorly it can lead to disaster. And transforming to an incorrect structure can be equally fatal. Before acting, the organization first must decide on its new structure and validate that structure as fully as possible. How can we achieve this?

Management consultants can be used to assist in these decisions. They base their advice on past experience in similar organizations and knowledge of the industry, or of similar industries. This experience is invaluable. But they do not have the detailed knowledge and experience held by managers of the organization to be restructured. It has been hard to communicate this knowledge in the past. But it is now accessible to managers and consultants alike: in the form of the strategic map and abstracted subject map.

These allow alternative organization structures to be identified, evaluated and validated: the strategic map represents the organization. Organizational groupings can be defined and tested, to assess: reporting and communication paths; audit controls; management responsibilities; and business opportunities. And information technology can be used to provide the information needed to manage the organization through the 90s and into the 21st century.

The following sections show how this can be achieved. We first examine the strategic and subject maps to identify potential functions. These functions are next mapped to relevant organization structures. These structures are evaluated using the strategic and subject maps. The final subject map for the XYZ Corporation, developed earlier in this chapter and in Chapter 13, is shown in Figure 14.8.

14.2.3 Step 5 – Identifying potential functions

A number of potential strategic functions are now apparent, indicated by intersecting entities in Figures 14.6 and 14.8. These functions are shown in Table 14.2, replacing the preliminary functions used in Table 13.1 to identify priority areas for modeling.

We can group these functions and implement them in any of the organization structures illustrated in Charts 14.1–14.5. But before we do this, it is important to emphasize an important benefit of strategic management planning: these functions have been directly identified from intersecting entities in the strategic map, which has (in turn) been directly developed from the refined strategic plan. The functions therefore reflect the organization's needs for the future; they do not just reflect the functions of the past.

The benefits discussed above for strategic management planning lead also to benefits in organization structure design (as we will shortly see), and to development productivity and maintenance benefits in strategic systems development (in Part 4). Contrast this with other development methods

Table 14.2 Functions identified from the strategic model

Intersecting Entity	Associated Function
Tactical Entities	**Tactical Functions**
MARKET NEED	Market Needs Analysis
ORGANIZATION NEED	Organization Needs Analysis
PRODUCT NEED	Product Needs Analysis
NEED SURVEY	Needs Survey and Analysis
MARKET SURVEY	Market Survey and Analysis
ORGANIZATION ROLE TRAINING PROGRAM	Organization Training
TRAINING FINANCIAL ANALYSIS	Training Financial Analysis
ORGANIZATION FINANCIAL ACTIVITY	Organization Financial Analysis
PRODUCT FINANCIAL ACTIVITY	Product Financial Control
PROJECT FINANCIAL CONTROL	Project Financial Control
PROJECT NEED TECHNOLOGY	Technology Monitoring and Analysis
PROJECT RESOURCE USAGE	Project Resource Usage
PRODUCT RESOURCE USAGE	Product Resource Usage
PRODUCT DESIGN PROJECT	Product Design and Development
PRODUCT ADVERTISING	Product Advertising
Generic Entities	**Generic Functions**
OBJECTIVE PERFORMANCE	Generic Performance Monitoring
OBJECT DATA DOCUMENTATION	Generic Documentation

that start by examining the existing functions or processes of the organization. They model data needed to support those functions. This approach works well for organizations in a stable environment, that do not contemplate significant change from their present organization structure, or from their present data bases and information systems. But as we discussed in Chapter 1, the only thing stable in the 90s and beyond will be change itself.

Strategic systems are being developed, and organizations are restructuring for the 21st century, not because they expect little change. The opposite will be the case. As Nolan comments: '*Transformation entails changing* **everything** (his emphasis) *about the business, while incorporating information technology at the same time*'. The refined strategic plan developed in Chapters 9–12, and the strategic map from Chapters 13 and 14, allows this restructuring of the organization and its systems to be assessed.

14.2.4 Evaluating organization structures

The functions in Table 14.2 map directly to the subject map in Figure 14.8 by allocating responsibility for each intersecting entity to a relevant functional area. This functional area responsibility can be specified to data modeling software as discussed in Chapter 17. That software then plots those entities as a data map of the function for the specific functional area. We will illustrate this conceptually next, by extracting relevant sections of the subject map in Figure 14.8.

For example, the Marketing function (at the strategic level) includes tactical functions, with intersecting entities in Table 14.2 shown in brackets, of: Market Needs Analysis (MARKET NEED); Needs Survey and Analysis (NEED SURVEY); and Market Survey and Analysis (MARKET SURVEY). Using the entity dependency rules (see Chapter 3), these intersecting entities depend on MARKET, NEED and SURVEY. These entities have been extracted from Figure 14.8 and are shown in Figure 14.9.

The association degree and nature specify that every NEED will be surveyed; there are (over time) many surveys for a need. So also with market surveys. A need may suggest many markets (see MARKET NEED above); a MARKET (to exist) will have one or many needs. These needs are determined by the Marketing function. Needs are evaluated in terms of existing, and possible future, products to satisfy those needs. Product Needs Analysis (PRODUCT NEED) also belongs to this function. It is dependent on PRODUCT and NEED and has been extracted in Figure 14.10. Note that PRODUCT will also shared with the Production function, however.

The Product Advertising function in Table 14.2 is indicated by PRODUCT ADVERTISING in Figure 14.8. This is dependent on PRODUCT NEED, ADVERTISING CAMPAIGN and on MARKET NEED. It has

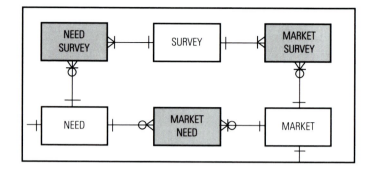

Figure 14.9 Data used by the marketing function.

been extracted as shown in Figure 14.11. This function also belongs to Marketing. It will have to coordinate with the Production, Product Development and the R&D functions to identify the needs of existing and planned future products: so that Marketing can establish appropriate advertising campaigns.

By now, you can see that we are using the subject map (and when we need more detail, the strategic map) to examine different functions and allocate responsibility for specific entities that represent data needed by those functions. This allows management to think through alternative strategies, and check that the appropriate audit and other controls are reflected in the associations joining related entities. Associations can also represent the reporting paths and communication paths between functions.

The omission of expected associations between related entities also highlights missing information that may be needed by a function, or missing audit controls, or identifies reporting or communication paths between functions that should be coordinated. We will see in Chapter 17 that software can be used to carry out strategic analysis of strategic, tactical or operational models: to identify potential associations that have not yet been defined between entities, that should be related for the above reasons.

We have so far discussed the Marketing, Production, Product Development and R&D functions. These functions can be directly mapped easily to a bureaucratic structure, as shown by Chart 14.2. But XYZ Corporation

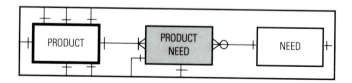

Figure 14.10 Data shared by the marketing and production functions.

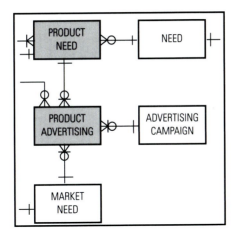

Figure 14.11 Data shared by the marketing, production, product development and R&D functions.

already has a bureaucratic organization structure. This is part of the reason for its difficulty today.

It can also be mapped to the divisional organization structure of Chart 14.3, perhaps with the Marketing (and also Sales) functions in a marketing division; and with the Production, Product Development and R&D functions in a manufacturing division. But the greater decision-making autonomy that a divisional structure offers represents a possible difficulty: we saw above that the marketing and the manufacturing divisions would need to communicate, and also coordinate, their activities from time to time. This and other needed coordination between different functions (as indicated by the subject map) would have to be explicitly designed into this divisional structure.

So it appears that the Coordinated organization structure in Chart 14.4 might be more appropriate to XYZ. Certainly XYZ could establish the marketing and manufacturing divisions in such a structure, coordinating them by product group (say). Each product group coordinator in Chart 14.4 is thus responsible for effective coordination between marketing, manufacturing and other divisions in his product group. Or a structure can be used with strategic business units (SBUs). This may be appropriate for resources or functions that are shared by many product groups, such as an Information Centre or other support groups. Or a combination of SBU and product group coordination might be more appropriate: this is the specific example illustrated in Chart 14.4.

But we saw earlier that both the divisional and the coordinated organization structures in Charts 14.3 and 14.4 are less adaptive to rapid change than a Participative or Matrix structure, as shown in Chart 14.5. And

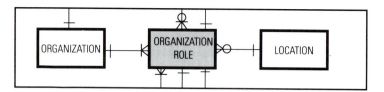

Figure 14.12   Great flexibility is offered by ORGANIZATION ROLE.

we know that the ability to change rapidly will be essential to survival and growth of organizations into the 21st century. So is the Participative or Matrix organization structure appropriate for XYZ Corporation? Let us evaluate the XYZ subject map further.

In Figure 14.8 we can see that ORGANIZATION NEED is dependent on NEED, and also on ORGANIZATION. Similarly ORGANIZATION ROLE depends on ORGANIZATION, and on LOCATION. Let us examine ORGANIZATION ROLE further.

Figure 14.7 shows the strategic map for ORGANIZATION ROLE, part of which is shown in the fragment of the subject map as Figure 14.12. Referring to Figure 14.7, we see that the secondary entities of ORGANIZATION, ORGANIZATION ROLE and also AGREEMENT are illustrated. This offers great flexibility to XYZ as an organization can have many roles: as a customer, supplier, competitor (or other roles still to be defined at the tactical and operational levels). We can provide predefined and expert knowledge of organizations and roles with ORGANIZATION STRUCTURE (in Table 13.3) and ORGANIZATION ROLE STRUCTURE (in Table 13.2).

Contrast this with our initial representation of customers in Figure 13.6. This considered private sector customers, personal customers and public sector customers; but we were restrictive in our thinking at that point. We focused only on the functional interpretation of the Sales function, from the present organization structure of XYZ as a bureaucracy. We did not also consider other roles that an organization may take as a supplier, or as a competitor, or its relationships with such other organizations. Our discussion in Tables 13.2 and 13.3 for the above structure entities highlighted the need for coordination in the dealings that XYZ has with all organizations.

Look again at the section of Figure 14.8 that relates to projects, extracted in Figure 14.13. Projects were initially introduced into the strategic model for product design purposes, reflected in the Product Design and Development function in Table 14.2 (see PRODUCT DESIGN PROJECT in Figure 14.13). But we can also see that projects can be established by the Project Need Technology function, as required, for specific technologies and needs (in PROJECT NEED TECHNOLOGY).

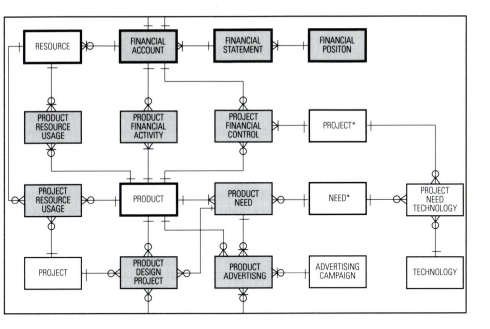

Figure 14.13 Projects can also be defined for the participative or matrix organization. Resources are allocated by PROJECT RESOURCE USAGE, and managed financially by PROJECT FINANCIAL CONTROL. Asterisk entities have been repeated.

Projects require resources (people, equipment, funds). This is the responsibility of the Project Resource Usage function in Table 14.2 (PROJECT RESOURCE USAGE). Projects are managed financially by the Project Financial Control function (PROJECT FINANCIAL CONTROL). As this is related to FINANCIAL ACCOUNT, the flexible financial reporting and budget control systems defined in the strategic plan and modeled in Chapter 13 can also be used for the financial and budgetary control of projects.

It is apparent that we have already defined the required resource and financial capability to establish and manage projects for any defined purpose. The strategic model thus supports the Participative or Matrix organization structure in Chart 14.5.

As we examine the subject map in Figure 14.8, and the more detailed strategic map, we can see that the strategic model has been designed to accommodate significant changes in the way that XYZ operates. It can respond rapidly, and easily, to business changes in the systems and information needed to run the business. But a flexible strategic model and flexible data bases and systems lose much of their competitive advantage when used by an organization that cannot adapt itself rapidly to change.

We saw in Chapters 9–12 that XYZ must change if it is to survive. We now know that the strategic model can be used for bureaucratic, divisional or coordinated organization structures, and also maps easily to the Participative or Matrix organization structure in Chart 14.5. This allows the strategic functions discussed above to be implemented as described next.

The Vice President–Marketing has vertical responsibility for the Marketing function (see Chart 14.5). The Vice President–Production similarly has vertical responsibility for the Manufacturing function. These VPs allocate marketing staff, or production staff, together with other resources under their control, across different projects as indicated by the horizontal responsibilities in that organization chart. These projects may take a product group focus as shown in Chart 14.5. Or they can take any other focus relevant to the changing environment in which XYZ finds itself. Staff, equipment and funds can be allocated as resources across any projects: approved either by corporate (staff) management or by line management. And priorities defined for projects avoid potential resource allocation conflicts.

It is now also apparent that the main coordination and control functions for operation of XYZ in this changed structure are the approval and management of projects. The steps to be followed for project approval and for project management can be defined in greater detail through tactical and operational modeling. Projects can also be established for the management and control of other projects. And performance criteria can be defined dynamically as described earlier in this chapter.

We are seeing significant changes in organizations as they prepare themselves for the competitive environment of the 90s and into the 21st century. According to Drucker [11]:

> 'The typical large business 20 years hence will have fewer than half the levels of management of its counterpart today, and no more than a third the managers. It is more likely to resemble the hospital, the university, the symphony orchestra. For like them, the typical business will be knowledge-based.
>
> Businesses, especially large ones, have little choice but to become information-based . . . . But as soon as a company takes the first tentative steps from data to information, its decision processes, management structure and work . . . . begin to be transformed . . . . The number of management levels can be sharply cut.
>
> The organization will go beyond the matrix, and may indeed be quite different from it. The best example of a large and successful information-based organization had no middle management at all.'

The role of middle management in the past has been to extract the information needed by senior management from the operational data used by the organization. This role is now increasingly being filled by information systems and computers. The other role of communicating and implementing the strategic plans set by management has not been carried out well at all. As these directions are incorporated in the information systems built to support the strategic plans, the role of middle management will become even more superfluous. With the discarding of unnecessary middle management layers, tomorrow's organization will be slimmer, less top-heavy, more streamlined, and able to change rapidly for competitive reasons [12]. It will *'dance like a butterfly, sting like a bee'* (attributed to Mohammed Ali).

Continuing this theme, Applegate, Cash and Mills [13] emphasize that tomorrow's organizations will have centralized control and decentralized decision-making, using Information Technology as a tool for downsizing and restructuring organizations. Computer systems will then provide the communication, coordination and control functions previously performed by middle managers.

They argue that this will offer the benefits of small scale and large scale simultaneously, so that even large organizations will be able to adopt flexible, dynamic structures. The distinction between centralized and decentralized control will blur. In tomorrow's organization they emphasize that *'the focus will be on projects and processes than on tasks and standard procedures.'* We can see that this flexibility is reflected in the strategic model we have developed for XYZ Corporation, with the ability to dynamically define projects and processes according to relevant criteria set by management.

Applegate *et al* conclude by discussing that sophisticated expert systems and knowledge bases will help capture decision-making processes; decision-making will be better understood; control will be separate from reporting relationships; computers will support creativity at all organization levels; and information and communication systems will retain corporate history, experience and expertise. By using the methods discussed in this book, we now know how these desires can be achieved.

We are now ready to continue our development of the strategic model. This is covered in the remainder of the chapter. It completes its definition for implementation in Part 4.

14.3 PREPARING FOR STRATEGIC IMPLEMENTATION

The strategic model entities now will be defined to attribute detail. This is the fifth strategic modeling step. We can use the strategic functions identified in Table 14.2 to focus on priority areas first.

14.3.1 Step 6 – Identify strategic attributes

Primary and foreign keys are defined to implement the associations in the strategic map. Additional strategic attributes, suggested by the strategies in Figure 13.1 or by objectives developed from those strategies, are also identified. Financial strategies are of highest priority for XYZ management. Using financial functions in Table 14.2, we will define attributes for the *Organization Financial Analysis, Product Financial Control, Project Financial Control and Training Financial Analysis* functions first.

Referring to Figure 14.8 we can see that the intersecting entities for these functions in Table 14.2 are all related to FINANCIAL ACCOUNT. This is dependent on PERIOD and FINANCIAL STATEMENT, which is dependent on FINANCIAL POSITION in turn. These entity dependencies are shown indented below, with the number of indents in brackets. (We will see in Chapter 17 that the indent number is the project phase number for implementation.) Each entity is dependent on those entities above it, with a lower indent number.

```
(1)  PERIOD
     (2)  FINANCIAL POSITION
          (3)  FINANCIAL STATEMENT
               (4)  FINANCIAL ACCOUNT
```

The indent number indicates the sequence that we will use to define attributes of these entities, starting with PERIOD.

PERIOD has a primary key of *period id#*, and contains attributes of: *period start date, period start time, period end date, period end time* – from which {*period duration*} is derived, expressed in time units defined by *period duration unit of measure*. (Or given a start date and time, and a duration, the end date and time can be derived.) Using entity list notation, PERIOD is documented as follows:

> PERIOD (period id#, period start date, period start time, period end date, period end time, {period duration}, period duration unit of measure)

The principal entity FINANCIAL POSITION (see Figure 14.8) has a primary key of *financial position id#*, with a foreign key of *period id#* (for the association to PERIOD). It has an alternative key of [*financial position reference*]. This is also referred to as a selection attribute: it is non-unique and is used for alternative access. The right bracket is left open, as additional attributes will be defined for this entity shortly.

> FINANCIAL POSITION (financial position id#, period id#, [financial position reference],

Type and structure entities (Figure 13.13) are defined fully. FINANCIAL POSITION TYPE has a primary key of *financial position type id#*, with a non-key attribute of *financial position type description*. A foreign key of *financial position type id#* is also added to FINANCIAL POSITION. FINANCIAL POSITION STRUCTURE has the primary keys of the type and principal entities, with these keys also duplicated as foreign keys – using the alias names: *related financial position id# and related financial position type id#*.

FINANCIAL POSITION TYPE   (financial position type id#, financial position type description)

FINANCIAL POSITION   (financial position id#, period id#, [financial position reference], financial position type id#,

FINANCIAL POSITION STRUCTURE   (financial position id#, financial position type id#, rel fin position id#, rel fin position type id#)

PERIOD TYPE is similarly defined with a primary key of *period type id#* and non-key attribute of *period type description*. A foreign key *period type id#* is added to PERIOD. PERIOD STRUCTURE is defined with *period id#*, *period type id#*, and alias foreign keys of *related period id#*, *related period type id#*.

PERIOD TYPE   (period type id#, period type description)

PERIOD   (period id#, period start date, period start time, period end date, period end time, {period duration}, period duration unit of measure, period type id#)

PERIOD STRUCTURE   (period id#, period type id#, rel period id#, rel period type id#)

Secondary entities BUDGET FINANCIAL POSITION and ACTUAL FINANCIAL POSITION (see Figure 13.13) have the same primary key *financial position id#* of the principal entity FINANCIAL POSITION. No additional attributes have been defined for these entities so far, but the right bracket is left open for attributes to be added later.

BUDGET FINANCIAL POSITION   (financial position id#,

ACTUAL FINANCIAL POSITION   (financial position id#,

Similarly secondary entities of ACCOUNTING PERIOD, REPORTING PERIOD and PERFORMANCE PERIOD have the primary key *period id#* of PERIOD. The right bracket is left open, for other attributes to be defined later if required.

ACCOUNTING PERIOD   (period id#,

REPORTING PERIOD   (period id#,

PERFORMANCE PERIOD   (period id#,

Attributes for the PERIOD entities to this point are summarized as follows:

PERIOD TYPE	(period type id#, period type description)
PERIOD	(period id#, period start date, period start time, period end date, period end time, {period duration}, period duration unit of measure, period type id#)
ACCOUNTING PERIOD	(period id#,
REPORTING PERIOD	(period id#,
PERFORMANCE PERIOD	(period id#,
PERIOD STRUCTURE	(period id#, period type id#, rel period id#, rel period type id#)

We have now defined the primary and foreign keys needed to implement associations for the PERIOD and FINANCIAL POSITION entities in the subject map of Figure 14.8, and in its strategic map in Figure 13.13. Next we will identify any strategic attributes suggested by defined strategies or objectives.

The *Budget Control* strategy in Figure 13.1 indicates:

'Establish and maintain strong budgetary controls for all expenditure, linked directly to revenue achievement. All financial statements must clearly show actual revenue and expenditure against budget, and indicate percentage change from the previous reporting period.'

The following attributes are therefore added to the secondary financial position entities: *budget financial amount* and *actual financial amount*. The attributes: *financial variance against budget* and *financial variance change from previous period* have been added to their principal entity. Additional attributes may later be defined during tactical and operational modeling. Attributes defined for FINANCIAL POSITION entities to this point are summarized as follows:

FINANCIAL POSITION TYPE	(financial position type id#, financial position type description)
FINANCIAL POSITION	(financial position id#, period id#, [financial position reference], financial variance against budget, financial variance change from previous period, financial position type id#)
BUDGET FINANCIAL POSITION	(financial position id#, budget financial amount)
ACTUAL FINANCIAL POSITION	(financial position id#, actual financial amount)
FINANCIAL POSITION STRUCTURE	(financial position id#, financial position type id#, rel fin position id#, rel fin position type id#)

Primary and foreign keys for the FINANCIAL STATEMENT entities (see Figures 13.13 and 14.8) are next defined, similar to the FINANCIAL POSITION on the previous page. This uses the secondary entities PROFIT AND LOSS STATEMENT and BALANCE SHEET STATEMENT.

FINANCIAL STATEMENT TYPE	(financial statement type id#, financial statement type description)
FINANCIAL STATEMENT	(financial statement id#, financial position id#, period id#, [financial statement reference], financial statement type id#)
PROFIT AND LOSS STATEMENT	(financial statement id#,
BALANCE SHEET STATEMENT	(financial statement id#,
FINANCIAL STATEMENT STRUCTURE	(financial statement id#, financial statement type id#, rel fin statement id#, rel fin statement type id#)

Notice that *financial position id#* and *period id#* have both been added to FINANCIAL STATEMENT as foreign keys, for the associations from PERIOD and FINANCIAL POSITION to FINANCIAL STATEMENT. (These may be defined as a compound primary key, if *financial statement id#* is not wholly unique.)

The *Financial Reporting* strategy in Figure 13.1 indicates:

'Implement flexible financial reporting systems able to be introduced at any organizational level, and which can provide profit and loss statements for any defined reporting frequency, with associated balance sheet statements.'

ORGANIZATION FINANCIAL ACTIVITY, an intersecting entity between ORGANIZATION ROLE and FINANCIAL ACCOUNT (see Figure 13.13) supports this strategy. No additional FINANCIAL STATEMENT attributes are required at the strategic level: more detailed attributes may be defined during tactical and operational modeling. We will define attributes for FINANCIAL ACCOUNT, and for ORGANIZATION ROLE, next.

Figure 13.13 shows that FINANCIAL ACCOUNT has secondary entities of REVENUE ACCOUNT, EXPENDITURE ACCOUNT, ASSET ACCOUNT and LIABILITY ACCOUNT. These entities are defined as for FINANCIAL STATEMENT. *Financial statement id#* and *period id#* have been added to FINANCIAL ACCOUNT as foreign keys (or as a compound primary key) to define associations with FINANCIAL STATEMENT and PERIOD.

FINANCIAL ACCOUNT TYPE	(financial account type id#, financial account type description)
FINANCIAL ACCOUNT	(financial account id#, financial statement id#, period id#, [financial account reference], financial account type id#)
REVENUE ACCOUNT	(financial account id#,
EXPENDITURE ACCOUNT	(financial account id#,
ASSET ACCOUNT	(financial account id#,
LIABILITY ACCOUNT	(financial account id#,
FINANCIAL ACCOUNT STRUCTURE	(financial account id#, financial account type id#, rel fin account id#, rel fin account type id#)

We saw that ORGANIZATION FINANCIAL ACTIVITY depends on FINANCIAL ACCOUNT and on ORGANIZATION ROLE. This is related to ORGANIZATION, AGREEMENT and also MARKET and LOCATION. We will define these next:

```
(1) FINANCIAL ACCOUNT
(1) ORGANIZATION
(1) AGREEMENT
(1) MARKET
(1) LOCATION
    (2) ORGANIZATION ROLE
        (3) ORGANIZATION FINANCIAL ACTIVITY
```

However we earlier saw that FINANCIAL ACCOUNT has other entity dependencies. When we include these dependencies, we find the following indented structure:

```
(1) PERIOD
    (2) FINANCIAL POSITION
        (3) FINANCIAL STATEMENT
            (4) FINANCIAL ACCOUNT
(1) ORGANIZATION
(1) AGREEMENT
(1) MARKET
(1) LOCATION
    (2) ORGANIZATION ROLE
            (5) ORGANIZATION FINANCIAL ACTIVITY
```

This indicates the data needed to satisfy the *Financial Reporting* and *Budget Control* strategies of Figure 13.2. The dependencies shown by the numbered indents above have provided a preliminary definition sequence. This can be used similarly to a Gantt Chart for project management purposes. We will define ORGANIZATION, AGREEMENT, MARKET and LOCATION entities, then ORGANIZATION ROLE, and finally the ORGANIZATION FINANCIAL ACTIVITY entity.

ORGANIZATION is first defined. As shown in Figure 13.9, it has secondary entities of PUBLIC SECTOR ORGANIZATION, PRIVATE SECTOR ORGANIZATION and PERSONAL ORGANIZATION. These entities are defined as follows:

ORGANIZATION TYPE	(organization type id#, organization type description)
ORGANIZATION	(organization id#, [organization reference], organization type id#)
PRIVATE SECTOR ORGANIZATION	(organization id#,
PUBLIC SECTOR ORGANIZATION	(organization id#,
PERSONAL ORGANIZATION	(organization id#,
ORGANIZATION STRUCTURE	(organization id#, organization type id#, rel organization id#, rel organization type id#)

Next, AGREEMENT is defined – again based on Figure 13.9. It has secondary entities of CUSTOMER SALES AGREEMENT, SUPPLIER PURCHASE AGREEMENT and SUPPORT SERVICES AGREEMENT.

AGREEMENT TYPE	(agreement type id#, agreement type description)
AGREEMENT	(agreement id#, [agreement reference], agreement type id#)
CUSTOMER SALES AGREEMENT	(agreement id#,
SUPPLIER PURCHASE AGREEMENT	(agreement id#,
SUPPORT SERVICES AGREEMENT	(agreement id#,
AGREEMENT STRUCTURE	(agreement id#, agreement type id#, rel agreement id#, rel agreement type id#)

MARKET has no secondary entities defined. It has a primary key of *market id#* and a secondary key [*market reference*]. We will leave the definition of other attributes until we address the *Market Research* strategies later in this chapter.

MARKET	(market id#, [market reference],

LOCATION is now defined with secondary entities of GEOGRAPHIC LOCATION, GRID LOCATION and LOGICAL LOCATION. The attribute *geographic location address* is added to GEOGRAPHIC LOCATION. The group attribute (*grid reference*) is added to GRID LOCATION (perhaps later to be defined with more detailed tactical attributes of *grid reference X coordinate, grid reference Y coordinate* and even *grid reference Z coordinate*). These entities are defined as follows:

LOCATION TYPE	(location type id#, location type description)
LOCATION	(location id#, [location reference], location type id#)
GEOGRAPHIC LOCATION	(location id#, geographic location address,
GRID LOCATION	(location id#, (grid reference),
LOGICAL LOCATION	(location id#,
LOCATION STRUCTURE	(location id#, location type id#, rel location id#, rel location type id#)

Following the definition of ORGANIZATION, AGREEMENT and LOCA-TION – on which ORGANIZATION ROLE is dependent – we can now proceed with the definition of ORGANIZATION ROLE itself. This is an intersecting entity which has a unique primary key of *organization role id#*, and foreign keys of *organization id#, agreement id#, period id#, market id#, location id#* – the primary keys of the entities on which it is dependent. It has four secondary entities (see Figure 13.9): CUSTOMER, SUPPLIER, COMPETITOR and SUPPORT.

Each of these entities allow us to define strategic attributes relevant to each role that an organization may take. For example, the CUSTOMER attribute {*customer total location sales this period*} is of interest. This is derived from ORGANIZATION FINANCIAL ACTIVITY, as we will see shortly. The SUPPLIER attribute {*supplier total location purchases this period*) is also important and is similarly derived. Further, attributes {*competitor total location sales this period*} and {*support total location sales this period*}, in COMPETITOR and SUPPORT respectively, are also significant.

ORGANIZATION ROLE TYPE	(organization role type id#, organization role type description)
ORGANIZATION ROLE	(organization role id#, [organization role reference], organization id#, agreement id#, period id#, market id#, location id#, organization role type id#)
CUSTOMER	(organization role id#, {customer total sales this period},
SUPPLIER	(organization role id#, {supplier total purchases this period},
COMPETITOR	(organization role id#, {competitor total sales this period},
SUPPORT	(organization role id#, {support total sales this period},
ORGANIZATION ROLE STRUCTURE	(organization role id#, organization role type id#, rel organization role id#, rel organization role type id#)

Finally, we can define the entity ORGANIZATION FINANCIAL ACTIVITY. This is an intersecting entity with a compound primary key: *financial account id#, organization role id#, period id#*. It contains a strategic attribute: *organization financial activity amount*. This indicates the amount charged to a financial account in a period according to a specific organization role. This attribute is used to calculate the derived attribute {*customer total sales this period*} in CUSTOMER as discussed in the previous page, and the similar attributes in SUPPLIER, COMPETITOR and SUPPORT.

ORGANIZATION FINANCIAL ACTIVITY   (organization role id#, financial account id#, period id#, organization financial activity amount)

For example, for an organization with an *organization role id#* for a CUSTOMER, where *financial account id#* references a REVENUE ACCOUNT, then *organization financial activity amount* represents 'total customer revenue this period'. When further accumulated by organization, agreement, market and location, the attribute {*customer total location sales this period*} in CUSTOMER is derived. Similarly, if *organization role id#* is a SUPPLIER and *financial account id#* is an EXPENDITURE ACCOUNT, then *organization financial activity amount* is 'total supplier purchases this period' – so deriving {*supplier total location purchases this period*} in SUPPLIER. The relevant amount is reflected in the appropriate financial account, and is included in the financial statement for the defined organization in the period.

Any organization unit can be defined in ORGANIZATION (as a public sector, private sector or personal organization) for any ORGANIZATION ROLE (customer, supplier, competitor or support) and AGREEMENT (either a customer sales agreement, supplier purchase agreement or support services agreement). This allows any customer, supplier or competitor of XYZ – or in fact any part of XYZ itself – to be defined. Thus financial statements can be produced for any of these organizations, for any accounting period and market. Further, an accounting period can be defined for any *period duration unit of measure*: either yearly, quarterly, monthly, weekly – or even daily, if relevant.

This is extremely flexible: it satisfies the strategy in Figure 13.1 for *Financial Reporting* at any organizational level of XYZ. It extends flexibility to customers and suppliers, also: XYZ can produce financial statements for revenue and profit generated by major customers; for purchases from major suppliers; and also for financial analysis of competitors based on their published financial reports, if sufficient information is available.

The *Budget Control* strategy in Figure 13.1 requires '. . . *strong budgetary controls for all expenditure, linked directly to revenue achievement . . .*': supported by *budget financial amount, actual financial amount, financial variance against budget, financial variance change from previous period* in FINANCIAL POSITION, and related to FINANCIAL STATEMENT. This not only supports *Budget Control* for XYZ, but it also supports XYZ revenue and expenditure budgets for customers and suppliers.

Close control can be placed on expenditure associated with major customers, to ensure that a profit is produced from revenue generated by those customers. This close control enables XYZ to offer special prices based on projected sales to major customers, which can be incorporated in the relevant customer sales agreement. Similarly, XYZ can use projected purchases from major suppliers to negotiate special prices for raw materials, and can monitor those purchases against budget. Entities defined to this point for the Financial strategies are summarized below.

PERIOD TYPE	(period type id#, period type description)
PERIOD	(period id#, period start date, period start time, period end date, period end time, {period duration}, period duration unit of measure, period type id#)
ACCOUNTING PERIOD	(period id#,
REPORTING PERIOD	(period id#,
PERFORMANCE PERIOD	(period id#,
PERIOD STRUCTURE	(period id#, period type id#, rel period id#, rel period type id#)
FINANCIAL POSITION TYPE	(financial position type id#, financial position type description)
FINANCIAL POSITION	(financial position id#, period id#, [financial position reference], financial variance against budget, financial variance change from previous period, financial position type id#)
BUDGET FINANCIAL POSITION	(financial position id#, budget financial amount)
ACTUAL FINANCIAL POSITION	(financial position id#, actual financial amount)
FINANCIAL POSITION STRUCTURE	(financial position id#, financial position type id#, rel fin position id#, rel fin position type id#)
FINANCIAL STATEMENT TYPE	(financial statement type id#, financial statement type description)
FINANCIAL STATEMENT	(financial statement id#, financial position id#, period id#, [financial statement reference], financial statement type id#)
PROFIT AND LOSS STATEMENT	(financial statement id#,
BALANCE SHEET STATEMENT	(financial statement id#,
FINANCIAL STATEMENT STRUCTURE	(financial statement id#, financial statement type id#, rel fin statement id#, rel fin statement type id#)
FINANCIAL ACCOUNT TYPE	(financial account type id#, financial account type description)
FINANCIAL ACCOUNT	(financial account id#, financial statement id#, period id#, [financial account reference], financial account type id#)

REVENUE ACCOUNT

(financial account id#,

EXPENDITURE ACCOUNT

(financial account id#,

ASSET ACCOUNT

(financial account id#,

LIABILITY ACCOUNT

(financial account id#,

FINANCIAL ACCOUNT STRUCTURE

(financial account id#, financial account type id#, rel fin account id#, rel fin account type id#)

ORGANIZATION TYPE

(organization type id#, organization type description)

ORGANIZATION

(organization id#, [organization reference], organization type id#)

PRIVATE SECTOR ORGANIZATION

(organization id#,

PUBLIC SECTOR ORGANIZATION

(organization id#,

PERSONAL ORGANIZATION

(organization id#,

ORGANIZATION STRUCTURE

(organization id#, organization type id#, rel organization id#, rel organization type id#)

AGREEMENT TYPE

(agreement type id#, agreement type description)

AGREEMENT

(agreement id#, [agreement reference], agreement type id#)

CUSTOMER SALES AGREEMENT

(agreement id#,

SUPPLIER PURCHASE AGREEMENT

(agreement id#,

SUPPORT SERVICES AGREEMENT

(agreement id#,

AGREEMENT STRUCTURE

(agreement id#, agreement type id#, rel agreement id#, rel agreement type id#)

MARKET

(market id#, [market reference],

LOCATION TYPE

(location type id#, location type description)

LOCATION

(location id#, [location reference], location type id#)

GEOGRAPHIC LOCATION

(location id#, geographic location address,

GRID LOCATION

(location id#, (grid reference),

LOGICAL LOCATION

(location id#,

LOCATION STRUCTURE

(location id#, location type id#, rel location id#, rel location type id#)

ORGANIZATION ROLE TYPE

(organization role type id#, organization role type description)

ORGANIZATION ROLE

(organization role id#, [organization role reference], organization id#, agreement id#, period id#, market id#, location id#, organization role type id#)

CUSTOMER	(organization role id#, {customer total sales this period},
SUPPLIER	(organization role id#, {supplier total purchases this period},
COMPETITOR	(organization role id#, {competitor total sales this period},
SUPPORT	(organization role id#, {support total sales this period},
ORGANIZATION ROLE STRUCTURE	(organization role id#, organization role type id#, rel organization role id#, rel organization role type id#)
ORGANIZATION FINANCIAL ACTIVITY	(organization role id#, financial account id#, period id#, organization financial activity amount)

The utilization of resources for products is important to management. They select the Product Resource Usage function in Table 14.2 as the next priority area for definition of strategic attributes.

This function is based on PRODUCT RESOURCE USAGE. This intersecting entity is dependent on PRODUCT and on RESOURCE. In turn, RESOURCE is dependent on the entities FINANCIAL ACCOUNT, FINANCIAL STATEMENT and FINANCIAL POSITION, which we defined earlier. These dependencies are all shown as follows:

```
(1) PERIOD
    (2) FINANCIAL POSITION
        (3) FINANCIAL STATEMENT
            (4) FINANCIAL ACCOUNT
                (5) RESOURCE
(1) PRODUCT
                (6) PRODUCT RESOURCE USAGE
```

We will define the last three entities in the sequence listed, starting with RESOURCE.

Figure 13.13 showed the RESOURCE secondary entities: PROPERTY RESOURCE, PLANT AND EQUIPMENT RESOURCE, HUMAN RESOURCE, INVENTORY RESOURCE and FUNDS RESOURCE. A resource is charged to a financial account, shown by the association between RESOURCE and FINANCIAL ACCOUNT. (A resource may actually be changed to more than one account – such as to an asset account for plant and equipment, and also to an expenditure account for depreciation purposes – but has been modeled for only one account in Chapters 13 and 14.) *Financial account id#* is thus added as a foreign key to RESOURCE.

RESOURCE TYPE	(resource type id#, resource type description)
RESOURCE	(resource id#, [resource reference], financial account id#, resource type id#)

PROPERTY RESOURCE	(resource id#,
PLANT & EQUIPMENT RESOURCE	(resource id#
HUMAN RESOURCE	(resource id#,
FUNDS RESOURCE	(resource id#,
INVENTORY RESOURCE	(resource id#,
RESOURCE STRUCTURE	(resource id#, resource type id#, rel resource id#, rel resource type id#)

Next we will define PRODUCT. This has secondary entities: STANDARD PRODUCT and CUSTOM PRODUCT. Quality control is important to management, defined by the *Quality Control* strategy in Figure 13.1: *'Establish and maintain stringent quality control over all production, to achieve a significant reduction in reject and recall levels.'* This shows a need to know the percentage of products rejected in each period; and the change in the percentage of products rejected, when compared to the previous period. This indicates strategic attributes for PRODUCT of: {*product reject percent this period*} and {*product reject change percent from previous period*}. These are derived from *product total accepted this period* and *product total rejected this period*. (These attributes were used earlier in this chapter – with Table 14.1 and Figure 14.4 – to discuss generic performance monitoring. Similar attributes may also exist for recalls as well as rejects: we will leave these for more detailed tactical and operational ·modeling, later.)

Each of these attributes is dependent on *period id#*, which is included as a compound primary key with *product id#*. Note that PRODUCT in Figure 14.8 is not shaded: no association was defined to PERIOD, earlier. The strategic attributes above now show the existence of this association, with *period id#* as part of the compound primary key.

PRODUCT TYPE	(product type id#, product type description)
PRODUCT	(product id#, period id#, [product reference], product total accepted this period, product total rejected this period, {product reject percent this period}, {product reject change percent from previous period}, product type id#)
STANDARD PRODUCT	(product id#,
CUSTOM PRODUCT	(product id#,
PRODUCT STRUCTURE	(product id#, product type id#, rel product id#, rel product type id#)

We can now define the intersecting entity PRODUCT RESOURCE USAGE. This has a compound primary key *product id#*, *resource id#*, *period id#*. It has the derived strategic attribute {*product resource total used this period*}.

```
PRODUCT RESOURCE USAGE    (product id#, resource id#, period id#, {product resource used this
                          period},
```

Not only can we determine the total amount of each resource used for a product, but – by the associations from RESOURCE to FINANCIAL ACCOUNT and FINANCIAL STATEMENT – financial statements can be produced for a product showing the profit contribution made by those resources to the product.

Management are vitally interested in the profitability of products. They focus on the Product Financial Control function in Table 14.2, next. This uses the intersecting entity PRODUCT FINANCIAL ACTIVITY. Indented dependencies for this entity are:

```
(1)  PERIOD
    (2)  FINANCIAL POSITION
       (3)  FINANCIAL STATEMENT
          (4)  FINANCIAL ACCOUNT
(1)  PRODUCT
             (5)  PRODUCT FINANCIAL ACTIVITY
```

We have defined all of these entities, except for PRODUCT FINANCIAL ACTIVITY. This has a compound primary key of *product id#*, *financial account id#*, *period id#* and a non-key attribute of *product financial amount this period*.

```
PRODUCT FINANCIAL ACTIVITY    (product id#, financial account id#, period id#, {product financial
                              amount this period},
```

This enables financial statements to be produced for any product and any accounting period – whether yearly, quarterly, monthly, weekly or daily. Revenue, expenditure and thus profitability for any product can be closely monitored; managed within defined budgets using FINANCIAL POSITION.

XYZ management now concentrate on the Market Analysis function in Table 14.2. This focuses on the Market Research strategies of Figure 13.1. The *Market Analysis* strategy in Figure 13.1 states:

> *'. . . establish and maintain a regular market analysis capability so we can determine current and potential size of markets that management identify, together with their projected growth.'*

This suggests strategic attributes in MARKET of *market current size, market potential size, market size unit of measure* and also *market growth rate* – as values monitored over time: *period id#* is thus a compound primary key with *market id#*. The definition of MARKET is updated:

MARKET   (market id#, period id#, [market reference], market current size, market potential size, market unit of measure, market growth rate,

The *Market Analysis* strategy continues:

'*Identify existing and potential competition in those markets, and their relative market shares.*'

This suggests strategic attributes in COMPETITOR of *competitor total sales* and *competitor percent market share*. The first of these attributes has already been identified: the second attribute is added:

COMPETITOR   (organization role id#, {competitor total sales this period}, {competitor percent market share},

The Market Needs Analysis function in Table 14.2 is first addressed. This is based on the intersecting entity MARKET NEED in Figure 14.8, which depends on MARKET and NEED as follows:

(1) MARKET
(1) NEED
     (2) MARKET NEED

MARKET has been defined above. NEED is a principal entity, defined as follows:

NEED   (need id#, [need reference],

MARKET NEED is shaded in Figure 14.8: it has an association with PERIOD – market needs are monitored over time. It therefore has a compound primary key of *market id#*, *need id#*, *period id#*.

MARKET NEED   (market id#, period id#, need id#,

What strategic attributes are needed? In Chapter 12, objectives were defined in Figure 12.11 for the Market Needs Analysis strategy: shown on the following page as Figure 14.14 for reference.

Objectives indicate the existence of attributes which contain data used to measure their achievement. As indicated in Figure 14.14, an objective has

Organization: ___XYZ Corporation___   Area: ___Industry SV___   Period: ___1991___
Responsible Manager: ___Market Research Manager___

Strategy: ___Market Needs Analysis___
Description: ___For potential markets selected by management for possible entry, and for all markets___
___where we operate, regularly determine the needs of existing and potential customers___
___in those markets.___

Objective	Description	Measure	Level	Time
Needs of Current Markets	• Within 1 month of the close of each quarter, report on the needs of existing and potential customers in markets where we currently operate.	Report completion date	• Report delivery	Qtr + 1 month
	• In each quarterly report, include percent revenue change from previous periods against key needs indicators.	Percent change in revenue	• Report delivery	Qtr + 1 month
Sales Campaign	• For group A in the CV Market, report within one month on total market sales – together with total sales and percent market share for each of XYZ and Competitor X.	Group A sales report completion	• Report delivery	< 1 mth
Needs of New Entry Markets	• For markets we are contemplating entering, report within 3 months on the identified needs of existing and potential customers in those markets.	Report completion date	• Report delivery	Reqst + 3 mths
	• In each new market, include five year projected sales growth rates of the market, and of each market player.	5 yr sales growth rate	• Report delivery	Reqst + 3 mths

Figure 14.14   **Market needs analysis objectives (see Figure 12.11).**

three characteristics: a measure (which suggests the attribute); a level for achievement; and a time to reach that level of achievement. We will address the first characteristic now; the other two characteristics relate to performance monitoring: covered shortly, during the definition of performance monitoring attributes.

The first objective in Figure 14.14 indicates: '*Within 1 month of the close of each quarter, report on the needs of existing and potential customers in markets where we currently operate.*' This requires that we identify not only the needs of existing customers, but also of potential customers. Figure 14.8 has an intersecting entity ORGANIZATION NEED, which represents the Organization Needs Analysis function in Table 14.2. It also requires an additional secondary entity of POTENTIAL CUSTOMER, for the principal entity ORGANIZATION ROLE.

```
ORGANIZATION NEED        (organization id#, period id#, need id#,

POTENTIAL CUSTOMER       (organization role id#,
```

These needs are determined through regular surveys. The Needs Survey and Analysis, and the Market Survey and Analysis functions in Table 14.2 address this area. They indicate intersecting entities NEED SURVEY and MARKET SURVEY respectively. These are both dependent on SURVEY. These three entities are defined as follows:

```
SURVEY           (survey id#, [survey reference],

NEED SURVEY      (need id#, period id#, survey id#,

MARKET SURVEY    (market id#, period id#, survey id#,
```

The results of these surveys must be reported '. . . *within 1 month of the close of each quarter.*' The objective has been defined to ensure these needs are reported promptly and the measure is '*report completion date*'. This requires establishment of a performance criterion, using Figure 14.6, to monitor the report delivery date of Needs Analysis Reports.

The next objective in Figure 14.14 is more interesting: '*In each quarterly report, include percent revenue change from previous periods against key needs indicators.*' The measure in Figure 14.14 for this objective is '*percent change in revenue*'. This suggests two additional attributes of NEED: *need total revenue this period* and also *need revenue percent change from prior period*. Both of these attributes are dependent on *period id#*, which is added to the primary key of NEED – updated as follows:

```
NEED     (need id#, period id#, need total revenue this period, need revenue percent change from
         prior period,
```

This revenue may be determined through survey questions for potential customers; for existing customers it requires financial analysis of needs. This suggests that an intersecting entity between NEED and FINANCIAL ACCOUNT should be added to support a *Needs Financial Analysis* function: called NEED FINANCIAL ANALYSIS:

```
NEED FINANCIAL ANALYSIS    (need id#, financial account id#, period id#, need financial activity
                           amount,
```

Where *financial account id#* refers to a REVENUE ACCOUNT, *need financial activity amount* indicates the revenue attributed to each identified need: this is accumulated in {*need total revenue this period*} as required by the objective. If an expenditure financial account is referenced, this will also allow the total expenditure associated with a need to be determined – a useful extension if management later decide that they want to identify the most profitable needs to satisfy.

This objective implies that revenue generated be apportioned to relevant needs. This would be difficult to do manually in conjunction with the sale of each product. Is there a better way? The Product Needs Analysis function in Table 14.2 relates to PRODUCT NEED. This is dependent on PRODUCT and NEED (see Figure 14.8). Each product is related to relevant needs that it satisfies. We will add the attribute *product need percent weighting* to PRODUCT NEED. This indicates the percentage of the applicable product sale price apportioned to each need: it is used to calculate *need financial activity amount* automatically, in NEED FINANCIAL ACTIVITY above.

> PRODUCT NEED   (product id#, need id#, period id#, product need percent weighting,

The third objective in Figure 14.14 states: '*For group A in the CV Market, report within one month on total market sales – together with total sales and percent market share for each of XYZ and Competitor X.*' We previously defined in MARKET, the attributes: *market current size, market potential size* and *market growth rate*. This objective has indicated a new attribute: *market total revenue*, which is dependent also on *period id#*.

> MARKET   (market id#, period id#, [market reference], market current size, market potential size, market unit of measure, market growth rate, market total revenue,

The last part of this objective relates to competitors. Each competitor ORGANIZATION takes an ORGANIZATION ROLE of COMPETITOR (Figure 13.9): including XYZ when it is competing against others. This suggests two attributes for COMPETITOR: {*competitor total sales this period*} and also {*competitor percent market share*}. This confirms the earlier definition:

> COMPETITOR   (organization role id#, {competitor total sales this period}, {competitor percent market share},

The fourth objective in Figure 14.14 is similar to the first, but instead of '. . . *markets where we currently operate*' it addresses '. . . *markets that we are contemplating entering*'. This new objective is fully supported by the entities defined for the first objective, with a different *market id#* value.

The final objective in Figure 14.14 states: '*In each new market, include five year projected sales growth rates of the market, and of each market player.*' In MARKET, the attribute *market growth rate* supports this, and is dependent on *market id#* and *period id#*. No other attributes are needed.

This objective requires performance criteria to be defined based on *period id#* – set for each of the next five years in the future to determine the five year projected sales growth rate measure for markets of interest. A 'market player' is defined as a competitor, a customer or a supplier – indicated by ORGANIZATION ROLE for the relevant *market id#*.

We will not complete the definition of attributes for the remaining entities in Figure 14.8. These are documented in the entity list on this and the following page. This updates the previous financial strategy entity list and is a summary of all the entities defined for the subject map in Figure 14.8.

Entity list for XYZ subject map in Figure 14.8

PERIOD TYPE	(period type id#, period type description)
PERIOD	(period id#, period start date, period start time, period end date, period end time, {period duration}, period duration unit of measure, period type id#)
ACCOUNTING PERIOD	(period id#,
REPORTING PERIOD	(period id#,
PERFORMANCE PERIOD	(period id#,
PERIOD STRUCTURE	(period id#, period type id#, rel period id#, rel period type id#)
FINANCIAL POSITION TYPE	(financial position type id#, financial position type description)
FINANCIAL POSITION	(financial position id#, period id#, [financial position reference], financial variance against budget, financial variance change from previous period, financial position type id#)
BUDGET FINANCIAL POSITION	(financial position id#, budget financial amount)
ACTUAL FINANCIAL POSITION	(financial position id#, actual financial amount)
FINANCIAL POSITION STRUCTURE	(financial position id#, financial position type id#, rel fin position id#, rel fin position type id#)
FINANCIAL STATEMENT TYPE	(financial statement type id#, financial statement type description)
FINANCIAL STATEMENT	(financial statement id#, financial position id#, period id#, [financial statement reference], financial statement type id#)
PROFIT AND LOSS STATEMENT	(financial statement id#,
BALANCE SHEET STATEMENT	(financial statement id#,
FINANCIAL STATEMENT STRUCTURE	(financial statement id#, financial statement type id#, rel fin statement id#, rel fin statement type id#)

FINANCIAL ACCOUNT TYPE   (financial account type id#, financial account type description)

FINANCIAL ACCOUNT   (financial account id#, financial statement id#, period id#, [financial account reference], financial account type id#)

REVENUE ACCOUNT   (financial account id#,

EXPENDITURE ACCOUNT   (financial account id#,

ASSET ACCOUNT   (financial account id#,

LIABILITY ACCOUNT   (financial account id#,

FINANCIAL ACCOUNT STRUCTURE   (financial account id#, financial account type id#, rel fin account id#, rel fin account type id#)

ORGANIZATION TYPE   (organization type id#, organization type description)

ORGANIZATION   (organization id#, [organization reference], organization type id#)

PRIVATE SECTOR ORGANIZATION   (organization id#,

PUBLIC SECTOR ORGANIZATION   (organization id#,

PERSONAL ORGANIZATION   (organization id#,

ORGANIZATION STRUCTURE   (organization id#, organization type id#, rel organization id#, rel organization type id#)

AGREEMENT TYPE   (agreement type id#, agreement type description)

AGREEMENT   (agreement id#, [agreement reference], agreement type id#)

CUSTOMER SALES AGREEMENT   (agreement id#,

SUPPLIER PURCHASE AGREEMENT   (agreement id#,

SUPPORT SERVICES AGREEMENT   (agreement id#,

AGREEMENT STRUCTURE   (agreement id#, agreement type id#, rel agreement id#, rel agreement type id#)

MARKET   (market id#, period id#, [market reference], market current size, market potential size, market unit of measure, market growth rate, market total revenue,

LOCATION TYPE   (location type id#, location type description)

LOCATION   (location id#, [location reference], location type id#)

GEOGRAPHIC LOCATION   (location id#, geographic location address,

GRID LOCATION   (location id#, (grid reference),

LOGICAL LOCATION   (location id#,

LOCATION STRUCTURE — (location id#, location type id#, rel location id#, rel location type id#)

ORGANIZATION ROLE TYPE — (organization role type id#, organization role type description)

ORGANIZATION ROLE — (organization role id#, [organization role reference], organization id#, agreement id#, period id#, market id#, location id#, organization role type id#)

CUSTOMER — (organization role id#, {customer total sales this period},

SUPPLIER — (organization role id#, {supplier total purchases this period},

COMPETITOR — (organization role id#, {competitor total sales this period}, {competitor percent market share},

SUPPORT — (organization role id#, {support total sales this period},

POTENTIAL CUSTOMER — (organization role id#,

ORGANIZATION ROLE STRUCTURE — (organization role id#, organization role type id#, rel organization role id#, rel organization role type id#)

RESOURCE TYPE — (resource type id#, resource type description)

RESOURCE — (resource id#, [resource reference], financial account id#, resource type id#)

PROPERTY RESOURCE — (resource id#,

PLANT & EQUIPMENT RESOURCE — (resource id#,

HUMAN RESOURCE — (resource id#,

FUNDS RESOURCE — (resource id#,

INVENTORY RESOURCE — (resource id#,

RESOURCE STRUCTURE — (resource id#, resource type id#, rel resource id#, rel resource type id#)

PRODUCT TYPE — (product type id#, product type description)

PRODUCT — (product id#, period id#, [product reference], product total accepted this period, product total rejected this period, {product reject percent this period}, {product reject change percent from previous period}, product type id#)

STANDARD PRODUCT — (product id#,

CUSTOM PRODUCT — (product id#,

PRODUCT STRUCTURE — (product id#, product type id#, rel product id#, rel product type id#)

NEED

(need id#, period id#, need total revenue this period, need revenue percent change from prior period,

SURVEY

(survey id#, [survey reference],

PROJECT

(project id#, [project reference],

ADVERTISING CAMPAIGN

(campaign id#, [campaign reference],

TECHNOLOGY

(technology id#, [technology reference],

ORGANIZATION FINANCIAL ACTIVITY

(organization role id#, financial account id#, period id#, organization financial activity amount)

MARKET NEED

(market id#, period id#, need id#,

PRODUCT RESOURCE USAGE

(product id#, resource id#, period id#, {product resource used this period},

PRODUCT FINANCIAL ACTIVITY

(product id#, financial account id#, period id#, {product financial amount this period},

ORGANIZATION NEED

(organization id#, period id#, need id#,

NEED SURVEY

(need id#, period id#, survey id#,

MARKET SURVEY

(market id#, period id#, survey id#,

NEED FINANCIAL ANALYSIS

(need id#, financial account id#, period id#, need financial activity amount,

PRODUCT NEED

(product id#, need id#, period id#, product need percent weighting,

PROJECT RESOURCE USAGE

(project id#, resource id#, period id#,

PROJECT NEED TECHNOLOGY

(project id#, need id#, technology id#,

PROJECT FINANCIAL CONTROL

(project id#, financial account id#, period id#,

PRODUCT DESIGN PROJECT

(design id, product id#, project id#, market id#, need id#,

PRODUCT ADVERTISING

(advertising id#, product id#, campaign id#, market id#, need id#,

14.3.2 Generic performance monitoring attributes

The Generic Performance Monitoring function in Table 14.2 is associated with the entity OBJECTIVE PERFORMANCE. In Figure 14.6 this is dependent on OBJECTIVE and PERFORMANCE CRITERION in OBJECT DATA. The indented dependencies are:

```
(1)  PERIOD
(1)  PERSON
     (2)  OBJECTIVE
(1)  DATA BASE
     (2)  DATA BASE TABLE
          (3)  DATA BASE COLUMN
               (4)  DATA BASE ROW
(1)  DATA BASE CONDITION
(1)  PROCESS
                    (5)  OBJECT DATA
                    (6)  OBJECTIVE PERFORMANCE
```

PERIOD has already been defined. The other entities are new. We will define primary and foreign keys for these entities; other attributes will be defined only if relevant. More detailed PERSON attributes are defined during tactical and operational modeling, for example. We only need the primary key, and perhaps a name for alternative access.

PERSON   (person id#, [person name],

OBJECTIVE has a primary key *objective id#* and secondary key [*objective reference*]. It is dependent on PERSON: *person id#* is a foreign key. The text required to describe the objective, as in Figure 14.14, will be defined when we address Generic Documentation function entities shortly.

OBJECTIVE   (objective id#, [objective name], person id#,

Next are the data base entities. This allows us to maintain the names of relevant data bases, tables, columns, rows and conditions for dynamic performance monitoring and documentation purposes, independent of the DBMS product used to implement relevant data bases. The attribute *data base condition statement* is also included in DATA BASE CONDITION. This is used to store the SQL WHERE clause, for example: defining the actual statement entered to control selection of rows which meet the selection criteria. The text of the Product Reject Monitoring condition described earlier in conjunction with Figure 14.4 would be stored in this attribute, for example.

DATA BASE	(data base id#, [data base name],
DATA BASE TABLE	(data base table id#, [data base table name], data base id#,
DATA BASE COLUMN	(data base column id#, [data base column name], data base id#, data base table id#,
DATA BASE ROW	(data base row id#, [data base row name], data base id#, data base table id#, data base column id#,
DATA BASE CONDITION	(data base condition id#, [data base condition name], data base condition statement,

We discussed PROCESS earlier in this chapter, in conjunction with secondary entities PROCEDURE and TASK (see Figure 14.3). These are defined next.

PROCESS TYPE   (process type id#, process type description)

PROCESS   (process id#, [process reference], process type id#)

PROCEDURE   (process id#,

TASK   (process id#,

PROCESS STRUCTURE   (process id#, process type id#, rel process id#, rel process type id#)

Figure 14.3 also shows that OBJECT DATA has a secondary entity PERFORMANCE CRITERION, which is associated with PROCESS: *process id#* is included in this entity as a foreign key. We will define a new primary key *performance criterion id#*, and will make *object data id#* a foreign key also.

OBJECT DATA TYPE   (object data type id#, object data type description)

OBJECT DATA   (object data id#, [object data reference], data base id#, data base table id#, data base column id#, data base row id#, data base condition id#, object data type id#)

PERFORMANCE CRITERION   (performance criterion id#, object data id#, process id#

We are now ready to define the attributes of OBJECTIVE PERFORMANCE. At this point you may find it helpful to review the discussion in conjunction with Table 14.1 and Figure 14.4.

OBJECTIVE PERFORMANCE has a primary key *objective id#*, *performance criterion id#*, *period id#* and a number of non-key attributes. These are indicated in Table 14.1: they are used to produce the decision early warning graph of Figure 14.4. They define the upper and lower boundaries of acceptable performance, the target value and early warning period. The attribute *early warning unit* is also defined, as it may be different to the *period duration unit of measure* in PERIOD. We may later wish to change *period duration unit of measure* from *weeks*, perhaps to *days* so we can monitor performance more closely – but we may wish to leave *early warning unit* still defined in *weeks*. Finally, the actual value calculated from *process id#* in PERFORMANCE CRITERION (based on *performance criterion id#*) is defined as a derived attribute.

OBJECTIVE PERFORMANCE   (objective id#, performance criterion id#, period id#, obj perf upper value, obj perf lower value, obj perf target value, obj perf early warning period, obj perf early warning unit, {obj perf actual value},

As the final section of this chapter we will define the Generic Documentation function in Table 14.2: associated with OBJECT DATA DOCUMENTA-TION. As discussed earlier in relation to Figure 14.6, this can be used to attach any form of documentation – whether textual, audio, video or graphical – dynamically to any defined object data of interest in any data base, table, column and row, and under any defined conditions. This has indented dependencies as follows:

```
(1)  PERIOD
(1)  DATA BASE
     (2)  DATA BASE TABLE
          (3)  DATA BASE COLUMN
               (4)  DATA BASE ROW
(1)  DATA BASE CONDITION
                    (5)  OBJECT DATA
(1)  DOCUMENTATION
                    (6)  OBJECT DATA DOCUMENTATION
```

All of these entities have been defined, except for DOCUMENTATION and OBJECT DATA DOCUMENTATION. We will define TEXTUAL DOCU-MENTATION as a secondary entity of DOCUMENTATION, with *textual documentation content*. (This is later defined, implemented as part of a Generic Documentation System, as a variable length character string to contain the relevant text documentation.) Other attributes may be appropriate for graphical, audio and video documentation, but will be left for later tactical and operational modeling.

DOCUMENTATION TYPE	(documentation type id#, documentation type description)
DOCUMENTATION	(documentation id#, [documentation reference], documentation type id#)
TEXTUAL DOCUMENTATION	(documentation id#, textual documentation content,
GRAPHICAL DOCUMENTATION	(documentation id#,
AUDIO DOCUMENTATION	(documentation id#,
VIDEO DOCUMENTATION	(documentation id#)
DOCUMENTATION STRUCTURE	(documentation id#, documentation type id#, rel documentation id#, rel documentation type id#)

The OBJECT DATA DOCUMENTATION intersecting entity is now defined. This is used to attach the relevant documentation (indicated by *documentation id#*) to any *object data id#*. This can be any column in any table of any data base: where each is named in its relevant data base entity.

OBJECT DATA DOCUMENTATION	(object data id#, documentation id#, period id#,

Entered documentation is attached to any rows in the specified column, according to the condition statement defined in the data base condition entity. As data base, table and column names can be entered as data, and as condition statements can also be entered as data, this documentation can be dynamically attached to any data of interest in a data base. This enables the textual definition of objectives in Figure 14.14, for example, to be dynamically defined and entered. We will now summarize all entities defined for the generic performance monitoring and documentation subject map in Figure 14.6.

Entities for the generic performance monitoring and documentation subject map in Figure 14.6

PERSON	(person id#, [person name],
OBJECTIVE	(objective id#, [objective name], person id#,
DATA BASE	(data base id#, [data base name],
DATA BASE TABLE	(data base id#, [data base table name],
DATA BASE COLUMN	(data base id#, [data base column name],
DATA BASE ROW	(data base id#, [data base row name],
DATA BASE CONDITION	(data base id#, [data base condition name], data base condition statement,
PROCESS TYPE	(process type id#, process type description)
PROCESS	(process id#, [process reference], process type id#)
PROCEDURE	(process id#,
TASK	(process id#,
PROCESS STRUCTURE	(process id#, process type id#, rel process id#, rel process type id#)
OBJECT DATA TYPE	(object data type id#, object data type description)
OBJECT DATA	(object data id#, [object data reference], object data type id#)
PERFORMANCE CRITERION	(performance criterion id#, object data id#, process id#
DOCUMENTATION TYPE	(documentation type id#, documentation type description)
DOCUMENTATION	(documentation id#, [documentation reference], documentation type id#)
TEXTUAL DOCUMENTATION	(documentation id#, textual documentation content,
GRAPHICAL DOCUMENTATION	(documentation id#,

AUDIO DOCUMENTATION	(documentation id#,
VIDEO DOCUMENTATION	(documentation id#,
DOCUMENTATION STRUCTURE	(documentation id#, documentation type id#, rel documentation id#, rel documentation type id#)
OBJECTIVE PERFORMANCE	(objective id#, performance criterion id#, period id#, obj perf upper value, obj perf lower value, obj perf target value, obj perf early warning period, obj perf early warning period unit, {obj perf actual value},
OBJECT DATA DOCUMENTATION	(object data id#, documentation id#, period id#,

14.3.3   Step 7 – Define purpose descriptions

The final strategic modeling step is the definition and documentation of purpose descriptions for every defined entity and attribute, and for each association in the relevant strategic map for these entities. A description for each entity can be clearly defined, based on a greater knowledge of the purpose of the entity and also on its attribute content. Similarly the purpose of each attribute is more evident: its purpose description can be defined more precisely. The purpose description of the entity OBJECTIVE PERFORM-ANCE follows, to illustrate.

Entity: OBJECTIVE PERFORMANCE

Purpose: This provides a dynamic capability for performance monitoring, based on a defined objective and performance criterion. For each period it allows the definition of upper and lower boundaries of acceptable performance, together with a target value for achievement. The actual value reached in the period is derived according to the performance criterion. The nominated manager for the objective is notified on an exception basis if the actual value falls outside these boundaries. An early warning period can also be provided, for early warning notification if an unacceptable performance trend becomes apparent.

The purpose description of the attribute *obj perf early warning period* is next illustrated.

Attribute: *obj perf early warning period*

Purpose: This defines a period for early warning notification in the event that an unacceptable performance trend based on the attribute: *obj perf actual value*, becomes apparent. It represents the lead time for resources needed to change the trend, based on the relevant performance criterion. It may also include the lag time for the allocated resources to take effect, and may include a further time for a safety margin.

It is essential that all purpose descriptions be completed before proceeding to tactical and operational modeling. Following this, we have now completed strategic modeling.

14.4 SUMMARY

In this and the previous chapters we have made substantial progress. We started in Chapter 8 with a definition of the mission statement of the XYZ Corporation. We used this, together with the management questionnaire, to obtain strategic input from the managers of XYZ. Responses from this questionnaire represented an informal strategic plan: they could have been used directly as a catalyst, to develop a strategic model as described in Chapters 13 and 14.

In Chapter 9 we applied goal analysis to these responses, to produce a refined strategic plan for XYZ. Again, this could have been used as a catalyst to develop a more refined strategic model. However in that chapter we realized that the strategic plan, defined to that point, was passive; it was reactive; it did not offer the competitive advantage required by XYZ management.

In Chapter 10 we carried out an internal appraisal of XYZ to identify its strengths and weaknesses. In Chapter 11 we carried out an external appraisal of competitors to identify opportunities and threats. These appraisals were examined in Chapter 12. We identified performance gaps. We considered various strategic alternatives to address these gaps. We selected appropriate alternatives. We documented the rationale and con-tingencies underlying the strategic plan. We refined the strategies accord-ingly, and then defined specific objectives for achievement. The result was a refined strategic plan: one which incorporated the strategies from Chapter 9, but also included additional strategies that offered significant competitive advantage to XYZ Corporation.

In Chapter 13 we used this strategic plan as a catalyst for strategic modeling. We first developed a preliminary strategic map from the mission model used in Chapter 8. We defined preliminary functions from this map to focus on priority interest areas for XYZ management. Using the strategic plan from Chapter 12, we defined entities to provide needed information. We built great flexibility into the strategic model, supporting the proactive focus of the plan.

In Chapter 14 we defined a performance monitoring and documenta-tion capability that was generic, and able to be used dynamically by manage-ment to monitor any areas of interest. We identified potential tactical functions from the strategic map, grouping them into strategic functions to focus further on priority areas.

We next used the subject map – and where greater detail was needed, the strategic map – to evaluate organization structures for XYZ: presently a bureaucratic organization. We saw that the strategic model could be used with any organization structure. We mapped functions from the strategic model to a Divisional, and also a Coordinated, organization structure. We considered whether these structures would be sufficiently responsive to change for XYZ in the 21st century. We discussed the flexibility of the Participative or Matrix organization structure. This dynamically allocates resources (people, equipment, funds) to projects, as identified by management for any required focus. We saw that the strategic model already provided required project management and financial controls, and mapped readily to such an organization structure.

We then completed the strategic model ready for implementation in Part 4. We defined primary and foreign keys in entities to implement associations in the strategic model. From the strategic plan and objectives of Chapter 12, we also defined other strategic attributes as required. Finally we documented purpose descriptions for each identified entity, attribute and association.

The result has been the development not only of a refined, proactive strategic plan, but also the development of a strategic model. This model represents the data and systems needed to provide the information required by management in support of that plan. It can be used to define organization structures. It is also part of a strategic systems plan: providing a basis for detailed tactical and operational modeling to implement the required systems. Part 4 now covers systems development, for the design and implementation of these systems.

References

[1] Galbraith, J. (1973). *Designing Complex Organizations*, Addison-Wesley: Reading, MA.

[2] Finkelstein, C. B. (1989). *An Introduction to Information Engineering*, Addison-Wesley: Reading, MA.

[3] McConnell, J. (1987). *Analysis and Control of Variation: Control Chart Techniques for TQC Practitioners*, Delaware Books: Sydney, Australia.

[4] Mintzberg, H. (1979). *The Structuring of Organizations*, Prentice-Hall: Englewood Cliffs, NJ.

[5] Kimberley, J. R. and Miles, R. H. (1980). *The Organizational Life Cycle*, Jossey-Bass: San Francisco: CA.

[6] Galbraith, J. R. and Kazanjian, R. K. (1986). *Strategy Implementation*, West Publishing Company: Los Angeles, CA.

[7] Rowe, A. J., Mason, R. O., Dickel, K. E. and Snyder, N. H. (1990). *Strategic Management: A Methodological Approach (Third Edition)*, Addison-Wesley, Reading: MA.

[8] Nolan, R. (1987). What Transformation Is, in *Stage by Stage*, Nolan, Norton & Co: Boston, MA Vol 7, No 5.

[9] A discussion on *Organization Design* appears in *Stage by Stage*, Nolan, Norton & Co: Boston, MA Vol 6, No 5 (1986).

[10] Discussions on *Information Technology Architecture* appear in *Stage by Stage*, Nolan, Norton & Co: Boston, MA Vol 7, Nos 2 and 4 (1987).

[11] Drucker, P. (1988). *The Coming of the New Organization*, Harvard Business Review: Boston, MA (Jan–Feb).

[12] Kanter, R. M. (1990). *When Giants Learn to Dance*, Unwin Hyman: London, UK.

[13] Applegate, L., Cash, J. and Mills, D. *Information Technology and Tomorrow's Manager*, Harvard Business Review: Boston, MA (Nov–Dec).

PART FOUR

Systems Development

CHAPTER 15

Strategic Modeling of a Priority Area

This chapter illustrates development of a strategic data model for a priority area selected by management. This will be expanded in the next chapters through tactical modeling and operational modeling, to develop an operational data model. This operational model will be used in later chapters to illustrate the design and development of systems.

We saw in Chapters 7 and 13 that a strategic model is initially defined from the mission of an organization. It is refined to address concerns, issues, strengths and weaknesses, and include the policies, goals and objectives and strategies of the organization. We will focus in this chapter on the mission of a priority area, selected by the management of XYZ Corporation following strategic planning in Part 3, to illustrate the general concepts of strategic modeling at a priority area level.

15.1 THE SELECTED PRIORITY AREA

As a priority area for initial systems development after strategic modeling in Chapters 13 and 14, the senior management of XYZ selected the Customer Support function: this addresses the Customer Satisfaction strategy as part of their emphasis on Total Quality Management (TQM) (see Chapters 9 and 13, and Figure 13.1). In particular, XYZ urgently needs new systems that support the resolution of customer complaints. When received, every complaint must be investigated. Is it a complaint which arose due to an error or problem on the part of XYZ? Or was it due to an error or a misunderstanding by the customer? Both sides of the situation must be investigated and evaluated.

In a small organization, complaints may be easy to evaluate and rectify. The customer's description of the problem is readily available. The organization's staff can also give their view. A decision can then be made. But a large organization may have difficulties. Some of these stem from its size: it is often difficult to determine who can best give the organization's view.

Another problem of size is visibility. Banks, airlines, insurance companies, health care organizations or hospitals, government departments or other large organizations can be vulnerable to media exposure and community or government pressure. If the complaint is not handled responsibly and resolved, its severity may escalate. The customer may approach the newspapers, radio or TV. If the complaint is directed to a government department, the customer may contact an Ombudsman whose function is to mediate in disputes between the community and government. Or the customer's representative in government may be contacted, to direct a public question to the Minister or political representative responsible for the relevant industry sector. The complaint will be forwarded by the Minister to the organization for explanation. A satisfactory and timely answer must be given. If the complaint is not justified and the customer is wrong, this must be clearly demonstrated. If the organization is at fault, a resolution of the problem which is acceptable to the customer must be proposed.

When a complaint escalates to this level, the damage in cost and time spent in resolution can be very high. If not resolved satisfactorily under this scrutiny its repercussions can be disastrous. The organization may have to respond differently, because of exposure, than it would in a less sensitive environment. Time is also an important factor in demonstrating its responsiveness: the complaint must be resolved in a reasonable amount of time.

We saw in Chapter 9 that XYZ Corporation is very weak in customer support. The Customer Satisfaction strategy was defined to address this weakness. As their present complaint resolution systems do not allow prompt and correct resolution of complaints, XYZ senior management have selected this as the priority area for initial systems development.

To ensure prompt and correct response to complaints, an organization may establish a formal complaint resolution function: called the Complaints Department. XYZ uses the term: Complaint Resolution for its complaints area. We will refer to it as **COMRES** in the following discussions.

The key responsibility of the COMRES function is management of the investigation process. The important issue is not so much in determining whether the complaint is valid, or whether the customer or the organization was at fault. Each case will be decided by the responsible manager based on the facts of the matter. The COMRES function ensures that all relevant facts known to the involved parties are made available for management decision-making. In effect, COMRES is concerned with management of cases and investigations, rather than in the resolution of complaints (as its name suggests). This is reflected in the mission of COMRES:

COMRES Mission

'Manage the investigation of cases, to result in their prompt and correct resolution.'

We will use this to develop a Complaint Resolution strategic model. We will then use more detailed management statements in following chapters to expand it to tactical and operational model detail, based on the data modeling concepts covered in Chapters 2–4.

15.1.1 Complaint resolution strategic map

The mission statement above provides a starting point for development of the strategic model. It refers to cases and investigations: the entities CASE and INVESTIGATION are therefore indicated. A case must result in at least one investigation: it may require more investigations if it is not resolved satisfactorily. One of the parties may provide additional information, make a further complaint or exercise a right of appeal which requires the case to be opened again and other investigations to be carried out. There is therefore a *mandatory one to mandatory many* association between the entities CASE and INVESTIGATION (see Chapters 2 and 3). This is illustrated in Figure 15.1.

The phrase *'prompt and correct resolution'* has been used in the COMRES mission statement. The correct resolution of a case can only be decided by the responsible manager when the relevant facts are considered: we discussed above that the decision itself is not the responsibility of COMRES. But COMRES is certainly responsible for obtaining all relevant information so a correct decision can be made.

Prompt resolution is affected by the time taken to gather the facts for a case: this is also the responsibility of COMRES. We can see therefore that

Figure 15.1 **A case must have one or many investigations.**

Figure 15.2 Prompt resolution of cases. There may be one or many cases in a period.

time is important. We will manage time at the strategic level by the entity PERIOD, where a period is measured in months, or weeks, or days depending on the circumstances. In a period there may be many cases which are managed by COMRES. Thus there is a mandatory one to optional many association between the entities PERIOD and CASE as shown in Figure 15.2.

A number of people are involved in an investigation. These include the customer, as well as staff of the organization itself. They also include representatives of COMRES, whose responsibility is to ensure the relevant facts are obtained from the customer and the organization staff. They include the manager who will make a decision based on the facts of a case, and also the minister or ombudsman who is interested in seeing that the case is resolved. We will refer to all of these people by the entity: INVOLVED PARTY.

There are many involved parties in an investigation. A specific involved party may also be involved in many investigations, particularly for representatives of COMRES. The resulting *many to many* association between INVESTIGATION and INVOLVED PARTY is resolved through the process of business normalization as two *one to many* associations with INVESTIGATION INVOLVED PARTY, which is an intersecting entity. The strategic data map now expands as shown in Figure 15.3.

The strategic map indicates that an investigation must have at least one involved party – the COMRES representative. There is a *mandatory one to mandatory many* association between INVESTIGATION and INVESTIGATION INVOLVED PARTY. Most people are never involved in an investigation: there is only a *mandatory one to optional many* association between INVOLVED PARTY and INVESTIGATION INVOLVED PARTY.

A case has associated with it certain text which describes the relevant facts. TEXT is a strategic entity. It may be text contained in customer correspondence describing the problem which gave rise to the case. It may be text from the minister or ombudsman relevant to the case. And it will include text from staff giving their understanding of the circumstances. A case therefore may have many instances of text: some text may also relate to more than one case. There is a *many to many* association between case and text,

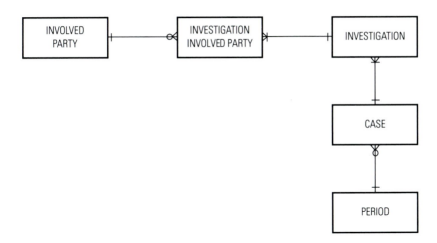

Figure 15.3 Many parties are involved in an investigation.

resulting in the intersecting entity CASE TEXT. Text may change over time, with a *mandatory one to optional many* association between PERIOD and TEXT.

A CASE has a *mandatory one to optional many* association between CASE and CASE TEXT. TEXT also has a *mandatory one to optional many* association between TEXT and CASE TEXT. This is shown in the strategic map in Figure 15.4. The text which is relevant to a case is gathered as a result of an investigation for that case. The parties involved in the investigation will

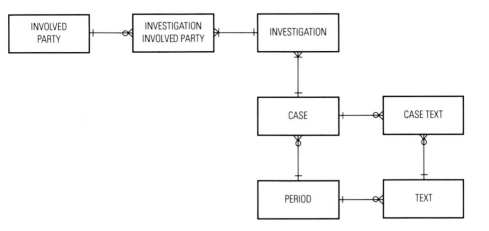

Figure 15.4 Many text documents are associated with a case.

mainly be the individuals who provide that text. However there may be other text relevant to the case. This can include text describing pertinent policies of the organization which may be used by the responsible manager to reach a decision.

An involved party can be contacted at a specific location. However there may be many locations relevant for an involved party. Similarly, a location may have many involved parties. The *many to many* association between the entity LOCATION and INVOLVED PARTY indicates an intersecting entity INVOLVED PARTY LOCATION.

An involved party must have at least one location, but may have many that are relevant. However a location need not have any involved parties located at it. A *mandatory one to mandatory many* association exists between INVOLVED PARTY and INVOLVED PARTY LOCATION. A *mandatory one to optional many* association exists between LOCATION and INVOLVED PARTY LOCATION as shown in Figure 15.5.

A case may comprise a number of topics which are relevant to its understanding, and its subsequent resolution. Similarly a topic may apply to more than one case.

The *many to many* association between CASE and TOPIC therefore leads to the intersecting entity CASE TOPIC. A case *must* have at least one topic: the association is *mandatory one to mandatory many* between CASE and CASE TOPIC. A topic may not initially relate to any case, but over time will likely be addressed in many cases: the association therefore is *mandatory one to optional becoming mandatory many* between TOPIC and CASE TOPIC. Both are related to PERIOD by a *mandatory one to optional many* association (see Figure 15.6).

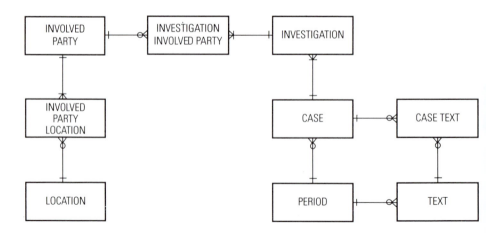

Figure 15.5 An involved party must have one or many locations.

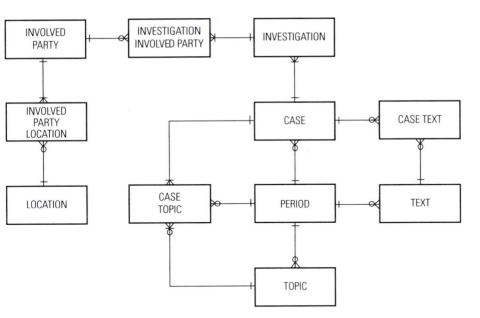

Figure 15.6 A case must comprise one or many topics.

A topic may relate to many locations, while a location may have many topics associated with it. This indicates a many to many association between TOPIC and LOCATION, with an intersecting entity TOPIC LOCATION. A topic will have many locations associated with it: the association between TOPIC and TOPIC LOCATION is therefore *mandatory one to optional becoming mandatory many*. A location may have many topics associated with it: the association between LOCATION and TOPIC LOCATION is *mandatory one to optional many* as illustrated in Figure 15.7.

Finally, we need to reflect in the COMRES strategic map the fact that a topic may also have text associated with it. Text describes a case, and a case can have many topics – each of which may have text describing circumstances relevant to that topic. Or the text may detail particular policies which apply to the topic, for reference by managers. This is all relevant information which is the responsibility of COMRES to obtain, so that a correct decision can be made for the case – as defined in its mission statement.

We therefore can see a *many to many* association between the entities TOPIC and TEXT, with an intersecting entity TOPIC TEXT. A topic may have text associated with it: the association between TOPIC and TOPIC TEXT is thus *mandatory one to optional many*. Text (such as a policy) may relate to many topics: the association between TEXT and TOPIC TEXT is also *mandatory one to optional many*. The strategic map which we have developed to this point is illustrated in Figure 15.7.

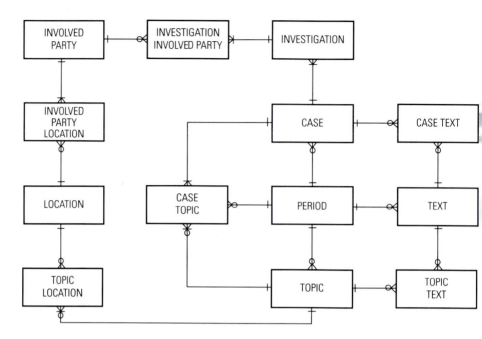

Figure 15.7 The COMRES strategic data map.

15.1.2 Resolution of strategic maps

In Part 3 we developed the strategic map for XYZ Corporation. The principal entity ORGANIZATION ROLE was identified, with the secondary entities of CUSTOMER, SUPPLIER, COMPETITOR and SUPPORT. This chapter focuses on a priority area: Complaints Resolution. **Involved party** is a collective term used by COMRES to refer to customers, suppliers, support staff or competitors involved in an investigation. The strategic map in Figure 15.7 therefore suggests that INVOLVED PARTY is a synonym for ORGANIZATION ROLE. Similarly, TEXT is a synonym for the entity TEXTUAL DOCUMENTATION in the XYZ strategic map. PERIOD and LOCATION are the same in both strategic maps. CASE and INVESTIGATION are unique to COMRES.

It is best to adopt a standard terminology, rather than use synonyms. COMRES should change its terminology to the agreed corporate term, or the corporate term should be changed to that used in priority areas such as COMRES. Thus it will use TEXTUAL DOCUMENTATION rather than TEXT. It can later use other documentation defined in the XYZ strategic map: audio, graphical and/or video documentation, where relevant. But where terminology is an accepted part of an industry, it may not be feasible to change to a different term: it may create future communication problems with customers and suppliers who use the industry term. We assume this is the case for COMRES, to illustrate resolution of this dilemma.

We will allow COMRES to continue with its use of INVOLVED PARTY. To ensure it is correctly represented at the corporate level, however, we will define it as another secondary entity of ORGANIZATION ROLE. This will allow us later to integrate the COMRES strategic map with the XYZ strategic map. We can utilize ORGANIZATION ROLE STRUCTURE (see Table 13.2) to relate it to the other secondary entities.

As we developed the strategic map, we decomposed each *many to many* association into two *one to many* associations – with an intermediate intersecting entity. These are illustrated in Figure 15.8 by shading. The two entities of the original *many to many* association are **principal** entities. At the strategic level, principal entities represent data bases: intersecting entities indicate tactical areas and application systems. Tactical areas are also referred to as **functional areas**. Principal and intersecting entities are defined further during tactical modeling. They may represent potential operational data bases and systems which are defined more fully during operational modeling.

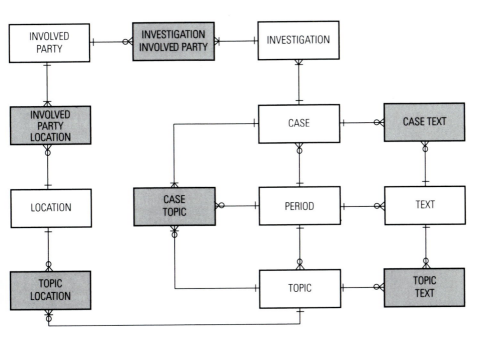

Figure 15.8 Principal and intersecting (shaded) entities.

15.1.3 Potential complaint resolution systems

Potential application systems represented by intersecting entities can be named by adding the word 'systems' to the intersecting entity name, to identify specific systems. CASE TEXT suggests the existence of possible 'Case Text Systems'. This name may be modified if necessary, such as in 'Case Documentation Systems'. Similarly, TOPIC TEXT indicates the existence of possible 'Topic Documentation Systems'. Both these systems are the responsibility of the functional area called **Case Investigations** by the Complaint Resolution managers.

Table 15.1 lists each intersecting entity from Figure 15.8, together with the functional area and potential systems it represents. We will use this table in Chapter 16 to select priority systems for more detailed tactical and operational modeling.

So far we have concentrated on development of the strategic data map. However we know from Chapters 2 and 3 that an entity list also exists for every data map. While the data map illustrates entities and associations schematically, the entity list details the attribute content of each entity. We will now develop the COMRES strategic entity list from its strategic data map.

15.1.4 Complaint resolution strategic entity list

Each entity must have at least one attribute: this is the primary key attribute which uniquely identifies it. Several key attributes may be needed to ensure uniqueness, as a compound key. These key attributes may also exist in other

Table 15.1 Potential systems from the strategic map

Intersecting Entity	Functional Area	Potential Systems
INVESTIGATION INVOLVED PARTY	Case Investigations	Investigation Reference Systems
INVOLVED PARTY LOCATION	Case Investigations	Location Reference Systems
TOPIC LOCATION	Case Investigations	Topic Reference Systems
CASE TOPIC	Case Investigations	Case Topic Analysis Systems
CASE TEXT	Case Investigations	Case Documentation Systems
TOPIC TEXT	Case Investigations	Topic Documentation Systems

entities as either primary or foreign keys. Key attributes are identified mainly during strategic modeling.

An entity may have many other attributes. These are defined during detailed tactical and operational modeling. Detailed data required by staff at tactical and operational levels of the business are uncovered: derived attributes whose values are calculated from other attributes; non key attributes which represent fundamental data; and selection attributes (secondary keys) for alternative access (see Chapter 2). Other key attributes may also be identified during tactical and operational modeling.

In developing the strategic map we identified entities and the associations by which they are related. These associations are based on common key attributes: at least one key must be common to two entities for them to be related by an association. There can be several keys in common between entities: either primary or foreign keys. The strategic entity list documents these entities and key attributes.

Figure 15.7 illustrates the COMRES strategic map. We will develop the strategic entity list which implements that data map. The rightmost bracket will be left open in each entity for additional attributes identified later, during tactical and operational modeling. We will start by defining attributes for each principal entity. These are: PERIOD, CASE, INVESTIGATION, INVOLVED PARTY, TOPIC, TEXT and LOCATION.

Time is an important factor, as indicated in the COMRES mission statement referring to prompt resolution of cases. This is represented in the strategic map by PERIOD. We will uniquely identify each period by the primary key *period id#*, which is abbreviated from *period identifier#*. As discussed in Chapter 2, the terminating # symbol indicates a key attribute; underlining indicates a primary key.

PERIOD   (period id#,

Each case is also uniquely identified. We will use the primary key *case id#*, abbreviated from *case identifier#*. CASE is dependent upon PERIOD. We will include *period id#* as part of the compound key. However management refer to a case by *case name* rather than *case id*. We will therefore include the attribute *case name* as a secondary key for alternative access purposes. A secondary key is surrounded by square brackets, as in [*case name*].

CASE   (case id#, period id#, [case name],

An investigation is uniquely identified by the primary key *investigation id#*. Although no association is shown between PERIOD and INVESTIGATION, time is important to investigations. Therefore we will include *period id#* also as part of a compound key of INVESTIGATION. INVESTIGATION is dependent on CASE: a case has many investigations. We will thus include a foreign key of *case id#* in INVESTIGATION. Foreign keys are not underlined, to distinguish them from primary keys.

INVESTIGATION   (investigation id#, period id#, case id#,

An involved party is uniquely identified by the primary key *involved party id#*. The history of an involved party is relevant to COMRES, indicating that *period id#* also exists as part of a compound key. Each involved party will be referenced by name rather than identifier: [*involved party name*] is included as a secondary key.

INVOLVED PARTY   (involved party id#, period id#, [involved party name],

(To integrate INVOLVED PARTY as a secondary entity of ORGANIZA-TION ROLE in the XYZ strategic map (see Chapter 13), we would also need to include organization *role id#* as a foreign key. We will not do that at this time: we must later add it prior to merging the COMRES strategic map automatically into the XYZ strategic map, using software.)

A case has many topics. Each topic is identified by *topic id#*, but is referenced by [*topic name*] as a secondary key. Time is also important, as indicated by the association between PERIOD and TOPIC: *period id#* is thus part of the compound key. This is of particular interest to COMRES management: they can determine the total references for each topic in a period. For topics with many references, management controls or other appropriate measures can be implemented. The attribute {*topic total refs this period*} is a strategic attribute which is of interest to management. It is a derived attribute (shown by surrounding braces), calculated by counting all instances of cases which refer to a specific topic in a period.

TOPIC   (topic id#, period id#, [topic name],
         {topic total refs this period},

TEXT is identified by the primary key *text id#*. The period to which specific text refers is often relevant: *period id#* is part of the compound key.

TEXT   (text id#, period id#,

LOCATION is uniquely identified by *location id#*. A secondary key of [*location name*] provides alternative reference.

LOCATION   (location id#, [location name],

We have now defined the key attributes and other attributes of interest at the strategic level for the principal entities in Figure 15.8. We will now address the intersecting entities.

An investigation has many involved parties: an involved party may participate in many investigations. The primary key of INVESTIGATION INVOLVED PARTY is a compound key of *investigation id#*, *involved party id#*, *period id#* – based on the primary keys of the principal entities it relates. At the strategic level, Table 15.1 indicates that this intersecting entity represents a group of **Investigation Reference Systems** based on the terminology of the Case Investigations functional area.

INVESTIGATION INVOLVED PARTY   (investigation id#, involved party id#, period id#,

An involved party has at least one location for contact purposes, but may have many locations which are relevant to an investigation. The compound key of *involved party id#*, *location id#*, *period id#* is used for INVOLVED PARTY LOCATION. This represents a group of **Location Reference Systems**, as indicated by Table 15.1.

INVOLVED PARTY LOCATION   (involved party id#, location id#, period id#,

A topic can relate to many locations: a location may have many topics associated with it. At the strategic level, senior management have said they are interested in total references for a topic in a period. At the tactical level, middle management may also be interested in the breakdown of topics by location. However we will not prejudge this. We will only define the compound key of TOPIC LOCATION as *topic id#*, *location id#*, *period id#*. This represents **Topic Reference Systems** (see Table 15.1).

TOPIC LOCATION   (topic id#, location id#, period id#,

A case has one or many topics: a topic may exist in many cases. Time is also relevant. The compound key of CASE TOPIC is therefore *case id#*, *topic id#*, *period id#*. This represents a group of **Case Topic Analysis Systems,** based on the terminology used by the Case Investigations functional area (see Table 15.1).

CASE TOPIC   (case id#, topic id#, period id#,

CASE TEXT has a compound primary key of *case id#*, *text id#*. As *period id#* is part of the compound key of both CASE and TEXT, we can already identify the period to which specific case documentation relates. At the strategic level we have chosen to omit *period id#* from the compound key. We will review this decision during tactical and operational modeling if time-dependent attributes of CASE TEXT are identified. Table 15.1 indicates that this entity represents a group of **Case Documentation Systems.**

CASE TEXT   (case id#, text id#)

Finally, a topic may have text associated with it: text may also relate to many topics. This intersecting entity represents **Topic Documentation Systems** at the strategic level. TOPIC TEXT has a compound key of *topic id#*, *text id#*. *Period id#* has been omitted for the same reasons as for CASE TEXT.

TOPIC TEXT   (topic id#, text id#)

We have now completed the definition of the strategic entity list for COMRES based on the data map in Figure 15.7. This is summarized next. We are now ready to commence tactical modeling.

The COMRES strategic entity list

PERIOD	(period id#,
CASE	(case id#, period id#, [case name],
INVESTIGATION	(investigation id#, period id#, case id#,
INVOLVED PARTY	(involved party id#, period id#, [involved party name],
TOPIC	(topic id#, period id#, [topic name], {topic total refs this period},
TEXT	(text id#, period id#,
LOCATION	(location id#, [location name],
INVESTIGATION INVOLVED PARTY	(investigation id#, involved party id#, period id#,
INVOLVED PARTY LOCATION	(involved party id#, location id#, period id#,
TOPIC LOCATION	(topic id#, location id#, period id#,
CASE TOPIC	(case id#, topic id#, period id#,
CASE TEXT	(case id#, text id#)
TOPIC TEXT	(topic id#, text id#)

15.2 SUMMARY

This chapter focused on a priority area selected from the XYZ corporate strategic model developed in Chapters 13 and 14. The *Customer Satisfaction* strategy of XYZ has been severely compromised by a pressing need for new systems to assist the *Customer Support* function in the prompt resolution of customer complaints. This was identified by management as the first area to be addressed for early development of systems from the strategic model.

Strategic modeling focused on the Complaints Department, which is responsible for the Complaints Resolution functional area (COMRES). Similar to strategic modeling at the corporate level, strategic modeling for the COMRES functional area involves senior and middle managers of that area, together with managers from other areas that provide information to, or receive information from, COMRES: called the clients of COMRES.

We saw that COMRES is responsible for the management of cases and investigations that are established on receipt of a customer complaint. COMRES does not resolve the complaint itself: that is the role of its clients, who deal directly with customers. Rather, COMRES is responsible for obtaining all of the relevant facts from the customer, from staff of XYZ, and any other individuals or organizations who can provide information pertinent to the specific case. Once all of the details of a case have been gathered, that information is given to the client manager who is responsible for making a decision to resolve that complaint.

We started strategic modeling with the mission statement of COMRES: 'Manage the investigation of cases, to result in their prompt and correct resolution'. We identified CASE and INVESTIGATION, and indicated time dependency with PERIOD. The people involved in a case were represented by INVOLVED PARTY. We saw that their LOCATION was important. A CASE has TOPIC entities, with TEXT that describes a case and relevant topics of that case.

The COMRES strategic map was then evaluated against the XYZ strategic map from Chapter 14. We saw that INVOLVED PARTY and TEXT (in the COMRES map) are both synonyms for ORGANIZATION ROLE and TEXTUAL DOCUMENTATION respectively (in the XYZ map). Unique to COMRES are CASE and INVESTIGATION, while we saw that PERIOD and LOCATION are the same in both maps. We discussed the need to adopt a standard data naming terminology throughout XYZ, using accepted industry terms if feasible. Where a change of terminology by COMRES was not feasible, we resolved data naming inconsistencies by defining INVOLVED PARTY as another secondary entity of ORGANIZA-TION ROLE. We can utilize ORGANIZATION ROLE STRUCTURE to relate INVOLVED PARTY to CUSTOMER, CLIENT and SUPPLIER.

We analyzed the COMRES strategic map to identify the Complaints Resolution tactical systems, to focus on priority areas during tactical model-ing. Finally, we developed a strategic entity list from the COMRES strategic map, preparatory to tactical modeling in the next chapter.

CHAPTER 16

Tactical Modeling

This chapter illustrates the development of a tactical data model, based on the strategic model in Chapter 15. This will be analyzed in Chapter 17, and expanded by operational modeling in Chapter 18. The resulting operational model will be used in later chapters to illustrate the design and development of systems.

Tactical modeling addresses a specific functional area, and focuses on its markets [1] and its products and services. It draws on the expert knowledge of functional area experts [2] to define the data relevant to this business focus, and needed to support systems which represent channels used by the functional area to deliver, support or provide products and services to its markets [3, 4]. In this chapter we will focus on the Case Investigations tactical functional area that was identified within the Complaints Resolution functional area in Chapter 15. We will establish this as a tactical project, for tactical modeling.

16.1 CASE INVESTIGATIONS FUNCTIONAL AREA

During tactical modeling the knowledge of functional area experts is used to identify markets of the functional area. These represent users, or customers, of the products and services produced or supported. Markets are identified by questions such as:

- Who are our customers?
- Where are they located?
- What do they consider value?
- What are they prepared to pay?

The products and services provided by a functional area should address the needs of its customers and markets. Only if their needs are satisfied effectively will customers continue to use the products and services. If a functional area no longer has a market, it has no reason for existence. For Complaint Resolution, its market is represented by customers, the minister or ombudsman, and management.

These people are all interested in *'prompt and correct resolution'* of cases, as indicated in the mission statement in Chapter 15. Products and services of the Case Investigations functional area of COMRES are therefore information obtained from investigation of cases, which will help in their resolution.

We will illustrate tactical modeling in the following pages by using a typical modeling session. Statements made by functional area experts are indented and shown in italics. We will use the data modeling concepts from Chapters 2 and 3 to expand the strategic map as appropriate, and will define attributes relevant to the tactical entities at this level. These attributes will be documented in a tactical entity list for that part of the data map illustrated, using principles of business normalization as discussed in Chapter 4.

Figure 15.8 illustrates the COMRES strategic map, with intersecting entities highlighted in Figure 15.9. These indicate potential application systems as summarized in Table 15.8. The entity list which implements the strategic map is summarized at the end of Chapter 15. We will use these as the starting point for tactical modeling.

Tactical modeling focuses first on those systems of highest priority to management. The systems in Table 15.1 have been prioritized in two groups – with A indicating high priority – as follows:

Potential Systems	Priority
Investigation Reference Systems	A
Location Reference Systems	A
Case Topic Analysis Systems	A
Topic Reference Systems	A
Case Documentation Systems	B
Topic Documentation Systems	B

16.1.1 Investigation reference systems

These systems are based on the entities PERIOD, CASE, INVESTI-GATION, INVOLVED PARTY and INVESTIGATION INVOLVED PARTY (see Figure 15.7). INVOLVED PARTY represents a number of people involved in a case. These include customers, the minister or ombudsman, management and COMRES staff. These represent the market of the Case Investigations functional area. They are all users of the information provided by it. An explanation from a functional area expert is appropriate.

> *Customers may contact a government organization (through the minister or the ombudsman) with a complaint which is to be investigated. A case is established to manage the investigation. Many involved parties – such as the government organization which was contacted, our staff, the customer or others may participate in the investigation.*

This statement indicates we are interested in several involved parties. These are shown as secondary entities related to the principal entity INVOLVED PARTY. The Case Investigations functional area uses the terms: CUSTOMER and CLIENT. A minister, ombudsman or manager who uses information from an investigation to resolve a case for a customer is known specifically as a CLIENT. Also relevant to an investigation may be details relating to suppliers: SUPPLIER is also needed.

A type entity INVOLVED PARTY TYPE is required for these secondary entities. On further discussion with the functional experts we find that they are also interested in the interrelationships between involved parties from our organization, from government organizations, suppliers, and clients, as well as the customer. A structure entity is suggested: INVOLVED PARTY STRUCTURE. This is represented as a data map in Figure 16.1.

(Note that when the COMRES strategic map is merged into the XYZ strategic map, both INVOLVED PARTY and CLIENT will become additional secondary entities of ORGANIZATION ROLE, together with the existing secondaries of CUSTOMER and SUPPLIER, all at the same level. These will all be interrelated by ORGANIZATION ROLE STRUCTURE (see Chapters 13 and 14). We saw earlier that INVOLVED PARTY is the COMRES term, not ORGANIZATION ROLE. For tactical and operational modeling in Part 4, therefore, we will interrelate them with INVOLVED PARTY STRUCTURE.)

Each of the secondary entities uses the same key *involved party id#* as the principal entity. This is its primary key. If other identifying keys are normally used, such as *customer id#* to indicate a unique customer identifier, *involved party id#* must still exist, but may become a foreign key. These type and structure entities are documented on the following page. The principal entity INVOLVED PARTY now includes a foreign key of *involved party*

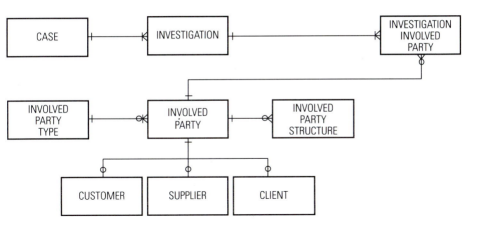

Figure 16.1 Investigation Reference Systems data map.

type id#. The structure entity contains characteristic duplicate primary and foreign keys as discussed in Chapters 2 and 4.

INVOLVED PARTY TYPE	(involved party type id#, involved party type description)
INVOLVED PARTY	(involved party id#, period id#, [involved party name], involved party type id#,
CUSTOMER	(customer id#, involved party id#,
SUPPLIER	(involved party id#,
CLIENT	(involved party id#,
INVOLVED PARTY STRUCTURE	(involved party id#, involved party type id#, involved party id#, involved party type id#)

We will now concentrate on identifying tactical attributes of interest. We progressively add these to the entity list, using business normalization and including also attributes earlier identified in the COMRES strategic entity list in Chapter 15. We find from the functional area experts that the following details are relevant.

> *We use a 'case file identifier' as alternative identification of a case. This helps us to locate correspondence or other relevant material filed elsewhere. The minister has his own reference identifier, which we must use in correspondence to him about a case. This also applies to the ombudsman. We call this the 'case foreign reference identifier'.*

These are secondary keys and are all wholly dependent on *case id#*. They have been included in CASE as follows:

CASE	(case id#, period id#, [case name], [case file id], [case foreign ref id],

We group cases into categories for subsequent analysis purposes. To manage each case, we need to know when the case was first received and the date when information is due to be provided to interested parties. When a case is finally completed we need to record that date, and also when the responsible manager has signed off on the case. He is referred to as the signatory. Of course we also need to know the customer who initiated the case.

[*Category identifier*] is also a secondary key. This and other attributes suggested above are all dependent on *case id#* and have been added to CASE:

CASE   (case id#, period id#, [case name], [case file id], [case foreign ref id], [category id], case date received, case date due, case date completed, case date signed, customer id#, signatory id#:alias involved party id#,

The foreign key *customer id#* refers to CUSTOMER. Notice that *signatory id#* is a foreign key also, but indicates with a colon that it is an alias name for *involved party id#*. The responsible manager, as signatory, is an involved party.

We need to know the target and actual completion dates for an investigation, as there may be more than one investigation carried out for a case. For each involved party we also need to know the relevant address and phone number.

INVESTIGATION   (investigation id#, period id#, investigation target completion date, investigation actual completion date, case id#,

INVOLVED PARTY   (involved party id#, period id#, [involved party name], involved party address, [involved party phone number],

The secondary key [*involved party phone number*] allows direct access. The tactical entity list for Investigation Reference Systems is summarized below. This documents the data map in Figure 16.1.

Investigation Reference Systems entity list

CASE   (case id#, period id#, [case name], [case file id], [category id], [case foreign ref id], case date received, case date due, case date completed, case date signed, customer id#, signatory id#:alias involved party id#)

INVESTIGATION   (investigation id#, period id#, investigation target completion date, investigation actual completion date, case id#)

INVOLVED PARTY TYPE   (involved party type id#, involved party type description)

INVOLVED PARTY   (involved party id#, period id#, [involved party name], involved party address, [involved party phone number], involved party type id#)

CUSTOMER	(customer id#, involved party id#)
SUPPLIER	(involved party id#)
CLIENT	(involved party id#)
INVOLVED PARTY STRUCTURE	(involved party id#, involved party type id#, involved party id#, involved party type id#)
INVESTIGATION INVOLVED PARTY	(investigation id#, involved party id#, period id#)
PERIOD TYPE	(period type id#, period type description)
PERIOD	(period id#, period start date, period start time, period end date, period end time, {period duration}, period unit, period type id#)

Many of the entities above use *period id#* as part of their compound key. We have thus included PERIOD in the entity list. This offers great flexibility with time, for analysis and management purposes. Rather than use date and time directly, we will instead use an automatically allocated period identifier (see Chapter 13) to which we can associate attributes of *start date* and *start time*, and *end date* and *end time*. This will enable us to derive *duration*.

As discussed in Chapter 13, by including the attribute *period unit*, we can express {*period duration*} in months, weeks, days, hours or any other time unit of interest. For example we may use a monthly time period for accounting purposes, but a weekly time period for reporting purposes and a quarterly period for performance analysis. Here we are interested in three types of period: accounting period; reporting period; performance period. PERIOD TYPE has also been included.

Furthermore we can easily vary the unit of these different periods, and also the end date and time (and hence duration). Thus we can change to weekly accounting periods, and monthly or daily reporting, or monitor annual performance, at will. This offers great flexibility to management for reporting and analysis purposes. PERIOD was omitted in the Figure 16.1 data map: we will see how this omission is detected in the next chapter.

16.1.2 Location reference systems

The location of each involved party is discussed in this section. We will focus on the intersecting entity INVOLVED PARTY LOCATION from Figure 15.7, and on the principal entities INVOLVED PARTY and LOCATION.

The location of an involved party who is part of the investigation is important, for contact and other purposes. This location may be a geographic location, or may be a grid location or a logical location.

There are three types of location which are of interest: GEOGRAPHIC LOCATION, GRID LOCATION and LOGICAL LOCATION. These secondary entities are all associated with LOCATION. A geographic location (such as a state) may contain other geographic locations (such as cities). This indicates a recursive association. It may also comprise grid locations, or a number of non-contiguous, logical locations. Or a logical location may include several geographic locations. These recursive associations, and associations between secondary entities, indicate the existence of the structure entity LOCATION STRUCTURE. Figure 16.2 illustrates the Location Reference Systems data map. The entity list with this figure is based also on the following comments by the functional area experts.

We often refer to locations by name, for alternative access to a location address. We also use grid reference for more detailed grid location coordinates.

This indicates location attributes for inclusion in the Location Reference Systems entity list. We also include PERIOD and the attributes we identified in the Investigation Reference Systems entity list for involved parties.

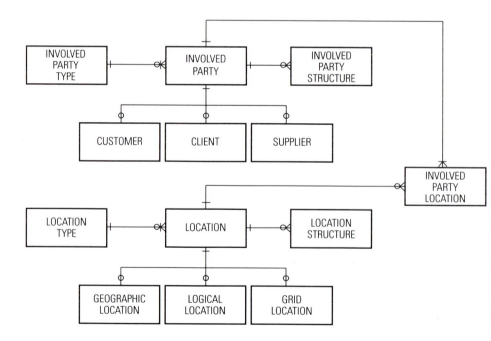

Figure 16.2 Location Reference Systems data map.

Location Reference Systems entity list for Figure 16.2

INVOLVED PARTY TYPE	(involved party type id#, involved party type description)
INVOLVED PARTY	(involved party id#, period id#, [involved party name], involved party address, [involved party phone number], involved party type id#)
CUSTOMER	(customer id#, involved party id#)
SUPPLIER	(involved party id#)
CLIENT	(involved party id#)
INVOLVED PARTY STRUCTURE	(involved party id#, involved party type id#, involved party id#, involved party type id#)
LOCATION TYPE	(location type id#, location type description)
LOCATION	(location id#, [location name], location address, location type id#)
LOCATION STRUCTURE	(location id#, location type id#, location id#, location type id#)
GEOGRAPHIC LOCATION	(location id#)
LOGICAL LOCATION	(location id#)
GRID LOCATION	(location id#, (grid reference))
INVOLVED PARTY LOCATION	(involved party id#, location id#, period id#)
PERIOD TYPE	(period type id#, period type description)
PERIOD	(period id#, period start date, period start time, period end date, period end time, {period duration}, period unit, period type id#)

16.1.3   Case topic analysis systems

Topics indicate specific situations or problems which lead to the customer's complaint. A case may have many topics associated with it. A topic may also be relevant to several cases. An investigation examines each topic for a case to determine the facts from all involved parties. The functional area experts describe typical topics:

> *A case may comprise a number of topics. These topics may relate to: an account or problem topic, or a policy topic, staff topic or an enquiry.*

These are secondary topic types associated with the principal entity TOPIC. Topics may be interrelated. For example, an enquiry may relate to a policy, or may be due to an account topic or a problem topic. A problem topic can also result in an account topic: because of a problem, incorrect charges may be made to an account. These show a need for a structure entity TOPIC

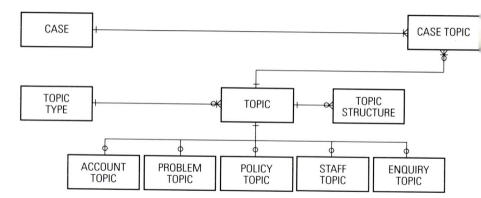

Figure 16.3 Case Topic Analysis Systems data map.

Case Topic Systems entity list

CASE	(case id#, period id#, [case name], [case file id], [category id], [case foreign ref id], case date received, case date due, case date completed, case date signed, customer id#, signatory id#:alias involved party id#)
PERIOD TYPE	(period type id#, period type description)
PERIOD	(period id#, period start date, period start time, period end date, period end time, {period duration}, period unit, period type id#)
TOPIC TYPE	(topic type id#, topic type description)
TOPIC	(topic id#, period id#, [topic name], {topic total references this period}, topic type id#)
TOPIC STRUCTURE	(topic id#, topic type id#, topic id#, topic type id#)
ACCOUNT TOPIC	(topic id#)
PROBLEM TOPIC	(topic id#)
POLICY TOPIC	(topic id#)
STAFF TOPIC	(topic id#)
ENQUIRY TOPIC	(topic id#)
CASE TOPIC	(case id#, topic id#, period id#, case topic date received, case topic due date, case topic completion date)

STRUCTURE. Figure 16.3 is the data map, followed by the relevant entity list as defined by the functional experts.

We are aware of the interest senior management have in the total references to a topic in a period. No other topic attributes have been further suggested by the functional area experts.

Each of the secondary topic entities uses the primary key *topic id#* of TOPIC. No other attributes of these secondary entities have been identified at this point, merely the types of topic. The Case Topic Systems entity list includes the CASE attributes and PERIOD attributes identified earlier. Each of these entities is also relevant to Case Topic Systems.

There is one remaining high priority system identified by management. This relates to Topic Reference Systems. It indicates the location of each topic.

16.1.4 Topic reference systems

Those locations with many references to a specific topic may need more investigation. For example, problems at a location due to incorrect use of products by customers may suggest a need for further customer training. We ask the functional area experts to discuss the entities TOPIC, LOCATION and TOPIC LOCATION in Figure 15.7:

> *The ability to determine the location of a topic is often of assistance to an investigation, and for other purposes. This location may be a geographic location, or may be a grid location or a logical location.*

The data map is shown in Figure 16.4, with the entity list on the following page.

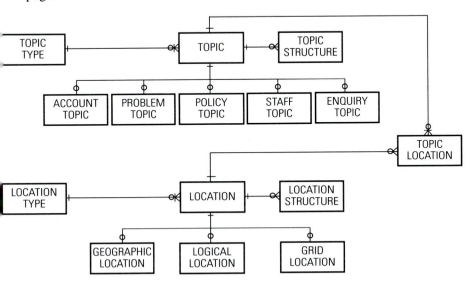

Figure 16.4 Topic Reference Systems data map.

Topic Reference Systems entity list

TOPIC TYPE	(<u>topic type id#</u>, topic type description)
TOPIC	(<u>topic id#, period id#</u>, [topic name], {topic total references this period}, topic type id#)
TOPIC STRUCTURE	(<u>topic id#, topic type id#, topic id#, topic type id#</u>)
PERIOD TYPE	(<u>period type id#</u>, period type description)
PERIOD	(<u>period id#</u>, period start date, period start time, period end date, period end time, {period duration}, period unit, period type id#)
LOCATION TYPE	(<u>location type id#</u>, location type description)
LOCATION	(<u>location id#</u>, [location name], location address, location type id#)
LOCATION STRUCTURE	(<u>location id#, location type id#, location id#, location type id#</u>)
TOPIC LOCATION	(<u>topic id#, location id#, period id#</u>, {total topic location references this period})

This entity list omits the secondary TOPIC and LOCATION entities as these are documented in the two earlier lists. {*Total topic location references this period*} is now added to TOPIC LOCATION, as COMRES calculates total location references to a topic.

We have now modeled the high priority systems. Next we model the lower priority Case Documentation Systems and Topic Documentation Systems.

16.1.5   Case documentation systems

All circumstances relating to a case must be documented. This includes correspondence as well as notes taken during an investigation, and specific written reports. It may also include textual documentation detailing policies of the organization in particular situations. This is needed so the relevant manager can arrive at a decision. In the words of the functional experts:

> *Cases are described by a textual record of the circumstances associated with the case. This textual documentation may comprise letters or notes in relation to the case, or may be text used to report the result of an investigation to the minister, the ombudsman or the customer.*

Standard paragraphs are often used to document a case or to compose letters. These are combined in different ways, or modified. A letter may use standard paragraphs as well as unique textual documentation for the case.

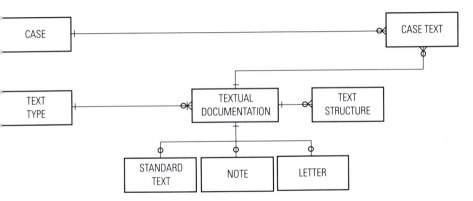

Figure 16.5 Case Documentation Systems data map.

It may be related to documentation on relevant policies. This suggests the entities NOTE, LETTER and STANDARD TEXT, and TEXT STRUCTURE in Figure 16.5.

The actual text is *text content* in the principal entity TEXTUAL DOCUMENTATION. When implemented, this may be defined as a variable length data field representing a line, or instead a page, of text. This is dependent on the capability of the software used for implementation. The Case Documentation Systems entity list is illustrated below.

Case Documentation Systems entity list

CASE	(case id#, period id#, [case name], [case file id], [category id], [case foreign ref id], case date received, case date due, case date completed, case date signed, customer id#, signatory id#:alias involved party id#)
PERIOD TYPE	(period type id#, period type description)
PERIOD	(period id#, period start date, period start time, period end date, period end time, {period duration}, period unit, period type id#)
TEXT TYPE	(text type id#, text type description)
TEXTUAL DOCUMENTATION	(text id#, period id#, text content, text type id#)
TEXT STRUCTURE	(text id#, text type id#, text id#, text type id#)
STANDARD TEXT	(text id#)
NOTE	(text id#)
LETTER	(text id#)
CASE TEXT	(case id#, text id#)

16.1.6 Topic documentation systems

There is also documentation on each topic. Text is used to define policies relevant to the topic, or may document standard paragraphs for specific topics. Topic Documentation Systems allow this text to be referenced in relation to each topic in a case.

Topics may also be described textually. This text may comprise letters or notes in relation to the topic, or may be text used in reporting to the minister, the ombudsman or the customer.

TOPIC TEXT is the intersecting entity which represents these systems. The data map is illustrated in Figure 16.6. TOPIC and TEXTUAL DOCUMEN-TATION secondary entities have been already defined earlier, and so have been omitted from the entity list on the following page.

We have now completed this tactical modeling example and are ready for operational modeling. First we need to document the tactical model formally, and analyze it so we can identify priority subject data bases and systems. We can then concentrate on their detailed definition in operational modeling, for early development and delivery of those priority systems. This is addressed in the next chapter.

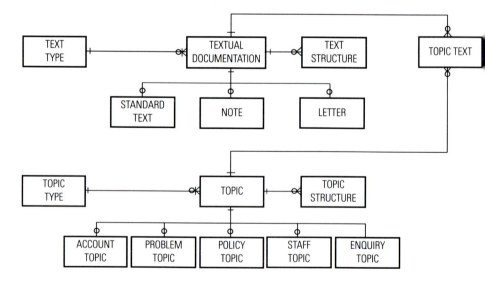

Figure 16.6 Topic Documentation Systems data map.

Topic Documentation Systems entity list

PERIOD TYPE	(period type id#, period type description)
PERIOD	(period id#, period start date, period start time, period end date, period end time, {period duration}, period unit, period type id#)
TOPIC TYPE	(topic type id#, topic type description)
TOPIC	(topic id#, period id#, [topic name], {topic total references this period}, topic type id#)
TOPIC STRUCTURE	(topic id#, topic type id#, topic id#, topic type id#)
TEXT TYPE	(text type id#, text type description)
TEXTUAL DOCUMENTATION	(text id#, period id#, text content, text type id#)
TEXT STRUCTURE	(text id#, text type id#, text id#, text type id#)
TOPIC TEXT	(topic id#, text id#)

16.2 | SUMMARY

In this chapter we covered tactical modeling of the Case Investigations priority tactical functional area within the Complaints Resolution strategic functional area, identified by analysis of the strategic map in Chapter 15. To manage this, a tactical project was established for tactical modeling of the Case Investigations project area.

We discussed that tactical modeling focuses on markets and customers of the project area. These are the client managers of COMRES, the customers they are responsible for, and external representatives; all of whom provide case details to, or receive information from, COMRES. This information represents products and services that are provided by COMRES. Products and services are received from, or provided to, COMRES markets and customers through channels.

The first step saw management prioritize the tactical systems identified in Chapter 15. This indicated the priority sequence that was to be followed for tactical modeling. The Investigation Reference Systems were identified as highest priority.

Business experts with detailed knowledge of the relevant tactical system were brought together for tactical modeling. They had already been trained in tactical modeling, and so participated actively in tactical modeling sessions that required their expertise. They also reviewed tactical models that were developed in areas that they interface with, in carrying out their duties.

We saw that greater detail emerges during tactical modeling; this is reflected in type, secondary and structure entities related to principal entities from the strategic model, as well as any new entities identified as also needed. All data is normalized as it is identified: schematically by decomposing all *many to many* associations in the tactical map; and also by business normalization of tactical attributes in the entity list, which is defined as the tactical map is progressively developed.

We saw the development of the Investigation Reference Systems tactical data map, together with its entity list. This identified secondary entities of INVOLVED PARTY as CUSTOMER, SUPPLIER and CLIENT. Tactical attributes indicating data needed in CASE and INVESTIGATION were identified during tactical modeling. These were normalized to 3BNF, 4BNF and 5BNF as required, and added to the entities where they belonged.

We modeled Location Reference Systems as the next highest priority area, identifying GEOGRAPHIC LOCATION, LOGICAL LOCATION and GRID LOCATION secondary entities of LOCATION, together with additional attributes as needed.

Modeling the Case Topic Analysis Systems indicated that TOPIC had secondary entities of ACCOUNT TOPIC, PROBLEM TOPIC, POLICY TOPIC, STAFF TOPIC and also ENQUIRY TOPIC. The first two of these topics relate to customer complaints. Additional attributes were identified.

In modeling Case Documentation Systems, we saw the need for secondary entities of STANDARD TEXT, NOTE and LETTER for TEXTUAL DOCUMENTATION. Topic Reference Systems related topics to locations, but no new secondary entities were identified. No other secondary entities were needed for Topic Documentation Systems, either.

The tactical model, comprising tactical maps and entity lists of the tactical project area, was documented ready for analysis by software in the next chapter.

References

[1] Drucker, P. (1974). *Management: Tasks, Responsibilities, Practices*, Harper & Row: New York, NY.

[2] Finkelstein, C. (1989). *An Introduction to Information Engineering*, Addison-Wesley: Reading, MA.

[3] Lorange, P. (ed), (1982). *Implementation of Strategic Planning*. Prentice Hall: Englewood Cliffs, NJ.

[4] Rowe, A. J., Mason, R. O., Dickel, K. E. and Snyder, N. H. (1990). Strategic Management: A Methodological Approach (Third Edition), Addison-Wesley, Reading: MA.

CHAPTER 17

Data Model Analysis

This chapter describes the analysis of data models using software. Principles discussed in this chapter apply to the analysis of strategic, tactical or operational models. We will use the strategic and tactical models from Chapters 15 and 16 to illustrate relevant concepts. After analysis, the tactical model will be used in Chapter 18 to develop an operational model. The operational model will be implemented as application systems in later chapters.

17.1 DATA MODELING CASE PRODUCTS

Data model analysis can be carried out manually for small data models with less than 50 entities, using the entity dependency concepts discussed in Chapter 3. Manual analysis of larger data models is impractical: software is needed because of their complexity.

Data model analysis, as described in this book, is carried out by two Computer-Aided Software Engineering (CASE) data modeling packages – IE: Expert (by IESC) [1] and ISM (by Infonetics) [2]. Both CASE products operate on IBM-compatible microcomputers. IE: Expert runs under DOS Windows 3.0 [3] or later, while ISM runs under control of SCO Xenix System V [4]. In addition, ISM is also available for various versions of UNIX, such as HP/UX V7.0 [5]. Both CASE products carry out data model analysis, producing analysis and documentation reports as detailed in Table 17.1. It is not the purpose of this chapter to discuss these products in detail,

Table 17.1   Documentation and analysis of IE: Expert and ISM

IE: Expert	ISM
Data Model Documentation	**Data Model Documentation**
• Planning Reports of single or selected sessions, users, statements or model views, as an outline or sorted by name or planning statement type, with all statement text, outline and data model dictionary links and time stamped session activity.	• Entity Definition Report with entities, associations and attributes.
• Model View Reports of single or selected users, sessions or model views, in structured outline or sorted by name, with purposes, time stamped session activity and family links.	• Enterprise, Application, and Functional Decomposition Charts, plus chart indexes.
• Entity Reports of single or selected sessions, model views and/or entities, sorted by name, type or implementation phase, with entities, associations and attributes plus details, views, purposes, statement links and time stamped session activity.	• Enterprise, Application and Functional Decomposition Usage Matrices. • Association Matrix. • Entity, Attribute, and Key Usage Permission Matrices.
• Attribute Reports of single or selected sessions and model views, sorted by name or type, including attributes with all details, entities, views, purposes, statement links and time stamped session activity.	• Entity Review Status and Security Matrices. • View Review and Security Matrices.
• Session Reports by title or type with session notes (such as attendees, session objectives) and time stamps.	• Indexes to all matrices. • Capacity Planning Report.
• History Log Reports of all session activity, for data model audit and security purposes.	
Data Model Analysis	**Data Model Analysis**
• Automatically generated and maintained data maps in implementation phase sequence.	• Automatically generated and maintained data maps in implementation phase sequence.
• Cluster Report of single or selected model views, showing application systems and data bases, with comparison to other cluster reports for impact analysis.	• Cluster Report, showing application systems and data bases.
• Model Completeness Report for consistency and quality assurance of entities, attributes, associations and planning statements.	• Loop Detection Analysis.
• Model Analysis Report for quality assurance validation of entities, attributes, associations, clusters and model views.	

but to use them only to illustrate the analysis and documentation that must be provided by any software tool which plans to support Information Engineering.

A number of other packages also provide similar documentation, but they do not directly support the business-driven variant of Information Engineering described in this book, and do not carry out all of the essential data model analysis described in this chapter. Instead they support the DP-driven variant. Three of these products are the Information Engineering Facility (IEF) from Texas Instruments [6], and the Information Engineering Workbench (IEW) and Application Development Workbench (ADW) products developed by KnowledgeWare [7]. However, IE: Expert provides a bidirectional bridge between it and IEW for analysis of IEW data models. Other CASE products also provide support for data modeling. Chapters 18 and 19 of my earlier book provide a comprehensive evaluation method for CASE products.

IE: Expert V5.0 uses a standard graphical user interface (GUI) based on DOS Windows 3.0. It supports all standard Windows facilities such as cut, copy and paste between applications. It presents a familiar look and feel to users, with ease of use. At the time of writing, ISM does not use a GUI. Instead it uses a text-based windowing facility built on Xenix and UNIX. Although ISM does not have the same ease of use as IE: Expert, it carries out much of the data model analysis described in this chapter. To illustrate principles of data model analysis and documentation, IE: Expert will be our focus in the following pages.

17.2 | DATA MODEL DOCUMENTATION

We will discuss data model documentation first. The correct documentation of data entities, attributes and associations is essential before any analysis can be carried out. The goal analysis statements developed in Chapter 9 and strategic and tactical modeling examples that we discussed in Chapters 15 and 16 will be used to illustrate relevant principles.

17.2.1   Model view documentation

IE: Expert uses the concept of model views. A data model always has at least one model view, called the root view. This comprises the entire model. Any subset of the data model can also be defined as a model view. Using our jigsaw puzzle analogy, the root view is the jigsaw picture, while other model views represent parts of the jigsaw. Thus priority areas of an organization are defined in a model view so they can be modeled and analyzed separately from other parts of the business of lower priority. The data bases and systems needed by these priority model views can then be defined, developed and delivered early.

Each model view is given a unique name. The root view, called THE MODEL by default, always exists. This default name can be changed if required, such as to 'XYZ MODEL' for the XYZ Corporation. A model view is also defined as a model view type. This may be a functional area (such as the Finance Department), or it may be a strategic, tactical or operational view, a process view of part or all of an application system, or a control group. As IE: Expert is extensible, other model view types also can be defined by a nominated systems administrator for use by IE: Expert, to reflect an organization's unique terminology. Full security control of users and passwords is enforced so that only authorized systems administrators can make these changes.

Model views are used to manage large data models. They allow several project teams to work concurrently on different model views, for development and delivery of priority systems. Model views are related in a hierarchy based on the root view, as illustrated in Figure 17.1 for the XYZ MODEL.

The XYZ MODEL in Figure 17.1 shows three model views below it. The bottom right corner of each model view box indicates the type of view, such as R (root view), F (functional area view) or W (operational view). The first functional area view is called GOAL ANALYSIS, defined for the planning statements from Chapter 9. The COMPLAINTS RESOLUTION view was defined for the XYZ COMRES strategic model in Chapter 15. The CASE INVESTGNS view was used for the tactical model in Chapter 16.

A model view hierarchy can include any number of views at any level, and any number of levels, limited only by the disk storage capacity available to IE: Expert. Figure 17.1 shows COMPLAINTS RESOLUTION with a dependent functional area view, INVESTGN REFERENCE SUBJECTS, below it. This allows principal and intersecting entities to be copied to this view to represent the subject map of Investigation Reference Systems (see Section 16.1.1). The tactical model CASE INVESTGNS is also a functional area view, with the operational view INVESTGN REFERENCE SYSTEMS below it. This will be used for the operational model to be developed in Chapter 18.

Model views can also be printed in report form, as shown in Figure 17.2. This shows all model views defined for the XYZ COMRES encyclopedia, using dot notation 1, 1.1, 1.2, 1.2.1 to indicate hierarchical dependencies.

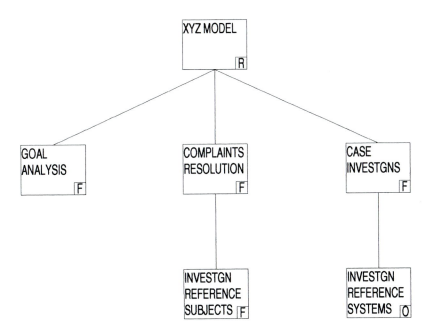

Figure 17.1 XYZ Model View Hierarchy, as printed by IE: Expert V5.0.

17.2.2 Planning statement documentation

IE: Expert allows textual planning statements to be defined and linked to entities, attributes and associations in a data model. Many statement types are supported, such as mission, critical success factor, goal, issue for resolution, objective, strategy, policy, tactic, systems design objective or business event. Planning statement types are also extensible; any other types can be added by a nominated systems administrator so that an organization's unique planning terminology can be used.

Each planning statement is given a unique name, and statements can be structured hierarchically as a planning outline. In Chapter 9 the XYZ mission and critical success factors were used first to define goals, then issues, strategies and objectives. This is shown next for Asset Growth and Profitability. The statement name is in capitals; the statement type is shown in brackets. The type has also been included in the name for uniqueness, abbreviated in some cases.

XYZ COMRES Model View Report
All Model Views
Thu Jun 13 14:36:59 1991 Page 1

XYZ MODEL

1 **XYZ MODEL**

Category:	Root View
Sub-views:	GOAL ANALYSIS
	COMPLAINTS RESOLUTION
	CASE INVESTGNS
Created:	Tue Jun 04 16:51:24 1991
	by CBF in session COMRES MODELING
Modified:	Thu Jun 13 09:05:56 1991
	by CBF in session COMRES MODELING

1.1 **GOAL ANALYSIS**

Category:	Functional Area
Parent View:	XYZ MODEL
Created:	Tue Jun 04 16:52:05 1991
	by CBF in session COMRES MODELING

1.2 **COMPLAINTS RESOLUTION**

Category:	Functional Area
Parent View:	XYZ MODEL
Sub-views:	INVESTGN REFERENCE SUBJECTS
Created:	Tue Jun 04 16:52:06 1991
	by CBF in session COMRES MODELING
Modified:	Thu Jun 13 09:09:48 1991
	by CBF in session COMRES MODELING

1.2.1 **INVESTGN REFERENCE SUBJECTS**

Category:	Functional Area
Parent View:	COMPLAINTS RESOLUTION
Created:	Wed Jun 12 16:21:27 1991
	by CBF in session COMRES MODELING
Modified:	Thu Jun 13 09:13:40 1991
	by CBF in session COMRES MODELING

1.3 **CASE INVESTGNS**

Category:	Functional Area
Parent View:	XYZ MODEL
Sub-views:	INVESTGN REFERENCE SYSTEMS
Created:	Tue Jun 04 16:52:06 1991
	by CBF in session COMRES MODELING
Modified:	Thu Jun 13 09:13:04 1991
	by CBF in session COMRES MODELING

Figure 17.2 Model View report for the XYZ COMRES encyclopaedia.

1.3.1 **INVESTGN REFERENCE SYSTEMS**

        Category: Operational View
    Parent View: CASE INVESTGNS
         Created: Wed Jun 12 16:05:36 1991
                  by CBF in session COMRES MODELING
       Modified: Thu Jun 13 09:06:49 1991
                  by CBF in session COMRES MODELING

Figure 17.2 (cont.)   **Model View report for the XYZ COMRES encyclopaedia.**

Statements are structured in the following outline form to show dependencies; this is called a planning outline by IE: Expert. Planning statements can be reported in this structured form, or instead may be reported alphabetically.

```
XYZ MISSION (Mission)
    CSF: ASSET GROWTH (Critical Success Factor)
        GOAL: ASSET GROWTH (Goal)
            ISSUES: ASSET GROWTH (Issue for Resolution)
                STRATEGY: MARKET EXIT (Strategy)
                STRATEGY: ASSET DISPOSAL (Strategy)
    CSF: PROFITABILITY (Critical Success Factor)
        GOAL: PROFITABILITY (Goal)
            ISSUES: PROFITABILITY (Issue for Resolution)
                STRATEGY: FINANCIAL REPORTING (Strategy)
                STRATEGY: BUDGET CONTROL (Strategy)
```

Figure 17.3 illustrates the planning session where these statements were defined. A number of windows are displayed, representing 'IE: EXPERT – XYZ COMRES' as shown on the top line. This is the name of the encyclopedia that has been allocated by IE: Expert to document and analyze the XYZ COMRES data model in this chapter. The top right window displays the 'Model View Hierarchy' of Figure 17.1. This has not been drawn manually, but has been generated automatically by IE: Expert. The dotted box around GOAL ANALYSIS indicates that this is the current model view to be acted upon. The bottom right window is 'Planning Outline: GOAL ANALYSIS'. Planning statements from Chapter 9 are displayed in outline form, showing the XYZ mission and the asset growth CSF and dependent statements, with part of the profitability statements.

The left window in Figure 17.3, showing 'Planning Statements: GOAL ANALYSIS', displays the statements for the current model view. In the Planning Outline window the line 'GOAL: ASSET GROWTH (Goal)' is highlighted in reverse white on black; this indicates that it is the current selected statement. Detail of this statement is displayed in the Planning Statement window, where we can see that the statement type is 'Goal'. The statement text is displayed over as many window pages as required. We

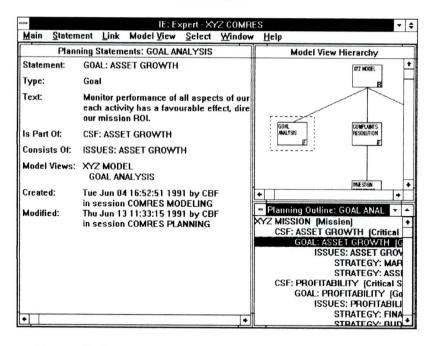

Figure 17.3 Goal analysis planning session, based on Chapter 9.

see that this goal is part of CSF: ASSET GROWTH, and also consists of ISSUES: ASSET GROWTH (as shown also in the outline window). It is used by model views XYZ MODEL and GOAL ANALYSIS. Finally the session and user where it was created, and later modified, are shown.

The planning statements in a selected model view, or in several views, are printed in a Planning Statement Report. This is directed to any printer supported by Windows 3.0, or can be displayed on the screen or stored in a file. Figure 17.4 shows part of the report with the XYZ mission statement, asset growth CSF and dependent statements. The report has been printed in structured form for the GOAL ANALYSIS model view so that the statement dependencies are clearly seen, using the dot notation 2, 2.1, 2.1.1 etc. (The notation 1, 1.1, 1.1.1 is used in the root view Planning Statement Report for the XYZ MODEL, as other statements may also be included in that view.)

The mission statement text is first printed, over as many pages as required. During goal analysis in Chapter 9 the mission statement was used to identify the data subjects CUSTOMER, MARKET, NEED, PRODUCT and PERFORMANCE (see Figure 9.2). Figure 17.4 shows dictionary links defined to these data subjects. It shows that the mission statement consists of the CSFs discussed in Chapter 9. These CSFs were attached to relevant data subjects in the mission model (see Figure 9.3). Figure 17.4 also shows on its second page that CSF: ASSET GROWTH has a dictionary link to PERFORMANCE.

In Chapter 3 we saw that groups of related entities represent policies or issues, and define boundaries of responsibility. Policies and issues are usually linked to entities by the Planning Statement window of IE: Expert. Quantified goals are long-term targets and objectives are short-term targets: these are generally linked to attributes. Associations are usually linked to strategies or tactics. We refer generically to linked entities, attributes and associations as linked data model objects. To accommodate variations in terminology and strategic planning in organizations, IE: Expert allows any defined planning statement type to be linked to any relevant data model objects. For example, a goal could also be linked to relevant entities or associations.

Because of these linkages, the data model objects defined from planning statements are readily apparent, as shown in Figure 17.4. These statements give clear management direction for the data bases or systems developed from these objects. We will see this when we discuss data dictionary reports next.

XYZ COMRES   Planning Statement Report
Planning Statement Report
Thu Jun 13 14:33:43 1991   Page 1

                                                              XYZ MISSION
2   **XYZ MISSION**

              Category: Mission
                  Text: Develop, deliver and support products and services which satisfy the needs
                          of customers in markets where we can achieve a return on investment at
                          least 20% pa within two years of market entry.
            Dict Links: CUSTOMER
                          MARKET
                          NEED
                          PERFORMANCE
                          PRODUCT
          Consists Of: CSF: ASSET GROWTH
                          CSF: PROFITABILITY
                          CSF: MARKET SHARE
                          CSF: INNOVATION
                          CSF: MARKET ANALYSIS
                          CSF: CUSTOMER SATISFACTION
                          CSF: PRODUCT QUALITY
                          CSF: PRODUCT DEVELOPMENT
                          CSF: STAFF PRODUCTIVITY
               Created: Tue Jun 04 16:52:56 1991
                          by CBF in session COMRES MODELING

Figure 17.4   Goal analysis planning statement report.

XYZ MISSION

        Modified: Thu Jun 13 10:23:12 1991
                    by CBF in session COMRES MODELING

2.1 CSF: ASSET GROWTH

        Category: Critical Success Factor
            Text: The Asset Growth CSF is the prime responsibility of PERFORMANCE areas
                    of XYZ.
      Dict Links: PERFORMANCE
       Is Part Of: XYZ MISSION
     Consists Of: GOAL: ASSET GROWTH
         Created: Tue Jun 04 16:52:52 1991
                    by CBF in session COMRES MODELING
        Modified: Thu Jun 13 10:24:46 1991
                    by CBF in session COMRES MODELING

2.1.1 GOAL: ASSET GROWTH

        Category: Goal
            Text: Monitor performance of all aspects of business so that each activity has a
                    favourable effect, directly or indirectly, on our mission ROI.
       Is Part Of: CSF: ASSET GROWTH
     Consists Of: ISSUES: ASSET GROWTH
         Created: Tue Jun 04 16:52:51 1991
                    by CBF in session COMRES MODELING
        Modified: Thu Jun 13 11:33:15 1991
                    by CBF in session COMRES PLANNING

2.1.1.1 ISSUES: ASSET GROWTH

        Category: Issue for Resolution
            Text: – High proportion of investments in declining markets.
                    – High market entry cost into markets later found to be marginal.
                    – High debt levels for assets in sunset markets.
       Is Part Of: GOAL: ASSET GROWTH
     Consists Of: STRATEGY: MARKET EXIT
                    STRATEGY: ASSET DISPOSAL
         Created: Tue Jun 04 16:52:54 1991
                    by CBF in session COMRES MODELING
        Modified: Thu Jun 13 10:36:14 1991
                    by CBF in session COMRES MODELING

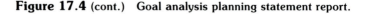

Figure 17.4 (cont.)   Goal analysis planning statement report.

STRATEGY: MARKET EXIT

2.1.1.1.1   **STRATEGY: MARKET EXIT**
      Category: Strategy
          Text: Identify markets which are unprofitable and in decline, and exit those markets
                  at the lowest possible cost.
      Is Part Of: ISSUES: ASSET GROWTH
        Created: Tue Jun 04 16:52:58 1991
                     by CBF in session COMRES MODELING
      Modified: Thu Jun 13 11:39:30 1991
                     by CBF in session COMRES PLANNING

2.1.1.1.2   **STRATEGY: ASSET DISPOSAL**
      Category: Strategy
          Text: Identify assets which cannot provide a return within two years consistent with
                  the mission ROI, and dispose of them at the best possible price.
      Is Part Of: ISSUES: ASSET GROWTH
        Created: Tue Jun 04 16:52:57 1991
                     by CBF in session COMRES MODELING
      Modified: Thu Jun 13 11:39:04 1991
                     by CBF in session COMRES PLANNING

Figure 17.4 (cont.)   **Goal analysis planning statement report.**

17.2.3   Data dictionary documentation

As well as the planning statements in an IE: Expert encyclopedia, the related
data model objects are defined in a data dictionary. This is illustrated
in the three windows of the modeling session shown in Figure 17.5. The
top right 'Model View Hierarchy' window shows that the current view is
COMPLAINTS RESOLUTION (see Figure 17.1). This view is displayed
in data map form as 'Data Map: COMPLAINTS RESOLUTION' in the
bottom right window. This data map has not been drawn manually, but
instead has been automatically generated and displayed by IE: Expert. We
will discuss this later in the chapter.

The current entity is surrounded by a dotted box on the data map.
Figure 17.5 shows that this is CASE. The left window displays the detail of
each entity as defined in the data dictionary for the current model view, or
for any other model view in the encyclopedia. We can see that the current
model view 'Data Dictionary: COMPLAINTS RESOLUTION' is displayed,
showing the CASE entity. This is a principal entity with a dynamic nature,
indicating that its values are defined during execution. The purpose of

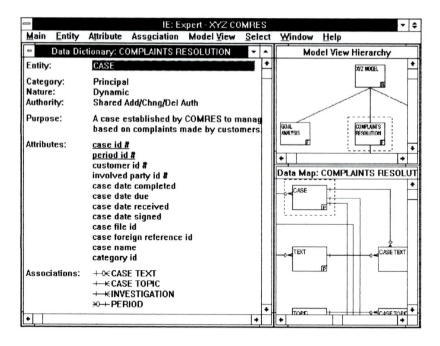

Figure 17.5   Modeling session for CASE (see Chapters 15 and 16).

the entity is also shown; this can extend over as many window pages as needed.

The data dictionary window in Figure 17.5 shows that the ownership authority of CASE is 'Shared Add/Chng/Del Auth'. This indicates that other model views may also add, change or delete this entity when it is later implemented as a data base table to be accessed and processed by systems developed from those model views. For security, audit or other control purposes, the authority of an entity may instead be defined as 'Sole Add/Chng/Del Auth', 'Change Only Auth', Read Only Auth' or 'Not Defined'. Any other control or authority status appropriate to an organization can also be defined by an authorized system administrator, using the extensibility features of IE: Expert.

Figure 17.5 shows the attributes defined for CASE. Key attributes are shown with a '#' suffix, with primary keys underlined using the conventions described in Chapter 2. The non-key attributes of CASE that we defined in Chapter 16 are also displayed. The data dictionary window in Figure 17.5 next shows that CASE has an association with PERIOD, INVESTIGA-TION, CASE TOPIC and CASE TEXT.

Figure 17.6 shows the next page of CASE in the data dictionary window. All model views of CASE are displayed, indented in outline form. The root view, XYZ MODEL, is always shown. We can also see that the

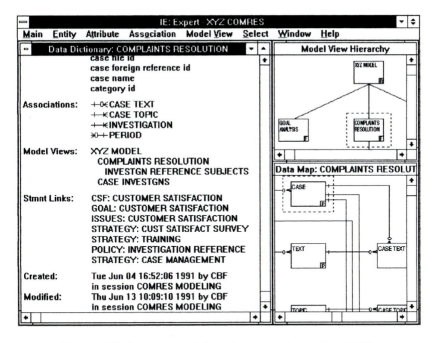

Figure 17.6   Additional data dictionary details for CASE.

INVESTGN REFERENCE SUBJECTS and CASE INVESTGNS views also share this entity with the COMPLAINTS RESOLUTION view.

The statements linked to this entity are displayed. As a case is established following a complaint from a customer, CASE is linked in Figure 17.6 to the CSF, goal and issue statements for CUSTOMER SATISFACTION, and also to strategy statements for CUSTOMER SATISFACTION SURVEY and for TRAINING. Other statements linked to CASE are the INVESTIGATION REFERENCE policy and CASE MANAGEMENT strategy. Finally sessions where the entity was created, and where it was last modified, are indicated with the relevant user.

The detailed definition of entities in a model view is printed in an Entity Report. Figure 17.7 shows part of the Entity Report for COMPLAINTS RESOLUTION, detailing the definition of CASE in the data dictionary. While not visible in the displayed section of the data dictionary window in Figure 17.5, we now see in Figure 17.7 that CASE should be implemented in Phase 3. The implementation phase number is dynamically (and transparently) derived by IE: Expert when each entity or association is defined or as each association is modified, based on the entity dependency concepts in Chapter 3. We will discuss this later in the chapter.

As well as listing in outline form the model views that share CASE, we also see that the authority defined for each view is 'Shared Add/Chng/Del

Auth'. The purpose is documented, with the statement links discussed for Figure 17.6. Attributes defined for CASE, and the associations between CASE and other entities, are listed in Figure 17.7 in summary form. These attributes can alternatively be documented in full detail, as discussed later in this section in relation to Attribute Reports.

XYZ COMRES   Entity Report
All Entities in Model View: COMPLAINTS RESOLUTION
Thu Jun 13 14:50:52 1991   Page 1

                                                                                CASE

Entity: **CASE**
    Category: Principal
       Phase: 3
   Model Views: XYZ MODEL   Shared Add/Chng/Del Auth
              COMPLAINTS RESOLUTION
                                        Shared Add/Chng/Del Auth
              INVESTGN REFERENCE SUBJECTS
                                        Shared Add/Chng/Del Auth
              CASE INVESTGNS   Shared Add/Chng/Del Auth
     Purpose: A case established by COMRES to manage investigations based on complaints made by customers.
  Stmnt Links: CSF: CUSTOMER SATISFACTION   (Critical Success Factor)
              GOAL: CUSTOMER SATISFACTION   (Goal)
              ISSUES: CUSTOMER SATISFACTION   (Issue for Resolution)
              STRATEGY: CUST SATISFACT SURVEY   (Strategy)
              STRATEGY: TRAINING   (Strategy)
              POLICY: INVESTIGATION REFERENCE   (Policy)
              STRATEGY: CASE MANAGEMENT   (Strategy)
   Attributes: case id#
              period id#
              customer id#
              involved party id#
              case date completed
              case date due
              case date received
              case date signed
              case file id
              case foreign reference id
              case name
              category id
 Associations: > O- - - - -|- PERIOD
              -|- - - - -|< INVESTIGATION
              -|- - - - -|< CASE TOPIC
              -|- - - - -O< CASE TEXT

Figure 17.7 Complaints resolution entity report for CASE.

The statement linkages in Figures 17.6 and 17.7 also appear as dictionary links in the Planning Statement Report for COMPLAINTS RESOLUTION, shown in Figure 17.8. To help you relate these links back to Chapter 16, I have taken the comments of the business experts from that chapter to illustrate statement linkage principles. Figure 17.8 thus documents informal comments from tactical modeling, rather than relevant strategic planning statements. The COMRES mission statement is printed first, followed by INVESTIGATION REFERENCE policy with dictionary links to CASE, INVESTIGATION, INVOLVED PARTY and INVESTIGATION INVOLVED PARTY. The CASE IDENTIFICATION strategy is linked to the attributes: *case file id*, *case id#* and *case foreign reference id*. We can see that the CASE MANAGEMENT strategy is linked to the same entities as the above policy, to the associations between those entities, and also to the attributes: *case date received*, *case date due*, *case date completed* and *case date signed*. We also see the objective statements for CASE CATEGORIZATION and CASE COMPLETION, together with linkages to the attributes used to measure achievement of these objectives.

XYZ COMRES   Planning Statement Report
Planning Statement Report
Thu Jun 13 14:32:17 1991   Page 1

                                                        COMPLAINTS RESOLUTION MISSION
1   **COMPLAINTS RESOLUTION MISSION**
            Category: Mission
               Text: Manage the investigation of cases, to result in their prompt and correct
                        resolution.
         Consists Of: POLICY: INVESTIGATION REFERENCE
                        POLICY: LOCATION REFERENCE
            Created: Thu Jun 13 13:39:59 1991
                        by CBF in session COMRES PLANNING

1.1   **POLICY: INVESTIGATION REFERENCE**
            Category: Policy
               Text: Customers may contact a government organization (through the minister or
                        the ombudsman) with a complaint which is to be investigated. A case is
                        established to manage the investigation. Many involved parties – such as the
                        government organization which was contacted, our staff, the customer or
                        others may participate in the investigation.
          Dict Links: CASE
                        INVESTIGATION
                        INVOLVED PARTY
                        INVESTIGATION INVOLVED PARTY
          Is Part Of: COMPLAINTS RESOLUTION MISSION

Figure 17.8 Complaints resolution planning statement report.

POLICY: INVESTIGATION REFERENCE

Consists Of:	STRATEGY: CASE IDENTIFICATION
	STRATEGY: CASE MANAGEMENT
Created:	Thu Jun 13 13:44:54 1991
	by CBF in session COMRES PLANNING
Modified:	Thu Jun 13 14:04:15 1991
	by CBF in session COMRES PLANNING

1.1.1 STRATEGY: CASE IDENTIFICATION

Category:	Strategy
Text:	We use a 'case file identifier' as alternative identification of a case. This helps us to locate correspondence or other relevant material filed elsewhere. The minister has his own reference identifier, which we must use in correspondence to him about a case. This also applies to the ombudsman. We call this the 'case foreign reference identifier'.
Dict Links:	case file id
	case id#
	case foreign reference id
Is Part Of:	POLICY: INVESTIGATION REFERENCE
Created:	Thu Jun 13 13:49:41 1991
	by CBF in session COMRES PLANNING

1.1.2 STRATEGY: CASE MANAGEMENT

Category:	Strategy
Text:	To manage each case, we need to know when the case was first received and the date when information is due to be provided to interested parties. When a case is finally completed we need to record that date, and also when the responsible manager has signed off on the case. He is referred to as the signatory. Of course we also need to know the customer who initiated the case.
Dict Links:	case date received
	case date due
	case date completed
	case date signed
	involved party id#
	customer id#
	CASE -|-----|< INVESTIGATION
	INVESTIGATION INVOLVED PARTY >|-----|- INVESTIGATION
	INVESTIGATION INVOLVED PARTY >○-----|- INVOLVED PARTY
	CASE
	INVESTIGATION

Figure 17.8 (cont.) Complaints resolution planning statement report.

STRATEGY: CASE MANAGEMENT

	INVOLVED PARTY
	INVESTIGATION INVOLVED PARTY
Is Part Of:	POLICY: INVESTIGATION REFERENCE
Consists Of:	OBJECTIVE: CASE CATEGORIZATION
	OBJECTIVE: CASE COMPLETION
	OBJECTIVE: INVOLVED PTY CONTACT
Created:	Thu Jun 13 13:50:39 1991
	by CBF in session COMRES PLANNING
Modified:	Thu Jun 13 13:54:52 1991
	by CBF in session COMRES PLANNING

1.1.2.1   **OBJECTIVE: CASE CATEGORIZATION**

Category:	Objective
Text:	We group cases into categories for subsequent analysis purposes.
Dict Links:	category id
	case name
Is Part Of:	STRATEGY: CASE MANAGEMENT
Created:	Thu Jun 13 13:55:15 1991
	by CBF in session COMRES PLANNING
Modified:	Thu Jun 13 13:57:56 1991
	by CBF in session COMRES PLANNING

1.1.2.2   **OBJECTIVE: CASE COMPLETION**

Category:	Objective
Text:	We need to know the target and actual completion dates for an investigation, as there may be more than one investigation carried out for a case.
Dict Links:	case date completed
	case date due
	case topic completion date
	case topic due date
	investgn actual completion date
	investgn target completion date
Is Part Of:	STRATEGY: CASE MANAGEMENT
Created:	Thu Jun 13 13:57:41 1991
	by CBF in session COMRES PLANNING

Figure 17.8 (cont.)   Complaints resolution planning statement report.

In Figure 17.5 we saw that CASE is a dynamic entity. Most entities are defined as dynamic: the values in data base tables implemented from these entities dynamically change based on applications that access those tables. Alternatively, an entity can be defined as having a static nature to indicate that its values are pre-defined. An example is a type entity, whose values are predefined based on the secondary entities controlled by it (see Table 2.1 in Chapter 2). IE: Expert allows the values for static entities to be entered into the data dictionary. When the data base table is later generated, IE: Expert also generates SQL INSERT statements to populate static tables with the defined values.

Type entities can be grouped together, to be physically implemented in one table that contains all type entities. This consolidated type table can be partitioned so that each type table can be referenced by name. Type identifiers and descriptions then define the name of each principal and secondary entity for the relevant type table. This is shown in Table 17.2 for INVOLVED PARTY TYPE and LOCATION TYPE.

Figures 17.3, 17.5 and 17.6 show only three windows. The number of windows that can be displayed concurrently by IE: Expert is limited only by the memory (real or virtual) available to Windows 3.0. These windows can be for the same or other model views, with any combination of model view hierarchy, planning statement, planning outline, data map, data dictionary or other windows of IE: Expert, or windows for any other software products that run under control of Windows 3.0. Data can be cut, copied or pasted between IE: Expert and any software products that also use Windows 3.0 facilities. For example, part of a data model that is to be the focus of a forthcoming modeling session can be copied directly into a letter that is prepared using a word processor, to notify participants of that session.

Figure 17.9 next shows part of the Attribute Report for COM-PLAINTS RESOLUTION, documenting *case date completed*. This is an

Table 17.2   Consolidated type table

TYPE TABLE	TYPE ID	TYPE DESCRIPTION
INVOLVED PARTY TYPE	0	INVOLVED PARTY
	1	CUSTOMER
	2	CLIENT
	3	SUPPLIER
LOCATION TYPE	0	LOCATION
	1	GEOGRAPHIC LOCATION
	2	LOGICAL LOCATION
	3	GRID LOCATION

---

                                                              case date completed

Attribute: **case date completed**
        Category: Elemental
        Data Type: Date
        Purpose: The date when the case was completed.
                    Entity: CASE
                    Type: Non-Key
                Edit Rule: Add later & modify later
                Nature: Mandatory
            Model Views: XYZ MODEL   Update Authority
                              COMPLAINTS RESOLUTION
                                                           Update Authority
                              INVESTGN REFERENCE SUBJECTS
                                                           Update Authority
                              CASE INVESTGNS   Update Authority
        Stmnt Links: GOAL: CUSTOMER SATISFACTION   (Goal)
                      OBJECTIVE: CASE COMPLETION   (Objective)
                      STRATEGY: CASE MANAGEMENT   (Strategy)
        Created: Tue Jun 04 16:52:13 1991
                      by CBF in session COMRES MODELING
        Modified: Tue Jun 04 17:15:33 1991
                      by CBF in session COMRES MODELING

Figure 17.9   Part of Complaints Resolution attribute report.

---

elemental attribute: it is not a group attribute, nor is it repeating. It is fully normalized and cannot be reduced further. Its data type is documented in Figure 17.9 as 'date', with its purpose and the entity in which it resides: CASE. This indicates that the attribute will be defined as a 'date' column when the SQL CREATE TABLE statement for the CASE data base table is generated. Other data types are system generated, numerical, character, money, time, real or flag. Data size and precision (number of decimals) are specified where relevant.

Edit rules are defined for each attribute, indicating how that attribute is to be initially entered or later modified by the application systems that process the data base column implemented from the attribute. We can see in Figure 17.9 that the edit rule for *case date completed* has been defined as 'add later & modify later', as the date when a case is completed will not be available until some time after the case has been established. Edit rules of 'not defined', 'add now & modify later', 'add now, cannot modify later', or 'add later, cannot modify later' may instead be selected. Other edit rules can be defined by an authorized systems administrator, using the extensibility features of IE: Expert.

This attribute is mandatory; every case must eventually have a completion date. We can also see that each of the model views with access to CASE have 'update authority': they are all authorized to update the attribute. Other attribute authorities are 'not defined' or 'read only authority'. The authorized systems administrator can extend IE: Expert to support additional attribute authorities. Finally, the statements that this attribute is linked to are listed, as documented also in Figure 17.8.

17.2.4   Association definition

In the entity details for CASE, shown in the data dictionary window in Figure 17.5 and in the Entity Report in Figure 17.7, the associations between CASE and its related entities have already been defined. The definition of these associations was specified to IE: Expert as shown in Figure 17.10. The Add Association window is used to select the relevant association between two related entities.

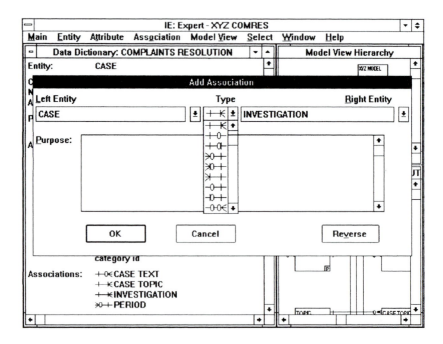

Figure 17.10   Defining associations to IE: Expert.

The 'Left Entity' initially displayed in the Add Association window is CASE. This is the current entity. The drop down list (indicated by the button with a down arrow to the right of the entity name) can be used to select any other entity for the association. The 'Right Entity' field also uses a drop down list to select the other entity to participate in the association. Figure 17.10 shows that INVESTIGATION has already been selected.

The association between these two entities is then presented in a drop down list of possible associations depending on the entity types to be related, so that the degree and nature of both ends of the association can be selected. IE: Expert determines the type of each entity in the association and first suggests the most likely degree and nature. For example, if a principal entity is associated with a secondary entity, a *mandatory one to optional one* association is suggested. If a type entity is to be associated with a principal entity, a *mandatory one to optional becoming mandatory many* association is instead suggested. This can be accepted, or any other association can then be selected.

In our example CASE and INVESTIGATION are both principal entities, so IE: Expert initially suggested the association for the two entities was *mandatory one to optional many*. The drop down list also displays below it other possible associations that may be used for these entities. The third listed association, *mandatory one to mandatory many*, more correctly applies. This was selected and replaced the suggested association between the two entity names. The three buttons at the bottom of the Add Association window are 'Add' (to add the association between these two entities to the data dictionary), 'Cancel' (to exit without adding the association), and 'Reverse'. The reverse button is used to switch left and right entity names, if necessary, based on the selected association.

Finally, the purpose of the association is defined. Text describes how (or why) the two entities are so related, or how the association will later be used for processing, or may instead describe the management or audit controls applying to the association. The association can later be linked also to planning statements that document the policies, strategies, objectives or other statements that apply to it, as described in Figure 17.8.

This association definition is simple, fast and accurate. The ease of use of the Add Association window also applies to modification. By double clicking on the association displayed in the data dictionary window for either of the related entities, this window is displayed for any required changes. Using this approach and the entity dependency concepts of Chapter 3, the need to draw data maps manually is eliminated. IE: Expert automatically generates the data map, as seen in Figure 17.5. If entities or associations are added or changed, IE: Expert automatically and transparently regenerates affected data maps to reflect those changes. Manual updating of data maps, required by other CASE tools (with the consequent possibility of errors), is also eliminated. These data maps are produced by data model analysis.

17.3 DATA MODEL ANALYSIS

The documentation of the data model so far provides a passive reporting capability of data as entities, associations and attributes, and related planning statements. This is the minimum level of software support that must be provided by data modeling CASE tools. However the data model provides far more information than this. In this section we will see how it is analyzed automatically to derive implementation phase data maps, used to define project plans for project management. It is used to derive and identify application systems and data bases. It is used for the automatic generation of data base creation statements for data base installation. Later chapters address systems design and implementation of the identified application systems and data bases based on these project plans, and using the generated data base statements.

17.3.1 Generating data maps

The implementation phase of each entity is automatically derived by IE: Expert based on defined associations between that entity and related entities, using the entity dependency concepts of Chapter 3. This is used to plot data maps automatically as implementation phase data maps, as shown at the bottom of Figure 17.11. This displays the data map generated for the INVESTGN REFERENCE SUBJECTS model view. This is the current model view, shown by the dotted box in the model view hierarchy window. The data map shows that this model view includes principal entities, shown by 'P' in the bottom right corner of each entity box. INVESTIGATION INVOLVED PARTY is an intersecting entity, shown by 'I' in its entity box. This data map is therefore a subject map. The dotted box surrounding INVESTIGATION indicates that it is the current entity. The data dictionary window for this entity is also shown in Figure 17.11.

In the Entity Report for CASE (see Figure 17.7), we saw that it is in phase 3. The phase number is also displayed in the data dictionary window, but was not visible in Figure 17.5. Phase 1 entities are plotted on the left of the data map, with higher phase number entities then plotted progressively to the right so that all entities in the same phase are aligned vertically. Type entities are generally phase 1 entities, as they normally do not depend on other entities. They therefore appear on the left of the data map. A principal entity associated with a type entity, if not also dependent on other entities, is therefore a phase 2 entity: it is plotted to the right of its related type entity.

No type entities were included in INVESTGN REFERENCE SUB-JECTS model view. Although PERIOD is in phase 2, the data map in Figure

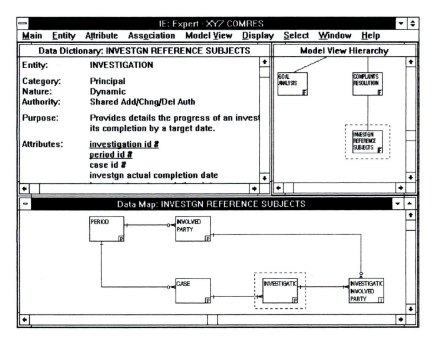

Figure 17.11   Data map for the INVESTGN REFERENCE SUBECTS view. This represents a subject map.

17.11 therefore shows PERIOD plotted on the left. INVOLVED PARTY and CASE are both vertically aligned in phase 3, while INVESTIGATION is in phase 4 and INVESTIGATION INVOLVED PARTY is plotted in phase 5. We will define a project plan based on these implementation phase numbers later in this chapter.

The subject map in Figure 17.11 is also printed in Figure 17.12. This shows the entity type in the bottom right corner of each box. The encyclopaedia name XYZ COMRES is printed above it, as well as the name of the model view for the data map. This data map can be produced by any plotter or graphics printer that is supported by Windows 3.0. It has been printed in Figure 17.12 using a Postscript laser printer.

The vertical phase alignment of entities is clearly shown in Figure 17.13. This shows how automatic derivation of implementation phase number for each entity is used to plot automatically the tactical map for the CASE INVESTGNS model view. This is the tactical map defined in Chapter 16. The type entities are plotted on the left in phase 1, with PERIOD in phase 2. CASE, surrounded by the dotted box, is in phase 3. We can print all entities as displayed in Figure 17.13, or instead select only some entities for printing as shown next in Figure 17.14. Only the principal and intersecting

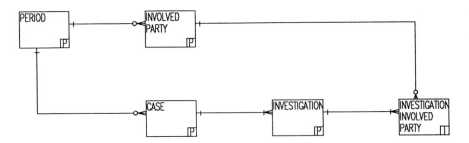

Figure 17.12   Printed subject map of INVESTGN REFERENCE SUBJECTS view.

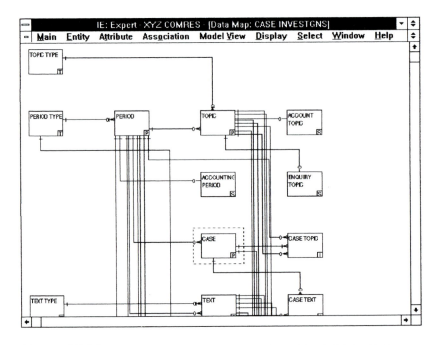

Figure 17.13   Generated tactical data map for CASE INVESTGNS view.

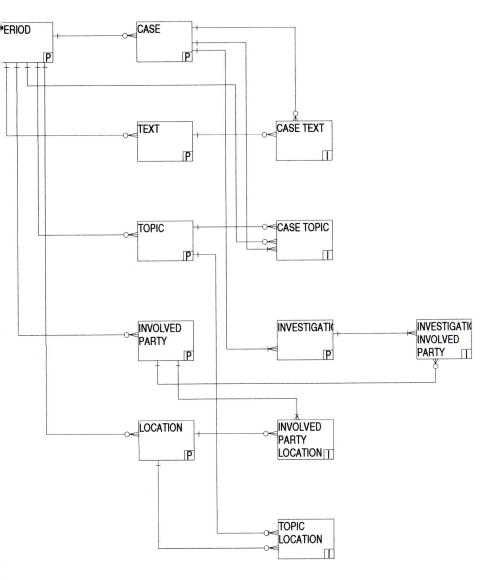

Figure 17.14 Data map of selected entities in the CASE INVESTGNS view.

entities were selected in this example. This now represents the strategic map developed in Chapter 15.

We have seen how IE: Expert derives the implementation phase of each entity to generate, display and print data maps automatically. This now leads us to identification of application systems and data bases also from the data model.

17.3.2 Identifying application systems and data bases

IE: Expert uses entity dependency, the derived implementation phase of all entities, and referential integrity concepts to group related entities into implementation clusters. An implementation cluster is part or all of an application system or systems, or of data bases, that depend on entities in that cluster. Clusters are printed in a **Cluster Report**; the Cluster Report for COMRES is in Appendix 2, and is discussed in this section. IE: Expert derives clusters automatically, as shown in brackets after each cluster name in Figure A2.1 of Appendix 2. Clusters are also derived based on referential integrity constraints. This is discussed shortly. Referential integrity constraints are implemented during data base design and installation, and later in the design of application systems.

Clusters are initially unnamed. The name of each cluster is determined by the last printed entity, called the **cluster end point**. If this end point is an intersecting entity, the cluster is an application system or systems. If instead the end point is a principal or secondary entity, the cluster represents a data base for that entity. If a structure entity is the end point of a cluster, however, the related systems that are suggested often indicate expert systems based around the principal entity for that structure entity. The report is printed alphabetically by cluster name. Clusters are numbered, based on alphabetical sequence, for reference purposes.

Clusters indicate potential application systems or data bases. The Cluster Report is thus also called the **Application Systems and Data Bases Report**. Priority systems or data bases can be identified from it, selected and then copied into separate model views in IE: Expert. This enables project teams assigned to these priority views to define, develop and deliver the relevant priority systems or data bases early. If the data model represents the entire jigsaw puzzle and the data map is the jigsaw picture in our earlier analogy, these priority views are those areas of the jigsaw that must be addressed first. Resources can be allocated to these priority views for early completion.

We saw in Chapter 14 that a data map can also be used for organizational planning, and for the design of organization structures. Clusters derived by IE: Expert provide a clear indication of dependent entities, based on the associations that implement defined policies, strategies or tactics. These associations represent communication or reporting paths. The data map of clusters in a defined view provides clear documentation of the data that the view is responsible for, or needs to access. The data map thus indicates boundaries of responsibility. Automatically generated data maps and derived clusters of IE: Expert therefore suggest to management alternative organization groups, units or organizational structures.

The complete XYZ COMRES Cluster Report of the COMPLAINTS RESOLUTION view is included in Appendix 2 as Figure A2.1. We will use clusters in the following pages extracted from this figure to discuss model analysis concepts further. The page in the full Appendix 2 Cluster Report of each relevant cluster is also referenced.

It was not appropriate to emphasize it at the time, but when we identified potential systems in Chapters 15 and 16 during strategic and tactical modeling we manually derived clusters using concepts similar to those applied by IE: Expert. Identification then was based on intersecting entities in strategic and tactical data maps. Refer to Table 15.1 developed from the strategic model. The second system in that table, Location Reference Systems, was determined from the intersecting entity INVOLVED PARTY LOCATION. This appears as cluster 12 in the Cluster Report (page 3 in Figure A2.1). It is repeated below, where we see that the intersecting entity appears as the last line of the cluster.

XYZ COMRES   Cluster Report
Model View: COMPLAINTS RESOLUTION
Thu Jun 13 15:04:25 1991   Page 3

                                                               New Clusters

12.   **LOCATION REFERENCE SYSTEMS** (derived)
      1) LOCATION TYPE
      1) PERIOD TYPE
         2) PERIOD
            3) LOCATION
      1) INVOLVED PARTY TYPE
            3) INVOLVED PARTY
               4) INVOLVED PARTY LOCATION (LOCATION REFERENCE SYSTEMS)

The right bracketed number beginning each cluster line is the derived phase number for the relevant entity. We can see that the intersecting entity is in phase 4. Refer now to the tactical map in Figure 16.2. Cluster 12 shows that LOCATION TYPE and INVOLVED PARTY TYPE are both in phase 1. However PERIOD TYPE has also been included in phase 1, with PERIOD in phase 2. Instead of LOCATION and INVOLVED PARTY being in phase 2 as suggested by Figure 16.2, they are instead in phase 3. Why is this?

Before the Cluster Report was produced, IE: Expert was used to analyze the data model. A Model Analysis Report was produced following this analysis. It showed that we had made a serious oversight during strategic and tactical modeling. Where was it?

Look at the tactical entity list for Location Reference Systems, below Figure 16.2. What do you notice about the primary key of INVOLVED PARTY? Part of this key is *period id#*. COMRES not only needs the current address and phone number of each involved party as suggested by the attributes in that entity, but it also needs access to past history of involved parties. This information is required before an investigation is finally completed. In fact, *period id#* was originally defined as part of the primary key in the strategic entity list of INVOLVED PARTY (see Section 15.1.4) based on the stated interest by COMRES managers in this involved party historical information.

The model analysis carried out by IE: Expert detected the existence of a potential association between PERIOD and INVOLVED PARTY. We had missed this in the strategic map, and also in the tactical map. In later chapters we will see that an Involved Party History System is indeed used to provide this information at the operational level of COMRES. In addressing this requirement we would most likely have seen the need for an association between PERIOD and INVOLVED PARTY during operational modeling. But IE: Expert detected the need for this association, in fact, during analysis of the strategic model. We will see the significance of this early detection in the following paragraphs.

Guided by this analysis, the association was therefore defined between PERIOD and INVOLVED PARTY as *mandatory one to optional many*. We can now see why PERIOD and PERIOD TYPE have been automatically included in Cluster 12 (see Figure A2.1) by IE: Expert. INVOLVED PARTY is dependent on PERIOD, which is in turn dependent on PERIOD TYPE in phase 1. PERIOD is thus in phase 2, with INVOLVED PARTY in phase 3. Finally we see that the intersecting entity INVOLVED PARTY LOCATION is in phase 4, as it in turn depends on both LOCATION and INVOLVED PARTY. Cluster 12, the Location Reference Systems, thus shows the definition and implementation sequence for these entities. We will see later in the chapter how a cluster can be used as a project plan.

In Figure 16.2 a number of secondary entities also appear in the Location Reference Systems tactical map. Cluster 12 has been derived from the associations between the intersecting entity and all other entities related to it: thus only principal and type entities have been included based on entity dependency. We will see shortly that other clusters are also derived from the secondary entities shown in Figure 16.2.

Look now at the first system in Table 15.1, the Investigation Reference Systems. This was indicated, after strategic modeling, by the intersecting entity INVESTIGATION INVOLVED PARTY. It is cluster 10 in the

Cluster Report (page 3 of Figure A2.1), where this intersecting entity is the last line of the cluster and is in phase 5.

XYZ COMRES   Cluster Report
Model View: COMPLAINTS RESOLUTION
Thu Jun 13 15:04:25 1991   Page 3

New Clusters

10. **INVESTIGATION REFERENCE SYSTEMS** (derived)
        1) INVOLVED PARTY TYPE
        1) PERIOD TYPE
            2) PERIOD
        1) LOCATION TYPE
            3) LOCATION
                4) INVOLVED PARTY LOCATION (LOCATION REFERENCE SYSTEMS)
            3) INVOLVED PARTY
        1) TOPIC TYPE
            3) TOPIC
                4) CASE TOPIC (CASE TOPIC ANALYSIS SYSTEMS)
            3) CASE
                4) INVESTIGATION
                    5) INVESTIGATION INVOLVED PARTY (INVESTIGATION REFERENCE
                        SYSTEMS)

Notice that other intersecting entities also appear in this cluster, in phase 4. These are INVOLVED PARTY LOCATION and CASE TOPIC. They represent Location Reference Systems, and the Case Topic Analysis Systems that were also identified in Table 15.1. The Location Reference Systems appear in cluster 12 as we discussed above. The Case Topic Analysis Systems also appear as cluster 4 (shown next, and in Figure A2.1 on page 1) where intersecting entities INVOLVED PARTY LOCATION and INVESTIGATION INVOLVED PARTY also appear. Why is this? The three systems appear to be interrelated in some way.

Look at the strategic map in Figure 15.8. We see that INVOLVED PARTY LOCATION is dependent both on LOCATION and also on INVOLVED PARTY (and on PERIOD as we saw above in relation to cluster 12). It does not depend on any other entities. But the same situation does not apply to INVESTIGATION INVOLVED PARTY. This intersecting entity depends on INVESTIGATION, which in turn depends on CASE and on PERIOD. It depends on INVOLVED PARTY, but we can also see that there is a *mandatory one to mandatory many* association in Figure 15.8 between INVOLVED PARTY and INVOLVED PARTY LOCATION: an involved party **must** have at least one location. Similarly there is a *mandatory one to mandatory many* association between CASE and CASE TOPIC, as a case **must** have at least one topic.

New Clusters

4. **CASE TOPIC ANALYSIS SYSTEMS** (derived)
    1) PERIOD TYPE
        2) PERIOD
    1) INVOLVED PARTY TYPE
    1) LOCATION TYPE
        3) LOCATION
            4) INVOLVED PARTY LOCATION (LOCATION REFERENCE SYSTEMS)
        3) INVOLVED PARTY
            5) INVESTIGATION INVOLVED PARTY (INVESTIGATION REFERENCE SYSTEMS)
        4) INVESTIGATION
        3) CASE
    1) TOPIC TYPE
        3) TOPIC
            4) CASE TOPIC (CASE TOPIC ANALYSIS SYSTEMS)

We can now see that the associations implement strategies where involved parties participate in investigations for specific topics in a case, according to relevant locations for those parties. Clusters 4 and 10 thus show interrelationships arising from these strategies. They highlight that a knowledge of involved parties and locations, as well as investigations, cases and case topics is needed to correctly define and implement these interrelated systems. People with this detailed business knowledge should be present during modeling sessions for these systems. This is also an example of referential integrity, rules–IE: Expert has automatically determined these knowledge interrelationships. Referential integrity is discussed further in later chapters.

But what of the secondary entities in the tactical map in Figure 16.2? Refer now to cluster 5 (page 2 of Figure A2.1), the Client Data Base for the CLIENT secondary entity. Similarly cluster 6 is the Customer Data Base for CUSTOMER. (The Supplier Data Base is cluster 26 in Figure A2.1.)

We can see in each case that INVOLVED PARTY LOCATION is also included in these clusters: data stored in the data bases is defined according to the information required by the Location Reference Systems. Each of these data bases and the intersecting entity are in phase 4: they all should be defined together. But if priorities do not permit this combined definition, then the same people must still come together again later, as part of the same project team, for separate detailed definition of the Location Reference Systems and relevant data bases when appropriate.

Now look at clusters 18–22 in Figure A2.1. These are all based on the structure entities in the data model. They are named according to the principal entity associated with each structure entity, and are related systems

New Clusters

5. **CLIENT DATA BASE** (derived)
     1) INVOLVED PARTY TYPE
     1) PERIOD TYPE
        2) PERIOD
     1) LOCATION TYPE
        3) LOCATION
           4) INVOLVED PARTY LOCATION (LOCATION REFERENCE SYSTEMS)
        3) INVOLVED PARTY
           4) CLIENT (CLIENT DATA BASE)

6. **CUSTOMER DATA BASE** (derived)
     1) INVOLVED PARTY TYPE
     1) PERIOD TYPE
        2) PERIOD
     1) LOCATION TYPE
        3) LOCATION
           4) INVOLVED PARTY LOCATION (LOCATION REFERENCE SYSTEMS)
        3) INVOLVED PARTY
           4) CUSTOMER (CUSTOMER DATA BASE)

that suggest potential expert systems. Cluster 18 represents Related Involved
Party Systems (page 4 in Figure A2.1). The last line of the cluster is
INVOLVED PARTY STRUCTURE, and is in phase 5. It is dependent on
the principal entity INVOLVED PARTY in phase 4. These two entities
suggest the name for the cluster, which represents potential expert systems
for involved parties.

The intersecting entity INVOLVED PARTY LOCATION also appears in this cluster in phase 4. This is also cluster 12, as we discussed
earlier. It suggests that location is important in relation to involved parties,
reflected by the *mandatory one to mandatory many* association between
INVOLVED PARTY and LOCATION. PERIOD also exists in this cluster:
time also appears to be important for involved party expert systems.

We discussed structure entities in Chapter 2, and again in Chapter 4.
We saw that occurrences of a principal entity, and also occurrences of its
secondary entities, may be interrelated based on common factors. These
interrelated occurrences are implemented in a structure entity in 5BNF.
Cluster 18 suggests that interrelationships may be based on common factors
of time or location. There may, of course, be many other factors that are also
important, but whose associations have not yet been identified. This cluster
enables people with expert knowledge of involved parties and common

New Clusters

18. **RELATED INVOLVED PARTY SYSTEMS** (derived)
    1) INVOLVED PARTY TYPE
    1) PERIOD TYPE
      2) PERIOD
    1) LOCATION TYPE
        3) LOCATION
          4) INVOLVED PARTY LOCATION (LOCATION REFERENCE SYSTEMS)
        3) INVOLVED PARTY
          4) INVOLVED PARTY STRUCTURE (RELATED INVOLVED PARTY SYSTEMS)

factors to focus on defining additional data, associations and expert rules that are needed to implement involved party expert systems using appropriate technology.

Related Location Systems and Related Period Systems also appear in the Cluster Report (page 4 in Figure A2.1). These follow as clusters 19 and 20 respectively. They suggest systems that require expert knowledge of locations and periods (or time) for proper investigation of cases. This knowledge may also exist in other parts of XYZ as part of its normal business activity. Cluster 19 also includes PERIOD, which suggests that expert knowledge needed for potential Location Expert Systems may also require an expert knowledge of time dependencies.

New Clusters

19. **RELATED LOCATION SYSTEMS** (derived)
    1) LOCATION TYPE
    1) PERIOD TYPE
      2) PERIOD
        3) LOCATION
          4) LOCATION STRUCTURE (RELATED LOCATION SYSTEMS)

20. **RELATED PERIOD SYSTEMS** (derived)
    1) PERIOD TYPE
      2) PERIOD
        3) PERIOD STRUCTURE (RELATED PERIOD SYSTEMS)

Clusters 21 and 22 (page 5 of Figure A2.1) are Related Text Systems and Related Topic Systems. They indicate the expert knowledge that COMRES investigators need to investigate cases effectively. Related text documentation or related topics may suggest related cases, involved parties or locations.

XYZ COMRES   Cluster Report
Model View: COMPLAINTS RESOLUTION
Thu Jun 13 15:04:25 1991   Page 5

                                                                New Clusters
21. **RELATED TEXT SYSTEMS** (derived)
     1) TEXT TYPE
     1) PERIOD TYPE
        2) PERIOD
           3) TEXT
              4) TEXT STRUCTURE (RELATED TEXT SYSTEMS)

22. **RELATED TOPIC SYSTEMS** (derived)
     1) TOPIC TYPE
     1) PERIOD TYPE
        2) PERIOD
           3) TOPIC
              4) TOPIC STRUCTURE (RELATED TOPIC SYSTEMS)

Although not immediately apparent from cluster 21, we can see other dependencies associated with text when we look at the intersecting entity CASE TEXT. This represents Case Documentation Systems in cluster 3 (page 1 of Figure A2.1). A knowledge of the Location Reference Systems, Investigation Reference Systems and Case Topic Analysis Systems discussed earlier is also relevant to Case Documentation Systems, as indicated by their automatic inclusion in this cluster by IE: Expert.

XYZ COMRES   Cluster Report
Model View: COMPLAINTS RESOLUTION
Thu Jun 13 15:04:25 1991   Page 1

                                                                New Clusters
3. **CASE DOCUMENTATION SYSTEMS** (derived)
     1) PERIOD TYPE
        2) PERIOD
     1) INVOLVED PARTY TYPE
     1) LOCATION TYPE
        3) LOCATION
           4) INVOLVED PARTY LOCATION (LOCATION REFERENCE SYSTEMS)
        3) INVOLVED PARTY
           5) INVESTIGATION INVOLVED PARTY (INVESTIGATION REFERENCE SYSTEMS)
        4) INVESTIGATION

```
XYZ COMRES                                                Cluster Report
Model View: COMPLAINTS RESOLUTION
Thu Jun 13 15:04:25 1991                                        Page 1
───────────────────────────────────────────────────────────────────────
      1) TOPIC TYPE
           3) TOPIC
                4) CASE TOPIC (CASE TOPIC ANALYSIS SYSTEMS)
           3) CASE
      1) TEXT TYPE
           3) TEXT
                4) CASE TEXT (CASE DOCUMENTATION SYSTEMS)
```

The Topic Documentation Systems are simpler, however, as shown in cluster 27 (page 6 of Figure A2.1).

```
XYZ COMRES                                                Cluster Report
Model View: COMPLAINTS RESOLUTION
Thu Jun 13 15:04:25 1991                                        Page 6
───────────────────────────────────────────────────────────────────────
                                                          New Clusters
     27.  TOPIC DOCUMENTATION SYSTEMS (derived)
          1) TOPIC TYPE
          1) PERIOD TYPE
               2) PERIOD
                    3) TOPIC
          1) TEXT TYPE
               3) TEXT
                    4) TOPIC TEXT (TOPIC DOCUMENTATION SYSTEMS)
```

In later chapters we will see how the design of application systems can draw on this identified expert knowledge of involved parties, locations, text and topics for the resolution of cases.

We can see that IE: Expert has provided much assistance in identifying potential application systems and data bases by expert cluster analysis of the data model. This analysis is objective: clusters are automatically derived that reflect the business rules of the organization as embodied in the associations between related entities. Additional clusters can also be defined, if required, by explicitly nominating specific entities in a derived cluster also to be cluster end points. This can be used to break down derived clusters into smaller subset systems for their definition, development and early delivery as operational systems: due to business priorities; or to interface with existing systems. These early delivered systems can thus be used immediately, before all of the systems represented by the complete cluster are implemented.

Other data modeling CASE tools use a different cluster analysis technique, called affinity analysis, which is more subjective. It requires the definition by data analysts of a threshold that is used to cluster entities into subject areas. Data bases and application systems are then identified by inspection. Depending on the threshold defined, and the data modeling experience and business knowledge of the data analysts, the data bases and application systems identified by different people using the same data model may vary. Affinity analysis is used by IEF, IEW and ADW.

Contrast this with the objective data model analysis carried out by IE: Expert based on entity dependency. Associations reflect defined strategies: the same clusters will always be automatically derived by IE: Expert while the business rules defined by the associations and strategies remain the same. Subjective interpretation by data analysts and business staff is thus eliminated.

We saw earlier how the Model Analysis Report helps to identify errors in the data model, or business rules may have been overlooked. The *Model Completeness Report* produced by IE: Expert also provides further quality assurance. This examines the data model to determine whether model view and entity authorities are consistent. It ensures that all required purposes have been defined in entities, attributes and associations. It checks that attribute edit rules have been validly defined, and that group attributes and repeating groups have been fully decomposed and normalized. Attributes are checked also to ensure that the data type has been defined, where relevant with an appropriate data size and precision. This definition is essential before data base creation statements can be generated automatically. For planning consistency, it checks that appropriate planning statement and dictionary links have also been established.

Following this analysis of the COMRES data model by IE: Expert, we can now use it to develop project plans to guide operational modeling in Chapter 18.

17.3.3   Developing project plans

Each cluster represents a separate potential implementation project. Indented phases allow the Cluster Report to be used similar to a Gantt Chart for project planning. We will see an example of this shortly. We earlier saw that data maps generated by IE: Expert show phase sequence through vertical alignment of entities in the same phase. These provide visual guidance for project planning.

The Cluster Report in Appendix 2 can also be used to support **functional analysis**. This determines business functions interested in the application systems or data bases represented by cluster end points. Business functions with an interest in each cluster end point can be listed in a right hand column of the Cluster Report. Some functions may create, delete or update relevant data, others may only reference data. A column can be included on this report to indicate the type of activity for each function, shown as a code (such as A: add, D: delete, R: read or U: update) against each function for a cluster end point. A Systems–Function Matrix, discussed in the next section, also achieves a similar result.

The significance of functional analysis *after* production of the Cluster Report cannot be over-emphasized. Some systems development approaches *start* with an analysis of the existing functions in an organization, then define data and systems based on those functions. In Chapter 14 we saw this assumes the future will be essentially the same as the present. However new systems are not developed because organizations are happy with today, but because they want to change. The future may be very different from today. New data and systems may be needed for tomorrow's competitive environment; new functions will be required to manage them. Data and systems for that future are defined not from today's functions (which reflect the needs of yesterday), but rather from the strategic plans for tomorrow. Data defined as strategic and tactical models, analyzed as described in this chapter, lead to identification of the application systems, data bases and functions needed to support the business. Some functions may not exist today. A new organization structure may be needed to manage them, as we saw in Chapter 14. This need may not have been seen, starting from today's functions.

The systems and functions determined from the Cluster Report can be presented as a **Systems–Function Matrix** (see Figure 17.15). Management use this to select priority systems and data bases for incremental development and delivery. This offers much benefit: people, funds, equipment and other resources are allocated to priority systems which are needed first, leaving lower priority systems to be developed later.

Figure 17.15 is developed from the Cluster Report in Figure A2.1. A subset of the clusters has been included based on the intersecting entities. The cluster name for each cluster end point has been used as the system name. The cluster number refers directly to Figure A2.1. A column has allocated for each business function: R&D, Operations, Financial Control, Management Services and Case Investigations. The interest that each function has in a system is shown by a '•' in the relevant system row. Alternatively an activity code ('A' for Add, 'U' for Update, 'R' for Read or 'D' for Delete) can be inserted in the matrix for each function interested in a system.

All functions interested in a system are apparent by reading across the relevant system row. All systems for a function can be identified by reading down the function column. A description of each system is also documented for management review. This can be defined as a planning statement, linked to the entity that represents the cluster end point. This may be a strategy or tactic, or instead a new statement type 'Application System' can be defined by an authorized systems administrator and linked to this entity and to relevant associations.

Complaint Resolution Tactical Model

Cluster Number (Figure A2.1)	POTENTIAL OPERATIONAL SYSTEMS AND DATA BASES BY FUNCTION		Function					
	Potential Systems and Data Bases	Project	Research & Development	Operations	Financial Control	Management Services	Case Investigations
3	Case Documentation Systems	COMRES		•		•	•
4	Case Topic Analysis Systems	COMRES		•		•	•
10	Investigation Reference Systems	COMRES		•	•	•	•
12	Location Reference Systems	COMRES		•			•
27	Topic Documentation Systems	COMRES		•			•
28	Topic Reference Systems	COMRES		•	•		

Figure 17.15   Systems–Function Matrix.

The Systems–Function Matrix enables management to select priority systems for early delivery. The Cluster Report defines the phase sequence of these priority clusters for project planning purposes. The data maps in Figures 17.12 and 17.14 are plotted in implementation phase sequence. These all provide input for project planning.

Figure 17.16 now shows selected clusters from the Cluster Report in Appendix 2 (Figure A2.1). These are Investigation Reference Systems, based on INVESTIGATION INVOLVED PARTY (cluster 10), the Client, Customer and Supplier data bases for the secondary entities of INVOLVED PARTY (clusters 5, 6 and 26), and Accounting Period, Performance Period and Reporting Period data bases for secondary entities of PERIOD (clusters 2, 15 and 23). This data map is plotted in implementation phase sequence in Figure 17.16 with secondary entities now under the principal entity, and will be used to develop project plans for operational modeling.

Entities in phase 1 (PERIOD TYPE and INVOLVED PARTY TYPE) are defined first: staff with expert knowledge of involved parties and time dependencies, are used to determine whether additional secondary entities are required for PERIOD and INVOLVED PARTY. Next, phase 2 entities are addressed. PERIOD is the only entity in phase 2. CASE and INVOLVED PARTY are in phase 3. Detailed attributes of cases are defined in this phase, with common involved party attributes in the principal entity. Attributes unique to customers, clients and suppliers reside in the relevant secondary

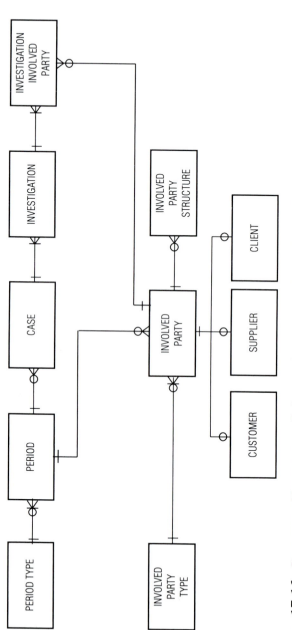

Figure 17.16 Data map of Investigation Reference Systems, together with associated secondary and structure entities.

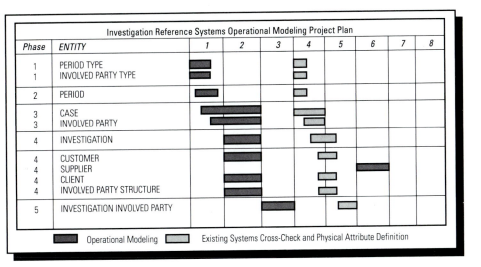

Figure 17.17 Gantt Chart for Investigation Reference Systems (from Figure 17.16 and Appendix 2).

entities (see clusters 5, 6 and 26 in Figure A2.1). These are all defined in phase 4, as are INVOLVED PARTY STRUCTURE attributes (see cluster 18 in Figure A2.1). Finally INVESTIGATION INVOLVED PARTY in phase 5 is defined (see cluster 10).

Implementation phase data maps can be used in this way for project planning of the next data modeling stage: operational modeling. Or they can be used to draw a Gantt Chart as shown in Figure 17.17. This chart is discussed briefly here, and in more detail in Chapter 18.

The time needed to define operational attributes in each entity of course depends on the complexity of the entity, the knowledge of that entity by functional area experts, and the other functional areas which share it. Where two or more areas share and update the same entity, additional time is needed to resolve conflicts which may exist. This is very important where more than one area considers it 'owns' the relevant entity.

Entity ownership is critical to resolve. Areas which create or delete occurrences of an entity have entity ownership status for that entity. Areas which only read or update attributes in the entity are said to have entity review status. The resolution of ownership can sometimes have complex political overtones: affected managers see the relevant data as part of their 'empire'. Higher-level managers may be needed to resolve these conflicts. This takes additional time, which should be allowed for in project planning. The results of this tactical modeling and analysis are presented for review by the managers who were involved in the prior strategic modeling.

17.4 MANAGEMENT REVIEW

The documentation and analysis reports introduced in this chapter are presented for review by management in a sequence other than used here. This enables them first to gain an overview of the relevant data model; then to evaluate in detail only those aspects of particular interest to them. A typical presentation sequence follows:

General Overview

- Model View Hierarchy Chart and Report
- Systems–Function Matrix and descriptions of priority functions or systems
- Data maps of priority application systems and data bases
- Cluster Report of priority views

Documentation Reports

- Planning Outline and Planning Statements Reports of priority views
- Entity and Attribute Reports of priority views
- Model Completeness Report of areas needing definition
- Model Analysis Report of situations needing resolution

The subject map format provides a very useful overview for large data models, as we saw in Chapter 13. We used the CASE INVESTGN SUBJECTS view to produce the subject map in Figure 17.12. We printed only principal and intersecting entities from the CASE INVESTIGATIONS view, so producing a subject map in Figure 17.14: this also represented the strategic map from Chapter 15. Both subject maps will be used for high-level review by management. They will also be used in later chapters for systems identification, project planning and development of process models through process modeling. Figure 17.14 is now reproduced here as Figure 17.18, in a format we will use extensively in those later chapters.

The entity list of the Case Investigations view is summarized below. We will use this in the next chapter during operational modeling when we will review attribute detail with functional area experts familiar with operational aspects of Case Investigations. We will cross-check the operational model also with existing systems.

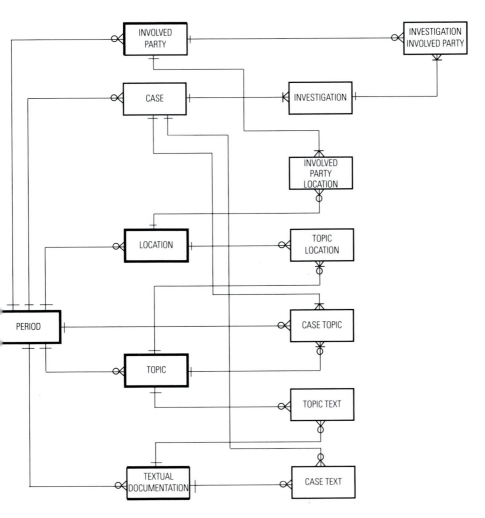

Figure 17.18 Subject map of CASE INVESTIGATIONS view.

Tactical model entity list

PERIOD TYPE	(period type id#, period type description,
PERIOD	(period id#, period start date, period start time, period end date, period end time, {period duration}, period unit, period type id#,
CASE	(case id#, period id#, [case name], [case file id], [category id], [case foreign ref id], case date received, case date due, case date completed, case date signed, customer id#, signatory id#:alias involved party id#,

Tactical model entity list (Cont.)

INVESTIGATION — (investigation id#, period id#, investigation target completion date, investigation actual completion date, case id#,

INVOLVED PARTY TYPE — (involved party type id#, involved party type description,

INVOLVED PARTY — (involved party id#, period id#, [involved party name], involved party address, [involved party phone number], involved party type id#,

INVOLVED PARTY STRUCTURE — (involved party id#, involved party type id#, involved party id#, involved party type id#,

CUSTOMER — (customer id#, involved party id#,

SUPPLIER — (involved party id#,

CLIENT — (involved party id#,

LOCATION TYPE — (location type id#, location type description,

LOCATION — (location id#, [location name], location address, location type id#,

LOCATION STRUCTURE — (location id#, location type id#, location id#, location type id#,

GEOGRAPHIC LOCATION — (location id#,

LOGICAL LOCATION — (location id#,

GRID LOCATION — (location id#, grid reference id,

TOPIC TYPE — (topic type id#, topic type description,

TOPIC — (topic id#, period id#, [topic name], {topic total refs this period}, topic type id#,

TOPIC STRUCTURE — (topic id#, topic type id#, topic id#, topic type id#,

ACCOUNT TOPIC — (topic id#,

PROBLEM TOPIC — (topic id#,

POLICY TOPIC — (topic id#,

STAFF TOPIC — (topic id#,

ENQUIRY TOPIC — (topic id#,

TEXT TYPE — (text type id#, text type description,

TEXTUAL DOCUMENTATION — (text id#, period id#, text content, text type id#,

TEXT STRUCTURE — (text id#, text type id#, text id#, text type id#,

STANDARD TEXT — (text id#,

NOTE — (text id#,

Tactical model entity list (Cont.)

LETTER	(text id#,
INVESTIGATION INVOLVED PARTY	(investigation id#, involved party id#, period id#,
CASE TOPIC	(case id#, topic id#, period id#, case topic date received, case topic due date, case topic completion date,
TOPIC LOCATION	(topic id#, location id#, period id#, {total topic location refs this period},
INVOLVED PARTY LOCATION	(involved party id#, location id#, period id#,
CASE TEXT	(case id#, text id#,
TOPIC TEXT	(topic id#, text id#,

17.5 SUMMARY

This chapter discussed software analysis of strategic, tactical and operational models. It used a typical CASE product, IE: Expert, to illustrate the analysis that should be carried out on data models. Model Hierarchy, Planning Outline and Planning Statement Reports documented the strategic statements supported by the data model. Data dictionary documentation was provided in Entity Reports, Attribute Reports and data maps.

Data model analysis reports were produced after software analysis of data models. This examined the strength of defined associations using entity dependency rules from Chapter 3, identifying data bases and application systems: documented in a Cluster Report. Systems were related back to project area functions (existing or planned) in a Systems–Function Matrix to identify systems for specified functions, or functions that should participate in more detailed, group modeling sessions for definition of data at the next modeling level.

Data maps were plotted in implementation phase sequence automatically. Project plans for the next level of activity were developed from these data maps or from the Cluster Report. Matrices, data maps, cluster and planning reports, data dictionary and model analysis and completeness reports were used for management review and later data modeling sessions.

References

[1] IE: Expert™ was developed by Information Engineering Systems Corporation (IESC) in Alexandria VA.

[2] ISM™ is Infonetics System Modeller. It was developed by Infonetics Pty Ltd in Sydney.

[3] Windows 3.0™ was developed by Microsoft Corporation in Redmond WA, and operates with MS-DOS™ as supplied by Microsoft, or with PC-DOS™ or OS/2™ V2.0 as supplied by IBM Corporation.

[4] SCO Xenix™ was developed by Microsoft Corporation and by The Santa Cruz Operation (SCO) in Santa Cruz, CA.

[5] UNIX™ was developed by AT&T Corporation. HP/UX™ is a version of UNIX supplied by Hewlett-Packard in Palo Alto, CA.

[6] Information Engineering Facility™ (IEF) was developed by Texas Instruments, Inc in Dallas, TX.

[7] Information Engineering Workbench™ (IEW) and Application Development Workbench (ADW) were developed by KnowledgeWare, Inc in Atlanta, GA. They are supported in the USA by KnowledgeWare, and world-wide by Ernst and Young.

CHAPTER 18

Operational Modeling

In Chapters 15 and 16 we discussed strategic and tactical modeling, both of which focus on identifying data needed for the future based on strategic directions defined by management. In contrast, operational modeling addresses existing systems, both manual and automated. These systems may currently be used, or may be new automated systems or application packages which are being considered for use.

18.1 OPERATIONAL MODELING STRATEGIES

Strategic and tactical modeling use a top-down approach based on strategic directions for the future. Operational modeling addresses a specific system or group of systems, and can use a top-down, a bottom-up or a sideways-in approach to data modeling.

18.1.1 Top-down data modeling

Top-down operational modeling continues the focus we used for strategic and tactical modeling, expanding both the tactical data map and entity list to operational detail for priority systems based on defined data needed for the future. This is appropriate for systems which do not exist today, or which need to change significantly from their present approach.

For example, systems which presently take a product-oriented

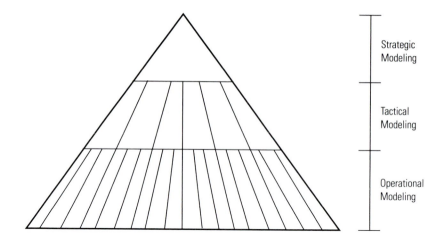

Figure 18.1 Top-down data modeling.

approach to processing may not be able to change readily to a new customer-oriented emphasis. Using existing systems as a starting point may severely inhibit consideration of alternative approaches. A top-down emphasis which focuses first on customers, their needs and other market-oriented data can result in more flexible systems which allow products or services to be supplied that more directly satisfy those needs.

Figure 7.3 (repeated here as Figure 18.1) shows the progressive top-down expansion of the strategic model. This identifies a number of functional (tactical) areas. A priority functional area is selected for tactical modeling. This expands the strategic data map and entity list with further entities and attributes, and indicates many potential operational systems. One system, or instead a group of systems of high priority are selected for operational modeling.

Many industries are becoming increasingly competitive. The organizations that prosper in the future will be those that can satisfy the needs of their customers and the market better than can their competitors. The operational systems needed for this competitive future may be quite different from the existing systems used by the organization.

Senior management of these organizations recognize that their DP staff do not have the knowledge of the business needed to develop strategic systems for the future. These managers could not previously provide essential direction, because of the complexity of traditional application systems development. Today however, they set those directions through the use of Information Engineering, applying it as described in this book. To ensure that all future systems are developed from a strategic and a business perspective, they may demand that these techniques be used by all staff – both DP and non-DP, as the standard for all systems development.

These managers use the top-down approach of Figure 18.1 to define strategic directions in the strategic model, using a facilitator who develops this model with them based on their strategic input. They view the strategic model from a business and a strategic planning perspective. They review the resulting tactical and operational models developed by their staff to ensure their directions are followed, and they benefit from the rapid feedback available as a by-product of this more detailed modeling.

Other senior managers do not realize that their input is needed and leave it entirely up to the DP department to develop any new systems.

18.1.2   Sideways-in data modeling

In this case the sideways-in approach can be used. Strategic, tactical and operational modeling are applied as before, but each stage now focuses on the same organizational level – moving to increasing levels of data detail, as illustrated from left to right in Figure 18.2. The same project team carries out each modeling stage, in turn.

Broad strategic directions are used by functional area experts to develop a preliminary strategic model. These directions draw on strategic plans or other documentation which have been separately produced. This strategic model will later change: senior managers have not been directly involved in its development and their input is essential. But it is a sufficient starting point for tactical and operational modeling as discussed below.

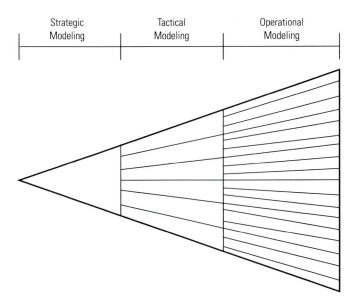

| Strategic Modeling | Tactical Modeling | Operational Modeling |

Figure 18.2   Sideways-in data modeling.

As these data models reflect the organization, with its specific terminology, they can be used to demonstrate the benefits of Information Engineering. When management realize that these techniques depend not on knowledge of computers, but instead require the detailed understanding of the business that they possess, they will become involved. They will apply the top-down approach of Figure 18.1, refining the preliminary strategic model developed by the functional area experts and providing the strategic direction missing from the sideways-in approach.

18.1.3 Data model evolution

With top-down and sideways-in data modeling, the data model expands in detail and complexity as shown in Figures 18.1 and 18.2, and summarized in Table 18.1. The strategic model typically identifies 50–90 entities and an average of two attributes per entity, mainly keys. A strategic model may cover approximately 20 tactical areas, which are defined further as tactical models. A tactical model includes typically 10–20 entities with an average of 5 attributes per entity which may also include non key attributes, derived attributes and secondary keys. At this stage the strategic model has expanded to 250–700 entities. There are approximately 3 operational systems for each tactical model. Each operational system in an operational model comprises 2–5 entities, now with an average of 10 attributes per entity. These provide the fundamental data needed by each operational system as discussed later in this chapter. The strategic model has resulted in 400–1,000 entities and indicates approximately 60 operational systems.

Table 18.1 Evolution of the data model

No of Models	No of Entities	Entity/Attribute Ratio
1 strategic model for each strategic area	50–90 entities per strategic model	1:2
approx 20 tactical models for each strategic model	10–20 entities per tactical model — 250–700 entities per strategic model	1:5
approx 3 operational systems for each tactical model	2–5 entities per operational system — 400–1000 entities per strategic model	1:10

18.1.4   Bottom-up data modeling

The third operational modeling strategy is a bottom-up approach. This is used by DP staff when both senior management and functional area experts do not participate. In this case the existing systems are used as the starting point, perhaps with some enhancements.

The DP staff do not have a detailed knowledge of the business and its future directions which would allow them to use strategic and tactical modeling to define the data needed by the systems under development. They can only refer to documentation of existing systems. This includes enquiries, reports, file or data base formats and relevant source documents, as well as data flow diagrams (DFDs) or other design material. Using this documentation as input, they apply the principles of business normalization described in Chapter 4. They develop a normalized operational model entity list. From this they develop an operational model data map.

The result is a data model and its associated operational systems which reflect the needs of yesterday, rather than the requirements of tomorrow. It is not easy to decide which of these are priority systems: management direction is not available. There is little alternative but to develop all of the indicated systems. It will be a very large project, with a long development time.

The bottom-up approach suffers from a lack of perspective of the organization. It is as if the DP staff are working on individual pieces of a jigsaw puzzle, with no idea of the overall jigsaw picture. Data bases and application systems represent the organization. They are complex components which must be fitted together precisely to be effective. But DP staff do not have the organizational understanding held by management and their staff to help them decide where the pieces fit. They cannot identify and concentrate on priority systems. They may develop prototypes using fourth generation languages (4GLs). But to be safe, they have no alternative but to delay the incremental delivery of priority systems until they can develop and deliver *all* systems for the entire project. This may take many years.

In contrast, the top-down approach gives this overall perspective: the strategic model represents the jigsaw picture. The tactical model provides more detail in priority areas. The operational model defines how pieces fit together. Analysis of these data models as described in Chapter 17 allows priority systems to be selected from the tactical model, defined and implemented. The organization benefits from early use of incrementally delivered systems. Lower priority systems are left for later development. Development resources are only used for the systems that are needed first.

18.1.5 Interfaces with existing systems and packages

Regardless of the strategy used for data modeling: whether top-down, sideways-in or bottom-up, operational modeling can be used to define interfaces with those systems or packages used at present, which will coexist with the new systems being developed.

We discussed earlier that bottom-up operational modeling uses source documents, enquiries, reports and file or data base formats for formal development of an operational model: as input to business normalization. The resulting data model allows interfaces to be defined between the new systems to be developed, and existing systems or packages which will coexist with those new systems.

We also saw that top-down and sideways-in modeling focus on directions set for the future, using business knowledge of functional area experts to define relevant entities and their attributes. In this environment operational modeling also uses source documents, enquiries, reports and file or data base formats as relevant input. However this input is used informally as a cross-check that all required data has been identified, rather than formal input to business normalization for bottom-up modeling.

Whether used for business normalization, or as an informal cross-check, this input results in operational models with interfaces defined by common entities that exist in both the new systems to be developed, and in existing systems or packages. These common interface entities enable those new systems to be integrated with the existing systems that must coexist with the new systems.

Using the analysis carried out in Chapter 17 on the tactical model, we will extract priority systems to develop to operational model detail. We will then cross-check the operational models for these systems against existing forms, enquiries and reports in the following pages. We will use process modeling in Chapter 19 to design new systems as needed.

18.2 | OPERATIONAL MODELING EXAMPLE

We will start with the first of the high priority systems identified by management in Chapter 16: Investigation Reference Systems. This is documented as cluster 10 in Figure A2.1 of Appendix 2, and is plotted as an implementation phase data map in Figure 17.16. It was used to develop the Gantt Chart in Figure 17.17 as a project plan for operational modeling of these systems. This has been included in this chapter for easy reference as Figure 18.3.

Investigation Reference Systems Operational Modeling Project Plan									
Phase	*ENTITY*	*1*	*2*	*3*	*4*	*5*	*6*	*7*	*8*
1	PERIOD TYPE	▰			▱				
1	INVOLVED PARTY TYPE	▰			▱				
2	PERIOD	▰			▱				
3	CASE		▰		▰				
3	INVOLVED PARTY		▰		▱				
4	INVESTIGATION			▰	▱				
4	CUSTOMER			▰	▱				
4	SUPPLIER						▰		
4	CLIENT			▰	▱				
5	INVESTIGATION INVOLVED PARTY			▰		▱			

▰ Operational Modeling   ▱ Existing Systems Cross-Check and Physical Attribute Definition

Figure 18.3 Project Plan (from Figure 17.17).

Note: This project plan shows that PERIOD TYPE and INVOLVED PARTY TYPE are modeled first.

We will carry out operational modeling using the business experts from the Case Investigations functional area. These people have no knowledge of computers, but are very experienced in investigating and resolving complaints. They were not present during earlier strategic and tactical modeling sessions of Case Investigations, and thus are not familiar with the models developed during those sessions. In the following discussion they will be introduced to terminology and data defined in these models and will cross-check these against their own experience.

18.2.1 Type entities

There are two steps carried out during operational modeling of type entities. The first step identifies the specific secondary entities relevant to the current operational system being modeled. These are modeled in detail only when their related principal entity is addressed, according to its phase number.

The second step next reviews the type entity attributes. In Chapter 2 we saw that type entities normally contain two attributes: a primary key *type id#* and a non key attribute *type description* (or instead a secondary key of [*type description*] if needed for alternate access). However other attributes may also reside in a type entity. These are typically derived attributes, containing summary data required in support of defined tactical or strategic management objectives. For example, the total number of involved parties of each type may be of interest to management: the derived attribute {*involved party type total*} is thus indicated. We have no stated requirements for additional derived type attributes in our current example; we will therefore concentrate only on step 1.

We defined a number of secondary involved party entities in the tactical model. These are included in the entity list following Figure 17.18 – as CUSTOMER, SUPPLIER and CLIENT. Functional area operational experts confirm their interest in each of these entities, except for SUPPLIER. The project plan showed that SUPPLIER can be left till later: it is not relevant to Involved Party Reference Systems (see Figure 18.3). We ask the operational experts for clarification:

> *We need to know about suppliers when we interview involved parties as part of an investigation. This is only necessary if a problem is traced back to inferior components from a supplier.*

This confirms that detailed definition of SUPPLIER can be left till later, when we model the Supplier Data Base (cluster 26 in Appendix 2).

When modeling PERIOD in Chapter 16 we discussed several period types. There was interest from management in having different accounting periods, reporting periods and performance periods. We confirm these now with the experts:

> *It would be useful to change the normal reporting period in certain cases, so that we can analyze some topics through more frequent reporting. Of course there is the normal accounting period, but sometimes we need to track specific financial aspects more closely. The ability to change the accounting period is useful. But the most important is performance. If an unacceptable trend develops we must monitor performance more closely in the affected areas. The ability to define a performance period different from other periods will be very helpful.*

This confirms the need for ACCOUNTING PERIOD, REPORTING PERIOD and also PERFORMANCE PERIOD as secondary entities of PERIOD. We will model these when we cover PERIOD. This would normally be addressed next, in phase 2 according to Figure 18.3. However we will defer this until after we have modeled CASE, which is in phase 3. We first need to confirm whether different types of cases are important. No case types were indicated during tactical modeling. The experts confirm that CASE TYPE is not needed.

The project plan of Figure 18.3 indicates that CASE should be defined next. This first appears in phase 2 – an association with PERIOD (based on the common primary key *period id#* in CASE and PERIOD) had not yet been defined: when defined, it moves CASE to phase 3. A separate CASE TYPE entity would also shift CASE to phase 3, but no case types were indicated during tactical modeling. The experts confirm that CASE TYPE is not needed:

> *We don't distinguish between different types of cases, but only according to the topics and the parties they involve.*

18.2.2   Principal entities

We will review with the operational experts the definition of CASE to this point:

CASE   (case id#, period id#, [case name], [case file id], [category id], [case foreign ref id], case date received, case date due, case date completed, case date signed, customer id#, signatory id#:alias involved party id#,

> *We could have a problem with this definition of CASE. It includes most of the attributes we need, but makes no provision for recording interim dates. A date prior to the due date is often defined, for review of an investigation to determine whether other people should participate. I suggest we cross-check this with the case records we keep now. And there is also another point. The definition here assumes only one customer, but a case sometimes involves several customers.*

Some refinement is needed. The last comment indicates that the *customer id#* foreign key is not correctly normalized: it is obviously a repeating group if more than one customer can be involved. We could define CASE CUSTOMER as a separate intersecting entity, but we already have that capability with INVESTIGATION INVOLVED PARTY: a customer is an involved party. We therefore remove *customer id#* from CASE here, and will define it in more detail when we review INVOLVED PARTY in phase 3.

Now let us review the other point above about interim dates. Figure 18.4 illustrates the Case Record form. This form is currently used to manage cases and investigations. The operational experts cross-check this form against the CASE entity.

> *Cases may be referenced by Case File Identifier, Case Name, Foreign Reference Identifier or by Category in the Case Record. These can sometimes change.*

These fields are used for alternative access, which confirms that the secondary keys of [*case file id*], [*case name*], [*case foreign ref id*] and [*category id*] in CASE are defined correctly. By using case id# as an internal unique primary key which never changes, performance will be improved in the final operational system: if these were defined as primary keys, much index

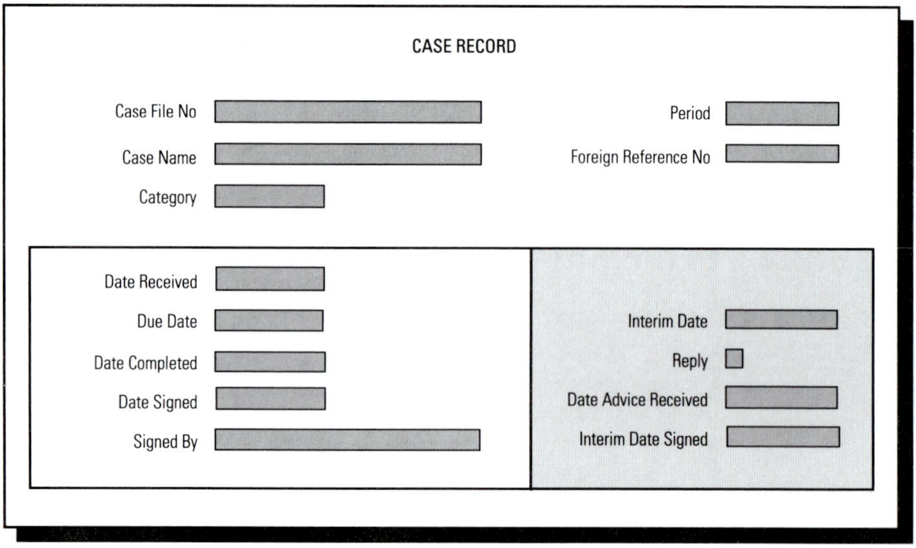

Figure 18.4 Existing Case Record Form.

maintenance would have otherwise been required. The other primary key of *period id#* is also confirmed by the form.

The fields Date Received, Due Date and Date Completed confirm *case date received*, *case date due* and *case date completed*. Date Signed confirms *case date signed*. The Signed By field provides for a name to be entered: the foreign key *signatory id#* is an alias for *involved party id#* in INVOLVED PARTY – the name of the relevant person can be extracted from that entity.

Now let us examine the shaded section of the Case Record. This indicates the Interim Date for review of a case and, by the Reply field, whether a reply is needed for advice. The Date Advice Received field shows when that reply is received, and the Interim Date Signed field acknowledges receipt of the advice. These attributes were missed earlier, but have now been identified during operational modeling. CASE, following operational modeling and existing systems cross-check, is now defined as follows:

CASE (case id#, period id#, [case name], [case file id], [category id], [case foreign ref id], case date received, case date due, case date completed, case date signed, case interim date, case reply, case advice date received, case interim date signed, signatory id#:alias involved party id#)

We have completed operational modeling for this entity. Referring back to the project plan in Figure 18.3 we have also completed an existing systems cross-check. We used both steps together with CASE above. However for new business opportunities there may be no existing systems to cross check. If the new systems are completely different from existing systems, no benefit may be felt to be gained by an existing systems cross-check. What do we do in this situation?

Both the Operational Modeling and the Existing Systems Cross-Check and Physical Attribute Definition steps are shown in the project plan for good reason. Even if the existing systems will be fully replaced, a cross-check can confirm that deficiencies in those systems are addressed by the new systems. Existing systems also help us define the physical characteristics (data type and size) of each defined attribute in an entity. If there are no existing systems to cross-check, this step concentrates only on physical attribute definition. We will discuss Physical Attribute Definition later, in Section 18.3 of this chapter.

PERIOD is in phase 2 according to the project plan, and is next to be modeled. This is followed by INVOLVED PARTY in phase 3, and INVESTIGATION in Phase 4. These are both principal entities.

PERIOD   (period id#, period start date, period start time, period end date, period end time, [period duration], period unit, period type id#)

We are intrigued by the concept of Period represented here. This means we can define different types of period, such as accounting periods, reporting periods and performance periods as we discussed earlier. We can then define different time units or durations for each. We can nominate a start date and time, and then an end date and time, and so derive duration – or we could specify a duration and so derive the end date and time. This offers us great flexibility. We can't think of any other period attributes that have been missed, but how can we define each period identifier?

The concern about having to specify each *period id#* value of PERIOD is resolved, as it is automatically allocated by the computer. In operation, application systems which use PERIOD will only require that the operator nominate the type of period and both dates (with times only if relevant), or instead one date and a duration. The computer then will allocate the next available period identifier.

We will briefly review INVESTIGATION now, leaving INVOLVED PARTY to be reviewed shortly in conjunction with its secondary entities.

INVESTIGATION   (investigation id#, period id#, investigation target completion date, investigation actual completion date, case id#)

The details for investigation are all OK. We need to know the target completion date for an investigation, and for management purposes when that investigation was actually completed. Case id# allows us to relate the investigation back to its case. There are no other attributes we need.

The definition of INVESTIGATION is confirmed as correct. We will now define the secondary PERIOD entities discussed in phase 1 in conjunction with PERIOD TYPE.

18.2.3 Secondary entities

When modeling secondary entities at the operational level we identify attributes unique to a single entity. Such attributes reside in the relevant secondary entity. If an attribute is common to all, it resides in the principal entity. If it is common only to a group of secondaries, but not all, an intermediate secondary entity is needed for that group: this typed secondary entity (see Chapter 2) is placed between the present secondary entities and the principal entity. Common attributes for a secondary group reside in the typed secondary entity.

In our example no unique attributes are needed for secondary PERIOD entities: only a primary key – which is *period id#*, taken from the principal entity. These secondary entities are now added:

ACCOUNTING PERIOD	(period id#)
PERFORMANCE PERIOD	(period id#)
REPORTING PERIOD	(period id#)

We have now modeled most entities in the first three phases of the project plan. INVOLVED PARTY still remains from phase 3. It is a principal entity, and is modeled in conjunction with its structure and secondary entities. We will discuss the type and principal entities first:

INVOLVED PARTY TYPE	(involved party type id#, involved party type description)
INVOLVED PARTY	(involved party id#, period id#, [involved party name], involved party address, [involved party phone id], involved party type id#)

We need to know whether an involved party is a customer, or one of our people. We also need the responsible manager, and a representative of the minister or ombudsman, who are our clients. We don't need to know about suppliers at this stage – that is only of interest later. We need the name and the main address of each involved party, and a contact phone number. Other locations for an involved party can be determined later.

We covered the type entity in phase 1. We use it for reference only here. The operational staff have confirmed that we only need the name, address and contact phone number of an involved party. Other locations of an involved

party will be addressed when we later model INVOLVED PARTY LOCA-
TION for the Location Reference Systems. Let us look at the secondary
entities next:

CUSTOMER   (customer id#, involved party id#)

CLIENT   (involved party id#)

SUPPLIER   (involved party id#)

*We identify customers by customer identifier as shown. We don't need any
other attributes specific to a secondary entity: merely the type of involved
party.*

The secondary entities are confirmed. What of the structure entity?

18.2.4   Structure entities

A structure entity normally has the form shown below. However other
attributes can be included. These may be specific to the interrelation-
ship indicated by a row in a structure entity: additional Bill of Material attributes in a PRODUCT STRUCTURE entity may be needed. In our example,
a date when the two involved parties became related, and the reason, might
be relevant: expressed as *involved party date of contact* and *involved party
relationship reason*. This would require all four keys below to be part of the
primary key. We now review INVOLVED PARTY STRUCTURE.

INVOLVED PARTY STRUCTURE   (involved party id#, involved party type id#, involved party id#,
                             involved party type id#)

*Now that is interesting. As we understand it, this will allow us to identify not
only a specific customer or customers involved in a case and investigation, but
also all relevant staff from our organization and government organizations.
We can thus get all the facts so a decision can be made by the client manager.*

*There is also an additional benefit offered here: interrelated customers, based
on common factors, will enable us to link otherwise unrelated cases. Sometimes we encounter malicious cases. This will help us expose possible fraud.*

INVOLVED PARTY STRUCTURE allows us to interrelate all involved
people in a case, and link them to other relevant cases. Quite apart from the
possibility of fraud discussed above, other relationships may be of interest.
For example all of the people involved in different cases with specific staff,
or managers, can be identified for analysis. But no additional structure
attributes are indicated, so the entity is confirmed as shown above.

18.2.5 Intersecting entities

As discussed in earlier chapters, intersecting entities represent potential high volume application processing. They appear last in the project plan: they are only covered when all related subject data bases in earlier phases have been confirmed. For instance, in our example INVESTIGATION INVOLVED PARTY is in phase 5: dependent on INVESTIGATION in phase 4 and INVOLVED PARTY in phase 3. Together with CASE in phase 3, they contain most of the data needed by the intersecting entity. We only need to confirm that all attributes which depend wholly on the compound key of the intersecting entity have been defined:

INVESTIGATION INVOLVED PARTY   (investigation id#, involved party id#, period id#)

We can determine when each involved party participated in an investigation, based on the specific period indicated. We don't need any other details.

No other attributes are warranted in INVESTIGATION INVOLVED PARTY. We have now finished the operational modeling step for Investigation Reference Systems. We will next define the physical characteristics of each attribute. These definitions are needed so we can implement the relevant entities and systems.

18.3 PHYSICAL ATTRIBUTE DEFINITION

Once again, we use the project plan in Figure 18.3 to determine the entity sequence in which we should define physical attribute characteristics. This is shown by the lighter shaded durations in the project plan. This step can be carried out together with existing systems cross-check, after operational modeling: the current source documents, enquiries, reports and file or data base formats are then readily available to determine the data type and size of each confirmed attribute. For example, we could have defined the physical characteristics of each CASE attribute immediately after we had confirmed those attributes using the Case Record form in Figure 18.4.

According to the project plan, we will define the data type and size of each attribute in PERIOD TYPE, INVOLVED PARTY TYPE and CASE first. This is shown in the form of an Application Group Contents Report in Figure 18.5. This report will be used in conjunction with the following discussion.

Date 31.10.91   Page 1

APPLICATION GROUP CONTENTS REPORT – PROJECT: COMRES

PERIOD TYPE

K	period type id	numeric	integer long	10
N	period type description	character	string	31

INVOLVED PARTY TYPE

K	involved party type id	numeric	integer long	10
N	involved party type description	character	string	31

CASE

K	case id	numeric	integer short	5
K	period id	numeric	integer long	10
K	signatory id	numeric	integer long	10
S	case name	character	string	31
S	category file id	character	string	31
S	category id	numeric	integer long	10
S	case foreign ref id	character	string	10
N	case date received	date	dd-mm-yy	8
N	case date due	date	dd-mm-yy	8
N	case date completed	date	dd-mm-yy	8
N	case date signed	date	dd-mm-yy	8
N	case interim date	date	dd-mm-yy	8
N	case advice date received	date	dd-mm-yy	8
N	case interim date signed	date	dd-mm-yy	8
N	case reply	character	string	1

K – Key Attribute   S – Secondary Attribute   N – Non Key Attribute

Figure 18.5   Partial. Application Group Contents Report.

The primary key of each type entity, *period id#* and *involved party type id#* has been defined as a long integer of 10 digits. This permits a key of 9,999,999,999 (sign is not relevant). In each case *type description* is a character string of 31 characters. This contains the name of each secondary entity controlled by the type entity: it references that entity directly. When implemented in an SQL environment it will contain a table name derived from the relevant entity name.

The primary and foreign keys of CASE (*case id#*, *period id#* and *signatory id#* – the alias for *involved party id#*) have been defined as integers of 5 digits (for cases) and 10 digits for the other keys. If 99,999 is not sufficient to identify all cases we can easily define more digits; or perhaps such a large number of cases is a symptom of a larger business problem?

The secondary keys of CASE are character strings of 31 characters ([*case name*] and [*case file id*]) or 10 characters ([*case foreign ref id*]). [*Category id*] is a long integer of 10 digits.

ENTITY NAME Key	Attribute Name	Data Type	Format	Size
PERIOD TYPE				
K	period type id	numeric	integer long	10
N	period type description	character	string	31
PERIOD				
K	period id	numeric	integer long	10
K	period type id	numeric	integer short	5
N	period start date	date	dd mm yy	8
N	period start time	numeric	integer short	5
N	period end date	date	dd mm yy	8
N	period end time	numeric	integer short	5
N	period duration	numeric	integer short	5
N	period unit	character	string	5
CASE				
K	case id	numeric	integer short	5
K	period id	numeric	integer long	10
K	signatory id	numeric	integer long	10
S	case name	character	string	31
S	case file id	character	string	31
S	category id	numeric	integer long	10
S	case foreign ref id	character	string	10
N	case date received	date	dd mm yy	8
N	case date due	date	dd mm yy	8
N	case date completed	date	dd mm yy	8
N	case date signed	date	dd mm yy	8
N	case interim date	date	dd mm yy	8
N	case advice date received	date	dd mm yy	8
N	case interim date signed	date	dd mm yy	8
N	case reply	character	string	1
INVESTIGATION				
K	investigation id	numeric	integer short	5
K	period id	numeric	integer long	10
K	case id	numeric	integer short	5
N	investgn target compln date	date	dd mm yy	8
N	investgn actual compln date	date	dd mm yy	8
INVOLVED PARTY				
K	involved party id	numeric	integer long	10
K	period id	numeric	integer long	10
K	involved party type id	numeric	integer short	5
S	involved party name	character	string	31
S	involved party phone number	numeric	integer long	10
N	involved party address	character	string	60
TOPIC				
K	topic id	numeric	integer short	5
K	period id	numeric	integer long	10
K	topic type id	numeric	integer short	5
S	topic name	character	string	31
N	topic total references this period	numeric	integer short	5

K – Key Attribute   S – Secondary Attribute   N – Non Key Attribute

Figure 18.6   **Physical attribute definitions.**

ENTITY NAME Key	Attribute Name	Data Type	Format	Size
TEXTUAL DOCUMENTATION				
K	text id	numeric	integer long	10
K	period id	numeric	integer long	10
K	text type id	numeric	integer short	5
N	text content	character	string	70
LOCATION				
K	location id	numeric	integer long	7
K	location type id	numeric	integer short	5
S	location name	character	string	31
N	location address	character	string	60
INVESTIGATION INVOLVED PARTY				
K	investigation id	numeric	integer short	5
K	involved party id	numeric	integer long	10
CASE TEXT				
K	case id	numeric	integer short	5
K	text id	numeric	integer long	10
INVOLVED PARTY LOCATION				
K	involved party id	numeric	integer long	10
K	location id	numeric	integer long	7
CASE TOPIC				
K	case id	numeric	integer short	5
K	topic id	numeric	integer short	5
K	period id	numeric	integer long	10
N	case topic date received	character	dd mm yy	8
N	case topic due date	character	dd mm yy	8
N	case topic completion date	character	dd mm yy	8
TOPIC LOCATION				
K	topic id	numeric	integer short	5
K	location id	numeric	integer long	7
K	period id	numeric	integer long	10
N	total topic location refs this period	numeric	integer short	5
TOPIC TEXT				
K	topic id	numeric	integer short	5
K	text id	numeric	integer long	10

K – Key Attribute   S – Secondary Attribute   N – Non Key Attribute

Figure 18.6 (cont.)   **Physical attribute definitions.**

The non key date attributes have been defined as date fields with a dd mm yy format. We will later implement the Investigation Reference Systems using ORACLE SQL. This will allow us to use features of ORACLE to present dates in a variety of formats. Finally, case reply is defined as a one character string. This normally contains Y or N (for Yes or No), but could be used for additional status codes of case replies.

Physical definitions for attributes of all of the entities in the Investigation Reference Systems are documented in Figure 18.6. These can be used to calculate the size of data bases for capacity planning. This is discussed in Chapter 22.

18.4 | SUMMARY

We discussed three strategies used for operational modeling: top-down, bottom-up and sideways-in. Top-down modeling occurs when various management levels participate as separate project teams for strategic, tactical and operational modeling in a project. Sideways-in modeling occurs when the same project team participates in each of the strategic, tactical and operational modeling stages of the project. Bottom-up modeling is carried out when source documents, reports, enquiries, file or data base formats, and other documentation is used: with business normalization used by DP staff to develop detailed, operational entity lists and data maps in the project. We discussed evolution of the data model as it progressed through each stage, and the interfaces between the operational model and existing systems and packages.

Operational modeling was carried out on the Investigation Reference Systems. These were the highest priority systems identified in Chapter 16 from the tactical model of the Case Investigations functional area. This modeling used the project plan developed from the data model analysis in Chapter 17.

We saw operational experts review the tactical model developed for the Investigation Reference Systems, identifying additional attributes based on required operational data, and normalizing these attributes to 3BNF, 4BNF and 5BNF as necessary. Additional entities and associations were defined where required.

After completion of operational modeling of each entity (or alternatively after completing operational review of all entities in the Investigations Reference Systems), the physical definition of attributes was completed. This specified the data type and size (and where appropriate, the displayed or printed format for each attribute) preparatory to physical data base generation in Chapter 20.

CHAPTER 19

Process Modeling

We have now completed operational modeling for the Investigation Reference Systems example in Chapter 18. We will next design the operational systems to be implemented with appropriate software. We will use the process modeling principles discussed in Chapters 5 and 6.

In Chapter 17 the tactical model was analyzed to identify priority application systems for implementation. These systems are shown as implementation clusters in the Cluster Report (see Figure A2.1 in Appendix 2). One, or a group of clusters may represent priority systems for development and early delivery. Figure 17.16 is an implementation phase data map of the Investigation Reference Systems. We will use these systems to illustrate process modeling and subsequent implementation.

19.1 DEVELOPING PROCESS MODELS

Process modeling is applied at two levels: high-level modeling, followed by detailed modeling of priority operational systems. An implementation phase data map illustrates many potential operational systems: high-level modeling allows priority systems to be identified for detailed modeling. It begins with Systems Identification.

19.1.1 Systems identification

Systems identification is the selection of priority operational systems by management. It uses the subject map of principal and intersecting entities, developed earlier for review by senior management. This is also used for project planning. Figure 17.18 shows the subject map developed for the Case Investigations view, repeated here as Figure 19.1. It includes six intersecting entities, plotted to the right. An intersecting entity is a group of

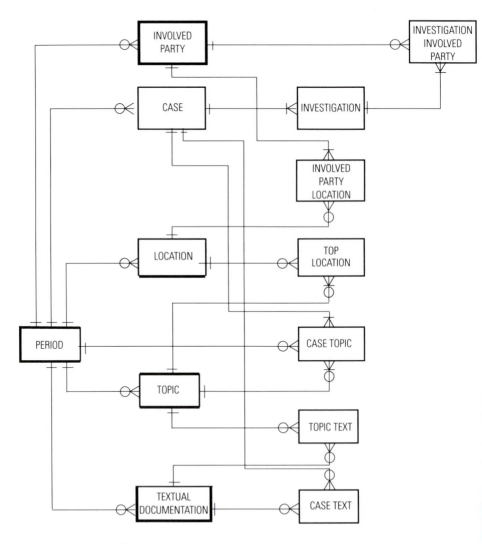

Figure 19.1 Case Investigations subject map.

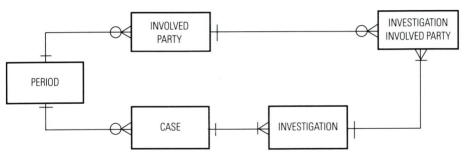

Figure 19.2 Investigation Reference Systems subject map.

potential operational systems. The first of the intersecting entities: INVES-
TIGATION INVOLVED PARTY, for example, represents the priority
Investigation Reference Systems. INVESTIGATION INVOLVED PARTY
is dependent on entities INVESTIGATION and INVOLVED PARTY,
which are in turn dependent on CASE and PERIOD. We will extract each
of these related entities into a separate Investigation Reference Systems
subject map as printed in Figure 17.12 and presented (slightly redrawn) in
Figure 19.2.

The subject map in Figure 19.2 shows the relevant implementation
phase for each entity. No type entities are included in a subject map, so phase
1 entities do not appear. PERIOD is implemented in phase 2: it represents
a fundamental Phase 2 System which all other systems may use. We will call
this the **Period Control System**. CASE and INVOLVED PARTY are both
implemented in phase 3: systems which use these entities are called Phase 3
Systems. INVESTIGATION thus is for Phase 4 Systems. INVESTIGA-
TION INVOLVED PARTY indicates Phase 5 Systems.

The associations between entities are next examined to identify the
operational systems in each phase. Each *one to many* association is a
potential system for the two entities related by the association. Starting with
PERIOD in phase 2, we see that it has a *one to many* association with CASE.
This is a Phase 3 System as we saw above. A potential name for this system
is suggested by the association. A period may have *one or many* cases: this
suggests the name of Cases (plural, for the *many* end of the association) in
a Period (singular, for the *one* end of the association), or perhaps **Period
Cases**.

This represents an existing system used in the Case Investigations area,
known as the Case History System. It is used for analysis purposes and also
for enquiries. If a new system contains significant changes from the existing
system it replaces, a new name should be chosen to highlight those changes.
Otherwise the existing name can continue to be used: we have adopted the
existing name in Figure 19.3.

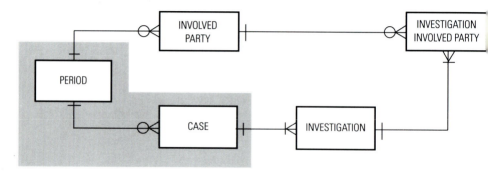

Figure 19.3 Case History System.

PERIOD has a similar association with INVOLVED PARTY. The association suggests the name: Involved Parties in a Period for this Phase 3 System. We will continue to use the current name, the **Involved Party History System**, to provide historical data on each involved party (see Figure 19.4). This system is based on an association between PERIOD and INVOLVED PARTY, as detected by IE: Expert in Chapter 17, that we had overlooked during strategic and tactical modeling. However management have said that it is of lower priority than other identified Investigation Reference Systems.

The *one to many* association between CASE and INVESTIGATION indicates the first of the Phase 4 Systems suggested by Figure 19.1 for the Case Investigations functional area. This system in fact uses the same name: it is called the **Case Investigations System** – from the association: CASE (*one*) and INVESTIGATION (plural, for *many*) in Figure 19.5.

Figure 19.6 next indicates a Phase 5 System called the **Involved Party Investigations System**. This is the first association we have examined with the intersecting entity: it identifies each investigation in which a specific involved party has participated, for subsequent analysis.

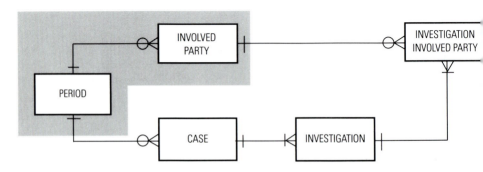

Figure 19.4 Involved Party History System.

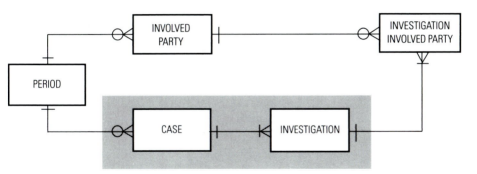

Figure 19.5   Case Investigations System.

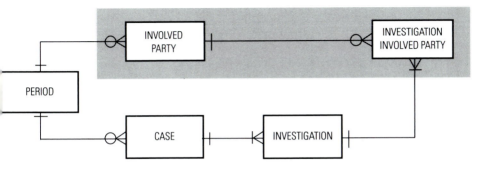

Figure 19.6   Involved Party Investigations System.

Most systems centred on an intersecting entity will also need to reference other principal entities on which that entity depends. This is essential, to extract descriptive attributes. For example, accessing INVESTIGATION INVOLVED PARTY from INVOLVED PARTY will identify the relevant investigations for an involved party. The name of the investigation and appropriate details of a case to which it belongs can only be obtained by access to INVESTIGATION and then CASE. We will see later in this chapter how more complex procedures are so designed from these initial operational systems.

Figure 19.7 shows a similar system based on the other association with the intersecting entity: called the **Investigation Contact System**. It identifies each of the involved parties who have participated in a specific investigation, to contact each for interviews. Notice that this system references both INVESTIGATION and INVOLVED PARTY to extract data. It may be further combined with the Involved Party Investigations System in Figure 19.6 for complex analysis procedures. For example an Involved Party

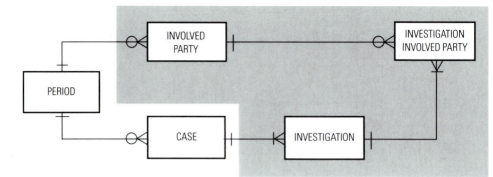

Figure 19.7 Investigation Contact System.

		Investigation Reference Systems Project Plan						
Phase	*Pty*	*Operational System*	*1*	*2*	*3*	*4*	*5*
2	High	Period Control System	▭				
3	High	Case History System	▭				
3	Low	Involved Party History System					▭
4	High	Case Investigations System		▭			
5	High	Involved Party Investigations System			▭		
5	High	Investigation Contact System				▭	

Figure 19.8 Investigation Reference Systems Project Plan.

Analysis System can examine all past investigations and cases for all involved parties in an investigation.

The systems identified in each phase are summarized in Figure 19.8, together with their relevant management priority. The phase and system priority indicate project sequence: the durations are dependent on the complexity of each system. This is used to manage development of relevant procedures and then operational systems. For example, the Involved Party History System, which management has said is low priority, has been scheduled last for development.

We will cover process modeling of these systems in the remainder of this chapter but will leave their implementation to later chapters. In practice, each system will move into implementation immediately after process modeling, and be delivered before later scheduled systems. We will apply high-level process modeling first, then detailed modeling for the priority systems in each phase.

19.1.2 Process modeling

During systems identification we covered Phase 2 Systems first. These are fundamental to systems developed for later phases. The Period Control System is the only Phase 2 Investigation Reference System. It is shown as a high-level procedure in Figure 19.9.

In Chapters 5 and 6 we discussed the development of generic procedures. Figure 5.17 shows a generic process procedure. Figure 19.10 expands the high-level procedure map in Figure 19.9 into the Process procedure and pseudocode for PERIOD: calling generic procedures for process actions.

As we included only principal and intersecting entity subject data bases in the subject map, the subject data base PERIOD also implies the entity PERIOD TYPE, on which the entity PERIOD is dependent. In Chapter 18 we saw that secondary entities ACCOUNTING PERIOD, PERFORMANCE PERIOD and REPORTING PERIOD are also dependent on PERIOD. Figure 19.11 shows the data map for PERIOD with the physical definition of each attribute (extracted from Figure 18.6).

We will use the data map in Figure 19.11 to develop a detailed procedure map for the high-level procedure 'Process PERIOD'. Each entity has a generic process procedure which controls processing activity against that entity: for add, read, change, delete and display. This is shown in Figure 19.12. Notice that data map dependencies indicated by the associations have been used to determine the procedure map execution sequence, as indicated by the arrows. PERIOD TYPE is referenced first, then PERIOD. PERIOD STRUCTURE is referenced only if the condition 'IF Related Period' is satisfied.

A relevant secondary entity is next referenced based on the foreign key *period type id* of PERIOD, indicated by PERIOD TYPE. For example, if *period type id* = 3 (say, for Reporting Period), the condition 'IF Reporting Period' is satisfied – REPORTING PERIOD may therefore be referenced.

Figure 19.9 Period Control System high-level procedure map.

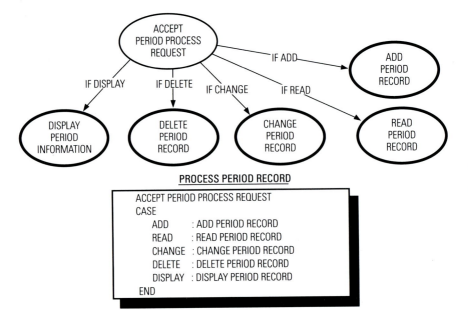

Figure 19.10 Process PERIOD procedure (from Figure 19.9).

However in this example no secondary entity has any unique attributes. Each contains a primary key only of *period id#* – no other data is available: merely the type of period. As PERIOD TYPE and PERIOD both contain *period type id*, these secondary entities need not be referenced at all. If, after process modeling, there is no procedure which explicitly accesses these secondary entities directly, but only need to know the type of period, these entities need not even be implemented physically in the data base: the data they represent – *period type id* – is available from the principal or the type entity.

We have seen how a high-level procedure map is developed from a subject data base represented in a subject map (see Figure 19.9). We have also seen how a detailed procedure map is then developed from the data map of the relevant subject data base. In the following pages we will show the high-level procedure maps developed for each of the systems identified in Figures 19.3–19.7.

The high-level procedure map for the Phase 2 Systems – the Case History System (see Figure 19.3) and the lower priority Involved Party History System (Figure 19.4) – is shown in Figure 19.13, overlaid on the subject map from Figure 19.2.

The operational data map for the PERIOD, INVOLVED PARTY and CASE subject data bases is illustrated in Figure 19.14, showing type,

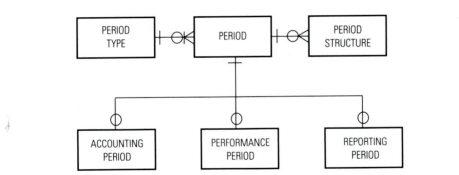

Figure 19.11 Data map and physical definitions for PERIOD.

ENTITY NAME				
Key	Attribute Name	Data Type	Format	Size
PERIOD TYPE				
K	period type id	numeric	integer long	10
N	period type description	character	string	31
PERIOD				
K	period id	numeric	integer long	10
K	period type id	numeric	integer short	5
N	period start date	date	dd mm yy	8
N	period start time	numeric	integer short	5
N	period end date	date	dd mm yy	8
N	period end time	numeric	integer short	5
N	period duration	numeric	integer short	5
N	period unit	character	string	5
ACCOUNTING PERIOD				
K	period id	numeric	integer long	10
PERFORMANCE PERIOD				
K	period id	numeric	integer long	10
REPORTING PERIOD				
K	period id	numeric	integer long	10

principal, secondary and structure entities. No intersecting entities are relevant for these systems.

The association between PERIOD and CASE, and between PERIOD and INVOLVED PARTY, is *one to many*: this indicates iterative processing. In a period there are many cases for review in the Case History System: similarly many parties are contacted in the Involved Party History System. This iterative processing is shown by a hooked arrow on the execution line between the relevant Process procedures. (An alternative hooked arrow

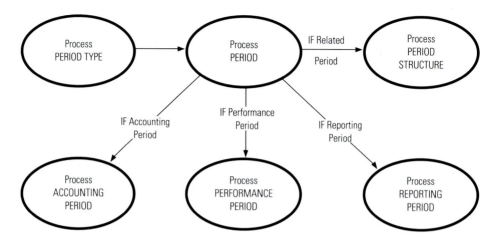

Figure 19.12 Period Control System detailed procedure map.

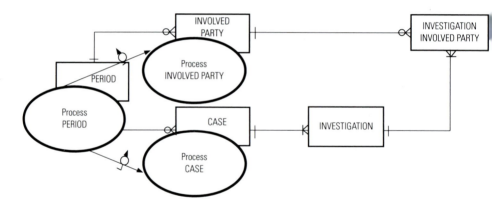

Figure 19.13 High-level procedure map for Phase 3 systems.

iteration notation has been used here, rather than the curved arrow notation used in Chapters 5 and 6.) As management have indicated that the Involved Party History System is of a lower priority, we will not develop it further: we will only address the Case History System. The detailed procedure map for this system is now shown in Figure 19.15.

As the association between PERIOD and CASE is *mandatory one to optional many*, it represents WHILE . . . DO iteration. This is shown as an optional hooked arrow: there may be no cases for a period. Figure 19.15 shows the iteration condition is 'While More Cases for the Period': on referencing a specific period, if there are no cases for that period the Process CASE procedure is never executed.

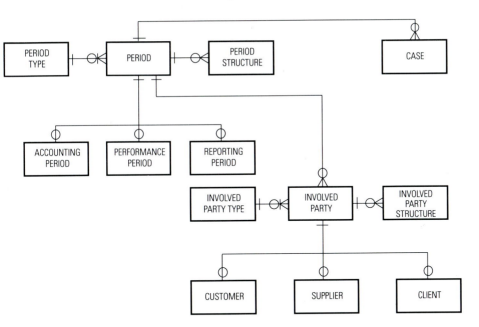

Figure 19.14   Operational data map for Phase 3 systems.

The high-level procedure map for the Phase 4 Case Investigations System is illustrated in Figure 19.16. There is a *mandatory one to mandatory many* association between CASE and INVESTIGATION. The iteration condition is thus shown as a mandatory hooked arrow, representing REPEAT . . . UNTIL: there is at least one investigation for a case, but there may be more. This is shown by the iteration condition 'Until No More Investigations for a Case'. As there are no secondary or structure entities for CASE or INVESTIGATION, the high-level procedure map is also the detailed procedure map.

Finally we will develop procedure maps for the Phase 5 Systems. Figure 19.17 shows the procedure maps for the Involved Party Investigations Systems – showing the high-level map (a) and the detailed procedure map (b): which reflects the secondary and structure entities contained in the INVOLVED PARTY subject data base.

The only data unique to the secondary INVOLVED PARTY entities is the primary key *customer id#* in CUSTOMER. The other entities indicate only the specific type of involved party. This exists as the foreign key *involved party type id#* in INVOLVED PARTY. If these secondary entities only contain the primary key *involved party id#* and no other attributes, we may later choose not to implement those entities physically at all.

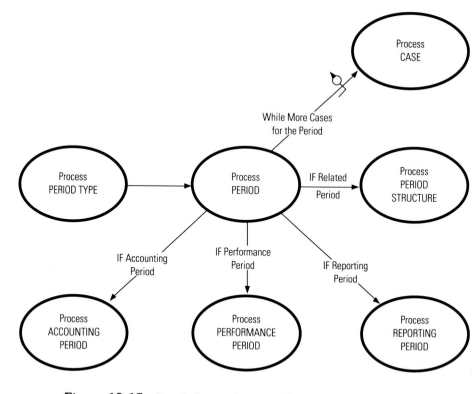

Figure 19.15 Detailed procedure map for Case History System.

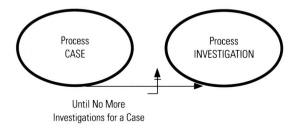

Figure 19.16 Case Investigations System procedure map.

The high-level procedure map for the Investigation Contact System in Figure 19.18(a) shows mandatory iteration from INVESTIGATION to INVESTIGATION INVOLVED PARTY then, for each involved party, unconditional access in the reverse direction to the related INVOLVED PARTY entity: for that person's name, address, contact phone number and involved party type (see the physical attribute definitions in Figure 18.6).

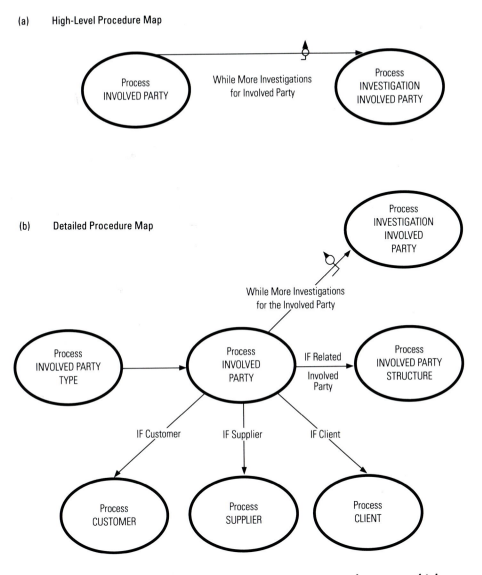

(a)   High-Level Procedure Map

(b)   Detailed Procedure Map

Figure 19.17 Involved Party Investigations System procedure maps: high-level and detailed.

Figure 19.18(b) next shows the detailed procedure map derived from the operational data map.

The Involved Party Investigations System (see Figure 19.17) has been further extended in Figure 19.19 to show similar reverse access from INVESTIGATION INVOLVED PARTY to INVESTIGATION, and then to CASE.

(a)   High-Level Procedure Map

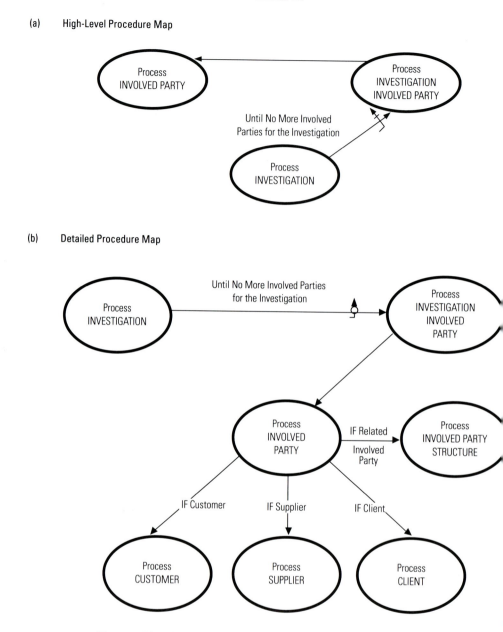

(b)   Detailed Procedure Map

Figure 19.18   Investigation Contact System procedure map.

This allows examination, for each involved party, of the details of each investigation and its associated case. It supports an involved party analysis system – called the Involved Party Case Analysis System – which illustrates

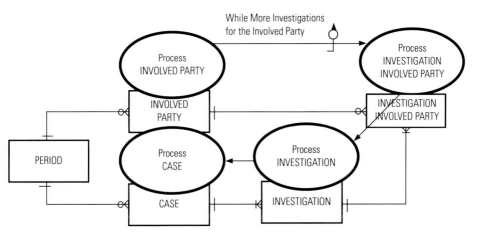

Figure 19.19   High-level procedure with referential integrity for Involved Party Case Analysis.

referential integrity: the included data map indicates (by *many to mandatory one* associations) other required entities which must exist. The procedure map overlaid on it clearly shows these reverse accesses from the intersecting entity to each of the entities on which it depends: to add, read, change, delete or display relevant data.

Several procedures may be combined to develop more complex application systems. Figure 19.20 shows each of the procedures in this chapter, numbered (in brackets) for reference. In Figure 19.20, for each case in a period (1) all investigations for that case can be determined (3). Then for each of these investigations, all of the involved parties (5) are identified. Next for each of these involved parties, other investigations in which they have been involved (4) – and their associated cases (6) – can be analyzed further. For a specific period, all involved parties can be identified (2), and for each of these involved parties, the investigations (4) and cases in which they have been involved (6) can again be analyzed. These systems can also be illustrated in an Application Systems Chart as shown in Figure 19.21. This indicates access paths taken through the data bases for processing purposes. These paths can also be used for performance analyses as discussed in Chapter 22.

19.1.3   Object-oriented programming

The high-level and detailed procedures developed in this chapter show the conditional logic which controls the sequence of execution of generic

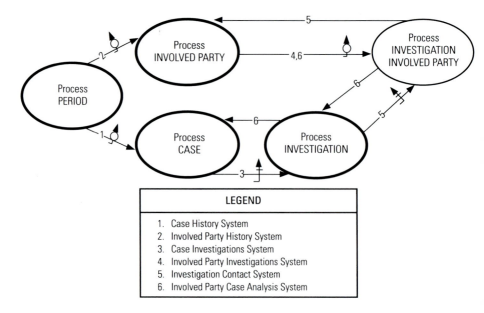

Figure 19.20   Procedures combine into application systems.

procedures derived from referenced entities. These conditions are expanded further by users to represent the complex interaction of systems based on different business conditions. In Chapters 20 and 21 we use ORACLE and SQL*Forms to develop screen forms and applications based on some of the procedures and systems defined in this chapter.

As discussed in Chapters 5 and 6, these procedures represent logic which has been derived directly from a data model. Each entity and its associated generic procedures is treated as an object, implemented with object-oriented programming principles [1]. These objects are executed by passing messages comprising the entity name and the specific action to be carried out.

High-level procedures offer the advantages of encapsulation: they can be executed without any knowledge of the logic within them. The detailed procedures within them support inheritance. Both are used as building blocks for larger systems as required. Process modeling, used in conjunction with data modeling is thus a user-driven method for analysis and design of high quality, maintainable systems developed using object-oriented programming techniques.

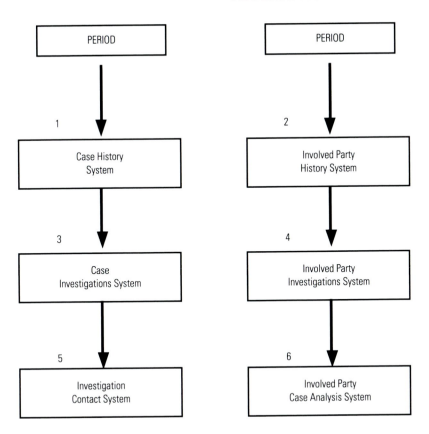

Figure 19.21   Application Systems Chart.

19.2 BENEFITS OF PROCESS MODELING

Process modeling, used for systems development with Information Engineering, offers many significant benefits over the traditional procedural development methods such as Business Systems Planning [2] (BSP), and Software Engineering using structured analysis and design [3, 4, 5, 6].

- Procedures are designed by functional area experts directly from data maps which they also develop. The resulting data bases, procedures and systems exhibit a higher quality than those designed by DP staff, on their behalf, using data flow diagrams and structure charts.

- Management can review the high-level process models, and also the data models on which they are based, to provide strategic direction for systems opportunities which are identified.

- Precise project plans are developed from data and process models for the early, incremental development and delivery of priority systems which have been identified by management.

- Interfaces with existing systems are readily identified for integration with, or replacement of, those systems as appropriate.

- Process modeling is a user-driven method for the analysis and design of high quality, maintainable object-oriented systems developed using object-oriented programming techniques.

- Systems maintenance is significantly lower because of the higher systems quality resulting from user-driven design, object-oriented programming and the ease in which changes can be made to data and process models.

- Data and process modeling lead to the automatic generation of complete, operational systems using today's relational data base management systems and associated software development tools. These systems are regenerated also automatically following any design changes.

19.3 | SUMMARY

We carried out process modeling of the priority Investigation Reference Systems that completed operational modeling in Chapter 18. We extracted the subject map of these systems, plotted in implementation sequence by the software used in Chapter 17. From this data map we used the associations between entities to identify separate operational systems. The data map was also used to develop a project plan, to manage process modeling and later implementation of each system.

We developed high-level and detailed procedure maps of each identified operational system. High-level procedure maps were developed from the Investigation Reference Systems subject map; this shows only principal and intersecting entities. The detailed procedure maps were developed from the complete operational model: including also type, secondary and structure entities.

We saw that this process modeling stage allowed operational experts to evaluate the business implications of alternative processing strategies, and ensure that all required conditional logic was represented on the procedure maps. The identified operational systems were summarized in an Application Systems Chart.

We then reviewed the implementation of procedure maps using either conventional or object-oriented programming techniques. We concluded the chapter by summarizing the benefits of process modeling: with higher quality systems designed by business experts; in a form that management can easily review; precise project plans for later implementation; easily identified interfaces with existing systems; a user-driven method for design and implementation of object-oriented systems; lower systems maintenance from these higher-quality systems; leading to automatic generation of data bases and operational systems using RDBMS and associated software development products.

References

[1] Cox, B. J. (1987) *Object Oriented Programming*, Addison-Wesley: Reading, MA.

[2] IBM Corporation. (1981) *Business Systems Planning: Information Systems Planning Guide*, White Plains, NY IBM Reference No. GE20-0527.

[3] Yourdon, E. and Constantine, L. L. (1979) *Structured Design, Fundamentals of a Discipline of Computer Program Systems Design*, Prentice-Hall: Englewood Cliffs, NJ.

[4] De Marco, T. (1982) *Software Systems Development*, Yourdon Press: New York, NY.

[5] Jackson, M. A. (1975) *Principles of Program Design*, Academic Press: New York, NY.

[6] Orr, K. T. (1977) *Structured Systems Development*, Yourdon Press: New York, NY.

CHAPTER 20

Software Tools for Implementation

We have now developed and reviewed the priority operational model, and are ready for physical data base implementation. We have also defined process models and priority operational systems from this operational model, ready to develop application screens and reports and link these together as application systems. But first we need to review some of the capabilities of software tools which can assist with this development.

20.1 DBMS PRODUCTS AND DEVELOPMENT TOOLS

The relational approach to data base management, first proposed by Dr Edgar Codd [1] in 1969-70, lead to development of several prototype Relational Data Base Management Systems (RDBMS) in the 1970s. Two of these are particularly important:

- System R, built at IBM San Jose Research Laboratory during 1974–77.
- University INGRES, built at the University of California at Berkely during 1973–75.

The System R prototype resulted in the later commercial release of the IBM DB2 and SQL/DS products. The university INGRES prototype saw the commercial release as a product by Relational Technology Inc (later called Ingres Corporation). INGRES was originally an acronym for Interactive Graphics and Retrieval System. Oracle Corporation released its first ORACLE RDBMS product before the IBM SQL/DS and DB2 products, or the INGRES product, however. See Chapters 4 and 21, and my earlier book, for discussions by Codd [2, 3, 8] and others, into relational theory.

We will discuss two RDBMS products in this chapter: ORACLE and INGRES. The principles described for these two products and their development tools can be applied to other RDBMS products and associated tools, and to other DBMS and 4GL products. We will review software tools provided with ORACLE (INGRES tools in brackets): SQL*Forms (INGRES/QBF) for the design, development and execution of screen-based, interactive applications; and also SQL*Menu (INGRES/MENU) and PL/SQL (INGRES ABF/4GL and INGRES/Windows 4GL), to produce customized screen-based and report-based systems integrated with other related applications. We will only touch briefly on SQL*ReportWriter (INGRES/RBF and INGRES Report-Writer) for report-based applications.

20.1.1 ORACLE relational DBMS

ORACLE was the first relational data base management system released in 1979 for DEC minicomputers [4, 5]. It has since been ported to a wide range of mainframes, minis and microcomputers. It not only offers advantages of portability of data bases and systems across this variety of hardware and operating system environments: systems can also be interconnected in a distributed data base environment with SQL*Net. Because of this strategy of interoperability, Oracle Corporation has experienced rapid growth: at the time of writing it is the largest data base software company in the world.

Oracle Corporation supports a superset of the SQL standard [6], called SQL*Plus. SQL*Forms Version 3.0 is a screen-based application generator with both prototyping and production execution capability. This operates in many window-based environments: using bit-mapped graphics terminals, character-mode terminals and also block-mode terminals (such as IBM 3270 terminals) based on Oracle Toolkit. This was developed by Oracle so that applications built for one operating system and windowing environment can be easily moved at the source code level to other environments. The environments supported by Oracle Toolkit include: DEC VMS with DECWindows; IBM OS/2 with Presentation Manager; UNIX with X-Windows; and Apple Macintosh.

SQL*ReportWriter is used for development and execution of report-based systems. SQL*Menu achieves menu-driven integration of SQL*Forms, SQL*ReportWriter, SQL*Plus and non-ORACLE applications. PL/SQL provides a procedural language capability for the above products.

SQL*Graph and ORACLE *Graphics offer graphics access to ORACLE data bases, while ORACLE Add-in for 1-2-3 provides access to ORACLE data bases from Lotus 1-2-3 spreadsheets.

20.1.2 INGRES relational DBMS

As for ORACLE, INGRES provides a comprehensive relational data base capability [7]. Released in 1981, it now operates on many mainframes and minis, under: DEC VMS and Ultrix (as Ultrix/SQL); IBM VM/CMS and MVS/XA; and UNIX. On microcomputers it runs under DOS. This offers portability across operating environments. It can operate in a distributed data base environment with INGRES/NET and INGRES/STAR for access to INGRES Gateways to access non-INGRES data bases. It provides two relational languages: QUEL (Query Language); and SQL. Ingres Corporation packages its tools for each operating environment. For example, INGRES Tools for DOS comprises:

- *Query-By-Forms (QBF)* to generate screen-based applications, with both prototyping and production execution capability.
- *Report-By-Forms (RBF)* to define and execute custom report formats.
- *Visual-Forms-Editor (VIFRED)* to modify forms generated by QBF for customized forms-based systems.
- *INGRES/MENU* to integrate QBF and RBF applications in a menu-driven execution environment.

INGRES Report-Writer is also available. This is used for the design and execution of more sophisticated report-based systems than can be developed using RBF. Ingres Corporation further offers two application development environments: INGRES ABF/4GL and INGRES/Windows 4GL. These are discussed next.

INGRES ABF/4GL offers comprehensive capability to create customized application systems, completely integrated with several Ingres products. INGRES/Windows 4GL extends this further. It operates in many window-based environments, taking on the native 'look and feel' of different graphical user interfaces. These include: DECWindows; OSF/Motif; X-Windows; OpenWindows; Windows/386; Windows 3.0; Presentation Manager; and Macintosh. This combines the INGRES 4GL capability with visual interface editors and object-oriented programming concepts: a frame editor interactively paints windows; a 4GL script editor encapsulates 4GL code with any visual interface component (such as windows, fields, menus, buttons, check boxes, text); and a menu editor designs menu bars and pull-down or pull-across menus.

Any number of windows can be active simultaneously. Windows can send messages to other windows, allowing users to switch rapidly between tasks. All common window toolkit interface elements (such as fields, buttons, bitmaps, and other visual elements), available in a windows palette, allow developers to place components in windows with 'point and click' simplicity. Text and bitmap displays can also be stored as documents, pictures or drawings in the INGRES data base; large bitmaps are displayed in scrolling regions within windows. OpenSQL can be used within the 4GL to access distributed data in INGRES and non-INGRES data bases. All application elements and objects, maintained in an INGRES data dictionary, are tracked within and across applications.

The remainder of this chapter, and also Chapters 21 and 22, illustrate implementation of systems from data models using examples based on ORACLE SQL*Forms. Where relevant, reference is also made to tools, techniques or terms used by INGRES. The rest of the book assumes a knowledge of SQL. Readers not familiar with this language may first wish to refer to Appendix 1.

20.2 RELATIONAL DATA BASE CONCEPTS

To illustrate some concepts of relational data bases [8, 9, 10] we will use the subject map for the Investigation Reference Systems (see Figure 19.2). We will focus on CASE and INVESTIGATION, for the Case Investigations System in Figure 19.5. This is repeated here as Figure 20.1.

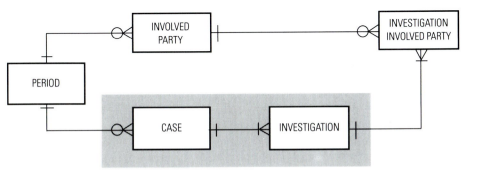

Figure 20.1 Case Investigations System.

Pg 193

```
create table CASE
    (  case_id                     NUMBER (5)      NOT NULL,
       period_id                   NUMBER (12)     NOT NULL,
       customer_id                 NUMBER (12)     NOT NULL,
       signatory_id                NUMBER (12)     NOT NULL,
       case_name                   CHAR (31),
       case_file_id                CHAR (31),
       category_id                 NUMBER (12),
       case_foreign_ref_id         CHAR (10),
       case_date_received          DATE,
       case_date_due               DATE,
       case_date_completed         DATE,
       case_date_signed            DATE,
       case_interim_date           DATE,
       case_advice_date_received   DATE,
       case_interim_date_signed    DATE,
       case_reply                  CHAR (1)                        );
```

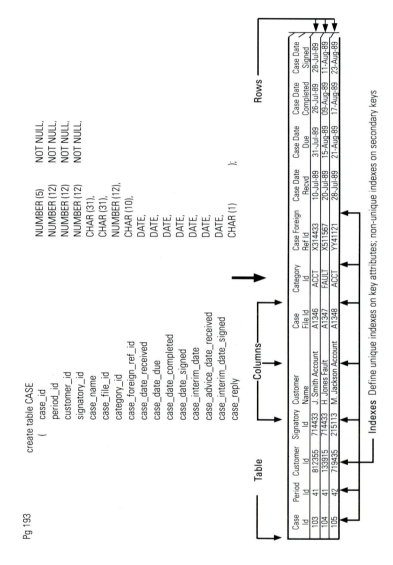

Case Id	Period Id	Customer Id	Signatory Id	Customer Name	Case File Id	Category Id	Case Foreign Ref Id	Case Date Recvd	Case Date Due	Case Date Completed	Case Date Signed
103	41	812355	714433	J. Smith Account	A1346	ACCT	X314433	10-Jul-89	31-Jul-89	26-Jul-89	28-Jul-89
104	41	133915	714433	H. Jones Fault	A1347	FAULT	X511567	20-Jul-89	15-Aug-89	09-Aug-89	11-Aug-89
105	42	719435	215113	M. Jackson Account	A1348	ACCT	YY41121	28-Jul-89	21-Aug-89	17-Aug-89	23-Aug-89

Table — Columns — Rows

Indexes Define unique indexes on key attributes; non-unique indexes on secondary keys

Figure 20.2 SQL table for CASE (from Figure 20.1).

20.2.1 Implementing entities as SQL tables

Figure 20.2 shows an SQL table, which is defined for CASE by the Create Table SQL command. As SQL table and column names can be only one word (see Appendix 1), each space between words in entity and attribute names is replaced by an underscore. The CASE entity is implemented directly as an SQL table: each attribute represents a column; each entity occurrence is a row in the table. Notice that key attributes are defined as SQL NOT NULL: all primary and foreign keys must have a value. As duplicate keys are not allowed, unique indexes are defined if more efficient access is required. However secondary keys can be null and duplicates are allowed: non-unique indexes can thus be defined for secondary keys. Physical attribute definitions of integer in Figure 18.6 are defined as NUMBER columns; the length is specified in digits. Character attributes are defined as CHAR columns to a maximum of 255 characters. Character attributes larger than this are defined as columns of data type LONG, to 65,535 characters. Date attributes, defined as DATE columns, can be directly manipulated using the advanced facilities of SQL*Plus. Time attributes can be defined as NUMBER columns, or integrated with date in SQL DATETIME columns.

SQL allows tables to be joined on common columns, regardless of whether they have been defined as associations. The following example illustrates:

```
SELECT      CASE.period_id, case_file_id, case_name, case_date_received,
            case_date_due, investigation_id, investgn_target_compln_date,
            investgn_actual_compln_date

FROM        CASE,INVESTIGATION

WHERE       CASE.case_id = INVESTIGATION.case_id

AND         CASE.period_id = INVESTIGATION.period_id

ORDER BY    CASE.period_id;
```

This shows that all investigations for each case in a period, sorted chronologically, are found by joining CASE and INVESTIGATION on common *case_id* and *period_id*, ordered by *period_id*.

Figure 20.3 shows that the CASE and INVESTIGATION SQL tables are joined on common keys. (The definition of SQL primary and foreign keys, and of SQL indexes, is discussed in Chapter 21.) We saw in Chapter 15 that these entities are linked by *case_id*: which is a primary key in CASE and a foreign key in INVESTIGATION. *Period_id* is also common to both. The association between these entities in Figure 20.1 represents these common keys.

```
create table CASE
    (    case_id                       NUMBER (5)     NOT NULL,
         period_id                     NUMBER (12)    NOT NULL,
         customer_id                   NUMBER (12)    NOT NULL,
         signatory_id                  NUMBER (12)    NOT NULL,
         case_name                     CHAR (31),
         case_file_id                  CHAR (31),
         category_id                   NUMBER (12),
         case_foreign_ref_id           CHAR (10),
         case_date_received            DATE,
         case_date_due                 DATE,
         case_date_completed           DATE,
         case_date_signed              DATE,
         case_interim_date             DATE,
         case_advice_date_received     DATE,
         case_interim_date_signed      CHAR (1)       );
         case_reply

create table INVESTIGATION
    (    investigation_id              NUMBER (5)     NOT NULL,
         period_id                     NUMBER (12)    NOT NULL,
         case_id                       NUMBER (5)     NOT NULL,
         investgn_target_compln_date   DATE,
         investgn_actual_compln_date   DATE           );
```

Case_id used to join CASE and INVESTIGATION Tables

Figure 20.3 SQL tables are joined on common keys.

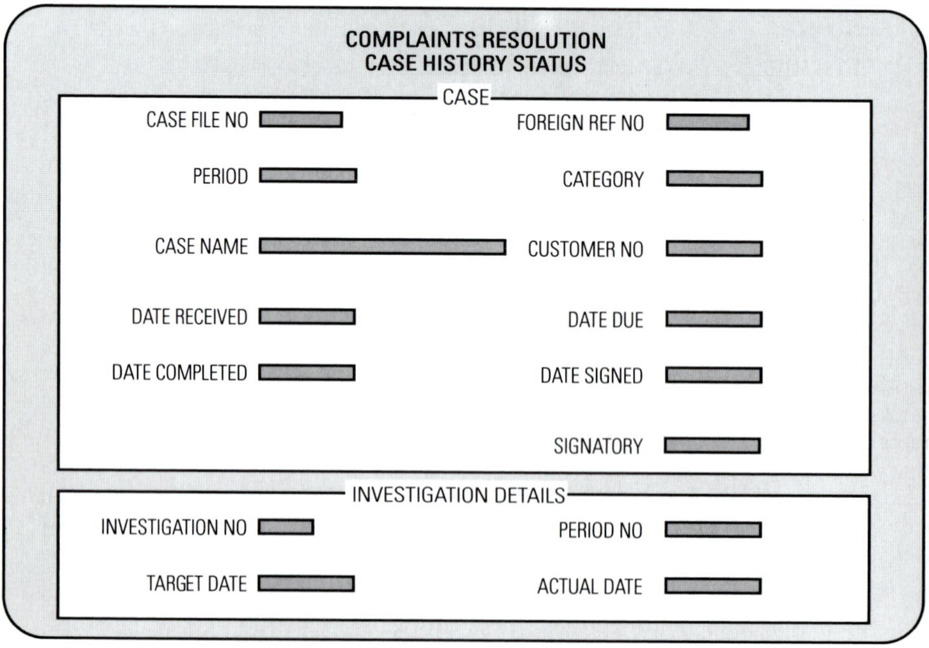

Figure 20.4 Case History Status Form.

Potential associations identified through model analysis in Chapter 17, but which have not yet been defined explicitly in the data map, can be implemented directly in SQL by joining the relevant tables on common keys.

20.2.2 ORACLE and INGRES forms concepts

To illustrate terminology used by ORACLE SQL*Forms, with relevant INGRES/QBF terminology shown in brackets, we will use SQL tables from Figure 20.3 and a form from the existing system used by Case Investigations: this is the Case History Status form, illustrated in Figure 20.4. This form does not include the interim dates defined during operational modeling in Chapter 18. It shows the status of an investigation carried out for a case. Each investigation for that case is displayed, in turn, in the Investigation Details part of the form.

Figure 20.5 uses this form to indicate the specific terminology used by SQL*Forms. A form contains one or more blocks. A block resides on a page:

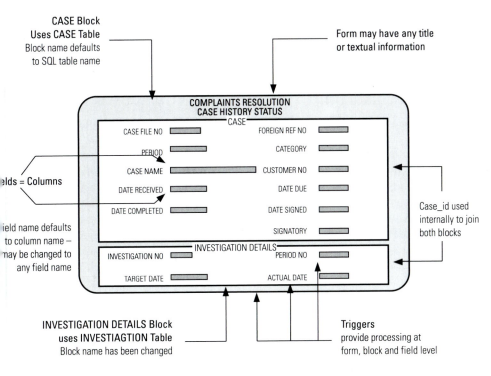

Figure 20.5 ORACLE SQL*Forms terminology.

several blocks can be included on a page. Pages can be larger or smaller than the screen size: defined to cover the entire screen; or to 'pop-up' over other displayed pages – disappearing when no longer needed; they are thus referred to as pop-up pages. (INGRES refers to the entire screen, made up of a displayed form and its menu line, as a **frame**.)

Each block represents one SQL table and hence one entity. This is called the **base table** for the block. It is given the same name as the base table by default, but this can be changed to any appropriate block name. For example, Figure 20.5 shows one page with two blocks. The CASE block is named by default from its base table: CASE. The default block name for the INVESTIGATION base table, however, has been changed to INVESTIGATION DETAILS.

Columns from one or more tables are included in a block as data fields (called **data windows** by QBF). Columns from the base table are included by default; columns from other related tables included in the block must be explicitly defined. The **field label (field title** in QBF) defaults to the column name; it can be changed to any relevant field label. Notice that the default field labels defined in Figure 20.5 have been changed: *case_date_received, case_date_due, case_date_completed* and *case_date_signed* were changed, for example, to DATE RECEIVED, DATE DUE, DATE COMPLETED and DATE SIGNED respectively.

Related blocks can be joined together, using common keys in the tables on which those blocks are based. For example Figure 20.5 shows that *case_id* is used as a common key to join the two blocks: for a particular CASE, only investigations for that case are presented in the INVESTIGA-TION DETAILS block. This is referred to as a **Master-Detail relationship** by SQL*Forms Master/Detail by QBF): CASE is called a **master block**; INVESTIGATION DETAILS is a **detail block**. This represents a *one to many* association between CASE and INVESTIGATION, as illustrated in Figure 20.1. A master block can have several detail blocks with relevant master-detail relationships; however SQL*Forms imposes a constraint that each detail block can have only one master block. INGRES/QBF uses the term **JoinDef** for joins between: Master/Master (a *one to one* association); or Master/Detail (*one to many*).

A join of related blocks is defined in a **trigger**. This allows specific logic to be defined for processing related data in those blocks. Triggers may be defined at three levels: form, block and field. A form-level trigger applies to all blocks and fields in the form, unless specifically overridden at a lower level. Similarly a block-level trigger applies to all fields in a block, unless it is overridden at the field-level. This implements object-oriented logic inheritance.

A block can be defined to display one row (or record) from a table at a time: called a **single-record block (simple fields** in QBF). For example, each block in Figure 20.5 is single-record. Or instead a number of rows can be

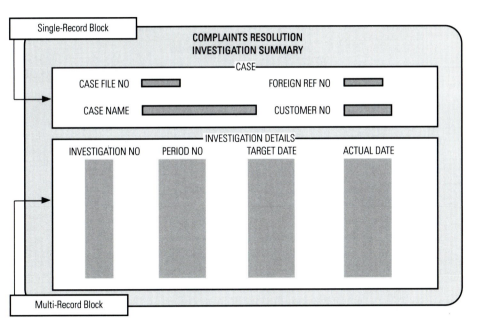

Figure 20.6   Single- and multi-record blocks.

displayed together: called a **multi-record block,** as shown in Figure 20.6
(table fields in QBF).

This allows *one to many* associations to be implemented as Master-
Detail relationships on one page: many of the investigations for a case can
be displayed in columnar form in this example. SQL*Forms, and also QBF,
automatically generate all of the trigger logic for Master-Detail relationships
to synchronize data displayed in a detail block with relevant data in its
related master block. For example, only those investigations for a specified
case are displayed in Figure 20.6.

A screen page can comprise master-detail blocks, as well as other
related blocks, that are needed to carry out a specific application function.
In this book we collectively refer to all blocks included on a screen page,
based on associations between their relevant entities, as an application
screen. Figures 20.4 and 20.6 show two design examples of application
screens for Case Investigations: using both single-record and multi-record
blocks. Figure 20.4 shows much detail about a case in the Case History
Status Form, using a master-detail relationship with single-record blocks. In
contrast, Figure 20.6 presents minimal data on the case so that many
investigations can be displayed in an Investigation Summary Form: the
master-detail relationship uses a multi-record detail block. The most
appropriate design, or both, depends on the application requirements.

20.2.3 Generic procedures with SQL*Forms and QBF

Blocks are used for query processing, or for data maintenance (to add, delete or update data). SQL*Forms and QBF generate SQL SELECT commands for queries, to extract requested data from rows of related tables for a block. New rows can be added for data entry: an INSERT command is generated to insert data from fields in the block displayed on screen into relevant columns of related tables. Rows are updated or deleted: UPDATE and DELETE commands are therefore generated by SQL*Forms.

We can see that each block thus provides all of the logic to add, read, display, change or delete data in a table. It represents one approach to implementing generic procedures for an entity, developed using process modeling as we saw in Chapter 19. Triggers implement the conditional logic which defines execution sequence from a procedure to other related generic procedures. This execution sequence can also be specified with ORACLE SQL*Menu. Triggers and SQL*Menu can both use PL/SQL (as discussed in following chapters) to link related application screens together to implement complex application systems. (Related INGRES applications screens are linked together using INGRES/MENU, INGRES ABF/4GL or INGRES/Windows 4GL.) In Chapters 21 and 22 we will use SQL*Forms to implement the procedures and application systems that we defined in Chapter 19.

20.3 USING ORACLE SQL*FORMS

This section shows the use of ORACLE SQL*Forms Version 3.0 for form design and execution. We will use a generated form for execution, and will then modify that form. (Similar concepts are also used by INGRES/QBF, but will not be explicitly detailed.) Actual screen snapshots from two SQL*Forms sessions are included in the following pages: one session used SQL*Forms running in a single-user environment with OS/2 on a Toshiba 5200/100 laptop microcomputer; the second session used SQL*Forms in a multi-user UNIX environment with HP/UX V7 on a Hewlett-Packard mini, and with IBM PC-compatible microcomputers emulating DEC VT100 terminals. A window environment is automatically emulated by SQL*Forms for these character-mode terminals.

An example of the SQL*Forms log-on screen for each environment is shown in Figure 20.7. This requests the username and password, to authorize access to SQL*Forms. The data base administrator (DBA) responsible for

(a) SQL*Forms Version 3.0 OS/2 Logon Screen

SQL*Forms Design: Version 3.0.14.0.1 – Beta on Fri Oct 05 09:47:51 1990

Copyright (c) Oracle Corporation 1979, 1989. All rights reserved.

Using Object*SQL Version 1.0.16.0.1 (Production)

Using PL/SQL Version 1.0.30.1.1 (Beta)

Username:

Password:

Press F1 at any time to show function keys.

Figure 20.7(a)   SQL*Forms log-on under OS/2.

(b) SQL*Forms Version 3.0 UNIX Logon Screen

SQL*Forms Design: Version 3.0.14.1.1 – Production on Wed Oct 10 11:13:04 1990

Copyright (c) Oracle Corporation 1979, 1989. All rights reserved.

Using Object*SQL Version 01.00.16.00.02 (Production)

Using PL/SQL Version 01.00.30.00.00 (Beta)

Username:

Password:

Press ^K at any time to show function keys.

Figure 20.7(b)   SQL*Forms log-on under UNIX.

managing ORACLE data bases and generated forms allocates a username
and password to each authorized user. Through this log-on procedure, the
user gains access to the ORACLE data bases and forms which have been
granted by the DBA to that registered username.

Figure 20.7 shows the message: *'Press F1 at any time to show function
keys'* for the OS/2 log-on screen, or *'Press ^K at any time to show function
keys'* for the UNIX log-on screen. SQL*Forms operates with many
terminals: the mapping of SQL*Forms control keys is displayed if Function
key 1 (F1) is pressed for an OS/2 PC keyboard, or if the 'Control' key is held
down while 'K' is pressed (indicated by ^K, or Ctrl-K) for a UNIX terminal.
To avoid confusion in different environments, ORACLE refers to each key
by its function, surrounding the relevant function name in square brackets.
Thus [Show Keys] in OS/2 (and also DOS) is F1, while with UNIX it is
^K (Ctrl-K). Pressing [Show Keys] displays other function keys for the
terminal environment being used. In Chapter 21, Tables 21.1–21.4 show the
function keys used by SQL*Forms for key mapping.

If the correct password has been given during log-on, the next screen
displays the main menu. This is a pull-down menu; used to select
SQL*Forms menu items. Figure 20.8 shows the *Action* pull-down menu.
Horizontally listed menu items are highlighted with [Left] or [Right] arrow
keys; vertically listed items with [Up] or [Down] arrow keys. Once highlighted, an item is selected by pressing the [Accept] key (discussed shortly).
The horizontally displayed menu items in Figure 20.8 are:

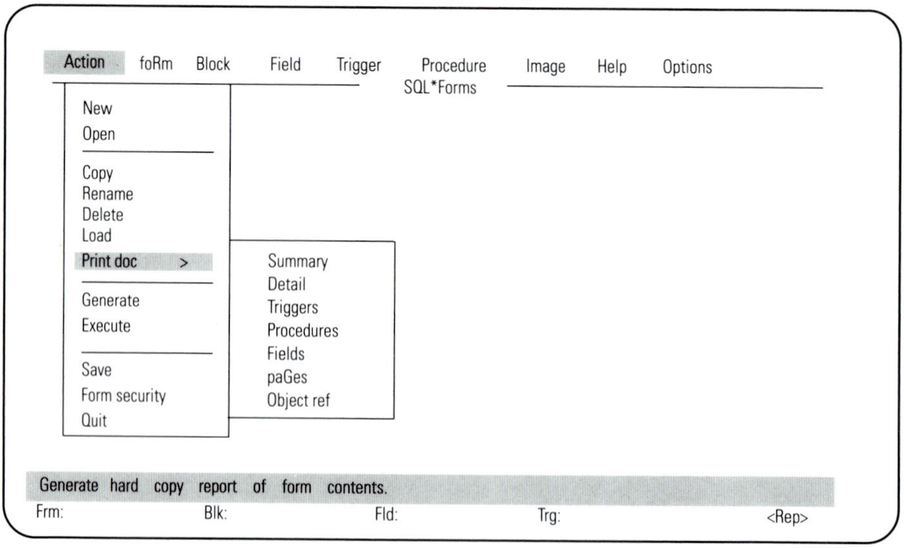

Figure 20.8 The Action menu choices.

Action	Perform global operations on forms.
foRm	Modify form level attributes and information.
Block	Modify an existing block, or create a new block from scratch.
Field	Edit or create a field definition.
Trigger	Create, edit, delete triggers.
Procedure	Create or edit PL/SQL procedures callable from any trigger.
Image	Edit an existing page definition, or create a new one.
Help	Invoke the on line help system.
Options	Set run time and design options.

Alternatively, typing the first capital letter in a name selects that item immediately: for example the *foRm* option is selected by typing R; the *Field* option by typing F. The vertical menu items for the *Action* menu in Figure 20.8 (displayed by typing A) are:

New	Create a new form.
Open	Open a form definition to edit it.
Copy	Copy a form to a new name.
Rename	Rename a form.
Delete	Delete a form from the database.
Load	Load a form definition into memory from a flat file.
Print doc >	Generate hard copy report of form contents.
Execute	Execute the form.
Save	Save the form in the database.
Form Security	Grant access to a form for object reference and copying.
Quit	Exit SQL*Forms.

Menu items with a > at the right of the name indicate that a SQL*Forms submenu exists. Figure 20.8 shows the Print doc > menu item with its submenu items displayed. These are:

Print doc >	Generate hard copy report of form contents.
Summary	Generate report summarizing the form.
Detail	Generate report showing all aspects of form.
Triggers	Generate report describing triggers and trigger text.

Procedures   Generate report describing procedures.

Fields   Generate report describing fields and field attributes.

paGes   Generate report describing pages and page attributes.

Object ref   Generate report listing places a particular object is listed in.

20.3.1   Executing a form

The following steps execute the CASE_STATUS form illustrated in Figure 20.9:

(1)   Select Open and type the name of the form.

(2)   Generate and execute the form (by selecting Generate and then Execute).

Figure 20.9 shows the Open Form dialog box, used to enter the name of the form to be opened in Step 1 above. Instead of typing the name, if several forms exist (indicated in Figure 20.9 by <List> in the bottom right corner of the screen), they can be displayed for selection by pressing the [List] key (discussed later). Once opened, the form is then generated and executed in Step 2: specifying through dialog boxes other details, such as the file name to be used to save the generated form.

In this example we invoked SQL*Forms first, and then specified the relevant form for execution. This is appropriate if we want to make changes

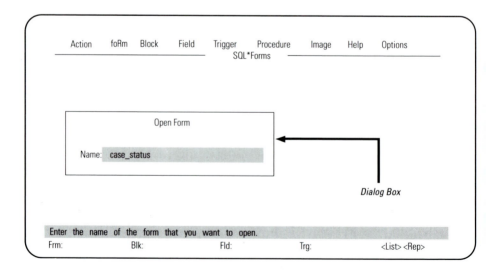

Figure 20.9   Executing the CASE_STATUS form.

to an existing form and then immediately test the modified form. If direct execution with no modification is instead required, the main menu is bypassed: the RunForms program of SQL*Forms is first invoked before log-on, or the form is directly executed using SQL*Menu as described in Chapter 22.

Regardless of whether a form is generated first and then executed, or directly executed, the form is displayed ready for processing – as illustrated by the Case History Status Form in Figure 20.4. New data, entered into fields of the form, are added to the data base; existing data are queried, updated, or deleted as designed for the form.

In the rest of this chapter we will discuss the initial design of a form: the execution of the designed form will be left for discussion in Chapter 21. In the next sections we will describe how default blocks in a form are designed and generated, and how these default blocks are initially refined.

20.3.2 Generating a default block

Each block in a form can be generated directly from the definition of its base table in the ORACLE catalog. The following pages describe generation of a new form with default blocks. Default blocks reflect screen layout and design decisions that are automatically taken by ORACLE (by default) for each block; these blocks are later refined as required by the designer. Generated default blocks can be further refined by addition of triggers and procedural logic as described in Chapters 21 and 22.

In brief, the designer specifies New and defines a new form to be generated. The form is then modified by generating default blocks; each block can then be further modified. To achieve this, the following steps are carried out:

(1)   Select New, and enter the name of the new form in a dialog box similar to that shown in Figure 20.9.

(2)   Select foRm, then Modify, to modify the new form.

The Form Definition screen is displayed, as illustrated in Figure 20.10. This requires definition of certain characteristics of the form. The validation unit can be specified as: Form, Block, Record or Field (see the Validation Unit pop-up list in Figure 20.10). This indicates whether SQL*Forms is to validate data in each new or changed field immediately (field validation), or whether this validation is to be deferred and carried out at the record, block or form level later. The normal validation unit is specified as Field. Validation is discussed in Chapter 21.

Figure 20.10 shows the terminology that is used with pop-up lists. The

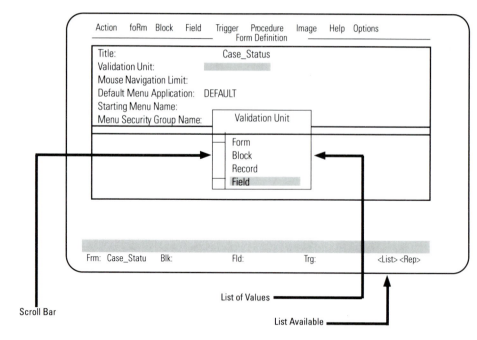

Figure 20.10 Defining a new form.

List Available (< List >) indicator is shown in the bottom right corner of the screen, as discussed with Open earlier: a *List of Values* exists for the current field (the Validation Unit field). The **Scroll Bar** is used to scroll up and down the list if more values exist than are displayed in the list: shown by an up (∧) and/or a down (∨) indicator in the boxes above or below the scroll bar, respectively.

The other specifications in Figure 20.10 are: the **Mouse Navigation Limit** (used for bit-mapped screens with a mouse; normally set to Field); the **Default Menu Application**; the **Starting Menu Name**; and the **Menu Security Group Name**. These associate specific menu characteristics with a form for use with SQL*Menu. This product is discussed in Chapter 22.

The lower part of the Form Definition screen in Figure 20.10 allows **Comments** to be entered. These describe the business purpose of the form: a general description of how that purpose is achieved, with other comments to any required level of detail. These comments are printed by SQL*Forms in any documentation produced for the form (using Action Print doc as shown in Figure 20.8).

Continuing with the steps for default block generation:

(3) Select Block, then Default, to define a default block.

The Default Block definition screen in Figure 20.11 is then displayed. The

Block Name is first entered, followed by the name of its **Base Table**. As we saw in Figure 20.5, the block can have a name different from its base table. The base table is optionally selected from a list of all tables that the designer is authorized to use, as shown in Figure 20.12.

Figure 20.11 shows buttons and check boxes used to specify characteristics of default blocks. These implement the selection of options in a windowing environment. Buttons display a list of choices; check boxes implement a single choice – either selected (ON: indicated by 'X') or deselected (OFF: shown by a blank). For example, the check box **Use Constraints** notifies SQL*Forms to generate triggers to use with any constraints defined for the base table in the ORACLE data base. These may be Check clauses used to enforce specific data values in certain columns of the table, or may specify referential integrity constraints. Referential integrity is discussed in Chapter 21.

Initially all columns in the base table are implicitly selected, ready to be generated as fields in the default block. By using the **Select Columns** button (see Figure 20.11), this implicit selection can be overridden: columns to be explicitly excluded from the block can be deselected.

Figure 20.12 next shows a search field, used to select the base table for the block.

A large displayed list (in this case, of tables authorized for the designer to use) can be reduced by entering a search criterion in the search field. This criterion can use the SQL '%' or the '_' wild card characters (see Appendix

Figure 20.11 is shown below as a screen layout:

```
 Action    foRm   Block   Field   Trigger   Procedure   Image   Help   Options
                                  Default Block

  Block Name:
  Base Table:

  Sequence Number:   1        (Select Columns)          (      ) use Constraints
  Records Displayed: 1        Page Number: 1            Base Line: 1

  Master Block:                                         (      ) Delete Details

                             Join Condition



  Button                                                        Check Box

 Enter  the  name  of  the  block.
 Frm:  Case_Statu       Blk:          Fld:          Trg:              <Rep>
```

Figure 20.11   Specifying a default block.

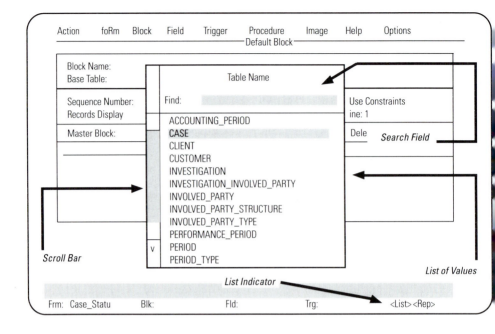

Figure 20.12 The search field used in a list of base tables.

1). For example, 'C%' (or just 'C') will display all tables beginning with 'C'; the search field '%PARTY%' displays all tables with 'PARTY' anywhere in the table name; the search field '___CASE%' displays any tables with 'CASE' in the fourth through seventh characters of the name.

Figure 20.13 shows the Default Block screen ready to generate the CASE block for the CASE base table. This is the first block of the CASE_STATUS form in Figure 20.5: specified in Figure 20.13 as *Sequence Number: 1* (block 1). The *Records Displayed: 1* specifies this as a single-record block on *Page Number: 1*, starting on the first line of the screen – *Base Line: 1*. If Records Displayed is greater than 1 a multi-record default block is generated for the specified number of records, starting at the indicated base line.

This default block automatically places each column from the table for that block in an appropriate location of the screen as shown in Figure 20.14. The default CASE block can then be immediately generated and executed as discussed earlier. Screens can thus be developed rapidly as prototypes for initial testing. The default block can be further modified, as described in Chapter 21, to refine the screen as required.

Figure 20.15 next shows the definition of the **Investigations block**, based on the base table INVESTIGATION. This has been defined as a

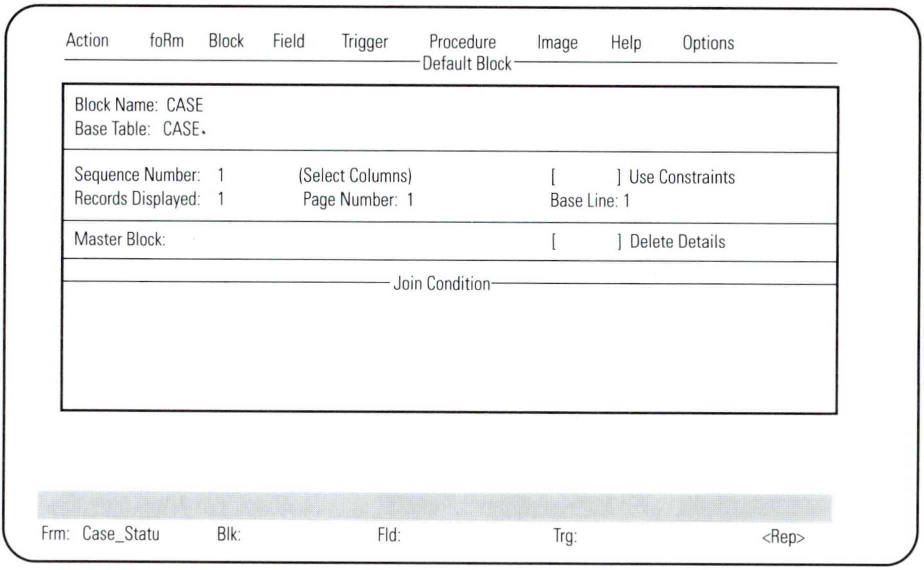

Action   foRm   Block   Field   Trigger   Procedure   Image   Help   Options
── Default Block ────

Block Name: CASE
Base Table: CASE.

Sequence Number: 1   (Select Columns)   [   ] Use Constraints
Records Displayed: 1   Page Number: 1   Base Line: 1

Master Block: [   ] Delete Details

──────────────────────────── Join Condition ────────────────────

Frm: Case_Statu   Blk: Fld: Trg: <Rep>

Figure 20.13   Specifying default single-record CASE block.

= = = = = CASE = = = = =

CASE_ID   PERIOD_ID

CUSTOMER_ID   SIGNATORY_ID

CASE_NAME   CASE_FILE_ID

CATEGORY_ID   CASE_FOREIGN_REF_ID

CASE_DATE_RECEIVED   CASE_DATE_DUE

CASE_DATE_COMPLETED   CASE_DATE_SIGNED

Frm: Case_Statu   Blk: CASE   Fld: Trg: <Rep>

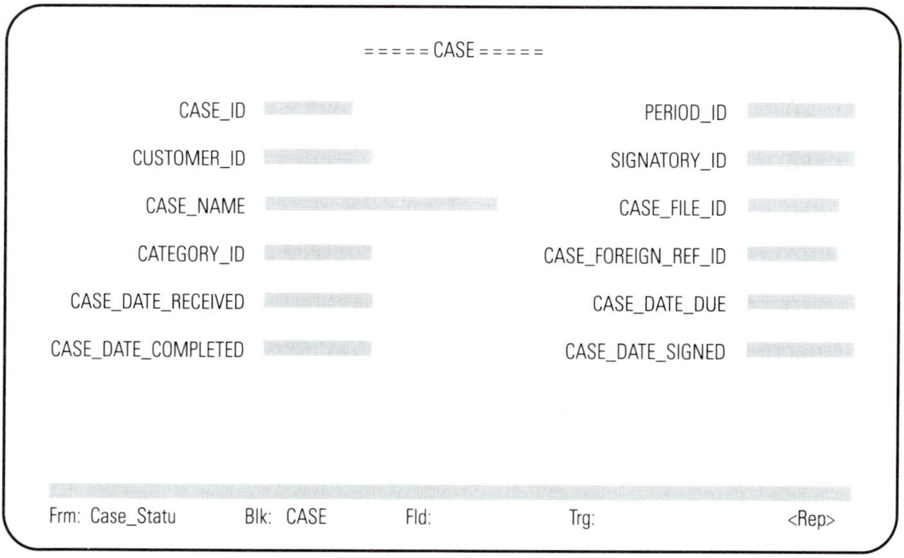

Figure 20.14   The default single-record CASE block.

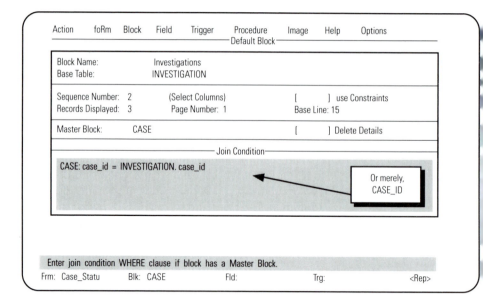

Figure 20.15 Specifying a default multi-record block.

multi-record block with *Records Displayed: 3* from *Base Line: 15* on *Page Number: 1.*

Notice that Figure 20.15 indicates *Master Block: CASE*; this indicates a Master-Detail relationship between the (master) Case block and the (detail) Investigations block, with a Join Condition of the underlying base tables of:

CASE.case_id – INVESTIGATION.case_id

Alternatively, as both base tables have the same named common key, *case_id* could be specified alone as shown in Figure 20.15. This Master-Detail specification results in the automatic generation of appropriate trigger logic to synchronize a specified CASE master record with its related INVESTIGATION detail records. Furthermore, if check box *Delete Details* is turned ON ('X'), additional integrity trigger logic is generated for the deletion of master records: any detail rows that exist for a master record are deleted automatically. If *Delete Details* is turned OFF (that is, blank) deletion is rejected to maintain data integrity, but the operator is notified of this rejection by a message.

Figure 20.16 shows the application screen for these two SQL*Forms Master-Detail blocks.

Notice that field labels for a multi-record block (see Figure 20.16) appear above the relevant field column, but the join field (*case_id*) is unlabelled during a Design session. This field is not displayed at all during

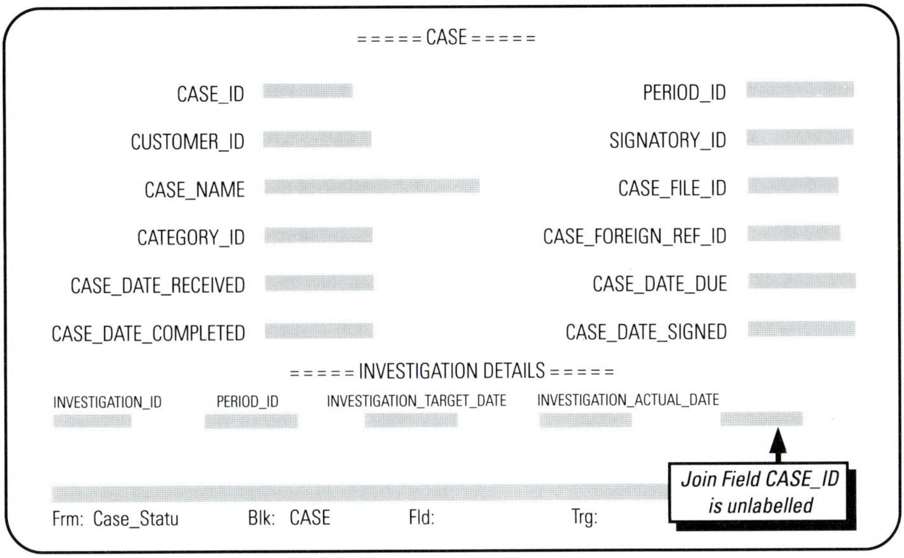

Figure 20.16   Default Master-Detail blocks.

execution: it is assumed that the master block will indicate the relevant join value for the detail block. It must exist in the block, but can be resized to a single column and placed anywhere as desired.

We have defined the default blocks in Figure 20.16. We can immediately generate them to evaluate the effectiveness of the SQL*Forms default screen design for execution: this is discussed in Chapter 21.

20.3.3   SQL*Forms context

Finally, we introduce the concept of SQL*Forms **context**. The context is shown by the current form, page, block, field and/or trigger; as illustrated by the object hierarchy in Figure 20.17. A field is defined within a block, which is defined within a page, and so within a form. This is particularly important for triggers, which are defined at the form, block or field level.

The current context is always shown on the status line: the last line of a screen below the message line. For example, the following context is the *Case_Status* form; in the *CASE* block; for the *customer_id* field and the *POST-CHANGE* trigger.

Frm: CASE_STATUS   Blk: CASE   Fld: customer_id   Trg: POST-CHANGE   < Rep >

Following the development of default blocks, some changes in screen design or layout may be needed. Some fields may not be required; other fields may

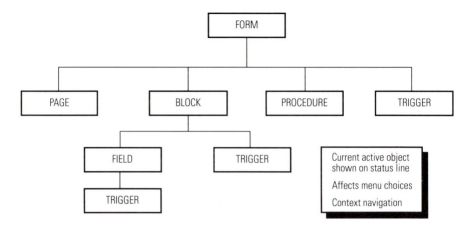

Figure 20.17 SQL*Forms object hierarchy indicates context.

have to be moved; still other fields may have to be resized (to increase or decrease the number of positions taken by those fields on the screen); there may be validation tests which must be applied against data entered or changed in fields; some additional fields may have to be defined, to display data from columns from other related tables.

We will discuss this refinement of default blocks in Chapter 21. In so doing, we will further see how SQL*Forms implements generic procedures as discussed in Chapters 5 and 19. In Chapter 22 we will combine these blocks into application screens based on the data map. We will then link screens together as complex procedures, to implement the application systems we earlier designed using process modeling.

20.4 SUMMARY

This chapter provided an overview of software tools that can be used to implement the systems defined in earlier chapters. We reviewed support provided by two relational DBMS products: ORACLE and INGRES.

We reviewed ORACLE products: SQL*Plus; SQL*Net; SQL*Forms; SQL*Menu; and SQL*ReportWriter. Oracle Toolkit provides source code portability across: UNIX and X-Windows; DEC VMS and DECWindows; IBM OS/2 and Presentation Manager; and Apple Macintosh for applications developed with SQL*Forms. We reviewed INGRES products: INGRES/NET, INGRES/STAR and INGRES Gateways; Query-By-Forms (QBF); Report-By-Forms (RBF); Visual-Forms-Editor (VIFRED); INGRES/MENU; and INGRES Report-Writer. We discussed the INGRES application development environments used for integrated customized application systems: INGRES ABF/4GL; and INGRES/Windows 4GL for graphical user interface environments. These provide application portability across operating system and user interface environments.

We discussed the implementation of entities as SQL tables, and used the Case Investigations System (identified in Chapter 19) to illustrate some of the concepts used by relational data bases. Each entity is implemented as an SQL RDBMS table: as a block in a form using SQL*Forms, or as fields in a QBF frame (comprising a form and its menu).

We saw that single-record blocks (simple fields for QBF) display only one row of its base table; multi-record blocks (table fields for QBF) display many rows at once. We discussed the concept of Master-Detail blocks (also called Master/Detail in QBF) used to implement *one to many*, or *one to one* associations: with SQL*Forms using triggers (or QBF using JoinDefs) to automatically synchronize the detail block with its relevant master block. We were able to generate default single- or multi-record blocks, and also default Master-Detail blocks, using screen snapshots from a typical SQL*Forms session to illustrate the concepts.

We saw that SQL*Forms blocks and function keys (QBF frames) relate generally to generic procedures in Process modeling, implementing procedure map conditional logic by using triggers at the form-level, block-level or field-level.

References

[1] Codd, E. F. (1970). *A Relational Model for Large Shared Data Banks*, CACM, 13 (6), pp. 377–387.

[2] Codd, E. F. (1979). *Extending the Database Relational Model to Capture More Meaning*, ACM Trans on Database Systems, Vol 4, No 4, pp. 397–434.

[3] Codd, E. F. (1988). *Domains, Keys, and Referential Integrity in Relational Databases*, InfoDB – Colin J. White Consulting: San Jose, CA.

[4] Koch, G. (1990). *ORACLE: The Complete Reference*, Osborne McGraw-Hill: Berkeley CA.

[5] Groff, R. and Weinberg, P. (1990). *Using SQL*, Osborne McGraw-Hill: Berkeley CA.

[6] Date, C. J. (1988). *A Guide to the SQL Standard*, Addison-Wesley: Reading, MA.

[7] Date, C. J. (1987). *A Guide to INGRES*, Addison-Wesley: Reading, MA.

[8] Codd, E. F. (1990). *The Relational Model for Database Management, Version 2*, Addison-Wesley: Reading, MA.

[9] Date, C. J. (1986). *An Introduction to Database Systems, Fourth Edition*, Addison-Wesley: Reading, MA.

[10] Date, C. J. and White, C. J. (1988). *A Guide to DB2, Second Edition*, Addison-Wesley: Reading, MA.

CHAPTER 21

Development of Data Entry Screens

In this chapter we will discuss development of data entry screens. These will be used to enter, retrieve, modify or delete data stored in ORACLE SQL tables generated from the data model. The concepts introduced in this chapter for SQL*Forms are also applicable to other DBMS and 4GL software products. We will see that each data entry screen represents the generic process procedures (discussed in Chapter 19) for the entities implemented as blocks on that screen. In Chapter 22 we will use these same principles to develop application screens, and link them together as application systems to address complex business processing and analysis. First we need to discuss the responsibilities of all of the participants involved in systems development. The following discussion applies to ORACLE, INGRES and any other DBMS development tools.

21.1 SYSTEMS DEVELOPMENT RESPONSIBILITIES

The emphasis throughout this book is that Information Engineering allows people who are experts in the business, rather than in computers, to analyze and design their own systems. With appropriate software tools they can build those applications, and change them later as dictated by business needs. These users become self-supporting: they can develop and maintain

504

their own application systems. Alternatively, DP staff can build the applications for them based on the more precise definition resulting from the users' active involvement in design. There are many benefits from this approach: an increase in software development productivity; development of high-quality systems based on the business knowledge of these experts; the availability of easily maintained systems; and a reduction in the application backlog of systems waiting to be developed by the DP department.

However there is also a need for control. Strategic, tactical and operational modeling allow common data, used throughout the organization, to be identified. The problem of data in different stages of processing because of redundant copies, disappears. The data are stored in data bases once only, yet able to be shared by all areas of the business authorized to access or update those data. But unless control is exercised, the benefits of non-redundant, consistent, up-to-date data are never realized. This control is provided by the Data Administration (DA) function in the organization.

Data base administration is a technical DP activity, and DBAs normally report to the DP department. In contrast, *data administration* is a business activity: typically carried out by the users themselves; or instead by business analysts, rather than DP analysts. The role of data administration is to provide central control and coordination, to develop and maintain data models on which the data bases and systems are built.

Thus the DA section is responsible for central control of the strategic model developed for each area in the organization. It is responsible for consolidation of the different models so developed, by merging them progressively together into a single, corporate strategic model. The strategic directions set by management can therefore be directly supported by information systems and data bases developed from this corporate strategic model.

The DA section is also responsible for control of the separate tactical and operational models that are developed for each area from its strategic model. This includes data model analysis using software as described in Chapter 17. Where different terminology is used in various parts of the organization, the DA section can help establish a standard terminology throughout the business. This is essential if common data are to be shared effectively: people must refer to this shared data consistently, using the same names.

A further DA role is the coordination of different projects throughout the organization, particularly where several projects may be underway concurrently. This ensures that the strategic, tactical and operational models that are developed in each project can be merged together progressively, producing consolidated tactical and operational models for each business unit as well, in addition to the consolidated corporate strategic model. Each of these project teams also has specific responsibilities. They must review the data models following software processing and analysis by the DA section.

They must set project plans as described in Chapter 17 for subsequent modeling and refinement based on this processing, and conduct those sessions. They must define purpose descriptions of all entities, attributes and associations in their area of interest. And finally, they must define the physical data types and sizes of all attributes in priority operational systems which are to be implemented. The DA section can then ensure that data bases generated from these data models are consistent, and can be physically installed either centrally, or instead distributed geographically, to be shared as needed.

As well as central coordination and maintenance, the DA section is also responsible for the generation of data bases and table indexes. Data base and index generation is carried out automatically by the CASE data modeling packages IE Expert [1] and ISM [2] that were discussed in Chapter 17. These generated data bases and indexes are delivered by the DA section to the project team as text files, for physical installation on the relevant hardware. The installed data bases are next used by the project team to develop default screens for initial data entry and prototyping against the generated data base. The project team refines these screens for final use in data entry – which is the subject of this chapter. They then build application systems as described in Chapter 22. We will discuss definition of primary and foreign keys, and of SQL indexes, first.

21.2 PRIMARY AND FOREIGN KEYS

Throughout this book we have seen the role of primary and foreign keys in establishing associations between entities. These associations define entity dependency, which leads to identification of systems from data models, derivation of implementation sequence and the development of project plans for those systems (see Chapters 17 and 19). The rules of entity dependency in Chapter 3 are based on the concept of 'referential integrity'. This is only one of five aspects of integrity which Codd [3] indicates should be supported by relational data base management systems; the others are **domain integrity, column integrity, entity integrity** and **user-defined integrity** [4]. The release of DB2 Version 2 by IBM (and also ORACLE Version 7.0 and INGRES Release 6.3) provided some of the required integrity support: through support for primary and foreign keys, and elements of referential integrity [5]. The following discussion relates specifically to DB2 Version 2.2.

Primary and foreign keys are normally defined when a table is created (with CREATE TABLE). However because earlier releases of DB2 did not support primary or foreign keys, they may be defined later (with ALTER TABLE) when migrating data bases used by earlier DB2 releases. A unique index must also be specified to enforce primary and foreign key uniqueness on all columns that make up the key, and to enforce entity integrity (whereby no component of a primary or foreign key is allowed to accept null values) [4].

An example of the definition of primary and foreign keys in the INVESTIGATION table follows. All keys are defined as NOT NULL, and the compound primary key: *investigation_id, period_id* is defined. One foreign key exists in this table: *case_id*. This is given the name *case_fk* (for DB2 diagnostic reference only), and references the CASE table. Finally, ON DELETE CASCADE specifies that all investigations with the same *case_id* are to be automatically deleted when the relevant case is deleted. (Alternatively, ON DELETE RESTRICT prevents this automatic deletion.) Further detail is provided in the IBM DB2 Reference manuals. We will discuss other logic for referential integrity later in this chapter.

```
CREATE TABLE INVESTIGATION
       (  investigation_id        NUMBER (12)             NOT NULL,
          period_id               NUMBER (12)             NOT NULL,
          case_id                 NUMBER (12)             NOT NULL,
          PRIMARY KEY             (investigation_id, period_id),
          FOREIGN_KEY case_fk     (case_id)
          REFERENCES              CASE
          ON DELETE               CASCADE        );
```

Following this discussion of primary and foreign keys, the remaining chapters of this book will assume that key definition has already been established in conjunction with SQL CREATE TABLE commands, according to the specific support offered by the RDBMS you will be using.

21.3 DEFINING SQL INDEXES

SQL indexes may improve performance in accessing SQL tables. The table for CASE will be used to illustrate the concepts for defining primary, foreign and secondary keys as indexes. The SQL CREATE TABLE and CREATE INDEX commands for CASE are documented in Figure 21.1.

The primary keys of an entity are defined as a **unique** index for its generated SQL table. This ensures that only one row will exist for each index value. Foreign keys must also be unique, but an index need only be defined if there is much activity in joining two or more tables based on common keys: a foreign key index can improve join performance. In contrast, a secondary

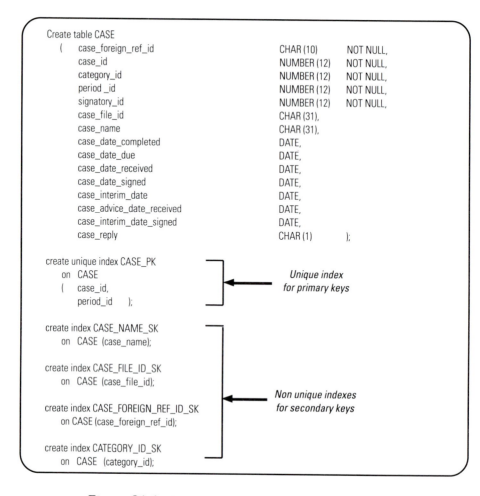

Figure 21.1 Definition of SQL tables, keys and indexes.

key may identify many rows with the same index value: secondary key indexes are therefore usually defined as non-unique.

We discussed during operational modeling, in conjunction with Figure 18.4, that keys whose value may change 'volatile keys' should be defined as secondary keys instead of primary keys. Thus [*case name*], [*case file id*], [*case foreign ref id*] and also [*category id*] were defined as secondary keys for CASE rather than primary keys, as operational experts agreed that they are volatile. Then we defined a unique primary key of *case id#*, an internally generated key which will never change. The reason is discussed next.

If a primary or foreign key value is changed, every index entry for that key value must be updated in every table where it is part of the index. This is called **index maintenance**. As these are common keys used to join related tables, index maintenance can thus have a severe performance impact. In contrast, secondary keys exist in only one table: as only one index must therefore be updated, index maintenance is low – there is less of a performance impact than for changing indexes based on primary or foreign keys.

When the DA section generates a table, it must define a unique index for all of the primary keys of that table. As a useful convention this index is given the same name as its table, suffixed by '_PK' (for primary key: see Figure 21.1). A secondary key index takes the name of the secondary key column on which it is based, suffixed by '_SK' (for secondary key). Foreign keys are suffixed by '_FK'. Additional indexes may also be needed for various performance reasons: for different combinations of keys; for non key columns used for access; for columns used in WHERE clause processing; for sorted columns of an ORDER BY clause; or for grouped columns with a HAVING clause – all can use indexes if higher performance is needed.

We can now discuss the use of data entry and application forms for processing against these tables. For the rest of the book we will use SQL*Forms to illustrate development concepts, referring to INGRES/QBF only where relevant.

21.4 DATA ENTRY AND APPLICATION FORMS

Oracle Corporation provides extensive software tools for the design, development and generation of screen-based, interactive application systems using SQL*Forms Version 3.0, with SQL*Menu Version 5.0 and PL/SQL [6, 7]. For readers new to these products, we will separate the steps involved in design and development of data entry screens from steps followed to design and develop application screens and application systems. We will initially use two forms for each system: one for data entry; the other for application screens and systems. (Later, when proficiency has been gained in the use of these products, these steps can be combined; then only one form is used both for data entry and for application systems.) The following pages discuss the use of two forms.

The first form is used for data entry: we will call this the **data entry form**. Each table occupies one screen page of the form as a single-record block. All columns of the table are defined as fields in the block for adding, querying, changing or deleting rows of the table. Whenever we use the term data entry we imply all of these processing actions.

The second form is for application processing: called the **application form**. It contains an application screen on each page with two or more blocks for related tables. These may be single-record or multi-record blocks, defined with Master-Detail relationships if appropriate, as discussed in Chapter 20.

We will describe the design and refinement of data entry forms in the remainder of this chapter. Chapter 22 then describes the design of application forms.

21.5 USING DEFAULT FORMS FOR DATA ENTRY

We first discuss data entry using the default data entry form. This will help us to refine default screens for production data entry use. Default blocks are generated as described in Chapter 20. All table columns included in a default, single-record block occupy one screen page of the data entry form. These default screens can then be used for initial data entry by the project team.

Earlier versions of SQL*Forms used the block menu during execution, for rapid access to the relevant data entry block for a table. This is illustrated in Figure 21.2 for Version 2.3 of SQL*Forms. All blocks in the data entry form for Case Investigations System tables are listed. Each block has been

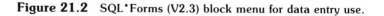

```
┌──────────────────────────────────────────────────────────────────────┐
│             COMPLAINTS RESOLUTION – ORACLE DATA BASE                    │
│                          MAIN MENU                                      │
│   BLOCK NAME                              APPID      APPLICATION NAME    │
│   ACCOUNTING_PERIOD                         2        COMRES             │
│   CASE                                      2        COMRES             │
│   CLIENT                                    2        COMRES             │
│   CUSTOMER                                  2        COMRES             │
│   INVESTIGATION                             2        COMRES             │
│   INVESTIGATION_INVOLVED_PARTY              2        COMRES             │
│   INVOLVED_PARTY                            2        COMRES             │
│   INVOLVED_PARTY_STRUCTURE                  2        COMRES             │
│   INVOLVED_PARTY_TYPE                       2        COMRES             │
│   PERFORMANCE_PERIOD                        2        COMRES             │
│   PERIOD                                    2        COMRES             │
│   PERIOD_TYPE                               2        COMRES             │
│   PERIOD_STRUCTURE                          2        COMRES             │
│   REPORTING_PERIOD                          2        COMRES             │
│   SUPPLIER                                  2        COMRES             │
│                                                                        │
│      v    Char Mode:  Replace         Page 1              Count:   15   │
└──────────────────────────────────────────────────────────────────────┘
```

Figure 21.2 SQL*Forms (V2.3) block menu for data entry use.

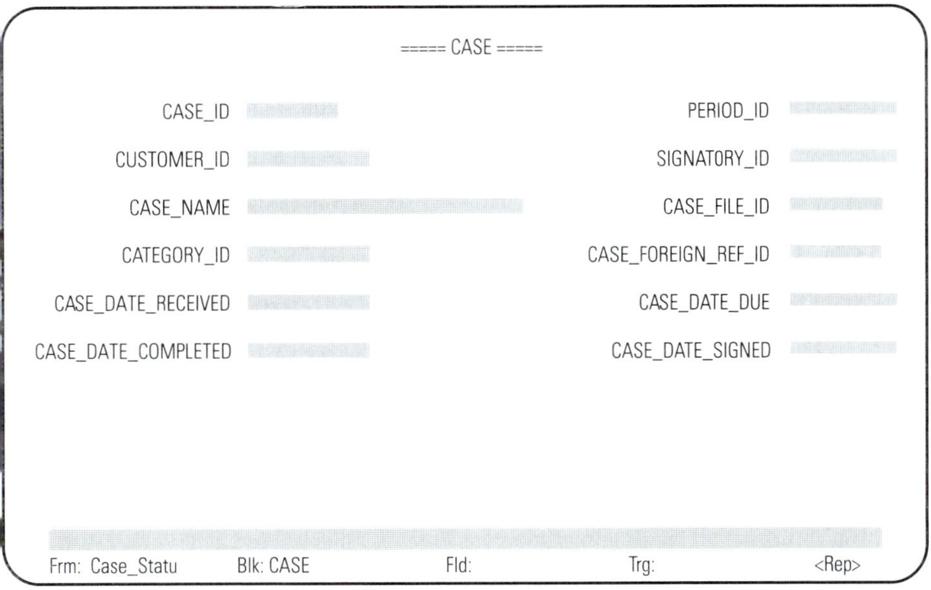

Figure 21.3   Default data entry screen for CASE.

given the exact name of its relevant table. Notice that this block menu is designed to present each block alphabetically. A required block is selected by moving the horizontal highlight bar using [Up] or [Down] arrow keys. This block menu approach is also supported by SQL*Forms Version 3.0; but each data entry screen is more readily invoked using SQL*Menu, as discussed in Chapter 22.

CASE is highlighted in Figure 21.2. The Return key is pressed to display the data entry screen for the selected block (and hence table). Figure 21.3 shows the default data entry screen generated for CASE. Each field on the screen has been given a default label, which is the name of the column used for that field. Although this form is not yet refined, it can be immediately used for data entry as described next.

21.5.1   SQL*Forms execution mode function keys

We discussed in Chapter 20 that Oracle uses function names to refer to keystrokes used for each SQL*Forms operating environment. The Execution Mode keys for OS/2 and DOS are next summarized in Table 21.1; and for UNIX with DEC VT100 terminals in Table 21.2. The Design Mode keys for OS/2 and DOS are summarized in Table 21.3; and for UNIX with DEC

VT100 terminals in Table 21.4. (From this point, any reference to the OS/2 version is also assumed to include the DOS version, unless explicitly stated otherwise.) We will discuss the use of the Execution Mode keys for data entry first, using the OS/2 keys in Table 21.1 to illustrate. (The dash '-' between keys shows that the first key is held down while pressing the second key.)

Table 21.1   SQL*Forms execution mode for DOS and OS/2

Cursor Movement Keys

Right	Right arrow	Left	Left arrow
Next Field	Tab	Previous Field	Shift-Tab
Next Block	Ctrl-PgDn	Previous Block	Ctrl-PgUp
Next Record	PgDn	Previous Record	PgUp
Next Set of Records	Alt-R	Next Primary Key	Shift-F3
Down	Down arrow	Up	Up arrow
Scroll Down	Ctrl-D	Scroll Up	Ctrl-U
Scroll Right	Ctrl-Right arrow	Scroll Left	Ctrl-Left arrow
Block Menu	F5		

Editing Keys

Delete Backward	Backspace	Delete Character	Del
Insert/Replace	Ins	Delete Line	Ctrl-Home
Clear Field	Ctrl-End	Clear Record	Shift-F4
Clear Block	Shift-F5	Clear Form/Rollback	Shift-F7
Beginning of Line	Home	End of Line	End
First Line	Alt-F	Last Line	Alt-L
Cut	Alt-X	Copy	Alt-C
Paste	Alt-V	Edit	Alt-E
Select	F2		

User Assistance Keys

Show Keys	F1 or Ctrl-K	Block Menu	F5
Display Error	Ctrl-F1	Duplicate Field	F3
Duplicate Record	F4	Exit/Cancel	Esc or Shift-F10
Help	Shift-F1	List	F9
Menu	Alt-F1	Print	Shift-F8
Refresh Page	Shift-F9 or Ctrl-L or Ctrl-R		

Query Processing Keys

Enter Query	F7	Execute Query	F8
Count Query Hits	Shift-F2		

Data Base Maintenance Keys

Insert Record	F6	Delete Record	Shift-F6
Commit/Accept	F10		

Block Mode Function Keys

Return	Enter

Table 21.2 similarly shows the function key mapping for SQL*Forms Execution Mode under UNIX, using DEC VT100 terminals. (The comma ',' between keys indicates that the first key is released before pressing the second, or subsequent, keys.)

Table 21.2 SQL*Forms execution mode for UNIX with VT100

Cursor Movement Keys

Right	Right arrow	Left	Left arrow
Next Field	Tab	Previous Field	PF1, Return or PF1, Tab
Next Block	Keypad--	Previous Block	Keypad-9
Next Record	PF1, Keypad--	Previous Record	PF1, Keypad-9
Down	Down arrow	Up	Up arrow
Scroll Down	PF1, Down	Scroll Up	PF1, Up
Scroll Right	PF1, Right	Scroll Left	PF1, Left
Block Menu	PF1, Keypad-0		

Editing Keys

Delete Backward	Delete	Delete Character	Ctrl-D
Insert/Replace	Ctrl-A	Delete Line	PF1, Delete
Clear Field	Keypad-4	Clear Record	Keypad-5
Clear Block	PF1, Keypad-4	Clear Form/Rollback	PF1, Keypad-5
Beginning of Line	PF1, PF1, Left	End of Line	PF1, PF1, Right
First Line	PF1, PF1, Up	Last Line	PF1, PF1, Down
Cut	PF1, Keypad-3	Copy	PF1, Keypad-.
Paste	PF1, Keypad-2	Edit	PF1, Keypad-1
Select	Enter or Ctrl-V		

User Assistance Keys

Show Keys	Ctrl-K	Block Menu	PF1, Keypad-0
Display Error	PF1, PF2	Duplicate Field	PF1, PF1, PF2
Duplicate Record	PF1, PF1, PF3	Exit/Cancel	PF4 or Ctrl-B
Help	PF2 or Ctrl-W	List	Keypad-. or Ctrl-F
Print	Ctrl-P	Refresh Page	Ctrl-R
Menu	Keypad-0 or Ctrl-G or Ctrl-N		

Query Processing Keys

Enter Query	Keypad-6	Execute Query	Keypad-,
Count Query Hits	PF1, PF3		

Data Base Maintenance Keys

Insert Record	Keypad-2	Delete Record	Keypad-3
Commit/Accept	PF3 or Ctrl-O		

Block Mode Function Keys

Return	Enter

21.5.2 SQL*Forms execution mode operation

The [insert record] key (see Data Base Maintenance Keys in Table 21.1) used to initiate entry of data values for a new row to be inserted in a table, is mapped to Function key 6 for OS/2 (F6). The [commit/accept] key indicates completion of entry of all values for the record: mapped to Function key 10 (F10). In the discussion which follows, square brackets indicate the SQL*Forms [named key]; curved brackets indicate the OS/2 and DOS (key equivalent).

We first initiate [insert record] mode by pressing (F6) and enter the data values of each field in turn for a new row to be inserted into the table. The cursor automatically moves to the first field on the screen ready for entry of data: the *case_id* field at the top left of Figure 21.3. Keying errors on data entry are corrected by the following keys: [delete backward] (backspace); [delete character] (Del); or [insert/replace] (Ins). The cursor can be moved non-destructively left or right in the field by the [left] (Left arrow) or [right] (Right arrow) keys. In Tables 21.1 and 21.2 these are called **Editing** keys.

A field is cleared by the [clear field] (Ctrl-End) key. This hyphenated combination of keys indicates that the Ctrl key and the End key are both held down at the same time. A field value from the previous record is duplicated by pressing the [duplicate field] key (F3). The entire previous record is duplicated for convenience by the [duplicate record] (F4) key.

A table column that is wider than its relevant field on the screen can be scrolled left by the [scroll left] (Ctrl-Left arrow) key, or right by the [scroll right] (Ctrl-Right arrow) key. Or the [edit key] (Alt-E) can be used to display a pop-up editing window, for word-processor editing of large fields (such as CHAR or LONG). The function keys used for OS/2 (and DOS) are displayed at any time by pressing [show function keys] (F1). The block menu (see Figure 21.2) is displayed by the [block menu] (F5) key. Help assistance is available at any time by pressing the [help] (Shift-F1) key.

The fields in the default screen are sequenced left to right, then top to bottom normally based on the original order of columns defined in the CREATE TABLE command used to generate the SQL table for the default block. These fields can be repositioned on the screen, and the sequence of execution changed, as described in *21.6 Refining Default Data Entry Screens*. The [next field] (Tab) key moves to higher sequence fields on the screen. [Previous field] (Shift-Tab) moves the cursor back to lower sequence fields. A description of a field is obtained by pressing [help] (Shift-F1).

We saw earlier that primary and foreign keys are defined in the CREATE TABLE command as NOT NULL columns. SQL*Forms defines each key field as **Required** (mandatory) for a default block generated from that table. This indicates that a value must always be entered in that field on the screen. If no value is entered, SQL*Forms displays an error message when the [next field] (Tab) key is pressed to move from that key field to the next field. The mandatory entry test is also carried out for key fields when the [previous field] (Shift-Tab) key is pressed.

When data has been entered into all fields on the screen, the [commit/accept] (F10) key is pressed to insert the record as a new row in the table for that block. If however a row already exists in the table with the same primary key values, the addition of a new row would result in a duplicate key. We saw earlier that primary keys are defined with unique indexes: SQL*Forms therefore rejects addition of a duplicate primary key row as an SQL error. Details of the error are displayed by pressing [display error] (Ctrl-F1). This can be refined by triggers (see *21.7.1 Validation of Unique Keys*), to present an error message as soon as an invalid key is entered.

The [insert record] (F6) and [commit/accept] (F10) keys are **Data Base Maintenance Keys** (see Table 21.1). Once data have been entered, they can be used for enquiries by first entering query mode. This is specified by pressing the [enter query] (F7) key: a **Query Processing Key** in Table 21.1. If the [execute query] (F8) key is next pressed, the first row of the table is displayed. Each row is then displayed in turn by pressing the [next record] (PgDn) key. Previous rows are displayed by the [previous record] (PgUp) key. Or instead, a value can first be entered into a key field: when the [execute query] (F8) key is pressed the row for that key value is displayed. [Next record] (PgDn) or [previous record] (PgUp) keys can then be used to move forward or backwards in the table from that point.

Values can also be entered into any fields on the screen to establish search criteria. The SQL wild card characters '%' and '_' can be used in character fields (as discussed in Chapter 20 for List of Values search criteria). The comparison operators may precede values entered in numeric fields; these operators include: $<$, $<=$, $>$, $>=$ and also ! $=$ or $\neg =$ for: less than, less than or equal, greater than, greater than or equal, and also not equal, respectively. A value with no preceding operator implies $=$, for equal to.

Variable names preceded by a colon ':' can also be entered in any character or numeric fields on the screen. SQL*Forms displays a window so that an SQL WHERE clause can be entered, referencing the variable names. For example, arbitrarily named variables of :DATE and :CAT entered in the CASE_DATE_RECEIVED and CATEGORY_ID fields respectively of Figure 21.3 can be used in a WHERE clause as follows:

```
WHERE :DATE > 31-DEC-91 AND :CAT IN ('A', 'B', 'E')
```

This displays those rows of the CASE table where the *case_date_received* column is greater than December 31, 1991 AND the *category_id* column contains A, B or E.

Once a record has been displayed as the result of a query, the data in selected fields can be changed by using the Editing keys. Once all relevant fields of the displayed block have been changed, that changed record is written back to the table as an updated row by pressing the [commit/accept] (F10) key. Again, if any key fields have been changed, unique values must exist in the relevant index; otherwise an SQL error will be notified. The operator corrects the error; or rejects the change with [exit/cancel] (Esc).

Alternatively, once a queried record has been displayed it can be deleted by pressing the [delete record] (Shift-F6) Data Base Maintenance Key. The deletion is confirmed by the operator pressing [commit/accept] (F10), or rejected by pressing [exit/cancel] (Esc).

21.5.3 Generic procedures with SQL*Forms

We can see from the above discussion that data entry screens generated by SQL*Forms contain logic to add, read, display, change and delete records as rows in a table. Each default block is generated from a single SQL table for an entity in the operational model. It is clear that SQL*Forms blocks are one example of a software implementation of generic procedures as discussed in Chapter 5. The default block for each SQL table represents one implementation of the Process ENTITY generic procedure discussed in that chapter.

We discussed that generic procedures represent object-oriented logic. Logic inherent in an SQL*Forms block is directly tied to the table used to generate that block. Blocks are logic objects: their processing is activated by messages. The block menu in Figure 21.2 defines the first part of the message: it identifies the relevant block. The block selected identifies the relevant Process ENTITY procedure (see Figures 5.7, 5.8 and 5.17). For example, we selected the Process CASE procedure when we chose the CASE block in Figure 21.2.

The specific keystrokes used are the other part of the message. They define the specific action: [insert record] and [commit/accept] for ADD; [enter query] with [execute query] for READ and DISPLAY; with any field changes and [commit/accept] for CHANGE; or with [delete record] followed by [commit/accept] for DELETE. An operator can reject a change, a deletion, or other actions if any error is found. Add, read, display, change or delete actions can be cancelled by the [exit/cancel] (Shift-F10 or Esc) key instead of the [commit/accept] (F10) key. These keystrokes implement the operator decision in the Process ENTITY procedure, to accept or reject a change or a deletion (see Figures 5.7 and 5.8 in Chapter 5).

The selection of blocks from a block menu (or by SQL*Menu), with keystroke-defined actions, is suitable for initial prototyping of default data entry screens. However this approach is not satisfactory for production data entry use: defining these actions using several keystrokes is cumbersome; the sequence and position of fields in a default block may not be optimum; data is not validated before storing it in a table. Instead SQL*Forms, using triggers and PL/SQL logic, can test the content of fields in a block for validity, or to evaluate process model conditions and so make an acceptance or rejection decision. To achieve this, default screens must first be refined for production data entry use. This is described next.

21.6 REFINING DEFAULT DATA ENTRY SCREENS

We discussed in Chapter 20 the steps involved in using SQL*Forms, logging-on as described in Figure 20.7. Figure 20.9 opened the form name for the default data entry form: COMRES in our example. We will use this form to describe typical design refinement steps for the CASE block. Blocks are refined in SQL*Forms Design mode.

21.6.1 SQL*Forms design mode function keys

We discussed mapping of function keys, used by SQL*Forms in Execution mode, in conjunction with Tables 21.1 and 21.2. Similar function key mapping is also available in DESIGN MODE. This is summarized in the following pages: in Table 21.3 for OS/2 and DOS; and in Table 21.4 for UNIX with DEC VT100 terminals.

Table 21.3   SQL*Forms design mode keys for OS/2 and DOS

Cursor Movement Keys			
Down	Down arrow	Up	Up arrow
Right	Right arrow	Left	Left arrow
Next Field	Tab	Previous Field	Shift-Tab
Next Block	Ctrl-PgDn	Previous Block	Ctrl-PgUp
Next Record	PgDn	Previous Record	PgUp
Next Page	Ctrl-N	Previous Page	Ctrl-P
Beginning of Line	Home	End of Line	End
First Line	Alt-F	Last Line	Alt-L
Scroll Down	Ctrl-D	Scroll Up	Ctrl-U
Scroll Right	Ctrl-Right arrow	Scroll Left	Ctrl-Left arrow

(cont'd)

Table 21.3 (Cont'd)   SQL*Forms design mode keys for OS/2 and DOS

Editing Functions

Down	Down arrow	Up	Up arrow
Right	Right arrow	Left	Left arrow
Beginning of Line	Home	End of Line	End
First Line	Alt-F	Last Line	Alt-L
Delete Backward	Backspace	Delete Character	Del
Delete Line	Ctrl-Home	Delete Record	Shift-F6
Insert/Replace	Ins	Insert Record	F6
Cut	Alt-X	Copy	Alt-C
Paste	Alt-V	Edit	Alt-E

General Design Functions

Screen Painter	Alt-P	Select	F2
Accept	F10	Exit/Cancel	Esc or Shift-F10
Change Diplay Type	Alt-D	Menu	Alt-F1
Copy Object	Alt-O	Help	Shift-F1
Show Keys	F1 or Ctrl-K	Insert Record	F6
Next Record	PgDn	Previous Record	PgUp
List	F9	Navigate	Alt-N
Menu	Alt-F1	Print	Shift-F8
Zoom In	Ctrl-Z	Zoom Out	Alt-Z
Refresh Page	Shift-F9 or Ctrl-L	Search	Alt-S
	or Ctrl-R	Bookmark	Alt-M

Screen Painting Functions

Down	Down arrow	Up	Up arrow
Right	Right arrow	Left	Left arrow
Cut	Alt-X	Paste	Alt-V
Define Field	F4	Resize Field	Shift-F4
Clear Field	Ctrl-End	Edit	Alt-E
Select	F2	Undo	F8
Next Field	Tab	Previous Field	Shift-Tab
Next Block	Ctrl-PgDn	Previous Block	Ctrl-PgUp
Next Record	PgDn	Previous Record	PgUp
Next Page	Ctrl-N	Previous Page	Ctrl-P
Return	Enter	Draw Box/Line	F7

Table 21.4   SQL*Forms design mode keys for UNIX with VT100

Cursor Movement Functions

Down	Down arrow	Up	Up arrow
Right	Right arrow	Left	Left arrow
Next Field	Tab	Previous Field	PF1, Return or PF1, Tab

Table 21.4 (Cont'd)   SQL*Forms design mode keys for UNIX with VT100

Next Block	Keypad--	Previous Block	Keypad-9
Next Record	PF1, Keypad--	Previous Record	PF1, Keypad-9
Next Page	PF1, Keypad-8	Previous Page	PF1, Keypad-7
Beginning of Line	PF1, PF1, Left	End of Line	PF1, PF1, Right
First Line	PF1, PF1, Up	Last Line	PF1, PF1, Down
Scroll Down	PF1, Down	Scroll Up	PF1, Up
Scroll Right	PF1, Right	Scroll Left	PF1, Left

Editing Functions

Down	Down arrow	Up	Up arrow
Right	Right arrow	Left	Left arrow
Beginning of Line	PF1, PF1, Left	End of Line	PF1, PF1, Right
First Line	PF1, PF1, Up	Last Line	PF1, PF1, Down
Delete Backward	Delete	Delete Character	Ctrl-D
Delete Line	PF1, Delete	Delete Record	Keypad-3
Insert/Replace	Ctrl-A	Insert Record	Keypad-2
Cut	PF1, Keypad-3	Copy	PF1, Keypad-.
Paste	PF1, Keypad-2	Edit	PF1, Keypad-1

General Design Functions

Screen Painter	PF1, PF3	Select	Enter or Ctrl-V
Accept	PF3 or Ctrl-O	Exit/Cancel	PF4 or Ctrl-B
Change Display Type	Keypad-1	Menu	Ctrl-G
Copy Object	Keypad-8	Help	PF2 or Ctrl-W
Show Keys	Ctrl-K	Insert Record	Keypad-2
Next Record	PF1, Keypad--	Previous Record	PF1, Keypad-9
List	Keypad-. or Ctrl-F	Navigate	Keypad-7
Menu	Ctrl-G	Print	Ctrl-P
Zoom In	PF1, Keypad-6	Zoom Out	PF1, Keypad-,
Refresh Page	Ctrl-R	Search	PF1, Enter
Bookmark	PF1, PF2	Change Display Type	Keypad-1

Screen Painting Functions

Down	Down arrow	Up	Up arrow
Right	Right arrow	Left	Left arrow
Cut	PF1, Keypad-3	Copy	PF1, Keypad-.
Paste	PF1, Keypad-2	Edit	PF1, Keypad-1
Define Field	PF1, Keypad-4	Resize Field	Keypad-5
Clear Field	Keypad-4	Return	Enter
Select	Enter or Ctrl-V	Undo	Keypad-,
Next Field	Tab	Previous Field	PF1, Tab or PF1, Return
Next Block	Keypad--	Previous Block	Keypad-9
Next Record	PF1, Keypad--	Previous Record	PF1, Keypad-9
Next Page	PF1, Keypad-8	Previous Page	PF1, Keypad-7
Draw Box/Line	Keypad-6		

We are now ready to refine the default blocks generated in Chapter 20. Menu selections in italics in the following pages refer to the SQL*Forms Design mode menu described in conjunction with Figure 20.8. The following steps are first carried out to prepare the CASE block for refinement:

(1)   *Open* the Case_Status form.
(2)   Select *Block Modify* and establish context at the CASE block.
(3)   Select *Image Painter* to invoke the screen painter.

Page 1, showing the CASE block, is then displayed as illustrated in Figure 20.16.

21.6.2   Stage 1 – Modifying the screen layout

The steps involved in modifying the layout of a default block are described next, using the CASE block as an example. The function keys in the following discussion are summarized in Table 21.3, with relevant OS/2 or DOS keystrokes shown in brackets.

Step 1.1 Removing fields and/or labels

A data entry block contains fields which are entered or changed by an operator. Figure 21.4 shows removal of the CASE_ID field. You will remember we defined *case_id#* as an internally generated primary key of CASE, which is never changed. We will later define a trigger to generate this key automatically when adding a new case. CASE_ID can therefore be removed from the data entry form.

The cursor is moved to the start of the screen area to be removed: the label CASE_ID in this example. This is marked by pressing [select] (F2): a **General Design Function** key in Table 21.3. The cursor is then positioned at the end of the field: delineated by pressing [select] (F2) once more. This marks the field and label, ready for removal. Pressing the [cut] (Alt-X) key removes the selected area into a temporary buffer: the **cut/paste buffer**. Information in this buffer can later be discarded for [cut]. Or it can be inserted in another part of the screen for [paste]; discussed shortly. An error can be corrected by pressing [undo] (F8): the area deleted is replaced back in the block, from the cut/paste buffer. (As we will use CASE_ID later in this chapter to illustrate system-generated keys, we will press the [undo] (F8) key and so leave CASE_ID in its original position in the CASE block.)

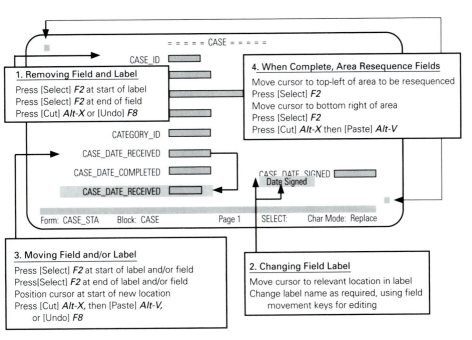

Figure 21.4 Changing or moving fields in a block (OS/2).

Step 1.2 Changing field labels

The default label – taken from the column name in the SQL table – can be changed if necessary. Figure 21.4 shows that this is achieved by typing over the current label, using editing keys for cursor movement and editing. The label CASE_DATE_SIGNED, allocated automatically by default, has been changed to 'Date Signed'.

Step 1.3 Moving fields and/or labels

This is the most common refinement for a default block. It involves moving data fields and labels to a more natural location on the screen, based on the sequence of data entry that is to be used by the operator. Fields are moved, similarly to removing fields, with the cut/paste buffer as described next.

Figure 21.4 illustrates moving the field: CASE_DATE_RECEIVED. The start of the label is defined with [select] (F2): the end of the field is delineated also with [select] (F2). The cursor is then moved to the first character position of the new label location. Both field and label are first removed by [cut] (Alt-X), into the cut/paste buffer. The [paste] (Alt-V) key next pastes it from this buffer to its new location. If that location is not correct, the cursor is first moved to the correct location. The [undo] (F8) key then deletes the incorrectly pasted label and field; the [paste] (F6) key next places it in its correct location.

Step 1.4 Area resequencing fields

Fields in a block are normally executed by SQL*Forms in the sequence: left to right, top to bottom. When all fields in the block have been moved to their correct location, the allocated sequence of fields, based on their original locations, may then need to be changed. For example, when CASE_DATE_RECEIVED is moved to its new location in Step 1.3, its sequence is automatically allocated by SQL*Forms to follow the last field in the block. Fortuitously, this happens to be the correct sequence in this example. But the last field sequence number is also allocated by default even if the field is moved to a lower sequence field position in the block. Once all fields have been moved to their final locations in a block, they must therefore be resequenced. The sequence number of each field may be explicitly defined as discussed in *Step 2.1 – Changing Field Sequence*. Or instead, a group of fields is resequenced to the normal left to right, top to bottom sequence as discussed next. This is called **area resequencing**.

Figure 21.4 shows that a group of fields to be resequenced in an area is first defined by moving the cursor to one corner of the area: such as the top left corner; the [select] (F2) key is pressed. The cursor is then moved to the diagonal corner: the bottom right; and [select] (F2) is pressed again. Moving the cursor back to the top left, the selected area is first [cut] (Alt-X), and then the [paste] (Alt-V) key is immediately pressed. This resequences all of the fields in the selected area to the desired sequence. As before, corrections can be made with the [undo] (F8) key.

Step 1.5 Resizing fields

Normally, fields are allocated an area on screen sufficient to contain all of the data in the relevant column. However some columns vary in width: such as CHAR columns with variable-length text. The default size of a field is taken as the length of its column. This size is changed (resized) by placing the cursor in the field and pressing [select] (F2), as shown in Figure 21.5. The cursor is placed at the required last field position to be displayed: the [resize field] (Shift-F4) key is then pressed. The size is increased or reduced accordingly. If the field is resized smaller than the number of characters to be contained in it, hidden characters in the field can be scrolled left or right in Execution Mode by pressing the [scroll left] or [scroll right] keys respectively.

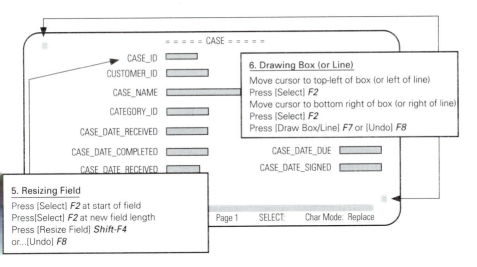

Figure 21.5   Resizing fields and drawing boxes or lines (OS/2).

Step 1.6 Drawing boxes or lines

When fields have been moved to their correct location, the appearance of the block can be improved by drawing boxes or lines. For example a block may be enclosed in a box (see the Case History Status Form in Figure 20.4). Related fields grouped in a specific area of the screen can also be enclosed in a box. In Figure 18.4 all date fields were grouped together into a box. Fields can be delineated from other parts of the screen by vertical or horizontal lines. In Figure 18.4 a vertical line separated the shaded section of interim dates from the other dates for a case.

A box is drawn similarly to area resequencing fields: by moving the cursor first to one corner of the desired box, such as the top left corner; press [select] (F2). The cursor is next moved to the diagonally opposite corner, the bottom right; [select] (F2) is pressed again. The box is drawn by pressing [draw box/line] (F7). A line is drawn by selecting each end before pressing [draw box/line] (F7). Both are corrected with [undo] (F8). The steps described above for refining screens are summarized in Box 21.1.

Fields are removed, labels are changed, fields are resized or moved until the data entry screen is satisfactory in appearance and utility for data entry purposes. All field labels must clearly indicate the purpose of their fields: additional descriptive text is included in the screen if necessary. This text is entered as for changing field labels in Figure 21.4. The block name, taken by default from its SQL table name and displayed at the top of the block, can also be changed if required.

Box 21.1
Refining the layout of blocks

---

1. *Changing a field label name:*

1. Move the cursor to the relevant location in the label and change the label as required.

2. *Removing a field and label:*

1. [Select] the start of the label.
2. [Select] the end of the field.
3. Press [Cut] to remove the label and field, or [Undo] to correct.

3. *Moving a field and label:*

1. [Select] the start of the label.
2. [Select] the end of the field.
3. Position the cursor at the new location of the first character of the label.
4. Press [Cut] to remove the label and field.
5. Press [Paste] to paste the label and field in the new location, or . . .
6. Press [Undo] to correct, reposition the cursor and repeat Step 5.

4. *Area resequencing fields:*

1. [Select] the top left corner of the area to be resequenced.
2. [Select] the bottom right corner of the area to be resequenced.
3. Press [Cut] to remove all labels and fields in the area.
4. Move the cursor back to the top left corner, then press [Paste] to paste and resequence all labels and fields, or . . .
5. Press [Undo] to correct, reposition the cursor and repeat Step 4.

Box 21.1 (cont.)
Refining the layout of blocks

5. *Resizing fields:*

1. [Select] the start of the field to be resized.
2. [Select] the position to be the new (resized) end of the field.
3. Press [Resize Field] to resize the field to the new field length, or . . .
4. Press [Undo] to correct, and repeat Steps 1–3.

6. *Drawing boxes and lines:*

1. [Select] the top left corner of the box, or the left end of the line, to be drawn.
2. [Select] the bottom right corner of the box, or the right end of the line, to be drawn.
3. Press [Draw Box/Line] to draw the box or line, or . . .
4. Press [Undo] to correct, and repeat Steps 1–3.

21.6.3 Stage 2 – Refining field attributes

Once the design and appearance of the screen is suitable, the definition and attributes of relevant fields can then be refined as discussed in the following pages in conjunction with Figures 21.7–21.8. Each field is selected for field definition as follows:

(1)   [Tab] to the relevant field and select it.
(2)   Press [Define Field] (F4), to display the Field Definition screen.

For example, Figure 21.6 selects the CASE_FOREIGN_REF_ID field for definition, and displays its **Field Definition** screen in Figure 21.7. This field refers to the column *case_foreign_ref_id* in its base table CASE.

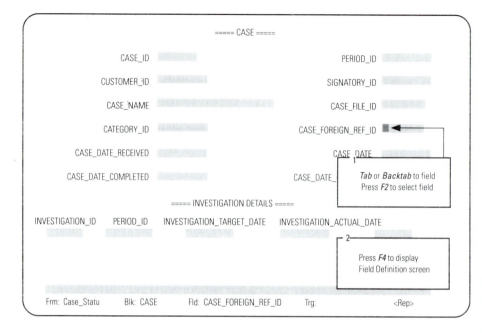

Figure 21.6 Selecting a field for definition (OS/2).

Data Type shows that the field is defined as CHAR in its base table. Its **Field Length** and the **Query Length** are both 10 characters. The **Display Length** is also 10 characters; no special formatting is indicated in the **Format Mask** that may require a longer display length. The X and Y coordinates of the field on the screen are also shown (X: 60, Y: 9) on Page: 1. The remaining field definitions relate to validation and are discussed in *21.6.4 Stage 3 – Defining Field Validation*.

The order of fields must be suitable, according to the sequence used for data entry. We earlier discussed area resequencing of a group of fields. The explicit resequencing of an individual field is described next.

Step 2.1 Changing field sequence

Sequence Number in the top left part of the Field Definition screen is the sequence of execution of a field in the block. Figure 21.7 shows that CASE_FOREIGN_REF_ID is **Sequence Number: 8**; it is the eighth field in the block. This sequence number is used by [next field] (Tab) or [previous field] (Shift-Tab) in Execution Mode. After moving fields as described in Step 1.3 above, the sequence of each field in the block is changed to another sequence number to indicate a different execution sequence for that field in the block, by typing over it.

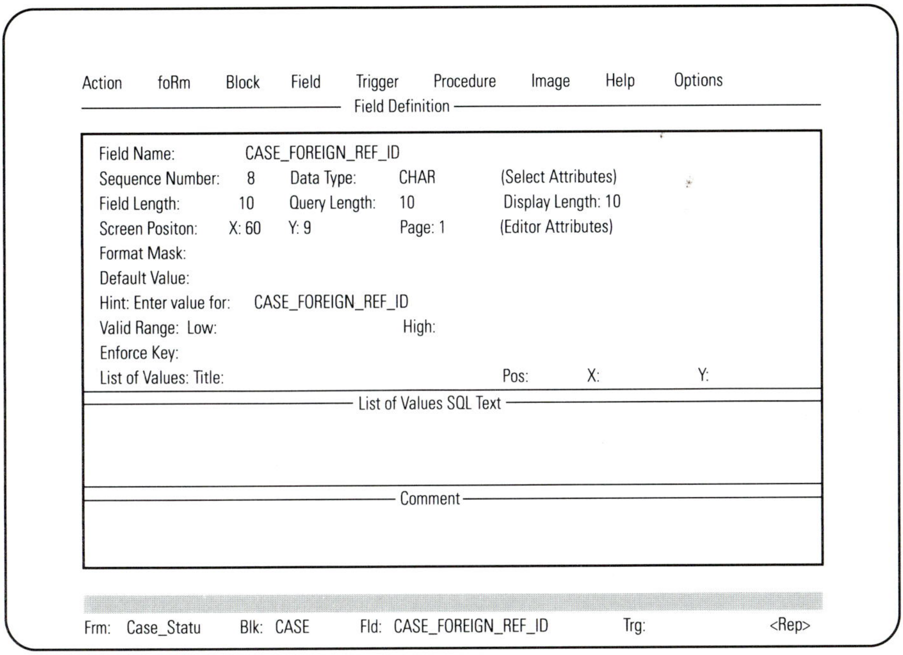

Figure 21.7 The Field Definition screen.

The Field Definition screen also shows a **Select Attributes** button in Figure 21.7. This displays other attributes for the current field: data base attributes; required; displayed; fixed length; automatic skip; automatic hint. This button displays a pop-up window as shown in Figure 21.8, to enable field attributes to be defined for the current field as discussed in the following sections.

Figure 21.8 shows a number of check boxes, defining attributes of the current field. This shows that CASE_FOREIGN_REF_ID is a **Base Table** field that is **Displayed** on the screen (that is, it is not hidden). Data can be entered, updated and queried in the field (**Input Allowed, Update Allowed** and **Query Allowed**). Data entered or updated in the field is to be displayed on the screen (**Echo Input**).

Step 2.2 Mandatory fields

If the current field is defined in its base table as NOT NULL, the check box **Required** is turned on ('X'). Fields which *must* be entered for a row are set to mandatory by this check box; optional fields have Required turned off. As with other check boxes, this field attribute is turned on by clicking

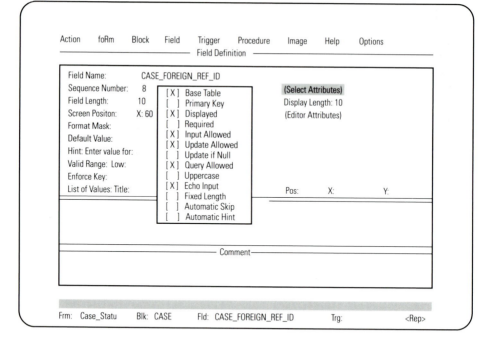

Figure 21.8 The Field Attributes screen.

on it with a mouse, or by typing any non-blank character in the square brackets. It is turned off by clicking again with a mouse, or by typing a space.

Step 2.3 Displayed, input, query, update attributes

Fields, whose values are to be shown, are specified as **Displayed**; those which accept input are specified as **Input Allowed**. Some data is displayed but never changed: Input Allowed is turned off for these fields. Echo Input displays information on the screen that is entered into the field: this input may be entered by the operator via the keyboard; or may be entered automatically by a trigger. For example, fields such as passwords allow input but the entered value is never shown for security reasons: Displayed and Echo Input are therefore both turned off. Similarly **Query Allowed** and **Update Allowed** are set on or off as required. These check boxes are all normally turned on initially for a Base Table field as shown in Figure 21.8.

Step 2.4 Other field attributes

Other attributes which can be selected are: **Update if Null**; **Fixed Length**; **Uppercase**; **Automatic Skip**; and **Automatic Hint**. For example, a help message is automatically displayed on the message line of the screen to assist the operator whenever the cursor is in an *Automatic Hint* field in Execution mode. A standard help message is displayed for the field, such as *'Enter value for: CASE_FOREIGN_REF_ID'* as shown in Figure 21.7. Or instead, a unique hint message is defined in conjunction with Step 3.6 below.

21.6.4   Stage 3 – Defining field validation

The Field Definition screen in Figure 21.7 is also used to specify required validation of relevant fields in the block. Typical validation or additional field processing steps are:

- Step 3.1: Default value fields
- Step 3.2: Formatting fields
- Step 3.3: Range checking fields
- Step 3.4: Mandatory fields
- Step 3.5: Table lookup fields
- Step 3.6: Automatic hint fields
- Step 3.7: Pop-up pages

Step 3.1 Default value fields

An initial value can be automatically displayed as a default value in a field: and accepted or changed by the operator, as required. This is specified in **Default Value** of the Field Definition screen (see Figure 21.7). This is useful when the same value is entered into a field for many rows in a table: such as a default zip code, or post code. We will see next that it can also be used to specify today's date as a default date, for example, or can be used to specify system generated keys.

Default dates   If today's date is normally entered into the CASE_DATE_RECEIVED field, the current date can be defined as its default value by using the SQL*Forms $$DATE$$ function. The *Format Mask* for the field can be defined (see Step 3.2 – Formatting Fields). A hint message to guide the operator can be included in the Field Definition screen (see Figure 21.9), such as:

To Change DATE RECEIVED, type a new date.

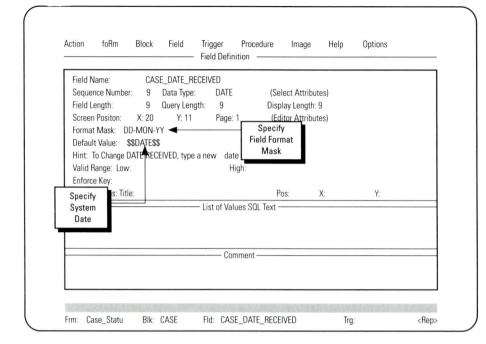

Figure 21.9 Default date field with formatting.

System generated keys The *Default Value* field of the Field Definition screen also enables system generated keys to be defined. In Chapter 18 we discussed that *case_id* in CASE should be system generated: each new case is automatically given the next case identification number. The following example assumes an ORACLE Version 6.0 sequence table for *case_id* has already been defined (using SQL*Plus, for example) as follows:

```
SQL > CREATE SEQUENCE CASE_ID;
```

A sequence table is given the name of the column to which it refers. As defined above, this statement will generate a sequence number for *case_id*: beginning with one (1), and incrementing by one (1) for each reference. The *Default Value* field of the CASE_ID Field Definition screen (see Figure 21.10) references this sequence table by:

```
:SEQUENCE.CASE_ID.NEXTVAL
```

NEXTVAL allocates the next sequence value, incrementing the sequence number in SEQUENCE.CASE_ID by one in this instance. Figure 21.10

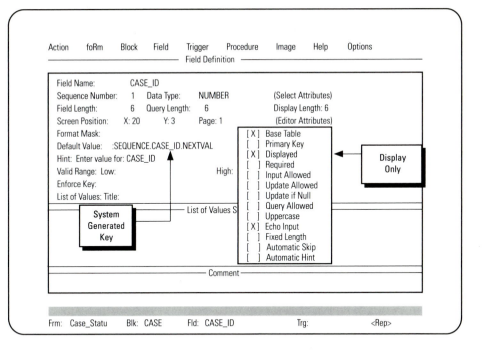

Figure 21.10   Using Default Value for System Generated Keys.

also shows the Field Attributes of CASE_ID: *Base Table; Displayed; Echo Input* – indicating that *case_id* is a column in base table CASE; and *Displayed* and *Echo Input* are both set ON, so displaying the system generated value automatically. Once generated, this value cannot be changed: *Input Allowed, Update Allowed* and *Query Allowed* are all turned OFF.

Step 3.2 Formatting fields

Format Mask in the Field Definition screen is used to define explicit formatting for a field based on SQL*Plus format conventions. To display dates as 'December 31st, 1991', for example, requires the format mask: Month" "DDth", "YYYY (with double quotes defining a space between month and day, and a comma and space before year); while the mask: DD-MMM-YY displays the date as "31-DEC-91" (see Figure 21.9). The mask for a United States Social Security Number is: 999"-"99"-"999. A telephone number with a bracketed area code is: "("999") "999"-"9999. A currency field, with a floating dollar sign, embedded commas and two decimal places is: $$,$$$,$$9.99.

Step 3.3 Range checking fields

The value of some fields must fall within a defined range. This is specified by lowest and highest values for range checking in the Field Definition screen (see *Valid Range: Low:* and *High:* in Figure 21.11).

If an entered value falls outside the defined range, an error message indicating the valid range of values for the relevant field is displayed for the operator.

Step 3.4 Mandatory fields

We saw in this chapter that primary and foreign keys in an entity are defined as NOT NULL columns in the SQL CREATE TABLE statement. The existence of these keys is mandatory in an SQL table: a value must be entered for every key. SQL*Forms therefore defines NOT NULL columns in a table as **Required** fields in the default block generated from that base table (see Figure 21.12): a value *must* be entered into these fields on initial data entry. If the operator tries to move the cursor out of the field (by pressing [next field] or [previous field]) an error message indicates that a value must be entered.

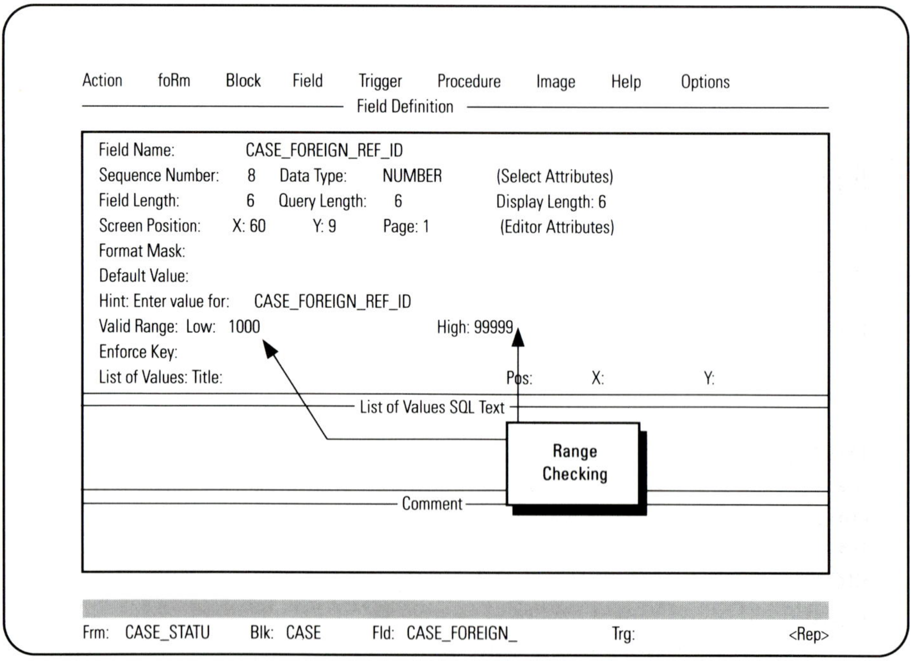

Figure 21.11 **Range Checking Fields.**

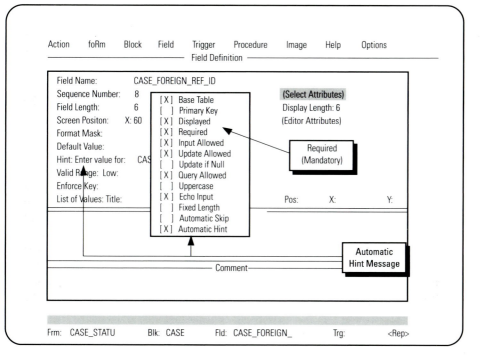

Figure 21.12 Mandatory Fields.

Step 3.5 Table lookup fields

Other fields may have to be validated against a list of values in another table: these are called **table look-up fields**. The relevant look-up table and column names are specified in *List of Values* in the Field Definition screen (see Figure 21.9).

For example, Figure 21.13 shows a refinement of the CASE data entry screen: the field SIGNATORY_NAME has been added. We saw in Chapter 18 that *signatory_id* is an alias for *involved_party_id*. The INVOLVED_PARTY table can thus be used as a look-up table to obtain the name of the signatory for a case. When the SIGNATORY_ID is entered, this value is used to access the relevant row in the INVOLVED_ PARTY table: the name of that involved party can then be displayed in the SIGNATORY_NAME field. SIGNATORY_ID is thus a look-up field in Figure 21.13.

Figure 21.14 shows how this table look-up field is specified, using *List of Values* in the Field Definition screen. The **List of Values Title** is SIGNATORIES: a pop-up list of ID values is displayed together with the

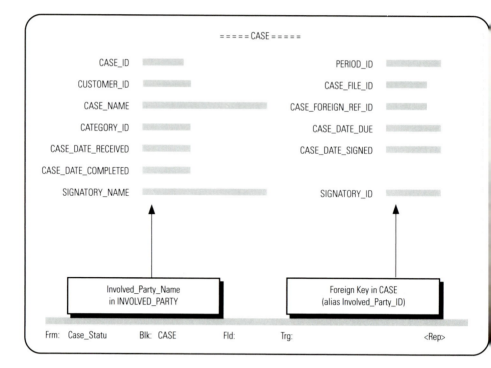

Figure 21.13   Table Lookup Field in CASE.

name of each signatory, ordered by name. This is defined by the following
List of Values SQL Text (see Figure 21.14):

```
SELECT      INVOLVED_PARTY_ID, INVOLVED_PARTY_NAME
INTO        :CASE.SIGNATORY_ID, :CASE.SIGNATORY_NAME
FROM        INVOLVED_PARTY
ORDER BY    INVOLVED_PARTY_NAME
```

The Hint field in Figure 21.14 also shows the message:

```
Press [LIST] to see valid SIGNATORIES.
```

If the Field Attributes window for the SIGNATORY_ID has *Automatic
Hint* turned ON (similarly shown in Figure 21.12), this message is automatically displayed for the operator. As *List of Values SQL Text* was defined
for SIGNATORY_ID, whenever the cursor moves into this field the
< List > indicator is displayed in the bottom right corner of the screen. The
message informs the operator to press the [List] key to display the list of valid
signatories. This is illustrated in Figure 21.15.

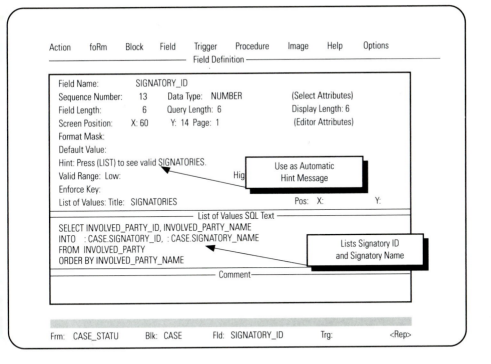

Figure 21.14 Defining Table Lookup Fields.

The operator uses the [Up] or [Down] keys, and [PgUp] or [PgDn] keys, to move the cursor through the displayed list. When the relevant signatory name is highlighted in Figure 21.15, it is accepted (by pressing [commit/accept]): the selected *signatory_id* and *signatory_name* are then automatically entered by SQL*Forms into their respective fields in the CASE block – as indicated by the INTO statement above. Alternatively, instead of pressing the [List] key, a value different from those displayed in the *List of Values* window can be entered, if valid.

If the operator is to be restricted only to selecting from the list of values, the **Display List of Values** execution option can instead be turned ON. This automatically displays the relevant *List of Values* when the cursor moves into a look-up field, just as if the operator had pressed the [List] key. On selecting from the list, the *signatory_id* value automatically entered into the look_up field will initiate an ON-CHANGE trigger (see shortly). This trigger then invokes the PL/SQL NEXT-FIELD packaged procedure to move the cursor automatically to the next field. The result: no value can be entered other than one selected by the operator from the displayed list of values.

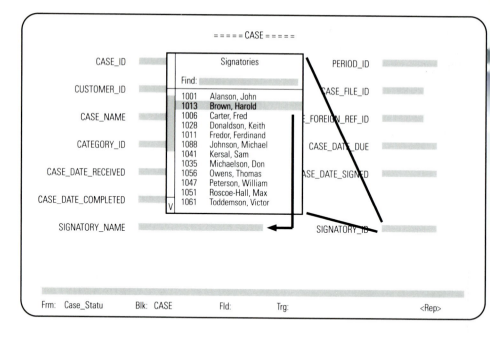

Figure 21.15 Result of table lookup for signatory name.

Step 3.6 Automatic hint fields

As we saw in Step 3.5, if the *Automatic Hint* attribute is ON in the *Field Attributes* screen (see Figure 21.12) a message entered in the *Hint* field of the *Field Definition* screen is displayed for the operator automatically, whenever the cursor is positioned in the relevant field.

Step 3.7 Pop-up pages

The ability to display a *List of Values*, described in Step 3.5, is a common application design requirement. The operator selects the relevant value from those available; a more effective person – machine interface is the result. Displaying other blocks in a **pop-up page** is another common design approach, leaving existing information still visible on the screen. For example, we may need to see information about an involved party (such as a signatory) to complete details about a case. The INVOLVED_PARTY block can be defined as a pop-up page to be displayed over part of the CASE block, for example. It disappears when finished, leaving the CASE details undisturbed underneath.

Figure 21.16 illustrates the terminology used in defining pop-up pages. A page may be larger than the physical dimensions of the screen. Only part of the page is to be viewed on the screen; this view may also be smaller than the screen. The page size and view size (see Figure 21.16) are defined by:

- Page Size (x) = total number of displayed positions along the page X-axis.
- Page Size (y) = total number of displayed positions along the page Y-axis.
- View Size (x) = total number of displayed positions along the view X-axis.
- View Size (y) = total number of displayed positions along the view Y-axis.

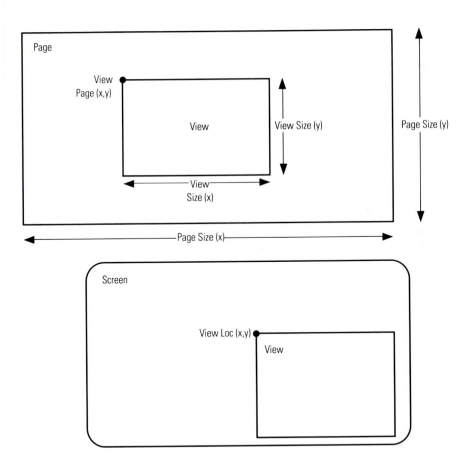

Figure 21.16   Terminology for pop-up pages.

The location of the view on the page, and of the view on the screen, is also defined. This is illustrated in Figure 21.16 and specified as:

View Page (x,y) = X- and Y- coordinate of top left corner of view on page.

View Loc (x,y) = X- and Y- coordinate of top left corner of view on screen.

The view forms a window on the screen. The full page is defined by **Page Size (x)** and **Page Size (y)**. The size of the view is defined by **View Size (x)** and **View Size (y)**. The rest of the information in the page is viewed by scrolling left or right, and up or down. The top left corner of the view on the page – defined by **View Page (x,y)** – is located on the screen according to **View Loc (x,y)**. A pop-up page can contain one block (as in our example with INVOLVED_PARTY), or can contain many blocks. These may be Master-Detail Relationships, or any single-record or multi-record blocks. Previously generated pages can be changed into pop-up pages at any time as described next.

The complete pop-up page definition is shown in Figure 21.17. A previously defined page is changed to a pop-up page by turning ON the **Pop Up** indicator. The page and view dimensions are then defined as shown on the left of Figure 21.16. A **Border** can be specified to surround the view; **Vertical Scroll Bars** (see Figure 20.11) and also **Horizontal Scroll Bars** can be defined to scroll up or down, left or right respectively. Turning ON **Remove on Exit** causes the pop-up page to disappear when the cursor exits the page, so displaying the information underneath; otherwise the pop-up

Figure 21.17   Definition of a pop-up page.

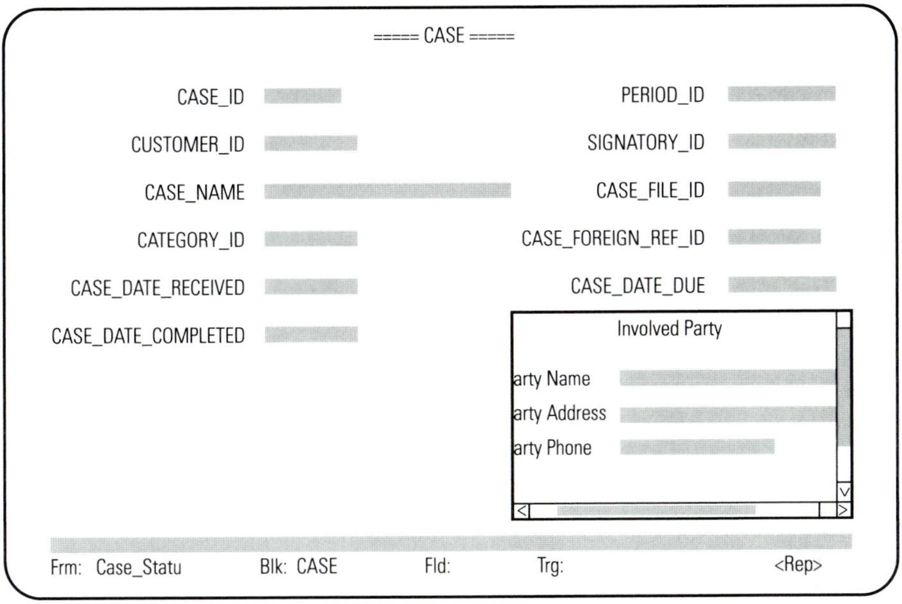

Figure 21.18   Result of pop-up page defined for involved party.

page is left on the screen. The **Title** (Involved Parties in Figure 21.17) is displayed at the top of the pop-up page. The result of this definition is illustrated in Figure 21.18.

We are now ready to define conditional logic to be executed in certain situations. In Chapters 5 and 6 we discussed the concepts of process modeling; we saw how logic can be derived from a data model. In Chapter 19 we applied these principles to the Case Investigations System. Procedures are executed based on conditions that are defined in the process model. The form and block concept that is utilized by SQL*Forms is one implementation of procedures generated from tables, that in turn are generated from a data model. Triggers and PL/SQL define the conditional logic required for execution of these forms. This leads us to Stage 4 of system implementation.

21.6.5   Stage 4 – Specifying conditional logic

Conditional logic in SQL*Forms is specified by triggers which are executed if defined conditions exist. Triggers may include SQL and/or PL/SQL commands. The following discussion provides an overview of the conditional logic defined through SQL*Forms. Refer to the SQL*Forms documentation [8, 9, 10] for further detail.

```
Action   foRm   Block   Field   Trigger   Procedure   Image   Help   Options
                              Trigger Definition

Trigger:   POST CHANGE                          For Key Triggers Only
Block:     INVOLVED_PARTY                 [  ] Show Keys
Field:     involved_party_id              Descrip:
Trigger Style: V3

                              Trigger Text
BEGIN
    SELECT involved_party_name
    INTO  : INVOLVED_PARTY.involved_party_name
    FROM  INVOLVED_PARTY
    WHERE INVOLVED_PARTY.involved_party_id = : INVOLVED_PARTY.involved_party_id;
EXCEPTION
WHEN NO_DATA_FOUND THEN
    MESSAGE ('INVALID INVOLVED PARTY.  USE [LIST].');
    RAISE FORM_TRIGGER_FAILURE;
WHEN TOO_MANY_ROWS THEN
    MESSAGE ('INVALID INVOLVED PARTY.  USE [LIST].');
    RAISE FORM_TRIGGER_FAILURE;
END;
                              Comment


Enter the trigger text.
Frm: Case_Statu     Blk: INVOLVED_P     Fld: involved_p     Trg: POST CHANG     <Rep>
```

Figure 21.19 Defining a trigger.

Triggers can be defined at the form-, block- or field-level (see Figure 20.17). For example, Figure 21.19 shows a field-level trigger in Form: Case_Status; defined in Block: INVOLVED_PARTY; and Field: *involved_party_id* (see the bottom status line of the figure). This is a POST CHANGE trigger: it is executed when data is entered, or changed, in the INVOLVED_PARTY_ID field of the INVOLVED_PARTY block, and is invoked when the cursor is about to leave the changed field; it is thus referred to as a POST CHANGE trigger.

This trigger checks that an INVOLVED_PARTY_ID field is valid, using a SELECT of the INVOLVED_PARTY table; the WHERE clause tests the :INVOLVED_PARTY_ID field in the block INVOLVED_PARTY for equality with INVOLVED_PARTY_ID as a column in the table INVOLVED_PARTY. The trigger succeeds if both are equal; the changed value is a valid involved party in the table. An error results in an exception.

An EXCEPTION occurs in two instances. Inequality results in NO_DATA_FOUND; the field value does not exist in the table. The message advises the operator: 'INVALID INVOLVED PARTY. USE [LIST].' The FORM_TRIGGER_FAILURE is raised: the cursor remains in the field so that the operator can select from a valid List of Values with the [List] key (defined as described in Figure 21.14).

The other exception: TOO_MANY_ROWS applies if the field value is not unique in the table; more than one row has the same value as the field. Again the operator is advised to use the [List] key. (This would never occur in this example: *involved_party_id* is the primary key of the INVOLVED PARTY entity; it is defined in a unique index so that only one value can exist.)

Figure 21.19 illustrates a PL/SQL procedure with BEGIN–END, and EXCEPTION, logic blocks. We can see that this example is one implementation of a generic VERIFY procedure, as discussed in Figures 5.11 and 5.12. Other software tools may implement generic procedures in a different way.

A form-level trigger is documented in Figure 21.20. This example is supplied as part of the SQL*Forms Order Entry tutorial application, documented by selecting *Action*, *Print doc*, *Procedure*: it defines a form-level trigger called CALCULATE_ITEM_TOTAL in the tutorial sample solution form called CHAPTER6.

This is another example of a simple PL/SQL procedure with a BEGIN–END logic block. It specifies that ITEMTOT (a field in the current block, as indicated by the colon preceding the name) is set to (indicated by ':=') the product ('*') of fields QTY and ACTUALPRICE. This procedure calculates the total price of an item by multiplying the quantity of an item by its unit price (actual price). This procedure is executed whenever it is invoked by name, shown by the ON-VALIDATE-FIELD trigger in Figure 21.21.

This is a Version 3.0 (V3) trigger (as distinct from V2 triggers, used in earlier versions of SQL*Forms). This ON-VALIDATE-FIELD trigger is defined on a QTY field of the SQL*Forms tutorial. It is invoked whenever

```
Application:     CHAPTER 6

Owner:

This form is used to enter, update, and query orders from customers.

Procedure Name:  CALCULATE_ITEM_TOTAL

    PROCEDURE CALCULATE_ITEM_TOTAL IS

       BEGIN
           :ITEMTOT :=:QTY* :ACTUALPRICE;
       END;
```

Figure 21.20   A form-level trigger.

```
Trigger Name: ON-VALIDATE-FIELD          Style: V3   Hide: Yes   Description:

Comment:

    Text: CALCULATE_ITEM_TOTAL;
```

Figure 21.21   Invoking a form-level trigger.

the item quantity has been validated and found to be correct; in turn it invokes CALCULATE_ITEM_TOTAL in Figure 21.20, multiplying the quantity by the unit price to determine the item total. A more detailed ON-VALIDATE-FIELD trigger (see Figure 21.22) is defined on the ACTUALPRICE field of the SQL*Forms tutorial, as discussed next.

The unit price of an item can be negotiated by the salesman: the agreed price becomes the ACTUALPRICE used in the form-level procedure in Figure 21.20. However this agreed price cannot be less than the minimum price approved for the item in the PRICE table. The ACTUALPRICE of each item must be validated against the PRICE table when it is first entered, and again whenever it is changed.

Figure 21.22 uses a PL/SQL DECLARE block to define a variable MINIMUM of data type NUMBER. The minimum price (MINPRICE) in the PRICE table is selected INTO the variable MINIMUM for the item WHERE the field :PRODID contains a valid item number in the table (PRICE.PRODID). There can be several rows in this table of earlier prices for the item: the WHERE clause also uses today's date (SYSDATE) to select the most recent price change.

The PL/SQL IF . . . THEN . . . ELSE construct checks IF the :ACTUALPRICE field is less than the price in MINIMUM. If it is, THEN the minimum price is converted to text by TO_CHAR (MINIMUM), concatenated (indicated by '‖') to the end of the message 'ACTUAL PRICE MUST BE GREATER THAN (MINIMUM).' and displayed for the operator. FORM_TRIGGER_FAILURE is raised: the cursor remains in the field so that the operator can enter a valid price. If the :ACTUALPRICE field is valid (that is, not less than MINIMUM) the ELSE statement invokes the form-level trigger in Figure 21.20 to calculate the item total.

An EXCEPTION occurs on NO_DATA_FOUND. The item is earlier validated in the SQL*Forms tutorial against the ITEM table and found to exist; this exception occurs if management have not yet set a minimum price – the item does not exist in the PRICE table. In this case the :ACTUALPRICE field value is accepted as valid: the form-level trigger is immediately invoked to calculate the item total.

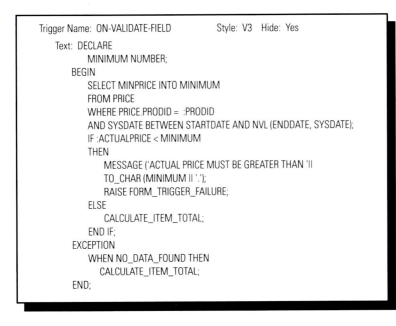

```
Trigger Name: ON-VALIDATE-FIELD          Style: V3   Hide: Yes
    Text: DECLARE
            MINIMUM NUMBER;
        BEGIN
            SELECT MINPRICE INTO MINIMUM
            FROM PRICE
            WHERE PRICE.PRODID = :PRODID
            AND SYSDATE BETWEEN STARTDATE AND NVL (ENDDATE, SYSDATE);
            IF :ACTUALPRICE < MINIMUM
            THEN
                MESSAGE ('ACTUAL PRICE MUST BE GREATER THAN 'II
                TO_CHAR (MINIMUM II '.');
                RAISE FORM_TRIGGER_FAILURE;
            ELSE
                CALCULATE_ITEM_TOTAL;
            END IF;
        EXCEPTION
            WHEN NO_DATA_FOUND THEN
                CALCULATE_ITEM_TOTAL;
        END;
```

Figure 21.22 A more detailed trigger.

We will finish this chapter by discussing some typical triggers which are defined for data entry screens. We will then test the modified data entry block.

21.7 | TYPICAL TRIGGERS FOR DATA ENTRY

A number of triggers are used for data entry screens. We have seen some examples, such as triggers for table look-up when the value in a field changes, or for validation purposes. Potential data base errors should also be tested first under control of a trigger – rather than be detected later as an SQL error only when committing insertions, updates or deletions to the data base. These triggers are used for: validation of unique keys in the data base; checking for valid foreign keys; or referential integrity concerns, such as checking other record dependencies before deleting records.

21.7.1 Validation of unique keys

This checks that an entered key does not already exist in the data base. For example, *case_file_id* is entered mandatorily as we saw above, and it must be unique. Although [*case_file_id*] is a secondary key, it can be defined with a unique SQL index. When a duplicate case file identifier is to be added to the data base, it is thus detected as an SQL error. However the error should ideally be detected during data entry, as soon as the [next field] key is pressed to move the cursor from the *case_file_id* field. Further, if the secondary key is changed, a trigger should check that the new *case_file_id* is still valid: it can confirm this by displaying the relevant CASE_NAME as shown in a form-level trigger called CHECK_CASE_FILE_ID, defined as follows:

```
Procedure Name:   CHECK_CASE_FILE_ID

PROCEDURE         CHECK_CASE_FILE_ID IS

    BEGIN

            SELECT   CASE_NAME

            INTO     :CASE_NAME

            FROM     CASE

            WHERE    CASE.CASE_FILE_ID = :CASE.CASE_FILE_ID;

    EXCEPTION

            WHEN     NO_DATA_FOUND THEN
                     MESSAGE ('INVALID CASE FILE ID. USE [LIST].');
                     RAISE FORM_TRIGGER_FAILURE;

            WHEN     DUP_VAL_ON_INDEX THEN
                     MESSAGE ('TWO OR MORE CASE FILE ID ALREADY EXIST.');
                     RAISE FORM_TRIGGER_FAILURE;

            WHEN     TOO_MANY_ROWS THEN
                     MESSAGE ('CASE FILE ID IS NOT UNIQUE. USE [LIST].');
                     RAISE FORM_TRIGGER_FAILURE;

    END;
```

This trigger checks the value in the *case_file_id* field of the CASE block (shown by the colon after the equal sign in the WHERE clause) for an equal value in that column of the CASE table. It then moves the CASE_NAME of the validated *case_file_id* into the :CASE_NAME field (see Figure 21.3). In this figure it would be appropriate to reverse the CASE_FILE_ID and CASE_NAME fields, and also change the field attributes of CASE_NAME: with *Displayed* and *Echo Input* set ON; and with *Input Allowed*, *Update Allowed* and *Query Allowed* set OFF.

The NO_DATA_FOUND exception indicates that the specified *case_file_id* does not exist: this is an error. The DUP_VAL_ON_INDEX exception may occur if two or more rows already exist with the same index value: *this should never arise* if the CASE_FILE_ID index was defined as unique; if it is detected the CASE table and/or index have been corrupted. Similarly, the TOO_MANY_ROWS exception indicates that more than one row in CASE exists with the same *case_file_id*: this error is detected if an index is not defined at all; it also indicates that the CASE table has been corrupted – more than one *case_file_id* of the same value exists in the data base.

This form-level trigger is called from a POST-CHANGE field-level trigger, both defined for *case_file_id* (discussed next), and also from a PRE-UPDATE block-level trigger.

FIELD-LEVEL TRIGGER   (POST-CHANGE)

    CHECK_CASE_FILE_ID;

A POST-CHANGE field-level trigger is executed immediately after a value is entered into the field that changes the file identifier for an existing case. The trigger verifies that the *case_file_id*, when changed, will still be unique. But until the changed CASE is committed to the data base, another operator (in a multi-user environment) may also store the same file identifier in the data base. An earlier validated *case_file_id* would no longer be unique, so corrupting the data base. A PRE-UPDATE block level trigger is essential to prevent this happening in a multi-user environment, as follows.

BLOCK-LEVEL TRIGGER   (PRE-UPDATE)

    CHECK_CASE_FILE_ID;

This block-level trigger checks that the validated *case_file_id* is still unique, before any changes in the details of a case are updated.

These triggers apply for changes made to an existing row in a table. They implement the VERIFY generic procedure logic for Read, Change and Delete actions as discussed in Chapter 5 (see Figures 5.11 and 5.12). The NO_DATA_FOUND exception and the DUP_VAL_ON_INDEX exception both indicate errors for these actions. But what about the Insert action in this procedure? For a new case to be added, the *case_file_id* should not already exist. Another form-level trigger is needed, as shown next.

```
Procedure Name:   NEW_CASE_FILE_ID

PROCEDURE         NEW_CASE_FILE_ID IS

   BEGIN

            SELECT   CASE_FILE_ID

            FROM     CASE

            WHERE    CASE.CASE_FILE_ID = :CASE.CASE_FILE_ID;
```

```
IF        SQL%FOUND THEN
          MESSAGE ('CASE FILE ID ALREADY EXISTS.');
          RAISE FORM_TRIGGER_FAILURE;

END IF;

EXCEPTION

WHEN     DUP_VAL_ON_INDEX THEN
         MESSAGE ('TWO OR MORE CASE FILE ID ALREADY EXIST.');
         RAISE FORM_TRIGGER_FAILURE;

END;
```

The existence of a case file identifier is tested prior to inserting a new CASE. PL/SQL provides the SQL%FOUND implicit cursor, which can be used for this purpose: if the (single-row) SELECT clause in the above form-level procedure returns a row, an error would occur if the new CASE was inserted: the message 'CASE FILE ID ALREADY EXISTS' notifies the operator. The FORM_TRIGGER_FAILURE exception is raised to prevent insertion of the new row.

Again, the DUP_VAL_ON_INDEX exception, if detected, indicates that not just one but several cases exist already in the CASE table with the same case file identifier: the index is not unique; the CASE table has been corrupted – the extent of this corruption is detailed by the 'TWO OR MORE CASE FILE ID ALREADY EXIST' message to the operator.

This form-level procedure is invoked from a field-level PRE-INSERT trigger defined for *case_file_id*, executed immediately after a value is entered into the CASE_FILE_ID field for a new case to be added. The trigger verifies that the new *case_file_id* does not exist. But until this new CASE is committed, as discussed earlier, another operator in a multi-user environment may attempt to store the same file identifier in the data base. The validated *case_file_id* would then no longer be unique, so corrupting the data base. A PRE-INSERT trigger at the block-level is also needed to prevent this happening in a multi-user environment.

```
FIELD-LEVEL TRIGGER    (PRE-INSERT)

  NEW_CASE_FILE_ID;

BLOCK-LEVEL TRIGGER    (PRE-INSERT)

  NEW_CASE_FILE_ID;
```

You have no doubt asked yourself why we should validate at the field-level, and again at the block-level. We could avoid potential concurrent corruption of the data base in a multi-user environment by locking the relevant CASE row until the first operator had completed all insert, update or delete activity to the CASE table and other related tables. Other operators would thus be unable to gain access to that table (or at least to the relevant row in the table); they would have to wait until all related processing for the locked row had been finished. So why should we validate twice?

Our reason: *data integrity in a high performance environment.* With low transaction volumes and short processing times, the wait delay may not present any problem for other operators. But the approach described above does not require that the CASE row be locked until all related insert, update or delete processing is completed. Using block-level triggers for revalidation offers better performance in a high transaction volume environment involving longer processing times.

21.7.2 Checking for valid foreign keys

A foreign key entered into a form must already exist also as a primary key in the data base. Similar form-level triggers check for the existence of a foreign key, and are also invoked at both the block level and the field level. In Chapter 15 we discussed that *signatory_id#* is an alias foreign key for *involved_party_id#*. The next example checks that the CASE block *signatory_id#* is a valid foreign key for *involved_party_id#* in the INVOLVED_PARTY table. This provides an alternative solution to the *List of Values* used in Figures 2.17 and 2.18 to select a valid signatory identifier.

```
Procedure Name:   CHECK_SIGNATORY_ID

PROCEDURE         CHECK_SIGNATORY_ID IS

   BEGIN

            SELECT    INVOLVED_PARTY_NAME

            INTO      :CASE.SIGNATORY_NAME

            FROM      INVOLVED_PARTY

            WHERE     INVOLVED_PARTY.INVOLVED_PARTY_ID =
                               :CASE.SIGNATORY_ID;

   EXCEPTION

            WHEN      NO_DATA_FOUND THEN
                      MESSAGE ('INVALID SIGNATORY ID.');
                      RAISE FORM_TRIGGER_FAILURE;
```

```
WHEN   DUP_VAL_ON_INDEX THEN
       MESSAGE ('TWO OR MORE SIGNATORIES HAVE SAME ID.');
       RAISE FORM_TRIGGER_FAILURE;

WHEN   TOO_MANY_ROWS THEN
       MESSAGE ('SIGNATORY ID IS NOT UNIQUE..');
       RAISE FORM_TRIGGER_FAILURE;

END;
```

The value entered into SIGNATORY_ID is validated against the INVOLVED_PARTY table. If it exists, the involved party name is displayed in the SIGNATORY_NAME field of the CASE block. Errors are detected as exceptions, similar to the earlier discussion for CASE_FILE_ID. Again for the multi-user performance reasons above, this form-level trigger is invoked both at the field-level and block-level as follows:

```
FIELD-LEVEL TRIGGER   (POST-CHANGE)

  CHECK_SIGNATORY_ID;

BLOCK-LEVEL TRIGGER   (PRE-UPDATE)

  CHECK_SIGNATORY_ID;
```

21.7.3   Checking for referential integrity

If rows in a table are deleted, rows in other tables may be affected – if required rows in that first table no longer exist. A check should be carried out to determine whether the key values of rows to be deleted exist as dependent foreign key values in other tables. This is called **referential integrity checking**. Earlier versions of SQL*Forms required that triggers be explicitly coded to check referential integrity. Data that is to be inserted or updated in tables should always be checked for validity before carrying out the insert or update. This is called **data integrity checking**. We discussed relevant trigger logic to achieve this earlier in the chapter.

Many relational DBMS products now provide automatic referential integrity checking before deletion, and automatic data validity checking of the values of specified columns to be inserted or updated in tables. This includes IBM DB2, ORACLE Version 7.0 and INGRES Release 6.3. Most referential integrity and data validity checking is now carried out automatically by SQL*Forms using ORACLE V7.0, as discussed next.

Automatic referential integrity checking

If a case is deleted, for example, its investigations may be affected. INVESTIGATION uses *case_id* as a foreign key to reference the relevant CASE.

Should the deletion of the case be rejected? This is specified using DB2 by the FOREIGN KEY definition ON DELETE RESTRICT (see Section 21.2 in this chapter). Or should deletion of a case cause every investigation for that case to be automatically deleted? This is defined to DB2 by ON DELETE CASCADE. Or instead should each investigation be explicitly deleted first – and only then allow the relevant case to be deleted?

We discussed this problem in Chapter 20, in part, during definition of a default detail block in a Master-Detail relationship. When the check box *Delete Details* is turned ON (see Figure 20.14), SQL*Forms V3.0 automatically generates all trigger logic required to synchronize the master and detail blocks. When a row in the master block is deleted, all of its related detail rows are also automatically deleted. This implements similar logic to the DB2 definition ON DELETE CASCADE.

Automatic data integrity checking

A **check clause** can be defined for columns in ORACLE V7.0 tables. This specifies data integrity checking that is to be carried out on inserting or updating values in the relevant column, when data is to be committed to the data base. Invalid data is thus detected and then rejected by this data integrity checking. The operator is notified that an SQL error has occurred.

But it would be more convenient to detect the error when the cursor moves out of the relevant field in the block, rather than when the block is committed to the data base after all data entry or data changes had been completed. This is the purpose of the check box *Use Constraints* (see Figures 20.12 and 20.14). If this check box is ON, SQL*Forms V3.0 automatically generates trigger logic from check clauses (in ORACLE V7.0) for columns in the base table of the relevant block. These triggers check the values of fields based on those columns, and notify the operator of an error before the cursor moves outside the relevant field. The error can then be corrected more readily.

21.8 COPYING AND REFERENCING OBJECTS

SQL*Forms allows an object (such as a block, field, trigger or procedure) defined in one form to be copied, or referenced, elsewhere in the same or a different form. The difference between copying an object, and referencing an object, is shown using form-level triggers as objects in the following discussion.

Form-level triggers, invoked by name as described in the examples above, can be referenced from other forms. The original trigger is the source trigger: other triggers referenced from it are called target triggers. Target triggers that are **referenced** cannot be changed. Instead, changes are made to the source trigger and are automatically applied by SQL*Forms to all target triggers that are referenced from that source. This reduces the impact of future changes that have to be made to trigger logic: trigger maintenance is reduced as the trigger is defined in only one place – the source trigger.

Target triggers can also be **copied** from a source trigger. This is used if a target trigger will have to be changed differently to the source trigger. In this instance, after copying the trigger SQL*Forms no longer maintains the links between the source and any target triggers copied from it. Each copied target trigger can thus be changed independently of its source and any other target triggers copied from the same source.

This concept can be extended further to establish installation standards: for definition of common triggers; for standard screen designs (common 'look and feel'); for common procedures defined with PL/SQL, or for other purposes. For example a standard page 'banner' can be defined in a form together with other common triggers and procedures. These standard definitions can then be referenced by all forms in an installation, to implement certain installation standards.

Figure 21.23 illustrates a typical standard page banner. This is referenced by each page in every form of every application. The code in the top left of the banner identifies each application, form and version (see AAAAAAFFVV in Figure 21.23). The first six characters (AAAAAA)

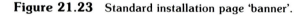

```
  ┌── AAAAAAFFVV ─────────────────────────────── PAGE NN OF XX ──┐
  │                          PAGE TITLE              DD-MON-YY     │
  │                                                               │
```

Figure 21.23   Standard installation page 'banner'.

indicate the application; the two characters (FF) that follow this identify the form within the application; the last two digits (VV) indicate the version of that form within the application. The specific page number (NN) of the total number of pages (XX) in the form is displayed in the top right of the banner. The title of the page and the current date are then displayed on the next line.

Defined in this way, each page is uniquely identified by the specific application, form, version and page number. The banner is a standard block that can now be referenced by each page in a form. Four tables are required: AUTHOR, SYSTEM_REGISTER, FORM_REGISTER and PAGE_REGISTER. We will discuss the last two tables; these are defined in a Master-Detail Relationship in Figure 21.24.

FORM_REGISTER is the master block; PAGE_REGISTER is the detail block (see Figure 21.24). Every application is registered and allocated a unique application code (see AAAAAA in Figure 21.23) and application name; these are stored and maintained in the SYSTEM_REGISTER. They are displayed in the FORM_REGISTER block as shown below. Each new form is allocated a unique form code (or a sequential number) in the application, and is allocated version number 01 (see FF and VV in Figure 21.23); later changes to the form are given the next sequential version number. The Contact and Location fields (from the AUTHOR table) identify who is responsible for maintaining the form. Finally, Total Pages is a field that always displays the total number of pages in the form; calculated by a field-level trigger that issues the COUNT-QUERY PL/SQL packaged procedure

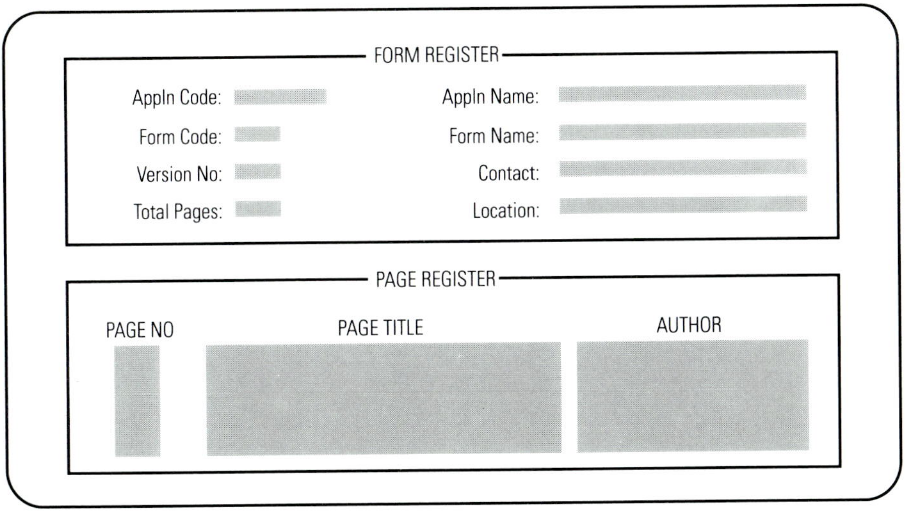

Figure 21.24 Form and page register for page 'banner'.

to count the number of rows in the PAGE_REGISTER table that are related to the current form in the FORM_REGISTER table.

The PAGE_REGISTER detail block then displays each page in the form, indicating the Page No, Page Title of the page, and its author (from the AUTHOR table).

The standard page banner in Figure 21.23 can now be automatically generated from this information. The Application Code, Form Code and Version Number in the form register are used to construct the AAAAAAFFVV code in the top left of the banner. The current page number (from the PAGE_REGISTER) and total number of pages (from the FORM_REGISTER) are displayed in the top right of the banner, replacing NN and XX. The current page title (from the PAGE_REGISTER) is displayed in the centre.

Each of the banner block fields has *Displayed* and *Echo Input* field attributes turned ON; *Input Allowed, Query Allowed* and *Update Allowed* are all turned OFF. Once referenced in a form these fields can only be displayed; they cannot be changed by the operator. Triggers are defined on each of these fields. These select the relevant columns from the FORM_REGISTER and PAGE_REGISTER tables. Each referenced banner, when included in its target form, must uniquely determine its current page number. The triggers defined for the NN and PAGE TITLE fields therefore obtain the current page number (of the referenced target form) by using the PL/SQL packaged function with the relevant field name as follows:

```
FIELD_CHARACTERISTIC (field_name, PAGE)
```

The current page number of the banner block referenced in the target form can now be used to select the relevant page number row from the PAGE_REGISTER table.

A number of advantages arise from this approach.

- The page number and page title can only be displayed in the standard banner if the form and every one of its pages have been registered in the relevant tables. Central control of all forms and pages can thus be maintained.

- By using object referencing, if the standard banner is changed, every form and all pages that reference the banner also change.

- Every page is uniquely identified: by application code, form code, version number and page number. If an operator requires assistance, or if a problem occurs, the relevant page can be easily determined.

- The author of each form and page in an application is readily identified, if that person also has responsibility for subsequent maintenance.

21.9 TESTING A MODIFIED BLOCK

The correct operation of a modified data entry block, changed field attributes, defined field validation checks or triggers can be tested at any time: by generating and executing the form from the Action menu (see Figure 20.8), or by using the RunForm program. The Execution Mode keys (see Tables 21.1 and 21.2) are used to test the operation of the block in different data entry conditions: adding, displaying, changing or deleting data to check that the application is functioning correctly.

We have now completed development of data entry screens. We have covered some of the more common triggers used with data entry forms. We are ready to develop application screens in the next chapter.

21.10 SUMMARY

We started this chapter with a discussion of the systems development responsibilities of data base administration, data administration and user project team groups. We next discussed Codd's five areas of integrity support for relational data base management systems: these are referential integrity; domain integrity; column integrity; entity integrity; and user-defined integrity. We discussed the specification of primary and foreign keys to allow RDBMS products to provide some of this required integrity support. We defined unique indexes for primary and foreign keys; non-unique indexes for secondary keys.

The rest of the chapter discussed development of data entry and application forms using ORACLE SQL*Forms V3.0. We saw key-mapping used by SQL*Forms for design mode and also for execution mode. We executed the default data entry form that was generated in Chapter 20, and discussed how SQL*Forms can implement the generic procedure concepts discussed in Chapters 5 and 6.

In refining default data entry screens: we first modified the screen layout; then refined editing and other specifications of data fields on screen; and next, the field validation to be applied to those fields. This included: default field values; system generated keys; field formats; range checking; mandatory fields; table look-up fields; automatic hint fields. We specified pop-up pages, to overlay parts of the screen with additional detail.

We defined conditional logic using triggers. We saw that these triggers can be defined at the form-level, block-level and/or field-level, using SQL and the Oracle PL/SQL procedural language. We described typical triggers that can be used for: the validation of unique keys; the checking of valid foreign keys; and automatic data and referential integrity checking. We saw how objects can be referenced and copied, illustrating this by designing an installation-standard page banner to present a standard 'look and feel' for all applications.

References

[1] IE: Expert is supported in the USA by Information Engineering Systems Corporation in Alexandria, VA and in Dallas, TX.

[2] ISM™ is supported in Sydney, Australia by Infonetics Pty Ltd.

[3] Codd, E. F. (1990). *The Relational Model for Database Management: Version 2*, Addison-Wesley: Reading, MA.

[4] Codd, E. F. (1988). *Domains, Keys and Referential Integrity in Relational Databases*, InfoDB, Colin White Consulting: San Jose, CA (Spring 1988).

[5] Date, C. J. (1988). *Primary and Foreign Key Support in DB2*, InfoDB, Colin White Consulting: San Jose, CA (Fall 1988).

[6] Koch, G. (1990). *ORACLE: The Complete Reference*, Osborne McGraw-Hill: Berkeley CA.

[7] Groff, R. and Weinberg, P. (1990). *Using SQL*, Osborne McGraw-Hill: Berkeley CA.

[8] Oracle. (1989). *SQL*Forms Designer's Tutorial Version 3.0*, Oracle Corp: Belmont CA, Oracle Part No. 3302-V3.0.

[9] Oracle. (1989). *SQL*Forms Designer's Reference Version 3.0*, Oracle Corp: Belmont CA, Oracle Part No. 3304-V3.0.

[10] Oracle. (1989). *PL/SQL User's Guide and Reference Version 1.0*, Oracle Corp: Belmont CA, Oracle Part No. 800-V1.0.

CHAPTER 22

Development of Application Systems

Once we have completed the refinement of data entry forms, we can apply the same principles to the refinement of application forms. We will develop application screens in this chapter – based on associations in the operational model, and guided by the systems and processes identified and defined in Chapter 19. We will link these application screens together as application systems, to address complex business processing and analysis. We will link these application screens also to the screens we developed earlier for data entry, so that data can be maintained as required by application processing. Finally we will design menus for these applications.

22.1 PRIORITY APPLICATION SCREENS

We will use the subject map for the Case Investigations functional area in Figure 17.18 to guide development of application screens and systems. We will first address high-priority Investigation Reference Systems, using the project plan defined in Figure 19.8, reproduced here as Figure 22.1.

22.1.1 Phase 2 Period control system

The Period Control System is in Phase 2, as most systems are dependent on it. This system only uses the PERIOD entity. The detailed procedure map

		Investigation Reference Systems Project Plan					
Phase	Pty	Operational System	1	2	3	4	5
2	High	Period Control System	▓				
3	High	Case History System	▓▓				
3	Low	Involved Party History System					▓
4	High	Case Investigations System		▓▓			
5	High	Involved Party Investigations System				▓▓	
5	High	Investigation Contact System				▓▓	

Figure 22.1 Priority Systems Project Plan (from Figure 19.8).

in Figure 19.12 is implemented mainly by the data entry screen developed for PERIOD, using the steps detailed in Chapters 21 and 22. However some further refinement is needed.

PERIOD uses *period_id* as a system generated primary key, calculated automatically as a default value. Many related entities use *period_id* as a foreign key. It is impractical for an operator to enter a system generated key. Instead, a form-level trigger is developed to accept a *period_start_date* (or a *period_end_date*). This trigger will look-up in PERIOD (or calculate) the relevant *period_id* for that date. The *period_id* is next inserted in a field of the current screen, to be written subsequently to its relevant table as a foreign key. Alternatively it can be saved in an SQL*Forms global variable of the application form. The *period_id* and its *period_type_id* are typically stored in global variables, together with other common key values such as the current *case_id*.

The Case History System, Case Investigations System and the Investigation Contact System are next in priority. These are shaded in Figure 22.2. We will design these application screens first, then discuss their refinement. We will link them together in application systems later in the chapter.

22.1.2 Screen 1 – Case history system

We saw in Chapter 19 that the association between PERIOD and CASE identified the Case History System. This is shaded and labelled as Application No. 1 in Figure 22.2. In a period there may be many cases: shown by a *one to many* association between PERIOD and CASE; and by the procedure map in Figure 19.15. This procedure is implemented by a screen which displays the start and end dates for a period, together with a multi-record list of the CASE fields *case_file_id*, *case_name*, *case_date_due*

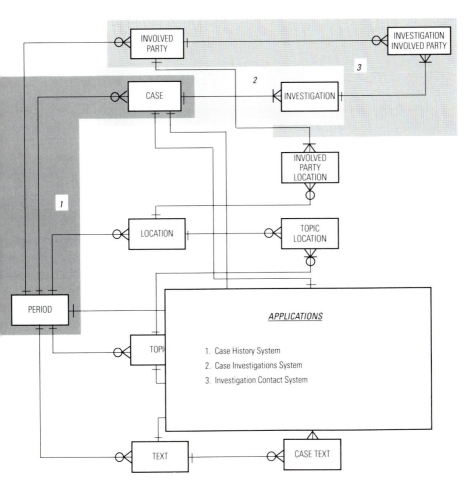

Figure 22.2 High-priority Investigation Reference Systems.

and *case_date_completed* for each case in a period. This is an application
screen for the Case History System, as illustrated in Figure 22.3.

This screen defines a Master-Detail Relationship between PERIOD
and CASE. Although not recommended, we could instead have used the
SQL CREATE VIEW command to define a view between PERIOD and
CASE, which we might call PERIOD_CASES_VIEW. We will refer to a
view created for an application screen as a **screen view**. It is defined as
follows (refer to Appendix 1 for a discussion of views).

```
create view      PERIOD_CASES_VIEW as

( SELECT         PERIOD.period_id, CASE.case_id, period_start_date, period_end_date,
                 case_file_id, case_name, case_date_due, case_date_completed
```

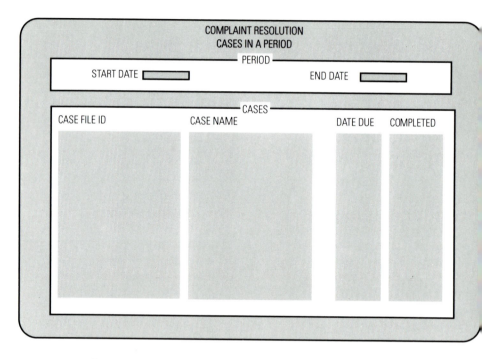

Figure 22.3 Application screen for Case History System.

FROM   PERIOD, CASE

WHERE   PERIOD.period_id = CASE.period_id);

The only columns in the view are those included as fields on the screen. The naming convention recommended for screen views is derived from the association that joins the two related entities. The owner table name (PERIOD, singular for the *one* end of the association) begins the name. This is suffixed by the member table name (CASES, plural for the *many* end of the association), and terminated by VIEW. The screen view name that results is then abbreviated if necessary, based on the maximum characters for a view name (29 for Oracle). This view can be used to generate the single-record block at the top of Figure 22.3, and again to generate the multi-record block at the bottom of that figure. All related table accessing is carried out by SQL through the join that implements the view. However, while straight-forward, this approach has a number of significant disadvantages relating to the updateability of views, as discussed next.

A view which joins two or more tables can only be used for query purposes: it cannot be used for data entry [1, 2, 3, 4]. Instead data is entered and updated using the data entry screens developed in Chapter 21. We can use SQL*Menu or function keys to link data entry screens to an application screen, as discussed later in this chapter.

Rather than define a view as above, we use Master-Detail Relationships to implement the *one to many* associations in an application screen. Figure 22.3 is developed using the steps described in Chapter 21. A default single-record master block is generated for PERIOD; a default multi-record detail block is generated for CASE – with only those columns in each block included as indicated in Figure 22.3. A form-level trigger is defined to save *case_id* and *period_id* as global variables for the form. This is invoked by a POST-QUERY trigger at the block level. These current keys can then be used by other application screens in the form.

22.1.3   Screen 2 – Case investigations system

The Case Investigations System is the next highest priority system in Figure 22.1. This is Application No. 2 in Figure 22.2. It is based on the *one to many* association between CASE and INVESTIGATION; and the procedure map in Figure 19.16. Two different screen designs are feasible: Version 1 (see Figure 22.4) includes the date fields for a case in a single-record CASE master block, with the INVESTIGATION detail block also defined as a single-record block.

Figure 22.4 displays the details of each separate investigation for a case in turn. Or many investigations for a case can instead be listed in a multi-

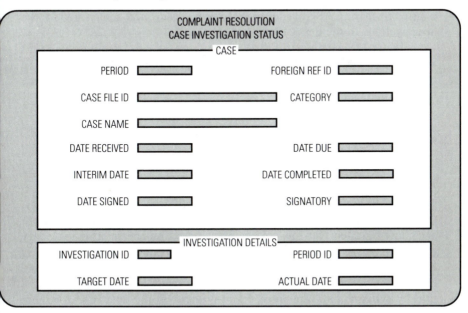

Figure 22.4   Case Investigations System screen (Version 1).

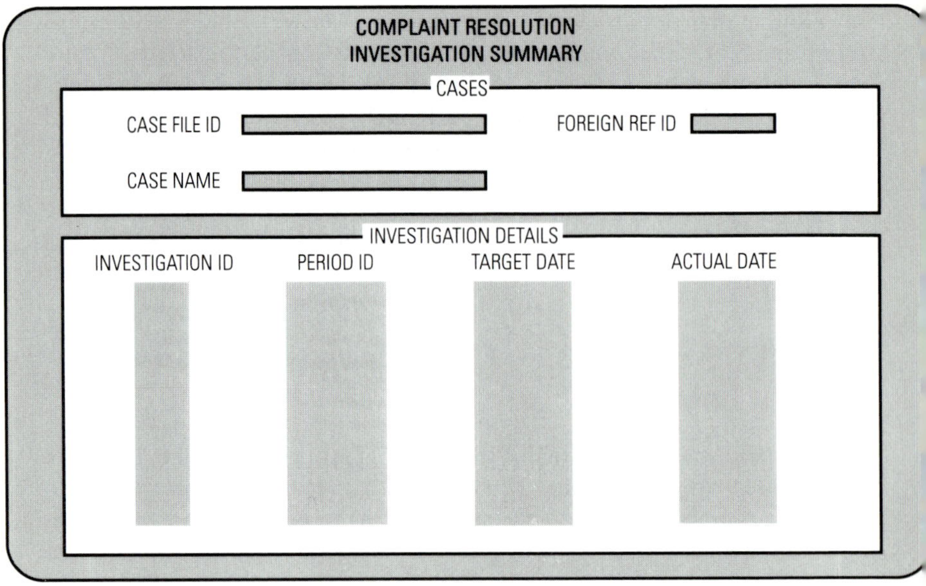

Figure 22.5   Case Investigations System screen (Version 2).

record detail block, shown as Version 2 in Figure 22.5. The date fields are omitted from the CASE master block to provide adequate screen area for the investigations in the detail block.

Figure 22.6 summarizes these two versions of the Case Investigations System. Other versions may be required for security or other reasons. These two screens are typical of some of the design decisions which can be made for each application screen.

22.1.4   Screen 3 – Investigation contact system

Although the Involved Party Investigations System is the next system according to Figure 22.1, we will defer it until after we discuss the Investigation Contact System. This is Application No. 3 in Figure 22.2. Both are phase 5 systems in the project plan, based on the intersecting entity INVESTIGATION INVOLVED PARTY: dependent on INVOLVED PARTY in phase 3 and INVESTIGATION in phase 4 (see Figure 19.1). We earlier developed and refined the data entry screens for all entities in the priority systems: data are entered and updated in the data base for these earlier phase entities. Thus either of these two intersecting entity systems can be implemented first depending on the business requirements.

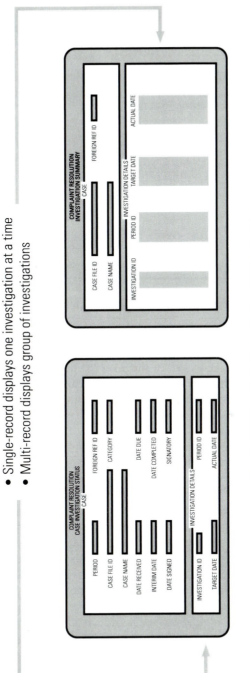

For a Case

- Single-record displays one investigation at a time
- Multi-record displays group of investigations

Figure 22.6   Application screen design decisions.

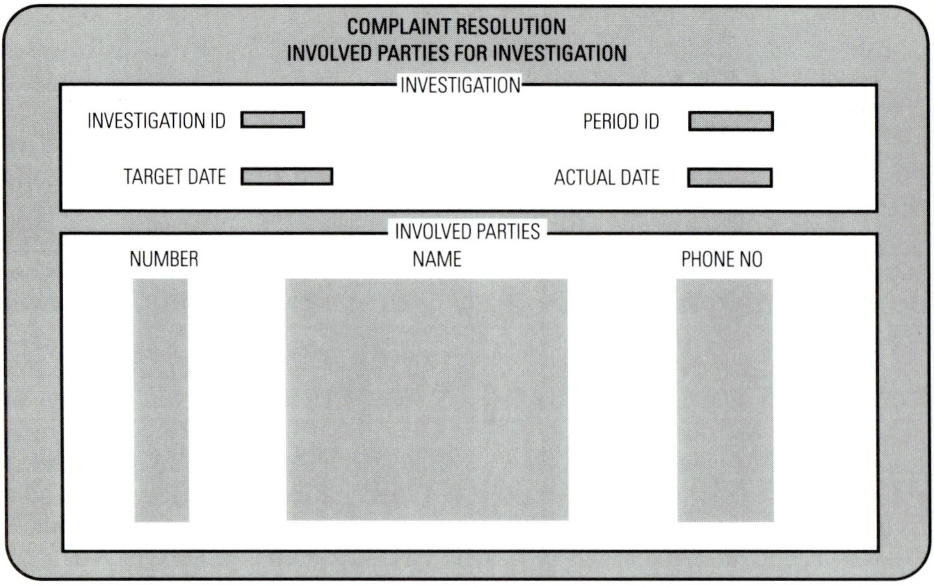

Figure 22.7 Investigation Contact Systems application screen.

The Investigation Contact System is based on the procedure map in Figure 19.18. This displays all of the involved parties who have participated in an investigation, or have otherwise been contacted. These contacts can be detailed in a multi-record block for an investigation as illustrated in Figure 22.7.

Once again, several screen designs may be appropriate. Figure 22.7 provides a useful telephone directory of all contacts for a case. Other fields may be included: either in this multi-record block; or all details for an involved party can be displayed in a single-record block as a separate pop-up page. For application screens based on intersecting entities, data from other related tables is often needed. Case and investigation details, for example, may be required as well as involved party details. Related tables can all be joined in a screen view if only queries will be made and performance is not a concern. Or alternatively, related tables can be defined as single-record blocks and implemented as pop-up pages as for the Involved Party page (see Figure 21.17) if optimum performance is important.

22.1.5 Refinement of application screens

To this point we have concentrated on the overall design of application screens, guided by the project plan developed during process modeling and based on associations in the subject map. Each default block, generated to include only those columns required by the application screen as described above, is refined as described in Chapter 21 for data entry screens: labels are renamed; fields are resized; fields and/or labels are moved as necessary; and boxes or lines are drawn.

Application screens based on two or more tables joined in a view cannot be used for data entry; only for queries. Screens designed using SQL*Forms V3.0 Master-Detail Relationship default blocks can be used both for data entry and for queries. Data entry screens normally display all columns in a base table as fields in the block. These fields are used for any data which is to be entered, updated or deleted. For security reasons, separate screens may be used for data entry and for queries. All fields are displayed for authorized data entry operators. Only certain authorized fields are displayed for queries, depending on the authorization level of the query operator. SQL*Menu is used here to maintain the different security control for data entry and query screens. We will later see how other data entry screens can be invoked directly from any application screen.

To prevent application screens being used also for data entry, the *Display* and *Query Allowed* field attributes are turned ON for each field, but the *Input Allowed* and *Update Allowed* attributes are turned OFF (see Figure 21.8). Most of the validation checks essential for data entry screens are therefore not relevant for application screens.

22.1.6   Triggers for application screens

Triggers are still needed in a number of circumstances. Only valid keys can be used to initiate a query: these keys should first be validated with a trigger. Columns extracted from related tables can be included in an application screen as a look-up field, using List of Values. Triggers also store common key values, such as *case_id* and *period_id*, in global variables of an application form for use by related application screens.

Checking for valid keys

A key entered to initiate a query should first be validated. For example, a *case_file_id* is entered to query the details of a case and display its investigations. This is shown as [1] in Figure 22.8 for the Case Investigations System. The form-level trigger is discussed in Chapter 21. A field-level POST-CHANGE trigger checks that the key is valid.

Including look-up fields

Figure 22.8 also shows other refinement to the application screen. In [2], the signatory is an involved party. We discussed in Figure 21.14 how the List of Values facility can be used to select the relevant involved party row for the

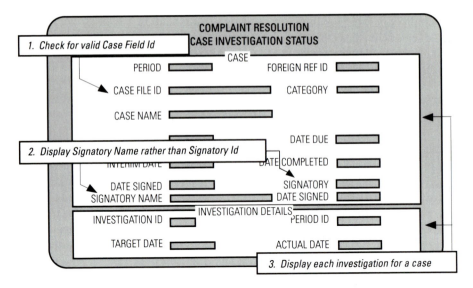

Figure 22.8 Typical refinement of application screens.

signatory_id of a case into the Signatory Name field. This approach is used if a look-up field is required in every instance. But a signatory name is only available if the case has been signed. The trigger logic in Figure 21.17 must therefore be modified to test for this situation: by including a PL/SQL IF . . . THEN . . . ELSE statement to test that *case_date_signed* is NOT NULL.

In [3] of Figure 22.8 the effect of the Master-Detail Relationship is illustrated: using *case_id* as the join field to include only investigations for the specific case.

22.2 OTHER APPLICATION SCREENS

Figure 22.9 shows additional application screens derived from the Case Investigations subject map. This illustrates a Case Topics System, a Topic Locations System, and a Location Contact System.

22.2.1 Screen 4 – Case topics system

Figure 22.10 illustrates an application screen designed for the Case Topics System (see [4] in Figure 22.9). This is based on the intersecting entity CASE TOPIC.

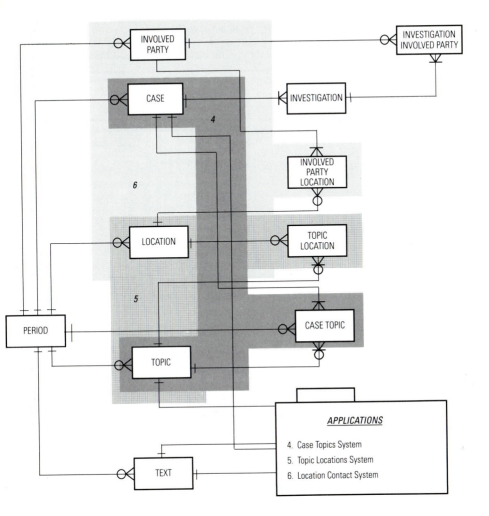

Figure 22.9   Other application screens from the subject map.

22.2.2   Screen 5 – Topic locations system

Figure 22.11 next illustrates an application screen for the Topic Locations System (see [5] in Figure 22.9), based on the intersecting entity TOPIC LOCATION.

22.2.3   Screen 6 – Location contact system

Figure 22.12 is an application screen for the Location Contact System (see [6] in Figure 22.9), based on the intersecting entity INVOLVED PARTY LOCATION.

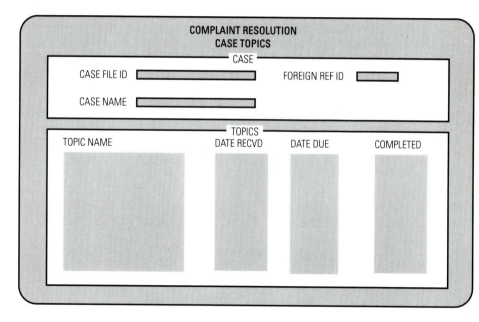

Figure 22.10 Case Topics System application screen.

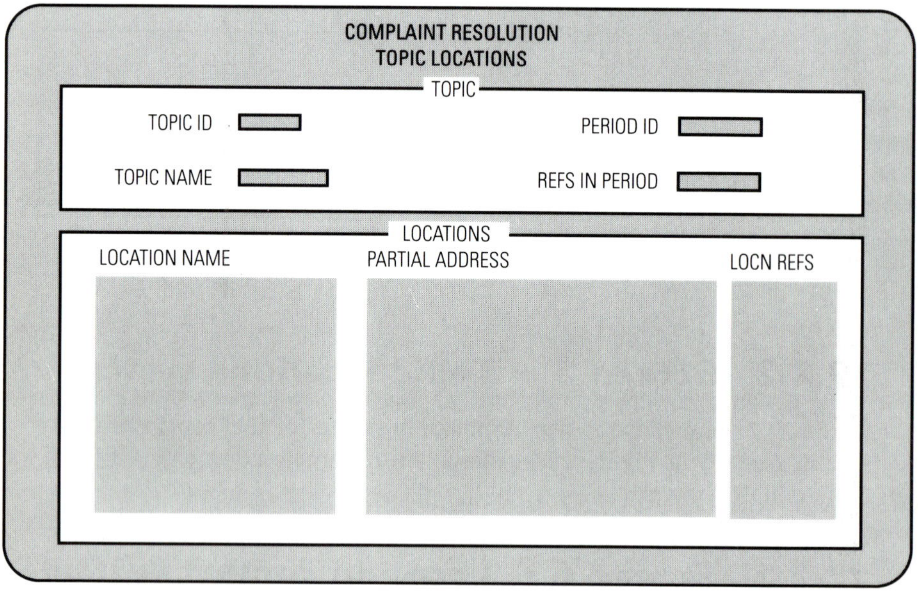

Figure 22.11 Topic Locations System application screen.

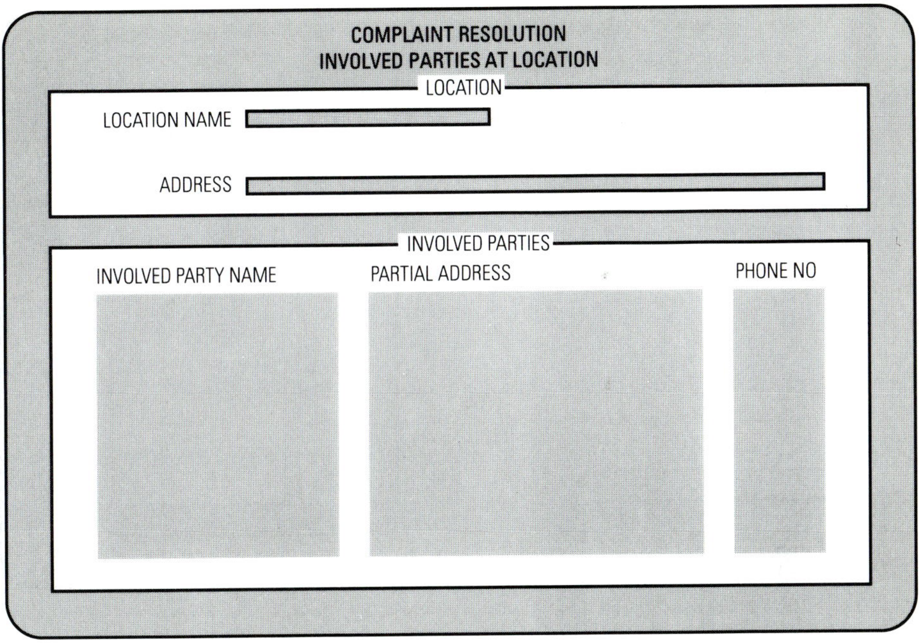

Figure 22.12   Location Contact System application screen.

We have designed a number of application screens based on the subject map in Figure 22.2. Designing screens as described in Chapters 21 and 22 allows data entry screens to be used independently also, as application screens. Application screens can be linked together as required, progressively building application systems. Similarly application systems can be linked together via application screens, or via SQL*Menu, to develop complex application systems. The development of application systems and of complex application systems are discussed next.

22.3 DEVELOPING APPLICATION SYSTEMS

As we developed application screens, it was apparent that many screens could be used also in conjunction with other screens. For example, when displaying all of the cases for a period in the Case History System (Figure 22.3), we may want to select a specific case and examine all investigations for that case. Version 2 of the Case Investigations System lists these investigations (see Figure 22.5). For each investigation we may then want to list all

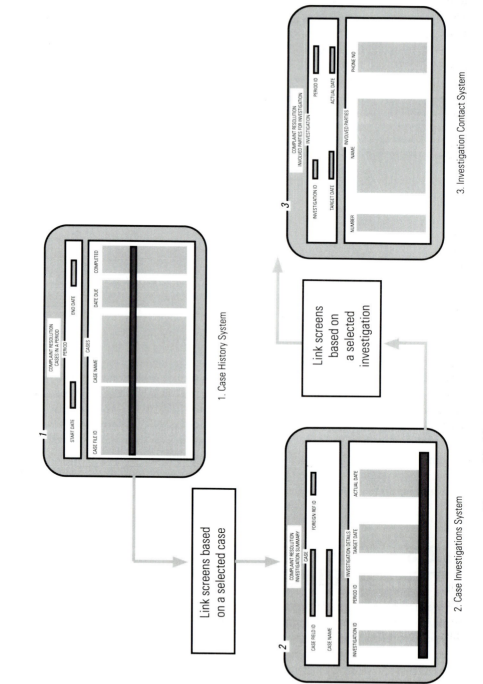

Figure 22.13   Investigation Reference application system

parties contacted, in the Investigation Contact System (see Figure 22.7). These three application screens can be linked together, as illustrated in Figure 22.13.

This represents Applications 1–3 of the Investigation Reference Systems in the Case Investigations subject map in Figure 22.2: identified through process modeling in Chapter 19, and scheduled as high-priority applications in Figure 22.1. Application screens are linked together to produce application systems by the use of triggers.

22.3.1 Linking application screens using triggers

If application screens appear as blocks in the same application form, we can link them together by triggers associated with the calling block. Two user-named triggers are used: the first clears the block to be called; the second issues the relevant PL/SQL commands (such as EXECUTE_QUERY) for actions to be carried out against the called block. An example that is based on a selected row in the CASES detail block of the Case History System (see [1] in Figure 22.13) will be used to illustrate. This identifies a case (by CASE_ID) to be used to link to the Case Investigations System (see [2] in Figure 22.13).

The first trigger is called CLEAR_CASE_INVESTIGATIONS. If a row in the (Case History) CASES block is selected (:CASES.CASE_ID is NOT NULL) a GO_BLOCK PL/SQL command transfers control to the CASE block (in the Case Investigations System). It clears that block and then returns to the CASES block. This trigger logic is shown in the following example.

```
Trigger Name:   CLEAR_CASE_INVESTIGATIONS

    IF    :CASES.CASE_ID IS NOT NULL THEN

          GO_BLOCK      ('CASE');

          CLEAR_BLOCK;

          GO_BLOCK      ('CASES');

    END IF;
```

The second trigger is called QUERY_CASE_INVESTIGATIONS. This uses similar logic to the first trigger as shown next, but also requires a change to the CASE block of the Case Investigations System. These are both discussed in the following paragraphs.

```
Trigger Name:   QUERY_CASE_INVESTIGATIONS

    IF    :CASES.CASE_ID IS NOT NULL THEN

          GO_BLOCK      ('CASE');
```

```
        EXECUTE_QUERY;

        GO_BLOCK       ('CASES');

    END IF;
```

If a row in the (Case History) CASES block is selected (:CASES.CASE_ID is NOT NULL) GO_BLOCK transfers control to the CASE block (in the Case Investigations System). A PL/SQL EXECUTE_QUERY command is then issued in that block. This displays the relevant CASE details for the selected CASE_ID (by enforcing a foreign key relationship to CASES – see below) as if a query for the case had been entered by an operator. In turn, related investigations are displayed in the INVESTIGATIONS detail block, as we specified in Chapter 21. The operator can use all facilities of that application screen, looking at other cases and their investigations as relevant. When the [exit/cancel] or the [accept/commit] key is pressed by the operator (or when the Exit menu option is selected), control is returned back to the CASES block in the Case History System by the last GO_BLOCK statement in the trigger.

However, for this second trigger to operate correctly, a change must also be made to the CASE_ID field in the CASE block of the Case Investigations System. Refer back to the Field Definition screen in Figure 21.7. This shows the field characteristic *Enforce Key*, which indicates to SQL*Forms the source of the value to be used to populate the field. The example in Figure 22.13 uses the selected CASE_ID in the CASES block (of the Case History System) as a foreign key to access the relevant CASE_ID in the CASE block (of the Case Investigations System). This must therefore be defined as a foreign key relationship in the CASE_ID field of the Case Investigations System CASE block as follows:

```
    Enforce Key:   CASES.CASE_ID
```

A foreign key relationship defined in this way is enforced by SQL*Forms when:

- A new record (for example, a new case) that contains the field is created.
- The block that contains the field is queried (as in the example above).
- A record that contains the field is inserted.

If the CASES block is in another form, the selected CASE_ID value must be stored in a global variable. Instead of GO_BLOCK, the PL/SQL procedure CALL (form_name) or CALL_QUERY (form_name) can be used to transfer control to the called form. (The CALL_QUERY procedure allows only queries to be made to the called form; the CALL procedure also allows data to be added, updated or deleted using the form. (Use of these procedures is discussed further below, in *22.3.2 Invoking Data Entry Screens*.) Finally, in the called form the global variable is then used to store the CASE_ID value in a target field of a block in that form. This value is enforced from that target field as shown above. Using the design approach in Chapters 21 and 22, full advantage is therefore taken of trigger logic automatically generated by SQL*Forms: for Master-Detail Relationships; for referential integrity and data integrity checking; and for foreign key enforcement.

Figure 22.14 next shows an application system that analyzes cases and locations. It shows the Case History System (Figure 22.3) linked to applications 4–6 of Figure 22.9; similar to our discussion above for applications 1–3 also in Figure 22.9.

A selected case calls the Case Topics System (Figure 22.10) to display all topics that are referenced by the case. A selected topic next displays all locations relevant to that topic, using the Topic Locations System (Figure 22.11). For a specific location, all involved parties at that location can be displayed using the Location Contact System (Figure 22.12). The result is the Case Location Analysis System in Figure 22.14.

We have seen how application screens can be linked together to implement application systems that support comprehensive queries. These screens may only display a subset of all of the fields in a block, tailored to satisfy specific types of queries. They may not therefore be suitable also for data entry purposes. The data entry screens in Chapter 21 were developed for this purpose. We will now discuss linking the data entry screens to the application screens.

22.3.2 Invoking data entry screens

We developed the data entry screens in a data entry form (called, say, CASEDATA) and the application screens in an application form (called, say, CASEQERY). (If form names are limited to 8 characters (an MS-DOS constraint) the designed systems can be easily ported across the different hardware and operating system platforms supported by SQL*Forms V3.0.) We will call CASEDATA from CASEQERY with a form-level procedure as follows:

```
Procedure Name:   LINK_CASEDATA

                  CALL      (CASEDATA, NO_HIDE, DO_REPLACE);
```

The CALL PL/SQL packaged procedure used here allows the called form to be used to add, query, update or delete data defined as blocks in that form. The CALL_QUERY procedure prevents the called form being used for data entry purposes; data can only be queried. Optional parameters can

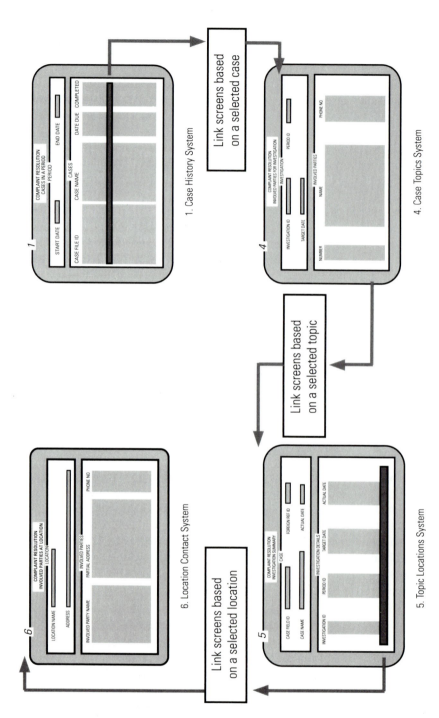

Figure 22.14   Case Location Analysis System.

be used with CALL and CALL_QUERY procedures. These specify that the calling form is to be hidden by the called form (HIDE). Or, if the called form is smaller than the calling form, NO_HIDE (used above) indicates that the calling form is to be displayed in the background – partly visible under the called form. Similarly, if SQL*Menu is also used during execution, DO_REPLACE (as used above) specifies that the execution menu used by the called form replaces the menu used by the calling form; NO_REPLACE is specified to retain the calling form menu for use also with the called form.

When this form-level procedure is invoked from the application form, the data entry form is called and application processing is suspended. Any valid data can be added, updated or deleted by CASEDATA, as defined in Chapter 21. On completion, data entry is terminated as normal by the [accept/commit] or [exit/cancel] key. Processing is resumed at the CASEQERY application form, from the point of earlier suspension.

Figure 22.15 shows the data entry screen used to add new cases, update existing cases or delete cases. This screen can be called from any relevant application screen. No modifications are required to the screen to add a new case. But if a *case_id* from the calling form is to be used to update details, or to delete the case, the *Enforce Key*: field must be defined in the CASE_ID *Field Definition* screen in the CASE block of the data entry form, as described earlier.

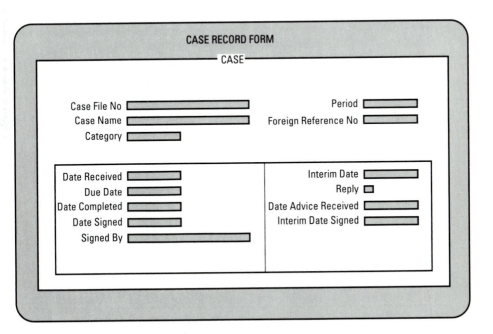

Figure 22.15   **Data entry screen called from an application.**

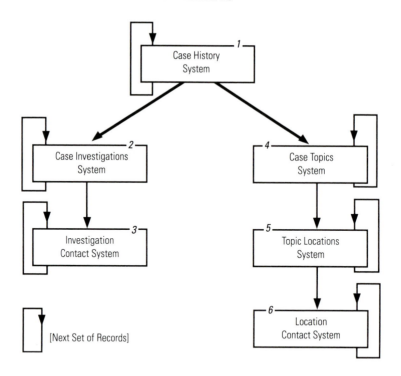

Figure 22.16 Application System Chart for applications 1–6.

22.3.3 Application systems chart

Figure 22.16 next summarizes the application systems from Figures 22.13 and 22.14 in an *Application Systems Chart*. This shows each application screen as a box, with the recursive execution within that screen shown as a right-angled loop. The number in the top-left of each application screen box is cross-referenced to the relevant application in Figure 22.2 (Applications 1–3) or Figure 22.9 (Applications 4–6).

22.4 DEVELOPING COMPLEX SYSTEMS

We will now discuss complex application systems, developed from application screens for each association or related group of entities. Figure 22.17 shows several application systems which are numbered for reference. These are indicated by access paths through the subject map. This shows the analysis of an involved party and the cases associated with that individual.

All investigations for an involved party, with details of those investiga-

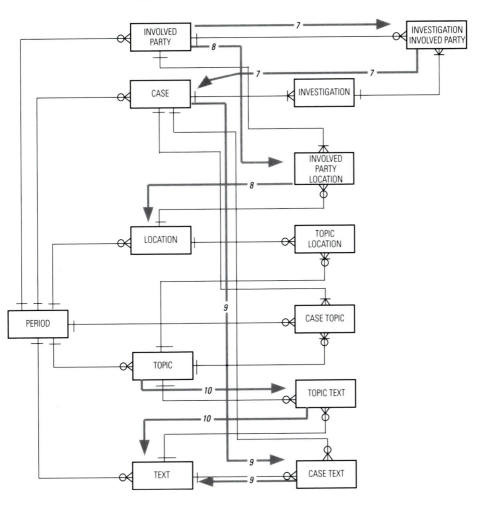

Figure 22.17 Complex involved party analysis systems.

tions and their relevant cases can be obtained from the Involved Party Cases System (application [7] in Figure 22.17). All locations for the involved party can be determined by the Involved Party Locations System [8]. For each case that an involved party has participated in, the Case Documentation System [9] provides all relevant textual documentation. For each topic in a relevant case, the Topic Documentation System [10] provides detail.

The Application System Chart for the analysis systems in Figure 22.17 is shown in the summary of application systems in Figure 22.20.

Figure 22.18 next shows a Location Analysis System. All topics for a specific location are determined in a Location Topics System [11]. For each topic at the location, all cases that refer to that topic are indicated by a Topic

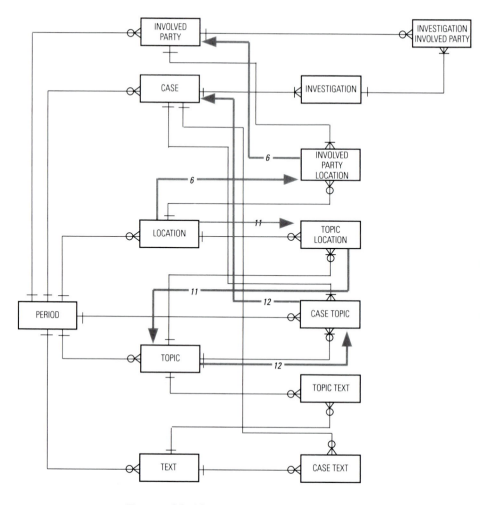

Figure 22.18 Location Analysis System.

Cases System [12]. All involved parties in those cases who also are at the specific location are identified by the Location Contact System [6] developed earlier. Problem locations can thus be used to determine if there is any correlation with specific involved parties, for investigation purposes.

Figure 22.19 shows a Topic Analysis System. For a given topic, all of the cases for that topic are determined by a Topic Cases System [12]. All locations for each of these topics are indicated by the Topic Locations System developed earlier [5]. Finally the involved parties at those locations who participated in cases related to these topics are identified by the Location Contact System [6], also developed earlier. The result is the correlation of involved parties and locations with problem topics.

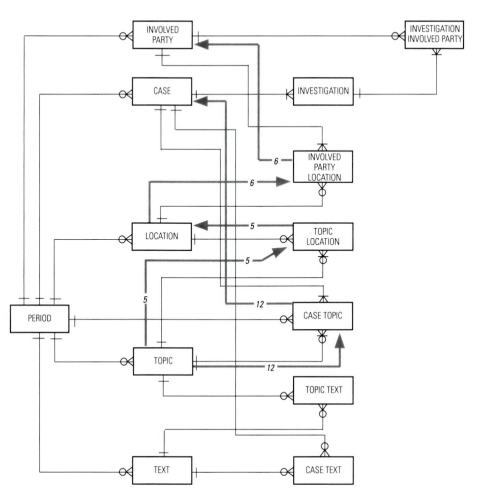

Figure 22.19 Topic Analysis System.

22.4.1 Complex analysis systems

A Case Analysis System is developed from the application systems discussed earlier in Figure 22.16. This is at the left of the Application Systems Chart in Figure 22.20, indicated by the CASE box at the top left of that figure. The Case Investigations System [2] identifies all investigations for a case. All involved parties who participated in those investigations are available from the Investigations Contact System [3]. Furthermore all of the topics in the relevant case are indicated by the Case Topics System [4].

Each of these topics can be analyzed further by the Topic Analysis System described in Figure 22.19. This is shown to the right of the Case

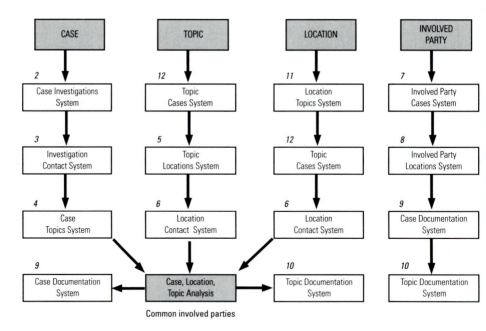

Figure 22.20 Complex integrated analysis systems.

Analysis System in Figure 22.20, starting from the TOPIC box. This identifies problem locations for each topic. For each of these locations, the Location Analysis System in Figure 22.18 can be used to determine involved parties also at those locations. This is shown in Figure 22.20 under the LOCATION box.

These three analysis systems can be further joined on common keys, in a complex Case, Location and Topic Analysis System. For example, some of the involved parties in a current case may have also been associated in the past with problem topics or locations in conjunction with other cases. These people can be readily identified by the common *Involved_party_id* keys, as shaded in Figure 22.20.

The Involved Party Analysis System developed in Figure 22.17 can now be used to examine all past cases for those indicated involved parties. This system is shown in the Application Systems Chart in Figure 22.20 at the right of the figure, under the box for INVOLVED PARTY. The documentation associated with these past cases and topics is available from the Case Documentation System [9] and Topic Documentation System [10]. These documentation systems can also be used for other cases indicated by the Case, Location and Topic Analysis shaded box.

The result is the development of complex analysis systems which are able to be used by management for decision support. Application systems can be progressively combined, using SQL*Forms and with SQL triggers, for the detailed examination of related tables based on common keys and for various conditions as defined in SQL WHERE clauses.

We are now ready to define the user interface for these applications, using SQL*Menu. We will start with an overview of the features of this product. The chapter then finishes with a discussion of a typical menu structure developed for the above applications.

22.5 LINKING APPLICATIONS WITH SQL*MENU

With SQL*Menu Version 5.0, Oracle Corporation has provided a product that can be used to integrate diverse applications. These may have been developed by SQL*Forms Version 3.0 or by SQL*Plus, SQL*ReportWriter, PL/SQL and other products. The menus developed with SQL*Menu are not limited to ORACLE-based applications; they can integrate ORACLE applications transparently with non-ORACLE applications that are normally invoked directly by the host operating system. Menus can be designed using three styles:

- Pull-down menus, for use with character-mode, block-mode or bit-mapped screens. The examples displayed in Chapters 20–22 illustrate typical pull-down menus.
- Bar style menus, as used by spreadsheet products such as Lotus 1-2-3.
- Full-screen menus, as used in many mainframe and mini-based systems.

SQL*Menu exhibits ease-of-use in menu development and menu operation:

- Menus can be designed with menu items that execute SQL*Menu functions and/or PL/SQL commands, implementing complex, conditional navigation between applications.
- Menus can prompt the operator at run-time for additional information that is passed as parameters to menu functions.
- Menu-driven execution of host operating system commands insulates the operator from complexity. Applications that do not use ORACLE products can be integrated transparently with ORACLE applications.
- Background menus can be designed for any part of the menu hierarchy, to provide the operator with 'accelerator keys' for frequently used commands.

- Security is enforced based on application security levels and each operator's user security level. Unauthorized menu items can be dimmed, or instead are dynamically removed from menus that are not authorized for that operator.

- Menus can invoke SQL*Forms Version 3.0 applications; these applications can also dynamically invoke or change menus from forms due to changing requirements during application processing.

To illustrate the utility of SQL*Menu, we will use it to implement the menu tree shown in Figure 22.21. This is based on the integrated analysis systems in Figure 22.20.

Each of the vertical application paths in Figure 22.20 is implemented in Figure 22.21 as a menu option, shown as: CASES, TOPICS, LOCATIONS and PARTIES. A further option is included to produce reports (such as developed using SQL*Plus, or instead with SQL*ReportWriter). Beneath each option are listed the menu items used to invoke application systems typically used by that option (discussed earlier for Figures 22.17–22.20). The operator can select individual applications using these menu items. When an application is selected, related applications are accessed directly as designed earlier for the linked screens. Or instead the application menu is used to select another relevant menu item. Complex, conditional navigation can be defined using PL/SQL procedures integrated with menu items in the menu structure.

Menus can be designed as pull-down style, bar style or as full screen menus. These menus can in turn can have sub-menus, to any depth. The tree structure menu shown in Figure 22.21 is used for menus with a limited depth.

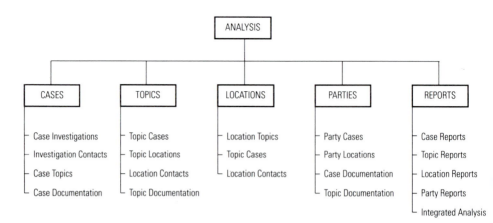

Figure 22.21 Menu tree for Analysis Systems.

```
ANALYSIS
  ├── CASES
  │       ├─ Case Investigations
  │       ├─ Investigation Contacts
  │       ├─ Case Topics
  │       └─ Case Documentation
  ├── TOPICS
  │       ├─ Topic Cases
  │       ├─ Topic Locations
  │       ├─ Location Contacts
  │       └─ Topic Documentation
  ├── LOCATIONS
  │       ├─ Location Topics
  │       ├─ Topic Cases
  │       └─ Location Contacts
  ├── PARTIES
  │       ├─ Party Cases
  │       ├─ Party Locations
  │       ├─ Case Documentation
  │       └─ Topic Documentation
  ├── REPORTS
  │       ├─ Case Reports
  │       ├─ Topic Reports
  │       ├─ Location Reports
  │       ├─ Party Reports
  │       └─ Integrated Analysis
  ├── UTILITIES
  │       ├─ SQL* Forms
  │       ├─ SQL* ReportWriter
  │       ├─ SQL* Plus
  │       └─ Operating System
  └── EXIT
```

Figure 22.22   Menu outline structure for Analysis Systems.

But where menus extend beyond two levels, an outline structure is more useful in showing complex menu options and items. This is shown in Figure 22.22, which illustrates an extension to the application menu with additional options.

The application menu in Figure 22.21 has now been extended with a UTILITIES and an EXIT option. The first invokes SQL*Forms, SQL*ReportWriter or SQL*Plus, or instead the host operating system, directly from the application menu. The second exits completely from application execution. A high security level must be defined for the first option, so that it can only be used by staff who are charged with the maintenance responsibility for these applications. This option will not appear at

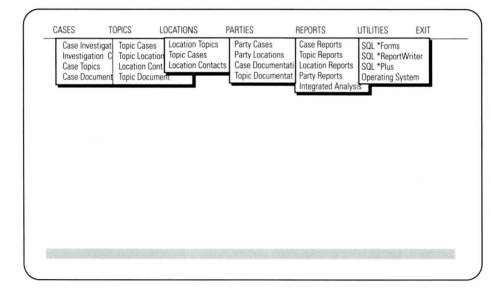

Figure 22.23   Application menus for Analysis Systems.

all for any operators with a lower security level that does not authorize them to carry out maintenance.

These menu options and items are now shown in Figure 22.23. This uses a pull-down menu style. When an option is selected, its pull-down menu appears for selection of menu items under that option. But to illustrate the various menu choices in the Case Analysis Applications in menus, Figure 22.23 shows all menus 'pulled-down'. If any sub-menus are defined below this level, they are shown by a '>' at the right of the item, as we saw earlier in Figure 20.8 with the *Action Print doc* sub-menu items shown in a sub-menu to the right of the *Action* menu.

If the operator has an approved security level, the UTILITIES menu option is visible; otherwise EXIT immediately follows the RE-PORTS option. UTILITIES allows ad-hoc reports to be defined using SQL*Plus or SQL*ReportWriter. On-line applications can be developed with SQL*Forms. Other processing is invoked from the operating system. And PL/SQL integrates the developed systems for pre-defined conditions. Or instead menu conditions are evaluated during operation; PL/SQL can change transition between applications dynamically. The result: we have now defined a menu structure that can be used by operators for data entry, enquiry or data maintenance of cases and associated information. A number of pre-defined reports can be selected and printed. And additional facilities are available for authorized operators.

22.6 | CAPACITY PLANNING AND PERFORMANCE

While application systems can today be designed, tested and evaluated on micros, these systems may require the power and capacity of larger computers to operate under production data and transaction volumes. With data bases and application languages now portable across hardware and software platforms as we have seen with ORACLE, INGRES and other DBMS application development products, the migration of systems to their final environment does not require significant change. But we need to calculate the size of data bases for capacity planning purposes, to ensure that adequate disk, optical or other storage capacity is available. We also need to evaluate whether response times for online systems, or processing times for batch systems, satisfy the time-demands of their users. Performance analysis is therefore also important to decide if sufficient CPU processing power is available.

Of course systems operating on micros, in one software environment, cannot be used as an exact guide to final production performance when operating on minis or mainframes in a different environment. But we can nevertheless subject these micro-based systems to loads that allow us to evaluate the *relative* performance of different transactions or programs against each other. This can help identify potential transaction or program performance problem areas where greatest benefit will be gained from the more detailed performance focus that follows.

22.6.1 Capacity planning

In Section 18.3 we covered physical attribute definition after operational modeling. We defined the data type and size of all attributes, documented in an Application Group Contents Report (see Figure 18.6). At that stage we can calculate the initial data storage volumes for capacity planning purposes, or we can leave calculation until this stage of systems development when the likely hardware and software environment to be used for implementation is more firm.

The number of occurrences of each entity must first be estimated. This becomes the number of data base rows, when the entity is later implemented as a data base table. Where occurrences change only slowly over time, such as with a product data base, an estimate of the average number of occurrences is adequate. But where occurrences are more volatile, such as in orders for products, the minimum and maximum number of occurrences are also needed. When transaction data is held online for enquiry purposes, such as for order enquiries, the total number of transactions in a defined enquiry period is also needed. If these transaction volumes are volatile then the average, minimum and maximum volumes in that period are needed to estimate corresponding data volumes.

With the data type and size of each attribute in an entity, the size of each column in the implemented data base table can be determined. If some columns contain variable-length text, implemented by VARCHAR in DB2 for example, an estimate of average, minimum and maximum number of characters in these columns must be made. The total of all columns in a table then indicates the total size of each data base row. To this is added additional data storage overhead for each row, such as for internally-generated row identifiers, depending on the specific data architecture used by the DBMS product utilized for implementation.

When the data base row size is multiplied by the average, minimum and maximum number of rows, determined as described above, the size of each data base table can then be calculated. This capacity planning is supported by ISM (see Table 17.1). Or a variety of spreadsheets can be used. For example, IE: Expert is able to direct the Entity Report with full attribute details to a file on disk (see Chapter 17). A macro in a spreadsheet program, written to extract each attribute name, data type and size from this report on disk can then be used to populate cells in a spreadsheet. The average, minimum and maximum data volume of each entity, separately entered into the spreadsheet, is used to calculate the size of the relevant data base table. As well as giving the average, minimum and maximum size of each table, changes can be made to estimates of variable-length column sizes, and also of volatile data volumes, for what-if capacity planning.

22.6.2 Performance analysis

After process modeling in Chapter 19, the access paths that procedures take in the data map can be determined. These will later represent data base access paths when the relevant entities are implemented as data base tables. Associations define procedures, implemented as application screens. When these screens are combined into application systems as discussed in this chapter, data base access paths along associations can be defined. These are used for performance analysis of transactions that utilize the application screens or for batch systems that process data in tables.

For example, *one to many* associations indicate Master-Detail application screens: many occurrences of a detail entity exist for each occurrence of a master entity. Given data volumes as calculated above, we can estimate average, minimum and maximum occurrences of detail entities for each master entity. This is an association frequency of occurrence, called the

association frequency. Where data volumes vary, the association frequency also varies: with average, minimum and maximum association frequencies.

Given association frequencies, we can now estimate the number of times that an application system will refer to data across these access paths. These are called **logical references**. Each access by a transaction across an association path, from a master to a detail entity, will eventually be a physical data base access between the related tables when implemented as a physical data base. Or instead, they may represent accesses to data in buffers held in memory.

The following example illustrates the concepts of performance analysis. We saw that the *one to many* association between PERIOD and CASE represents the Case History System in Figure 19.3. This is access path 1, shown on the shaded arrow parallel to the association in Figure 22.24. In each period we are told that there is an average of ten cases. This indicates an association frequency of 1 at PERIOD, and a frequency of 10 at the *many* end of the association at CASE. These are written at the relevant ends of the association as shown in Figure 22.24.

Let us now assume that there is an average of five Case History enquiries in an hour, shown as bold, italic numbers '*1(5)*' on the shaded arrow entering PERIOD. The '*1*' is a single transaction; the bracketed number '*(5)*' is the total number of transactions in the hour. A total of five accesses per hour are made to PERIOD, called the **total references** as shown in the legend of Figure 22.24. For each access to PERIOD, the association frequency indicates that there are 10 logical references to CASE. For five hourly transactions at PERIOD there are thus 50 total references per hour to CASE. This is shown in the figure as '*10(50)*' below the shaded arrow head at CASE.

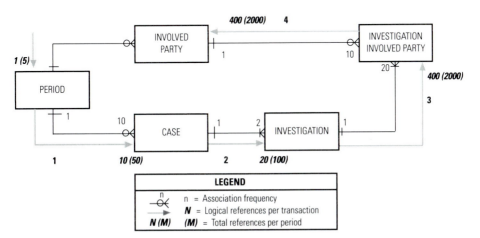

Figure 22.24

The Case Investigations System in Figure 19.5 is now shown by the *one to many* association between CASE and INVESTIGATION. This is path 2 of Figure 22.24, which shows there is an average of two investigations for each case: the association frequency is 2 at INVESTIGATION. Therefore for every 10 references to CASE there are 20 total references to INVESTIGATION. For every 50 total references per hour to CASE there are thus 100 total references per hour to INVESTIGATION.

The Investigation Contact System in Figure 19.7 is next shown in Figure 22.24 by two paths: path 3 between INVESTIGATION and INVESTIGATION INVOLVED PARTY, a *one to many* association with a frequency of 20, and then by path 4. This is the *many to one* association from INVESTIGATION INVOLVED PARTY to INVOLVED PARTY, with an association frequency of 1 at INVOLVED PARTY. For 20 references to INVESTIGATION, there are thus 400 logical references along path 3, and also 400 logical references along path 4. For every 100 total references per hour to CASE there are thus 2000 total references per hour along path 3, and 2000 per hour also along path 4.

These references are all summarized in Table 22.1. We see that the target entity of path 1 is CASE, with 10 logical references and 50 total references. CASE is the source entity for path 2, whose target is INVESTIGATION. The product of the logical references of CASE (10, in path 1), and the association frequency of path 2 (2, in path 2) indicates that 20 logical references are therefore made along path 2. Similarly the product of the total references per hour of CASE (50, in path 1) and the association frequency of path 2 (2, in path 2) calculates the total references per hour along path 2 as 100. By summing each column at the bottom of the table, we also see that 831 logical references are made for a single transaction, with 4155 total references for the five enquiries made in each hour.

Table 22.1 Transaction performance calculations

Access Path	Type of Access	Association Frequency	Logical References	Total References
Entry : PERIOD	R	1	1	5
1. PERIOD : CASE	R	10	10	50
2. CASE : INVESTIGATION	R	2	20	100
3. INVESTIGATION : INVESTIGATION INVOLVED PARTY	R	20	400	2000
4. INVESTIGATION INVOLVED PARTY : INVOLVED PARTY	R	1	400	2000
TRANSACTION TOTALS			831	4155

Given the definition of access paths for a transaction, with association frequency and total transactions in a period, the column values and column totals of Table 22.1 can be calculated by any spreadsheet. This performance analysis, when carried out for all relevant transactions, can be used to identify those transactions that involve the greatest number of logical references. The response-time needs of users also help in identifying response-critical transactions that involve many logical references in their processing. It may be possible to consider alternative access paths for processing some transactions, to reduce the total number of logical references and so improve potential performance.

The calculated total references of 4155 per hour does not represent much data base processing for a mini or mainframe, but it may be significant for a micro. However, rather than five enquiries per hour, if instead the transaction volume was 50 enquiries per second, the data base processing load would be 41,550 total references per second. This may now be a significant workload even for a mini or a mainframe. The data base design may be critical, if each enquiry requires a response within a few seconds. There are many data base design factors that must be considered to optimize performance for these transactions in an online environment, or for program processing performance in a batch environment.

22.6.3 Data base design performance considerations

In Table 22.1 we considered only one transaction operating along an access path against rows of data base tables. But in a production multi-user environment there may be many transactions operating concurrently. Some are enquiries against data, able to operate concurrently without any danger of data base corruption. But other transactions may need to add, update or delete data. There is a potential danger of data corruption with concurrent data base processing in these cases. Of course today's DBMS products use data locking to protect against data corruption from concurrent update processing. For example, concurrent transactions that all need to process the same row in a data base table will be locked automatically so that only one transaction at a time is permitted to access and change the relevant data. However this has a performance impact as discussed next.

You will notice that Table 22.1 shows an additional column, 'Type of Access', for each path. This indicates 'A' (for Add), 'R' (for Read), 'U' (for Update) and 'D' (for Delete). We used an enquiry transaction in our example, so all accesses are shown as 'R' in the figure. There are no performance impacts arising from data locking in this example. In a multi-user environment with high update activity, however, transaction performance can be affected by data locking: only one transaction at a time can update the same data base row. Other transactions must wait until the first transaction has completed its data base update processing before they are also allowed to proceed, so delaying the response time.

Logical and total reference calculations for each transaction provide input for data base design to be used by a DBA. A logical reference may result in physical accesses to indexes and tables stored on disk, or maintained in memory buffers by the DBMS product that is used. The translation of these logical references to physical accesses depends on many factors: the DBMS product and its architecture; indexes defined for access to tables; access methods used by the DBMS for indexes and tables; the size of buffer areas allocated in memory; the performance of disk drives used; the allocated space on disk and the distribution of disk drives across channels; the CPU processing path length for DBMS activity, the speed and power of the CPU itself, and of course other concurrent CPU activity.

These calculations are complex: estimates can only be made based on assumptions in each of these areas. However an analysis of performance as described in this section can help to identify those transactions that contribute most to the data base performance load. Where many concurrent transactions also access the same path, estimates of their cumulative access path load is important for data base design purposes. The allocation of DBMS and machine resources, and the data base design for high-load transactions, can have a greater impact on overall performance than will data base design and tuning for low-load transactions.

22.7 SUMMARY

In this chapter we discussed the progressive implementation of application screens and systems with ORACLE SQL*Forms, using the project plan developed for process modeling in Chapter 19. When designing application systems, we saw that each association in a data map represents a potential application screen; related entities are implemented together as blocks on the same SQL*Forms screen page. Similar design principles also apply to INGRES and other DBMS application development products. We used the subject map to determine access paths through the data map. These access paths helped us to identify potential application systems.

We discussed different design alternatives for application screens, and saw that we can link these application screens into defined application systems: by using triggers to call an application screen block in the same form, or to call an application screen in a different form. These triggers can use PL/SQL to include quite complex procedural logic, as needed. We saw that we can also invoke data entry screens from application screens.

We saw that the interaction of different application screens in application systems can be illustrated by Application Systems Charts. We then used these charts to illustrate that application systems can in turn be linked together as complex application systems. We discussed SQL*Menu, and showed how this product could be used to invoke application screens, data entry screens and application systems.

We concluded the chapter with a discussion of capacity planning and performance analysis. We calculated physical data base sizes, and estimated the relative performance of different transactions by calculating their logical references along access paths. These size and performance results provide invaluable input for data base design and tuning.

References

[1] Codd, E. F. (1990). *The Relational Model for Database Management: Version 2*, Addison-Wesley: Reading, MA.

[2] Date, C. J. (1986). *An Introduction to Database Systems, Fourth Edition*, Addison-Wesley: Reading, MA.

[3] Date, C. J. and White, C. J. (1988). *A Guide to DB2, Second Edition*, Addison-Wesley: Reading, MA.

[4] Date, C. J. (1987). *A Guide to INGRES*, Addison-Wesley: Reading, MA.

CHAPTER 23

Information Engineering in Context

We have now completed the main topics of this book: Part 1 provided an overview; Part 2 introduced Information Engineering concepts; Part 3 discussed strategic planning; Part 4 then showed how strategic plans are used in systems development. This chapter concludes the book by reviewing how each component of Information Engineering is used for strategic systems development. It provides a concise summary of key concepts [1].

23.1 INFORMATION ENGINEERING REVIEW

Competitive pressures, business opportunities and technological change inexorably press in on senior management and information technology staff alike. The computer industry provides some of the most fertile ground in the world for innovation and development. But unless this technology can be harnessed for competitive advantage, organizations can only react to change – rather than control their own destiny. This book has shown how Information Engineering can be used to integrate information technology with strategic planning. It provides a roadmap for navigation through what has often been a fog of too much information and jargon in the computer industry. In this chapter we will first review the Information Engineering methodology. We then conclude by discussing current issues in systems development and strategic planning, describing their relationship with Information Engineering.

23.1.1   The information engineering phases

Figure 23.1 summarizes the phases of Information Engineering, emphasizing two distinct stages: a **technology-independent** stage; and a **technology-dependent** stage. The starting point is strategic business planning. Part 3 described the strategic management planning steps (Chapters 8–12), that are used for strategic business planning in Figure 23.1. Chapters 13–14 used data modeling principles to develop a corporate strategic model. Part 4 next described how data modeling is used in a functional area for strategic, tactical and operational modeling (Chapters 15–18). Chapter 19 discussed process modeling to identify application systems. All of these chapters addressed the *technology-independent* stage of Information Engineering.

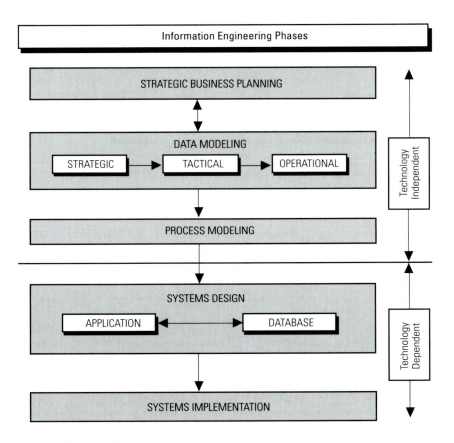

Figure 23.1   The information engineering phases in review.

The *technology-dependent* stage was described in Chapters 20–22, using ORACLE and INGRES as typical relational data base management systems and development tools. This illustrated the systems design of applications and data bases, for systems implementation in different hardware and software environments.

Figure 23.1 shows that strategic business plans are incorporated in technology-independent data and process models, so allowing a clear separation from technology-dependent application and data base designs. We have seen that productivity gains are achieved in strategic planning, systems development and maintenance, resulting also in high quality plans and systems. This is due to a four-level architecture, which allows us to place the business-driven variant of Information Engineering in context.

23.1.2   Four-level information engineering architecture

We now see that Information Engineering addresses four architectural levels, as shown in Figure 23.2. This architecture clearly separates data and process, and enables organizations to build data bases and applications that

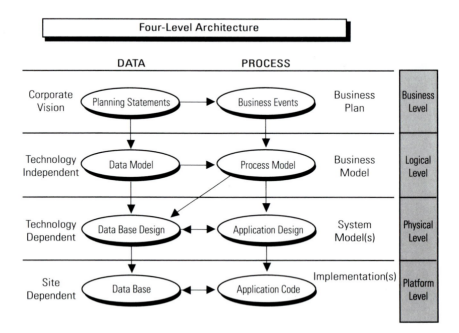

Figure 23.2   The information engineering four-level architecture.

can change rapidly to achieve competitive advantage. Level 1 is the business level which represents the corporate vision as captured in the business plan, and other business information. Level 2 is the logical level, which is technology-independent and represents a precise model of the business. Level 3 is the physical level, which is technology-dependent and represents system models. Level 4 is the platform level, which is site-dependent and represents implementations.

Level 1 – the business level   This reflects the corporate vision in clear, concise strategic planning statements defined at all management levels. Business events are stimuli, either internal or external to the business, which cause it to react in some way. Both these components are written in business language.

Level 2 – the logical level   The business model is one cohesive, comprehensive representation of the business. As described earlier in this book, the data model is developed from strategic planning statements. The process model is developed based on the data model; sharing the sequence of business activities required in response to a business event. The business model is captured in the rich, yet rigorous 'language' of modeling techniques.

Level 3 – the physical level   Together, data and process models provide input to technology-dependent data base designs. Each of these models of a system, normally consisting of data base designs, optimizes a subset of the business model for implementation in a specified environment. Many designs may be required, based on the capabilities and constraints of available technology, to implement any one subset.

Level 4 – the platform level   The data base design is physically implemented as site-dependent data bases. These data bases and the application design are implemented as application code which operates against the data bases. Data bases and applications can then be implemented on specific platforms that utilize the best available hardware, software and communications technologies. Any one design may be implemented in multiple sites, again based on the performance characteristics of the target environment.

This four-level architecture thus isolates changes at the business and logical levels from changes at the physical and platform levels. Because business rules are modeled as data the business can change easily and rapidly. And new hardware, software or communication technologies can also be introduced easily without requiring major redevelopment of systems. The massive systems development projects of the past, based on the traditional systems development methodologies, are replaced by incremental development and rapid delivery of priority systems and data bases as an organization fine-tunes its data, information and knowledge resources for its competitive march into the future.

The components of a data model, linked to the management statements that drive that model, identify redundant data in an organization. This data resource and its derived information resource can be managed for business advantage. Organizations now realize that they must gain control over the information needed to make critical business decisions about their financial, material and people resources to achieve any strategic advantage. Even more valuable is their knowledge resource: this is reflected in the business rules that are captured in the data model and enforced in the process model. Information Engineering enables this knowledge resource to be used for competitive advantage. We will review how this is achieved in the following sections.

23.1.3 The strategic data model

The strategic data model (see Figure 23.3) not only defines the scope of systems development projects; it also represents a picture of the business. Strategic statements provide a textual definition of strategic plans. These provide input for development of the strategic data model: comprising the strategic data map; planning outline; planning statements; model views; data dictionary and associated reports (see Chapter 17). We saw how these are used to design and build systems and data bases based on the plans. We also saw (in Chapter 14) how they are used to design organization structures to implement those plans. The strategic data model is thus the jig-saw picture that allows an organization to identify priority areas to be implemented first. This identification of priorities for implementation ensures that resources are optimally allocated.

The strategic data model is the first view at the logical level, based on input from the business level as discussed earlier in Figure 23.2. The tactical and operational data models, and the process models, that are also built at this logical level then represent the technology-independent business model.

23.1.4 Process modeling

We saw in Chapters 5–6 that process modeling derives process models from data models, based on business events. This is illustrated in Figure 23.4. A business event will result in a business process, that may use other processes. The business process may also respond to many other business events. A

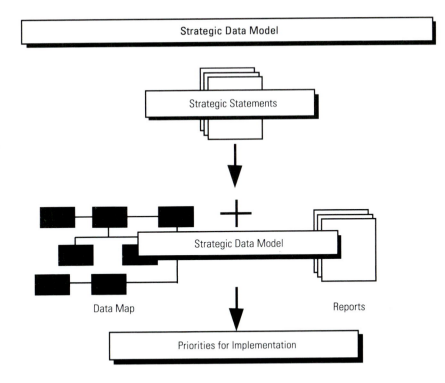

Figure 23.3 The Strategic Data Model allows resources to be optimally allocated to high priority areas, for both organizational planning and for systems development.

business process may interface with many users, who must use many business processes.

Figure 23.4 shows that a business process may use many data access processes: these are the generic procedures discussed in Chapters 5–6 and used in Chapters 21–22. A data access process will be used by many other business processes, and may use other data access processes. A data access process accesses data model components: these are entities, associations and attributes. These data model components will result in many data access processes. This separation of data access processes from the business processes that invoke them and control user interfaces ensure reusability of processes. Redundancy in process logic is eliminated in the process model just as redundancy in data is eliminated in the data model. By increasing the quality of the business model in this way, its usability for the organization is further enhanced.

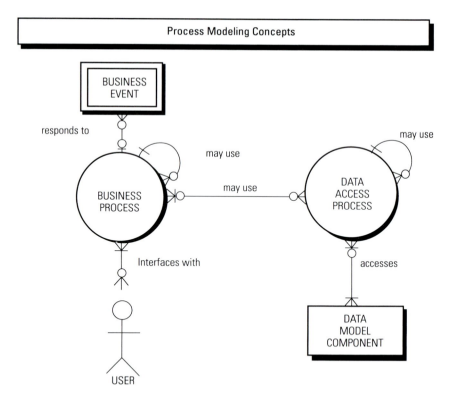

Figure 23.4 Process models, responding to business events, interface with users. They use data access processes derived from data model components.

23.1.5   The business model

The business model is based on the business plans, business rules, strategic and tactical statements, and business events of the project area (see Figure 23.5). Through tactical and operational modeling, we saw that the strategic model expands to greater data detail. Process modeling uses the data models, business rules and business events to derive processes: these data and process models thus represent the business model.

Because the business model exists at the logical level, it can be used to develop new systems or evaluate commercially available packages. An organization can thus analyze and plan migration from, or integration with, its current systems: both automated and manual (see Figure 23.5). It can also integrate new systems with packages for added functionality. Thus new systems, needed for tomorrow, can be fine-tuned to work also with the current systems and packages needed for today. Development resources

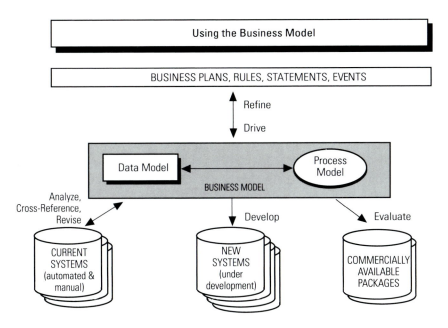

Figure 23.5   Using the Business Model in Systems Development.

can be concentrated on priority new systems, integrating them with current systems or packages where required. This allows an organization to change its systems rapidly for competitive advantage, as discussed in the next section.

23.2 | SYSTEMS DEVELOPMENT ISSUES

We have seen throughout this book how Information Engineering leads to gains in the productivity and quality of systems development; gains that are often dramatic. To conclude this chapter, we will first discuss some of the significant issues relating to systems development in the 90s:

- Data administration and IRM
- Productivity and system quality
- Change management and evolution
- Migrating to alternative architectures
- Rule modeling to allow rapid business change

- Reverse engineering and re-engineering
- Object-oriented development

23.2.1 Data administration and IRM

Information Engineering is a powerful vehicle to establish the data admin-istration and information resource management (IRM) functions of an organization. We saw that data administration is a function that establishes standards, stewardship and control of the information in an organization. Information resource management has a similar purpose to data admin-istration, but also includes the planning, organizing and control of both technology-independent and technology-dependent data and process models and designs, as well as the configurations of hardware and software, and training of the people required to support the information systems of the organization. Establishing an information resource management function invariably leads to implementation of an information encyclopaedia to manage the meta-data involved. This encyclopaedia is the most important development issue affecting organizations today. Software is becoming available to manage this encyclopaedia: examples include IBM's Reposi-tory Manager and AD/Cycle, and DEC's Cohesion. We have seen in this book that the definition of the encyclopaedia is achieved by Information Engineering.

23.2.2 Productivity and system quality

Much has been written in recent years regarding quality. Increased produc-tivity with poor quality will not achieve the desired result: productivity and quality must both improve together. Because Information Engineering captures business requirements before creating solutions, quality is assured at every step of the process. The rigour in the techniques and phases of the methodology ensure that this initial quality is carried through to implementation. Use of the four-level Information Engineering architecture for change management (see Figure 23.2) then ensures that quality is maintained over time. Although it certainly costs an organization precious resources to establish and maintain the IRM function described earlier, the increase in the productivity of systems development using Information Engineering more than compensates this investment.

23.2.3 Change management and evolution

The four-level architecture used by Information Engineering provides a mechanism to manage change in an organization: both impact analysis and 'what-if' planning can be carried out. Establishing and maintaining the architecture as part of the IRM function ensures that change can be managed in a controlled fashion. Traditional methodologies had maintenance as a separate phase. Now, however, we recognize that maintenance is a required response to some change in the business. Changes in technology or systems requirements require modifications to systems designs and implemented systems. The addition, deletion or revision of a business rule requires evaluation from a broader perspective of the data and process models: this may cascade to modifications in many systems. But we now see that by separating the technology-independent aspects of change management from technology-dependent implementations, maintenance is an evolutionary process that allows an organization to control its own destiny.

23.2.4   Migrating to alternative architectures

Once technology-independent data and process models have been developed for a functional area, they provide the basis for systems design and implementation. In some cases the target environment for implementation of a particular functional area may have already been specified. In many situations, however, the data and process models become the baseline to evaluate alternative technologies. This allows an organization to select the optimum configuration of hardware and software, based on the budget they have available, to meet their needs. It may be that more than one target environment will be required to satisfy the business needs depicted by the data and process models. Rather than merely interfacing these different environments, however, they can be fully *integrated*: so taking advantage of the key features of each environment.

23.2.5   Rule modeling to allow rapid business change

We have glimpsed some of the power of modeling business rules as data. There are still more powerful extensions of rule modeling that are beyond the scope of this book. These allow business experts to capture details precisely as data, rather than in process logic: so permitting rapid business change for strategic advantage. By modeling the rules that govern the business logic that controls capture of business facts, two clear advantages are realized. First of all, rule modeling refines the data model so ensuring that business data is precisely modeled. Secondly, a change in the business rules can be immediately accommodated when it occurs, with a fraction of the maintenance impact required by the traditional methods. By implementing the rules as data, business users quickly and easily implement business changes by changing the data rules; so avoiding the time-delay and the expense of program modifications to systems.

23.2.6 Reverse engineering and re-engineering

The top-down approach to building data and process models described in this book is sometimes also referred to as **forward engineering**. It yields high quality results in a short period of time, while also ensuring user understanding and buy-in of the end result. However it is not always an achievable starting point. For organizations with current systems that are not well-documented, a bottom-up approach may be necessary: called **reverse engineering**. Information Engineering uses business normalization and reverse engineering principles to extract data base designs from data structures and program code. These can be further abstracted to the level of technology-independent data and process models. Essentially, reverse engineering also follows the four-level architecture (see Figure 23.2), but in a backwards sequence. This technique can be further combined with systems design and used to build systems for different technology-dependent platforms.

Migrating from one technology to another without changing business requirements is termed **re-engineering**. This is feasible for those organizations that are not subject to business change because of regulatory or other constraints. But it is not recommended where business plans or rules are changing, as it invariably takes more time than the top-down, forward engineering approach. Both approaches, however, still lead to the development of integrated data bases and easily maintained systems through object-oriented development.

23.2.7 Object-oriented development

The emergence of object-oriented analysis, design and programming has lead to a review of the traditional information systems development methodologies. The distinct sequencing of data, then process, inherent in the business-driven variant of Information Engineering ensures that objects important to the business are identified, defined well, and linked to the strategic management statements that govern their existence. We saw that the characteristics of object-oriented systems and data bases (including abstraction, inheritance, identity and encapsulation) are fundamental characteristics of Information Engineering. We saw that the object-oriented approach and Information Engineering have both conceptually arrived at the same point, but from two different directions. The Information Engineering methodology evolved from a business-driven perspective, while the object-oriented approach evolved from increasingly sophisticated attempts to structure systems development.

This means that object-oriented data base management systems and programming languages are particularly well suited to implement the data and process models developed during the technology-independent stage of Information Engineering. But we also saw the ease of implementation in a relational environment; using Information Engineering, many of these productivity and quality gains can also be realized in a non-relational environment. In an object-oriented environment, design and implementation can potentially be even easier than in these relational and non-relational environments.

Information Engineering thus enables an organization to maximize the advantages gained from emergent technologies. The benefits realized range from new insights into the strategic business vision of the organization, to detailed planning and optimization of new technologies. Both short- and long-term benefits are attained. Once established, the returns from implementing Information Engineering ensure competitive advantage and long-term success for the organization.

23.3 STRATEGIC PLANNING ISSUES

We conclude by discussing a number of issues relating to strategic planning and organizational design:

- Strategic planning and refinement
- Information-based organizations
- Knowledge-based organizations
- Future organization structures

23.3.1 Strategic planning and refinement

We saw the development and refinement of strategic business plans, carried out at the corporate, business unit and functional area levels, in Chapters 8–12. In Chapters 13–14 we discussed development of a strategic model for a typical organization, based on those plans. The strategic, tactical and operational data models, and process models, also provide immediate feedback to management for refinement of the plans. They identify information-based and knowledge-based restructuring opportunities.

23.3.2 Information-based organizations

An organization's information resource is vital. The definition and management of this resource is essential for organizations to be able to compete in the turbulent years ahead, as was emphasized by Drucker in Chapter 14 [2]:

> *'We are entering a period of change: a shift from command-and-control organizations to information based organizations of knowledge specialists.'* He commented that: *'Businesses, especially large ones, will have little choice but to become information-based . . . But as soon as a company takes the first tentative steps from data to information, its decision processes, management structure and work . . . begin to be transformed.'*

Applegate, Cash and Mills [3] indicated that top management will have centralized control with decentralized decision-making in such information-based organizations: by using Information Technology to downsize and restructure the organization so that computer systems provide the communication, coordination and control functions that were previously performed by middle managers. They emphasized that sophisticated expert systems and knowledge bases will help capture decision-making processes, so moving the business eventually to a knowledge-based organization.

23.3.3 Knowledge-based organizations

Drucker continued this theme by saying that: *'To remain competitive – maybe even to survive – businesses will have to convert themselves into organizations of knowledge specialists.'* We saw that Information Engineering is used to capture an organization's knowledge resource in data models and process models, implemented as information systems and data bases, or as expert systems and knowledge bases: so making this knowledge available to all who are authorized to access it. Drucker went on to say:

> *'The typical large business 20 years hence will have fewer than half the levels of management of its counterpart today, and no more than a third the managers. It is more likely to resemble the hospital, the university, the symphony orchestra. For like them, the typical business will be knowledge-based.'*

Such organizations, to utilize their information and knowledge resources more effectively and to operate with fewer management levels, will be structured differently than organizations today.

23.3.4   Future organization structures

We saw in Chapter 14 that the bureaucratic, divisional and coordinated organization structures are not very adaptable. Information systems and procedures, both automated and manual, developed to support organizations like these do not readily accommodate change. The participative or matrix structure, in contrast, is designed for change. An organization's existing systems, if developed using traditional methods, often have difficulty surviving these organizational changes: they may need to be redeveloped. Information systems developed from data and process models using methods in this book, however, enable organizations to navigate changes easier. But Drucker points to a future even beyond these structures, when he says: *'The organization will go beyond the matrix, and may indeed be quite different from it.'* For we have no doubt that opportunities open to organizations that move to an information-based and knowledge-based environment will suggest even more effective organization structures than we can imagine today.

23.4 | THE CRITERIA FOR SUCCESS

We have focused our attention on strategic systems development, discussing systems development and strategic planning issues; showing how the methods presented in this book address those issues. But, although rigorous, these methods cannot guarantee project success. Eventual success in strategic planning and systems development depends on two criteria that are fundamental to any business project, not only strategic systems development projects. Indeed, without meeting the first criterion any project will certainly fail. But satisfying this criterion, only, does not guarantee success: to succeed the second criterion is also essential. These criteria are:

- Executive sponsorship and commitment
- Project management

23.4.1   Executive sponsorship and commitment

A strategic systems development project, whether for strategic planning, or for systems development, or both, requires a significant commitment of people and time. The allocation of these and other resources by an organization over the duration of a project is essential. Apart from the full-time participation of a core project team of two or three business experts and an experienced project manager in the technology-independent stage, others participate only when needed according to the project plan. Strong management support is required to allocate these resources initially, and to ensure that they continue to be available throughout the project. People who are needed for a strategic systems development project are the most experienced individuals in an organization; these people are almost always difficult to release from their present commitments (which confirms their experience). But the directions to be taken in the future should be based on an organization's most experienced people: who are not readily available as they are also in demand elsewhere. The project cannot use those who may be readily available because of their lack of experience.

A project may likely also identify changes that are required. People resist change. Strong management support is thus needed to ensure required changes are introduced. And political barriers may also be encountered in these requests for resources and in the need for change. Strong management support is absolutely vital here: internal politics often represent the most dangerous threat to project success. Without this executive sponsorship and commitment, therefore, a project is certain to fail: the only unknown is when, and how spectacular will be the eventual disaster. The only decision that can be taken, when this sponsorship is missing, is not to start! This criterion thus becomes the overriding factor in deciding where to begin a project in an organization: choose a project area where this management support is assured.

The management support provided through this executive sponsorship and commitment must be active, not passive. This is demonstrated by the personal endorsement of the manager through introductory speeches and letters to all full-time and part-time project staff, and by attendance at strategic review sessions. To be effective, the executive sponsor must have the responsibility and authority to allocate resources to the project and ensure that they stay allocated, and to 'clear the calendars' for experienced staff so that they can participate.

But executive sponsorship and commitment are not sufficient to ensure success: when this criterion has been satisfied, the second criterion then becomes important.

23.4.2 Project management

With even the most committed level of management support, a project will not succeed if it is not properly managed. We have seen throughout this book how project plans can be derived from a data model: manually using entity dependency principles (see Chapter 3), or by automated data model analysis (see Chapter 17). Because a derived project plan reflects all data model changes, it provides up-to-date guidance for project management. This is the second criterion for success. It ensures that executive sponsorship and commitment is well-placed: in the allocation of people and resources; and in the management support that is needed to overcome political obstacles as they arise. Together, these two criteria establish a strong environment for success.

23.5 CONCLUDING REMARKS

Information Engineering has evolved dramatically since its original development in the 70s, and its refinement during the 80s. It is now an integrated set of techniques which extend from strategic planning at the highest management levels to the analysis, design and implementation of information systems, decision support systems and executive information systems which implement the vision of management. The data bases and systems that are developed address the needs of managers and their staff more precisely than those built by traditional methodologies. With its use now by thousands of organizations and by people in the management and user communities, and also by data processing staff, Information Engineering will continue to evolve in the 1990s and into the 21st century.

References

[1] The figures in this chapter are based on visuals that were kindly provided by Information Engineering Systems Corporation in Alexandria, VA. These figures summarize the main concepts introduced earlier in the book. Their permission to use the figures, as well as the assistance of Tim Rinaman of IESC, are acknowledged with thanks.

[2] Drucker, P. (1988). *The Coming of the New Organization.* Harvard Business Review, Boston, MA (Jan–Feb).

[3] Applegate, L., Cash, J. and Mills, D. (1988). *Information Technology and Tomorrow's Manager.* Harvard Business Review, Boston, MA (Nov–Dec).

APPENDICES

APPENDIX 1

SQL Overview

SQL (Structured Query Language) is a fourth generation language which has been adopted as a standard 4GL by the American National Standards Institute (ANSI) [1]. A tutorial approach has been used in this Appendix. This is not intended to be a complete presentation of the language: it is sufficient only to provide an overview of SQL. Refer to the references for more detail [2, 3, 4, 5].

A1.1 | INTRODUCTION TO SQL

SQL was developed in the 1970s by IBM as a non-procedural fourth generation language (4GL) for use with relational Data Base Management Systems (DBMS). It was adopted in October 1986 by the American National Standards Institute (ANSI) as a standard language for relational DBMS products. It was first supported on a commercial basis by Oracle Corporation in 1979 initially on DEC minis, and then on a variety of mainframes, minis and micros. It was supported by INGRES in 1981, and by IBM in 1982 with SQL/DS, and in 1984 with IBM's DB2 relational DBMS.

The basic introduction to SQL in this Appendix uses part of an operational model. This relates to a hypothetical company, XYZ Corporation. Initial development of the XYZ strategic model was discussed in Chapters 13 and 14. This was refined to operational detail, and part is reproduced as figures and tables in this appendix. One area of this operational model will be used: the Customer Service functional area. This includes two application systems: the Product History System and the Customer Product

Application Systems Report for Clusters 1 and 2

Cluster	Application System	Functional Area
1. (1) PRODUCT TYPE		
(2) PRODUCT		
(3) PRODUCT HISTORY	Product History System	Customer Service
2. (1) CUSTOMER TYPE		
(2) CUSTOMER		
(1) PRODUCT TYPE		
(2) PRODUCT	Customer Product	Customer Service
(3) CUSTOMER PRODUCT REQUEST	Request System	

Figure A1.1 Application systems report.

Request System, represented in the Application Systems Report in Figure A1.1.

The implementation phase data map for these systems is reproduced for reference as part of Figure A1.2. Each entity in this map is documented in entity list form following Figure A1.2. An entity represents an SQL table. This table is made up of SQL columns, where each attribute in the entity defines a separate column of the table. Each SQL row of the table is an occurrence of the entity. For example, the entity CUSTOMER TYPE in Figure A1.2 represents a type entity, the Customer Type table: this indicates three types of customers of interest to XYZ Corporation as shown in Table A1.1.

The primary key of CUSTOMER TYPE is *customer type id#*. This is one of the columns of the table, labelled by the attribute name. The rows in

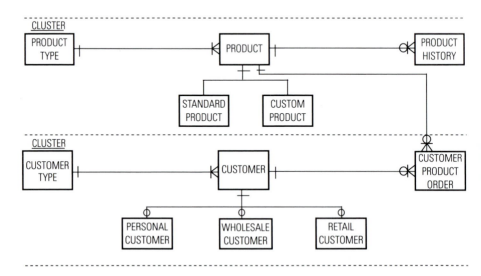

Figure A1.2 Implementation phase data map for systems of the Customer Service functional area.

CUSTOMER TYPE	(customer type id#, customer type description)
CUSTOMER	(customer number#, [customer name], customer address, customer type id)
RETAIL CUSTOMER	(customer number#, period number#, {retail customer total revenue}, {retail customer gross profit})
WHOLESALE CUSTOMER	(customer number#, period number#, {wholesale customer total revenue})
PERSONAL CUSTOMER	(customer number#, period number#, {personal customer total revenue})
PRODUCT TYPE	(product type id#, product type description)
PRODUCT	(product number#, [product name], product type id)
STANDARD PRODUCT	(product number#, period number#, {standard product total revenue}, {standard product total units}, standard product price, standard product lead time)
CUSTOM PRODUCT	(product number#, period number#, {custom product total revenue}, {custom product total units}, custom product price, custom product lead time)
PRODUCT HISTORY	(product number#, period number#, product type id#, {product total revenue}, {product total units})
CUSTOMER PRODUCT REQUEST	(customer number#, product number#, request number#, customer product date requested, customer product time requested, customer product date provided, customer product time provided)

Table A1.1   Representation of the entity
CUSTOMER TYPE

Customer Type Id	Customer Type Description
1	Retail Customer
2	Wholesale Customer
3	Personal Customer

Table A1.1 are sequenced in ascending order based on *customer type id#*. Each *customer type id#* exists only once: it is a unique key. The attribute *customer type description* represents the second column of the table, again labelled according to the attribute name. The relevant customer type description for each unique *customer type id#* is defined by the table. (The '#' suffix for each key has been excluded in the key columns shown in Table A1.1 and the following tables.)

Let us look at the entity CUSTOMER. This is a typed secondary entity, represented by Table A1.2. Again, each of the attributes of the entity is used as the label of the column: that is, the column heading. The table is organized in ascending sequence based on the primary key *customer number#*.

Table A1.2 Customer table, based on the entity CUSTOMER

Customer Number	Customer Name	Customer Address	Customer Type Id
104	First XYZ Bank	318 Wayward Ave, Lower Falls	1
105	XYZ Corporation	133 Fork Ct, Wester Walk	1
106	BBX Corporation	3361 Alwyn Cr, Middleton	2
107	Fordam, Ken	203 Elmsford Ave, South Park	3
108	Wexlo Ltd	161 Koolonga Ave, Calder	2
109	Walls, Janet	402 Talwood Rd, Wexby	3

Although Figure A1.2 indicates that there are several 4BNF Customer secondary entities, we will not include tables for these entities in this overview.

Returning to the example, PRODUCT TYPE is another type entity represented by Table A1.3. The primary key is *product type id#*, with *product type description* as the other column.

Table A1.3 Product type table, based on PRODUCT TYPE

Product Type Id	Product Type Description
31	Standard Product
32	Custom Product

XYZ Corporation offers a number of different products, within each of these product types. Table A1.4 represents the principal entity PRODUCT. Each attribute of PRODUCT is a column heading, indicating the name of the product and the relevant product type to which it belongs. We will ignore 4BNF PRODUCT entities in Figure A1.2 in this overview.

The final table we are interested in represents the entity PRODUCT HISTORY. This is an intersecting entity (see Table A1.5) sequenced on *product number#* and *period number#*. *Product number#* is not unique: only the compound key is unique – *product number#* and *period number#*.

Table A1.4 The product table, based on PRODUCT

Product Number	Product Name	Product Type Id
211	A–Lo	31
212	Wender	31
213	Wesley	31
311	Wender–S1	32
312	Wender–S2	32
313	Wender–S3	32
314	Wender–S4	32
315	Wender–S5	32
316	Wender–S6	32
411	Wesley–S1	32
412	Wesley–S2	32
413	Wesley–S3	32
414	Wesley–S4	32

Table A1.5 The product history table

Product Number	Period Number	Product Type Id	Product Total Revenue	Product Total Units
211	1	31	503,000.00	3,125
211	2	31	551,000.00	3,200
211	3	31	503,000.00	3,550
212	1	31	650,000.00	5,110
212	2	31	580,000.00	4,900
212	3	31	720,000.00	5,500
213	1	31	3,200,000.00	24,000
213	2	31	4,350,000.00	33,000
213	3	31	5,650,000.00	44,550
311	1	32	0.00	0
311	2	32	0.00	0
311	3	32	0.00	0
312	1	32	325,000.00	2,500
312	2	32	0.00	0
312	3	32	650,000.00	5,500
411	1	32	280,000.00	15,500
411	2	32	350,000.00	19,500
411	3	32	390,000.00	21,000
412	1	32	354,000.00	15,600
412	2	32	465,000.00	23,000
412	3	32	315,000.00	12,500
413	1	32	230,000.00	11,000

(cont'd)

Table A1.5 (Cont'd) The product history table

Product Number	Period Number	Product Type Id	Product Total Revenue	Product Total Units
413	2	32	380,000.00	26,000
413	3	32	430,000.00	29,000
414	1	32	24,500.00	1,050
414	2	32	212,000.00	10,850
414	3	32	128,000.00	6,100

We will use the tables in Tables A1.1–A1.5 to discuss some of the facilities offered by SQL. We will introduce the language progressively, starting first with simple commands for queries and for table and index definition. We will then cover more detailed queries. Following this, we will introduce commands which change data in SQL tables.

A1.2 THE SELECT COMMAND

The SELECT command is used by SQL to retrieve data from a table. This is used to query the data held in a table for enquiry or reporting purposes, or for later processing or analysis. The SELECT command is made up of two parts – SELECT followed by an SQL FROM clause:

SELECT data [by naming a relevant attribute (or attributes) – that is, column(s)].

FROM table ; [by naming a relevant entity (or entities) – that is, table(s)].

Example Conventions: An SQL command and associated details can be entered either in capitals or lower case. Each command is terminated by a semicolon (;) as illustrated above. We will use the following documentation conventions for examples in this Appendix.

- Each required SQL word is printed in CAPITALS in a bold typeface: shown above with **SELECT** and **FROM**. This must be entered exactly as spelled (but can be entered either in upper or lower case).

- Table names entered by the user are shown in CAPITALS and take the name of the relevant entity. They are printed in a plain typeface (not bold). They can however be entered either in upper case or lower case. Two or more words in an entity name are combined into one word by inserting an underscore character (_) between each word (such as CUSTOMER_TYPE).

- Column names entered by the user are shown in *lower case* and take the name of the relevant attribute. They are printed in a plain typeface (not bold). They can however be entered either in upper case or lower case. Two or more words in an attribute name are combined as one word by inserting an underscore character (_) between each word (such as *customer_type_id*).

- Each SQL command can be entered on one or several lines, until terminated by a semicolon (;).

For example, we can use the SELECT command to extract data from Table A1.2, the CUSTOMER table. Examples in this Appendix display column headings on two lines (as for Customer Number below). The column size in the defined table is the column width: the column name is truncated to this width if it is longer. A displayed result may extend over more than one line. We will display all columns (attributes) as follows:

User Input:

SELECT   customer_number, customer_name, customer_address, customer_type_id

FROM   CUSTOMER;

SQL Output:

Customer Number	Customer Name	Customer Address	Customer Type Id
104	First XYZ Bank	318 Wayward Ave, Lower Falls	1
105	XYZ Corporation	133 Fork Ct, Wester Walk	1
106	BBX Corporation	3361 Alwyn Cr, Middleton	2
107	Fordam, Ken	203 Elmsford Ave, South Park	3
108	Wexlo Ltd	161 Koolonga Ave, Calder	2
109	Walls, Janet	402 Talwood Rd, Wexby	3

Instead of explicitly naming every column to be displayed, we can refer to all columns implicitly by following the word SELECT by an SQL asterisk (*) in place of the column names. For example:

User Input:

SELECT   *

FROM   CUSTOMER_TYPE;

SQL Output:

Customer Type Id	Customer Type Description
1	Retail Customer
2	Wholesale Customer
3	Personal Customer

A1.3 | DEFINING SQL TABLES

Each table is explicitly defined by the CREATE TABLE command. After definition of a table in an SQL data base, it can be used to store temporary (or permanent) results of processing carried out against other tables. Tables are created as described in the next section.

A1.3.1   The CREATE TABLE command

The table called RESULT (see the following table) may be defined with three columns: called respectively *result number*, *result description* and *total value*. The first column is an INTEGER number. The second column is text of a maximum number of characters, defined as CHAR. The third column is a decimal number defined as FLOAT.

Note that DB2 SQL and ORACLE SQL use different column type definitions. FLOAT is referred to by ORACLE as NUMBER (p,q) and by DB2 as DECIMAL (p,q). For example, in entity list notation RESULT appears as:

RESULT   (result number#, result_description, total_value)

Result Number	Result Description	Total Value
INTEGER	CHAR (characters)	FLOAT

This table is defined explicitly by the CREATE TABLE command by first naming the table and then all columns enclosed in left and right brackets. Note that DB2 and SQL/DS support SQL table names to a maximum of only 18 characters; ORACLE supports 29 characters. Each table name must be a **unique** name. References to DB2 in the following discussion include SQL/DS.

Each column name is defined, followed by the physical format for implementation as INTEGER, CHAR or FLOAT. INTEGER and SMALLINT are supported by DB2 and ORACLE. FLOAT is supported by DB2 and ORACLE; DECIMAL (p,q) is also used with ORACLE. VARCHAR (n) is used with both DB2 and ORACLE for strings containing greater than 0 and less than 16K bytes (where n is the maximum number of characters in the string). ORACLE also supports CHAR (n). For example:

User Input:

```
CREATE TABLE   RESULT   ( result_number     INTEGER,
                          result_name       CHAR (10),
                          total_value       FLOAT );
```

SQL Output:

Table created.

If a column cannot be empty (for example, a mandatory attribute), it is defined as NOT NULL. Otherwise an optional attribute can be defined as NULL: if empty it will not take up any space. If omitted, NULL is assumed. For example, the PRODUCT_TYPE table (see Table A1.3) can be created by:

User Input:

CREATE TABLE	PRODUCT_TYPE	
	(product_type_id	**INTEGER NOT NULL**,
	product_type_description	**CHAR** (20) **NOT NULL**);

SQL Output:

Table created.

A1.3.2   The ALTER TABLE command

Once created, a table can be changed to add additional columns (attributes) following previously defined columns, by the ALTER TABLE command as shown below. This example adds another column: *result_status* to the RESULT table.

User Input:

ALTER TABLE	RESULT
ADD	result_status INTEGER;

SQL Output:

Table altered.

A1.3.3   The CREATE INDEX command

SQL allows an index to be defined on any one, or several, column(s) of a table. This index is automatically used by SQL during execution to optimize performance. An index should be defined for each of the primary keys defined in an entity, when that entity is specified for installation using SQL/DS, DB2 or ORACLE, and for secondary keys and foreign keys (if required). If additional indexes are needed, they can be explicitly defined as indicated by the CREATE INDEX command described here.

If duplicate values cannot exist in a column (such as for a primary key), the index defined on that column is specified as UNIQUE. Several columns can be included as part of the index and are specified in sequence of the major sort column first, followed by successive minor sort columns. Each column in the index is defined as either ascending (ASC) or descending (DESC) sequence in the SQL ORDER BY clause (see shortly). If neither ASC or DESC is specified, SQL assumes ASC.

For example, to create the index (called RESULT_NAME) on unique ascending *result_name* (major) by descending *result_status* (minor) values of the RESULT table (see SQL ALTER TABLE command above which added the *result_status* column to the RESULT table), the following command would be used:

User Input:

CREATE UNIQUE INDEX RESULT_NAME

ON RESULT (result_name, result_status DESC);

SQL Output:

Index created.

A1.3.4 The INSERT command

A table, defined explicitly by the CREATE TABLE command above, must contain data before it can be used for selection or other processing. Data is loaded into a table by the INSERT command. For example, to load data into the RESULT table created above, the following INSERT statements can be used to add three rows of the table.

User Input:

INSERT INTO RESULT **VALUES** (1,'Result 1', 10.0, 3);

INSERT INTO RESULT **VALUES** (2,'Result 2', 50.0, 1);

INSERT INTO RESULT **VALUES** (3,'Result 3', 80.0, 2);

SQL Output:

3 records created.

We will later find that rows can be added to a table based on extraction or calculation from rows in the same (or other) tables by using the SELECT command in conjunction with the INSERT command. This is discussed in *A1.7 Modifying SQL Tables* later in this Appendix.

A1.3.5 DROP TABLE and DROP INDEX commands

Once a table and indexes on that table have been created, it is available for processing until it is no longer required. At that time a table or an index can be deleted by the DROP TABLE and DROP INDEX commands as shown below:

User Input:

> **DROP TABLE**   RESULT;
>
> **DROP INDEX**   RESULT_NAME;

SQL Output:

> Table dropped.
> Index dropped.

A1.4 ADDITIONAL SELECT COMMAND OPTIONS

We will now cover additional options associated with the SELECT command. These allow us to select specific columns from a table, to select only specific rows according to a condition which is satisfied, or to combine several, nested SELECT commands.

A1.4.1 Selecting specific columns from a table

We may want to select only some columns of a table. This is achieved by explicitly naming in the SELECT command only those columns required, in the same order in which they are to appear in the final displayed output report. For example, only the *customer number* and *customer name* (in that order) from the CUSTOMER table (see Table A1.4) are requested by the SELECT command in the next example.

User Input:

> **SELECT**   customer_number, customer_name
>
> **FROM**   CUSTOMER;

SQL Output:

Customer Number	Customer Name
104	First XYZ Bank
105	XYZ Corporation
106	BBX Corporation
107	Fordam, Ken
108	Wexlo Ltd
109	Walls, Janet

A1.4.2 Selecting specific rows with WHERE clause

The selection of particular rows from a table is achieved by the WHERE clause of the SELECT command, which follows the FROM clause. Additionally we can select only those columns to be displayed that we are interested in, as above. For example, only the *product number*, *period number*, *product total revenue* and *product total units* (in that order) from the PRODUCT_HISTORY table (see Table A1.5) are provided by the following SELECT command. The WHERE clause includes only those rows that satisfy the specified condition (that is, *product number* = 212 below).

User Input:

SELECT	product_number, period_number, product_total_revenue, product_total_units
FROM	PRODUCT_HISTORY
WHERE	product_number = 212;

SQL Output:

Product Number	Period Number	Product Total Revenue	Product Total Units
212	1	650,000.00	5,110
212	2	580,000.00	4,900
212	3	720,000.00	5,500

A1.4.3 Multiple WHERE clause search conditions

More than one search condition can be included in the WHERE clause so that only those rows which satisfy the specified conditions are selected. Each search condition is combined with the other relevant conditions by connector words, such as: AND, OR, NOT. (Other connectors are described shortly.) By combining different conditions in the same WHERE clause with these connectors, a large variety of selection conditions can be specified. A condition is specified in the form:

column_name   (operator)   value

The operators can be: = (equal); > (greater than); < (less than); >= (greater than or equal); <= (less than or equal). The negative condition is specified by preceding each of these with a logical not operator ($\neg$), such as: $\neg$ = (not equal); $\neg$ > (not greater than – which is less than or equal); $\neg$ < (not less than – which is greater than or equal). This is illustrated by the following example using the PRODUCT_HISTORY table (see Table A1.5).

User Input:

SELECT	product_number, period_number, product_total_revenue, product_total_units
FROM	PRODUCT_HISTORY
WHERE	(product_number = 212
AND	product_total_units > 5000)
OR	product_number = 411;

SQL Output:

Product Number	Period Number	Product Total Revenue	Product Total Units
212	1	650,000.00	5,110
212	3	720,000.00	5,500
411	1	280,000.00	15,500
411	2	350,000.00	19,500
411	3	390,000.00	21,000

This command selects only those rows where the (product number is 212 AND the product total units column is greater than 5000) OR where the product number is 411.

A1.4.4   Selecting a list using the IN operator

Several values used for selection can be specified in a list. This is achieved by means of the IN operator, shown next based on the PRODUCT_HISTORY table (Table A1.5).

User Input:

SELECT	product_number, period_number, product_total_revenue
FROM	PRODUCT_HISTORY
WHERE	product_number **IN** (211, 213, 411);

SQL Output:

Product Number	Period Number	Product Total Revenue
211	1	503,000.00
211	2	551,000.00
211	3	503,000.00
213	1	3,200,000.00
213	2	4,350,000.00
213	3	5,650,000.00
411	1	280,000.00
411	2	350,000.00
411	3	390,000.00

The negative of the IN operator can also be used, as in the example:

WHERE	product_number **NOT IN** (311, 312);

A1.4.5 Selecting in a range using BETWEEN operator

Several values in a range can be specified for selection. This uses the BETWEEN operator, shown following for the PRODUCT_HISTORY table (see Table A1.5).

User Input:

SELECT	product_number, period_number, product_total_units
FROM	PRODUCT_HISTORY
WHERE	product_total units **BETWEEN** 15000 **AND** 25000;

SQL Output:

Product Number	Period Number	Product Total Units
213	1	24,000
411	1	15,500
411	2	19,500

Product Number	Period Number	Product Total Units
411	3	21,000
412	1	15,600
412	2	23,000

The negative of the BETWEEN operator can also be used, as in the example:

WHERE product_total_units **NOT BETWEEN** 10000 **AND** 20000;

A1.4.6 Selecting by character matching using LIKE

Rows can be selected based on the presence of a defined character string in each value of a specified column name. This is achieved by the LIKE operator, as shown in the following example based on the CUSTOMER table (see Table A1.2).

User Input:

SELECT customer_number, customer_name, customer_address

FROM CUSTOMER

WHERE customer_name **LIKE** ('%XYZ%')

OR customer_address **LIKE** ('_ _ _ _ Elm%');

SQL Output:

Customer Number	Customer Name	Customer Address
104	First XYZ Bank	318 Wayward Ave, Lower Falls
105	XYZ Corporation	133 Fork Ct, Wester Walk
107	Fordam, Ken	203 Elmsford Ave, South Park

The % wild card in the character string indicates that zero or any number of characters which precede (or follow, according to the example) the specified character string are to be ignored. Thus customers 104 and 105 are both selected. On the other hand, each underscore (_) included represents one character position to be ignored. Hence a customer with any four characters, numbers or spaces at the beginning of the customer address, 'Elm' as the next three characters and any characters following, would be selected. Only customer 107 satisfies this condition in the CUSTOMER table.

The negative of the LIKE operator can also be used, as in the example:

WHERE customer_name **NOT LIKE** ('%Ford%');

A1.4.7 Sorting rows with the ORDER BY clause

Once rows have been extracted by the SELECT and WHERE clauses, those rows can be presented in a defined sequence by specifying one or several columns in an ORDER BY clause, as sort keys. For example the following command selects rows from the CUSTOMER table (see Table A1.2) in alphabetical order on customer name.

User Input:

SELECT	customer_name, customer_address, customer_number
FROM	CUSTOMER
ORDER BY	customer_name;

SQL Output:

Customer Name	Customer Address	Customer Number
BBX Corporation	3361 Alwyn Cr, Middleton	106
First XYZ Bank	318 Wayward Ave, Lower Falls	104
Fordam, Ken	203 Elmford Ave, South Park	107
Walls, Janet	402 Talwood Rd, Wexby	109
Wexlo Ltd	161 Koolonga Ave, Calder	108
XYZ Corporation	133 Fork Ct, Wester Walk	105

To select rows from the PRODUCT_HISTORY table and display them in ascending order on *period number*, then descending order on *product total revenue*, the latter column is followed by DESC as for the example using the PRODUCT_HISTORY table in Table A1.5, which follows:

User Input:

SELECT	product_number, period_number, product_total_revenue
FROM	PRODUCT_HISTORY
WHERE	product_type = 31
ORDER BY	period_number, product_total_revenue **DESC**;

SQL Output:

Product Number	Period Number	Product Total Revenue
213	1	3,200,000.00
212	1	650,000.00
211	1	503,000.00

Product Number	Period Number	Product Total Revenue
213	2	4,350,000.00
212	2	580,000.00
211	2	551,000.00
213	3	5,650,000.00
212	3	720,000.00
211	3	503,000.00

If any indexes are defined on columns specified in the ORDER BY clause, those indexes are used for performance improvement by SQL during processing.

A1.4.8   Selecting only rows with DISTINCT values

The SELECT command presents all rows that satisfy the specified conditions. Several rows with the same value in a specific column may satisfy the defined conditions. If only different values in those columns are required, this can be achieved by specifying the DISTINCT clause before the column name in the SELECT command, as shown below for the PRODUCT table in Table A1.4.

User Input:

SELECT   DISTINCT product_type_id

FROM   PRODUCT;

SQL Output:

Product Type Id
31
32

Although the PRODUCT table contains details of 13 products (it has 13 rows, see Table A1.4), they represent only two distinct product types.

A1.5   JOINING SQL TABLES

SQL tables can be combined together based on the existence of common values in defined columns. This operation is called a JOIN operation, and can bring together two or more tables. While this is appropriate for entities (tables) interrelated by the same primary and/or foreign keys, SQL can be used to join tables based on common values in any column, not only a key column.

A1.5.1 Selecting from more than one table

The SELECT command can be applied against two or more tables at the same time. All of the columns of the specified tables are available for presentation in the result. These tables are combined based on the existence of a common value in a specified column of each table. For example, consider the CUSTOMER_TYPE table in Table A1.1, and the CUSTOMER table in Table A1.2. Both contain the column *customer type id*. These two columns can be used to combine relevant rows in each table which have the same customer type id value as follows:

User Input:

SELECT	customer_number, customer_name, CUSTOMER.customer_type_id, customer_type_ description
FROM	CUSTOMER_TYPE, CUSTOMER
WHERE	CUSTOMER_TYPE.customer_type_id = CUSTOMER.customer_type_id
ORDER BY	customer_name;

SQL Output:

Customer Number	Customer Name	Customer Type id	Customer Type Description
106	BBX Corporation	2	Wholesale Customer
104	First XYZ Bank	1	Retail Customer
107	Fordam, Ken	3	Personal Customer
109	Walls, Janet	3	Personal Customer
108	Wexlo Ltd	2	Wholesale Customer
105	XYZ Corporation	1	Retail Customer

As we can see, the two tables have been joined together: the result now appears as one table. Thus this form of the SELECT command is referred to as a JOIN, as discussed above. The WHERE clause defines the JOIN condition based on identified columns in each table. Expressed in narrative form, the above command requests the following:

'Select from the CUSTOMER and the CUSTOMER TYPE tables every row where the customer type id column in the CUSTOMER TABLE has the same

value as the customer type id column of the CUSTOMER TYPE table. Discard any rows which do not have the same customer type id value in each table. Present the result as a combined table with the columns: customer number, customer name, customer type id and customer type description, alphabetically sorted by customer name.'

Notice in the above WHERE clause that the join column of each table is qualified by prefixing it with the table name. This table name is concatenated with a period and then the relevant column name, as in CUSTOMER.*customer_type_id* (and in the SELECT list). This avoids ambiguity, particularly with key columns which may appear in several tables and so interrelate those tables. Another example for the PRODUCT table in Table A1.4 and PRODUCT_HISTORY table in Table A1.5 follows:

User Input:

SELECT	product_name, period_number, product_total_revenue
FROM	PRODUCT, PRODUCT_HISTORY
WHERE	PRODUCT.product_number = PRODUCT_HISTORY.product_number
AND	PRODUCT.product_number **IN** (211, 212)
ORDER BY	product_total_revenue DESC;

SQL Output:

Product Name	Period Number	Product Total Revenue
Wender	3	720,000.00
Wender	1	650,000.00
Wender	2	580,000.00
A-Lo	2	551,000.00
A-Lo	1	503,000.00
A-Lo	3	503,000.00

A1.5.2   Use of the UNION clause

We have seen how two or more tables can be combined together, by joining them based on common values in defined columns. Additionally, two or more SELECT commands (against the same or different tables) can be combined by the UNION clause as shown on page 628. This statement also illustrates another facility of SELECT: the inclusion of text strings (enclosed in brackets) in the SELECT command, to form a descriptive part of the output.

User Input

SELECT	product_number, 'First Selection: ', product_total_units
FROM	PRODUCT_HISTORY
WHERE	product_total_units > 25000
UNION	
SELECT	product_number, 'Second Selection: ', product_total_units
FROM	PRODUCT_HISTORY
WHERE	product_total_units BETWEEN 5000 AND 10000
ORDER BY	product_number;

SQL Output:

Product Number		Product Total Units
212	Second Selection:	5,110
212	Second Selection:	5,500
213	First Selection:	33,000
213	First Selection:	44,550
312	Second Selection:	5,500
413	First Selection:	26,000
413	First Selection:	29,000
414	Second Selection:	6,100

The above example of UNION uses the same table. Different tables can also be combined with the UNION clause. However they must be **union-compatible**: that is, each table *must* have the same number of columns, and every *corresponding* column in each table *must* be of the same defined data type. Redundant duplicate rows are eliminated in the result. Finally, if the result is to be ordered (as in the example above) any ORDER BY clause must appear as part of the last SELECT only.

A1.5.3 Arithmetic expressions in a SELECT command

All columns in the earlier examples had been previously defined as attributes in an entity, or as text constants. However we may wish to carry out certain calculations against values in some columns and present those calculations as a separate column of the result. The following example illustrates this using the PRODUCT_HISTORY table in Table A1.5 to increase *product_total_units* by 10% for some products.

User Input:

SELECT	product_name, period_number, product_total_units, product_total_units * 1.1
FROM	PRODUCT, PRODUCT_HISTORY
WHERE	PRODUCT.product_number = PRODUCT_HISTORY.product_number
AND	PRODUCT.product_number **IN** (211, 212);

SQL Output:

Product Name	Period Number	Product Total Units	Product Total Units * 1.1
A-Lo	1	3,125	3,437
A-Lo	2	3,200	3,520
A-Lo	3	3,550	3,905
Wender	1	5,110	5,621
Wender	2	4,900	5,390
Wender	3	5,500	6,050

The operators which are able to be used in an arithmetic expression as above are:

+, −, * and /   for add, subtract, multiply and divide respectively.

SQL/DS and DB2 support these arithmetic operators. ORACLE supports these as well as several other operators.

A calculated column has no defined column name. If a calculated column is to be used in a WHERE clause for a selection condition, the column is referred to by its column number – according to the sequence of column names listed in the associated SELECT command. To illustrate, the following variation of the previous example only presents those rows where the calculated value in the fourth column exceeds 5000:

User Input:

SELECT	product_name, period_number, product_total_units, product_total_units * 1.1
FROM	PRODUCT, PRODUCT_HISTORY
WHERE	PRODUCT.product_number = PRODUCT_HISTORY.product_number
AND	PRODUCT.product_number **IN** (211, 212)
AND	4 > 5000;

SQL Output:

Product Name	Period Number	Product Total Units	Product Total Units * 1.1	
				) that is,
				) 4th Column
Wender	1	5,110	5,621	
Wender	2	4,900	5,390	
Wender	3	5,500	6,050	

In addition to the use of arithmetic expressions as described above, SQL allows the use of the built-in expressions of MAX, MIN, SUM, AVG and COUNT. Examples using these expressions are discussed in the following section.

A1.5.4 Use of GROUP BY and built-in functions

Grouping is used to summarize a group of rows based on one or several common factors. For example, we may wish to use the PRODUCT table in Table A1.5 to identify the product which generated the greatest revenue for each *product type id*. This is achieved by the GROUP BY clause as illustrated below. This clause allows 'control breaks' to be specified; any number of columns can be defined in the GROUP BY clause. For example, all products with the same *product type id* can be grouped together and the maximum value of product total revenue can be extracted by using the built-in expression MAX (*total_product_revenue*) as shown below.

User Input:

SELECT	product_type_id, MAX (product_total_revenue)
FROM	PRODUCT_HISTORY
GROUP BY	product_type_id;

SQL Output:

Product Type id	MAX (Product Total Revenue)
31	5,650,000.00
32	650,000.00

The use of MAX above invokes a built-in function which determines the highest value of product total revenue for all products of the same product type id, as indicated by the GROUP BY clause. When the *product type id* changes, the SELECT command displays the highest value found. A number of built-in functions are provided. These are listed as follows:

- SUM   Calculate the total value of a specified column within a defined group.

- AVG   Calculate the average value of a specified column within a defined group.

- MAX   Calculate the highest value of a specified column within a defined group.

- MIN   Calculate the lowest value of a specified column within a defined group.

- COUNT   Count the number of values in a specified column within a defined group.

SQL/DS, DB2 and ORACLE support all of the functions listed above. ORACLE also supports a number of built-in and arithmetic functions in addition to those listed above. Another example illustrating the use of these built-in functions follows. This uses a join query:

User Input:

SELECT	product_type_description, COUNT (*), SUM (product_total_revenue), AVG (product_total_revenue)
FROM	PRODUCT_HISTORY, PRODUCT_TYPE
WHERE	PRODUCT_TYPE.product_type_id = PRODUCT_HISTORY.product_type_id
GROUP BY	PRODUCT_TYPE.product_type_id;

SQL Output:

Product Type Description	COUNT (*)	SUM (Product Total Revenue)	AVG (Product Total Revenue)
Standard Product	9	16,707,000.00	1,856,333.00
Custom Product	18	4,533,500.00	251,861.11

A1.5.5   Selecting specific groups with HAVING clause

The WHERE clause, as we saw earlier, is used to select rows whose columns satisfy one or several conditions. However the WHERE clause cannot be used for selection of groups of rows. Instead the HAVING clause is used, which must follow the GROUP BY clause. An example which uses the previous query to eliminate any groups with less than $5,000,000 product total revenue follows:

User Input:

SELECT	product_type_description, COUNT (*), SUM (product_total_revenue), AVG (product_total_revenue)
FROM	PRODUCT_HISTORY, PRODUCT_TYPE
WHERE	PRODUCT_TYPE.product_type_id = PRODUCT_HISTORY.product_type_id
GROUP BY	PRODUCT_TYPE.product_type_id
HAVING	3 > 5000000;

SQL Output:

Product Type Description	COUNT (*)	SUM (Product Total Revenue)	AVG (Product Total Revenue)
Standard Product	9	16,707,000.00	1,856,333.00

This example specifies in the HAVING clause that the third column in the SELECT list above – which is SUM (*product_total_revenue*) – is to be evaluated: only those groups which exceed $5,000,000.00 in total product revenue are to be included.

A1.6 | THE USE OF SUBQUERIES

We have seen the use of single SELECT commands in each of the examples presented so far. However SQL offers considerably greater power than this through the use of multiple, nested SELECT commands included as part of a WHERE clause. These are subqueries, where several SELECTs can be nested as shown below. In evaluating nested SELECT commands, SQL proceeds from the inner-most SELECT to the outer-most SELECT. The following example lists all products which exceeded the average product total revenue for a period.

User Input:

SELECT	product_name, period_number, product_total_revenue
FROM	PRODUCT, PRODUCT_HISTORY
WHERE	PRODUCT.product_number = PRODUCT_HISTORY.product_number
AND	product_total_revenue >
	(**SELECT** AVG (product_total_revenue)
	FROM PRODUCT_HISTORY);

SQL Output:

Product Name	Period Number	Product Total Revenue
Wesley	1	3,200,000.00
Wesley	2	4,350,000.00
Wesley	3	5,650,000.00

Subqueries can be as complex as main queries. They can join one or several tables together and use simple or complex WHERE clauses for selection, which may include other nested SELECT subqueries. All subqueries can use the ORDER BY, GROUP BY and HAVING clauses, and can use arithmetic or built-in functions as described above. However subqueries cannot be combined by UNION. They can also be used in conjunction with INSERT, UPDATE or DELETE commands as described shortly.

A1.6.1   Use of alias names

In a group of nested subqueries the same table name may be referenced in the FROM clause of the same (or several different) SELECT command(s). Furthermore, the same column name may appear in more than one table (as with primary or foreign keys). To avoid ambiguity, an alias name can be attached to each table name in the FROM clause. An alias name can prefix a column name to relate it to one table (of several tables where it also exists). This alias name is used in the SELECT and WHERE clauses for explicit reference. The following example illustrates use of alias names to join the PRODUCT table (Table A1.4) to itself. This identifies interrelated products of the same *product type id*, such as for analysis of (5BNF) structure entities.

User Input:

SELECT	S1.product_number, S1.product_name, S2.product_number, S2.product_name
FROM	PRODUCT S1, PRODUCT S2
WHERE	S1.product_number < S2.product_number
AND	S1.product_type_id = 31;

SQL Output:

Product Number	Product Name	Product Number	Product Name
211	A-Lo	212	Wender
211	A-Lo	213	Wesley
212	Wender	213	Wesley

This example uses two alias names (S1 and S2) in the FROM clause to refer to the same table. Each alias immediately follows its relevant table name, with an intervening blank – and before the comma which signifies a new table name. The alias names are then used explicitly in the SELECT and WHERE clauses.

A1.6.2 Use of the EXISTS clause

SQL allows the existence or non-existence of certain conditions to be evaluated. This is often used to determine whether specified rows are present (EXISTS) or are missing (NOT EXISTS) based on a defined column. The following example identifies products in the PRODUCT table (see Table A1.4) for which there exists no activity in the PRODUCT_HISTORY table (see Table A1.5). Aliases are used to further illustrate their use.

User Input:

```
SELECT    SO.product_number, SO.product_name

FROM      PRODUCT SO

WHERE     NOT EXISTS

          ( SELECT    *

            FROM      PRODUCT SI, PRODUCT_HISTORY SH

            WHERE     SI.product_number = SH.product_number);
```

SQL Output:

Product Number	Product Name
313	Wender-S3
314	Wender-S4
315	Wender-S5
316	Wender-S6

In this example the subquery evaluates each row of the PRODUCT table (alias SI) for which there is a corresponding row in the PRODUCT_ HISTORY table (alias SH), based on the *product_number*. The outer-most query (using table PRODUCT – alias SO) accepts only those rows which do not satisfy the subquery, that is, a corresponding row does NOT EXIST in both the PRODUCT and the PRODUCT_HISTORY tables. Refer to Date's book on DB2 for additional examples of EXISTS and NOT EXISTS. It is recommended that EXISTS and NOT EXISTS clauses be used instead of using the ANY clause and ALL clauses in SQL. ANY and ALL can lead to ambiguous queries.

A1.6.3   Use of the NULL clause

We may wish to select rows based not on existence (or non-existence) as described above, but on whether a specified column is NULL or instead, NOT NULL. Unless a column is specified as NOT NULL when its relevant table is created, NULL values may exist. For example, columns where some values have not been explicitly added by the INSERT clause (see shortly) will contain a NULL value as in the next example.

User Input:

SELECT	*
FROM	PRODUCT_HISTORY
WHERE	product_total_revenue IS NOT NULL
AND	product_number = 312;

SQL Output:

Product Number	Period Number	Product Type Id	Product Total Revenue	Product Total Units
312	1	32	325,000.00	2,500
312	2	32	0.00	0
312	3	32	650,000.00	5,500

Note that one of the rows for product number 312 in Table A1.5 is explicitly zero in the *product total revenue* column. This is different from NULL – that is, 'does not exist'. Hence it has been selected above.

So far we have concentrated on the use of SQL for querying SQL tables. We will now cover the commands for modifying SQL tables.

A1.7 MODIFYING SQL TABLES

While the SELECT command is used to retrieve a set of rows from one or several tables, SQL also allows a set of rows of a table to be added to, updated or deleted. The commands which follow are used.

UPDATE	Changes the values stored in defined columns of a table.
DELETE	Deletes rows from a table.
INSERT	Adds rows to a table.

A1.7.1 The UPDATE command

The UPDATE command includes a SET clause followed by an optional WHERE clause. The following example illustrates an increase of the *product total units* in the PRODUCT_HISTORY table (Table A1.5) by 15% for product numbers above 400.

User Input:

> **UPDATE**   PRODUCT_HISTORY
>
> **SET**   product_total_units = product_total_units * 1.15
>
> **WHERE**   PRODUCT_HISTORY.product_number > = 400;

SQL Output:

> 12 records updated.

The UPDATE command first names the table to be updated (PRODUCT_HISTORY above). It then specifies in the SET clause the calculations to be carried out against the defined column (using arithmetic and built-in functions as required) according to the conditions specified in the WHERE clause (if included).

A1.7.2 The INSERT command

We previously discussed how to add rows to a table by explicitly inserting values into specified columns. We defined those values as a group of constants – with one INSERT command for each row to be added. Alternatively, we can select relevant columns from one table, use the arithmetic or built-in functions to manipulate them in a defined way, and insert those calculated values in another table.

The following example illustrates creation of a new table called NEW_PRODUCTION, and the insertion in that table of a subset of columns from the PRODUCT_HISTORY table (see Table A1.5) for products above 400. An UPDATE is also included, to reflect an increase in the new product total units by 20%.

User Input:

> **CREATE TABLE** NEW_PRODUCTION   (product_number **INTEGER,**
>   new_product_units **INTEGER**);
>
> **INSERT**
>
> **INTO**   NEW_PRODUCTION **VALUES** (product_number, new_product_units)

SELECT	product_number, product_total_units
FROM	PRODUCT_HISTORY
WHERE	product_number > = 400;
UPDATE	NEW_PRODUCTION
SET	new_product_units = new_product_units * 1.20;

SQL Output:

Table created.
12 records created.

A1.7.3 The DELETE command

Complete rows of a table can be removed by the DELETE command. Once again, individual rows or a set of rows can be selected for deletion by the WHERE clause, which may include complex conditions or subqueries to whatever depth is necessary. The following example illustrates the deletion of all rows of the PRODUCT_HISTORY table (Table A1.5) where the product total revenue is zero.

User Input:

DELETE

FROM	PRODUCT_HISTORY
WHERE	product_total_revenue = 0.00;

SQL Output:

4 records deleted.

A1.7.4   GRANT and REVOKE commands

Obviously, security controls must be in place before data may be deleted or updated as described in the above section. SQL (as supported by SQL/DS, DB2 and ORACLE) provides the GRANT and REVOKE commands to control such operations.

A1.7.5   COMMIT and ROLLBACK commands

SQL supports the COMMIT and ROLLBACK commands for recovery and integrity purposes in a multi-user environment. Changes made to tables can be indicated as permanent by entering a COMMIT command. This is known as a COMMIT point. In the event of a machine or power failure, processing can be reversed (rolled back) to its status at the most recent COMMIT point, by entering the command ROLLBACK.

A1.8 DEFINING ALTERNATE VIEWS OF TABLES

In all of the foregoing material we have referred to real tables which contain data. SQL also allows 'virtual' tables to be defined. These are tables which do not exist in real-life, but instead reflect different views of real tables. A person using a table may be interested in (or be authorized to see) only part of a larger table: this is called a **view**. Only that part of the table defined in the view is available to the user: to all intents and purposes the rest of the real table does not exist.

A1.8.1 The CREATE VIEW command

A view is created from a real table by use of the CREATE VIEW command together with the SELECT command. This may include all of the SELECT command facilities covered so far. Each table view is explicitly named, and appears as if it is a real table. It can be operated on by all of the SQL commands as if it is a real table. The CREATE VIEW command defines a view of the PRODUCT_HISTORY table (Table A1.5) in the following example. This view contains only a subset of columns and a subset of rows based on the SELECT command included as part of the view.

User Input:

```
CREATE VIEW    PRODUCTION
AS          (  SELECT    product_number, product_total_units
               FROM      PRODUCT_HISTORY
               WHERE     product_number > = 400);
```

SQL Output:

```
View created.
```

This creates a subset of PRODUCT_HISTORY which contains the *product number* and *product total units* columns, and only includes rows where *product number* is greater than or equal to 400. The PRODUCTION view can now be operated on directly. The following example extracts those rows where the product total units is greater than 30,000.

User Input:

SELECT	
FROM	PRODUCTION
WHERE	product_total_units > 30000;

In resolving a command against a view, such as in the above example, SQL combines the user's commands with the definition of the view in the CREATE VIEW command. The above query is modified automatically and transparently by SQL as if the user had instead entered the following SELECT command.

User Input:

SELECT	product_number, product_total_units
FROM	PRODUCT_HISTORY
WHERE	product_total_units > 30000
AND	product_number > = 400;

Both the original SELECT command above, and its translated equivalent, produce the output result which follows.

SQL Output:

Product Number	Product Total Units
213	33,000
213	44,500

As can be seen above, views can be used for any operation which is valid against real tables. Sensitive columns or rows in real tables can be excluded from unauthorized personnel by defining a view. Note that some views (for example, joining two or more tables) cannot be used with UPDATE or DELETE commands (see *References*).

A1.8.2 The DROP VIEW command

When a view is no longer required, it is removed by the DROP VIEW command. Once created, a view cannot be altered as with the ALTER

TABLE command discussed earlier. Instead, the view must be dropped, and a new CREATE VIEW command defined. The following example illustrates the DROP VIEW command.

User Input:

DROP VIEW   PRODUCTION;

SQL Output:

View dropped.

We have now completed this overview SQL. See the references for further detail.

References

[1] Date, C. J. (1988). *A Guide to the SQL Standard*, Addison-Wesley: Reading, MA.

[2] Codd, E. F. (1990). *The Relational Model for Database Management: Version 2*, Addison-Wesley: Reading, MA.

[3] Date, C. J. and White, C. J. (1988). *A Guide to DB2, Second Edition*, Addison-Wesley: Reading, MA.

[4] Date, C. J. (1987). *A Guide to INGRES*, Addison-Wesley: Reading, MA.

[5] Sachs, J. (1987). *SQL*Plus Reference Guide – Version 2.0*, Oracle Corporation: Belmont, CA, Oracle Part No: 3203–V2.0.

APPENDIX 2

Data Model Analysis

This appendix documents the complete Cluster Report produced by IE: Expert, following analysis of the strategic and tactical models developed in Chapters 15 and 16.

A2.1 CLUSTER ANALYSIS OF DATA MODELS

The analysis of the strategic and tactical models that were developed in Chapters 15 and 16 is discussed in Chapter 17. This analysis was carried out by IE: Expert V5.0. Section 17.2 of that chapter discusses the documentation of these models. Section 17.3 describes data model analysis, and includes a number of data maps automatically generated by IE: Expert. Section 17.3.2 discusses the identification of systems and data bases from the data model using automatic cluster analysis. It uses a number of clusters derived in this way to identify relevant systems and data bases. This appendix documents the full Cluster Report produced for the Complaints Resolution view of the COMRES encyclopaedia. This appears for reference purposes as Figure A2.1, over six pages.

New Clusters

1. **ACCOUNT TOPIC DATA BASE** (derived)
    1) TOPIC TYPE
    1) PERIOD TYPE
        2) PERIOD
            3) TOPIC
                4) ACCOUNT TOPIC (ACCOUNT TOPIC DATA BASE)

2. **ACCOUNTING PERIOD DATA BASE** (derived)
    1) PERIOD TYPE
        2) PERIOD
            3) ACCOUNTING PERIOD (ACCOUNTING PERIOD DATA BASE)

3. **CASE DOCUMENTATION SYSTEMS** (derived)
    1) PERIOD TYPE
        2) PERIOD
    1) INVOLVED PARTY TYPE
    1) LOCATION TYPE
        3) LOCATION
            4) INVOLVED PARTY LOCATION (LOCATION REFERENCE SYSTEMS)
        3) INVOLVED PARTY
                5) INVESTIGATION INVOLVED PARTY (INVESTIGATION REFERENCE SYSTEMS)
            4) INVESTIGATION
    1) TOPIC TYPE
        3) TOPIC
            4) CASE TOPIC (CASE TOPIC ANALYSIS SYSTEMS)
        3) CASE
    1) TEXT TYPE
        3) TEXT
            4) CASE TEXT (CASE DOCUMENTATION SYSTEMS)

4. **CASE TOPIC ANALYSIS SYSTEMS** (derived)
    1) PERIOD TYPE
        2) PERIOD
    1) INVOLVED PARTY TYPE
    1) LOCATION TYPE
        3) LOCATION
            4) INVOLVED PARTY LOCATION (LOCATION REFERENCE SYSTEMS)
        3) INVOLVED PARTY
                5) INVESTIGATION INVOLVED PARTY (INVESTIGATION REFERENCE SYSTEMS)
            4) INVESTIGATION
        3) CASE

Figure A2.1   Cluster Report for COMPLAINTS RESOLUTION view.

4. **CASE TOPIC ANALYSIS SYSTEMS**

   1) TOPIC TYPE
      3) TOPIC
         4) CASE TOPIC (CASE TOPIC ANALYSIS SYSTEMS)

5. **CLIENT DATA BASE** (derived)
   1) INVOLVED PARTY TYPE
   1) PERIOD TYPE
      2) PERIOD
   1) LOCATION TYPE
      3) LOCATION
         4) INVOLVED PARTY LOCATION (LOCATION REFERENCE SYSTEMS)
      3) INVOLVED PARTY
         4) CLIENT (CLIENT DATA BASE)

6. **CUSTOMER DATA BASE** (derived)
   1) INVOLVED PARTY TYPE
   1) PERIOD TYPE
      2) PERIOD
   1) LOCATION TYPE
      3) LOCATION
         4) INVOLVED PARTY LOCATION (LOCATION REFERENCE SYSTEMS)
      3) INVOLVED PARTY
         4) CUSTOMER (CUSTOMER DATA BASE)

7. **ENQUIRY TOPIC DATA BASE** (derived)
   1) TOPIC TYPE
   1) PERIOD TYPE
      2) PERIOD
      3) TOPIC
         4) ENQUIRY TOPIC (ENQUIRY TOPIC DATA BASE)

8. **GEOGRAPHIC LOCATION DATA BASE** (derived)
   1) LOCATION TYPE
   1) PERIOD TYPE
      2) PERIOD
      3) LOCATION
         4) GEOGRAPHIC LOCATION (GEOGRAPHIC LOCATION DATA BASE)

9. **GRID LOCATION DATA BASE** (derived)
   1) LOCATION TYPE
   1) PERIOD TYPE
      2) PERIOD

Figure A2.1 (cont.)   Cluster Report for COMPLAINTS RESOLUTION view.

9. **GRID LOCATION DATA BASE**

          3) LOCATION
              4) GRID LOCATION (GRID LOCATION DATA BASE)

10. **INVESTIGATION REFERENCE SYSTEMS** (derived)
       1) INVOLVED PARTY TYPE
       1) PERIOD TYPE
          2) PERIOD
       1) LOCATION TYPE
          3) LOCATION
              4) INVOLVED PARTY LOCATION (LOCATION REFERENCE SYSTEMS)
          3) INVOLVED PARTY
       1) TOPIC TYPE
          3) TOPIC
              4) CASE TOPIC (CASE TOPIC ANALYSIS SYSTEMS)
          3) CASE
              4) INVESTIGATION
                  5) INVESTIGATION INVOLVED PARTY (INVESTIGATION REFERENCE SYSTEMS)

11. **LETTER DATA BASE** (derived)
       1) TEXT TYPE
       1) PERIOD TYPE
          2) PERIOD
              3) TEXT
                  4) LETTER (LETTER DATA BASE)

12. **LOCATION REFERENCE SYSTEMS** (derived)
       1) LOCATION TYPE
       1) PERIOD TYPE
          2) PERIOD
              3) LOCATION
       1) INVOLVED PARTY TYPE
          3) INVOLVED PARTY
              4) INVOLVED PARTY LOCATION (LOCATION REFERENCE SYSTEMS)

13. **LOGICAL LOCATION DATA BASE** (derived)
       1) LOCATION TYPE
       1) PERIOD TYPE
          2) PERIOD
              3) LOCATION
                  4) LOGICAL LOCATION (LOGICAL LOCATION DATA BASE)

Figure A2.1 (cont.)   Cluster Report for COMPLAINTS RESOLUTION view.

XYZ COMRES   Cluster Report
Model View: COMPLAINTS RESOLUTION
Thu Jun 13 15:04:25 1991   Page 4

New Clusters

14. **NOTE DATA BASE** (derived)
    1) TEXT TYPE
    1) PERIOD TYPE
        2) PERIOD
            3) TEXT
                4) NOTE (NOTE DATA BASE)

15. **PERFORMANCE PERIOD DATA BASE** (derived)
    1) PERIOD TYPE
        2) PERIOD
            3) PERFORMANCE PERIOD (PERFORMANCE PERIOD DATA BASE)

16. **POLICY TOPIC DATA BASE** (derived)
    1) TOPIC TYPE
    1) PERIOD TYPE
        2) PERIOD
            3) TOPIC
                4) POLICY TOPIC (POLICY TOPIC DATA BASE)

17. **PROBLEM TOPIC DATA BASE** (derived)
    1) TOPIC TYPE
    1) PERIOD TYPE
        2) PERIOD
            3) TOPIC
                4) PROBLEM TOPIC (PROBLEM TOPIC DATA BASE)

18. **RELATED INVOLVED PARTY SYSTEMS** (derived)
    1) INVOLVED PARTY TYPE
    1) PERIOD TYPE
        2) PERIOD
    1) LOCATION TYPE
            3) LOCATION
                4) INVOLVED PARTY LOCATION (LOCATION REFERENCE SYSTEMS)
            3) INVOLVED PARTY
                4) INVOLVED PARTY STRUCTURE (RELATED INVOLVED PARTY SYSTEMS)

19. **RELATED LOCATION SYSTEMS** (derived)
    1) LOCATION TYPE
    1) PERIOD TYPE
        2) PERIOD
            3) LOCATION
                4) LOCATION STRUCTURE (RELATED LOCATION SYSTEMS)

Figure A2.1 (cont.)   Cluster Report for COMPLAINTS RESOLUTION view.

New Clusters

20. **RELATED PERIOD SYSTEMS** (derived)
    1) PERIOD TYPE
       2) PERIOD
          3) PERIOD STRUCTURE (RELATED PERIOD SYSTEMS)

21. **RELATED TEXT SYSTEMS** (derived)
    1) TEXT TYPE
    1) PERIOD TYPE
       2) PERIOD
          3) TEXT
             4) TEXT STRUCTURE (RELATED TEXT SYSTEMS)

22. **RELATED TOPIC SYSTEMS** (derived)
    1) TOPIC TYPE
    1) PERIOD TYPE
       2) PERIOD
          3) TOPIC
             4) TOPIC STRUCTURE (RELATED TOPIC SYSTEMS)

23. **REPORTING PERIOD DATA BASE** (derived)
    1) PERIOD TYPE
       2) PERIOD
          3) REPORTING PERIOD (REPORTING PERIOD DATA BASE)

24. **STAFF TOPIC DATA BASE** (derived)
    1) TOPIC TYPE
    1) PERIOD TYPE
       2) PERIOD
          3) TOPIC
             4) STAFF TOPIC (STAFF TOPIC DATA BASE)

25. **STANDARD TEXT DATA BASE** (derived)
    1) TEXT TYPE
    1) PERIOD TYPE
       2) PERIOD
          3) TEXT
             4) STANDARD TEXT (STANDARD TEXT DATA BASE)

26. **SUPPLIER DATA BASE** (derived)
    1) INVOLVED PARTY TYPE
    1) PERIOD TYPE
       2) PERIOD

Figure A2.1 (cont.)   **Cluster Report for COMPLAINTS RESOLUTION** view.

XYZ COMRES Cluster Report

Model View: COMPLAINTS RESOLUTION

Thu Jun 13 15:04:25 1991 Page 6

---

26. **SUPPLIER DATA BASE**

1) LOCATION TYPE
        3) LOCATION
            4) INVOLVED PARTY LOCATION (LOCATION REFERENCE SYSTEMS)
        3) INVOLVED PARTY
            4) SUPPLIER (SUPPLIER DATA BASE)

27. **TOPIC DOCUMENTATION SYSTEMS** (derived)

1) TOPIC TYPE
1) PERIOD TYPE
    2) PERIOD
        3) TOPIC
1) TEXT TYPE
        3) TEXT
            4) TOPIC TEXT (TOPIC DOCUMENTATION SYSTEMS)

28. **TOPIC REFERENCE SYSTEMS** (derived)

1) TOPIC TYPE
1) PERIOD TYPE
    2) PERIOD
        3) TOPIC
1) LOCATION TYPE
        3) LOCATION
            4) TOPIC LOCATION (TOPIC REFERENCE SYSTEMS)

New clusters saved in file: COMRES.CLU

Figure A2.1 (cont.) **Cluster Report for COMPLAINTS RESOLUTION view.**

INDEX